Gerasim Petrinski

The Image of the Demon in Byzantium
Philosophical and Mythological Origins

With a foreword by Prof. Georgi Kapriev

STUDIES IN HISTORICAL PHILOSOPHY

Editor: Alexander Gungov

Consulting Editor: Donald Phillip Verene

ISSN 2629-0316

1 *Dustin Peone*
  Memory as Philosophy
  The Theory and Practice of
  Philosophical Recollection
  ISBN 978-3-8382-1336-1

2 *Raymond Barfield*
  The Poetic Apriori:
  Philosophical Imagination
  in a Meaningful Universe
  ISBN 978-3-8382-1350-7

3 *Jennifer Lobo Meeks*
  Allegory in Early Greek
  Philosophy
  ISBN 978-3-8382-1425-2

4 *Vanessa Freerks*
  Baudrillard with Nietzsche
  and Heidegger: Towards a
  Genealogical Analysis
  ISBN 978-3-8382-1474-0

5 *Thora Ilin Bayer and
  Donald Phillip Verene*
  Philosophical Ideas
  A Historical Study
  ISBN 978-3-8382-1585-3

6 *Jeffrey Andrew Barash*
  Shadows of Being
  Encounters with Heidegger in
  Political Theory and Historical
  Reflection
  ISBN 978-3-8382-1485-6

7 *Donald Phillip Verene*
  The Philosophic Spirit
  Its Meaning and Presence
  ISBN 978-3-8382-1781-9

8 *Geoffrey Dean*
  The Orphic I
  A Philosophical Approach to
  Musical Collaboration
  ISBN 978-3-8382-1629-4

9 *Gerasim Petrinski*
  The Image of the Demon in
  Byzantium
  Philosophical and
  Mythological Origins
  With a foreword by Prof.
  Georgi Kapriev
  ISBN 978-3-8382-1785-7

10 *Donald Phillip Verene*
   Philosophical Self-Knowledge
   Two Studies
   ISBN 978-3-8382-1880-9

Gerasim Petrinski

THE IMAGE OF THE DEMON IN BYZANTIUM

Philosophical and Mythological Origins

With a foreword by Prof. Georgi Kapriev

Bibliografische Information der Deutschen Nationalbibliothek
Die Deutsche Nationalbibliothek verzeichnet diese Publikation in der Deutschen Nationalbibliografie; detaillierte bibliografische Daten sind im Internet über http://dnb.d-nb.de abrufbar.

Bibliographic information published by the Deutsche Nationalbibliothek
Die Deutsche Nationalbibliothek lists this publication in the Deutsche Nationalbibliografie; detailed bibliographic data are available in the Internet at http://dnb.d-nb.de.

ISBN-13: 978-3-8382-1785-7
© *ibidem*-Verlag, Hannover • Stuttgart 2024
Alle Rechte vorbehalten

Das Werk einschließlich aller seiner Teile ist urheberrechtlich geschützt. Jede Verwertung außerhalb der engen Grenzen des Urheberrechtsgesetzes ist ohne Zustimmung des Verlages unzulässig und strafbar. Dies gilt insbesondere für Vervielfältigungen, Übersetzungen, Mikroverfilmungen und elektronische Speicherformen sowie die Einspeicherung und Verarbeitung in elektronischen Systemen.

All rights reserved. No part of this publication may be reproduced, stored in or introduced into a retrieval system, or transmitted, in any form, or by any means (electronic, mechanical, photocopying, recording or otherwise) without the prior written permission of the publisher. Any person who does any unauthorized act in relation to this publication may be liable to criminal prosecution and civil claims for damages.

Printed in the EU

For my parents

Contents

ABBREVIATIONS 11
FOREWORD 13
INTRODUCTION 21

Part One
BYZANTINE HAGIOGRAPHY: RHETORICAL ASPECTS, FORMS, AND TYPOLOGIES

CHAPTER 1.
EPIDEICTIC AND HAGIOGRAPHICAL EPIDEICTIC 37
1. Byzantine hagiography between rhetoric and literature 37
2. Typologies 52

CHAPTER 2
SCHOOLS, AUTHORS, AND TEXTS 67
1. Biographical hagiography in the sixth and seventh centuries 67
2. The Great Lavra of St. Sabbas in Palestine (seventh–ninth century) 79
3. Polemical iconodule hagiography 82
   3.1. Patriarch Germanos 83
   3.2. Stephen the Deacon and his pupils 84
4. The hagiographical school of Bithynia 93
5. Semi-secular hagiography 101
6. Ignatios the Deacon (c. 770–mid-ninth century) and Pseudo-Ignatios the Deacon 103
7. The "historical" hagiography during the ninth century 107
8. The hagiography of Constantinople from the late ninth to the mid-tenth century 109
9. The hagiography of Sicily and Southern Italy 117
10. Greece and Macedonia: from St. Theodora of Thessalonica to St. Nikon Metanoeite 127

Part Two
THE DEMON: ORIGINS AND TRADITIONS

CHAPTER 1
THE PRE-CHRISTIAN DEMON 139
1. The Homeric demon 140
2. Objectivizations of the notion demon 144
   - 2.1. Hesiod 144
   - 2.2. The demons of the dead 147
   - 2.3. The Demon-Paredros: the personal guardian demon and the myth of Doctor Faustus 152
   - 2.4. The Neoplatonic tradition: from the "bad" to the "evil" demon 180

CHAPTER 2
THE DEMON AND THE CHRISTIAN TRADITIONS 195
1. The origin and the nature of Evil 196
   - 1.1. The Devil 196
   - 1.2. The demons and the evil spirits 199
2. Demons in the sacred history of humankind 209

Part Three
FORMS, TRANSFORMATIONS, AND INFLUENCE OF THE DEMONS

INTRODUCTION POLARIZATION" AND PARODY IN THE IMAGE OF THE DEMON 229

CHAPTER 1
THE ELEMENTS OF THE DEMONIC IMAGE 233
1. Organismic: the demonic body 234
   - 1.1. The metamorphoses of ugliness 234
   - 1.2. Disproportions: excess and deficiency 237
   - 1.3. Impurity and filth 245
2. Clothing and jewelry 249
3. Kinesics 255
   - 3.1. Facial expression and gestures 255
   - 3.2. Levitation 263
4. Vocalization, speech, and divination 267
   - 4.1. Languages and stereotypical phrases 268
   - 4.2. Ventriloquism and divination 279

CHAPTER 2
COMPLEX ANTHROPOMORPHIC IMAGES 285

1. The black man: symbolism and transformations
   of darkness 286
   1.1. Origins 286
   1.2. Visions and dreams 293
   1.3. The black demon in the human world 298
2. Arabs 305
3. The general and his soldiers 307
4. The female demon 312
   4.1. Gello: the Child-killer 313
   4.2. The Temptress 320
   4.3. The Child-killer and the Temptress: a reconstruction of
        the image and its origins 323
   4.4. Why did Byzantine writers avoid female demons? 327
5. Demons disguised as saints and angels 329
   5.1. Demonic fire and angelic light 330
   5.2. Lack of persistence 332

CHAPTER 3
ANIMALS AND PLANTS 335

1. Snakes and scorpions 338
   1.1. Origins 338
   1.2. Appearance and influence 346
2. Dragons 352
3. Birds 360
   3.1. Ravens 360
   3.2. "Birds" of the night: bats and owls 365
   3.3. Other images 367
4. Mammals 369
   4.1. Mice: plague, filth, and death 369
   4.2. Pigs, swine, and boars: aggression and homosexuality .. 373
   4.3. Dogs and wolves 378
5. Insects 380
6. Plants 383
7. Conclusion 384

Part Four
THE DEMONIC SPACE

CHAPTER 1
THE INVISIBLE WORLD 389
1. Humankind besieged 389
2. Trial: the demons of the air 390
   2.1. The "tollhouses" 392
      2.1.1. Origins 393
      2.1.2. St. Athanasios the Great, St. Ephraem Syrus, and St. Cyril of Alexandria 397
      2.1.3. The early hagiography and St. Anastasios Sinaita 401
      2.1.4. George Hamartolos and the Life of St. Basil the Younger: Demon-sins in Byzantine hagiography 406
   2.2. The Ladder to Heaven 418
3. Punishment: the demons of Hell 420

CHAPTER 2
THE VISIBLE WORLD 427
1. The uncivilized space 431
   1.1. The open wilderness 431
   1.2. Caves 437
   1.3. Rivers 440
2. Decivilized space 442
   2.1. Graves, relics, and hidden treasures 442
   2.2. Desecrated churches 454
   2.3. Wells 457
3. Civilized space 459
   3.1. Streets and buildings 459
   3.2. Baths 461
4. The bridge between worlds 464
5. Confining and controlling the demon 466

CONCLUSION 471

BIBLIOGRAPHY 487
   I. PRIMARY SOURCES 487
   II. SECONDARY SOURCES 514

ABBREVIATIONS

AASS: Acta Sanctorum, 68 vols (Paris: Palmé, 1870).

BS: Bibliotheca Sanctorum, ed. Filippo Caraffa and Giuseppe Morelli, 12 vols (Vatican: Istituto Giovanni XXIII, 1961–1970).

BHG: Bibliotheca Hagiographica Graeca, ed. François Halkin [Subsidia Hagiographica 8a], 3 vols (Brussels: Société des Bollandistes, 1957).

DOHD: Dumbarton Oaks Hagiography Database (https://www.doaks.org/research/byzantine/resources/hagiography/database/dohp.asp?cmd=AList)

LSJ: Greek-English Lexicon. With a Revised Supplement, ed. Henry Liddell, Robert Scott, and Henry Jones (Oxford: Clarendon Press, 1996).

MPG: Patrologiae cursus completus. Series Graeca, ed. Jacques Paul Migne, 161 vols (Paris: Migne, 1857–1866).

MPL: Patrologiae cursus completus. Series Latina, ed. Jacques Paul Migne, 217 vols (Paris: Migne, 1841–1855).

ODB: Oxford Dictionary of Byzantium, ed. Alexander Kazhdan, 3 vols (Oxford: Oxford University Press, 1991).

PLRE: The Prosopography of the Later Roman Empire, ed. John Martindale et al., 3 vols (Cambridge: Cambridge University Press, 1971–1992).

PGM: Papyri Graecae Magicae, ed. and comm. Karl Preisendanz, 2 vols (Leipzig: Teubner, 1928–1931).

TIB: Tabula Imperii Byzantini, ed. Johannes Koder, 15 vols (Vienna: Verlag der Österreichischen Akademie der Wissenschaften, 1976–2022).

A NOTE ON THE CITATIONS OF BIBLICAL TEXTS

All references to the Old and New Testaments are based on the following editions:

Septuaginta, ed. Alfred Rahlfs, 2 vols (Stuttgart: Württemberg Bible Society, 1971).

The Greek New Testament, ed. Kurt Aland, Bruce Metzger, and Allen WIkgren (Stuttgart: Württemberg Bible Society, 1968).

The Holy Bible, New International Version (NIV) (Grand Rapids, MI: Zondervan, 2011).

FOREWORD

The Eastern Roman Empire, misleadingly referred to as "Byzantium", provides the modern researcher with innumerable accounts of the demon both as an abstract concept and as the concrete material image of the incarnation of Evil. During the past hundred years, the complexities of this image have attracted the interest of specialists in the fields of theology, literature, philosophy, and the history of culture. These studies, however comprehensive and thorough some may be, usually focus either on the period following the eleventh century, when a whole set of demonological traditions developed, or on particular texts and concepts, like the journey of the soul in the afterlife.

The main subject of Gerasim Petrinski's book is the image of the demon in the hagiographic tradition between the reign of Emperor Justinian I and the epoch of Symeon Metaphrastes. The foundations and supporting framework of high Byzantine culture were laid during this long period, marked and defined by countless political, economic, religious, and philosophical conflicts, culminating in the Iconoclast Controversy in the eighth and the first half of the ninth century. These complex and ambiguous processes resulted in the golden era of tenth- and eleventh-century classicism when the heritage of antiquity, once the natural enemy of Christianity, was already "disarmed" and selectively assimilated, and when the works of the early Fathers of the Church were reconsidered, re-evaluated, and approached from a new perspective. The evolution of the image of the demon during this epoch is an essential and fascinating element in the processes of Byzantine cultural formation.

The hagiographic literature is a unique literary and cultural niche. The authors of the saints' *Lives* were to some extent theologically educated, but they were not necessarily strictly constrained by formulated doctrinal positions. This particularity explains the relatively free blending of high dogmatic matters with concepts containing pagan remnants and elements of contemporary folklore with its corresponding local distinctive features. In addition, the hagiographic texts reveal educative or contextually assimilated cultural deposits displaying a sense and sensibility of Hellenic mythological and narrative culture and perspectives not typical of classical Greek culture and mentality. Taking this into account, Petrinski offers a brief overview of demonology, as it unfolds in Western cultural space from the medieval and post-medieval times up to the present, in order to establish and outline both the similarities and the differences between the cultural domains formed around the two "foci" of the "ellipse" of Christian culture, namely the Western Catholic and the Eastern Orthodox worlds, each of which laid the foundations of their own European cultures – distinct but interwoven.

In the first chapter, the author provides an analysis of the rhetorical aspects of the hagiographic genre and an overall survey of the texts and the "schools" to which they belong, in this way introducing the reader to the literary and historical context of the main subject of the book. He highlights the distinctive features of each period from a literary, political, cultural, and philosophical point of view, emphasizing the various patterns of ideological demands fulfilled by the texts during the age of Justinian, the epoch of the Arab conquest, the Iconoclast crisis, and, ultimately, the Golden era of Byzantine classicism and elitist encyclopedism of the second half of the ninth and the tenth centuries. The perspective chosen by Petrinski demonstrates the processes that structure and form the hagiographic tradition, its evolution and trends, proposing that "some of the most interesting demonic images and narratives come from texts written before the last Seventh Ecumenical Council in 787". This is a natural conclusion for a period in which standards and clichés had not yet been established, or, at least, had not acquired and solidified a normative character that would allow for the emergence of a universally accepted "Orthodox tradition". Petrinski's thorough analysis of the demonic images and narratives in the hagiographic texts under consideration demonstrates the complex dynamics behind the formation of Byzantine culture, and this undoubtedly is one of the many merits of the book.

Another significant contribution is the intertextual manner of approaching and developing the theme. The author rightly notes that an approach that regards the Byzantine evil spirit solely as a historical, or cultural, or mythological, or theological phenomenon oversimplifies the problem, leading to misleading interpretations. Petrinski relies on various and valuable sources and uses different methodological approaches to produce a comprehensive and detailed analysis that encompasses the philosophical and mythological origins and aspects of the notion. Byzantine demonology emerges from the multifarious and syncretic cultural environment of the late Roman Empire. Though covered with a thin veil of Christian dogma, Byzantine demonology before the tenth century still echoes the roar of late antique cities and the sober conversations of the academicians in the schools of philosophy and rhetoric in Athens, Alexandria, and Antioch. The book's second part encompasses and analyzes these various cultural layers that lie behind the notion of "demon", skillfully leading the reader through the complexities of its formation and engaging them with new perspectives and interpretations of classical and post-classical texts. Petrinski traces the philosophical and mythological origin of the demon back to the so-called "Homeric" and "Hesiodic" traditions, pointing out the ambivalence of the notion. In the Homeric epics, *demons* appear as an irrational, chaotic, and unknown power bringing fateful and usually baneful turns in human life. About a century later, Hesiod conceptualizes and objectifies them as higher beings of human origin, namely the souls of the "pure" and "blessed" dead who lived during the Golden Age of humanity. In the sixth century B.C., the Pythagoreans transformed this concept, enriching it with elements of South Italian folklore and traditions, shaping their own idea of demons as the ghosts of the dead floating restlessly in the aerial spaces above the human world, influencing human life both as guardians of mortals and as harbingers of doom.

These threads can be traced in the literature and philosophy of the following epochs: in the poetry of Pindar, the mythological approach of Plato, the philosophical speculations of the Neoplatonists, and the viewpoints and reflections of early Christian authors. Remarkably, the authors of the saints' *Lives* rarely refer to the works of the Church Fathers and the theologians. Neither, often, do they bother to develop theoretical concepts about demons' origins, functions, and purposes. Ultimately, Byzantine hagiography develops a non-systematic demonology that borrows elements from the standard concept of demons as fallen angels, Mediterranean mythologies, and contemporary folklore. This eclectic mental structure influenced the Medieval Orthodox world and still significantly impacts modern concepts of the supernatural.

The idea that demons are inherently evil is a product of the syncretic world of Late Antiquity. This concept is found both in the Neoplatonic tradition and, naturally, in early Christian beliefs. This book takes readers on a captivating journey through the urban legends of Late Antique cities, filled with stories of powerful supernatural guardians granting their masters' wishes. Additionally, it offers a comprehensive and rigorous analysis of the treatises by prominent Neoplatonic philosophers, who created intricate hierarchies of gods and demons while attempting, with varying degrees of success, to define the ontological notion of "Evil".

In the second chapter of this study, Christian "sacred history" and the role of the Devil (also known as Beelzebul, Satan, Beliar, etc.) are presented. The Gospels portray the fallen angels not as powerful allies of Satan but as weak and wretched creatures who fear the mere mention of Christ's name. These beings are commonly referred to as "demons", and the synonym "spirits" is frequently used, often accompanied by adjectives like "unclean" or "evil". Demons lack a stable material form, being naturally bodiless, and they constantly seek to possess a host. They can take various material forms and exert different harmful influences, but their power is always deceptive and imaginary. They lack really transformative or even magical powers, since for hagiographers, the only force capable of performing miracles and wonders is the power of God. The difference between angels and demons is evident in the type of light they emit. While the Devil's servants sometimes pretend to be saints or angels, their light is burning, non-illuminating, and repulsive, unlike the angelic light, unburning, pure, peaceful, and enlightening. However, discerning between the two types lies within the power of saints and holy persons alone, not the ordinary human sensibility. Another distinction between angelic and demonic natures is the permanence of the angelic presence and the transience, fleetingness, and brevity of demonic visions and influence.

Another essential feature of the images of demons and angels in many, mostly vernacular, hagiographical texts is the somewhat paradoxical blending of their elements to form a unified image of the supernatural that does not easily fit into the inherent Christian dualism. Not infrequently, the outer appearance of materialized Good (the angels) and Evil (the Devil and the demons) share similar characteristics, like a large stature, fearful eyes, and exceptional physical power, but, as always, "the Devil is in the details". Holy men and women are presented as the only "specialists" able to tell the difference between the two sides of the supernatural world. However, as much as demons may vary in different descriptions, a few stereotypical identifying characteristics can be identified. Among the surest is their abnormal ugliness, which lacks a stable form and instead stems from human perception. It is evident in various forms of disproportion, deformity, excess, and social impropriety, observable in their physical form, clothing, accessories, tone of voice, manner of speaking, and body language. Usually assuming a male form, the demons are almost always described as overdressed or clad in luxurious garments. Their gestures, facial expressions, and intonation reflect the excessiveness of the negative and sinful emotions they embody (such as anger, envy, and bitterness). Moreover, they often use stereotypical strange and incomprehensible words and phrases, sometimes even speaking in an unknown language. These and similar attributes explicitly emphasize the "otherness" of the demons, culminating in the image of the "black Ethiopian": strong and sexually potent, yet evil, beast-like, and uncivilized. He personifies a great variety of sins and represents death and the underworld. This image is set in stark contrast with the white, gentle, ethereal, fragrant, and harmonious angel, creating the philosophical and religious basis for the inherent "racism" of pre-modern European societies. Additionally, evil spirits occasionally take various zoomorphic forms, such as snakes, dragons, birds, insects, pigs, and other "unclean" animals.

The hagiographic literature displays a natural interest in the fate of the human soul after physical death. The corresponding descriptions demonstrate this genre's connection with apocryphal Christian texts, para-religious piety, and the superstitious imagery prevalent in the period under study, especially in the late ninth and tenth centuries. It is worth noting that the Eastern Orthodox tradition views such ecstatic experiences with suspicion, whether they occur in dreams or not. Excluding the long-discussed "didactic visions", such dreams and journeys to other worlds are typically attributed to demonic influence. However, hagiography abounds in extensive descriptions of the Underworld. While earlier hagiographies linked the latter less to the torments and sufferings inflicted by demons but instead to the horrors of darkness, with occasional and brief mentions of a "river of fire", the later hagiographies more frequently feature various evil spirits punishing sinners dramatically and spectacularly.

Characteristically, hagiography in the period under study interprets the invisible world through a four-part framework, which deviates from orthodox theological teachings and instead incorporates ideas borrowed from Neoplatonism and other non-Christian doctrines. God's heavenly kingdom is accessible only to righteous souls; there, they can unite with God and bask in perfect bliss and harmony. Just below lies the "air", where demons examine the dead for various mortal sins and stop the impure from ascending the "heavenly ladder". Beneath this heavenly realm is the visible world of the living, situated above the Earth's depths, where Satan's kingdom thrives. John Climacus (*c.* 650 A.D.) presented the metaphor of the "heavenly ladder" in its most elaborate form, which intriguingly intertwines with the metaphor of the "river of fire". This fiery river is crossed by a narrow bridge, allowing only select righteous souls passage to the opposite shore from whene they can proceed to God's Kingdom, while all others are condemned to burn in darkness and horror.

Christian beliefs about the torments of sinners in Hell, inflicted by dreadful demons, appeared as early as the birth of Christianity – for instance, in various apocryphal gospels and the Book of Revelation, only one of which found a place in the New Testament. Nevertheless, as Petrinski demonstrates, in Byzantine hagiography, descriptions of Hell are relatively rare and, at least before the tenth century, are usually not associated with the presence of demons but instead with darkness and fire. Petrinski's analysis of sources convincingly points to the increasing prevalence of these descriptions and themes, rooted in ancient culture and the Western Christian tradition of the early and High Middle Ages. During the ninth and tenth centuries, the interest of the Byzantine intellectual elite in ancient literature was very great. The ninth century was also a period of intensive but not necessarily friendly contact between the clergy of Constantinople and the Franks (especially around the baptism of the Bulgarians).

Given the peculiarities of the genre, hagiographical texts focus not only on demons in the fearsome aerial regions and the Underworld but also on their presence and harmful influence in the world of the living. The visible world is the battleground on which the forces of Evil try to regain and impose their power, defeated by Christ's incarnation. After Christ's victory, the Devil cannot win the war, and his power is nothing but an apparition, a nightmarish illusion, unable to harm physically those who genuinely believe in God. Still, through their deceptions and temptations, the Fallen Angel and his demons can lead people to sin and destruction. No place in the world is secure from their presence; but, most commonly, the saints' *Lives* describe them haunting the wilderness, the uncivilized and uninhabited space where only holy men and women dare to set foot. Yet even inhabited spaces are not immune to being haunted by malevolent forces. With astonishing mastery of language and imagery, the hagiographers vividly describe the demonic presence in monasteries, monks' cells, deserted churches, wells, bathhouses (associated with magical practices and sin), pagan shrines, tombs, cemeteries, and inhabited and uninhabited houses. In their skillful narratives, astute readers can discern echoes of Greco-Roman and Near Eastern mythological traditions, ancient literature, and contemporary folklore. Ultimately, there is no place in the visible world that is indisputably safe from the invasion of evil spirits. Restraining their malevolence and controlling them requires the presence and actions of holy persons or saints blessed with divine grace emanating from their relics and tombs. Occasionally, the hagiographers refer to demons confined in a particular space or an inanimate object, subjected them to excruciating pain, rendering them harmless.

Even this limited overview of the themes in *The Image of the Demon in Byzantium: Philosophical and Mythological Origins* demonstrates the significance and innovation of Gerasim Petrinski's research. Deliberately narrowing the subject of study to Byzantine hagiography between the sixth and the tenth centuries allows him to present these themes in their historical dynamics, taking into account the local specifics of different schools and enriching the analysis with details, some of which are unique to a school or even a single text. This hagiography demonstrates a pronounced character, one displaying a powerful syncretism, drawing from a "toolbox" of late antique concepts and mythological narrative, the living folklore of the time, as well as high and low theological discourses, and canonical and apocryphal texts. The period under study witnessed the consolidation and systematization of divergent demonological concepts, which would continue to be developed by subsequent authors in the following centuries. Despite the tendency towards stereotyping, Petrinski's interpreted texts provide a well-structured image of syncretic Byzantine culture, revealing its unique characteristics, but also its commonalities with Western cultural tropes. The development of an everyday religiosity, along with the integration of elements of apocryphal and superstitious beliefs, are particularly evident, and their continuation can be traced to the present day. The popularity of the Byzantine hagiographical texts has preserved them and established them as a part of Orthodox culture into our own time. They must now be recognized as an essential element of the European cultural heritage as well.

Prof. Georgi Kapriev, Ph.D., Dr. Sc.

INTRODUCTION

On June 13, 2014, the worldwide media published a "revolutionary" report. Pope Francis officially recognized the International Association of Exorcists[1] and thus legalized the necessity of appointing "professionals" to exorcise evil spirits. The stately tone of this proclamation is simply a continuation of a tendency in the development of the Church's attitude to demons and the Devil during the second half of the twentieth century. As Robert Moushembled points out, fifteen years before this announcement, Pope John Paul II introduced a reformed ritual for exorcism and increased the number of priest exorcists from fifteen to 120 in France alone.[2]

To properly understand this gradual recognition of the material existence of demons over the last decades, we must distinguish between the demon as a real, material subject and the evil spirit as a metaphor. In Ancient Greek, this distinction is apparent on a terminological level. The Bad/Evil (τὸ κακόν) is a substantive adjective without an image of its own, an abstract category whose *eidos* Plotinus found so difficult to define. The Evil or the Deceitful One (ὁ Πονηρός), on the other hand, is a prominent epithet for the Devil; this is the substantialized, materialized, external power that intentionally leads humans into temptation and destroys their souls. For the medieval as for the modern intellectual, innate human sinfulness, the imperfection of the human being, vigorously opposes such substantiation. The "Evil" is a spirit, the plague of materiality that necessarily infects the soul in its mortal shell during our brief earthly life. Everyone should fight against their imperfection and irrationality, objectified as the Devil, the invisible Enemy within, through knowledge and reason, with no external circumstances and supernatural creatures

---

[1] Carol Glatz, "Vatican formally recognizes international association of exorcists", National Catholic Reporter, July 3, 2014. https://www.ncronline.org/news/vatican/vatican-formally-recognizes-international-association-exorcists (accessed June 14, 2023).

[2] Robert Muchembled, *Une Histoire du Diable. XIIe-Xxe siècle* (Paris: Éditions du Seuil, 2000), 9.

allowed as excuses. In Western Europe, this concept paved the way for the Renaissance and the Enlightenment, the great development of the sciences and philosophy, and the gradual emancipation of intellectual life from the Church. Ideologically, it was fruitful as well. It provided the means for the psychological subjectivization of social issues, thus strengthening modern power structures. As an example of this discursive strategy, we could mention so-called "anger issues". According to some clinical psychologists, whose theories are useful as propaganda, social exclusion is not the result of objective factors, e.g., low income or the lack of a social welfare system, but of internal, medically explainable psychosis. The discourse of madness, so brilliantly defined and studied by Michel Foucault in the context of the paradigm of reason, replaces the old discourse of the "Evil within". The ideology of (neo)liberalism puts Agent in the place of Scene — in the terms of Kenneth Burke's dramatic Pentad — and, in this way, again puts personal will above circumstances in European history. Such an arrogant attribution of all responsibility to the human being is elitist and intellectual. Yet it is simultaneously condemned to unpopularity by depriving us of the ability to blame someone/something else for our misfortunes.

On the other hand, the concept of actual, material incarnations of Evil differs markedly from the metaphorical Devil. Deformed or too beautiful, dangerous or tempting, demons' bodies are a convenient "depository" for every human weakness and for everything in the world we do not understand. The name of the materialized evil spirit is Legion. It constantly changes shape, and its wicked deeds reflect everyone's deepest fears. However, it is the necessary manifestation of Chaos and absolute irrationality that the enlightened intellectual tried so feverishly to escape after the Great Witch-hunt (from the fifteenth to the seventeenth centuries).

Both images of the Devil, the metaphorical and the material, blend peculiarly in the context of Western civilization. During the Middle Ages, the demon discriminates. It possesses persons belonging to marginalized groups: heretics, lepers, Muslims, destitute old women. In France, the British Empire, Spain, Germany, and the Americas, the upper classes joined forces with the Church to produce a robust and extensive power structure, possessing well-developed theoretical means to detect and recognize the incarnated demon. This oppressive system fulfilled two social and political functions. The first was to restore the Church's authority, which had been seriously shaken by Savonarola and the Reformation in the late fifteenth and early sixteenth centuries. The second was to strengthen the emerging power of the central government by providing it with an external enemy to fight. The demon Chaos, proud and magnificent, rose up as an antagonist of state Order.

In 2000, Robert Muchembled published *A History of the Devil*. About seven years earlier, *The X-Files* was first broadcast and continued on the air until 2011. Since the late twentieth century, "demons" have been all around us in such series as *Supernatural* (2005–20, fifteen seasons), *Buffy, the Vampire Slayer* (1997–2003, seven seasons), *The Collector* (2004–6, three seasons), *Sleepy Hollow* (2013–17, four seasons), and many others. Of course, horror movies enjoyed great popularity from the first years of motion pictures, but TV series create an atmosphere of presence. In the latter, the supernatural is always next to us, and its "reality" overflows the screen into our world. The average viewer lives with the demons of Dana Scully and Fox Mulder, the Winchester brothers, and Morgan Pimm. Moreover, the belief in the materialized demon, so different from the intellectuals' metaphorical evil spirit, has probably been a part of folklore for tens of thousands of years; however, specific conditions are necessary for it to come to public light. After the collapse of the Soviet Union, the United States lost its eternal enemy, the "Evil Empire". Numerous discursive strategies were used from the early 1990s to the present to resolve this problem. The struggle against supernatural evil spirits and demons in movies and novels is only one part of these strategies, but by no means the least important one. The significance of *The X-Files* does not lie simply in its marking a turning point in Western popular culture. Its propaganda message is even more crucial. In however fantastic, simplistic, and infantilizing ways, through figures of FBI agents Mulder and Scully, the State declares its ability to cope with all sorts of enemies — including supernatural ones. Since 9/11, the dominance of the discourse on terrorism has contributed to developing a "fear syndrome", that feeling of constant threat and menace that enhances interest in the materialized demon.

We are paying so much attention to the Western European demon because of the enormous popularity and propaganda use of the images produced by Gothic novels and Hollywood cinema in modern popular culture. The concept of the demon as both a powerful and constantly hidden creature reflects the West's culture of guilt and the constant fear of Evil lurking with the human being and society. However, this image misleads us where the Orthodox world is concerned. The purpose of this book is to present another demon, one whose information is drawn from the Byzantine hagiographical literature from the time of Emperor Justinian I (mid-sixth century) to the epoch of Symeon Metaphrastes (mid-tenth century). Unlike its Western European "counterpart", in Gothic novels and Hollywood movies, the Byzantine demon can only conceal itself with difficulty and never very successfully. Its outer appearance is distinctive and recognizable. It is difficult to defeat, but the instruments for the struggle are clear to every Christian. The origin of its image is heterogeneous, but its type is obvious. The evil spirit is either too tall or too short; it is physically deformed; its color is almost always black; and it can take the form of a certain number of animal and human images. These are the elements that we will find in almost every hagiographical text. In addition, the demonization of sin-possessed emperors, dignitaries, and political figures is a powerful strategy for promoting the Iconodule dogma in the eighth and ninth centuries.

* * *

The image of the demon in Byzantine hagiographical literature has not yet been subjected to a comprehensive independent study. There has been research on the term "demon" before the Renaissance, but mainly in Antiquity from Homer to the dawn of the Hellenistic era. In the middle of the twentieth century, two voluminous studies were devoted to this problem: Marcel Detienne's *La notion de DAÏMÔN dans le pythagorisme* *ancienne*³ and Gilbert François's *Le Polythéisme et l'emploi au singulier des mots θεός, δαίμων dans la litterature grecque d'Homère à Plato*.⁴ These provide essential methodological guidelines for studying the demon in the narrow chronological period from Homer to Plato. We will use these books and articles as a basis for the presentation of the historical development of the Byzantine δαίμων, to which the second part of the present study is devoted. Such a short survey is necessary for several reasons. The Christian evil spirit (πονηρὸν πνεῦμα) is simply the final stage in the development of an idea of the supernatural, which probably preceded Homer. Many of the meanings expressed in the word δαίμων remain intact not only in medieval but also in modern thinking. We will pay special attention to the opposition between the Homeric demon as an unknown and incomprehensible force, an impersonal influence on human life, and the tendency to objectify this concept in literature. We will present the Hesiodic, the Pythagorean/Neo-Pythagorean, the Platonic/Neoplatonic, and the (Orthodox) Christian definitions of this complex notion.

Medieval demonology aroused the interest of scholars of high Christian theology. In 1896–97, Frederick Conybeare published his extensive study "Christian Demonology". Its first part focuses on the demon in the New Testament, and the second deals with the views of early apologists (especially Origen).⁵ Relying on a comprehensive survey of source material, Conybeare's study is still a valuable guide to the Christian concept of the world of Evil, despite the availability of much more recent research on the subject. As regards the doctrine of the Devil and demons officially accepted by the Church today, works on general theo-

---

3   Marcel Detienne, *La notion de DAÏMÔN dans le pythagorisme ancienne* [Bibliothèque de la Fac. de Philos. et Lettres de l'Univ. de Liège, Fasc. clxv.] (Paris: Les Belles Lettres, 1963).
4   Gilbert François, *Le Polythéisme et l'emploi au singulier des mots θεός, δαίμων dans la litterature grecque d'Homère à Platon* [Bibliothèque de la Faculté de Philosophie et Lettres de l'Université de Liège, fasc. CXLVII] (Paris: Les Belles Lettres, 1957).
5   Frederick Conybeare, "Christian Demonology I", *Jewish Quarterly Review* 8, no. 4 (July 1896): 576–608; and Conybeare, "Christian Demonology II", *Jewish Quarterly Review* 9, no. 1 (October 1896): 59–114.

logy, such as Christos Androutsos's *Δογματικὴ τῆς Ὀρθοδόξου Ἀνατολικῆς Ἐκκλησίας* can also be helpful.[6] Scholars like Thomas Provatakis, Richard Greenfield, and Charles Stewart, also pay much attention to this topic; their studies will be discussed below.

Old Testament demonology and the Judaic demonological tradition are the focus of numerous studies that shed light on the origins of many images in Byzantine hagiography. The so-called Testament of Solomon and the tradition related to it are also crucial to this book. This mysterious text was first published in the Patrologia Graeca series under Michael Psellus. The actual origins of the text and late antique demonological concepts are studied by Charles McCown in his critical edition of 1922.[7] Various studies are devoted to certain evil spirits in the Old Testament tradition, like Beelzebub.[8] The classic study of Alfons Barb, "Antaura, the Mermaid and the Devil's Grandmother"[9] and Raphael Patai's voluminous *The Hebrew Goddess*[10] are dedicated to the roots of the female demonic images in Jewish and early Christian literature. The Greek scholar Dimitrios Oikonomides presents the development of the wicked evil spirit Gello in great detail.[11] Numerous studies address the elements of the demonic images in Byzantium. To take one example, Gay Byron's *Symbolic Blackness and Ethnic Difference in Early Christian Literature*[12] deals with the black demon.

---

[6] Christos Androutsos, *Dogmatics of the Eastern Orthodox Church* [Greek: Χρῆστος Ανδροῦτσοσ, *Δογματικὴ τῆς Ὀρθοδόξου Ἀνατολικῆς Ἐκκλησίας*] (Athens, 1907).

[7] *The Testament of Solomon* [*Untersuchungen zum Neuen Testament* 9], ed. Chester McCown (Leipzig, 1922).

[8] W. E. M. Aitken, "Beelzebul", *Journal of Biblical Literature* 31, no. 1 (1912): 34–54; E-van MacLaurin, "Beelzebul", *Novum Testamentum* 20, no. 2 (April 1978): 156–60.

[9] Alfons Barb, "Antaura, the Mermaid and the Devil's Grandmother", *Journal of the Warburg and Courtauld Institutes* 29, no. 1 (1966): 1–23.

[10] Raphael Patai, *The Hebrew Goddess* (Detroit, Wayne State University Press, 1990).

[11] Dimitrios Oikonomides, "Gello in Greek and Romanian Literature" [Greek: Δημήτριος Οἰκονομίδης, "Ἡ Γελλὼ εἰς τὴν Ἑλληνικὴν καὶ Ῥουμανικὴν λαογραφίαν"], *Journal of the Greek Folklore Society* 30 (1975): 246–78.

[12] Gay Byron, *Symbolic Blackness and Ethnic Difference in Early Christian Literature* (London: Routledge, 2002).

The Byzantine image of the demon is a vast field of study that initially attracted the interest of French scholars in the second quarter of the twentieth century. One of the first attempts to shed light on this problem is "Contribution à l'étude de la démonologie Byzantine",[13] an article by Armand Delatte and Charles Josserand, based primarily on the above-mentioned Testament of Solomon, the Church Fathers (among them Basil the Great and Theodoret of Cyrrhus), and the works of Michael Psellus. The two scholars make some references to the philosophy of Iamblichus and to Greco-Roman mythology.[14]

Périclès-Pierre Joannou's *La démonologie populaire à Byzance au XIe siècle* is dedicated specifically to the image of the demon in hagiography.[15] In this text, Joannou attempts to draw a clear distinction between folklore and the so-called "critical demonology" developed by Michael Psellus in the mid-eleventh century. Joannou's method has many advantages. The *Lives*, compiled between 565 and 1000, hardly constitute a careful theoretical system of evil creatures, in contrast to the great eleventh-century humanist who laid the foundations for late Byzantine demonology. In Joannou's view, the evil spirit is not a systematic idea but principally a collection of elements (external manifestations, acts, methods of exorcism) scattered through the vast hagiographic corpus. We must consider, however, that Joannou fails to include a large number of important hagiographic texts in his study — the *Lives* of St. Peter of Atroa, St. Elias Speleotes, St. Phantinos the Younger, among others.

In the 1980s and early 1990s, several important books on the Byzantine demon were published. These relied on different types of sources and therefore applied different methodologies. The approach of the Greek scholar Thomas Provatakis, who in 1980 published his voluminous work *The Devil in Byzantine Art* (Ὁ Διάβολος εἰς τὴν βυζαντινὴν τέχνην),

---

[13] Armand Delatte and Charles Josserand, "Contribution à l'étude de la démonologie byzantine", in *Mélanges Bidez*, ed. Georges Mathieu [Annuaire de l'institut de philologie et d'histoire orientales, vol. II] (Brussels, 1934), 207–32.
[14] Delatte and Josserand, "Contribution", 219ff.
[15] Périclès-Pierre Joannou, *La démonologie populaire à Byzance au XIe siècle. La vie inédite de S. Auxence par M. Psellos* (Wiesbaden: Otto Harrassowitz, 1972).

draws on archeology and art theory.[16] He studies the Devil's servants as part of an iconographic type that remained relatively stable in Byzantium; for him, the demon is a phenomenon outside of time and space. The images of the ugly Ethiopian, the temptress, the snake, or the dragon, remain almost unchanged. The elements of deformation that we will meet so often in hagiographic texts, i.e., disproportions, squinting eyes, sinister grimaces, and the scars left by disease on the material bodies of demons, are also stable.

Radically different is the approach of Richard Greenfield in his book *Traditions of Belief in Late Byzantine Demonology*.[17] He recognizes the need to place the Byzantine conception of the demon in specific literary and folkloric contexts.[18] According to him, biblical literature, both Jewish and Christian, as well as Greco-Roman literature and mythology are the essential factors in the formation of a system of "traditions". Greenfield distinguishes only two such traditions: the "Standard Orthodox tradition" and "Alternative traditions". The period he has chosen significantly facilitates building such abstract systematizations of the supernatural. The Paleologian era has created an extraordinarily detailed corpus of texts, both canonical works and demonological treatises, which construct consolidated belief systems, whether or not accepted by the Church.[19] Concerning the Late Byzantine period, we can only agree with Greenfield's conclusions. By the thirteenth century, the troubled times of the great heresies, which ended with the Iconoclast crisis of 726–843, were long gone, and the disputes with Rome were about liturgical rather than dogmatic matters. Late Byzantine society had a well-defined corpus of theological works sanctioned by the Church, which allows us to speak of an "orthodox tradition" regarding demons and many other beliefs. Moreover, after the early eleventh century, the intelligentsia had access to

---

[16] Thomas Provatakis, *The Devil in Byzantine Art* [Greek: Θωμάς Προβατάκης, Ὁ Διάβολος εἰς τὴν βυζαντινὴν τέχνην], (Thessalonica, 1980).

[17] Richard Greenfield, *Traditions of Belief in Late Byzantine Demonology* (Amsterdam: Hakkert, 1988).

[18] Ibid., xi – xii.

[19] On this corpus of texts, see Greenfield, *Traditions of Belief*, 3–6.

such a corpus of texts and knew them well. Michael Psellus (1017/18–c. 1078) and Pseudo-Michael Psellus (mid-thirteenth century), the authors of the most popular demonological texts in Byzantium,[20] were highly educated people thoroughly familiar with both the biblical texts and their officially accepted reception by the Church. The situation was quite different in the second half of the first millennium AD, whose hagiographic production will be the primary source for the present study. During this period, despite the Arab invasions, Byzantium was still a world empire stretching from the Tyrrhenian Sea to the Euphrates. Within this area there coexisted various poorly homogenized ethnic groups and communities, loosely fused by the Christian religion and the official Greek language of the imperial administration. Countless heresies and teachings constantly shook the Church, which was still far from assembling a generally accepted and consolidated corpus of theological works that would eventually form an orthodox demonological tradition. During the Middle Byzantine era, the provinces created a rich literature in which the supernatural played an important role. Palaeologian Byzantium, the focus of Greenfield's study, was a small state, even for its time, wielding hardly any power west and south of Thessalonica, north of the Rhodopes, or east of Bithynia. Its literary tradition was mainly a creation of Constantinople and was, therefore, highly consolidated from a dogmatic, linguistic, and stylistic point of view. In this case, the "Orthodox tradition" was undoubtedly a real phenomenon.

The situation regarding the concept of the so-called "alternative traditions" in Greenfield's book is different. It is not simply that it is inapplicable to the epoch we will study — worse, it is unscientific. "Alternative" is simply a fine-sounding synonym for "other", and "other traditions" is a term that refers to almost nothing. "Other traditions" include ancient mythology and literature, Neoplatonic teachings, Jewish Apocrypha, various remnants of Eastern religions, various folklore elements of Slavic and Celtic origin, and probably many other beliefs. Could these

---

[20]   See Paul Gautier, "De daemonibus de Pseudo-Psellos", *Revue des Études Byzantines* 38 (1980): 128–30.

"fossilized" remnants of the past be classified as "traditions", even less as a single "alternative tradition"? For the hagiographic literature of the period 565–1000, our answer to this question must be entirely negative.

The Christianization of ancient mythological, literary, and folklore images and motifs has become almost a commonplace. Greenfield presents this highly complex process as a set of traditions. In Byzantine hagiography, the focus of the present study, the picture of the supernatural is neither orderly nor coherent. In many cases, the thin veneer of Christian dogmata covering various images and motifs, well known to the classical philologist, cannot conceal the millennial traditions underlying them. One of the principal subjects of research here is the specific "conservatism" that the hagiographers demonstrate in constructing the image of the Devil and his servants; for this purpose, they make use of different remnants from the Greco-Roman world in standard ways. At the outset, we could say that the hagiographers employed the same strategy that the ideological architect of the Byzantine Middle Ages, Emperor Justinian I, applied when constructing Hagia Sophia in Constantinople. Justinian ordered various architectural elements from ancient monuments be incorporated into his building. Following a similar model, the hagiographers carefully removed characters, plots, and motifs from their religious and philosophical context. In this manner, they create a superficially homogeneous Christian image of the demon, an image that can more easily be traced back to texts rather than to authentic folklore. The comparison to church architecture is neither accidental nor simply a metaphor. The Christian way of thinking, whether concerning the construction of a temple or a literary image, follows the same tactics. It takes the exquisite Corinthian capital from an ancient temple, incorporates it into the solid brick wall of a cross-domed Church, deprives it of its architectural function, and thus "seals" it as a beautiful ornament in a temple structure dedicated to Christ, the new Pantocrator. This system is simple; it can be applied anywhere throughout the ancient Eastern Roman Empire; and it works flawlessly. It is much more difficult to discern the authentic, living folklore of the Middle Byzantine period. Here, however, the very peculiarities of hagiography as a genre come to our aid. A saint's

Life is a popular text whose function is mainly propagandistic and rhetorical. It must reach as many readers as possible to fulfill this function; therefore, its conceptual system must be comprehensible to a broad audience. As a result, we can assume that the ancient motifs, images, and stories used by hagiographers were not selected at random. The authors presumably chose only those that were present in some form in the beliefs prevalent among their readers. This method is highly rhetorical. The authors consider the opinions and the needs of their particular audience as in some way influential.

The third approach we need to consider is the ethnographic. Charles Stewart applies this method in his book *Demons and the Devil: Moral Imagination in Modern Greek Culture*,[21] published shortly after Greenfield's study. He is interested in the demonic and supernatural creatures in contemporary Greek folklore, mainly on the island of Naxos. In the fifth chapter of his book, Stewart draws attention to the official Orthodox concept of Evil and its creations. However, he disregards the definition of "alternative traditions" proposed by Greenfield and limits his analysis to various aspects of the beliefs held by some closed twentieth-century Greek communities.

To the three great studies of the 1980s, we must add the doctoral thesis of Stelios Lambakis, published in 1982 under the title "Descent into the Underworld in Byzantine and Post-Byzantine Literature" ("Οι καταβάσεις στον Κάτω κόσμο στη βυζαντινή και στη μεταβυζαντινή λογοτεχνία").[22] The second part of this work is dedicated to early Christian and Byzantine apocryphal writings and has proved very useful to our study. It focuses on a specific literary motif, namely the descent into Hell in ancient, apocryphal, and satirical Byzantine and post-Byzantine literature. Such a motif is inescapably connected to the image and role of the demon in Byzantium.

---

[21] Charles Stewart, *Demons and the Devil: Moral Imagination in Modern Greek Culture* (Princeton: Princeton University Press, 1991).

[22] Stelios Lambakis, "The Descents into Hell in the Byzantine and Post-Byzantine Literarure" [Greek: Στέλιος Λαμπάκης, "Οι καταβάσεις στον Κάτω κόσμο στη βυζαντινή και στη μεταβυζαντινή λογοτεχνία", PhD diss (University of Ioannina, 1982).

Some light on the Byzantine demon is also shed by Cyril Mango. In the seventh chapter of his book *Byzantium: The Empire of New Rome* — "The Invisible World of Good and Evil"[23] — he studies the earthly Empire and its hierarchy, headed by the Emperor, modeled on the kingdom of Heaven as a prototype. In this way, the world of Evil becomes a distorted, perverted simulacrum of God's creation, and demons become anti-angels with the Devil as their Antichrist-Emperor. This concept allows Mango to draw some essential general conclusions about the world of Evil and medieval ideas of the demon. Central to his theory is the idea of parody. The evil spirit is a pathetic and weak creature with no true power, easily defeated by merely pronouncing the name of God. This is the main difference between the Byzantine demon and the proud, mighty fallen angel that Western civilization inherited from the era of the so-called "wars of religion" between Protestants and Catholics (in the sixteenth and seventeenth centuries). The descriptions of the Devil and his servants in Byzantine literature very often approach parody and are able to make even the modern reader smile.[24] Another of Mango's objects of interest is the so-called "aerial tollhouses" (τελώνια), already studied as a literary phenomenon as early as Franz Cumont's 1922 book *After Life in Roman Paganism*.[25] The problem posed by the origin of this concept will constitute one of the main topics in the fourth part of this study. The primary source on which Mango bases his conclusions is a short hagiographical text, probably composed in the 930s, and titled "The Terrible and Useful Vision of the Monk Cosmas". We should note that Mango uses only the short, Synaxarion version of this text and not the original form, published by Christine Angelidi in 1983. He does not reference other essential works that describe such visions, e.g., the "Short Chronicle" of George Hamartolos or the *Life* of St. Phantinos the

---

[23] Cyril Mango, *Byzantium: The Empire of New Rome*, (London: Scribner's, 1980), 151–65.
[24] Alexander Kazhdan, *A History of Byzantine Literature*, vol. 1: 650–850 (Athens: Institute for Byzantine Research, 1999), 300ff.
[25] Franz Valery Marie Cumont, *After Life in Roman Paganism: The Funeral Rites, Gods and Afterlife of Ancient Rome* (New Haven: Yale University Press, 1922).

Younger. Mango's 1992 article "Diabolus Byzantinus"[26] adds almost nothing new to his contributions on a theoretical level. However, he extends his research into some hagiographical sources, e.g., the *Lives* of St. Anthony the Younger and St. Nikon Metanoeite.

* * *

Whatever their strengths, the books and articles enumerated above leave gaps in the Byzantine concepts of the supernatural, in the first place regarding the sources. Serious research on the hagiographic material has been made only by Joannou in a brief introductory study that is at most forty pages long, which can hardly be said to place the *Lives* of the period between the fourth and the eleventh centuries in any particular literary, cultural, or religious context. On the other hand, Greenfield deals with the Palaeologian period, which is both very distant and very different from the Middle Byzantine era. The main subject of Steward's research is primarily modern Greek folklore, even though he tries to discover its ancient and early Christian roots. These authors, despite making use of an impressive corpus of sources, rarely refer to a single hagiographical text. The *Lives* of the saints between the eighth and the tenth centuries are almost entirely omitted. Their methodologies prove unsuitable for a period when Byzantium was still a vast and thriving cosmopolitan empire. The images and stories that will form the subject of the following pages must be studied along with the peculiarities of the hagiographical genre. They have to be placed in the context of ancient mythological and philosophical systems. The pictures drawn by the hagiographers were a realistic reflection of the Byzantine beliefs of this troubled time of brutal wars and religious controversies, and a genuine and exciting representation of a distant and exotic era.

---

[26]   Cyril Mango, "Diabolus Byzantinus", *Dumbarton Oaks Papers* 46 (1992): 215–23.

Part One
BYZANTINE HAGIOGRAPHY: RHETORICAL ASPECTS, FORMS, AND TYPOLOGIES

CHAPTER 1
EPIDEICTIC AND HAGIOGRAPHICAL EPIDEICTIC

1. Byzantine hagiography between rhetoric and literature

Before proceeding to this book's main subject, i.e., the images and incarnations of demons in Byzantium, we must first briefly circumscribe our research in terms of genre, history and geography. The corpus of sources — the Saints' *Lives* — suggests a distinctly interdisciplinary approach to the problem of the world of Evil. From a modern point of view, hagiography can be perceived as a literary genre with its own internal rules and "mechanisms of expression", as Alexander Kazhdan defines them.[27] These mechanisms were standardized in a particular, well-studied rhetorical matrix. However, we must remember that neither Ancient/Medieval Greek nor Latin have a word for imaginative literature.[28] No theory of literature of any kind existed in either Antiquity or the Middle Ages. As George Murphy points out, "there was not any single denominative term which could be applied to the collection of percepts for the instruction of those interested in preparing non-oratorical discourse".[29] Ancient and medieval novels, which by today's standards belong to fiction, undoubtedly existed: shorter works like *The Romance of Alexander the Great*, famous ancient Greek novels like *Daphnis and Chloe*, and the late Byzantine romances were an essential part of Ancient literature. However, such texts were not classified together, and no branch of criticism in Antiquity or the Middle Ages studied them. A theoretical system like that found in the rhetorical treatises that scrutinized every little detail of oratorical discourse was not constructed even

---

[27] Kazhdan, *History of Byzantine Literature*, 1: 5.
[28] George Murphy, *Rhetoric in the Middle Ages: A History of Rhetorical Theory from Saint Augustine to the Renaissance* (Berkeley and Los Angeles: University of California Press, 1974), 136ff.
[29] Ibid., 27.

by the Alexandrian scholars, who studied the classical heritage with such thoroughness. The term "literature" proves even more problematic when discussing hagiography. A saint's *Life* is a complex text that fits into the paradigm of the three main functions of an oratorical text (*officia oratoris*) as defined by Cicero: it has to entertain (*delectare*), to teach (*docere*), and to move emotionally (*movere*).[30]

These days, the biography of a saint is commonly regarded as boringly didactic. For the modern reader not drawn to Byzantine literature professionally, it is only a simple (even simplistic) and not very interesting story about some semi-legendary holy person, replete with old-fashioned Christian morality. To gain a proper understanding of any information provided by hagiography, we must shed this impression entirely; in other words, we must endeavor to read sacred biographies like the Byzantines. A saint's *Life* is not just a relic of the past but often involves events nearly contemporary to both the author and the reader. In the Byzantine world, full of monasteries and churches, the strait path to holiness that the biography describes so vividly is not only didactic and moralistic; it also excites and entertains its audience, just as Cicero advises the orator to do.[31] The hagiography of the period under study bears some comparison to today's spiritual literature, published by various biblical societies as modern bestsellers. The plots, with their numerous adventures and journeys, with the struggles of various demonic creatures or evil emperors, remind us of horror novels. The tradition of the ancient adventure romance is alive in these texts.

Hagiography successfully fulfills the second of Cicero's *officia oratoris* as well. It teaches and conveys a didactic message of a religious or political nature. In other words, it has a strategic and tactical propaganda function. As a propaganda tool, "the Byzantines, in particular, turned

---

[30] See Cicero, *De oratore*, ed. E. H. Warmington, trans. E. W. Sutton, H. Rackham, vol. 1: Books I, II (Loeb Classical Library 348) (London: William Heinemann, 1967), 2:27.115. See George Kennedy, *A New History of Classical Rhetoric* (Princeton: Princeton University Press, 1994), 142.

[31] See Kazhdan, *History of Byzantine Literature*, 1: 2.

hagiography into an industry", says Oliver Thomson.[32] For example, the hagiographies of the Iconoclast period, with very few exceptions, aim to discredit the policies of the emperors Leo III, Constantine V, Leo V, and Theophilos in the eyes of the public and to entrench the monastic authority challenged by the central government. The adventure novel here becomes a rhetorical work that uses a fascinating plot to "change or reinforce its audience's opinions, beliefs, convictions, and actions".[33] The ethos of the Saints, of their character and behavioral patterns, are constructed in a deliberate (and, as we shall see, standardized) way to erect a paradigm of the "ideal" Orthodox Christian. The distinctiveness of this paradigm lies in the fact that it is practically unattainable for laypeople and challenging even for those who have devoted themselves to monastic life. However, as Quintilian says, if something has not yet been achieved, it may still be achieved in the future.[34] In any case, even attempting to emulate the ideal ethos of the Saint has a beneficial effect on the audience of hagiographic discourse.

The hagiographic text is rhetorical not only in terms of its primary functions. It has a rhetorical structure and a strict set of rules. Every Saint's *Life* is an encomium, a eulogy, and the matrix of this genre was established as early as the late Hellenistic period through the corpus of rhetorical exercises (the so-called *Progymnasmata*),[35] used in schools

---

[32] Oliver Thomson, *Easily Led: A History of Propaganda* (Stroud: Sutton Publishing, 1999), 35.

[33] Donka Alexandrova, *Metamorphoses of 20th-century Rhetoric* [Bulgarian: Донка Александрова, *Метаморфози на реториката през XX в.*] (Sofia: Sofia University Press, 2013), 33.

[34] Quintilian, *The Institutio Oratoria*, ed. and trans. Harold Butler, (London and New York: G. P. Putnam's Sons, 1921), XII.11.25.

[35] The four treatises called *Progymnasmata* (Προγυμνάσματα) were written between the late first century B.C. and the fifth century A.D. by Theon of Alexandria (*Theonis Progymnasmata*, ed. Leonhard von Spengel, *Rhetores Graeci*, vol. 2, (Frankfurt am Main: Minerva, 1966), 59–130; see *Progymnasmata. Greek Textbooks of Prose Compilation and Rhetoric*, ed. and trans. George Kennedy [Atlanta: Society of Biblical Literature, 2003], 3–74), Pseudo-Hermogenes (Hermogène, "Exercices préparatoires", ed. Michel Patillon, *Corpus Rhetoricum*, vol. 1 (Paris: Les Belles Lettres, 2008), 180–206; for an English translation, see *Progymnasmata*, 73–88), Aphthonios (Aphthonios le Sophiste, "Exercices préparatoires", *Corpus Rhetoricum*, 1: 112–62; for an English

throughout the Greco-Roman world in Late Antiquity and then in the Middle Ages. The ancient theory of epideictic (ceremonial) oratory was powerful enough to impose its rules even on the hagiographers who formally rejected the ancient art of rhetoric, and there is a relatively stable textual structure in both sacred biographies and secular eulogies. In his book *Hagiographische Topos: Griechische Heiligenviten in Mittelbyzantinischer Zeit*, Thomas Pratch reconstructs the specific commonplaces (*topoi*) used by the authors; his comparison between the two matrices, the secular/rhetorical and hagiographical, shows a clear continuity. We will present them briefly below, along with their respective terminology in Greek, Latin, and German.

Undoubtedly, the most "rhetorical" part of both secular and hagiographic praise is the **introduction** (*exordium*, προοίμιον). Its structure is

---

translation, see *Progymnasmata*, 89–127), and Nicholas of Myra (*Nicolai progymnasmata*, ed. Joseph Felten [Rhetores Graeci 11] (Leipzig: Teubner, 1913), 1–79; for an English translation, see Kennedy, *Progymnasmata*, 129–72). The standard schoolbook on the subject after the fifth century is the work of Aphthonius The bibliography on the "Progymnasmata" is extensive: see, in general, George Kennedy, *A New History of Classical Rhetoric*, 202–8; Michel Patillon, *Corpus Rhetoricum*, 1:52–103; Gerasim Petrinski, *Late Antique and Byzantine Rhetoric* [Bulgarian: Герасим Петрински, *Късноантична и византийскаканонична реторика*] (Sofia: Sofia University Press, 2014), 144 and 178–80, with bibliography and references to primary sources. The first category of fourteen standard exercises includes commentaries on different types of literary and quasi-literary texts: *mythos* (fable, fictional story), *diēgēsis* (narrative, plausible story), *chreia* (a sentence of a famous and respected author), *gnōmē* (anonymous maxim), *anaskeuē* (a refutation of the plausibility of a given narrative), *kataskeuē* (approbation, confirmation of a given narrative), *topos* ("commonplace", or accusation against an abstract vice), *encomion* (praise), *psogos* (invective), *synkrisis* (comparison, or "double encomium"), *ēthopoieia* (personification), *ekphrasis* (description), *thesis* (argument, or essay), and *nomou eisphora* (introduction of a law). On the *encomion*, see in particular Hermogène, "Exercices préparatoires", VII.1-14; Aphthonios le Sophiste, "Exercices préparatoires", VIII.1-3; Kennedy, *A New History of Classical Rhetoric*, 205; Patillon, *Corpus Rhetoricum*, 1:83–86; Henri Marrou, *A History of Education in Antiquity*, trans. George Lamb (London and New York: Sheed and Ward, 1956), 198ff; Petrinski, *Late Antique and Byzantine Rhetoric*, 144 and 178–80.

rigorous.³⁶ The text begins with a maxim, usually a quote from Holy Scripture (χρεία/γνώμη, *sententia*).³⁷ The author must then display his modesty by questioning his ability to successfully present the great deeds of the Saint (*rerum magnitudo, Größe des Gegenstands*). Finally, the reasons for writing the work are given (*causa scribendi, Begründungstopos*). They are also standardized: the deeds of the holy person should not be forgotten (*oblivionis remedium, Mittel Gegen das Vergessen*), they should serve as an example for others (*exemplum, Erbaulicher Zweck*) and should hold an attraction because they have not been told before (*non prius audita, Ich bringe noch nie Gesagtes*). In this part, some authors also include the topos of "rejection of the ancient art of rhetoric" (*reiectio rhetoricae, Ablehnung der antiken Rhetorik*); they assiduously deny using any manipulative sophisms in their works.

The standard structure of the hagiographical prooemium meets the essential functions of the introduction according to the ancient rhetorical treatises. The initial maxim aims to attract the reader's interest (*attentum parare*). The "modesty" topos focuses on winning goodwill (*benevolum parare, captatio benevolentiae*) through a display of the author's ethos. By setting down his reasons for writing, the hagiographer endeavors to make the audience docile (*docilem parare*).

The introduction, both in secular and religious biographies, is followed by the detailed presentation of the protagonist's life and deeds; this part is called **narratio**.³⁸ The narration in the secular eulogy usually begins with the external circumstances (the background) that influenced the hero's life. Firstly, the noble origin (*nobilitas*, εὐγένεια) and the homeland (*patria*, πατρίς) of the subject are described. Since encomia usually refer to public figures and, above all, to rulers, this topos is vital to justify

---

[36] Thomas Pratsch, *Der hagiographische Topos. Griechische Heiligenviten in mettelbyzantinischer Zeit* [Millennium-Studien zu Kultur und Geschichte des ersten Jahrausends n. Chr., Band 6] (Berlin: De Gruyter, 2005), 19–56.

[37] On the *chreia* and *gnome* as rhetorical exercises see Petrinski, *Late Antique and Byzantine Rhetoric*, 129–34.

[38] For alternative terms like *prothesis* (πρόθεσις), see, among others, Heinrich Lausberg, *Handbook of Literary Rhetoric*, trans. Matthew Bliss, Annemiek Jansen, and David Orton (Leiden: Brill, 1998), 136ff.

their power and right to rule. Noble descent is relatively unimportant for a saint, so this part is frequently either omitted or modified in hagiography. As an essential component of a saint's background, the homeland is almost always described in both secular and religious biographies. Especially in hagiological texts, the "earthly home" topos (*Irdische Heimat*) is opposed to the "heavenly home" (πατρίς οὐράνιος, *Himmlische Heimat*) that awaits the holy person after death.[39] The description of the homeland is usually followed by a short account of the protagonist's parents. They could be rich and famous or poor and uneducated, but the orator must always be capable of bringing forward and emphasizing their virtues. In a saint's *Life*, material wealth is less important than it is in a secular biography; if present, the hagiographer must give a detailed account of the charity of his hero. The wealthy family's sudden loss of prosperity and status could be used as a turning point in the life of the future Saint, who then dedicates himself to God. In secular and hagiographic encomia, the hero's birth and childhood are marked by signs and omens indicating future greatness or holiness. For example, a sign could be the long period of childlessness in the family and the many prayers addressed by the parents to God, as a result of which the desired child is born.[40] The baptism and its surrounding events include a specific set of omens for the future of the holy man or woman. This topos can be found not only in encomia but also in invectives (ψόγοι). For example, in his colorful description of the baptism of the infant Constantine (the future iconoclast emperor Constantine V), son of Emperor Leo III, Theophanes Confessor relates that the little heir to the throne defecated in the baptismal font and treats this as a sign of his future sinfulness.[41] Childhood signs of future virtue, greatness, and holiness also appeared in secular and religious biographies. One such sign could be unnatural wisdom (*puer maturus* and *puer*

---

[39] Pratsch, *Der hagiographische Topos*, 56–58.
[40] Pratsch, *Der hagiographische Topos*, 72–74 (*Kinderlosigkeit der Eltern und Geburt nach Gebet*).
[41] *Theophanis chronographia*, ed. Carl de Boor, vol. 1 (Hildesheim: Olms, 1963), 400.7-10.

sapiens, *Fruhe Reife* and *Hohe Begabung*).[42] The "education" topos (παιδεία, *educatio*, *Bildung*) is also present in both types of biographies, but in hagiographic eulogies, its application is much more complicated. The saint does not need too much secular education to achieve sacred goals; the only fundamental knowledge required is that of God's Truth, revealed in the Holy Scriptures. For this reason, the authors carefully draw a distinction between three types of education:

- Secular education (Weltliche Bildung), which the future Saint often rejects;
- Spiritual education (*Geistliche Bildung*), which is the essential topos in this category;
- Self-education (*Autodidaktische Bildung*), which is relatively rare.

After covering education, secular eulogies frequently describe the hero's wealth (πλοῦτος), both earned and inherited. This topos does not aim simply to show the hero's abilities and resourcefulness, or his family's eminence. In Latin, the word *fortuna* means both *luck* and *riches*; if somebody is lucky and wealthy, this is treated as a clear sign that the gods have blessed him and, presumably, that they will also bless the subjects of such a fortunate individual. This topos is a critical component in the justification of the right to rule, especially in the Roman and then in the Byzantine Empire. In hagiographies, material wealth and worldly power are treated quite differently. They are opposed to the real purpose of the holy person's life, which is to gain spiritual riches and ultimately to enter the Kingdom of God. Gregory, the obscure author of the *Life* of St. Basil the Younger (mid-tenth century), gives an excellent example of this opposition between mundane and divine opulence. The Saint himself was

---

[42] Both secular and hagiographical encomia abound with such motifs, and the imagination of the authors is often really astonishing. For example, according to the *Life* of Empress Theophano, the future Saint refused to suck the breast of the wet nurse after her mother's death. Her mother tried hard to find a suitable woman to feed her daughter, but all her efforts were in vain. Finally, one of the servants, who was childless, tired from the baby's constant crying, gave the little girl her breast to soothe it. Miraculously, the barren woman began breastfeeding little Theophano (Empress Theophano, §4).

very poor, and all his life needed the financial support of wealthy residents of Constantinople. He had, however, a female servant, a slave called Theodora. When she died, Gregory, who knew both Basil and Theodora, asked God in his prayers to reveal to him the fate of the woman's soul. God sent him two angels, who led him through the narrow streets of the capital city. At some point, he realized that the alley had become very lofty, and the group walked through the air. Shortly afterwards, Gregorius and his companions reached a vast and imposing gate. The angels knocked on the door, and from inside emerged the dead Theodora herself. Smiling, she explained to the terrified Gregory that behind the gate and the wall lay St. Basil's palace.[43] In his hagiography, the material poverty of the future Saint is opposed to his spiritual and heavenly wealth.

After describing the Saint's background, the hagiographer had to expound on his subject's physical and spiritual virtues (*Beschreibung der Personlichkeit*).[44] In this part, the influence of the ancient rhetorical matrix is clearly discernible. The idea of *kalokagathia*, i.e., the harmonious combination of bodily, moral, and spiritual virtues, is pivotal for ancient Greek philosophy, mentality, and political ideology. However, Plato contrasts it with the image of the old and ugly Socrates. In secular biographies, the standard components of this ideal are health (ὑγεία), bodily strength (ῥώμη), height (ἡλικία), and physical beauty (κάλλος). Christian authors applied the ancient *Kalokagathia* topos very carefully and with mixed feelings in their eulogies. In secular biographies, the strong and handsome male body is crucial for the creation of a positive image of rulers and other political figures. On the other hand, tyrants and heretics are frequently described as physically weak, ugly, and repulsive. One of the best examples of such "black propaganda" can be found in the diplomatic report of Bishop Liutprandus of Cremona, who was sent in 968 as an emissary of his master, the German Emperor Otho I, to the court of Emperor Nikephoros II. Liutprandus was very displeased by the cold recep-

---

[43] Basil the Younger, Part II, §4.1-4.
[44] Pratsch, *Der hagiographische Topos*, 106–8.

tion he received from the Byzantine authorities and the poor living conditions provided for him in Constantinople. Bitterly, he describes Nikephoros in a very humiliating way. The ruler's appearance is downright disgusting:

> He was a rather monstrous man, a Pygmy, with a fat head and small eyes like a mole. His graying beard was short, broad, and thick. A neck as thin as a finger deformed his appearance. He looked like a pig with a thicket of hair on his head and was as black as an Ethiopian – someone you would not want to meet in the middle of the night. He had a swollen belly, a tiny bum, and legs too long for his stature. His shoulders were narrow and his feet were as big as his legs. He wore Sikyonic sandals and was clad in a purple[45] tunic, but it was old, worn out, and its spoiled decoration hideous to behold. His tongue was careless, his mind cunning as a fox, and his treacherous and deceitful nature made him a veritable Ulix.[46]

The Emperor's physical repulsiveness reflects his equally despicable soul. A wicked spirit resides in a hideous body.

Physical appearance is also an essential element of hagiography, but the usage of this topos is more complicated. The beauty (ὡραιότης, κάλλος, Schonheit der Gestalt) and the bodily harmony (ἁρμονία σωματική, körperlichen Harmonie) of the Saint reflect spiritual virtues, both in male and in female personages.[47] In general, the holy person is never ugly or physically deformed. As a typical example of a saint's *kalokagathia*, Pratch quotes a passage from the *Life* of St. Ioannikios the Great:

---

[45] The editor of the text suggests that *villinus* is an error in the manuscript, and that the original word is *visinus*.

[46] "Liutprandi Relatio de legatione Constantinopolitana", ed. Immanuel Bekker, *Die Werke Liutprands von Cremona* [Scriptores rerum Germanicarum in usum Scholarum ex Monumentis Germanicis Historicis separatism editi] (Hanover and Leipzig: Hahnsche Buchhandlung, 1915), §3: "*hominem satis monstruosum, pygmaeum, capite pinguem atque oculorum parvitate talpinum, barba curta, lata, spissa et semicana, foedatum, cervice digitali turpatum, proxilitate et densitate comarum satis hyopem, colore Aethiopem, cui per mediam nolis occurere noctem, ventre extensum, natibus siccum, coxis ad mensuram ipsam brevem longissimum, cruribus parvum, calcaneis pedibusque aequalem, villino sed nimis veternoso vel diuturnitate ipsa foetido et pallido ornamento indutum, Sicioniis calceamentis calceatum, lingua procacem, ingenio vulpem, peiurio seumendacio Ulyxem*".

[47] See Petrinski, *Late Antique and Byzantine Rhetoric*, 18–27.

> [Ioannikios] surpassed everyone in mind and strength. Still, he also looked pleasant and wonderful to everyone, and not only because of the charm of his blossoming physical beauty, but also because of his wisdom, moderation, and praiseworthy temperament...[48]

In contrast, it is common for hermits and monks to be attired in socially unacceptable, dirty, and ragged clothes. Their hygiene is frequently wanting, and their bodies could even be ridden with ulcers and worms from long months or years of seclusion far from civilization. This appearance, which generally would provoke disgust, is a sign of holiness.

Physical appearance is an essential element in the depiction of sinfulness as well. As a consequence of his downfall, the demon is out of proportion, deformed, and ugly; this ugliness is the physical reflection of absolute corruption. Unlike his counterpart in modern Hollywood movies, the demon rarely appears in Byzantine literature as a wealthy, handsome man or attractive woman. We will discuss this unholy hideousness of body and soul in the third part of this study.

The next sub-topos of the rhetorical matrix, both in hagiographies and secular biographies, concerns the moral virtues of the subject (γενικαί ἀρεταί, Kardinaltugenden).[49] Four of these are common to laypeople and religious figures: prudence or practical wisdom (φρόνησις, prudentia, Klugheit), justice (δικαιοσύνη, iustitia, Gerechtigkeit), bravery and courage (ἀνδρεία, fortitudo, Tapferkeit) and temperance (σωφροσύνη, prudentia, Besonnenheit). Thomas Pratch calls another four "theological" virtues (theologischen Tugenden),[50] which are typically exclusively for religious figures. These are piety (εὐσέβεια, pietas, Frömmigkeit), faith (πίστις, Glaube), love (ἀγάπη, Liebe) and hope (εὐελπισία, Hoffnung).

---

[48] Ioannikios (Peter), §4: πάντων μὲν κατεκράτει τῇ τε γνώμῃ καὶ ῥώμῃ, πᾶσί τε ἡδὺς καὶ ὡραιότατος κατεφαίνετο, οὐ μόνον διὰ τὸ ἐπανθοῦν αὐτῷ εὐειδὲς τῆς ἡλικίας καὶ τῇ τοῦ κάλλους στιλπνότητι, ἀλλ' ἤδη καὶ διὰ τὸ εὐσταθὲς καὶ εὔτακτον καὶ ἐπαινετὸν τοῦ τρόπου καὶ τῆς ἀναστροφῆς τούτου φιλοσοφώτατον. See Pratsch, Der hagiographische Topos, 107.

[49] On the usage of the four main rhetorical virtues in hagiography, see Pratsch, Der hagiographische Topos, 206–8. The author cites passages from the Lives of St. Theodore Studite, St. George of Amastris, St. Theophanes the Confessor, St. Patriarch Ignatios, and others.

[50] Pratsch, Der hagiographische Topos, 208ff.

Only occasionally could other virtues be added to this standard "set",⁵¹ — e.g., moral purity (ἁγνεία, puritas, Reinheit), tranquility (ἀπάθεια, apathia, Gelassenheit), mortification of the flesh (νέκρωσις, mortificatio, Abtötung), humility (ταπείνωσις, humilitas, Bescheidenheit), wakefulness (ἀγρυπνία, Schlaflosigkeit).⁵² The latter are variations of the general and theological virtues. For example, tranquility is a particular case of temperance, mortification of the flesh is an act of extreme faith, and wakefulness shows practical wisdom.

The **description of the deeds** is the next part of the encomium. In secular biographies, this part is usually based on a relatively simple complex of topoi reflecting the physical and spiritual virtues described in the preceding section of the text. The worthy politician must act selflessly and consistently in the public interest, take significant risks, and make great efforts to achieve his noble goals against all odds and with no help. His decisions must be innovative, intelligent, and far more effective than anybody else's.⁵³ This simple model of narration, invented as early as the Hellenistic period and clearly discernible in historical and rhetorical works, remains the same today. If we take a close look at modern electoral campaigns, we find the very same pattern in the representation of political leaders. Of course, the PR specialists of the twenty-first century have many more technological resources than their ancient counterparts, the rhetoricians. However, the means of persuasion and, more surprisingly, the expectations of modern audiences remain very much the same as in ancient Rome and Byzantium.

On the other hand, the hagiographical matrix is more elaborate than the rhetorical one, but the difference between the two models is not only in the details. The romance, the adventure novel, and the mythological tale have a much larger influence on the religious than on the

---

⁵¹ Ibid., 208 and 209-212.
⁵² Ibid., 208.
⁵³ Gerasim Petrinksi, *The Bride-Shows in Byzantium: Rhetoric, Literature, Propaganda* [Bulgarian: Герасим Петрински, *Конкурсите за красота във византийския императорски двор: реторика, литература, пропаганда*] (Haskovo: Poliraph-Jug, 2015), 25-27.

secular biography. The astute observer could trace its elements back to the *monomyth* studied so thoroughly by Joseph Campbell in his book *The Hero with the Thousand Faces* (1949). According to Pratch, the future saint's active life would begin with a *call to adventure* (κλῆσις, vocatio, Berufung),[54] which, in contrast to the hero of the fairy tales, he or she rarely rejects. The adventure itself is the continuous struggle with the Devil and his servants, both demons and evil humans (magicians and heretics [ἐχθροί, adversarii, Gegenspieler]). The scene of this battle could be the monastery, the secluded hermitage in the desert (ἀναχώρησις, *reclusio, Rückzug*), the stylite's tall column, or even the streets of some city. The Saint could also start a long journey (ἀποδημία, peregrinatio, Wanderschaft), full of deadly perils, trials, and devilish temptations (πειρασμός, temptatio, Versuchung),[55] just like some ancient mythological hero.[56] This part of the hagiographical text is the primary source of information for the image of the demon in Byzantium. Behind many of the supernatural creatures that the holy traveler defeats so fearlessly, we will discern the slight shadow of ancient Greek mythological monsters, Slavic river dragons (the so-called *zmey*), and many other popular images.

After the "road of trials", teeming with action, the Saint is ready to begin the contemplative life of a shepherd and teacher (ποιμὴν καὶ διδάσκαλος, pastor et doctor, Hirte und Lehrer). At this stage of the narrative, the fight against Evil does not cease, and the holy person continues to perform miracles (θαύματα, miracula, Wunder) until death comes.[57]

The last topos, common to both secular and religious biographies, is *euthanasia* (εὐθανασία). The Greek term, of course, has nothing to do with the English sense of "euthanasia", but instead means "worthy death". The good ruler is usually represented as dying heroically in battle, like Constantine X in 1453, or passing away peacefully, surrounded by his relatives and friends, like Constantine the Great in 337. In contrast, the

---

[54] See Joseph Campbell, *The Hero with a Thousand Faces* [Bollingen Series XVII] (Princeton: Princeton University Press, 2004), 45–54.
[55] Pratsch, *Der hagiographische Topos*, 160–70.
[56] See Campbell, *The Hero*, 89–100 ("The Road of Trials").
[57] Pratsch, *Der hagiographische Topos*, 244–48 (exorcism).

tyrant — murdered by an enraged mob, poisoned by rivals or by his wife, or perishing slowly and painfully from some venereal disease — always deserves a humiliating death. In secular biographies, the demise of the main character is certainly an essential element. However, the rhetorical matrix gives the authors considerable freedom to represent it as they wish. Yet, since death is the passage to the Kingdom of God, this occupies a much more important place in a Christian Saint's life. The holy person's demise (θάνατος, *obitus*, *Tod*) is usually described in great detail and includes numerous sub-topoi. If not a martyr, the future Saint would first fall sick (*Letzte Krankheit*), knowing that death is coming (*Wissen um den nahen Tod*), would give final instructions (*Letzte Verfügungen*), and would bid farewell to all (*Abschiedsgemeinschaft*). The hagiographer would record the precise day and the hour of death (*Lebensalter und Todeszeitpunkt*) and describe the burial in detail (*Beisetzung*). The last two sub-topoi, the translation of the relics and the posthumous miracles, are so important that they frequently become the subject of separate voluminous works and collections of texts.

The above two matrices, the rhetorical and the hagiographical, are neither thoroughly accurate nor entirely applicable to all secular and religious biographies. Despite their shortcomings, they provide a relatively good picture of the standard stages in the development of the main characters and the strategies for building the ethos of these characters as political and spiritual leaders. However, they show significant differences. When composing their secular eulogies, students of rhetoric were supposed to abide strictly by rules of the matrix, but fully developed authors had the right to alter the rhetorical model in a manner that best suited the specifics of their chosen genre. The topoi in ancient and medieval biographies enumerated above (homeland and family, birth and education, physical and moral virtues) are rather the variously colored pieces of an ancient mosaic than a completed picture. In order to reach the goal and create the desired persuasive image of the main character, the hagiographer could reassemble the pieces of the rhetorical pattern, accentuate some of the colors of the Saint's ethos, even omitting a topos entirely. This metaphor is all the more suitable since the words "color" and "χρῶμα" in ancient rhetorical treatises are used both in Latin and Greek as technical terms for the "argument from the character".

By contrast, the hagiographical matrix, as reconstructed by Thomas Pratch, has never been formulated so explicitly, probably because it was just a logical extension of the well-known rules of the secular encomium. The authors of religious biographies and eulogies used the standard model much more freely than their secular colleagues. In addition, they made some significant changes to this model following the Christian hagiographical discourse. The image of the secular political figure rests on certain features, e.g., noble origin, learning, wealth, physical beauty and strength, and dress.[58] When any of these topoi failed to suit the subject, the good orator or biographer had to find a way to apply them nevertheless, even if by sheer falsification. A typical example is the "noble origin" of Emperor Basil I invented by his son Leo VI in a long encomium for his father. On the other hand, the subject of the hagiographical encomium is almost the complete opposite of the political leader praised in secular encomia. The features which are a source of popularity and respect for the politician are simply an unbearable burden for the holy monk who had utterly refused worldly power and wealth for the sake of a godly life in Christ. Despite this, noble origins and wealth are not omitted in hagiographical texts — quite the contrary. As relatively well-educated people, the hagiographers were acquainted with the rhetorical matrix that was a part of formal rhetorical training.[59] They could disregard neither their education nor the expectations of their audiences. For this reason, they re-elaborated the rhetorical model and sometimes reversed the meaning of a particular topos to make it suitable for their specific subject. Where the secular biographer would typically describe the ruler's wealth, the author of a saint's *Life* would praise his hero's extreme poverty. Instead of being dressed in beautiful, expensive clothes, the monk would be clad in a single worn, ragged,

---

[58] Clothing appears intermittently in eulogies of laypeople. See, e.g., the vivid description of the attire of Emperor Nikephoros II Phocas, whose *worn-out cerise garment, braided with old and dirty ornaments*, is compared to the beautiful, rich clothing of the Holy German Emperors Otto II and Otto III ("Liutprandi Relatio", §3).

[59] Petrinksi, *Late Antique and Byzantine Rhetoric*, 142–46.

and dirty cassock. In place of the well-educated intellectual, the hagiographer would depict a humble, holy man completely disinterested in worldly knowledge.[60] Instead of the healthy, strong, and victorious general, the author would describe the selfless monk who despises his mortal body and mortifies it in every possible way. In fact, from the point of view of classical rhetoric, the hagiographer composes not a serious panegyric but an "adoxographical"[61] one, a sort of "encomium of Poverty," "encomium of Simplicity," or even "encomium of Death." Some authors go to extremes, as in the *Life* of St. George Chozebites (sixth century), in which the future Saint forbids his servants to wash his filthy and stinking dishes.[62]

All these extremes in the image of the holy monk led to an interesting but superficial parallel with the image of the demon. The evil spirit is frequently dirty and stinky, but this results from its primordial sinfulness, which is impressed on its material body. The Saint often has the same outer appearance, but this is a consequence of rejecting of everything worldly, a reflection of the Saint's absolute purity of soul. The two images are similar but by no means identical. The ugliness of the demon is always physical; its material body is deformed and repulsive. In contrast, the foulness of the holy monk, nun, or hermit relates only to clothing, accessories, and personal hygiene; because the body is the mirror of the soul, there is never real bodily ugliness or deformation. Both the rhetorical topoi and the ancient ideal of the *kalokagathia* remain intact; they

---

[60] See, e.g., John the Psichaites, §4, where the secular art of rhetoric is presented as equal to the veneration of demons.

[61] "Adoxography" and "paradoxography" are subgenres of epideictic eloquence. The two terms could be translated roughly as *parody*. The "adoxological" encomium praises things, ideas, and persons so ugly, dangerous, or vicious that they are in themselves unworthy of praise (ἄδοξοι ὑποθέσεις). The standard example of such discourse is Gorgias' *Encomium of Helen*, where the sophist tries to defend Helen of Troy. The a-doxographical tradition is widespread and includes works like the *Encomium of Death* by Polydamas, the *Encomium of Baldness* by Synesius of Cyrene, and the *Encomium of Poverty* by the Cynic philosopher Proteas. On the other hand, "paradoxography" praises objects so trivial or useless that they do not merit mention. To this group belong, e.g., works like the *Encomium of the Fly* by Lucian of Samosata and the *Encomium of the Hair* by Dio Chrysostomus. On this subject, see Arthur Pease, "Things without Honor", *Classical Philology* 21, no. 1 (January 1926): 27–42.

[62] George of Choziba, §2.6.

have simply been reconsidered, transformed, and embedded in the new hagiographic matrix.

2. Typologies

Byzantine hagiography attracts scholarly interest as early as the seventeenth century. In 1643, in Brussels, the Jesuit Jean Bolland or Bollandus (1596–1665) and his assistant Godfrey Henschen or Henschenius edited the first two volumes of the new corpus, which would eventually include all existing Latin and Greek Saints' *Lives*. The so-called "Bollandists" continued their work during the next three centuries, and the third and final edition of the *Acta Sanctorum* series was published in 1940. This voluminous corpus still includes the only editions of some important Byzantine texts, like, e.g., the *Lives* of St. Germanos of Kosinitza, St. Elias Speleotes, and Bishop John of Gotthia. Hagiography became an object of even greater interest in the second half of the nineteenth century. In 1882 the *Analecta Bollandiana* series was founded as a supplement to the *Acta Sanctorum*. In the twentieth and the twenty-first centuries numerous *Lives* were edited separately, along with comprehensive commentaries: *La Vie merveilleuse de saint Pierre d'Atroa* by Vitalien Lorraine (1956), *Saint Anastase le Perse et l'histoire de la Palestine au début du VIIe siècle* by Bernard Flusin (1992), *La vita di San Fantino il Giovane* by Enrica Folieri (1993), *The Life of St. Basil the Younger* by Alice-Mary Talbot (2014), and many others.

Probably the first typology of hagiography as a genre was proposed by the German literary scholar Karl Krumbacher (1856–1909) in his seminal book *A History of Byzantine Literature from Justinian until the Fall of the Eastern Empire* (*Geschichte der byzantinischen Literatur von Justinian bis zum Ende des Oströmischen Reiches*, 1897). Krumbacher's classification can be summarized in a diagram:

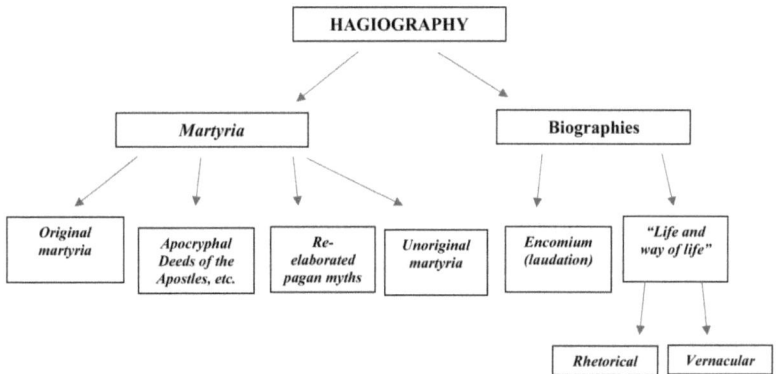

According to Krumbacher, the two main categories of the hagiographical genre are *martyrion* and *biography*. The *martyrion* (μαρτύριον) focuses on the martyrdom of the first Christians who shed their blood for Christ. The first such texts were compiled as early as the second half of the first century A.D. Their apparent goal was to present good examples and inspire fervent devotion among the adepts of the new religion. The so-called "original *martyria*" subcategory includes martyrs until 313. Almost all of these were written before the end of the fourth century. However, the core texts were repeatedly revised and adapted for new audiences until the epoch of Symeon Metaphrastes (late tenth century). The second subcategory in Krumbacher's classification is the apocryphal "Deeds of the apostles and other personages of the Old and the New Testament". They were very popular before the end of the fourth century, but the tradition continued until the ninth and tenth centuries. The third subcategory includes "re-elaborated pagan myths". These played an important role in the initial adaptation of the Christian religion to the needs and the traditional beliefs of the cosmopolitan Eastern Roman Empire. To these texts, we owe many syncretic images of "martyrs" who were not actual historical figures. Finally, the fourth subcategory consists of the so-called "unoriginal *martyria*", based on older texts and various folk legends. They are dedicated to characters from different epochs, and their authors are usually very distant chronologically from the events described. In the ninth and tenth centuries, the interest in this type of literature intensified. Typical representatives of this trend are Niketas-

David of Paphlagonia[63] and, of course, Symeon Metaphrastes with his "translations" (μεταφράσεις) of older texts into the standardized Attic Greek used by the intellectuals of the tenth century.

The *martyria*, dedicated to early Christian martyrs, could only provide sparse information (if any) on the historical persons they described and on the main subject of this study, i.e., the image of the demon. Objectivity demands that we use this type of hagiography only as a secondary source. Our main corpus will include the second category of Krumbacher's typology, namely the Saints' *Lives* (Βίοι ἁγίων). These began to emerge around the mid-fourth century with the famous biography of the Egyptian hermit Anthony the Great, written by the Patriarch of Alexandria, St. Athanasios the Great. In contrast to the *martyria*, the authors of these religious biographies are often known at least by name and are relatively close in time to their heroes. Therefore, they could provide relatively accurate chronological information or specific *termini post* and *ante quem*. Usually, unlike the authors of the *martyria*, biographers had direct information about the life and personality of the characters described, or some written accounts of them. The zeitgeist reflected in their texts is also completely different from the *martyria*. The martyrs for the Faith had material enemies; they did not fight demons or evil spirits but pagan tyrants. It is only logical that the stories of their martyrdom should focus less on the image of supernatural Evil than on Satan's destructive influence on humans. In the time of St. Anthony the Great and his followers, persecution against the Church had already ceased. Martyrs still existed, especially during the Iconoclast era. However, hagiographers' interest focused chiefly on the Saint's life and not on the moment of self-sacrifice for Orthodoxy. The authors of such biographies occupy the crossroads between the pursuit of plausibility, which would make their texts persuasive, and the need to idealize a holy person whose life should serve as an example to others. To what extent the biographer will adhere to the principles of accuracy or to those of elaborate and beautiful elo-

---

[63] See Alexander Kazhdan, *A History of Byzantine Literature*, vol. 2: 850–1000 (Athens: Institute for Byzantine Research, 2006), 95ff.

quence depends on his desire, goals, and literary abilities. This problem certainly affects the description of the supernatural. Some biographers prefer to stick to the original material, like the authors of the *Lives* of St. Theodore Sykeotes, St. Ioannikios the Great, St. David, Symeon, and George of Lesbos; these texts are among the most valuable and picturesque sources for the image of the demon. Other hagiographers deliberately avoid materialized Evil because, in Byzantine intellectual circles and among the higher clergy, superstition (δεισιδαιμονία) was despised at least as much as it is today. To this category belong various texts, usually written by educated Constantinopolitans and dedicated to political figures, e.g., St. Theodore Studite, Empress Theodora, Patriarch Euthymios, and Patriarch Ignatios. A similar attitude to the demonic is evident in the works of theologians like St. John of Damascus, who flatly refutes the widespread superstitions about demonic dragons and the evil witch Gello.[64] Finally, some authors distance themselves from the superstitions of their less educated contemporaries but give objective information about such beliefs nevertheless. A typical example of this can be found in the works of Ignatios the Deacon, especially his biography of Patriarch Tarasios.

The hagiographic text, whether produced in Abbasid-ruled Palestine or the imperial capital, is, in most cases, written in Greek.[65] Whether this Greek is Attic or vernacular, ornate or free of tropes and figures constitutes an essential criterion for its classification. According to this criterion, *Lives* are divided into two subcategories displaying stylistic and functional differences. The first is "laudation" or "praise" (ἐγκώμιον or ἔπαινος). Such texts are for oral delivery at the feast of a saint. For this reason, they are burdened with various rhetorical devices. Usage of this

---

[64] Joannes Damascenus, "De draconibus et strigibus", in MPG, vol. 94 (Paris, 1864), 1604.

[65] For example, the short *Life* of St. Romanus, a monk at the St. Sabbas monastery in Palestine and martyr (†780), was initially written in Arabic and later translated into Georgian (see Ihor Ševčenko, "Hagiography of the Iconoclast Period", in *Iconoclasm: Papers Given at the Ninth Spring Symposium of Byzantine Studies*, ed. Antony Bryer and Judith Herrin [Birmingham: University of Birmingham, 1975], 114). Such cases are extremely rare.

"high" style distorts accurate information and impairs objectivity, just as metrical translation diminishes the correct transmission of meaning of a poetic text.

Krumbacher calls the second subcategory of sacred biography "Life and way of life (βίος καὶ πολιτεία)". We will use the briefer term "*Life*" or "sacred biography" for this case. The first component, the Βίος, is the chain of events and circumstances that make up the life of the saint. Πολιτεία refers to the saint's dynamic behavior towards these circumstances, towards other people, towards God, and, of course, towards the Devil and his servants. This type of biography has strong roots in the Greco-Roman literary tradition, especially in the novel and in the ancient biography developed by authors like Plutarch. On the other hand, as mentioned above, its structure and system of topoi reflect the ancient rhetorical matrix, reworked to suit the needs of the new Christian world. The rapid development of this type of hagiography after the sixth century is a consequence of a phenomenon that Alexander Kazhdan calls "historiographical fatigue".[66] The long chain of monumental historical works in Late Antiquity came to an end with the great challenge of the Arab invasion in the second quarter of the seventh century. During the so-called "Dark Centuries" (the seventh to the ninth), these were replaced by sacred biographies. Saints' *Lives* had many advantages, which made them much more suitable for the new epoch. They were relatively short and full of exciting stories of adventures and miracles. Their language was relatively simple and close to everyday speech. Last but not least, they were more capable of effectively conveying an ideological, political, and religious message. Only a small circle of intellectuals could read and understand the voluminous works of authors like Dio Cassius, Socrates Scholasticus, Zosimus, or Procopius. The audience for the short biographies of saints was much broader, and this popularity made them a mighty ideological weapon, unparalleled in the Ancient world. Some of the sacred biographies of this subcategory use a very ornate style and their authors make an effort to employ classical Attic Greek. Krumbacher

---

[66] KAZHDAN, *A History of Byzantine Literature*, 1: 19–21.

calls such *Lives* "rhetorical".⁶⁷ Good examples of these are the biographies written by Ignatios the Deacon and by Niketas-David of Paphlagonia.⁶⁸ By contrast, the so-called "vernacular" *Lives* were written in the spoken language of the epoch and their syntax is relatively simple. Their authors usually lack deep theological knowledge and rarely engage in complicated dogmatic issues. The saints that they praise so vividly are frequently almost their contemporaries. Such texts provide us with countless stories of miracles and struggles against the Devil's servants and are among the most informative sources on the Byzantine demon. In the seventh century, such vernacular biographies were still relatively long texts, written by well-educated authors. As a typical example, we could mention Bishop Leontius of Cyprus (mid-seventh century) who wrote the *Lives* of St. Symeon the Fool (mid-sixth century), and Patriarch John the Merciful of Alexandria (late sixth to early seventh century). The heyday of the vernacular hagiography, however, was the period of the Iconoclast crisis (726–842), when Iconodule propaganda flourished, fulfilling its aim of establishing and promoting the veneration of the defenders of the icons. During the first iconoclast period (726–788), the persecution of Orthodox monks and clergy was severe; therefore, hagiographical production combined elements of the old *martyrion* and the newly emerging biography. The prototype of a this holy martyr was St. Stephen the Younger, who was executed under Emperor Constantine V in 764/765. The policy of the heretic rulers against Orthodoxy during the second iconoclast period (715–743) was much more moderate, and thus gave rise to a different image of the saint. Holy men like St. Ioannikios the Great (754/5 or 762–November 3, 846) and St. Peter of Atroa (773–837) chose to live mostly as wandering adventurers and as brave champions against evil spirits in western Asia Minor. Vernacular biographies were produced in other parts of the Empire as well. In the ninth and tenth centuries, the monastic communities in the distant island of Sicily, and in Italy, con-

---

[67] On the "rhetorical" ("rhetorischen") and the "vernacular" ("volkstümlichen") *Lives* see Karl Krumbacher, *Geschichte der byzantinischen Literatur von Justinian bis zum Ende des Oströmischen Reiches*, (München: C. H. Beck, 1897), 181.

[68] On them, see Part One, Chapter Two, §6 and §7.

stantly threatened by Muslim invasion, founded a flourishing hagiographic school, to which we owe the important *Lives* of many local monks and hermits like St. Elias the Younger, St. Elias Speleotes, St. Phantunus the Younger, and St. Sabbas the Younger. During this period, the Empire restored its full control of the Peloponnese and mainland Greece after the Slavic invasions of the sixth and seventh centuries. In these territories, until recently inhabited mostly by pagan Slavic tribes, the influence of the Church was enhanced by prominent local figures like St. Athanasia of Aegina, St. Luke of Steiris, St. Nikon Metanoeite, and others. Their "vernacular" biographies were highly popular.

Some of the most important saints were praised in encomia and vernacular biographies. For example, two encomia, one biography, and several collections of miracles were dedicated to St. Anastasios of Persia. In such rare cases, the differences between the different hagiographic categories become very apparent. St. Anastasios's *Life* is full of valuable and informative accounts of the image of the demon in seventh-century Palestine. On the other hand, the encomium to him by the famous poet George of Pisidia shimmers with its elegant style but fails to provide any information on the supernatural: it is very poor in any concrete biographical details.

Short and reworked versions of original vernacular *Lives* are often included for liturgical purposes in collections called *Menologia* or *synaxaria*. The most important compilation of this kind is the *Menologion*[69] prepared by Symeon Metaphrastes, probably in the 980s.[70] Symeon Metaphrastes was a typical Byzantine intellectual of his age. His efforts to find, re-elaborate, and systematize the previous hagiographers' works followed the same tracks as many other encyclopedic collections of the tenth century, when Emperor Constantine VII (913–959), his associates,

---

[69] On the content and the style of the *Menologion* of Symeon Metaphrastes, see Kazhdan, *A History of Byzantine Literature*, 2: 236–47.

[70] On Symeon Metaphrastes see Krumbacher, *Geschichte der byzantinischen Literatur*, 200–203; Paul Lemerle, *Le premier humanisme byzantine. Notes et remarques sur enseignement et culture à Byzance des origins au Xe siècle* [Bibliothèque Byzantine. Études 6] (Paris: Presses Universitaires de France, 1971), 293ff; Kazhdan, *A History of Byzantine Literature*, 2: 231–47 (esp. 233–34).

and their pupils struggled to gather all available information on subjects like diplomacy, geography, history, agriculture, and even veterinary medicine.[71] The collection compiled by Symeon was subjected to a strict "translation" from spoken language to the artificial Attic dialect of educated circles. The style of the original texts, too simple for the tastes of the epoch, was reworked to meet the highest rhetorical standards. Many *Lives* survived only in their Metaphrastian version. The popularity of the *Menologion* caused the loss of many authentic sources. An ornate style and artificial language are not the only shortcomings of these revisions. Not uncommonly, Symeon significantly changes the content and mercilessly censors everything that does not fit his moral values and worldview. This censorship deeply affects the representation of materialized Evil that interests us here. A good example is the *Life* of St. Ioannikios the Great. According to the two original versions of this vernacular text, during one of his adventures in the mountains of western Asia Minor, his outer appearance frightened an elderly couple. He was extraordinarily tall, his clothes were ragged, and his eyes blazed with inner power. To them, Ioannikios was a supernatural creature, a spirit (πνεῦμα) or a ghost (φάντασμα). However, they could not decide if he belonged to the realm of Heaven or of Hell.[72] The Metaphrastian version completely omits any supernatural element. The reader has the impression that the couple took him for a common bandit and was intimidated by the prospect of being robbed and murdered.[73] In the worldview of the erudite audience of the tenth century, there was no place for old wives' tales about ghouls and demonic monsters because Evil always lurked within a mortal's soul.

The last category of hagiographical texts consists of popular collections of miracles. As already mentioned, miracles (θαύματα) are an integral part of every sacred biography since the holy person has the *authority to trample on snakes and scorpions*, i.e., to defeat the powers of Evil. Such stories, sometimes almost contemporary with their author, provide

---

[71] On the encyclopedic works associated with Emperor Constantine VII and his circle, see, in general, Lemerle, *Le premier humanism*, 267–300.
[72] Ioannikios (*Peter*), §42; Ioannikios (*Sabbas*), §11.
[73] Ioannikios (*Metaphr.*), 48B.

this study with invaluable information about the image of the demon. The miracles attributed to some very popular saints grew over time and were compiled in voluminous collections. A typical example of this specific hagiographic category is the rich tradition around St. Anastasios of Persia, which includes a whole collection of miracles and a whole pamphlet dedicated exclusively to his *Roman miracle*.[74] Between the sixth and tenth centuries, many of these compilations were usually written long after the events described and can hardly be admitted as reliable and accurate sources. Like the synaxaria, they will be used here mainly as comparative material.

* * *

Krumbacher's typology is based on two main criteria: language and style. This approach is practical from a literary point of view since it outlines the characteristics of the hagiographic genre. However, the texts must be placed in their proper context to serve effectively as sources for the demonic image. During the twentieth century, scholars like Khrisanf Mefodievich Loparev, Germaine da Costa-Luillet, and Ihor Ševčenko analyzed the geographical distribution and the historical context of Byzantine hagiography from the seventh until the tenth century as criteria for typology. In our second chapter, we will rely on this methodology in our short survey of the primary hagiographical schools in Palestine, Constantinople, Asia Minor, Greece, Sicily, and Southern Italy.

In terms of chronology, our corpus of texts has a reasonably clear time frame. The period begins with an event representing a milestone in the political and cultural development of Byzantium, i.e., the death of Emperor Justinian I (527–565). Often referred to as the last truly Roman emperor, Justinian was tireless in his effort to give his Empire at least an essential religious unity. He fought fervently to defend Orthodoxy from the remnants of the old pagan cults and heresies. His victory over Monophysitism was by no means decisive. However, he successfully purged the

---

[74] On these texts, see Part One, Chapter 2, §1.

Empire of the old consolidated religious and philosophical systems, cults, and mysteries during his reign. When he ascended to the throne, the Neoplatonic school in Athens and the schools in Alexandria were still flourishing. At the time of his death, the auditoria where the voice of Proclus Diadochus once sounded were long closed, a vast basilica proudly stood in the courtyard of the famous Library of Hadrian in Athens, and the last prominent Neoplatonic teacher in Alexandria, Olympiodorus the Younger, lived his final years. In 527, the magical practices common throughout the Late Antique world were seldom considered a felony, and learned pagans were still free to teach their philosophy, sprinkled with mysticism. In these final years of the dying Ancient world, the word "demon" had different meanings for heathens and Christians.[75] By 565, and not without the active efforts of the imperial propaganda machine, the demonization of all that the conceptual system of Chalcedonian Orthodoxy could not explain was almost complete. After Justinian's reign, the ancient myths, deities, and practices survived only as flotsam of the distant past, emptied of their deeply religious and philosophical meaning, and loosely held together by the abstract Christian idea of Evil. In the *Life* of St. Theodore Sykeotes (late sixth–early seventh century), where this transitional period is very well described, "Artemis" is just one of the names of the so-called "noon demon" of the Old Testament, which haunted an unnamed place in the province of Galatia.[76] In this text, nothing remained of the ancient goddess but her name and her relationship with the wilderness. This is the beginning of the epoch that will be the focus of the present study.

Of course, the year 565 as a turning point is relative. Numerous popular saints were born during Justinian's reign and died after he did; we cannot omit their biographies. One of these essential texts is the *Life* of St. Symeon Stylites the Younger (521–592),[77] whose battles with various evil spirits the author vividly describes. The already-mentioned exor-

---

[75] On the evolution of the term "demon" in the Neoplatonic and Christian traditions, see Part Two.
[76] Theodore Sykeotes, §16.4. On the "noon demon", see also Ps. 90:6.
[77] For this Saint, see Part One, Chapter 2, §1.

cist St. Theodore Sykeotes (†613) lived under Justinian; in the course of his long biography, one can hardly find a single paragraph without some demonic story.

The studied period ends with the epoch of Symeon Metaphrastes. In the course of the tenth century, vernacular hagiography gradually declined and learned intellectuals, educated in the best rhetorical manner, replaced the humble biographers of the seventh to tenth centuries, with their spoken language and their taste for exciting and entertaining stories of adventures and demonic possessions. The stylistic re-elaboration of the texts and their "translation" into Attic Greek is a process which reveals important trends. The Byzantine culture of the Dark Ages was not so much associated with classicism as a system of grammatical rules, stylistic requirements, and a lexical apparatus. In this context, hagiographic texts written in a vivid and understandable language found a harmonious and dignified place. In addition, amid the general insecurity of the Arab invasions, they served a propaganda role in complex religious and political conditions. In the second half of the ninth century, and during the tenth, the long battle for the very survival of the Empire was won. The Abbasid caliphate, once such a significant threat, was in decline. The border with the Muslim world held steady, and the victories of generals and emperors like John Kourkouas, Nikephoros II Phocas, and John II Tzimiskes secured the Empire's core. Mainland Greece and the Aegean islands, including Crete, were once again controlled by Constantinople, and trade flourished. The nightmare of the Iconoclast heresy was long gone, and religious unity was formally restored. Of course, the seeds of future crises were already sown, but the Golden Age of Patriarch Photius, Aretas of Caesarea, Constantine VII, was now at its peak. The texture of Byzantine society, especially the Byzantine elite, had also changed. The Iconoclast Emperors and reasonable Orthodox rulers like Nikephoros I had struggled without mercy against the emerging class of the big landowners (*dynatoi*), who were gradually destroying the defensive system of the Empire. Now, a new proud aristocracy took the place of the free peasant-soldiers (*stratiotai*),[78] and a new generation of educated intellectuals replaced the old popular hagiographers.

Of course, these changes did not affect every corner of the Empire equally. The "translation" of the old hagiography is predominantly a Constantinople phenomenon. The Muslim military threat was still very real on the periphery, especially in Southern Italy, Sicily, and the Aegean islands. The Imperial administration in mainland Greece was gradually restored after the victories over the Slavic populations. However, the Church still had to fight the remnants of paganism through significant figures and preachers like St. Luke of Steiris, St. Germanos of Kosinitza, and St. Nikon Metanoeite. In these regions, the vernacular hagiographic tradition was alive at least until the end of the tenth century. The *Lives* produced there are among the most important sources for the image of the demon. For this reason, the period on which we will focus ends with the death of St. Nikon in the late tenth or early eleventh century.

Geography is an essential criterion for the typology of Byzantine hagiography as well. The scope of action of the most significant holy figures of Byzantium almost always coincides with the zones affected by the most severe conflicts. Great figures emerged in Palestine, Syria, Eastern Asia Minor, and Egypt from the late sixth century to the conclusion of the wars with Sasanian Persia (the Battle of Nineveh, 627). These areas were not only fields of constant military action and atrocities against Christians but hotspots of religious conflict as well. Large populations of Monophysites and Nestorians still inhabited them, and these groups were actively opposed to official Orthodoxy. The voluminous biographies of saints like St. Symeon Stylites the Younger, St. Symeon the Fool, St. Golinduch, and St. John the Merciful, who fought both against Zoroastrianism and the heresies, reflect the cultural, religious, and political developments of the Byzantine East just a few decades before the loss of these territories. Evil spirits play a crucial role in these *Lives*, and the many demonic stories are highly informative not only about contemporary folk-

---

[78] The *stratiotai* (στρατιῶται) were free peasants who had their own land in exchange for military service.

lore and beliefs but also about these images' philosophical and mythological origins. In addition, during this period, the imperial capital and the central parts of the Empire proved much less productive than the Eastern provinces: the only preserved text from central Asia Minor is the *Life* of St. Theodore Sykeotes. Palestine, already under Arab rule, continued to be a significant literary center in the eighth and even in the early ninth century. In the ancient Great Lavra of Saint Sabbas (*Mar Sabbas*) near Jerusalem, the *Lives* of hermits like St. Stephen the Sabbaite and St. Theodore of Edessa were written. This monastery gave John of Damascus the relative security he needed to write his polemical works against the Iconoclast heresy.

During the Iconoclast crisis, hagiography ceased to represent a phenomenon of the imperial periphery. In the eighth century, Constantinople and the nearby territories had become an arena of fierce religious and political struggles. The capital produced iconodule polemical texts like the *Lives* of St. Stephen the Younger, Patriarch Tarasios, Patriarch Nikephoros, and many others. Another iconodule stronghold was Bithynia in northwestern Asia Minor. The local monastic schools produced the biographies of saints like Ioannikios the Great, Eustratius of Agauros, Makarios of Pelekete, and Peter of Atroa. We will often refer to their struggles with Satan's servants in this study.

In the ninth and tenth centuries, Muslim invasions grew into a permanent threat to Byzantine possessions in Sicily and Southern Italy. In these distant parts of the Empire, monasticism flourished, and the *Lives* of local saints like Elias the Younger, Elias Speleotes, Sabbas the Younger, and Phantinos the Younger tell the story of the heroic Christian defense against the incursions of the Fatimid Caliphate of Egypt and the Aglavid emirate of Kairouan. These texts remind the modern reader of adventure novels with tales of sieges and pirate raids, long journeys, distant exotic countries, and haunted caves and towers.

As mentioned above, the Greek mainland was the last focal point of hagiographic activity in the period under study. While the holy monk of Italy and Sicily is predominantly a leader and sometimes even a warrior, the Greek saint of the ninth and tenth centuries is a builder and a Christian missionary. The regions of Macedonia, Attica, Peloponnese, Thessaly, and Boeotia were gradually gaining importance politically, economically, and culturally. On the other hand, for more than two centuries (late sixth– early ninth century), imperial control over these territories was very weak, even merely formal. The local Slavic tribes were left to govern themselves according to their own customs, even though the Orthodox Church was still relatively strong in cities like Athens. Following the re-establishment of the imperial administration, in many rural areas of the Greek mainland, especially the central Peloponnese, the Christian religion had to be restored, pagan cults and customs eradicated, and new churches built. These were the main tasks of the local holy leaders, and it is evident from their *Lives* how well they accomplished their mission.

Above we presented the texts that will be the focus of this study, and outlined the characteristics of their genre. As we will see, many political, ideological, religious, and cultural factors influenced the image of the Byzantine demon during this long period. During the sixth and seventh centuries, the demon still reflected ancient mythological and philosophical traditions of belief. During the Iconoclast crisis, in the imperial capital and on the periphery of the great Empire, there was no theoretical system that could produce an entirely coherent and consistent image of the evil spirit, beyond some very general references to the Scriptures and the writings of the Church Fathers. The outer appearance of the demon was still highly dependent on local beliefs. Nevertheless, the elements of the demonic image still reflect the philosophy and the folklore of the Ancient world, though through the prism of Christian theology. In the tenth century, the intellectual circles of Constantinople were already on the path to the formation of a solid and durable conceptual system that would lead to the treatises of Michael Psellus in the eleventh century and of Pseudo-Psellus two centuries later.

CHAPTER 2
SCHOOLS, AUTHORS, AND TEXTS

1. Biographical hagiography in the sixth and seventh centuries

The period from the death of Justinian I (565) until the demise of Heraclius I (641) marks the conclusion of a whole epoch. At the beginning of this period, the Empire was a world state spread over three continents. Its only rival was Sasanian Persia. By the mid-seventh century, it was a devastated country that had lost Egypt, its breadbasket, and all its Asian provinces southeast of Cilicia. Slavic tribes poured over the Byzantine European territories, and the only relatively secure strongholds were Asia Minor, Constantinople, and isolated Sicily. The literature of these troubled times, especially the hagiographic literature, reflects the sunset of the cosmopolitan world of Late Antiquity, marked by terrible disasters like Justinian's plague, the devastating earthquakes in Antioch, the invasions of the Persian Shahs Khosrow I Anushirvan (531–579) and Khosrow II Parviz (590–628), and finally the first Arab conquests. As mentioned above, the hagiography of this period is related predominantly to Saints who lived and were active in Eastern and Central Asia Minor (the provinces of Galatia and Cilicia) and especially in Syria and Palestine. Constantinople, Rome, Egypt, and Sicily appear sporadically in these texts, while the southern part of the Balkan Peninsula is absent. Most of the texts belong to the category of biography, especially the vernacular subcategory (βίος καὶ πολιτεία), even though many were later re-elaborated. These territories were the most critical zones of political, religious, and military conflict. The demonization of invaders and heretics is very clear, and the Devil and his servants play a crucial role in them.

Two lengthy biographies written during this period are devoted to stylites. The term "stylite" (στυλίτης) denotes a specific type of ascetic who dwelled on top of a column (στῦλος, κίων). This pillar was a relatively complex structure, large,[79] built upon a high base (βάσις, ὑποπόδιον) with the support of special technical devices (μηχαναί) (μηχαναί).[80] A platform of about two square meters,[81] surrounded by iron bars (τὰ σίδηρα τοῦ καγγέλλου),[82] allowed the hermit to lie down for a while and accept visitors. The pillar of the first well-known stylite, Symeon Stylites the Elder (c. 390–September 2, 459), had no shelter,[83] but Symeon Stylites the Younger (521–596/597) had something like a leather tent spread over the iron parapet. The author of his *Life* says that the Saint decided to change his first shelter, which had a small window (θυρίς) and admitted a little by sunlight, for a new one, which was completely dark. In this way, his ascetic feat grew even greater.[84]

The two stylite saints of the late sixth and early seventh centuries were Alypius Stylites and Symeon Stylites the Younger. The former[85] was born around 515 in the Paphlagonian town of Adrianople (Asia Minor). He lost his father when he was three years old, and his mother put him under the care of an old monk called Theodore to make him a priest. The future saint was ordained oeconomus and deacon of the Church in his native town. In his thirtieth year, Alypius decided to become a hermit and settled in a small cell near Adrianople. Shortly afterward, pious local inhabitants built a column for him, and he lived on it for the rest of his life. Alypius died when he was ninety-nine years old, during the reign of Emperor Heraclius (610–641). According to his biography, a monastery and nunnery formed around the pillar while the stylite was still alive. Alypius was a very popular saint in Byzantium. His skull was one of the

---

[79] On the στῦλος see Paul Van Den Ven, *La Vie ancienne de saint Syméon Stylite le Jeune (521 – 592)*, vol. 1: *Introduction et texte grec* [Subsidia hagiographica 32] (Brussels: Société des Bollandistes, 1962), 134–46*. For a summarized description of the device, see also *ODB*, vol. 3, s.v. "Stylite", 1971.

[80] Van Den Ven, 1:138*ff.

[81] Ibid., 1:140*.

[82] Symeon Stylites the Younger, §39.18.

[83] Hippolyte Delehaye, *Les Saints Stylites* (Brussels: Société des Bollandistes; Paris: Librarie Auguste Picard, 1923), xxviii, clviii.

[84] Symeon Stylites the Younger, §37.1-3.

[85] On St. Alypios Stylites and his *Life* see *BS*, vol. 1, s.v. "Alypio"; Delehaye, *Les Saints Stylites*, lxxxiiI and 148ff.

most valuable treasures of the Koutloumousiou Monastery on Mount Athos, and a monastery was named after him in the imperial capital.[86] An original biography, a Metaphrastian "translation," and a panegyric by St. Neophytos Enkleistos (1134–1214) were dedicated to him. The first of these texts was vernacular, with an extremely short exordium. It includes numerous miracles and a fascinating account of a haunted graveyard near the Paphlagonian town of Euchaita.[87]

The next sixth-century stylite Saint, who became extremely popular was St. Symeon Stylites the Younger (521–592). Thanks to the detailed research of Paul van den Ven (1962–1970), his biography is much more studied than that of St. Alypius. Even though only about thirty years of his lifetime (565–594) formally belonged to the period after the death of Justinian I, his biography is one of the most important sources for the image of the demon in the late sixth century, and we cannot omit it here. The Saint was born into a family of perfumers from the Syrian city of Edessa. Very early on, his parents moved to Antioch,[88] and his father died during the earthquake that struck the Syrian capital on May 29, 526, razing great sections of the city to the ground.[89] As a result of a divine vision, the six-year-old Symeon became a hermit and, during his travels, God led him to a small monastery near the city of Seleucia. Its abbot, John, became his mentor, and after a while, both retired as stylites. During his first stay on a column (528–541/2), the future Saint had to repel the attacks and temptations of many demons. He gained popularity by predicting the capture of Antioch by the forces of Shah Khosrow I Anushirvan in 540. He spent the next ten years (until mid-551)[90] as a hermit on the

---

[86] *BS*, vol. 1, s.v. "Alipio".
[87] Alypios Stylites, §9.4ff. and §9.18-26.
[88] For the principal events of the biography of St. Symeon Stylites the Younger, see Van den Ven, *La Vie ancienne*, 1: 108*–24* (a summary of the *Life*) and 124*–30* (datation); cf. *BS*, vol. 11, s.v. "Simeone Stilita il Giovane", 1141–57; *ODB*, vol. 3, s.v. "Symeon Stylite the Younger", 1986ff.
[89] See, for this disastrous event, Glanville Downey, *A History of Antioch in Syria: From Seleucus to the Arab Conquest* (Princeton: Princeton University Press, 1961), 521–24.
[90] The reference in *ODB*, vol. 3, s.v. "Symeon Stylite the Younger", 1986, is inaccurate. St. Symeon Stylites the Younger ascended the grand column in 551, not 541 (Van den Ven, *La Vie ancienne*, 1: 118*ff. and 126*).

Admirable Mountain southwest of the Syrian capital.⁹¹ In this period of his life, he foresaw the Great Plague of 541 and spiritually supported the local populace during this appalling trial. His followers built him a pillar and a large monastery complex around it.⁹² On Pentecost (June 4), 551, Symeon ceremonially ascended to the column where he would spend the rest of his life. The future Saint became one of the symbols of Orthodoxy, and despite his reclusion, he exercised significant influence even in Constantinople.⁹³ Symeon predicted important events like the death of Justinian I in 565, his succession by Justinus II (565–578), the coronation of Tiberius II (578–582), and the ascension to the throne of Mauritius (582–602). He managed to expel a powerful demon from the daughter of Justinus II with nothing more than a letter, and even dared to scold the Emperor for having a ventriloquist witch in his court.⁹⁴ Symeon died old in 592.

St. John of Damascus believes the author of St. Symeon Stylite the Younger's *Life* (BHG [1689]) to be Arcadios, Bishop of Constantia (ancient Salamis) in Cyprus. Van den Ven rejects this suggestion, arguing that the real author was a contemporary of the Saint, well acquainted with the topography of Antioch and the political situation in both the Empire and Persia, and considers the text anonymous.⁹⁵ The *Life* itself is a vernacular biography (βίος καὶ πολιτεία) and, unlike that of St. Alypius Stylites, begins with a lengthy introduction that includes most of the standard hagiographical topoi. The text was reworked in the late tenth

---

⁹¹ For the location of the Admirable Mountain (Θαυμαστόν Ὄρος), the modern-day Saman dağı, southwest of Antioch, near the estuary of the Orontes River, see Van den Ven, *La Vie ancienne*, 1: 191* ff.

⁹² For the monastery and the remains of the base of the original column, see Van den Ven, *La Vie ancienne*, 1: 191*–224*.

⁹³ For the accounts which hint that St. Symeon Stylites the Younger was very well connected to the Church and State leaders in Constantinople, see Symeon Stylites the Younger, §§202ff. (Symeon predicts the ascension of Justinus II to the imperial throne), §207 (Symeon uses a letter to exorcise the demon that had possessed the Emperor's daughter). See also Van den Ven, *La Vie ancienne*, 1: 107*ff. and 121*–23.

⁹⁴ Symeon Stylites the Younger, §209.

⁹⁵ Van den Ven, *La Vie ancienne*, 1: 101* ff.

century by the Byzantine general and encyclopedist Nikephoros Ouranos (BHG [1690]). There is a Georgian translation of the text as well.[96]

Another important saint of the seventh century was St. George of Choziba.[97] He was born in Cyprus. When his parents died, he followed in the footsteps of his brother Heraclides who became a monk at the Kalamon monastery near Jerusalem.[98] Since George was still a little boy, the monastic community decided that its rules were too harsh for him. The abbot sent him as a novice to another monastery called Choziba.[99] His mentor, an elderly native of Mesopotamia, was so austere that his severity forced George to return to Kalamon. He lived there with his brother until the latter's death. Due to disagreements with the other monks, he went again to Choziba, where Abbot Leontius welcomed him. This is the point where the hagiographer gives the only clearly-dated event in the biography, namely the Persian attack of 614, which forced the monks of Choziba to abandon the monastery and its surroundings. George used the occasion to visit Jerusalem and, after the invasion, returned to the devastated monastery, where he died shortly afterward. With its descriptions of guardian demons, demon-inspired predictions, and zoomorphic forms, the text is an important source for the image of the evil spirit.

The most dangerous political and ideological opponent of the Empire in the late sixth the early seventh century was Sasanian Persia. In this period, two martyr saints symbolized Christian supremacy over Persian "idolatry" and "sorcery". The *Lives* of St. Golinduch-Maria and St. Anastasios of Persia are among the essential sources for the relations between the two world empires, but also for the Byzantine demon.

---

[96] For this version, see Van den Ven, *La Vie ancienne*, 1: 53*–67*.
[97] For him and his *Life*, see Siméon Vailhé, "Répertoire alphabetique des monastères de Palestine", *Revue d'Orient Chrétien* 4 (1899): 526ff.; "Les Saints Kozebites", *Échos d'Orient* 1, no. 8 (1898): 229–33; *BS*, vol. 6, s.v. "Giorgio il Chozibita", 534–36.
[98] Vailhé fixes the date of the foundation of the monastic community in Kalamon in the early fourth century ("Répertoire alphabetique", 519ff.).
[99] The thriving monastery of Choziba was founded in the late fifth century by St. John of Choziba. It was located on the left side of the road from Jerusalem to Jericho, in the region of the modern Wadī-el-Kelt (Vailhé, "Répertoire alphabetique", 519ff.)

The Persian aristocrat Golinduch (Golindukht, Golindokht, or Dolindokht)[100] (†July 13, 591) was an extremely popular personage in Byzantine literature of the late sixth and early seventh centuries. The ecclesiastical historians Evagrius Scholasticus (late sixth century) and Nikephoros Kallistos Xanthopulos (fourteenth century), the historiographer Theophylact Simocatta (seventh century), and the chronicler John of Nikiû (late seventh century) mention her.[101] She was a noble Zoroastrian, introduced to Christianity by her husband's Byzantine captives. After his death, Golinduch was baptized and took the name "Maria". After an unsuccessful attempt to force her to renounce God and return to Zoroastrianism, Shah Khosrow I Anushirvan (531–579) imprisoned and tortured her. Even more cruel in his treatment of Golinduch-Maria was his successor Hormizd IV (579–590), who sentenced her to death. According to legend, after Hormizd died in 590,[102] she miraculously escaped from prison shortly before the sentence was to be carried out and went to Byzantine territory, where people venerated her as a *living martyr* (according to Evagrius Scholasticus)[103] until her demise on July 13, 591.

The author of the Greek vernacular version of her *Life*'s (*BHG* [700–701]) was called Eustratius,[104] a close friend and associate of Patriarch Eutychius of Constantinople (552–565; 577–582). According to Peeters, the text was written shortly after January 12, 602.[105] The introduction focuses on the topos "reiectio rhetoricae". Eustratius polemicizes against the supercilious and arrogant authors of standard rhetorical en-

---

[100] Her name derives from the Persian Golan-Dokt – *daughter of the flowers*. For more about her, see Paul Peeters, "Sainte Golinduch, martyre perse († 13.7.591)", *Analecta Bollandiana* 62 (1944): 74–125.

[101] For all of these texts, see Peeters, "Sainte Golinduch", 76–79 (Euagrios), 94–100 (Theophylact Simmocata), 100–102 (John of Nikiu), and 102ff. (Nikephoros Kallistos); and, for a reconstruction of the main events of her life, see 103–25.

[102] See Peeters, "Sainte Golinduch", 112.

[103] *The ecclesiastical history of Evagrius with the scholia*, ed. Joseph Bidez and Léon Parmentier (London: Methuen, 1979), 235.5.

[104] On him see Peeters, "Sainte Golinduch", 79–89. The text is summarized on 82-92.

[105] On the datation, based on the death of the Archbishop of Melitene Domitian (†January 12, 602), see Peeters, "Sainte Golinduch", 81.

comia, who pompously praise their heroes, regardless of whether these persons have performed real exploits or not.

Much more important for the subject of this study is the biography of the other Persian saint, Magundates-Anastasios (†January 22, 628). Thanks to Bernard Flusin's exhaustive and detailed study (1992),[106] we have a critical edition of all the known *Lives* and collections of miracles related to this fascinating person. Flusin reconstructs the main events of his biography and puts them in their historical context.[107] Magundates was born in a village called Rasnuni in Aramea, south of modern-day Teheran.[108] He was the son of the Zoroastrian priest (magus) Bau and received religious education under the supervision of his father. In his youth, he enlisted in the Persian army. He was present at the official ceremony in which the victorious Shah Khosrow II Parviz triumphantly presented the captured Holy Cross in the Sasanian capital Ctesiphon.[109] Seeing the holy object, the young soldier became interested in the Christian religion. Magundates took part in the military expedition led by General Shāhēn Vahūmanzādagān in western Asia Minor and, after the unsuccessful siege of Chalcedon (614), returned to the East. He deserted from the Persian army and settled first in Hierapolis (near the Euphrates). Around 619/620, he moved to Jerusalem, where he was baptized with the Christian name Anastasios. His baptism was not easy to acquire. Magundates had to beg his employer, a Christian jeweler, to become his godfather for a long time before he finally accepted the dangerous honor. The reluctance of this reasonable businessman was not surprising. According to Persian laws, if somebody betrayed Zoroastrianism, both the perpetrator and his helpers were subject to the death penalty.[110] Despite the danger, however, he finally agreed. Eight days after his conversion,

---

[106] Bernard Flusin, *Saint Anastase le Perse et l'histoire de la Palestine au début du viie siècle*, 2 vols. (Paris: Centre National de la Recherche Scientifique, 1992).

[107] It is relatively easy to date the main events of St. Anastasios of Persia's life. See Flusin, *Saint Anastase*, 2: 7–9 and 221–63; cf. also *BS*, vol. 1, s.v. "Anastasio Magundat", 1054–56.

[108] For the location, see Flusin, *Saint Anastase*, 2: 222ff.

[109] The Holy Cross was captured by the Persian Shah in 614, after the capture of Jerusalem.

[110] Flusin, *Saint Anastase*, 2: 227–31.

Magundates-Anastasios became a monk at a nearby monastery.[111] In 627, Anastasios saw in a vision that his destiny was to be a martyr. To fulfill his fate, he left the monastery and went to Caesarea,[112] where a Persian garrison was quartered. There the future martyr visited the local Zoroastrian priests and accused them of veneration of demons. Baffled by the irrationality of such utterly unprovoked behavior, they simply sent him away. But Anastasios did not give up. He then reviled the soldiers of the cavalry guard and was escorted to the marzban — the Persian military governor of the province. Like the priests, this esteemed official was more puzzled than angry about the strange and wholly aberrant behavior of Bau's prodigal son. Unwilling to enforce the law himself, he shrugged off the responsibility and sent Anastasios to the residence of the Shah in Bethsaloe near Dasdagerd.[113] The Shah politely urged the future Saint to denounce his new religion and return to Zoroastrianism, but he firmly refused. He was tortured and finally decapitated on Khosrow's orders on January 22, 628.

The author of the original *Life* (*BHG* [84]) was a contemporary and associate of the Saint, who accompanied him on his last journey to Bethsaloe. The text combines elements of biography and martyrologium (βίος καὶ μαρτύριον). It was written between 629–630[114] and includes many interesting accounts of demons and evil spirits. The Zoroastrian religion is a standard subject of demonization. Two epideictic versions of the *Life* are preserved as well. One of them (*BHG* [87]) was anonymous, and the other (*BHG* [86]) was written by the famous poet George of Pisidia in the mid-seventh century.[115]

Two other texts related to this extremely popular person are even more important than the encomia. The *Miracles of St. Anastasios of Per-*

---

[111] For the so-called "Monastery of Anastasios", to which the Saint retired, and for the Abbot Justin, see Flusin, *Saint Anastase*, 2: 185–88.
[112] Caesarea Palestinae/Maritima, an important port and the capital of the province of Palestine.
[113] Flusin, *Saint Anastase*, 2: 244 and n. 123. The city of Dasdagerd, ninety kilometers northeast of modern-day Bagdad, was one of the capitals of Shah Khosrow II.
[114] For the dating of the *Life*, see Flusin, *Saint Anastase*, 2: 185–93 (esp. 191–93).
[115] For these two texts, see Flusin, *Saint Anastase*, 2:381–84.

sia (*BHG* [89g-90]) are preserved in numerous manuscripts, but they all include events chronologically close to the death of the Saint. The author of Miracles № 1-14 was an anonymous contemporary of St. Anastasios. The author and the date of Miracles № 15-18 are unknown.[116] The *Roman miracle of St. Anastasios of Persia* (*BHG* [89]) is a relatively long text of more than thirty pages in Flusin's edition. It describes the exorcism of the daughter of a wealthy bishop of eastern origin, who lived in Rome with her family. According to the author, the event occurred between October 1 and November 1, 713.[117] The *Roman miracle* provides valuable theoretical concepts regarding the nature and the harmful influences of evil spirits, their manner of speech, their preferred images, and the limitations of their power.

* * *

Only a few hagiographers are known to have written more than one text. One of them was Leontius, bishop of the city of Neapolis on the south coast of Cyprus (modern-day Lemesos or Limassol). There is scarce information about his own life.[118] Since his literary career peaked in the 640s, he was likely born in the early seventh century. Supposedly, he came from an aristocratic family of Neapolis, just like Patriarch John the Merciful of Alexandria, to whom he dedicated a lengthy biography. Maybe this hagiographer was the Leontius of Neapolis who took part in the Lateran Council of 649, which condemned the Monothelite heresy.

---

[116] Ibid., 2: 337.

[117] Anastasios of Persia, *Roman miracle*, §1.15-20; Flusin, *Saint Anastase*, 2: 378.

[118] For the life and works of Leontius of Neapolis, see Derek Krueger, *Symeon the Holy Fool: Leontius's Life and the Late Antique City* (Berkley and Los Angeles: University of Califonia Press, 1996), 14-18 (with a detailed biography). See also Krumbacher, *Geschichte der byzantinischen Literatur*, 190ff.; André-Jean Festugière, *Léontios de Néapolis. Vie de Syméon le Fou et Vie de Jean de Chypre. Édition commentée par A. Festugière en collaboration de L. Rydén* [Bibliothèque Archéologique et Historique 95] (Paris: Librairie Orientaliste Paul Geuthner, 1974), 1ff. (with a short biography); Cyril Mango, "A Byzantine Hagiographer at Work: Leontios of Neapolis", in *Byzanz und der Westen: Studien zur Kunst des Europäischen Mittelalters*, ed. Irmagard Hutter, (Vienna: Osterreichischen Akademie, 1984); *ODB*, vol. 2, s.v. "Leontios of Neapolis", 1213ff.

Krueger suggests that Leontius was among the high officials who escaped Cyprus in 649 or 653 after the Arab governor of Syria, the future caliph Mu'awiya, captured the island. According to him, Leontius died in exile during the reign of Emperor Constans II (641–668).[119] Beyond the still extant *Lives* of St. Symeon the Fool and St. John the Merciful, he wrote a biography of St. Spyridon, now lost, and a treatise in defense of icons.

The *Life* of St. John the Merciful (*BHG* [886 — 886f]) was written around 640/1.[120] John himself is relatively well-known. He was a Melkite[121] patriarch of Alexandria in Egypt between 610 and 619/620. Born the son of the imperial governor of the island, he was trained for a secular career. When his wife and children died early, he dedicated himself to God. With the support of Emperor Heraclius, he was appointed Patriarch of Alexandria in 610 and, with the aid of the local monks, fought against Monophysitism and the remnants of pagan cults. Leontius left the city shortly before the Persian occupation of 619/620 and returned to his native Cyprus. The style of his *Life* is highly rhetorical. It gives detailed and interesting information about the role of demons in the journey of the human soul in the afterlife.

The biography of St. Symeon the Fool (*BHG* [1677–1677b])[122] is one of the most scandalous hagiographical texts written in the Medieval world. Leontius details the life and deeds of a "holy fool", i.e., one supposedly mad or possessed by a demon, whom God inspires to prophesy and coerce others to become aware of their sins and repent. The text contains vivid and sometimes disgustingly naturalistic descriptions of Late

---

[119] Krueger, *Symeon the Holy Fool*, 16.
[120] For St. John the Merciful, see *BS*, vol. 6, s.v. "Giovanni l'Elemosiniere", 750–57; Festugière, *Léontios de Néapolis*, 257–67; Mango, "A Byzantine Hagiographer", 33; *ODB*, vol. 2, s.v. "John Eleemon", 1058ff.; Krueger, *Symeon the Holy Fool*, 4ff. (n. 6) and 71–88.
[121] The term "Melkite" (from the Arabic root *mlk* – *king, ruler*) denoted the Orthodox Patriarchs of Alexandria. They were usually appointed by the emperor himself and had military and administrative power. Their most important task was to oppose the Monophysite Patriarchs of the Egyptian capital. See Festugière, *Léontios de Néapolis*, 258ff., with bibliography
[122] For St. Symeon the Holy Fool, see, in general, Krueger, *Symeon the Holy Fool*, 1–19.

Antique urban life, even including defecation in the streets. Leontius wrote it after the *Life* of St. John the Merciful between 642 and 649.[123]

A chronologically accurate reconstruction of St. Symeon's life is almost impossible. Leontius says that the Saint predicted an earthquake during the reign of Emperor Mauricius. We know that such an event occurred in 588. On the other hand, the ecclesiastical historian Evagrius Scholasticus[124] mentions the same prophecy, but dates the tremors thirty years earlier, in 551. According to Krueger, Leontius used written sources and his dating of this natural disaster is more accurate.[125] Like the *Life* of St. John the Merciful, the text is a very important source of information about urban legends in the Byzantine East in the late sixth century; these legends inevitably include many demonic images.

* * *

There were two great exorcists in Byzantine hagiography. The first was St. Auxentius the Great (†473), whose *Life* was compiled by the famous humanist Michael Psellus in the third quarter of the eleventh century. The other was St. Theodore Sykeotes (†613), whose biography (*BHG* [1748]) was written by the Saint's pupil George, and is one of the most interesting sources for evil spirits in Byzantium.[126] There is almost no paragraph in this text of more than a hundred and sixty pages that does not mention the words "demon" or "evil spirit". One reason for the important role played by demons in his biography is the specific rhetorical situation in which Theodore lived and worked. The saints of Syria and Palestine and the Persian martyrs fought against strong and entrenched enemies — heresies and, above all, the Zoroastrian religion, supported by the strong Sasanian Empire. Theodore, on the other hand, operated in a

---

[123] Ibid., 4ff. and n. 7, with a bibliography.
[124] *The ecclesiastical history of Evagrius*, §184.14-28.
[125] Krueger *Symeon the Holy Fool*, 21ff.
[126] For the main events of the life of St. Theodore Sykeotes, see *BS*, vol. 12, s.v. "Teodoro il Siceota", 263-65; André-Jean Festugière, *Vie de Théodore de Sykéôn*, vol. 1 [Subsidia hagiographica 48] (Brussels: Société des Bollandistes, 1970), v; *ODB*, vol. 3, s.v. "Theodore of Sykeon", 2045ff.

completely different environment and the very tone of his *Life* is serene and even, with none of the sharp twists and the feeling of constant insecurity that we find, for example, in the biographies of Leontius of Neapolis. The Saint was born during the reign of Justinian I in the village of Sykeon, located in Western Galatia, Asia Minor.[127] Life in this part of the Empire, mostly unaffected by Persian invasions and cataclysmic natural disasters, was almost idyllic. His mother Maria was the daughter of a wealthy female innkeeper, working without any compunction as a *hetaera*[128] (basically, a prostitute) in her mother's business along with her sister Despoinia. His father Kosmas was an imperial official, who in his youth distinguished himself in the Hippodrome in Constantinople for his excellent skills in camel dressage. He remained extremely pleased both with the young girl's sexual services and with the news of her pregnancy. Theodore was raised in a tranquil village by his loving grandmother, mother, and aunt. Between the ages of eight and twelve, already a student, he was visited by St. George, who cured him of bubonic plague and gave him the ability to cast out demons. After graduating from school, Theodore retired as a hermit first to an underground cave, then to an iron cage. His ecclesiastical career was extremely successful. He was ordained a priest, founded a monastery, and later became bishop of the town of Athanasiupolis near his native village. Theodore gained influence even in Constantinople, where he performed exorcisms on both high officials and ordinary citizens, and was a close friend of Patriarch Cyriacus (596–606).

 The majority of the demonic stories of the *Life* of St. Theodore, however, are set in his native province Galatia Prima,[129] where he spent the greater part of his life. There weren't many heretics in this area, at least before the great military expedition of general Shāhēn in 614; there, the life-and-death struggle with the Persians was but a distant echo. St. Theodore's demonic enemies were very different from those fought by

---

[127]   For the location, see *TIB*, vol. 4, 228ff.
[128]   Theodore Sykeotes, §3.9ff.
[129]   For Galatia Prima (capital Ancyra) and Galatia Secunda/Salutaria (capital Pessinous) see *TIB*, vol. 4: *Galatien und Lykaonien*, ed. Claus Belke (1984), 55.

saints like Symeon Stylites the Younger and the Persian martyrs. In his biography, we find vivid descriptions of evil wolves roaming the wilderness, of people possessed by demons in various animal shapes, but especially of haunted ancient graveyards and pagan shrines. This is an obvious sign that the most dangerous enemy of the Faith in Inner Asia Minor in the late sixth and early seventh centuries were the remnants of paganism.

2. The Great Lavra of St. Sabbas in Palestine (seventh–ninth century)

Arduous struggles for the very survival of the Empire marked the period from the death of Emperor Heraclius (641) until the mid-eighth century and the new deadly threat — the Arab invasion. In less than two decades, the political and intellectual centers of the ancient Roman East in Syria, Palestine, and Egypt became part of the powerful Arab caliphate. In the 660s, the capital of this new empire moved from the holy city of Mecca to the Syrian metropolis of Damascus, where the Umayyad dynasty ruled its vast territories. Asia Minor, the new heart of the Byzantine Empire, was subjected to annual raids. Two Umayyad rulers, Caliph Mu'awiya in 674 and Prince Maslama Abd al-Malik in 717 managed to besiege Constantinople. During this period, intellectual life in the Empire largely died out. There were practically no original hagiographic texts created on the Empire's territory in this epoch.

In contrast to the imperial mainland, in the First Iconoclast crisis (726–797), a stable Orthodox monastic community was established on the territory of the Umayyad and later of the Abbasid Caliphate. In all likelihood, the new Muslim rulers of these lands encouraged this Orthodox iconodule movement, which presumably opposed the heretical regime of the emperors in Constantinople. The Great Lavra of St. Sabbas near Jerusalem became one of the ideological centers of this movement. To this impressive monastery, John of Damascus himself retired in the first half of the eighth century. At the end of the same century, the local monastic community produced numerous hagiographical texts. They are a significant source for relations between Muslims and Christians under the Caliphate during this period and include elements of the vernacular biography and the *martyrion*. While in the third and fourth centuries, the original *martyria* focused on the very act of martyrdom, the later authors provided considerable information about the general life and work of the praised saint.

The first representative of the Palestinian hagiographic school was the monk St. Stephen the Sabbaite (725–794), also called "Thaumaturge" (Θαυματουργός). The dating of his major hagiographic work, *The Martyrion of the Sabaites* (BHG [1200]), and the Arab attack he described are still controversial. However, a Muslim raid occurred in the late eighth century. The first manuscripts of the text are from the tenth century, and this supplies a certain *terminus ante quem*.[130]

The *Life* of St. Elias of Heliopolis (759–779) belongs to the same mixed genre. It includes elements both of biography and *martyrion*. The Saint was born to a local Christian family of Heliopolis (Baalbek, in modern Lebanon). When he was a child, he moved with his parents to Damascus, where he became a carpenter. One night he got very drunk and accepted conversion to Islam, but in the morning repented and returned to the Christian faith. Since this was a capital crime, liable to the death penalty according to Sharia, he left the city and fled to his hometown. A few years later, he returned to Damascus and became a saddler but was discovered and persecuted. He was condemned by the famous jurist Al-Layth ibn Said (712/713–791/2) and by the Emir of Damascus Muhammad ibn Ibrahim (739/40–801), again refused to accept Islam, and was beheaded on February 1, 779.[131] The *terminus post quem* for the text (*BHG* [578–79]) is the tenth century, the first date of the manuscript. The

---

[130] Kazhdan, *History of Byzantine Literature*, 1: 169–71.

[131] For dating, see Chrisanf Loparev, *Greek Saints' Lives of the eighth and ninth centuries: An attempt at a scientific classification with an overview from a historical and historical-literary point of view* [Russian: Хрисанф Лопаревъ, *Греческія житія святыхъ VIII и IX вѣковъ. Опытъ научной классификаціи памятниковъ агіографіи съ обзоромъ ихъ съ точки зрѣнія исторической и историко-литературной*], vol. 1, (St. Petersburg, 1914), 406–10 (who dates his death to 795); *BS*, vol. 4, s.v. "Elia il Giovane", 1046ff.; Kazhdan, *History of Byzantine Literature*, 1: 174.

accurate chronological information provided by the author makes fixing the dates of the main events possible. The *Life* of St. Elias of Heliopolis is one of the most important sources for the relations between the Arabs and the local Christian groups in Syria. Information on demonic creatures is scarce, which is typical for the genre of the *martyria*.

Much more important for the present study are the *Lives* of St. Stephen the Sabbaite himself, and the *Life* of Bishop Theodore of Edessa. The former ([*BHG* 1670–70b]) was written by the monk Leontius of Damascus, a younger contemporary of the Saint, who knew him personally and, in all likelihood, was active in the first quarter of the ninth century.[132] According to him, Stephen was born around 725 and was probably a nephew of St. John of Damascus. The future Saint entered the Great Lavra as a novice in 735 and became a monk at the age of thirty-seven years in 762. He retired as a hermit to the caves near the monastery, maybe because of a conflict with the leading "St. Sabbas" party. His famous uncle and Iconoclasm are rarely mentioned, but the heretic Emperor Constantine V is bitterly vituperated. According to the text, the Saint died on April 2, 794.[133] The style and disposition of the *Life* is peculiar. The text comprises many short stories narrated directly by the leading personages. The biography of St. Stephen the Sabbaite, with its vivid depictions of the last journey of the human soul and the demons of the deadly sins, is one of the crucial sources for the image of Evil in the period under study.

Bishop Theodore of Edessa lived in Syria and Palestine in the ninth century. He was born in the city of Edessa (modern-day Urfa, in southeastern Turkey) around 776. His family was noble. At twenty years of age,

---

[132] For the *Life* of St. Stephen the Sabbaite, or Thaumaturge, and its author Leontius of Damascus, see Loparev, *Greek Saints' Lives*, 389–403; *BS*, vol. 12, s.v. "Stefano Sabbaita, il Taumaturgo", 14ff.; Kazhdan, *History of Byzantine Literature*, 1: 171ff.; *ODB*, vol. 3, s.v. "Stephen Sabaites", 1954ff.; Marie-France Auzépy, "De la Palestine à Constantinople (VIIIe – IXe siècles): Etienne le Sabaïte et Jean Damascène", *Travaux et Mémoires* 12 (1994): 183–218; John Lamoreaux, "Some Notes on a Recent Edition of the Life of St. Stephen of Mar Sabas", *Analecta Bollandiana* 113 (1995): 117–26.

[133] Stephen the Thaumaturge, §183. For different theories about the date of St. Stephen's death, see Kazhdan, *History of Byzantine Literature*, 1: 171.

he was accepted as a monk in the Great Lavra of St. Sabbas and later became its abbot. Around 836, Theodore was ordained as a bishop in his hometown. During the reign of Emperor Michael III and his mother, Empress Theodora (842–855), he visited Constantinople. Theodore died in the Lavra and was buried there. The *Life* includes many legendary events of the late eighth and the first half of the ninth centuries, e.g., the conversion to Christianity of the "master of Babylon Mauna". This imaginary person was probably an echo of the first caliph of the Umayyad dynasty Mu'awiya I, who lived some 200 years before the mid-ninth century. The author names himself Basil and claims that he was a nephew of the Saint, but, in all likelihood, the text was compiled in the tenth century. The first known manuscript dates from the year 1023, and this is the *terminus ante quem*.[134] According to the text, this legendary Saint's life was an endless struggle with the demons, but its images of evil spirits are all very standard and abstract.

3. Polemical iconodule hagiography

The rule of the first two emperors of the Syrian dynasty Leo III and his son Constantine V (717–765), is extremely interesting from an ideological point of view. Their reigns were undoubtedly prosperous. They managed to deal with the most significant military threats, i.e., the Arab invasions in Asia Minor and the Bulgarian attacks in Thrace and Macedonia. After their successes, the Caliphate was never again a danger to the very existence of the Empire. The main goal of their internal policy was to support the so-called *stratiotai*, or soldiers who received land for military service. These "middle-class" landowners were the most vital protective force of the new core of the Empire in Asia Minor. This drew the central government into a constant, endemic struggle against the growing aristocracy of big landowners (*dynatoi*). The reasonable internal policy of the first emperors of the Syrian dynasty had to face another enemy as well. This was the Church and the large monasteries with their enormous eco-

---

[134] Loparev, *Greek Saints' Lives*, 410–35; *BS*, vol. 12, s.v. "Theodoro di Edessa", 250; *ODB*, vol. 2, s.v. "Theodore of Edessa", 2043.

nomic power. The new Iconoclast heresy was formally directed against images and sacred relics, but it pursued clear political and financial objectives. Iconoclasm and the politico-economic doctrine lurking behind it provoked Orthodox circles, supported by the emerging aristocracy, to create a wide-ranging propaganda machine to discredit the otherwise successful rulers. A vital element of this propaganda strategy was hagiography. For about a century (at least until 842), one of the main characters in religious biographies was the saint who fought for Orthodoxy against the heretical emperors. As in Palestine, martyrological works reappeared on the territory of the Empire.

3.1. Patriarch Germanos

The texts, which refer to the earliest saints and martyrs who fought against the Iconoclast heresy and the Emperors Leo III, Constantine V, Michael II, and Theophilos, are either obscure or very late. The *Life* of Patriarch Germanos I (BHG [697]), who held the patriarchal throne in Constantinople from 715 to 730, has provoked much controversy among scholars and was probably composed long after the Saint's death; it was influenced by Theophanes the Confessor (eighth century) and perhaps even by George Kedrenos.[135] According to his biography, the future patriarch was the son of a high-ranking dignitary of Emperor Constantine II (641–688) named Justinian, who was executed on charges of conspiracy by his son Constantine IV (668–685). Germanos, not yet twenty years old, was castrated and became a monk. In 705/706, he was made bishop of Cyzicus. He ascended to the patriarchal throne during the reign of Emperor Anastasios II (713–715). After the iconoclastic decree of Emperor Leo III (726), he refused to support the new dogmatic line and was forced to abdicate. He probably died around 740.[136]

---

[135] For the different dates of the text, see Kazhdan, *History of Byzantine Literature*, 1: 55ff.
[136] For more on Patriarch Germanos, see *BS*, vol. 6, s.v. "Germano, Patriarca di Constantinopoli", 243–53; Ševčenko "Hagiography", 114; *ODB*, vol. 2, s.v. "Germanos I, patriarch of Constantinople", 846ff.; Kazhdan, *History of Byzantine Literature*, 1: 55–58.

3.2. Stephen the Deacon and his pupils

The most influential polemical iconoclastic *Life* dates from the first half of the ninth century. This is the *Life* of St. Stephen the Younger (BHG [1666]), written by Stephen the Deacon. This text had a massive impact on the Byzantine literature of the ninth century. It was the first Constantinopolitan polemical panegyric of an iconodule saint in Byzantium, and is a highly informative source for the history of the second and third quarters of the eighth century. The Saint was born in Constantinople during the patriarchate of Germanos I (715) to the family of a craftsman. After he finished elementary school, his parents took him from *heretical* Constantinople to the monastery of St. Auxentius (in western Bithynia, Asia Minot), where the boy lived with his mentor, Abbot John, and was ordained a monk at the age of ten. After the death of his mentor, Stephen succeeded him as abbot of the monastery and lived in the capital for some time. He refused to accept the decisions of the iconoclastic Council of Hieria (754), and his monastery was destroyed by an army unit led by the imperial favorite George Sincletus. The Saint himself was exiled to the island of Proconnesus (in the Sea of Marmara), imprisoned in Constantinople, and finally tortured and killed (November 28, 764 or 765). It is possible that his fate was related to a conspiracy against the Emperor rather than to the veneration of icons. According to the author, the text was written forty-two years after the Saint's martyrdom — in 806/807.[137]

---

[137] The bibliography on the *Life* of St. Stephen the Younger is extensive. See (with bibliography): Loparev, *Greek Saints' Lives*, 119–47; *BS*, vol. 11, s.v. "Stefano il Giovane", 1420ff.; Ševčenko, "Hagiography", 114ff.; *ODB*, vol. 3, s.v. "Stephen the Younger", 1955ff.; Kazhdan, *History of Byzantine Literature*, 1: 183–97; Alice-Mary Talbot, "Life of St. Stephen the Younger: Introduction and Translation", in *Byzantine Defenders of Images: Eight Saints' Lives in English Translation*, ed. Alice-Mary Talbot [Byzantine Saints' Lives in Translation, 2] (Washington D.C.: Dumbarton Oaks Research Library and Collection, 1998), 9ff. (includes a translation of the short version of the text); Marie-France Auzépy, *L'Hagiographie et l'iconoclasme Byzantin. Le cas de la Vie d'Étienne le Jeune* [Birmingham Byzantine and Ottoman monographs 5.] (New York: Routledge, 1999), 7–93; Marie-France Auzépy, *La Vie d' Étienne le Jeune par Étienne le Diacre*, [Birmingham Byzantine and Ottoman monographs 3.] (New York: Routledge, 2016), 5–42.

The *Life* of St. Stephen the Younger is vital to the study of the Byzantine demon and political demonization in general. The heretic Emperors Leo III and Constantine V are associated with evil spirits. These rulers are called *dragons, snakes, lions,* and *servants of Satan.* The text describes the ritual of making a contract with the Devil and mentions some very interesting demonic forms, e.g., the owl. Despite this increased interest in various exotic incarnations of Evil, Satan acts mainly through his human servants, i.e., through the heretic rulers.

The story of St. Stephen became a model for generations of hagiographers in their efforts to describe and praise the struggle of their heroes against heretical emperors and demonic creatures. In contrast to Stephen the Deacon, though, his followers showed less interest in the demonization of rulers and much more in the material forms in which evil spirits appear. The reasons for this tendency in ninth-century hagiography, especially during the Second Iconoclast period (815–843), are complex and require extensive analysis. Probably the most important reason was the change in the rhetorical situation itself. During the reign of Constantine V (741–765), there were real persecutions of icon-worshipers and especially of monks. These oppressive measures revived and introduced the image of the holy martyr in Byzantine society and Byzantine literature; in these circumstances, the saint's struggle is not against demons and passions but against real people, i.e., the heretics who unlawfully sat on the throne of the Empire. On the other hand, the emperors of the Second Iconoclast period (Leo V, Michael II, and Theophilos) did not persecute icon-worshipers on the scale of Constantine V in the times of St. Stephen the Younger. For this reason, the *Lives* written in the second quarter of the ninth century and later represent less the image of the martyr who dies for Orthodoxy than the image of the humble monk and ascetic, who only occasionally falls to the blows of malice and the envy of heretics. Miracles, struggles against evil spirits and passions, and exorcisms gradually took the place of martyrdom.

One of the earliest hagiographical texts, which imitated the *Life* of St. Stephen the Younger was the anonymous biography of St. John, Bishop of Gotthia (Crimea) (†*c.* 792–800). The Saint (a native of the village of Parthenitai in Crimea) was an icon-worshiper. Nevertheless, the iconoclastic church authorities respected the beliefs of the Orthodox population in his native province. With their consent, John took the vacant episcopal throne shortly after the heretical Council of Hieria (754). The bishop traveled to Palestine, Armenia, and Constantinople and participated in the Seventh Ecumenical Council, which triumphantly restored the icons in 787. His death was as quiet as his life. The text, preserved in a shorter and longer version (BHG [891–891b]), was composed before the Second Iconoclast Period (815–843).[138]

Two other polemical texts are related to the Medikion monastery in western Asia Minor.[139] The oldest is the *Life* of Abbot Nikephoros, who died in 813 (BHG [2297–99]). Unlike St. Stephen the Younger, this Saint was by no means a martyr. He spent his life relatively quietly, took part in the Seventh Ecumenical Council (787), and died before the restoration of iconoclasm as state policy in 815. The Saint's *Life* was written between 824 and 845. Its style is highly rhetorical and offeres very little historical data.[140] The text would contribute almost nothing to the study of Byzantine demonology since it barely mentions any materialized form of Evil. Nevertheless, the anonymous author comments on some general biblical ideas. Far more informative is the *Life* of the disciple and heir of Nikephoros, St. Niketas of Medikion (c. 760–April 3, 824), a native of Caesarea in Bithynia. The Saint was well-educated and had good relations

---

[138] Loparev, *Greek Saints' Lives*, 238; *BS*, vol. 6, s.v. "Giovane, vescovo dei Goti", 814ff.; Ševčenko, "Hagiography", 115; Kazhdan, *History of Byzantine Literature*, 1: 199ff., with bibliography.

[139] The Monastery Medikion was located in the region of Triglia (Τρίγλια, present-day Zeytinbağı), on the south coast of the Sea of Marmara, about twenty kilometers west of ancient Apamea. Cf. Raymond Janin, *Les églises et les monastères et les grands centres byzantins (Bithynie, Hellespont, Latros, Galèsios, Trébisonde, Athènes, Thessalonique)* (Paris: Institut français d'études byzantines, 1975), 165–68.

[140] Loparev, *Greek Saints' Lives*, 359; *BS*, vol. 9, s.v. "Niceforo, fondatore del monasterio di Medikion in Bittinia", 855; François Halkin, "S. Nicéphore de Médikion d'après un synaxaire du mont Sinaï", *Analecta Bollandiana* 88 (1970): 13–16; Warren Treadgold, "The Bulgars' Treaty with the Byzantines in 816", *Rivista di Studi Bizantini e Slavi* 4 (1984): 213–20; Ševčenko, "Hagiography", 118 and n. 43; Janin, *Les églises et les monastères*, 165; *ODB*, vol. 2, s.v. "Medikon Monastery", 1328; Kazhdan, *History of Byzantine Literature*, 1: 198.

with the high iconodule clergy between the First and the Second Iconoclastic periods. He took the monastic habit from none other than Patriarch Tarasios (782–806) and was made abbot by Patriarch Nikephoros (806–815). Niketas renounced Orthodoxy during the reign of Emperor Leo V but later repented and was sent into exile by the iconoclast authorities. He was liberated by Michael II in 820 and died shortly afterward. His *Life* (BHG [1341–42b]) was written by his pupil Theosteriktos between 824 and 844/5, when the dethroned Michael I Rangabe (d. 844/5) was still alive. The author gives detailed accounts of important political events and demonizes Emperor Leo V.[141] The text provides abundant descriptions of various exorcisms performed by the Saint. Demons often appear as spirits who possess monks and laypeople, and in various materialized forms.

The next text is the *Life* of the three Saints David, Symeon, and George (BHG [494]).[142] Their biography is a vital source, especially for the Second Iconoclastic period, but covers more than 130 years. The oldest of the three was born c. 717/8 and the youngest died in 845/6. According to the texts, the Saints were brothers, but this is biologically impossible for the Byzantine eighth century. According to Ševčenko's calculations, their mother would have had to give birth to David (c. 717/8–783/4) at the age of twelve or thirteen and must have been in her mid-fifties when Symeon (764/5–844/5) and George (763/4–845/6) were born.[143] The account of David's life is relatively short (chapters 3–9) and all but confined to describing the exploits of the Saint, who left his native Mytilene and settled on Mount Ida near ancient Troy. In this part of the

---

[141] Loparev, *Greek Saints' Lives*, 357–59; *BS*, vol. 9, s.v. "Niceta, egumeno del monasterio di Medikion in Bittinia", 890–92; Janin, *Les églises et les monastères*, 166ff.; Ševčenko, "Hagiography", 118 and n. 42; Treadgold, "The Bulgars' Treaty", 213–20; *ODB*, vol. 2, s.v. Niketas of Medikion, 1482; Kazhdan, *History of Byzantine Literature*, 1: 198ff.

[142] On the *Life* of St. David, Symeon and George cf. *BS*, vol. 4, s.v. "David, Simone (Simeone) e Giorgo", 519ff.; Ševčenko, "Hagiography", 117ff.; *ODB*, vol. 1, s.v. "David, Symeon, and George of Mytilene", 589; Dorothy Abrahamse and Douglas Domingo-Forasté, "Life of David, Symeon, and George", in *Byzantine Defenders of Images. Eight Saint's Lives in English Translation*, 143–47; Kazhdan, *History of Byzantine Literature*, 1: 200–202, with bibliography.

[143] Ševčenko, "Hagiography", 117.

text, iconoclasm is almost omitted. David is the founder of the St. Cyricus and Julita monastery, where he became a mentor to his younger "brother" Symeon. The Saint died peacefully and had no problems with the iconoclast Emperors of his time.

Much more adventurous is the story of Symeon, who returned to Lesbos after his teacher's death and spent many years as a stylite on a column erected near the southern port of Mytilene. This part of the text describes the Saint's struggles with the iconoclastic bishop of the island during the reign of Emperor Leo V (813–820); the heretic prelate tried to set the Saint's column on fire and subsequently sent him into exile. According to the text, Symeon became one of the prominent iconodule leaders during Emperor Michael II's reign and was exiled again by his son Emperor Theophilos (829–842), this time on the island of Aphousia in the Sea of Marmara. In 843, at the invitation of Empress Theodora, he went to the imperial court, where he took part in a dispute with Patriarch John Grammaticus and played an essential role in the final restoration of the icons in the same year.

The account of the third "brother", George, has fewer details and is directly related to the biography of Symeon, who persuaded him to become a monk. After his brother's exile, George became an abbot, and his monastic life was full of struggles with various demons. According to the text, in 843, he was invited to the court and sided with the moderate Patriarch Methodius I. He returned to Lesbos as a bishop, dedicated himself to charity, and performed numerous miracles.

The activities of David, Symeon, and George, and their dates, are very ambiguous. The hagiographical text does not give any information about the author except that he was somehow connected with the island of Lesbos. The *Life* is written in a moderately high style with few references to classical authors and many quotations from Holy Scripture. In addition, it mentions some buildings in the imperial capital that were erected as late as the tenth and eleventh centuries,[144] an apparent anach-

---

[144] Cf. David, Symeon, and George, §30 (on the Christ the Savior church in Constantinople, built in the tenth century) and §27 (on the Peribleptos monastery, built in the

ronism. The problem is made even more complicated by the fact that, in the Middle and Late Byzantine period, our St. George of Lesbos was frequently confused with another George. The latter lived c. 776–821 and, like his namesake, was bishop of Mytilene. His short *Life* (*BHG* [2163]) is available today in the edition of Ioannis Fountoulis.[145]

Despite its unreliability as a historical source, the *Life* of David, Symeon, and George is one of the most informative texts for the image of the demon in Byzantium. The author eagerly describes haunted places, possessed people, struggles with evil spirits, and exorcisms.

Another polemical iconodule biography is the *Life* of St. Nikephoros of Sebaze (*BHG* [2300]). The Saint lived during the reign of Leo V (813–820) and was subjected to persecution by this Emperor. He was abbot of the Antimaure monastery, supposedly located in Bithynia (northwestern Asia Minor). No other source mentions him.[146] The panegyric was written long after the death of Nikephoros, and the author himself says that his subject and his deeds had been forgotten. The *terminus ante quem* is from the mid-tenth century when the first manuscript was dated.[147]

A short but interesting biography is dedicated to the almost unknown monk St. John the Psichaites. He was ordained as a deacon by Patriarch Tarasios in the late eighth century and afterward became oeconomus and then abbot of one of the monasteries in the imperial capital. He was persecuted as an iconodule by Emperor Leo V and was subsequently exiled to Kherson (Crimea) where the Saint died around 825. The *Life* (*BHG* [896]) was written probably in the late ninth or early

---

eleventh century). On the anachronisms in the *Life*, see Abrahamse and Domingo-Forasté, "Life of David, Symeon, and George", 146 and n. 11.

[145] Ioannis Fountoulis, "The Saints Georges, Archbishops of Mytilene" [Greek: Ιωάννης Φουντούλης, "Οἱ ἅγιοι Γεώργιοι, ἀρχιεπίσκοποι Μυτιλήνης"], *Lesviakon Eortologion* [Greek: Λεσβιακὸν Ἑορτολόγιον] 1 (1959): 33–43. Cf also Kazhdan, *History of Byzantine Literature*, 1: 200ff.

[146] Janin, *Les églises et les monastères*, 101.

[147] Cf. *BS*, vol. 9, s.v. "Nicefore, fondatore del monasterio di Sebazé", 887ff.

tenth century.[148] The anonymous author overtly reveals his contempt for secular literacy, which is rather unexpected in the age of Byzantine encyclopedism. The text abounds with demonic stories and focuses primarily on the malignant influence of evil spirits on their victims.

* * *

Saints like Stephen the Younger, Nikephoros of Medikion, Niketas of Medikion, and John the Psichaites are not political figures. Their struggle with iconoclasm is deadly, but their involvement in social life is minimal. Their field of action is not the capital but the province. The next holy person we will present here could not be more different than these semi-legendary exorcists and martyrs. St. Theodor, the abbot of the great Monastery of Studios, forever influenced and changed Byzantine society and political life in the late eighth and the early ninth century.[149] Despite the almost utter lack of material demons in his biography, some general remarks about his activities are still necessary for this study; without them, we would hardly be able to understand the conditions which determined the further general development of Byzantine hagiography. The future abbot of one of the wealthiest and most influential monasteries of the Empire and leader of the Zealot party was born in 759. His family belonged to the highest aristocracy of Constantinople and was closely con-

---

[148] Cf. Loparev, *Greek Saints' Lives*, 231–37 (with a detailed account of the Saint's life); *BS*, vol. 6, s.v. "Giovanni lo Psichaita", 872ff.; Germaine da Costa-Louillet, "Saints de Constantinople aux VIIIe, IXe, et Xe siècles", *Byzantion* 24, no. 1 (1954): 256–63.

[149] The bibliography on St. Theodore Studites is extensive. See Alexander Dobroklonskiy, *The Venerable Theodore, confessor and Abbot of the Stoudios Monastery* [Russian: Александръ Доброклонскій, *Преп. Феодоръ, исповедникъ и игуменъ Студійскій*], 2 vols. (Odessa: "Экономическая" типография, 1913-14); Irénée Hausherr, *Théodore Studite: l'homme et l'ascète (d'après ses catéchèses)* [Orientalia Christiana Analecta 22] (Rome: Pontificium institutum orientalium studiorum, 1926); Charles Frazee, "St. Theodoros of Stoudios and Ninth-Century Monasticism in Constantinople", *Studi monastici* 23 (1981): 27–58; Božidar Vidov, *St. Theodore the Studite* (Toronto, 1985); Patricia Karlin-Hayter, "A Byzantine Politician-Monk: Saint Theodore Studite", *Jahrbuch der Österreichischen Byzantinistik* 44 (1994): 217–32; *ODB*, vol. 3, s.v. "Theodore of Stoudios", 2044ff. For a short biography of the Saint, see Kazhdan, *History of Byzantine Literature*, 1: 236–39.

nected to Emperor Constantine V and his administration. Theodore's father, Photinus, was a high official in the imperial financial agency. Theodore received the best possible *encyclopedic* education (ἐγκύκλιος παιδεία), one of whose most crucial disciplines was rhetoric. His uncle Plato, a provincial monk with unshakable iconodule persuasions, who was never subject to any persecutions, was the young man's great inspiration. There is no indication that Theodore's illustrious family ever fought against the official dogmatic line of the iconoclast government; his relatives joined Plato probably as late as the early 80s of the eighth century, shortly after the death of Emperor Constantine V. At that point, Empress Irene was already busy with preparations for the restoration of the icons. Under these favorable circumstances, Plato and Theodore founded the Monastery of Sakoudion in Bithynia. This institution quickly became an influential religious and political center, which obviously enjoyed the Empress's good graces. Theodore became its abbot in 794 and was accepted as the undisputed leader of the Zealots; the aim of this faction of intransigent and radical monks was to combat every interference of the State in the Church's affairs. He inspired and took an active part in the so-called "moechian schism", caused by the second marriage — unsanctioned by the Church — of Emperor Constantine VI (780–797). This bitter controversy and the young ruler's military failures in the war against the Abbasid caliphate in the early 790s cost him his throne in 797. For their intransigent position against the decision of the Emperor to divorce his first wife, Maria of Amnia, Plato and Theodore were exiled. Still, after his dethronement, Empress Irene reversed the verdict, and they triumphantly returned to Sakoudion.

After the devastating Arab raid of 798–99, Theodore managed to persuade Irene, who was already the sole ruler of the Empire, to fund the restoration of the old monastery of Studios in the capital and to give it to his monastic community. The new abbey became the fortress of the Zealot party against the moderates — led by the Patriarchs Tarasios (until 806) and Nikephoros (until 815) — whose aim was to reconcile the Church and the State. The influential leader of the Studite monks continued to destabilize the imperial government during the reign of Emperor

Nikephoros I (802–811) and add fuel to the fire of the moechian schism. He strenuously opposed the ruler's financial reform, which aimed to curtail the privileges and influence of the big landlords, the monasteries, and the business elite. What could be called stubborn and short-sighted attitude on the part of the Zealots and their leader paved the way for the restoration of iconoclasm as the official state policy by Emperor Leo V in 815. Theodore fought against the heresy but also his old enemy, the moderate church party. He died in exile in 829. The Zealots continued to play an essential political role long after the death of their leader.

Four biographies (BHG [1754–1755m]) are dedicated to Theodore Studite, both in prose and verse. They share evident similarities, and probably the version written by Michael the Monk (BHG [1754]) is closest to the lost original. It was compiled after the mid-tenth century, but the *terminus post quem* cannot be established. The other main version is associated with the name of Theodore Daphnopates (BHG [1755]), who was a monk at the Monastery of Studios in the late tenth century.[150]

The *Lives* of St. Theodore make almost no mention of materialized demons. Nevertheless, they are an essential source for demonization as a propaganda strategy in Byzantium in the ninth and tenth centuries.

* * *

As an epilogue to Byzantine polemical iconodule hagiography, we will offer a short account of the *Life* of Empress Theodora, who finally restored the icons in 843. The dating of the text (BHG [1731]) raises many problems that remain unresolved today. It was probably written after 867, when Emperor Basil I assassinated his predecessor, Michael III; this is the last event mentioned by the anonymous author of the biography. There are many similarities between the *Life* of St. Theodora and the Chronicle of George Hamartolos, written in its original form probably a few months before the coronation of Basil I. Kazhdan and Athanasios Markopoulos suggest that the chronographer revised his text around 872

---

[150] For the *Lives* of St. Theodore Studite see Loprev, *Greek Saints' Lives*, 161–84; *BS*, vol. 12, s.v. "Teodoro Studita", 265–70; Kazhdan, *History of Byzantine Literature*, 1: 235ff.

and drew information from the biography of Empress Theodora.[151] Martha Vinson disagrees and hypothesizes that the anonymous hagiographer was influenced by George Hamartolos, and not vice versa. Vinson associates the *Life* of St. Theodora with the struggle between the supporters of Patriarch Ignatios and Patriarch Photius in the late ninth and the early tenth centuries. She suggests that the text was compiled c. 895/896. In her opinion, the author was an educated layman, well-disposed towards both Emperor Michael III and Patriarch Ignatios. He tried to acquit Michael's father, Emperor Theophilos, and restore his memory by saying that the heretic ruler denounced iconoclasm shortly before his death in 842.[152]

4. The hagiographical school of Bithynia

Above we gave a brief account on the two leading holy figures of the era of the First Iconoclastic Crisis and the troubled times that immediately followed. These figures are the martyr St. Stephen the Younger, who was executed by the heretic Emperor Constantine V, and the intellectual St. Theodore Studite, who refused to accept the second marriage of Constantine VI and was subsequently repressed by Leo V and Michael II. By contrast, during the Second Iconoclastic period (815–843), persecutions against the Orthodox clergy were limited and lacked the intensity of the

---

[151] Alexander Kazhdan, "The Chronicle of Symeon Logothetes" [Russian: Александр Каждан, Хроника Симеона Логофета], *Vizantiyskiy Vremennik* 15 (1959): 126ff.; Athanasios Markopoulos, "*Life* of the Empress Theodora (BHG 1731)" [Greek: Αθανάσιος Μαρκόπουλος, "Βίος της αυτοκράτειρας Θεοδώρας (BHG 1731)"], *Byzantina Symmeikta* 5 (1983): 254.

[152] See Martha Vinson, "The Terms ἐγκόλπιον and τενάντιον and the Conversion of Theophilus in the *Life of Theodora* (BHG 1731)", *Greek, Roman and Byzantine Studies* 36 (1995): 89–99, where she analyzes the specific terms ἐγκόλπιον and τενάντιον, which, according to her, refer to the epoch of Photius and Ignatios; Martha Vinson, "Gender and Politics in the Posticonoclastic Period: The *Lives* of Antony the Younger, the Empress Theodora, and the Patriarch Ignatios", *Byzantion* 68, no. 2 (1998): 468–85. For the *Life* of Empress Theodora, see also *BS*, vol. 12, s.v. "Teodora, imperatrice di Constantinopoli", 222–24; Warren Treadgold, "The Bride-Shows of the Byzantine Emperors", *Byzantion* 49 (1979): 402–6; Lennart Rydén, "The Bride-Shows at the Byzantine Court – History or Fiction?", *Eranos Jahrbuch* 83 (1985): 183–88; *ODB*, vol. 3, s.v. "Theodora, empress", 2037ff.

second quarter of the eighth century. Martyrs like St. Stephen the Younger were practically nonexistent. The most severe consequence for Orthodox monks actively defending their beliefs was exile. A typical example of such moderate measures was the case of St. Symeon of Lesbos, mentioned above.

The relative tolerance on the part of the Iconoclast authorities gave birth to another hagiographic image, whose model was one of the most prominent saints of the ninth century. Ioannikios the Great (754/5 or 762–November 3, 846) has been given little credit for the enormous popularity that he gained after his death. He did not fight against iconoclasm, nor was he subjected to severe persecutions. Instead of ending in martyrdom, his life was full of adventures, travels, and struggles against evil spirits and creatures, materialized in numerous and various forms. The two versions of his *Life*, composed by the monks Peter and Sabbas,[153] are among the most important sources for studying the Byzantine image of the demon. The *Peter* version (BHG [936]) is characterized by more picturesque descriptions of events and a much more eloquent style; on the other hand, the author seems not very well acquainted with the political situation in the Empire and does not mention important events such as the ascension to the throne of Emperor Theophilos in 829. The *Sabbas* version (BHG [935]) is exceptional from a chronological point of view, but the dates of the events, provided by its author, often differ from those found in *Peter*. Both authors claim to have personally known Ioannikios himself and his close friend Eustratius of Agauros, whose life will be discussed below. Kazhdan[154] argues against a too early date of the *Peter* version, which, according to Mango, was written less than two months after

---

[153] For the two versions of the *Life* of St. Ioannikios the Great, see Loparev, *Greek Saints' Lives*, 293–315; Vitalien Lurent, *La Vie merveilleuse de saint Pierre d'Atroa*. [Subsidia hagiographica 29] (Brussels: Société des Bollandistes, 1956), 15ff. (exclusively on the "Sabbas" version); *BS*, vol. 6, s.v. "Giovanniccio, Monaco di Bittina", 1065ff.; *ODB*, vol. 2, s.v. "Ioannikios", 1005ff.; Kazhdan, *History of Byzantine Literature*, 1: 329–36; Cyril Mango, "Two Lives of St. Ioannikios and the Bulgarians", *Harvard Ukrainian Studies* 7 (1983): 393–404; Denis Sullivan, "Life of St. Ioannikios", in *Byzantine Defenders of Images. Eight Saints' Lives in English Translation*, 243–54.

[154] Kazhan, *History of Byzantine Literature*, 1: 329.

the Saint's demise. Kazhdan believes the two versions are based on the same sources (oral and written) but differ stylistically and politically.

The dates of the events given by the two *Lives* of St. Ioannikios are frequently precise but often do not match. Since they are directly related to the numerous miracles of the Saint and are not satisfactorily represented in modern research, we will here underake (to the extent possible) a short reconstruction of his biography. The Saint was born in 754/5 (*Sabbas*)[155] or 762 (*Peter*) in a village called Marikatou, located in Southern Bithynia, Asia Minor. His family name was Voilas (Βοΐλας), which probably indicates Slavic and Bulgarian origins.[156] In his youth, he was powerful physically and was accepted into the elite corps of the Byzantine army, the Excubitors (τάγμα τῶν Ἐσκουβιτῶν), whose headquarters were in Constantinople. This event occurred during the reign of the iconoclast Emperor Leo IV, and the future Saint most likely was an iconoclast himself.[157] In 792, during the disastrous battle of Markellai, when the Bulgarian khan Kardam defeated the young Emperor Constantine VI, Ioannikios saved the life of a high officer (*Sabbas*) or of the Emperor himself (*Peter*).[158] Despite the great honors and gifts that were lavished on him, the young soldier left the army and his career, rejected the Iconoclast heresy, and retired to the Antidion Monastery (Μονὴ Ἀντιδίου)[159] on Mount Olympus, in Southern Bithynia. Two years later, Ioannikios be-

---

[155] Sullivan, "Life of St. Ioannikios", 243.

[156] For the supposed Slavic or Bulgarian origin of St. Ioannikios, see Speros Vryonis, "St. Ioannicius the Great (754-846) and the 'Slavs' of Bithynia", *Byzantion* 31 (1961): 245ff; Faidon Malingoudis, "Slavonic Names from Byzantine Bithynia" [Greek: Φαίδων Μαλιγγούδης, "Σλαβικά ονόματα από τη Βυζαντινή Βιθυνία"], *Hellenika* 31, no. 2 (1979): 495.

[157] See Ioannikios (*Sabbas*), §5; Walter Kaegi, "The Byzantine Armies and Iconoclasm", *Byzantinoslavica* 27 (1966): 60ff.; Sullivan, "Life of St. Ioannikios", 245; Kazhdan, *History of Byzantine Literature*, 1: 330.

[158] Ioannikios (*Peter*), §5; Ioannikios (*Sabbas*), §6. See also Dennis Sullivan, "Was Constantine VI 'Lassoed' at Markellai", *Greek, Roman and Byzantine Studies* 35 (1994): 290ff.

[159] Ioannikios (*Peter*), §8; Ioannikios (*Sabbas*), §8. On the Antidion monastery, which was located on Mount Olympus, see Janin, *Les églises et les monastères*, 135ff. Whether or not Ioannikios became a monk during his stay there is controversial (see Sullivan, "Life of St. Ioannikios", 244 and n. 7, with bibliography).

came a hermit. He lived for thirteen years in a small cell on Olympus, during which time he made long trips throughout northwestern Asia Minor. Afterward, he settled in the district of the Thracesians (θέμα Θρακησίων), located in Central western Asia Minor, along the Aegean coast,[160] probably in the mountains close to the ancient city of Myra in Lycia.[161] There he remained during the first five years of the rule of Emperor Nikephoros I (802–811). Around 807, God ordered him to return to Bithynia,[162] where he performed numerous miracles. He predicted the battle of Varbitsa Pass (July 26, 811), when the armies of the Bulgarian khan Krum defeated and slaughtered the emperor and mortally wounded his son and heir, Stauracius. The reign of Nikephoros's successors Stauracius (811) and Michael I Rangabe (811–813), was unstable, and the next ruler, Leo V (815–820), chose to restore the Iconoclast heresy. Ioannikios was forced to flee again, this time to a mountain called Alsos (Ἄλσος) in Lydia.[163] There he lived almost until the emperor's bitter end; shortly before the violent death of Leo V on Christmas Eve, 820, the future Saint returned to Olympus, saving a village from a terrible evil dragon on the way.[164] During the reign of Michael II (820–829) and his son Theophilos (829–842), he lived in Southern Bithynia, making frequent trips to the nearby monasteries. In 821, he officially met some of the high-ranking iconodule clergy and personally spoke with Theodore Studite.[165] Ioannikios performed numerous miracles and died on November 23, 846. This serene monk, who remained untouched by the

---

[160] According to Ioannikios (*Peter*), §10, the "theme" (province, district) of the Thracesians in this period included the ancient regions of Ionia, Lydia, and parts of Caria and Phrygia, in western Asia Minor (see *ODB*, vol. 3, s.v. "Thrakesion", 2080).
[161] Ioannikios (*Sabbas*), §12.
[162] Ioannikios (*Peter*), §11; Ioannikios (*Sabbas*), §13.
[163] Ioannikios (*Peter*), §19; Ioannikios (*Sabbas*), §18. The exact location of Alsos is controversial. It was located in Lydia, southwest of Olympus (Janin, *Les églises et les monastères*, 150; Sullivan, "Life of St. Ioannikios", 274 and n. 167). This mountain is probably identical to Lisos in *Peter*, where the same events are dated much earlier, in 810.
[164] Ioannikios (*Peter*), §29; Ioannikios (*Sabbas*), §24.
[165] Ioannikios (*Peter*), §36; Ioannikios (*Sabbas*), §28. This dating follows Kazhdan, *History of Byzantine Literature*, 1: 328.

moderate persecutions of the Second Iconoclast period, lived to see the restoration of the icons in 843 and became, almost by chance, one of the symbols of his troubled epoch.

The two *Lives* of St. Ioannikios are among the most interesting and informative sources for the Byzantine demon. There is no other hagiographical text in the period under study with so many detailed descriptions of battles with demonic dragons. Sabbas and Peter give numerous accounts of miracles, magical practices and objects, and levitation.

* * *

Some other essential ninth-century texts belong to the hagiographical school of Bithynia. The monk Sabbas, the author of one of the *Lives* of St. Ioannikios, wrote two biographies of St. Peter of Atroa.[166] One (*BHG* [2364]) was probably compiled between 847–850.[167] The other, the so-called *vita retractata* (*BHG* [2365]), is usually dated between 858/60 and 865, despite the objections of Ivan Dujčev.[168] There are very few factual discrepancies between the two versions. The author had personal contact with the Saint and frequently participated actively in many episodes of his hero's life, but rarely gave accurate dates. St. Peter of Atroa resembles St. Ioannikios both in his origins and way of life.[169] The Saint, whose

---

[166] On the *Life* of St. Peter of Atroa see Loparev, *Greek Saints' Lives*, 315ff; Laurent, *La Vie merveilleuse*", 1-61; Ivan Dujčev, *The Bulgarian Middle Ages: Studies on the Political and Cultural History of Medieval Bulgaria* [Bulgarian: Иван Дуйчев, *Българско средновековие. Проучвания върху политическата и културната история на на средновековна България*] (Sofia: Nauka i Izkustvo, 1972), 134 and 139–45; *BS*, vol. 10, s.v. "Pietro d'Atroa", 668ff.; *ODB*, vol. 1, s.v. "Atroa", 228; Kazhdan, *History of Byzantine Literature*, 1: 336–40.

[167] See Laurent, *La Vie merveilleuse*, 14ff., who argues that the *Life* was written between 847 and 850. According to Laurent, the text could not have been compiled before the death of St. Ioannikios the Great (November 3, 846) since the latter is called "Saint" ("ὁ ἐν ἁγίοις"), a title never given to one living. Despite this persuasive argument, Kazhdan (*History of Byzantine Literature*, 1: 337) claims that the text was written soon after the death of Peter.

[168] Dujčev, *The Bulgarian Middle Ages*, 134 and 139–45.

[169] For the main events of St. Peter's life and their dates, see Laurent, *La Vie merveilleuse*, 24–35.

secular name was Theophylact, was born in 773 in Elea, a village near Pergamon in Mysia (in western Asia Minor). He was raised in the local Holy Mother of God church and, at twelve years of age, was ordained priest by the bishop. In 791/2, St. Peter was inspired by the Virgin Mary to travel to Mount Olympus. During this journey, he met his tutor Paul, who ordained him a monk in 794. His life was full of miracles but poor in public activity. Around 800, St. Peter helped Paul to found the St. Zacharias monastery and, in 805/6, succeeded him as abbot.[170] During the reign of the Iconoclast Emperor Leo V (815–820), he followed the example of St. Ioannikios and simply fled Bithynia. For a few years, he wandered around Lydia and visited Cyprus. After Leo's death, the persecutions against the iconodules temporarily abated. St. Peter returned to Mount Olympus, where the local monastic community did not receive him very well because of his reluctance to sacrifice himself for Orthodoxy; he was even accused of magical practices. The future Saint managed to win over St. Theodore Studite and gained back his influence. During the persecutions of Emperor Theophilos (832/3 and 835/6), he traveled again to northwestern Asia Minor and died on January 1, 837. The *Lives* of St. Peter of Atroa are like other texts produced by the Bithynian monks. They provide detailed accounts of numerous demonic images: snakes, pigs, dragons, and humans, among others.

A much more determined and active champion of Orthodoxy was Makarios (†c. 840), abbot of the monastery of Pelekete, located on the southern coast of the Sea of Marmara and west of Apamea. He came from a Constantinopolitan family of some social status. At the end of the eighth century, he entered the Pelekete monastery and was ordained a deacon by Patriarch Tarasios (782–806) himself.[171] Later he became an abbot and, unlike Ioannikios the Great and Peter of Atroa, actively fought against iconoclasm. He refused a high position offered by Leo V, and was arrested and exiled. Five letters of his correspondence with Theodore Studite are extant. St. Makarios died in 840, before the restoration of the

---

[170] *ODB*, vol. 1, s.v. "Atroa", 228; Janin, *Les églises et les monastères*, 151.
[171] Makarios of Pelekete, §7.

icons. The author of his *Life* (BHG [1003]), called Sabbas, claims to have known the Saint personally but does not provide much biographical information. Unlike other texts of the Bithynian hagiographical school, this text has the typical structure of a *martyrion*. It is organized around an *agōn* or public dispute with the heretical emperor.

The *Life* of Eustratios of Agauros is one of the last Bithynian biographies of the Iconoclast period. The Saint was born in the village of Biztiniana in northern Bithynia in the late eighth century. At the age of twenty, he entered the Agauros monastery (μονὴ τῶν Ἀγαύρου or τῶν Αὐγάρων), located in the vicinity of Prousa (modern-day Bursa), becoming its abbot during the reign of Emperor Theophilos (829–842). Like St. Ioannikios the Great and St. Peter of Atroa, he was forced by the persecutions to leave his monastery and travel around western Asia Minor in 815–20 and the 830s. The author of his *Life* (BHG [645]) had no personal contact with the Saint but claimed to have met his acquaintances. Some details indicate that the text was written after 900. For example, after 856, the Saint had healed a five-year-old boy who, at the time of the author's writing, had reached an advanced age. Use of written sources like, e.g., the *Lives* of St. Ioannikios the Great and St. Philaretos the Merciful, is obvious.[172]

* * *

The relocation of the core of the Empire from Asia Minor to mainland and insular Greece undoubtedly influenced the literature of the late ninth and tenth centuries. As a consequene of this change, the hagiography of Bithynia, which produced a large number of texts during the era of iconoclasm, gradually declined. During this period, there are only two hagiographical texts set in the area of the old monastic communities

---

[172] For the parallels with the *Life* of St. Philaretos the Merciful, see Kazhdan, *History of Byzantine Literature*, 1: 290. For general information about the *Life* of St. Eustratius of Agauros, see Loparev, *Greek Saints' Lives*, 318–32; *BS*, vol. 5, s.v. "Eustrazio il Taumaturgo", 313; Janin, *Les églises et les monastères*, 132–34; Kazhdan, *History of Byzantine Literature*, 1: 340ff.

of western Asia Minor, the *Lives* of St. Thomas Dephourkinos and St. Paul of Latros.

St. Thomas Dephourkinos is a little-known Byzantine saint, and the only specific information about him comes from his short Synaxarion *Life* (BHG [2453]).[173] He was born on Mount Kyminas in Bithynia to a middle-class family in the ninth century. He spent most of his life as the abbot of two monasteries along the river Sangarius in Bithynia, where he fought demons and became famous for his healing. Due to his contacts with Emperor Leo VI (886–912), mentioned in the text, Henri Grégoire believes that this is the priest who blessed the emperor's fourth marriage to Zoe Carbonopsina in 906. This identification cannot be considered certain.

The biography of St. Paul of Latros (early tenth century–December 15, 955) is far more informative. Like St. Peter of Atroa, he was born in Elea near Pergamum, as the son of the naval commander Antiochus, who lost his life in the unsuccessful expedition against the Arabs on the island of Chios in 912.[174] His mother moved with him and his brother Basil to Bithynia, where she soon died. After her death, Paul was forced to become a shepherd, but subsequently, with the help of Basil, entered the monastery of Karya (Καρύα)[175] on Mount Latros near Miletus.[176] His biography is full of hermitages and miracles, but the events cannot really be dated. Paul was very popular even during his lifetime. He was in contact

---

[173] For more on him and his life, see *BS*, vol. 12, s.v. "Tomaso Defurkino", 605ff.; Janin, *Les églises et les monastères*, 102; Henri Grégoire, "Thomas Dephourkinos du monastère de Kyminas et le quatrième mariage de Léon le Sage", *Byzantion* 32 (1962): 381–86.

[174] Alexander Vasiliev, *Byzance et les Arabes*, vol. 2: *La dynastie Macedonienne (867 – 959)* (Brussels: Éditions de l'Institut de philologie et d'histoire orientales et slaves, 1968), 214. His opinion is accepted by Kazhdan (*History of Byzantine Literature*, 2: 215).

[175] For the Karya monastery, founded by Peter, St. Paul's tutor, see Janin, *Les églises et les monastères*, 232–33, who argues that it was located near the ancient city of Myus, north of Mount Latros. A monastery of the same name was still in existence in 1049.

[176] Paul of Latros I, §4; cf. Kazhdan, *History of Byzantine Literature*, 2: 216. For the great monastic center of Latros or Latmos, which developed in the seventh and eighth centuries north of the river Maeander, see Janin, *Les églises et les monastères*, 216–40.

with Emperor Constantine VII (912–959), who planned to visit him,[177] and with the Bulgarian Tzar Peter.[178] Foreign peoples — the Arabs from Crete, the Russians, and the Romans — also knew about him.[179] To avoid this unwanted popularity, Paul is said to have twice escaped to the island of Samos.[180] He died in the monastery he founded on Mount Latros on December 15, 955. His *Life*[181] was written shortly after the Saint's demise and was probably based on his personal diary (οἴκοθεν βίβλος τῶν ἑαυτοῦ πράξεων).[182] The last emperor mentioned in the text is Nikephoros II Phocas, who assumed the throne in 963, the *terminus post quem*. The earliest manuscripts of the text date from the eleventh century.[183] The biography was greatly influenced by the legend of St. Ioannikios the Great. Paul's family moved to the vicinity of the Marikatou village, the homeland of Ioannikios, and the future Saint bcame a swineherd, like his great predecessor. Like most of the Bythinian *Lives*, Paul of Latros' is rich in miracles and demonic stories. Evil spirits often appear in various human forms or as wild animals.

5. Semi-secular hagiography

Several texts, quite different in style and date, are classified by Kazhdan as "semi-secular hagiography". The holy persons to whom these texts are dedicated spent most of their lives as laymen. The authors are interested in political events but tend almost wholly to omit the struggle between iconodules and iconoclasts.

---

[177] Paul of Latros, I, §28.1-5.
[178] Paul of Latros, I, §27.20–22.
[179] Paul of Latros, I, §27.19ff.
[180] Paul of Latros, I, §§24-26 and §35ff. For the first journey, see Kazhdan, *History of Byzantine Literature*, 2: 216ff.
[181] For Paul of Latros and his *Life*, see *BS*, vol. 10, s.v. "Paolo il Giovane", 258–60; *ODB*, vol. 3, s.v. "Paul of Latros", 1068; Kazhdan, *History of Byzantine Literature*, 2: 211–18. Janin refers to some of the events of his life related to the foundation of monasteries (*Les églises et les monastères*, 217–40).
[182] Paul of Latros I, §20.14.
[183] For the dating, see Kazhdan, *History of Byzantine Literature*, 2: 211.

The life of St. Philaretos the Merciful (BHG [1511z–1512b]) was the earliest semi-secular biography. It doesn't mention demons and evil spirits but gives interesting information about the Byzantine idea of beauty. The Saint himself is rather atypical. He was a Paphlagonian aristocrat who lost his wealth in an Arab raid on his homeland in the 780s but retained his piety and compassion. His impoverished family was involved in the high politics of the Empire when his granddaughter Maria won the beauty contest organized by Empress Dowager Irene and married her son Emperor Constantine VI (780–797). The only saintly virtues of Philaretos, who never became a monk, were, according to his *Life*, his patience and mercy. The text, preserved in two versions, was written by his grandson Niketas in 821, probably as a wedding present for Euphrosyne, daughter of Constantine VI and Maria, who married Emperor Michael II (820–829).[184]

A much more important source for the Byzantine demon is the other semi-secular hagiographical text of the ninth century, the *Life* of St. Antony the Younger (c. 785–865?). Antony is very different from the standard martyr or hermit. The biography begins with the story of John — a powerful robber who repented and became a monk in the monastery of St. Sabbas near Jerusalem. It was to this strange person that little Antony's parents entrusted their son. John predicted the successful career of his pupil and his future monastic exploits. A considerable part of the text is dedicated to Antony's worldly life. He moved to Asia Minor, won the favor of a Byzantine naval commander; subsequently, the iconoclast emperor Michael II made him the deputy (ἐκ προσώπου) of the governor of the province (theme) of the Cibyrrhaeots in southern Asia Minor. Antony's physical qualities (tall stature, extraordinary strength) and his military exploits against the rebel Thomas the Slav (821–823) and against

---

[184] For the *Life* of St. Philaretos the Merciful, see Loparev, *Greek Saints' Lives*, 440–50; *BS*, vol. 5, s.v. "Filarete l'Elemosiniere", 681–83; Ševčenko, "Hagiography", 126–27; Alexander Kazhdan and Lee Sherry, "The Tale of a Happy Fool: the *Vita* of St. Philaretos the Merciful (BHG 1511z – 1512b)", *Byzantion* 66 (1996): 351–62; *ODB*, vol. 3, s.v. "Philaretos the Merciful", 1650; Kazhdan, *History of Byzantine Literature*, 1: 281–91; Petrinski, *The Bride-Shows*, 37–40 and 52–66.

Arab raids are described extensively. Despite his successful career, Antony decided to become a monk. The story of his atypical resignation of his office gave rise to the assumption that the future Saint simply fell out of favor with the emperor. According to the text, the future Saint invited his subordinates to a feast, waited for them to get drunk, and fled to the monastery. The rest of the text describes Antony's travels and adventures. His confrontations with secular authorities, both with Michael II and his son Theophilos, had nothing to do with his iconodule leanings but rather concerned his previous actions as an imperial official. Antony died probably in 865 at the age of eighty. His *Life* (BHG [142-143a]) was written probably soon afterward by an unknown author and is preserved in several manuscripts.[185]

6. Ignatios the Deacon (*c.* 770–mid-ninth century) and Pseudo-Ignatios the Deacon

One of the most prolific religious writers of the eighth and ninth centuries is the excellent scholar Ignatios the Deacon (*c.* 770–mid-ninth century), a pupil of Patriarch Tarasios.[186] The peak of his career came after the 820s. Ignatios was a grammarian (teacher of grammar and rhetoric), a *skeuophylax* (keeper of the sacred vessels) of the St. Sofia church in Constantinople, and bishop of Nicaea. His literary production includes hagi-

---

[185] Loparev, *Greek Saints' Lives*, 332–47; *BS*, vol. 2, s.v. "Antonio il Giovane", 147–49; François Halkin, "Saint Antoine le Jeune et Pétronas le vainqueur des Arabes en 863", *Analecta Bollandiana* 62 (1944): 187–225 and *Analecta Bollandiana* 64 (1946): 256; *ODB*, vol. 1, s.v. "Antony the Younger", 126; Kazhdan, *History of Byzantine Literature*, 1: 291–94.

[186] For Ignatios the Deacon and his writings, see Elena Lipschitz, *Essays on the History of Byzantine Society and Culture. 8th – first half of the 9th century* [Russian: Елена Липшиц, *Очерки истории византийского общества и культуры. VIII-первая половина IX века*] (Moskow and Leningrad: Publishing House of the Academy of Sciences of the USSR, 1961), 302–9; Ševčenko, "Hagiography", 121–25; Cyril Mango and Stephanos Efthymiadis, *The Correspondence of Ignatios the Deacon* [Dumbarton Oaks Texts 11; Corpus Fontium Historiae Byzantinae, 39] (Washington, DC: Dumbarton Oaks Research Library and Collection, 1997), 3–18; Stephanos Eftymiadis, "On the Hagiographical Work of Ignatius the Deacon", *Jahrbuch der Österreichischen Byzantinistik* 41 (1991): 73–83; Kazhdan, *History of Byzantine Literature*, 1: 344–66.

ography, epistolography, and hymnography. During the reign of Emperor Leo V, he accepted iconoclasm and afterward asked for forgiveness from Patriarch Tarasios for this sin. It isn't easy to assign a specific date for all of these events since almost the sole source is the lemma in the *Suda* lexicon.[187] Ignatios was the author of the *Lives* of the Patriarchs Tarasios (784–806) and Nikephoros (806–815), who led the Orthodox Church between the First and the Second Iconoclast period. The biography of the latter (*BHG* [1335])[188] was almost certainly written shortly after 829. The *Life* of the former (*BHG* [1698])[189] was probably compiled late in the life of Ignatios. The two texts have so many similarities that Kazhdan calls them "two patriarchs and a single fabula".[190] The two Patriarchs were both greatly influenced by their mothers. They both had early careers as imperial secretaries, and both were invited by emperors to occupy the highest post in the Church. The *agōn* plays a vital role in the plots. For Nikephoros, who was forced to resign in favor of the iconoclast Theodotus Kassiteras, the protracted dispute with the heretic Emperor Leo V forms part of a logically coherent chain of events. Still, the bitter argument of Tarasios with Constantine VI about the latter's second marriage sounds slightly artificial given that the Patriarch himself allowed this wedding. The martyrdom of Nikephoros is real, while, accord-

---

[187] *Suidae lexicon*, ed. Ada Adler, [Lexicographi Graeci, vol. 1], Part 2: Δ-I, (Stuttgart: Teubner, 1994), s.v. I.84.

[188] For the *Life* of Patriarch Nikephoros, see Loparev, *Greek Saints' Lives*, 109–14; Lipschitz, *Essays on the History of Byzantine Society*, 85–105; *BS*, vol. 9, s.v. "Niceforo, patriarca di Constantinoipoli", 871–74; Ševčenko, "Hagiography", 125; da Costa-Louillet, "Saints de Constantinople", I, 245ff.; Efthymiadis, "On the Hagiographical Work", 73–83; *ODB*, vol. 3, s.v. "Nikephoros I, patriarch of Constantinople", 1477; Kazhdan, *History of Byzantine Literature*, 1: 344ff. and 352–56.

[189] For the *Life* of Patriarch Tarasios, see Stephanos Efthymiadis, *The Life of the Patriarch Tarasios by Ignatios the Deacon (BHG 1698)* [*Birmingham Byzantine and Ottoman monographs* 4] (New York: Routledge, 2016), 6–52; Loparev, *Greek Saints' Lives*, 99–109; *BS*, vol. 12, s.v. "Tarasio, patriarca di Constantinoipoli", 127-131; da Costa-Louillet, "Saints de Constantinople", I, 217–29; Romilly Jenkins, *Byzantium: The Imperial Centuries, A.D. 610–1071* (London: Weidenfeld & Nicolson, 1966), 93–100; Efthymiadis", On the Hagiographical Work", 73–83; *ODB*, vol. 3, s.v. "Tarasios", 2011; Kazhdan, *History of Byzantine Literature*, 1: 345 and 352–56.

[190] Kazhdan, *History of Byzantine Literature*, 1: 352.

ing to the text, Tarasios merely *admired* the exploits of the martyrs. In these two biographies, the supernatural seldom assumes material form. The texts are pretty rhetorical, significantly different from the *Lives* of provincial saints, like St. Ioannikios, in which Evil frequently appears in animal or human shape. On the other hand, the two texts are classic examples of the demonization of emperors, using certain features belonging to the classical image of the demon. Leo V is a lion, a dragon, and a wolf, who voluntarily puts himself in the service of demons and becomes their instrument. The *Life* of Patriarch Tarasios also mentions the female demon Gello, and this is the only account of the folklore beliefs related to this evil witch in the ninth century.

Two more hagiographic texts from the ninth century are attributed to Ignatios the Deacon. They differ in style and plot from the *Lives* of Tarasios and Nikephoros. The first is the biography of the "wandering saint"[191] Gregory of Dekapolis (*c.* 797–November 20, 842?), a native of the city of Irinopolis in Isauria (southeastern Asia Minor). "In the prime of his youth",[192] the future Saint rejected the marriage arranged for him by his parents, Sergios and Maria, and entered a monastery.[193] Since the usual age for a boy from a good family to marry in Byzantium was between sixteen and eighteen, it is logical to assume that Gregory was born *c.* 797 and became a monk *c.* 813–15. This dating is further confirmed by the episode of the rift between the young monk and the abbot caused by the latter's disinterested position towards the iconoclasts (τοῖς αἱρεσιώταις ἀδιαφόρως συμπεφυρμένου).[194] In 815, Emperor Leo V restored iconoclasm, and it was only logical for the young Gregory to find an iconodule monastery. He chose one in the region of Decapolis, in Isauria (Asia Minor),[195] whose abbot was his uncle Symeon. He spent

---

[191] The expression "wandering saint" belongs to Kazhdan (*History of Byzantine Literature*, 1: 356).
[192] Gregory of Dekapolis, §3.1ff.
[193] Gregory of Dekapolis, §5.
[194] Gregory of Dekapolis, §5.
[195] For this region, see *TIB*, vol. 5.1: *Kilikien und Isaurien*, ed. Friedrich Hild and Hansgerd Hellenkemper (Vienna: Verlag der Österreichischen Akademie der Wissenschaften, 1990), 235ff.

fourteen years there[196], until *c.* 829–30. Afterward, he decided to become a hermit in the wild mountains and caves of Decapolis, where his enemies were many various demons in different forms.[197] As we already mentioned, these stories are among the most informative sources for the image of the Byzantine evil spirit. During the persecutions of the iconoclast Emperor Theophilos (829–842), St. Gregory traveled a lot; among his destinations were cities like Ephesus, Aenus, Thessalonica, Rome, Syracuse, and Otranto. At the end of his life, he also visited Constantinople and Mount Olympus in Asia Minor. St. Gregory probably died before the restoration of the icons, in 842 or a little earlier.[198] The authorship of Ignatios the Deacon, accepted by Mango,[199] is spurious, even though most of the manuscripts refer to his name. Wanda Wolska-Conus and Kazhdan take up the opposite position.[200] The two scholars argue that the text's real author was another hagiographer of the same name. There are significant differences between the genuine biographies of Ignatios the Deacon and the *Life* of St. Gregory. The language is much more vernacular, and the text is full of miracles and demonic images, like dragons, mice, and snakes. Haunted buildings and caves are also described in detail, which is not typical of Ignatios. References to ancient authors and theologians are scarce.[201]

The last text, which is attributed to Ignatios the Deacon, is the *Life* of St. George of Amastris.[202] The Saint was born in the mid-eighth century in a small town near the city of Amastris, on the Paphlagonian shore of the Black Sea. His family belonged to the local nobility. George spent some years in the Church administration and around 790 was appointed

---

[196] Gregory of Dekapolis, §6.
[197] Gregory of Dekapolis, §§7–9.
[198] Cyril Mango, "On Re-Reading the Life of St. Gregory Gregory the Decapolite", *Byzantina* 13, no 1 (1985): 633–56; Kazhdan, *History of Byzantine Literature*, 1: 356.
[199] Mango, "On Re-Reading", 635.
[200] Wanda Wolska-Conus, "De quibusdam Ignatiis", *Travaux et mémoires* 4 (1970): 340ff. and 359; Kazhdan, *History of Byzantine Literature*, 1: 356–60.
[201] Kazhdan, *History of Byzantine Literature*, 1: 357.
[202] For the dating of the events in the *Life*, see Kazhdan, *History of Byzantine Literature*, 1: 360; *ODB*, vol. 2, s.v. "George of Amastris", 837.

bishop of Amastris by Patriarch Tarasios. He died between 802 and 807. Both the date of his *Life* and Ignatios the Deacon's authorship are very problematic. The text itself is very important from a historical point of view since it mentions the first Russian raid on Byzantine soil.²⁰³ Like the biography of St. Gregory of Dekapolis, this hagiographical work describes various miracles, demons, and exorcisms in detail, which is very unusual for Ignatios the Deacon.²⁰⁴ The author makes significant efforts to use classical Attic language, but with little success. Along with very difficult archaic forms like, e.g., dual number, he adopts the vernacular παιδί. The original Ignatios could never be accused of such semi-literate composition. According to Ševčenko, the *Life* of St. George of Amastris is one of the few surviving examples of pro-iconoclast hagiography. There is no mention of icons in the text and the numerous miracles are performed either directly by the power of God or through the sign of the cross. Ševčenko lays stress on the fact that the text is preserved in only a single manuscript, which leads to the conclusion that it was not considered very appropriate reading after the restoration of the icons in 843.²⁰⁵

7. The "historical" hagiography during the ninth century

The term "historical hagiography" comes from Alexander Kazhdan.²⁰⁶ It includes two texts of spurious date but similar in style, content, and context. The first is the *Life* of St. Michael the Synkellos (761–January 4, 846), a native of Palestine, who was a *synkellos* (a high-ranking Church official) of the Patriarch of Jerusalem. In 814, he was sent by Patriarch Thomas

---

[203] On this dispute, see Ševčenko, "Hagiography", 120–26; Kazhdan, *History of Byzantine Literature*, 1: 360–66. For general information about the *Life* of St. George of Amastris, other than the researches of Ševčenko and Kazhdan, see Loparev, *Greek Saints' Lives*, 238–58; *BS*, vol. 6, s.v. "Giorgio, vescovo di Amastri in Paflagonia", 533; Wolska-Conus, "De quibusdam Ignatiis", 329–60; Efthymiadis, "On the Hagiographical Work", 73–83; *ODB*, vol. 2, s.v. "George of Amastris", 837.
[204] Kazhdan, *History of Byzantine Literature*, 1: 361–66.
[205] Ševčenko, "Hagiography", 122–25.
[206] Kazhdan, *History of Byzantine Literature*, 2: 206.

(807–820) as an envoy to the iconoclast Emperor Leo V and shortly afterward was thrown in jail.[207] The Saint was given his freedom by the next emperor, Michael II (820–829), and retired as a hermit on Mount Olympus in Bithynia. Still, a few years later, Emperor Theophilos imprisoned him again in much harsher conditions[208]. After restoring the icons, Empress Theodora considered his nomination for Patriarch of Constantinople, but, ultimately, Methodius' candidacy prevailed. Nevertheless, the new Patriarch recompensed Michael for his suffering under iconoclast rule and for his defeat in the competition for the Ecumenical throne, giving him the great Chora monastery in Constantinople. The future Saint passed away quietly in 846.[209]

The date of the *Life* of St. Michael the Synkellos (*BHG* [1296])[210] is unclear. Since the text shows a positive attitude towards Emperor Michael III (842–867), Ševčenko argues that the author was a younger contemporary of the Saint, who wrote before the overthrow of the last emperor of the Amorian dynasty in 867 by Basil I the Macedonian. This argument is doubted by Kazhdan, who points to an anti-Macedonian trend in the 920s and the mid-tenth century. The definitive *terminus ante quem* is the first surviving manuscript, dated in the early eleventh century.

The other semi-secular text is the *martyrion* of the forty-two soldiers of Amorion. The city of Amorion in Phrygia, the capital of the Anatolic theme, was captured by Caliph Al-Muʻtasim (833–842) in 838.[211] Forty-two of the captives, both soldiers and officers, refused to convert to Islam. They were taken to the Abbasid capital Samara, tortured, and finally executed on March 6, 845. This text gives very little information about the image of the demon in Byzantium and we will not discuss the complex issue of the date and the authorship of its versions (*BHG* [1209–

---

[207] The text (Michael the Synkellos, §14) mentions the summer of the seventh *indiction* (i.e., of the year 815).
[208] Michael the Synkellos, §16.
[209] See Kazhdan, *History of Byzantine Literature*, 2: 204.
[210] On him see Loparev, *Greek Saints' Lives*, 213-224; *BS*, vol. 9, s.v. "Michele il Sincello", 452-457; Ševčenko, "Hagiography", 116 and note 19; *ODB*, vol. 2, s.v. "Michael Synkellos", 1369ff; Kazhdan, *History*, vol. 2, 204ff.
[211] On this important event see Vasiliev, *Byzance et les Arabes*, vol. 1, 144-177.

1214c]).²¹² There are two main redactions. One was compiled by the monk Euodios, otherwise unknown, and survives in two versions (short and long). This is a typical *martyrion* with an extensive *agōn*. The author is very critical of Emperor Theophilos, which indicates that the text was probably written in the first decades after the final restoration of the icons. The other redaction is preserved in numerous versions which bear the names of different authors, e.g., Michael, Sophronios of Cyprus (*c*. 858–890), Ignatios (early tenth century).²¹³

8. The hagiography of Constantinople from the late ninth to the mid-tenth century

The second half of the ninth century is when Byzantine literature is associated with Patriarch Photius and the so-called "Photian Renaissance". This was the period in which the specific socio-political conditions for the development of humanism and the interest in ancient rhetoric and philosophy were established. This tendency affects only a few hagiographical texts of the time, in which the demonic rarely appears in material form. In the *Lives* of the patriarchs Ignatios (847–858), Antony II Kauleas (893–901), and Euthymios I (907–912), only abstract demonological terminology is used, and some examples of the demonization of political figures appear.

The works of the great scholar, Niketas-David of Paphlagonia (first half of the tenth century) are highly rhetorical. They include encomia, epistolography, and homilies.²¹⁴ He is interested in patriarchs who were forced to abdicate, like St. Gregory of Nazianzus and St. John Chrysostom. His main hagiographical text is the *Life* of Patriarch Ignatios (847–858, 867–877). The Saint (whose secular name was Niketas) was

---

[212] For the forty-two martyrs of Amorion, see Loparev, *Greek Saints' Lives*, 76–91; *BS*, vol. 1, s.v. "Amorio, XLII martiri", 1018–20; *ODB*, vol. 2, s.v. "Forty-Two Martyrs of Amorion", 800ff.; Wolska-Conus, "De quibusdam Ignatiis", 334 and n. 28; Kazhdan, *History of Byzantine Literature*, 2: 206–9.

[213] Kazhdan, *History of Byzantine Literature*, 2: 207ff.

[214] For the biography of Niketas-David, see Kazhdan, *History of Byzantine Literature*, 2: 91–102.

one of the most significant church figures of the ninth century. He was the grandson of Nikephoros I (802–811) and the son of the emperor Michael I Rangabe (811–813). After his father was overthrown, he was castrated and forced to take the monastic order. Following the death of Patriarch Methodius (843–847), he was chosen by the empress regent Theodora to take his place. He was removed by Caesar Bardas and Emperor Michael III in 858 and replaced with Photius (858–867). Basil I, the founder of the Macedonian dynasty, returned him to the patriarchal throne in the first months of his reign (fall of 867). Ignatios died on October 23, 877, but his followers fought Photius and his supporters until the beginning of the tenth century. Niketas-David wrote his life (BHG [817–818]) in all probability in the early tenth century.[215] The text, which combines elements of eulogy for Ignatios and invective against Photius and Bardas, is not a standard biography. There is no mention of demons in any material form, but there are plenty of examples of the political demonization of Bardas, Photius, and other anti-heroes. There are also evil spirits associated with certain sins, like vain glory and posthumous miracles.[216]

Very little is known about the activities and life of the Patriarch of Constantinople Antony Kauleas (893–901). According to his biography, he grew up and was educated in the capital, taking monastic vows at the age of twelve, and later became abbot of an unknown monastery. Emperor Leo VI (887–912) appointed him patriarch and he tried to reconcile the supporters of Photius and Ignatios. He died on February 12, 901. His encomium (BHG [139])[217] was written by Niketas the Philosopher, whose identity has given rise to various conjectures. It is possible (al-

---

[215] For more on Niketas-David, see Loparev, *Greek Saints' Lives*, 265–90; da Costa-Louillet, "Saints de Constantinople", I, 461–78; *BS*, vol. 7, s.v. "Ignazio, patriarca di Constantinopoli", 665–72; *ODB*, vol. 2, s.v. "Ignatios, Patriarch of Constantinople" 983ff.; Kazhdan, *History of Byzantine Literature*, 2: 97–102 (for the dating, see 98).

[216] Patriarch Ignatios, §42, and §50. Kazhdan (*History of Byzantine Literature*, 2: 101) inaccurately claims that such miracles are entirely lacking from the text.

[217] For more on Antony Kauleas, see Loparev, *Greek Saints' Lives*, 148–52; *BS*, vol. 2, s.v. "Antonio II Cauleas", 202; *ODB*, vol. 1, s.v. "Antony II Kauleas", 125; Kazhdan, *History of Byzantine Literature*, 2: 89ff.

though unproven) that he is the Nikephoros with whom Patriarch Photius corresponded in 873–75.[218] The text is highly rhetorical and very rarely mentions the image of the demon. The only exceptions are one interesting account on demonic ghosts and a few posthumous miracles.

* * *

The *Life* of Patriarch Euthymios (*BHG* [651])[219] was probably written by a monk of the Psamatia monastery. He knew the Saint well and was well-acquainted with the political struggles in the Empire. This makes the text one of the essential sources for Byzantine history in the last quarter of the ninth and the first quarter of the tenth centuries. The biography was written shortly after the death of the Saint, *c.* 920, according to P. Karlyn-Hayter, or 932, according to D. Sophianos.[220] The anonymous author was a well-educated former civil servant influenced by the rhetorical style of Aretas of Caesarea.[221]

The future Patriarch Euthymios I (907–912) was born *c.* 832 in Seleucia, Isauria (in southeastern Asia Minor). He became a monk very young and afterward retired as a hermit on Mount Olympus in Bithynia. During the reign of Basil I, he settled in Constantinople and supported the crown prince Leo. After Leo acceded to the throne, he funded the construction of the Psamathias monastery (in the southwest corner of the capital) and appointed Euthymios its abbot and a member of the Senate. In 907, the crisis surrounding the emperor's fourth marriage reached its peak, and the removal of the disgraced patriarch Nicholas I Mystikos (901–907) opened the way for the Psamathian abbot to assume the high-

---

[218] This is the opinion expressed by the editor of the text, P. Leone. On this point, see Kazhdan, *History of Byzantine Literature*, 2: 90.

[219] The bibliography on Patriarch Euthymios is extensive. See Loparev, *Greek Saints' Lives*, 203ff.; *BS*, vol. 5, s.v. "Eutimio, patriarca di Constantinopoli", 327ff.; *ODB*, vol. 2, s.v. "Euthymios, patriarch of Constantinople", 755ff.; Kazhdan, *History of Byzantine Literature*, 2: 103–11.

[220] On these two hypotheses, see Kazhdan, *History of Byzantine Literature*, 2: 104ff.

[221] On the different suggestions about the datation and the author of the text, see Kazhdan, *History of Byzantine Literature*, 2: 103–5.

est order in the Orthodox Church. As patriarch, Euthymios legitimized the birth of Constantine (the future emperor Constantine VII) as heir to the throne, and thus satisfied the wishes of Leo VI. After the death of his brother, Emperor Alexander restored Nicholas I to his throne, and Euthymios was tortured and sent into exile for a time. He died on August 5, 917, having previously rejected the empress regent Zoe's offer to reassume the patriarchal throne.

In contrast to the *Life* of Patriarch Ignatios, which is a combination of encomium and invective, the biography of Patriarch Euthymios is much closer to the historical genre. Kazhdan even edited it under the title *Psamathian Chronicle*,[222] and not solely for the reasons of the ideological peculiarities of Soviet humanist studies. The narrative is constructed as a single and coherent chain of events, whereas the classical hagiographical text usually consists of discrete, relatively independent stories. Many of the episodes are presented in a pictorial, almost cinematic manner. The characters of personages like Basil I, Theophano, the mad Alexander, Zoe Carbonopsina, Aretas of Caesarea, and Niketas-David are not stereotyped. Unlike the standard *Lives*, the text doesn't mention any miracles performed by the Saint. For the study of Byzantine demons, the text is less interesting for the (minimal) information it provides on this particular subject but rather for the large number of situations in which, surprisingly, an evil spirit is not present. The author shows an amazing ability to describe human emotions. In hagiographical literature, such emotions, especially unbridled anger, are usually associated with demonic influence. Still, the anonymous author of the *Life* of Patriarch Euthymios avoids explanations of this kind and tries to gain real insight into the human soul. Evil spirits and demons are hardly mentioned, and human feelings harmonize with the character of each person. The emotional character of Leo VI and the misfortunes of his family give rise to his frequent tan-

---

[222] "The Psamathian chronicle" [Russian: "Псамафийская хроника"], ed. Alexander Kazhdan, in *Two Byzantine Chronicles* [Russian: *Две византийские хроники*] (Moscow: Publishing House of Oriental Literature, 1959), 7–139. Kazhdan (*History of Byzantine Literature*, 2: 105) points out that the chronicle is "closer to the genre of chronicle than to the 'encomion' of a saint".

trums, and the pride and boundless ambition of the Emperor's father-in-law Stylianos Zautzes quite naturally result in his outbursts against everything and everyone on his daughter's path to the throne. Unlike his predecessors, the author of the *Life* of St. Euthymios does not need to lean on demons to make the story and the characters plausible.

* * *

The *Life* of St. Irene "in Chrysobalanto" (*BHG* [952]) is an encomium for the abbess of the Chrysobalanton monastery in Constantinople.[223] According to the text, Irene was born in the late 840s or the early 850s and belonged to a noble Cappadocian family.[224] In 855, she took part in the bride show organized for the young Emperor Michael III (842–867). Her biographer says that she arrived in the capital late, and before she had got there, the youth had already chosen his bride Eudokia Dekapolitissa. Taking this as a sign from God, she entered the Chrysobalanton monastery, distinguished herself, and finally became abbess. According to her *Life*, she died at ninety-seven in the 940s or 950s.

The biography was written long after the Saint's death. The author informs us that the ruling Macedonian dynasty was in its fifth generation, which means the reign of either Basil II (976–1018) or Constantine VIII (1018–1025).[225] The biographer demonstrates astonishing ignorance of the political situation and events in the second half of the ninth and the first half of the tenth centuries. For example, her mentor before the bride show, which occurred in 855, was identified as St. Ioannikios the Great, who died on November 3, 846. Patriarch Methodius, who with such solemnity blessed her as the new abbess of Chrysobalanton,[226] passed away on June 14, 847, at least fifteen years before this event.

---

[223] For more on Irene, see *ODB*, vol. 2, s.v. "Irene of Chrysobalanton", 1010; Treadgold, "The Bride-Shows", 404–6; Rydén, "The Bride-Shows", 189ff. For some of the aspects of the demonic image in the *Life*, see Joannou, *Démonologie*, 14ff.
[224] *ODB*, vol. 2, s.v. "Irene of Chrysobalanton", 1010.
[225] Irene of Chrysobalanton, §12.
[226] Ibid., §7.

Despite the shortcomings of the text, which make it practically unusable as a historical source, it provides quite interesting information about the image of the Byzantine demon. This is one of the few hagiographical texts to develop some demonological system with a theoretical explanation of the actions of evil spirits. Some magical practices and rituals for breaking black love magic are described in detail.

* * *

Among the most informative texts of the late ninth and early tenth centuries are the *Life* of Basil the Younger (†March 26, 944 or 952) and the *Vision* of the monk Cosmas. These two works are among the most fascinating and detailed sources for the role of demons in the afterlife journey of the soul during the period under study.

The manuscript tradition of Basil's *Life* (*BHG* [263–264f]), probably the lengthiest hagiographical texts produced in Byzantium, is highly complex.[227] Until recently, the only available editions were partial, the most complete belonging to Alexander Veselovskij (1889 and 1891) and Sergey Vilinskij (1911–13).[228] In 2014, Alice-Mary Talbot published a complete edition of the text, based on the Moscow manuscript, with exhaustive introduction and commentary. Basil is a very obscure figure,[229] and his *Life* is the only source for any information about him. He was not included in the Synaxarion of Constantinople, no other author mentions

---

[227] For the manuscript tradition, see Christine Angelidi, *The Life of St. Basil the Younger* [Greek: Χριστίνα Αγγελίδη, *Ο Βίος τοῦ ἁγίου Βασιλείου τοῦ Νέου*], PhD diss (University of Ioannina, 1980), 1–17 and 22–51 (on the seven manuscript families); Basil the Younger, 53–58; Alice-Mary Talbot, "Some observations on the Life of St. Basil the Younger", in *Byzantine Hagiography: Texts, Themes & Projects*, ed. Antonio Rigo, Michele Trizio, and Eleftherios Despotakis [Studies in Byzantine History and Civilization 13] (Turnhout: Brepols Publishers, 2018), 314–19.

[228] On the earlier editions of the text, see Angelidi, "The Life of St. Basil", 18–21.

[229] For the main events of Basil's life and career, see Angelidi, "The Life of St. Basil", 58–63 (with a chronological table); *ODB*, vol. 1, s.v. "Basil the Younger", 270ff.; Kazhdan, *History of Byzantine Literature*, 2: 186–89; Talbot, "Some observations", 313ff.; Basil the Younger, 13–15 and 27–30.

him, and there is no surviving icon or depiction.²³⁰ The author, the pious layman Gregory, claims that he knows nothing about his origin, early career, or how he became a monk.²³¹ He begins his narration with Basil's arrest by imperial agents. In 896 or 906,²³² he was accused of espionage, brought to Constantinople, and tortured by order of the influential *patrikios* Samonas. Thrown into the sea, he was miraculously saved by two dolphins and delivered to Constantinople. The monk preferred to live the rest of his life in various private houses, rather than seek admittance to a monastery. He settled first in the home of John and Hellen, a "middle-class" couple, and then, probably after 928,²³³ he moved to the mansion of a high-ranking official, the *primikerios* Constantine. Basil performed various miracles, exorcized demons, and predicted the future,²³⁴ thus building an impressive reputation for himself. He had good connections to the imperial court, but also demonstrated deep sympathy to marginalized members of society.²³⁵ He died probably on March 26, 944 (or 952).²³⁶ The author of the *Life*, Gregory, was a moderately-endowed landowner, probably an extremely pious secular celibate, who lived in a small community of like-minded people and became the favorite disciple of Basil.²³⁷ He was well-acquainted with the political situation in the Empire and hostile to Emperor Romanos II Lekapenos.

The *Life* of Basil the Younger is one of the most informative and interesting sources for the image of the demon in Byzantium. The second

---

230   Talbot, "Some observations", 314; Basil the Younger, 13ff.
231   Angelidi, "The Life of St. Basil", 59; Kazhdan, *History of Byzantine Literature*, 2: 189; Basil the Younger, 12; Talbot, "Some observations", 314.
232   Although the text mentions the tenth year of the emperors Leo VI (886–912) and Alexander (co-emperor with his brother from 886 until 912 and sole ruler in 912), Talbot argues that the year 906 is more probable, since in 896 Samonas had not yet become a leading political figure and a *parakoinomenos* (Basil the Younger, 28). For the dating, see also Angelidi, "The Life of St. Basil", 60 and n. 8.
233   For the dating, see Angelidi, "The Life of St. Basil", 61–63.
234   See, for example, his prediction of the Russian invasion in 941 in Basil the Younger, Part III, §23.5–8.
235   Ibid., 12.
236   Ibid., 13; Angelidi, "The Life of St. Basil", 62ff.
237   For Gregory, see Basil the Younger, 15–19.

part of Talbot's edition, the *Vision of Theodora*, describes in detail the last moments of human life, death, and the journey past the aerial tollhouses, where black and terrible demons intensely examine the soul for the sins committed in life and block her passage to Heaven. This story became extremely popular in medieval Bulgaria and Russia and influenced the early development of the Bogomil heresy. Below, we will analyze the complex philosophical, mythological, and theological traditions that led to the sophisticated concept of the posthumous journey and trials in the mid-tenth century.[238]

Another interesting source for the journey of the human soul is the *Vision of the Monk Cosmas*. This text is focused not on the whole life of a saint, but on a particular event. The main character is one of the officers responsible for the royal chambers (εἷς ὢν τῶν ἐκ τοῦ βασιλικοῦ κοιτῶνος)[239] of Emperor Alexander (912), who *c.* 933 became the abbot of an unknown monastery in the Sangarios River valley in East Bithynia.[240] The anonymous author gives a detailed account of the descent of his soul into Hell and of the innumerable evil spirits there. The original version of the text was edited by Christine Angelidi.[241] A short version was included in Synaxarion of Constantinople in the eleventh century.[242]

* * *

During the Iconoclast epoch, hagiography was produced mainly in Constantinople and Bithynia, where numerous monastic communities flourished. Historically, this predominance of the capital and northwest-

---

[238] See Part Four, Chapter 1, §2.1.
[239] "La version longue de la vision du moine Cosmas", ed. Christine Angelidi, *Analecta Bollandiana* 101 (1983): 79.23.
[240] The text mentions the thirteenth year of the rule of an emperor called "Romanos". In all likeliness, this is Emperor Romanos I Lekapenos (December 17, 920–December 16, 944).
[241] Cod. marc. gr., 346, edited and translated into French by Christine Angelidi, "La version longue", 73–99. For this text, see Kazhdan, *History of Byzantine Literature*, 2:192ff.
[242] The shorter, synaxarion version of the text is translated with commentary by Mango (*Empire*, 151–53).

ern Asia Minor is easily explained. This was the relatively peaceful core of the Byzantine Empire, almost untouched by Slavic-Bulgarian and Arab invasions. At the end of the eighth and at the beginning of the ninth centuries, the "Reconquista" of the Peloponnese and mainland Greece had just begun with the marriage of Leo IV and the Athenian noble Irene, and with the great campaign of Emperor Nikephoros I against the Slavic tribes in 805. Sixty years later the political situation was quite different. In the last quarter of the ninth century, this region was already a flourishing center of sericulture. It is the word μοριά (mulberry, whose leaves are used as food for silkworms) that gives the medieval name of the Peloponnese peninsula, Morea. Silk farming and large-scale agriculture, as well as the relative tranquility of Thessaly and the territories to its south before the campaigns of the Bulgarian ruler Samuel at the end of the tenth century, made these lands one of the most important parts of the Empire.

9. The hagiography of Sicily and Southern Italy

The accession of Sicily and southern Italy to the Empire in the middle of the sixth century was the result of the policy of Emperor Justinian I (527–565) against the Goths who had occupied these territories after the fall of the Western Roman empire. Sicily, conquered by the armies of the Byzantine generals Narses and Belisarius, remained untouched by the great wars with the Persians, which completely ravaged Syria, Palestine, and a large part of Asia Minor. The Slavic tribes, whose settlements reached the southernmost Balkan possessions of Byzantium, did not affect it. Caliph Mu'awiya's mighty fleet barely reached the island, and the first Umayyads accomplished little more than occasional raids along its coast. This relatively peaceful period of Sicily's history, soon to be disturbed by great Arab invasions, produced very few hagiographical texts. Until the first half of the ninth century, the dating of the local saints' *Lives* is highly uncertain and even legendary. We know practically nothing about the abbot of the St. Sabbas monastery in Rome, Leontius, who wrote the biography of Gregory, Bishop of Agrigento. It is unclear whether the Saint lived during the time of Justinian II (685–695; 705–711) or a century and a half earlier, under Justinian I.²⁴³ The other biography, the *Life* of the legendary Bishop Leo, refers to events probably in the late seventh century. The information it provides is of the greatest importance for the study of the Byzantine demon. According to the legend, Leo was the extremely pious Bishop of Catania in northern Sicily. However, the narrative focuses less on him than on the anti-hero, the devilish magician Heliodorus. Despite his noble origin, when this young and ambitious local aristocrat failed to become the eparch (governor) of the city, he made a contract with the Devil, and began terrorizing the residents with his magical practices. When the situation became intolerable, the governor asked for assistance from the central authorities in Constantinople, but the imperial envoy failed to deal with the sorcerer. Despite his efforts, the bishop could not persuade the sorcerer to return to the bosom of the Church. He then hauled Heliodorus physically to the place where executions were usually carried out and where a great stake was lit. Leo entered the flames with the magician and came out intact. The fire consumed Heliodorus. In this way, the city of Catania was saved.

This strange, obviously legendary story is preserved in the three versions of the *Life* of St. Leo of Catania (*BHG* [981], *BHG* [981b], and *BHG* [981c]).²⁴⁴ The author is unknown, and the only information we can extract from the text is that he was very familiar with the topography of both Catania and Constantinople. The date of the *Life* is very unclear as well. The longer version (*BHG* [981]), edited by Vasily Latyshev,²⁴⁵ mentions the co-emperors Constantine IV (668–685) and Justinian II (685–695; 705–711). This would fix the date of the events somewhere between

---

[243] For Gregory of Agrigentum and his *Life*, see *ODB*, vol. 2, s.v. "Gregory of Akragas", 879ff.

[244] For the *Life* of St. Leo of Catania, beyond the sources cited below, see Loparev, *Greek Saints' Lives*, 492–96; Germaine da Costa-Louillet, "Saints de Sicile et d'Italie méridionale aux VIIIe, IXe et Xe siècles", *Byzantion* 29–30 (1959–60): 89-95; *BS*, vol. 7, s.v. "Leone, vescovo di Catania", 1223–26; *ODB*, vol. 2, s.v. "Leo of Catania", 1214; Kazhdan, *History of Byzantine Literature*, 1: 296–302.

[245] "The Life and Way of Life of Our Holy Father Leo, Bishop of Catania" [Greek: "Βίος καὶ πολιτεία τοῦ ὁσίου πατρὸς ἡμῶν Λέοντος ἐπισκόπου Κατάνης"], in Vasilij Latyshev, *Unpublished Greek Hagiographical Texts* [Russian: Василий Латышевъ, *Неизданные греческіе агіографическіе тексты*] (St. Petersburg, 1914), 12–28.

681, when the crown prince Justinian was crowned by his father[246] and the death of Constantine IV in 685. On the other hand, the shorter version (*BHG* [981b]), edited by Augusta Acconcia-Longo,[247] refers to the rulers "Leo and Constantine". The editor of the text and Marie-France Ausépy disagree about the identity of these two emperors, and their dating of it varies between the early eighth century and the second decade of the ninth centuries.[248] These theories relate mainly to the dating of the *Life* and less to the described events. Both scholars ignore these events almost completely (as no more than legendary) and focus on the author of the text. The historical context, however, and the main characters are consistent with the third quarter of the seventh century. In the first place, the text does not mention any Arab threat. The provincial city of Catania is described as a thriving trade center[249] in undisturbed direct contact with the imperial capital.[250] This means that no foreign fleet endangered

---

[246] The Emperor Justinian II ascended to the imperial throne after crushing the rebellion of his uncles, Heraklios and Tiberius, and after the official closing of the Sixth Ecumenical Council on September 16, 681 (see Aikaterine Christophilopoulou, *Byzantine History* [Greek: Αικατερίνη Χριστοφιλοπούλου, *Βυζαντινή Ιστορία*], vol. II.1 [=B'1]: 610–867 (Thessalonica: Vanias, 1993), 65ff.). See Kazhdan, *History of Byzantine Literature*, 1: 296.

[247] Augusta Acconcia-Longo, "La vita di s. Leone vescovo di Catania e gli incantesimi del mago Eliodoro", *Rivista di Studi Bizantini e Neoellenici* 26 (1989): 3–98.

[248] Ausépy dates the text between 730 and 843, during the Iconoclast crisis (Marie-France Auzépy, "A propos des vies de saints iconoclasts", *Rivista di Studi Bizantini e Neoellenici* 30 [1993]: 3–5). Acconcia-Longo identifies the "Emperor Leo" with Emperor Leo V (813–820) and Constantine with his son Sabbatios-Constantine (Augusta Acconcia-Longo, "A proposito di un articolo sull'agiografia iconoclasta", *Rivista di Studi Bizantini e Neoellenici* 29 (1992): 3–17; Augusta Acconcia-Longo, "Di nuovo sull'agiografia iconoclasta", *Rivista di Studi Bizantini e Neoellenici* 30 (1993): 7–15). For more on this matther, see Kazhdan, *History of Byzantine Literature*, 1; 296.

[249] According to the text, Catania's economy was not based on agriculture but on trade, and the story about the diabolical magical practices performed by Heliodorus (Leo of Catania, §15) supports this suggestion. For example, the wicked mage fooled the traders into seeing common rocks as precious stones and useless objects as necessary items. All of the city's inhabitants were so desperate and panic-stricken that they gave up all trade, which doomed them to poverty.

[250] According to the text, the governor of the city (ὕπαρχος), Loukios, exchanged letters with the emperor with no physical obstacle to hinder the communication (Leo of Catania, §16). The imperial envoy Heraclides has no difficulty traveling by sea from Constantinople to Sicily, despite the short time of only thirty-two days given to him to

Byzantine Sicily's integrity or maritime access to the island. Such tranquility in the Adriatic and the southern parts of the Aegean Sea seems unlikely as early as the eighth century. After the secession of the North African emirates from the Abbasid caliphate during the reign of the caliphs al-Mansur (754–775) and Harun al-Rashid (786–809), when the Aglavid raids in the Mediterranean commenced, it is already wholly unthinkable.[251] Dating the events after the beginning of the eighth century seems further groundless because of Catania's strong municipal government, despite the fact that the city was of only secondary importance. After the start of the Arab incursions into Sicily, the Empire created an exceptionally centralized system of government both on the island and in the Byzantine possessions in southern Italy. Almost all power was concentrated in the hands of a *patrikios* whose seat was in Syracuse.[252] On the other hand, according to the *Life*, Catania had an *eparch* or *hyparch* (the Greek term for the Latin *praefectus*) of its own, and this official asked for help not from his superior on the island but directly from the central government. The name of the imperial envoy Heraclides (Ἡρακλείδης), who was sent to arrest Heliodorus, also suggests that the events happened during the reign of the Heraclian dynasty (610–711). This name was extremely rare after the disgraceful fall of the dynasty in 711. And finally, Kazhdan points out that, after the early eighth century, the provincial town ceased to be the scene of action in hagiography, the monastery or the wilderness taking its place. At the same time, in the *Life* of St. Leo, almost everything happens in Catania.[253] All these suggestions are circumstantial but make dating the events in the core of the text to the third

---

make the journey, arrest Heliodorus, and deliver him to the capital (Leo of Catania, §21). This is circumstantial evidence that he did not need to consider any eventual complications, such as encounters with enemy warships or the need to avoid dangerous points around the islands in the Aegean basin and the Adriatic Sea.

[251] For the historical events in the Adriatic Sea and Sicily during this period, see Vasiliev, *Byzance et les Arabes*, 1: 61–64.

[252] Vera von Falkenhausen, *Untersuchaugen über die Byzantinische Herrschaft in Suditalien vom 9. bis ins 11. Jahrhundert* (Wiesbaden: O. Harrassowitz, 1967), 4–12.

[253] Kazhdan, *History of Byzantine Literature*, 1: 300.

quarter of the seventh century (the reign of the emperors Constantine IV and Justinian II) highly probable.

According to Alexander Kazhdan, the *Life* of St. Leo of Catania is one of the few hagiographical texts belonging to the comic genre.[254] Kazhdan pays close attention to the medieval sense of humor. On the one hand, laughter is perceived as evil ("Christ never laughed", says a proverb). But, on the other hand, it could serve as a way to understand something sacred better. It is difficult for the modern reader to grasp the meaning of the Byzantine sense of humor, which in hagiographical texts is based mainly on the parody of serious theological matters and helps clarify them.

* * *

After the *Life* of St. Leo of Catania, we have no hagiographical information about Sicilian saints until the second quarter of the ninth century. The lack of a local literary tradition in Sicily and southern Italy is fully explicable by the hard times experienced by this region, isolated from the Empire's core. Although the Arabs were temporarily unable to invade its interior until 827, their fleet constantly threatened communications in the eastern and central Mediterranean, even penetrating sporadically into the core of Byzantine trade, the Aegean basin. The province of Sicily was left to its fate. In these troubled times, it remained for many years apart from the revival of literary activity in Byzantium from the end of the eighth and the beginning of the ninth centuries.

The massive Arab invasion of Sicily and southern Italy, so vividly described by the ninth- and tenth-century hagiographers, officially and ceremonially began on June 17, 827, in Kairouan in North Africa, the capital of the dynasty of the Aglavides.[255] From that moment on, a continuous war for domination of the island began, which did not stop even with the fall of Taormina, the last Byzantine fortress, in 902. The Sicilian and Calabrian saints lived in an environment that differed completely

---

[254] Ibid., 1: 295ff.
[255] Vasiliev, *Byzance et les arabes*, 1: 73.

from the humble monks of Bithynia and Constantinople. They were part of a militarized society with little room for hermit exploits. St. Elias the Younger, the first of them, simply ran away from his homeland and spent most of his life wandering. The following generations, however, remained in Byzantine Italy and provided spiritual support to the local population and the imperial troops.

St. Elias the Younger (823–903)[256] was born in the town of Enna (Έννη; modern-day Castrugiuvanni). He belonged to the noble family of the Rachites, which still existed in Sicily as late as the thirteenth century.[257] In 830, when the future Saint was seven years old, the constant Arab raids forced his parents to escape to the northern part of the island, choosing the fortress of St. Mary as a refuge.[258] There the little boy was captured by Arab pirates and was sold as a slave in North Africa. After his release, he traveled for years to Palestine, Greece, and Rome. In the end, St. Elias settled in Byzantine Calabria, where he founded the first Greek monastery near the town of Salina, 22 kilometers south of Regium.[259] During the great Arab invasions, he also traveled to Greece, dying in Thessalonica on August 17, 903, on his way to Constantinople, where he was invited by Emperor Leo VI (886–912) himself. The *Life* of St. Elias the Younger (*BHG* [580])[260] is preserved in a manuscript of a

---

[256] The main events in the biography of St. Elias the Younger are summarized in da Costa-Louillet, "Saints de Sicile et d'Italie", 96–108; Jules Gay, *L'Italie méridionale et l'Empire Byzantin depuis l'avénement de Basile Ier jusqu'à la prise de Bari par les Normands (867 – 1071)*, vol. 1 (Paris: Fontemoing, 1904), 260ff.

[257] Da Costa-Louillet, "Saints de Sicile et d'Italie", 96.

[258] Elias the Younger, §3. A town of the same name (Santa Maria) is today located in the northern part of the island, west of Messina, but we do not have enough evidence to identify it with the "Hagia Marina" of the *Life* of St. Elias the Younger. However, it seems only logical for the family of the Rachites to have escaped to northern Sicily, which in this period was undisturbed by the Arab invasion. On the dating of this event, see Gay, *L'Italie méridionale*, 260; da Costa-Louillet, "Saints de Sicile et d'Italie", 96.

[259] Gay, *L'Italie méridionale*, 257.

[260] For more on Elias, see Loparev, *Greek Saints' Lives*, 499–513; *BS*, vol. 4, s.v. "Elia di Enna", 1043–45; André Guillou, "Grecs d'Italie du Sud et de Sicile au moyen âge: les moines", *Mélanges d'archéologie et d'histoire* 75, no. 1, (1963): 92; da Costa-Louillet, "Saints de Sicile et d'Italie", 95ff. and 108ff.; Nicola Ferrante, *Santi italogreci in Calabria* (Reggio Calabria: Rexodes Magna Grecia, 1981), 111–22; *ODB*, vol. 1, s.v. "Elias

relatively late date (1307-8) but was probably written not long after the Saint's death, during the fourth or the fifth decade of the tenth century, by an author who knew him well. Da Costa-Louillet's hypothesis that the anonymous hagiographer was Elias' pupil Daniel is unprovable.

St. Elias Speleotes (860/70–September 11, 960) belongs to the next generation of Sicilian and southern Italian saints.[261] He came from a wealthy family and was born in Regium (modern-day Reggio di Calabria), the capital of Calabria. At eleven years of age, he lost a finger of his hand in an accident and decided to become a hermit. In order to do so, he and one of his friends left Calabria for Sicily. This information sheds light on the conditions particular to this region, so isolated from the Empire's core. Around Elias' native town, there was still no monastic community that could allow the pious boy to follow the established practices, that is, to spend some time as a novice and, subsequently, as a monk at a monastery, then to obtain permission from the abbot or his spiritual father to go into the wilderness as a hermit, and eventually found a new monastery himself. Instead, the two little monks-to-be needed to go to the relatively more developed south. After a short stay in Sicily, Elias returned to his homeland as a monk under the spiritual guidance of a man called Arsenios. In 888, the great Arab raid against the city of Regium forced him and many other monks to emigrate to the Peloponnese.[262] A few years later, the situation in Calabria was somewhat stabilized. Elias could return and finally found a monastery in a cave near the village of

---

the Younger", 687. Cf. and Enrica Follieri, *La vita di San Fantino il Giovane. Introduzione, testo greco, traduzione, commentario e indici*, [Subsidia hagiographica, 77], (Brussels: Société des Bollandistes, 1993), 96-110.

[261] For the main events of the biography of St. Elias Speleotes, see da Costa-Louillet, "Saints de Sicile et d'Italie", 113-24.

[262] Elias the Younger, §38; Elias Speleotes, §20. For this raid, see da Costa-Louillet, "Saints de Sicile et d'Italie", 115 and n. 2; Vasiliev, *Byzance et les Arabes*, 2: 134-35; Gay, *L'Italie méridionale*, 146. For the stay of St. Elias the Younger and St. Elias Speleotes near the city of Patra, see Konstantinos Triandaphyllou, "Greeks from Southern Italy who escaped to Patra during the 9th century", [Greek: Κωνσταντίνος Τριανταφύλλου, "Έλληνες τῆς Νότιας Ἰταλίας καταφυγόντες εἰς Πάτρας τὸν θ' αι."], in *La chiesa greca in Italia dall' VIII al XVI secolo. Atti del convegno storico interecclesiale*, ed. Michele Maccarrone, vol. 3 (Padua: Antenore, 1973), 1085-94.

Seminarion (the modern-day town of Seminara in southwestern Calabria). He died at the age of ninety-six, on September 11, 960.

The *Life* of St. Elias Speleotes (*BHG* [581])[263] was written by a monk called *Quiriacus* in the Latin version of the text — obviously a Latinized version of the Greek name Κυριακός. Despite his claim that he knew the Saint, he speaks of many posthumous miracles and relates information given to him by older people. In all likelihood, Kyriakos belonged to the second or even the third generation of monks in the monastery founded by St. Elias and compiled the text relatively long after the Saint's death, towards the end of the tenth century. His style is somewhat peculiar. The author describes terrible atrocities in surprisingly vivid detail. God's punishments for sins are cruel and merciless. Despite being reprimanded by Elias and his mentor Arsenios, a prominent Roman nobleman embezzled land belonging to a nunnery. Consequently, he died, and the corrupt judge's body swelled so much that his stomach would have burst if he hadn't changed his verdict in favor of the nuns in time.[264] The author pays much attention to the passions, including their darkest sides. The boy with whom the young Elias departed for Sicily couldn't endure the life of a hermit and returned to their homeland; his punishment came soon, and he was murdered during an Arab invasion. Another peculiarity of the text is its mixture of the features of the powers of Good with those of Evil. The characters are often uncertain whether a vision comes from God or the Devil. A woman, who had sinned, was visited by a frightful angel, and she felt *demonic* fear.[265] In addition, the *Life* of St. Elias includes one of the most dramatic and detailed stories about a haunted tower that reminds the modern reader of a Gothic novel[266].

* * *

---

[263] For Elias, see *BS*, vol. 4, s.v. "Elia Speleota", 1052ff.; da Costa-Louillet, "Saints de Sicile et d'Italie", 113; Ferrante, *Santi italogreci*, 131–40; ODB, vol. 1, s.v. "Elias Speleotes", 687. Cf. Follieri, *La vita di San Fantino*, 101–14 (esp. 102ff., with a chronological table of the main events).

[264] Elias Speleotes, §15.

[265] Ibid., §25.

[266] Elias Speleotes, §21.

Thanks to the work and effort of Enrica Follieri, St. Phantinos the Younger (902–974) is one of the most studied Italian saints.[267] He was born in an unknown town in Calabria, to the family of the pious and wealthy George and Briena. At eight years of age, around 910/911, his father gave him to a monastery where the future Saint proved himself an exemplary monk for the following two and a half decades, until 935/936. When he turned thirty-three, he departed and spent the next eighteen years as a hermit, wandering in the mountains of Lucania. In 952/3, he founded a monastery. Already a respected abbot, he saw in a vision the fate of the human soul after death and the great ordeals it had to undergo to enter the Kingdom of God. This vision so influenced him that the old man decided to leave the monastery and once again retire as a hermit in the wilderness for four years (c. 958–962). Immediately after that, in 962,[268] Phantinos departed for Greece, where he visited Larisa and foretold with sorrow the capture of this illustrious city by the army of the Bulgarian king Samuel in 985 or 986.[269] The Saint died in Thessalonica in 974.

The *Life* of St. Phantinos (*BHG* [2367]) was written by an anonymous, well-educated monk from Thessalonica. The *terminus post quem* is the above-mentioned capture of Larisa, and the *terminus ante quem* is the end of the tenth century when the first known manuscript is dated. Follieri suggests that the text was compiled before the Byzantine general Nikephoros Ouranos

---

[267] For the timelines of St. Phantinos' life, see Follieri, *La vita di San Fantino*, 129ff. For his biography, see ibid., 76–131. See also *BS*, vol. 5, s.v. "Fantino il Giovane", 452ff.; da Costa-Louillet, "Saints de Sicile et d'Italie", 165ff.; Ferrante, *Santi italogreci*, 147–52; *ODB*, vol. 3, s.v. "Phantinos the Younger", 1646.

[268] For the dating of this event based on synaxarion sources, supported by hints in the text itself, see Follieri, *La vita di San Fantino*, 77–79.

[269] The exact date of the capture of Larisa is uncertain. See Srđan Pirivatrić, *Samuilo's State: Its Extent and Character* [Serbian: Срђан Пириватрић, *Самуилова Држава. Обим и карактер*] [Serbian Academy of Sciences and Arts Studies, 21] (Belgrade: Institute for Byzantine Studies, 1997), 88ff. and n. 50; Follieri, *La vita di San Fantino*, 78ff., dates the event to 986, accepting the opinion of Paul Lemerle, *Prolégomènes à une édition critique et commentée des "Conceils et Récits" de Kekaumenos* [Académie Royale de Belgique, Classe des Lettres et des Sciences Morales et Politiques, Mémoires, vol. LIV, fasc. 1] (Brussels: Académie Royale de Belgique, 1960), 25–58.

recaptured the city in 996 because this event is not mentioned. An argument *ex silentio*, though, can never be accepted unreservedly.²⁷⁰

* * *

The only hagiographical text of southern Italy and Sicily, relatively poor in demonic stories, is the *Life* of St. Sabbas the Younger. Here the evil spirits are standardized and appear but rarely in material form. The biography is replete with vivid descriptions of this region's everyday life, Arab and German raids, and various travels and adventures. Nevertheless, hardly a single event of the Saint's life can be positively dated.²⁷¹ He was born into a wealthy family in the early tenth century in the Sicilian town of Collesano. His father, Christophoros, left his wife and children and retired to the nearby monastery of St. Philipp. The pious man was soon followed by his two sons, Sabbas and Makarios. After a savage Arab incursion on Collesano, the young Sabbas persuaded his family to seek safety from the atrocities and emigrate to southern Italy. He spent his life as a monk, traveling in Calabria, Lucania, and Rome. Sabbas died in

---

²⁷⁰ For the author and the dating of the text, see Follieri, *La vita di San Fantino*, 273–92 (esp. 273).

²⁷¹ For the main events in the biography, see da Costa-Louillet, "Saints de Sicile et d'Italie", 133–39, who pays special attention to the death of St. Sabbas the Younger. Given the insignificance of the text as a source for the Byzantine demon, we will not deal with the dating of these events here. Nevertheless, it enables us to point out some information in the biography, which could eventually be helpful for a more accurate dating of this valuable source for the Byzantine territories in southern Italy in the tenth century. The *patrikios* Malakinos (Μαλακεινός), who defeated the Arabs in Calabria (Sabbas the Younger, §9), in all likelihood, is the *patrikios* Malakinos (Μαλακηνός) who was sent to Calabria by Emperor Constantine VII (sole ruler between 944 and 959) according to Scylitzes (*Ioannis Scylitzae Synopsis Historiarum*, ed. Ioannes Thurn [*Corpus fontium historiae Byzantinae* V] [Berlin: De Gruyter, 1973], §7). The "Frankish" raid against the province of Langobardia could be dated to the reign of Emperor Nikephoros II Phocas (963-969) when the coronation of Otto I as Emperor of the newly founded Holy Roman Empire (961) seriously affected the relations between the two great powers.

Rome between 990 and 995. His *Life* (*BHG* [1611])[272] was written by Patriarch Orestes of Jerusalem (986–1006), who was a monk in Calabria for a few years.

10. Greece and Macedonia: from St. Theodora of Thessalonica to St. Nikon Metanoeite

Most provincial hagiographers from the ninth to the tenth centuries refer to saints who lived in Greece, Macedonia, and the Aegean islands. The earliest of these were two married women originating from the island of Aegina who, after their husbands' deaths, took monastic vows: St. Athanasia of Aegina and St. Theodora of Thessalonica.

The *Life* of St. Athanasia of Aegina does not provide any precise chronological data except for a rather dubious prediction by St. Ioannikios the Great[273] about her future glory. However, Lee Sherry and Kazhdan date her life from *c.* 805 to the third quarter of the ninth century.[274] During her first marriage, she used to give alms generously to the so-called *athiggani* (ἀθίγγανοι) — a group of heretics considered the ancestors of modern gypsies.[275] They were greatly favored during the reign

---

[272] See *BS*, vol. 4, s.v. "Cristoforo di Collesano", 346–48, and vol. 11, s.v. "Saba il Giovane", 432; da Costa-Louillet, "Saints de Sicile et d'Italie", 133ff.; von Falkenhausen, *Untersuchaugen über die Byzantinische Herrschaft*, 80ff.; Ferrante, *Santi italogreci*, 153–55.

[273] There is no mention of St. Ioannikios the Great traveling to Aegina or the Aegean islands in his *Lives* or by any other known source, which makes it rather odd that neither Sherry nor Kazhdan pays attention to this very dubious moment in the biography of St. Athanasia of Aegina.

[274] For Ioannikios and her *Life*, see Loparev, *Greek Saints' Lives*, 450–55; *BS*, vol. 2, s.v. "Atanasia di Egina", 521; Lee Sherry, "Life of St. Athanasia of Aegina", in *Holy Women of Byzantium*, ed. Alice-Mary Talbot (Washington, DC: Dumbaron Oaks, 1996), 137–40; Kazhdan, *History of Byzantine Literature*, 2: 122ff. The English translation is based on the more recent edition of the text ("Vie de sainte Athanasie d'Egine", ed. François Halkin, *Six inédits d'hagiologie Byzantine* (Brussels: Société des Bollandistes, 1987), 179–95).

[275] On the Untouchable (Greek ἀθίγγανοι, *athigganoi*) in Byzantium and their origin, see Ilse Rochow, "Die Häresie der Athinganer im 8. und 9. Jahrhundert und die Frage ihres Fortlebens", in *Studien zum 8. und 9.Jjahrhundert in Byzanz*, ed. Helga Köpstein and Friedhelm Winkelmann [Berliner Byzantinische Arbeiten 51] (Berlin: De Gruyter, 1993), 163–78; Ioannis Panagiotopoulos, *On the Athiggani: Politics and Religion in the*

of Emperor Nikephoros I (802–811) and were allowed to settle wherever they wished throughout the Empire. This information could help us place the *Life* of St. Athanasia in a historical context.[276] During an Arab raid, dated by Vasiliev c. 825.[277], the future Saint lost her first husband.[278] Some time afterward, the emperor, probably Theophilos, issued an order that all single women had to marry, and Athanasia remarried, this time to a foreigner.[279] Soon she managed to persuade her new husband to take monastic vows with her. During her monastic life, her spiritual mentor Matthew played a primary role. The detailed posthumous miracles of St. Athanasia are an essential source for the image of the Byzantine demon. Her *Life* (BHG [180]) was probably written shortly after 900 because it is preserved in a manuscript of 916. The author, certainly a man, seems to have been relatively remote from the era of Athanasia, whose memory he wishes to save from oblivion. He claims to write in the fashionable tenth century high style, but his references are mainly to Holy Scripture, and his rhetorical devices are relatively poor.[280]

A slightly younger contemporary of St. Athanasia was St. Theodora of Thessalonica (812–892).[281] She came from a wealthy family of Aegina, who arranged her betrothal and marriage. After an Arab attack on the island in 825, she was forced to flee with her husband to Thessalonica, where she lost two children and was left a widow at the age of twenty-five. She gave her little daughter Theopiste as a novice and retired herself

---

Byzantine Empire [Ιωάννης Παναγιωτόπουλος, *Περί Αθιγγάνων: πολιτική και θρησκεία στη Βυζαντινή Αυτοκρατορία*] (Athens: Herodotos, 2000).

[276] *Theophanis chronographia*, 488.21-33.
[277] Vasiliev, *Byzance et les Arabes*, 1: 57ff. This date was accepted by Kazhdan (*History of Byzantine Literature*, 2: 122) without reference to Vasiliev's study.
[278] Athanasia of Aegina, §3.11-14.
[279] Ibid., §4.2-5. See also Sherry, "Life of St. Athanasia", 139 and 143 n. 22; Kazhdan, *History of Byzantine Literature*, 2: 122.
[280] Sherry, "Life of St. Athanasia", 139ff.; Kazhdan, *History of Byzantine Literature*, 2: 123.
[281] For Theodora and her *Life*, see Loparev, *Greek Saints' Lives*, 457-66; *BS*, vol. 12, s.v. "Teodora di Tessalonica", 226-27; *ODB*, vol. 3, s.v. "Theodora of Thessalonike", 2038ff.; Kazhdan, *History of Byzantine Literature*, 2: 119-22; Alice-Mary Talbot, "Life of St. Theodora of Thessalonica", in *Holy Women of Byzantium. Ten Saints' Lives in English Translation*, ed. Alice-Mary Talbot (Dumbarton Oaks: Dumbarton Oaks Research Library and Collection, 1996), 159-62.

in 837 to the monastery of St. Stephen in Thessalonica, which was later renamed after her.[282] She spent the rest of her life as an exemplary nun but did not perform miracles during her lifetime, nor did she indulge in extreme asceticism. St. Theodora died in 892 and was proclaimed a saint. It is commonly accepted that the author of her *Life*'s two versions (*BHG* [1737–8]), which are very close to each other, is the same person.[283] There is no evidence about her cult until the thirteenth century, and she is not mentioned even in the famous work of Eustathios of Thessalonica *On the Capture of Thessalonica*.[284] Kazhdan stresses the interest of the author Gregory in the family history of St. Theodora, who was a relative of Archbishop Antony. One of the central themes around which the *Life* itself is organized is the great love of Theodora for her only living daughter, Theopiste. This affection, which disturbed the ascetic fervor of the two women, forced the abbess Anna to forbid all conversation between mother and daughter for fifteen years. It is logical to assume that the author of the text is a relative of Theodora and wrote the *Life* to enhance the authority of his illustrious family. For several centuries, she remained a not particularly popular saint, coexisting with the cult of another local saint of the same name, a maiden and dragon-slayer. At a certain point, the image of Gregory's heroine absorbed that of her namesake.[285] For the study of the Byzantine concept of the demon, the text is helpful mainly for its descriptions of posthumous miracles.

* * *

One of the first important saints of mainland Greece was St. Euthymios the Younger (823/4–898).[286] This is one of the fascinating religious figures of the Middle Byzantine Period, whose checkered life and

---

[282] See Janin, *Les églises et les monastères*, 374ff. and 411.
[283] For the arguments in favor of this suggestion, see Kazhdan, *History of Byzantine Literature*, 2: 119; Talbot, "Life of St. Theodora", 160ff.
[284] Kazhdan, *History of Byzantine Literature*, 2: 119ff.
[285] Kazhdan, *History of Byzantine Literature*, 2: 120ff.
[286] The year of his birth, explicitly mentioned in the text, is 6332, i.e., AD 823/834 (Euthymios the Younger, §4.13–15).

innumerable travels remind the modern reader of an adventure novel. While hermits and monks like St. Ioannikios, St. Peter of Atroa, and St. Paul of Latros were forced to wander for years in the mountains of western Asia Minor due to the persecutions and repressions of heretic emperors, St. Euthymios was a restless person who yearned for adventure. The Saint, who bore the secular name Niketas, came from the village Opso in Galatia, Asia Minor, and was born into a wealthy family.[287] In his youth, he fulfilled his mother's wish that he marry and have children. Having done that, at eighteen (841/2), he retired to Mount Olympus in Bithynia and, in January 942, became a monk. In 859, his mother and wife also took vows but allowed his daughter Anastaso to marry and eventually bear three daughters and one son.[288] Euthymios spent seventeen years on Mount Olympus (until 859) and subsequently settled as a hermit on Mount Athos (859–863, 863–864, 865–866), playing a crucial role in the early history of the monastic community there. For two years (864–866), he lived as a stylite in the vicinity of Thessalonica. Afterward, he spent some years on the uninhabited island of Nei (modern-day Agios Eustratios or Ai-Stratis) in the central part of the Aegean Sea.[289] Between September 24, 870, and August 31, 871, he rebuilt the Church of St. Andreas south of Thessalonica, which can be seen today, and founded the famous Peristere monastery, to which he attached a nunnery in 885–89. About a year before his death, Euthymios left the monastery to his grandson Methodios and the nunnery to his granddaughter Euphymia. He died on the island of Hiera in 898.

---

[287] On the events of the biography of his life, we follow here the dating of Denise Papachryssanthou, "La vie de Saint Euthyme le Jeune et la métropole de Thessalonique à la fin du IXe et au début du Xe siècle", *Revue des Études Byzantines* 32 (1974): 234–42 (esp. 241ff.). See also Kazhdan, *History of Byzantine Literature*, 2: 118ff.

[288] Euthymios the Younger, §16.

[289] The island was located about thirty kilometers southwest of Limnos and about seventy kilometers northeast of Skyros (*TIB*, vol. 10: *Aigaion Pelagos (Die nördliche Ägäis)*, ed. Johannes Koder (Vienna: Verlad der Österreichischen Akademie der Wissenschaften, 1998), 240–42).

The author of the *Life* of St. Euthymios (*BHG* [655])[290] was called Basil and wrote the text probably in the early tenth century. He often addresses the reader and refers to various details of his own life.[291] According to his account, Basil became a monk in 875 and subsequently left the monastery to dedicate himself to a career as a high-ranking priest.[292] The Greek word ἀρχιερεύς, though, does not indicate his exact position in the Church hierarchy, and Denise Papachryssanthou rejects the older suggestion that he was identical to Archbishop Basil, known from other sources.[293] Basil was moderate politically and did not indulge in the controversy between the patriarchs Ignatios and Photios, which disturbed the Church in the late ninth century. His remoteness from the capital is a probable explanation for this indifference.

The *Life* of the monk-traveler Euthymios the Younger includes some fascinating accounts of the image of the demon. Aside from the vivid depiction of the problems around the restoration of the above-mentioned Church of St. Andreas, Basil describes evil spirits in the form of barbarians, Arabs, scorpions, dragons, and many others.

* * *

One of the less-known Byzantine saints was active in Aegean Macedonia, probably in the second half of the ninth century. His name was Germanos, and he was the founder of the monastery of Panagia Eikoksifoinissa (Bulg. *Kosinitza, Kušniš*) on the northern outskirts of Mount Pan-

---

[290] On the *Life* of St. Euthymios the Younger see Loparev, *Greek Saints' Lives*, 468–76; *BS*, vol. 5, s.v. "Eutimio il Giovane", 329; Papachryssanthou, "La vie de Saint Euthyme le Jeune", passim, esp. 225ff; *ODB*, vol. 2, s.v. "Euthymios the Younger", 757; Kazhdan, *History of Byzantine Literature*, 2: 118ff.

[291] Euthymios the Younger, §44, where the fixed date of the event is the fourth year after the rebuilding of the Church of St. Andreas. See also Papachryssanthou, "La vie de Saint Euthyme le Jeune", 226–34 and 242.

[292] Euthymios the Younger, §34.6-8 and §35.15-17; Papachryssanthou, "La vie de Saint Euthyme le Jeune", 228.

[293] Papachryssanthou, "La vie de Saint Euthyme le Jeune", 228–34; cf. Kazhdan, *History of Byzantine Literature*, 2: 118.

gaios.²⁹⁴ He was born far away, in Palestine, where he became a monk and dedicated himself to the most severe ascesis.²⁹⁵ In the thirteenth year of his life as a hermit, an angel appeared to him and admonished him to go to the mountains of Macedonia. The future Saint was to build a church dedicated to the Holy Mother of God. After a long journey, Germanos arrived successfully in the woody country north of the town of Drama, where he constructed the temple with his own hands. When the deed was finished, the angel appeared to him again and commanded the erection of another church on a mountain called Matikia. Germanos obeyed and began construction in an impenetrable forest in the vicinity of a village named Černista. But at this point, the holy man met an unexpected obstacle. He had collected only sixteen gold coins in alms from the local peasants, and the builders demanded a hundred in payment. When the building was finished, and the monk did not have the total amount, the angry workers seized him and departed for Drama, probably to sue him. But on the way, a miracle happened. By chance, the party met the esteemed Neophytos and Nicholas, imperial envoys to the Serbs. They gladly provided the necessary funds, saved the monk from trouble, and became monks themselves. The rest of the future Saint's life was full of holy exploits, but not with adventures. The biography is incompletely preserved, but the missing parts probably included only the closing of Germanos' final admonishments to the Eikosifoinissa monks just before his death.

The above story, though certainly very amusing, unfortunately gives practically no specific clue as to the time of the events. Theophylact of Ohrid (c. 1050/60–c. 1108), the famous Byzantine biblical scholar and exegete, mentions "the holy Germanos" who arrived in Bulgaria during the reign of Knyaz Boris (844–886).²⁹⁶ On the basis of this account, Loparev dates the life of the Saint to the second half of the ninth century.

---

²⁹⁴ The main events of St. Germanos' life are summarized in Loparev, *Greek Saints' Lives*, 480–84.
²⁹⁵ Germanos of Kosinitza, §§5–7. The anonymous author uses the name Kosinitra (Κοσινίτρα) instead of Kosinitza (Κοσινίτζα). For the location of the monastery, see Loparev, *Greek Saints' Lives*, 483.
²⁹⁶ *MPG*, vol. 120, 201C.

Ivan Dujčev accepts this hypothesis and speculates that the Byzantine mission to the Serbs, mentioned in the the texts, took place in 886.[297] The *Life* (*BHG* [698]) was compiled long after the death of the Saint, and most scholars date it to the twelfth century or later.[298]

* * *

One of mainland Greece's most famous religious figures of the tenth century is St. Luke of Steiris, the founder of the great Hosios Loukas monastery,[299] renowned for its magnificent eleventh-century mosaics.[300] All data specific to his life can only be obtained from his *Life*.[301] Like St. Theodora of Thessalonica, Luke came from a wealthy Aeginian family who fled the island to escape the Arab raids. His grandparents lived in different locations on the southern shore of the Phocis region. His parents, Stephen and Euphrosyne, finally settled in the small town of Kastrion near ancient Delphoi, where Luke was born in 896. At thirteen years of age, he lost his father and decided to become a monk (in 910/911). The boy left his home, retired on

---

[297] Ivan Dujčev, "Une ambassade byzantine auprès des Serbes au IXe siècle", *Zbornik radova Vizantoloskog Instituta Srpske akademije nauka* 7 (1961): 53–60.

[298] See *BS*, vol. 6, s.v. "Germano, fondatore del monasterio di Cosinizza", 240–43.

[299] The Hosios Loukas (Ὅσιος Λουκᾶς) monastery was probably built over the old monastic cell of the Saint and is today one of the best-preserved monuments of Byzantine monastic architecture of the eleventh century. See Dimitrios Pallas, "Zur Topographie und Chronologie von Hosios Lukas: eine kritische Übersicht", *Byzantinische Zeitschrift* 78 (1985): 94–107; Demetrios Sophianos, "The Monastery of Hosios Loukas: a survey and critical analysis of the reliability of the sources ", [Greek: Δημήτριος Σοφιανός, "Ἡ μονὴ τοῦ Ὁσίου Λουκᾶ: ἔλεγχος καὶ κριτικὴ τῆς ἀξιοπιστίας καὶ ἑρμηνείας τῶν πηγῶν"], *Mesaionika kai nea ellinika* (=Μεσαιωνικὰ καὶ Νέα Ἑλληνικά) 4 (1992): 23–80.

[300] The bibliography on the biography, the *Life*, and the monastery of St. Luke of Steiris, is considerable. For the main events of his life, see the detailed account of Demetrios Sofianos, *The Life of St. Luke of Steiri* [Greek: Δημήτριος Σοφιανός, Ὁ βίος τοῦ ὁσίου Λουκᾶ τοῦ Στειριώτη] (Athens: Akritas, 1989), 35–56 (for a chronological table, see 38). See also Loparev, *Greek Saints' Lives*, 439ff (on the first years of the Saint's life only); *BS*, vol. 8, s.v. "Luca il Giovane", 222ff; Germaine da Costa-Louillet, "Saints de Grèce aux VIIIe, IXe et Xe siècles", *Byzantion* 31 (1961): 332–43 (for a chronological table, see 343); *ODB*, vol. 2, s.v. "Loukas the Younger", 1254.

[301] See Luke of Steiris, §99, where the anonymous author summarizes the most important events of St. Luke's life.

nearby Mount Ioannitsa, and built a small hut. Luke spent seven years there, and during this period (until 918), grew famous throughout the Empire. As a result of the devastation of this region by the Bulgarian Tsar Symeon (probably in 918),[302] Luke moved to the vicinity of modern-day Xylokastro near Corinth, where he spent ten years with a famous local stylite. On May 27, 927, the fearsome Bulgarian ruler died, and his successor, Tsar Peter (927–969), finally signed a long-term peace treaty with Emperor Romanos I Lekapenos (929–944) on November 8 of the same year. This enabled the famous hermit to return safely to his homeland. He settled again on Mount Ioannitsa, probably in early 928.[303] Between 928 and 946, the future Saint lived as a hermit in his old cell, then traveled around the southern coast of Phocis, and finally, in 946, settled in the Steiris (Στείριον) region. Thus began the most crucial part of his life — here, he founded the famous monastery which bears his name today. Luke died peacefully on February 7, 953, and was buried under the floor of his cell. His grave became the kernel of the monastery, most of which was built in the mid-eleventh century.[304]

The *Life* of St. Luke of Steiris (*BHG* [994–994b])[305] was written by an anonymous author who didn't know the Saint personally. However, since he draws information from eyewitnesses, like his sister Kale, the text can be considered a reliable source. The text, which probably was written a few decades after Luke's death, is one of the essential sources for the image of the Byzantine demon.

---

[302] On the dating, see Sofianos, *The Life of St. Luke*, 47 and n. 79–81. Sofianos hypothesizes that the Bulgarian tsar could not have reached Phocis less than ten months after the Battle of Achelous (August 20, 917).

[303] Sofianos, *The Life of St. Luke*, 36ff.

[304] The mosaics of the Hosios Loukas monastery are among the most outstanding examples of Byzantine art of the late eleventh century. See, among others, Nikos Veis, *The monastery of St. Luke of Steiris and the monastic community of Panagia Naupaktiotissa, John Apokaukos, and Kyriakos of Ankon* [Greek: Νίκος Βέης, Ἡ Μονὴ τοῦ Ὁσίου Λουκᾶ τοῦ Στειριώτου καὶ ἡ ἐκκλησιαστικὴ κοινότης τῆς Παναγίας τῆς Ναυπακτιωτίσσης, ὁ Ἰωάννης Ἀπόκαυκος καὶ Κυριάκος ὁ ἐξ Ἀγκῶνος], (Athens, 1935); Nikolaos Oikonomides, "The First Century of the Monastery of Hosios Loukas", *Dumbaarton Oaks Papers* 46 (1992): 245–55.

[305] See Sofianos, *The Life of St. Luke*, 29–35.

* * *

The second great religious figure of tenth-century Greece is the famous (or notorious) St. Nikon Metanoeite. His nickname means *Repent!* This was the message that this righteous person strived to propagandize all his life. He definitely deserved this aggressive epithet for his uncompromising missionary activity and his narrow-minded hatred of anything that did not fit his worldview and for anybody who opposed his opinion even in the slightest. Nikon is so very different from the humble monks of the pages above that his biography may be considered a logical epilogue to the Byzantine hagiography of the period under study.

The main events of St. Nikon's life have been relatively well-studied and dated.[306] He was born *c.* 930 in the eastern Pontus (in North Asia Minor). As a monk, he spent twelve years in the monastery of Chryse Petra on the border of Pontus and Paphlagonia. For at least three years he wandered as a hermit in *the eastern lands*,[307] struggling with demons and spreading the call for repentance, to which he owed his nickname. In 961, the illustrious general and future Emperor Nikephoros Phokas, who had recently liberated the island of Crete from a long Arab occupation, invited many Christian missionaries. The task of these pious men was to preach throughout the island, which for almost a century and a half had been exposed to Muslim influence. Nikon selflessly responded to this appeal and spent seven years erasing *the unclean and shameful habits* of the island's inhabitants.[308] Initially, his behavior was so aggressive that, at one point, the Cretans threatened to lynch him. Nikon changed his tactics in time and managed to win some authority. In 968, he left Crete, traveling

---

[306] See Romilly Jenkins and Cyril Mango, "A Synodicon of Antioch and Lacedaemonia", *Dumbarton Oaks Papers* 15 (1961): 238ff; da Costa-Louillet, "Saints de Grèce", 350–65; Denis Sullivan, *The Life of Saint Nikon: Text, Translation, and Commentary* [The Archbishop Iakovos Library of Ecclesiastical and Historical Sources 14] (Brooklin, MA: Hellenic College Press, 1987), 1 and 18ff; *ODB*, vol. 3, s.v. "Nikon 'Ho Metanoeite'", 1484.

[307] The text's author claims that, in the third year of his wanderings, the future Saint was given the power to defeat demons (Nikon Metanoeite, §18ff.).

[308] Nikon Metanoeite, §20.15ff.

for some time in Central Greece, especially in Attica, and probably in 970, settled in the ancient town of Sparta, where he continued his missionary activities. The future Saint arrived during a plague and immediately discovered the "culprits" behind this dreadful illness, the local Jews. Consequently, the entire Jewish community was isolated in a ghetto outside the town's walls. The author does not inform his readers whether the spread of the disease stopped after this pious act, but one thing is certain — the local Christian traders were rid of their Jewish colleagues' competition. Nikon declared the only defender of the Jews, John Aratos, possessed by demons; according to the text, shortly afterward, John was severely punished by two angels, who beat him to death.[309] In Sparta, the future Saint founded a monastery, which modern researchers have attempted to locate (more or less successfully). St. Nikon Metanoeite played an essential political role in the Peloponnese until his death in the last years of the tenth or the beginning of the eleventh century. One of the versions of his *Life*, edited by Sullivan, includes many miracles around the Saint's grave.[310]

The biography of St. Nikon Metanoeite (*BHG* [1366–1368])[311] was written by an anonymous monk in the monastery the Saint founded. The hagiographer himself fixes the year (6650=A.D. 1141/1142) and the eleventh *indiction* in the text, but the two dates do not match. According to Jenkins and Mango,[312] the *Life* was compiled in 6656 (=A.D. 1148). Sullivan accepts their opinion and arguments.

---

[309] Ibid., §33.19–23 and §35.58–137. For more on John Aratos, see Alexios Savvides, "The Laconian John Aratos and the Jews in the Late Tenth Century A.D." [Greek: Ἀλέξιος Σαββίδης, "Ὁ Λάκων Ἰωάννης Ἄρατος καὶ οἱ Ἰουδαῖοι τῆς Σπάρτης στὰ τέλη τοῦ 10 μ. Χ. αἰ."], *Byzantinai Meletai* [Βυζαντιναί μελέται] 6 (1995): 201–9.

[310] Nikon Metanoeite, §§75–77. See esp. §77.5–8, where the author refers to the Saint's posthumous miracles.

[311] For more on Nikon, see da Costs-Louillet, "Saints de Grèce", 346–50; Sullivan, *The Life of Saint Nikon*, 1–18.

[312] Jenkins and Mango, "A Synodicon of Antioch", 238ff.

Part Two
THE DEMON: ORIGINS AND TRADITIONS

CHAPTER 1
THE PRE-CHRISTIAN DEMON

Before we begin with the detailed study of the demonic creatures in Byzantine hagiography, we need to pay attention to the meanings of the term *demon* itself and the different stages of its evolution. Two "trends" coexist in Greek literature. The first them could be called "Homeric" because its first appearance is in the Homeric *epos*. Here, the demon is an unknown, faceless, and unnamable power that influences human life either favorably or unfavorably in critical situations. This "fate" is not related to a transcendental Evil or Good; its impact could be positive or negative, but it is always unexpected and decisive. The second "trend" could be called "Hesiodic" or "objectivizing". The notion of the demon attracts the attention of many poets, philosophers, and other intellectuals, as early as the epoch of Hesiod's monumental *Works and Days*. They try to give demonic power specific characteristics, to objectivize it, and transform it from object to subject. In other words, if we use Marcel Detienne's definition , their goal was to define not what it is to *have* a demon but what it means to *be* one.[313] The most crucial objectivization of the term was undoubtedly by the Christians. Gradually, the theologians of the Church made the demon the absolute personification of Evil. However, the dogmatic postulates, which define the outer appearance of the demon and its functions, never managed entirely to erase the "Homeric" aspects of the notion, and in the Byzantine hagiography of the period between the second half of the sixth and the beginning of the eleventh centuries the demon continued to signify the unknown and faceless power that always tries to destroy or at least to disrupt the order established by God, the power that always sinisterly laughs at humans and their efforts, and constantly throws awry their plans and expectations in many odd ways. When influenced by this fateful power, one acts like the ancient hero Di-

---

[313] Detienne, *La notion de DAÏMÔN*, 112.

omedes who once dared to stand against the god Apollo himself, according to Homer.[314]

1. The Homeric demon

The various usages of the notion *demon* in the *Iliad* and the *Odyssey* will remain virtually unmodified in later Greek literature. A changeable outer appearance, a fatal and usually harmful influence upon human life, and the infliction of certain natural disasters, like illnesses and storms, will be among the features and the functions of the demon in the Christian and especially the hagiographic tradition.

In Homeric epic poetry, the *demon* (δαίμων) means *supernatural power* in general. On rare occasions, this term could be used for a particular deity, but usually it designates a nameless and vague influence on human life — just like the Latin *numen*.[315] For this reason, sometimes the most suitable translation of the word is *fate*.[316] Since fate is, above all, the fate of the body for Homer, δαίμων becomes the connection between the human soul and body, being the tangible manifestation of the divine principle and power within the limits of the human world.[317] However, though divine, demons are different from gods. Only Apollo, Aphrodite, and probably Athena are occasionally called demons in the *Iliad*.[318] "De-

---

[314] Homer, *The Iliad*, ed. and trans. Augustus Murray, vol. 1 (Cambridge, MA: Harvard University Press, 1924), V.431–44.

[315] Joseph-Antoine Hild, *Étude sur les demons dans la litterature et la religion des Grecs* (Paris: Librairie de L. Hachette, 1881), 47ff.

[316] On the demon-fate, see Hild, *Étude sur les demons*, 45–51; Joseph-Antoine Hild, "Daemon", in *Dictionnaire des antiquités Grecques et Romaines*, vol. 2.1 (Paris: Librairie de L. Hachette, 1892), s.v. "Daemon", 12–14. On the concept in the Homeric *epos* in particular, see Samuel Bassett, "ΔΑΙΜΩΝ in Homer", *The Classical Review* 33, no. 7/8 (November–December 1919): 134–36; F. A. Wilford, "ΔΑΙΜΩΝ in Homer", *Numen* 12, no. 3 (September 1965): 217ff. and 223. Homer uses δαίμων meaning *fate* in, e.g., *Iliad*, VIII.166.

[317] Petar Plamenov, *The Body Text* [Bulgarian: Петър Пламенов, *Тялото текст*], Sofia: Sofia University Press, 2018, 122.

[318] Hild, "Daemon", 10; Bassett, "ΔΑΙΜΩΝ in Homer", 134–36; Wilford, "ΔΑΙΜΩΝ in Homer", 218ff; Walter Burkert, *Greek Religion, Archaic and Classical*, trans. John Raffan (Oxford: Blackwell, 1985), 180.

mon" and "god" are sometimes interchangeable terms. "Whenso a warrior is minded against the will of a demon to fight with another whom a god honoureth, forthwith then upon him rolleth mighty woe", says Menelaus to himself, profoundly doubting that he was allowed to fight Hector and the Trojans for the dead body of Patroclus.[319]

However, in early epic poetry, there exist some substantial differences between a god and a demon. These differences presuppose the further evolution of the latter term as a personification of ultimate Evil.

Unlike the humanlike gods of Olympus, who have their names and well-defined functions and represent "intelligent, sensitive, passionate divinity",[320] the demon is nameless, unknown, and, above all, irrational. For Odysseus, the power that struck his ship with a thunderbolt is evident — it was the god Zeus. In the same passage, however, Odysseus was led to the island of Ogygia by a nameless demon, who in this way caused him many troubles.[321] Heroes are often in doubt about the name of the deity which influences their destiny and causes them harm; for this reason, the word "demon" usually appears in direct speech.[322] For instance, during the battle for the ships in the *Iliad*, Zeus breaks the bowstrings of the hero Teucer and diverts his arrow away from Hector; this is explained to the hearer by the poet himself. However, for Teucer himself, the power that

---

[319] Homer, Iliad, XVII.98ff: ὅππoτ' ἀνὴρ ἐθέλῃ πρὸς δαίμονα φωτὶ μάχεσθαι ὅν κε θεὸς τιμᾷ, τάχα οἱ μέγα πῆμα κυλίσθη. The expression "against the will of a demon" (πρὸς δαίμονα) is inaccurately translated by Murray as "against the will of heaven".

[320] Hild, *Étude sur les demons*, 39.

[321] Homer, *The Odyssey*, ed. and trans. Augustus Murray, vol. 1 (Cambridge, MA: Harvard University Press, 1919), VII.248–50: Ἀλλ'ἐμὲ τὸν δύστηνον ἐφέστιον ἤγαγε δαίμων οἷον, ἐπεί μοι νῆα θοὴν ἀργῆτι κεραυνῷ Ζεὺς ἐλάσας ἐκέασσε μέσῳ ἐνὶ οἴνοπι πόντῳ.

[322] The theory that Homer uses the term *demon* predominantly in direct speech was proposed for the first time by Ove Jörgensen, "Das Auftreten der Gotter in den Büchern ι-μ der Odyssee", *Hermes* 39 (1904): 357ff, and further developed by Gerald Else, "God and Gods in Early Greek Thought", *Transactions and Proceedings of the American Philological Association* 80 (1949): 26. According to Else, the poet himself always knows exactly *who* is the god who influences the fate of the hero, but the hero himself is often aware only that *some* god has intervened, calling this anonymous deity a "demon". Wilford ("ΔΑΙΜΩΝ in Homer", 218ff) calculates that Homer uses the singular form of the noun δαίμων fifty-nine times, of which only eleven are in indirect speech.

robbed him of the glory of murdering the greatest Trojan hero is simply an unknown and harmful demon.[323] Before his arrival on Helios's island, Odysseus does not know which god has turned against him; the only thing he knows of is that "some demon was assuredly devising ill".[324] In the *Iliad*, the demon has neither a face nor a cult nor a shrine[325] and is described only through its deeds and influence upon human lives. In this way, as early as the Homeric epoch, the concept of the demon took shape as an unknown, foreign supernatural power that mostly brings misfortune.[326] It is usually defined as "hateful" (στυγερός) and "tormenting" (χαλεπός).[327] In the *Odyssey*, the demon inflicts illnesses,[328] brings storms,[329] causes deceitful or dreadful dreams and illusions[330] and instigates fateful mistakes through rushed, unreasonable decisions.[331] The occasions on which this power is favorable are extremely rare and occur ex-

---

[323] Homer, *Iliad*, XV.467ff: ὢ πόποι ἦ δὴ πάγχυ μάχης ἐπὶ μήδεα κείρει δαίμων ἡμετέρης, ὅ τέ μοι βιὸν ἔκβαλε χειρός.

[324] Homer, *Odyssey*, XII.295: ὃ δὴ κακὰ μήδετο δαίμων. The Greek word δαίμων is inaccurately translated by Murray as "god".

[325] On this point, see Burkert, *Greek Religion*, 180.

[326] Homer, *Iliad*, XV.467ff and XXI.93, where Lycaon, the son of Priam, complains that a "demon" forced him again to test his strength against Achilles; Homer, *Odyssey*, XI.587, XII.295, XVI.370, and XVIII.256. At the beginning of the past century, Finsler tried to prove that the Homeric demon is an entirely evil being, almost identical to the Christian evil spirit. While Bassett ("ΔΑΙΜΩΝ in Homer" 134ff) persuasively rejects this hypothesis, he agrees that the influence of the demon on human fate is mostly negative. On demons as agents of misfortune, see Wilford, "ΔΑΙΜΩΝ in Homer", 221 and 223, who defines them as "undefined external powers".

[327] See, e.g., Homer, *Odyssey*, V.396 (στυγερὸς δέ οἱ ἔχραε δαίμων) and XIX.201 (χαλεπός τις ὤρορε δαίμων). Cf. Hild, *Étude sur les demons*, 59; Hild, "Daemon" 9ff; Burkert, *Greek Religion*, 180.

[328] Homer, *Odyssey*, V.395ff, where Odysseus rejoices like the children of a man whom the gods have rescued from a disease-carrying demon. See Hild, *Étude sur les demons*, 61; Hild, "Daemon", 10.

[329] Homer, *Odyssey*, XIX.201.

[330] Homer, *Odyssey*, XX.87, where a demon sends Penelope a tormenting dream. Here, the demon himself appears in the shape of Odysseus and, in this way, sharpens her grief and longing for her absent husband.

[331] Hild, *Étude sur les demons*, 50 and 61.

clusively in the *Odyssey*; in this case, the demon could inspire bravery or a good idea, just like the Roman *genius* or "guardian spirit".[332]

The demon is usually a lesser power compared to the gods of Olympus. They are surrounded by numerous supernatural beings, defined as δαίμονες.[333] A man who unsuccessfully and recklessly confronts some god whom he could not possibly defeat could be "equal to a demon" (δαίμονι ἶσος); among the most popular examples of this are the three attempts of Diomedes to overpower Apollo mentioned above.

According to Wilford, another important aspect of the term "demon" in Homer is preserved in later Greek literature. This supernatural power is associated with irrationality, as opposed to the rational divinity of the Olympian pantheon. Any action that cannot find a reasonable explanation in the eyes of others and that leads to disastrous consequences can be perceived as demonic. This is where the dividing line between a god and a demon lies. As he fought valiantly with the Trojans shortly before his death, displaying both superhuman bravery and intelligence, Patroclus was likened to a god, the swift Ares. A few lines later, however, when he dares to attack for the fourth time and encounters the battle frenzy of Apollo himself, he is already "demonlike". It was his irrational hybris that led to his death.[334] Again, Diomedes is demonlike when he confronts Apollo three times before realizing his folly.[335] In the passages where the expression δαίμονι ἶσος is used, the demon is opposed to the

---

[332] See, e.g., Homer, *Odyssey*, XII.169, where a demon puts the sea tides "to sleep", when Odysseus reaches the Sirens. A demon inspires bravery in Odysseus' friends shortly before the blinding of Polyphemus (*Odyssey*, XIX.381). A demon inspires Penelope and she lights upon the idea of avoiding an undesired marriage by weaving and unweaving the shroud for her father-in-law Laertes (*Odyssey*, XIX.138). For more on this and the typology of the demon's functions according to Homer, see Wilford, "ΔΑΙΜΩΝ in Homer", 221ff.

[333] Homer, *Iliad*, I.216 and I.221ff: χρὴ μὲν σφωΐτερόν γε θεὰ ἔπος εἰρύσασθαι... ἡ δ'Οὐλυμπον δὲ βεβήκει δώματ'ἐς αἰγιόχοιο Διὸς μετὰ δαίμονας ἄλλους.

[334] Homer, *Iliad*, XVI.784–92 (esp. 784 and 786). See also Wilford, "ΔΑΙΜΩΝ in Homer", 224; Hild, *Étude sur les démons*, 56.

[335] Homer, *Iliad*, V.432-442. See Wilford, "ΔΑΙΜΩΝ in Homer", 221, where he stresses the fact that the expression δαίμονι ἶσος, used nine times in the *Iliad* (and not a single time in the *Odyssey*), belongs to the oldest stratum of the *epos*.

gods. The address δαιμόνιε, not only in epic poetry but in Plato's dialogues as well, also expresses astonishment and misunderstanding — a person uses it when they do not understand the purpose and the reason for another's actions and attributes them to the influence of a demon.[336]

This opposition of the terms θεός (rational, organized, supreme and eternal power) and δαίμων (the insane, unknown and harmful supernatural being) will persist almost unchanged for more than a millennium. There are countless examples of the irrationality of demons and their victims in Byzantine hagiography. Suffice it to mention the eerie uncontrollable laughter of one of the evil spirits in the *Life* of St. Theodore Sykeotes, who encourages the villagers to beat and torture him more and more;[337] or the phrase, both frightening and comical, "I rejoice in my deeds" (ἐπιχαίρομαι τοῖς ἔργοις μου), used by the king of the demons to announce his three murders in Spain according to the *Roman Miracle of St. Anastasios of Persia*.[338]

2. Objectivizations of the notion demon

The Homeric demon is a shapeless and nameless force without a definite origin and abode in the world. Like human destiny, this power is ever-changing and characterized only by its actions, not by its material form. On the other hand, later Greek authors made efforts to clarify the concept, to give the demon various concrete images and functions, and finally to place it within the framework of numerous typologies that influenced the Christian theological tradition.

2.1. Hesiod

While the Homeric demon is a force of utterly unknown origin, a faceless influence on human life, Hesiod created, for the first time in Greek literature, a specific "demonogony", which influenced the Pythagoreans and

---

[336] Burkert, *Greek Religion*, 180. On the meaning of δαιμόνιος, see also Hild, *Étude sur les demons*, 58–61. Hild also points out that δαιμόνιος is a person struck by a supernatural power ("Daemon", 10).
[337] Theodore Sykeotes, §116.15–22.
[338] Anastasios of Persia, *Roman Miracle*, §7.6.

other philosophical systems. According to *Works and Days*, demons are of human origin. After the end of the Golden Age of the world, the people who belonged to this generation became *pure demons* (ἀγνοὶ δαίμονες) "dwelling on the earth ... kindly, delivering from harm and guardians of mortal men"[339] Hesiod only uses the word δαίμονες to refer to this highest category of souls, and calls those who lived during the Silver Age "blessed spirits of the underworld" (ὑποχθόνιοι μάκαρες θνητοί). In this way, Hesiod creates the first Greek hierarchy of the supernatural world:

GODS

|

DEMONS

|

BLESSED SPIRITS OF THE UNDERWORLD

|

MORTALS

Further clues about the Hesiodic concept of the supernatural can be found in his version of the myth of Phaethon. According to the *Theogony*, the goddess Aphrodite made him, still a boy, "a keeper of her shrine by night, a divine demon" (δῖος δαίμων).[340] The son of Eos became, in this manner, the so-called δαίμων πρόπολος, or a demon in the service of

---

[339] Hesiod, *Works and Days*, ed. and trans. Hugh Evelyn-White, *Hesiod: Homeric Hymns, Epic Cycle, Homerica* [Loeb Classical Library, Volume 57] (CambridgeMA: Harvard University Press, 1982), l. 122ff: τοὶ μὲν δαίμονες ἁγνοὶ ἐπιχθόνιοι τελέθουσιν ἐσθλοί, ἀλεξίκακοι, φύλακες θνητῶν ἀνθρώπων. See also Georg Luck, *Arcana Mundi. Magic and the Occult in the Greek and Roman Worlds. A Collection of Ancient Texts* (Baltimore: John Hopkins University Press, 2006), 123–25.

[340] Hesiod, *The Theogony*, ed. and trans. Hugh Evelyn-White, *Hesiod: Homeric Hymns, Epic Cycle, Homerica*, ll. 990ff. See Hild, "Daemon", 11; Burkert, *Greek Religion*, 180. For the version in which Phaethon was the son of Eos and not of Helios, see *The Theogony*, ll. 986ff.

some god, who helps mortals and instructs them how to worship the Olympians in the right way.[341]

Hesiod's interpretation of the origin of the demons represent the first intellectual objectivization of the concept in the Greek literary tradition. While the Homeric *epos* renders the δαίμονες as unidentified fateful forces with a fatal influence on man, Hesiod gives them a definite abode by calling them *earthly* (ἐπιχθόνιοι) and a definite origin as the spirits of the people who lived in the Golden Age. At the same time, he defines them as entirely benevolent beings, guardians of humans, and *protectors from Evil* (ἀλεξίκακοι). The word *demon* in the sense of "undefined, fatal force" occurs only once in the Hesiodic corpus. In the *Shield of Heracles*, the greatest Greek hero speaks sorrowfully about his destiny to his faithful friend and charioteer, Iolaus. Heracles is convinced that a *demon* laid the heavy *labors* on him.[342] This "supernatural sovereign power", as Gilbert François defines it,[343] is the driving force behind his extraordinary exploits.

The semantic difference in the term *demon* in the works of the earliest Greek epic poets is so striking that the two concepts seem to be based on entirely different folklore traditions or even that the Hesiodic concept is mostly Hesiod's own invention. Homer does not give the slightest hint that the δαίμονες are the spirits of *the* dead, much less the souls of *certain* dead. In the famous description of Odysseus' underworld experience, he simply calls the hero's deceased friends and relatives "the spirits of those that are dead" (ψυχαὶ νεκύων κατατεθνηώτων).[344] It is quite possible that Hesiod simply applied the concept of the δαίμων to already existing myths about people of the Golden Age.

---

[341] On the δαίμων πρόπολος, see Hild, "Daemon", 11ff; François, *Le Polythéisme*, 337–39.
[342] Hesiod, *The Shield of Heracles*, in *Hesiod. Homeric Hymns, Epic Cycle, Homerica*, l. 94: αὐτὰρ ἐμοὶ δαίμων χαλεποὺς ἐπετέλλετ' ἀέθλους.
[343] See François, *Le Polythéisme*, 56 and 335 n. 5. François defines the demon in this case as "une Puissance surnaturelle suveraine".
[344] Homer, *Odyssey*, XI.37.

The Pythagoreans adopted the concept of "pure" demons.[345] The philosopher Cornelius Alexander Polyhistor (mid-first century B.C.), cited by Diogenes Laertius (third century A.D.), is the first known Greek author who places these spirits in the aerial regions above the Earth. According to Polyhistor, the god Hermes takes the souls of the deceased and guides them all to the place they merited: the *impure* (ἀκάθαρτοι) are doomed to be chained and tortured by the Erinyes, the dreadful chthonic goddesses of vengeance, and the *pure* are allowed to dwell in the sky as *heroes* (ἥρωες) and *demons* (δαίμονες).[346]

In his dialogue *Cratylus*, probably under the Pythagorean influence,[347] Plato refers to the famous lines (122–23) of *Works and Days*[348] and tries to place the demon's origins and functions in a philosophical perspective. According to him, every wise and good mortal shares the fate of the blessed people of the Golden Age and becomes a pure demon after death.[349] To this idea, Plato applies his etymology of the word *demon*, which he claims to derive from the verb δαῆναι (to learn, to know) and from the adjective δαήμων (skilled, experienced).[350] The Hesiodic concept of demons as guardians and benefactors of humans can also be found in other of the great philosopher's dialogues.[351]

2.2. The demons of the dead

Hesiod introduced a new concept of the demon; for him, it denoted the pure spirits of the great ancients after death. As we learn from the preserved fragments, the Pythagoreans included the demons of the dead in

---

[345] See Detienne, *La notion de DAÏMÔN*, 93–117 (esp. 104), with bibliography. Detienne's hypothesis is accepted by Burkert, *Greek Religion*, 180.

[346] *Diogenis Laertii vitae philosophorum*, ed. Miroslav Marcovich, vol. 1: *Libri I–X* (Berlin: De Gruyter, 2008), VIII.31.4–32.6.

[347] Detienne, *La notion de DAÏMÔN*, 95–102 (esp. 96 and 100).

[348] Plato, "Cratylus", ed. John Burnet, *Platonis opera*, vol. 1 (Oxford: Clarendon Press, 1967), 397e–398a.

[349] Ibid., 398a-c. For the Pythagorean influence in this particular case, see Detienne, *La notion de DAÏMÔN*, 98ff.

[350] Ibid., 398b.

[351] See for example Plato, "Leges", ed. John Burnet, *Platonis opera*, vol. 5 (Oxford: Clarendon Press, 1967), 713c-e. See Detienne's analysis (*La notion de DAÏMÔN*, 102ff).

their philosophical system and defined their functions, outer appearance, and dwellings. However, their idea differs from the Hesiodic notion of pure demons. Some researchers[352] claim that the local cults strongly influenced the small Greek communities of southern Italy, where Pythagorean teaching was born. If this hypothesis is correct, we must accept that ancient Italian folklore of the sixth century B.C. played a crucial role in the formation of a concept that remained more or less unchanged for the next fifteen hundred years. In addition, information about the Pythagorean demons and their connection to the dead is largely provided by Late Antique secondary sources, mainly from Diogenes Laertius and Iamblichus. On the one hand, the late date of most of these sources casts doubt on the accuracy of the original teaching of Pythagoras and his direct pupils centuries earlier. On the other hand, these texts locate the idea of the demonic soul in the cultural and theological context in which the Christian religion developed. Many of the evil spirits in the New Testament and especially in the writings of the Church Fathers reflect certain beliefs and traditions widespread in the Greco-Roman world of Late Antiquity and pass practically unchanged into Byzantine hagiography.

On the basis of Cornelius Alexander Polyhistor's text, for the Pythagoreans, "demons" were not exclusively the spirits of the dead ancients of the Golden Age but the souls of distinguished and eminent mortals as a whole.[353] One passage clearly shows the characteristics and the functions of these supernatural creatures:

> They believe that the whole air above the earth is full of souls and that these souls are called "demons" and "heroes"; they admit also that these spirits are sending various dreams to the mortals, and omens, and illnesses; with different diseases, they strike not only the humans, but also the animals, domestic or not.[354]

---

[352] See Detienne, *La notion de DAÏMÔN*, 33.
[353] See Detienne, *La notion de DAÏMÔN*, 93.
[354] *Diogenis Laertii vitae philosophorum*, VIII.32.1–4 (= *Die Fragmente der Vorsokratiker*, ed. Hermann Diels and Walther Kranz, vol. 1 (Berlin: Weidmann, 1966, 58) (Pythagoreische Schule, fr. B1a. 57–60).

Therefore, the functions of demons, according to Polyhistor, are ambivalent, both favorable and harmful to mortals. The first is to send dreams, which is by no means an original idea. Homer mentions the dream sent by a "demon" to Penelope, but she is said to have clearly distinguished between delusions seen in sleep and a real revelation. By contrast, for the Pythagoreans, visions and dreams were not something imaginary but rather a different reality, in which one visits the nether world and speaks to the souls of the dead and the demons that inhabit it.[355] Thus was born the religious and philosophical idea of so-called *ecstasis* (ἔκστασις), namely the state in which the soul leaves the body and ascends temporarily to Heaven, descends to Hell, or travels to distant parts of the earthly world. The relationship between demons and visions is discernible in Byzantine hagiography, but not undistorted. This motif became extremely popular in the ninth and especially the tenth centuries with such texts as the *Lives* of St. Basil the Younger and St. Phantinos the Younger, the *Vision of the Monk Cosmas*, and others. In these cases, however, demons do not send visions but play an active role in them.

Another primary function of the demonic souls of the dead, presented by Polyhistor as a Pythagorean concept, is to spread diseases among humans and cattle. This idea was widespread in the Greco-Roman world[356] and remained almost intact in Christian theology.[357] Ac-

---

[355] See Detienne, *La notion de DAÏMÔN*, 42–46 and 91. Detienne provides many examples to support the hypothesis that, according to Hesiod, dreams were journeys to other worlds where the dreaming person could communicate with the souls of the dead and with various demons.

[356] See, for example, Hippocrate, "De la maladie sacrée", ed. and trans. Émile Littré, *Oeuvres complètes d'Hippocrate*, vol. 6 (Paris: Baillière; Amsterdam: Hakkert, 1962), §1.90–93. Hippocrates claims that people with the so-called "sacred disease" or epilepsy describe the seizures caused by the illness (the so-called *grand mal* and *petit mal* seizures) as *attacks of the goddess Hecate and skirmishes of heroes*. See Julius Tambornino, *De antiquorum daemonismo* (Gießen, 1909), 57ff. Tambornino summarizes the primary sources for various diseases associated with demonic influence. See also Detienne, *La notion de DAÏMÔN*, 46–48.

[357] The demons that cause illness were extremely popular in Byzantine hagiography. See, for example, for the demon of mutism: Theodore Sykeotes, §94; Patriarch Tarasios, §66.30–33, where the holy Tarasios is called "spiritual doctor" (πνευμάτων ἰατήρ); Peter of Atroa, §20; Eustratios of Agauros, §46; Niketas of Medikion, §17. For the demon

cording to Iamblichus, the Pythagoreans believed that the gods were not to blame for illnesses and that their real cause was human sin.[358] We cannot be sure about the origin of this reference, ascribed to the philosopher Heraclitus of Pontus (c. 390– c. 310 B.C.), and there is no specific evidence that this idea belonged to the oldest stratum of Pythagorean teaching. It seems obvious, however, that the Christians simply integrated an already existing and very popular concept into their theological system. In the Byzantine hagiography of the period between the sixth and the tenth centuries, the bodily sufferings to which mortals were subject under the influence of demons were caused chiefly by their sinfulness, which attracted the evil spirits to them and made their bodies susceptible to harmful impact, deforming them.

Another common idea, which was apparently part of Pythagorean philosophy, is that the demonic soul appears in non-material human form — this is the so-called εἴδωλον (phantom, ghost). Homer uses the latter term in the same sense, but it is not associated with demons in the *Iliad* and the *Odyssey*.[359] According to the Pythagoreans, these apparitions displayed the same outer appearance as when they were alive, but they looked like obscure reflections in a mirror and could not be touched.[360] Because the demons could be both benevolent and harmful, the Pythagoreans believed they had to be appeased with various gifts and ceremonies.[361] While these supernatural creatures were not associated

---

of blindness, see, e.g., Symeon Stylites the Younger, §137.13–16. For the demon of Leprosy, see, e.g., Peter of Atroa, §70ff. For other diseases, see, e.g., Theodore Sykeotes, §86 (heart conditions); Symeon Stylites the Younger, §188ff (paralysis); Symeon Stylites the Younger, §§114 and 115.14 (diseases of the excretory system); Luke of Steiris, §69 (diseases of the digestive system); Athanasia of Aegina, §29.

[358] Iamblichus, *De vita Pythagorica liber*, ed. Ludwig Deubner, (Leipzig: Teubner, 1975), §32.218.14–15. Cf. ibid., §32.217.5ff on the demons which cause diseases (νόσοι καὶ ὅσα πάθη σώματος ἀκολασίας ἐστὶ σπέρματα).

[359] Homer, *Iliad*, XIII.72; Homer, *Odyssey*, XI.83. See Burkert, *Greek Religion*, 195.

[360] Detienne, *La notion de DAÏMÔN*, 90ff; Burkert, *Greek Religion*, 195ff. Cf. and Homer, *Odyssey*, XI.206-208, where Odysseus reaches out to his mother's shadow three times, unable to touch her.

[361] Detienne, *La notion de DAÏMÔN*, 36ff; Burkert, *Greek Religion*, 195; Luck, *Arcana Mundi*, 99-101.

with specific rituals in the Homeric *epos*, they became an object of veneration in the Pythagorean system.

Information on the demonic souls of the dead can be found not only in the Pythagorean teachings, where the concept is integrated into a coherent philosophical system, but in various literary sources as well. Authors like Pausanias, Plutarch, and Lucian frequently use the term *demon* for the spirits of specific dead people. Who are these people, however? The classical Greek tragic poets believed they were the souls of the great and distinguished who perished heroically.[362] Euripides calls the diseased wife of Admetus, the king of Thessaly, a *blessed demon*[363] because she exchanged her life for that of her husband. The same author refers to the king of Thrace, Rhesus, as a *human demon* (ἀνθρωποδαίμων) after his death.[364] Again, according to Aeschylus, the king of Persia, Darius, appears as a demon near his grave.[365] Pausanias uses the same term for the ghosts of soldiers who fell heroically in the battle of Marathon and could still be seen fighting on the ancient battlefield with their rattling weapons and neighing horses. These demons were neither good nor harmful; according to the author, it was dangerous for somebody to watch them for a long time as a spectacle, but they never turned their battle frenzy on those who just happened to be there.[366]

The souls of executed felons and those who passed away violently leave this world with difficulty and grief; like the unburied, they often haunt the places of their death or graves. However, before the second century A.D., the authors refrain from using the term *demon*. Plato, for

---

[362] Burkert, *Greek Religion*, 181.
[363] Euripides, "Alcestis", ed. James Diggle, *Euripidis fabulae*, vol. 1, (Oxford: Clarendon Press, 1984), l. 1003: Αὕτα ποτὲ προύθαν' ἀνδρός, νῦν δ' ἔστι μάκαιρα δαίμων·
[364] Euripides, "Rhesus", ed. James Diggle, *Euripidis fabulae*, vol. 3, (Oxford: Clarendon Press, 1994), ll. 970ff: κρυπτὸς δ' ἐν ἄντροις τῆς ὑπαργύρου χθονὸς ἀνθρωποδαίμων κείσεται βλέπων φάος.
[365] Aeschylus, "Persae", ed. Gilbert Murray, *Aeschyli septem quae supersunt tragoediae*, (Oxford: Clarendon Press, 1960), ll. 620ff: ...τόν τε δαίμονα Δαρεῖον ἀνακαλεῖσθε·... On the demon of King Darius and its cult see Lily Taylor, "The Daimōn of the Persian King", *The Journal of Hellenic Studies* 48 (1928): 6.
[366] *Pausaniae Graeciae descriptio*, ed. Maria Helena Rocha-Pereira, vol. 1: *Libri I-IV*, (Leipzig: Teubner, 1989), I.32.3.4-8. Cf. Luck, *Arcana Mundi*, 238–40.

example, calls them *shadowlike apparitions* (σκιοειδὴ φάσματα).³⁶⁷ By contrast, ghostly demons are mentioned, though rarely, by Byzantine hagiographers. An example is the sinister ghosts of two executed criminals who appeared before Patriarch Antony Kauleas in a Constantinople graveyard in the late ninth century.³⁶⁸

2.3. The Demon-Paredros: the personal guardian demon and the myth of Doctor Faustus³⁶⁹

Late in Queen Elizabeth I's long reign, around 1595, Cristopher Marlowe presented on the stage his famous play *The Tragicall History of the Life and Death of Doctor Faustus*.³⁷⁰ In this play, a great scholar, who had penetrated the very depths of knowledge, summoned the Devil, rejected Christ and his Christian faith, and signed a contract with the Evil One in his blood. In the sixteenth and seventeenth centuries, the notorious Witch Hunt was a reality; hence, Marlowe's audience was well-acquainted with the idea of a pact with the Devil. A different situation occurred in the 1820s when Goethe composed and put on stage his own "Faustus". By then, almost a century had passed since the great burnings at the stake in Europe.

Nevertheless, the fascinating story of the man who sold his soul to the Devil is known today mainly in this literary, romantic form. In reality, though, behind the myth of Faustus lies an enormous philosophical, theological, political, and ideological tradition; its roots are visible in the literary production of Late Antiquity and the early Byzantine Empire.

---

[367] Plato, "Phaedo", ed. John Burnet, *Platonis opera*, vol. 1, (Oxford: Clarendon Press, 1967), 81c-d.

[368] Antony Kauleas, §20.

[369] The following text (§2.3.) was partially published in the *Sofia Philosophical Review* in 2020: see Gerasim Petrinski, "Faustus Byzantinus: The Legend of Faust in Byzantine Literature and Its Neo-Platonic Roots", *Sofia Philosophical Review* 13, no. 1 (2020): 48–76.

[370] The first edition of the play (the so-called "A-text") was published for the first time in 1604 by Valentine Simmes (see Cristopher Marlowe, *Doctor Faustus: A- and B- Texts (1604, 1616)*, ed. David Bevington and Eric Rasmussen [Manchester: Manchester University Press, 1993], 62).

The sources that provide information on the contract with the Devil were partially edited in 1927 by Ludwig Radermacher.[371] The texts incorporated in this collection date from the fourth to the seventh centuries. In the West, the Latin versions of the legend of Theophilos (the Church *oeconomus* or "manager" of the city of Adana, who reportedly sold his soul to the Devil) were translated and rewritten several times between the ninth and the thirteenth centuries. We also still have records of Byzantine variations of this narrative topos, in which it assumed political and religious dimensions and was probably interwoven with some urban legends of the cosmopolitan imperial capital between the eighth and tenth centuries.

The theme of the contract with the Devil in Late Antiquity and the Byzantine tradition is a complex phenomenon that combines elements from literature, folklore, politics, and philosophy. The core idea probably evolved as a Christian reaction against widespread magical practices (a flourishing business in the eastern Roman cities) and as an attempt to demonize them. In addition, as we will see below, in the late fourth century, Neoplatonism had already developed an elaborate demonological system, including the so-called *demon-paredros*, i.e., a "patron demon" or "protector demon".[372] In our opinion, early Christian authors of hagiographical texts borrowed this idea from the great Eastern philosophical schools of Athens, Antioch, and Alexandria, combined it with numerous urban legends, and created, in this way, the image of the evil spirit that accompanies and helps the devilish and cunning magician in his harmful deeds.

The theme of the Devil's contract was used in different anonymous hagiographical texts. In the late eighth and the early ninth centuries, Stephen, deacon of St. Sophia in Constantinople and founding father of iconodule hagiography, used it to create the image of Emperor Constantine V (741–775) — one of the most hated and demonized Byzantine rul-

---

[371] Ludwig Radermacher, *Griechische Quellen zur Faustsage* (Vienna and Leipzig: Hölder-Pichler-Tempsky in Komm, 1927).
[372] *PGM*, vol. 1 (1928), 8.

ers. Obviously, the legend of the emperor who signed a contract with the Devil enjoyed huge popularity among the populace of the imperial capital and was employed in the late ninth and the first half of the tenth centuries by the chronographer George Hamartolos, by the encyclopedists of Emperor Constantine VII's intellectual circle, and by the anonymous author of the *Suda* lexicon.

We can only make suggestions about the origin of the pact with the Devil before the period between the fourth and the sixth centuries when it first appears in a relatively elaborate form. It is vaguely reminiscent of the founding principle of the relationship between humans and gods in ancient Rome — *do, ut des* ("I give so that you may give"). Before some critical event, in cases of illness or difficulty, a person would promise a higher power particular reward for its help. Votive offerings (usually figurines representing the injured part of the body) are frequently found in ancient temples.[373] This tradition was not related to either mysticism or theurgy in the ancient Greek poleis and Rome. The pact with the deity was considered an actual contract, similar to the contracts made by mortals. In the eclectic Hellenistic world, and especially in Late Antiquity, where magical practices of Egyptian, Babylonian and Syrian origin mixed with Greco-Roman mythological traditions, the summoning of supernatural powers for the sake of a client became a profitable business for professional "magicians" in the great metropolises. These practices constituted a significant obstacle for Christianity on its path to universal power and were therefore subjected to intense propagandistic "demonization".[374] They became criminalized as early as the mid-fourth century under Emperor Constantius II (337–361). Ammianus Marcellinus mentions accusations of magical practices as a powerful weapon in political

---

[373] Cf. Annamaria Comella, *I rilievi votivi greci di periodo arcaico e classico: diffusione, ideologia, committenza* (Bari: Edipuglia, 2002).
[374] The term "démonization de la magie" is used by Jean-Benoît Clerc in his thorough analysis of the treatises of St. Augustine, St. John Chrysostom, and other early Christian theologians (Jean-Benoît Clerc, *Homines magici. Etude sur la sorcellerie et la magie dans la société romaine impériale* [Bern: Peter Lang, 1995], 248 and 246–78).

struggles.³⁷⁵ Supernatural aid, unauthorized by the Church, was perceived as dangerous for society.³⁷⁶

The judicial measures against widespread magical commerce were insufficient to deal with such practices, deeply rooted in the Greco-Roman and Middle Eastern social and religious traditions. The Christian Church needed propaganda to change public opinion and attitudes towards pagan cultism. Under these circumstances, along with the formation of the new religion's ethical and theological system, a new narrative emerged. The pivotal points in the plot and the main characters are clear from the beginning and, at least until the tenth century, were almost identical — the differences usually lying in the details and the background. A wealthy and powerful man (a Faustian type, we would say), typically young, is driven by ambition, lustful passion, or a thirst for revenge. But some obstacle stands in his way. In his frustration, he turns to a famous (or, from the Christian point of view, notorious) magician. This magician promises to fulfill his wish, but the supernatural powers summoned to this end require something in return. The price is great: the client has to sign a contract (usually in his own blood) promising his soul. In the end, the sinner usually confesses and is saved by a holy man.

This relatively simple and basic topos is very convenient for conveying a didactic message, which is the primary goal of hagiography. In addition, to be successful, every propaganda tool needs specific "anchors"

---

³⁷⁵ According to the same author, people were accused of magic and executed merely for being caught passing in the vicinity of graveyards early in the afternoon or in the evening. See Ammianus Marcellinus, *History. Books 14-19*, ed. and trans. John Rolfe [Loeb Classical Library 300] (Cambridge, MA: Harvard University Press; William Heinemann, 1935), XIX.12.14: *For if anyone was accused by the testimony of the evil-disposed of passing by a grave in the evening, on the ground that he was a dealer in poisons, or a gatherer of the horrors of tombs and the vain illusions of the ghosts that walk there, he was condemned to capital punishment and so perished*; Anastasia Vakaloudi, *Magic as a Social Phenomenon in Early Byzantium (4ᵗʰ – 7ᵗʰ centuries)* [Greek: Αναστασία Βακαλούδη, *Η μαγεία ως κοινωνικό φαινόμενο στο πρώιμο Βυζάντιο (4ος-7ος αι.)*] (Athens: Enalios, 2001), 192.

³⁷⁶ Vakaloudi, *Magic*, 193.

— values, beliefs, attitudes — already accepted by the one persuaded.[377] The storyline of the pact with the Devil was probably inspired by the urban legends of Antioch, Adana, and Constantinople, well known to the populace. These legends would have made the story more plausible.

2.3.1. The Platonic tradition and the concept of the demon-paredros

The concept of the hero's divine protector can be traced back to Homer. The classic example of this concept is the goddess Athena, who took Odysseus and his son Telemachus under her wing.[378] In the *Odyssey*, even the secondary hero, Autolycus, had a guardian, his father Hermes.[379] In some cases, another deity can oppose them, like Poseidon, who acts against Odysseus and "his" Athena,[380] or, as we learn from the tragic poet Euripides, a divine protector may abandon their protégé, like Artemis, who left Hippolytus. Nevertheless, these protectors are gods, not *daimones*. They are not identified with the hero himself, like the Roman *genius*. However, these guardians of heroes are thoroughly objectified forces. They are specific gods (θεοί), they act for specific reasons, and, of course, are in no way identified with the person whom they choose to help — their relationship to him is (in Arthur Nock's words) "ad hoc".[381]

Personal demons that accompany somebody throughout their life are mentioned for the first time in the sixth century BC. According to Pindar, there are two kinds of demons: one good and "the other demon, who brings a man to harm" (δαίμων δ'ἕτερος ἐς κακὸν τρέψαις).[382] In his *Elegies*, the poet Theognis mentions the "brave" (ἐσθλός) and the "cow-

---

[377] Garth Jowett and Victoria O'Donnel, *Propaganda and Persuasion* (Los Angeles: SAGE Publications, 2012), 35.
[378] Homer, *Odyssey*, XIII.300ff and XIII.393ff.
[379] Ibid., XIX.398.
[380] Ibid., IX.528-536.
[381] Arthur Nock, "The Emperor's Divine Comes", *Journal of Roman Studies* 37 (1947): 109ff.
[382] Pindar, "Pythia", ed. Herwig Maehler and Bruno Snell, *Pindari carmina cum fragmentis*, vol. 1: *Epinicia* (Berlin and New York: De Guyter, 2008), III.108ff. See Burkert, *Greek Religion*, 181.

ardly" (δειλός) demon, both of whom could determine one's life.[383] Because of one's inability to choose and control his demon, in Greek εὐδαίμων means *happy*, and κακοδαίμων means *unhappy*. Nevertheless, this concept of determination was not entirely fatalistic. Mortals could change their fate by willingly choosing to follow their "brave" guardian and avoid the vicious deeds inspired by the "other" one. This idea appears among the Pre-Socratic philosophers Heraclitus, one of whose famous sentences says "character is for man a daimon" (ἦθος ἀνθρώπῳ δαίμων), and Democritus.[384] On the basis of such examples, we may assume that the concept of guardian demon was quite common as early as the Archaic Period.

Plato and the Platonic tradition contributed significantly to the development of the philosophical idea of the personal demon. In the dialogue *Phaedo*, Plato says that every human being receives by lot their demon. This demon accompanies the person he took into charge throughout their entire life and, after death, leads them to the place in the kingdom of Hades where the dead are put on trial. According to the philosopher, one is not entirely dependent on their demon; one can always follow the path of virtue and is obliged to do so, even against the will of this personal genius.[385] Another well-known account on this subject is that of the "divine and demonic creature" (θεῖόν τι καὶ δαιμόνιον), whose voice Socrates heard since childhood. This voice never incited the philosopher to do anything but rather always prevented him from acting.[386] Because of this, Socrates was charged with attempting to introduce "new deities" (καινὰ δαιμόνια)[387] in Athens and eventually lost his life.

---

[383] Theognis, "Elegiae", ed. Ernestus Diehl, *Theognis*, (Leipzig: Teubner, 1971), I.161–64.
[384] See Hild, "Daemon", 14ff; Burkert, *Greek Religion*, 181; Nock, "The Emperor's Divine Comes", 109ff and n. 69–77.
[385] Plato, "Phaedo", 107d–e and 113d; Plato, "Respublica", ed. John Burnet, *Platonis opera*, vol. 4 (Oxford: Clarendon Press, 1968), 617b–618a.
[386] Plato, "Apologia Socratis", ed. John Burnet, *Platonis opera*, vol. 1 (Oxford: Clarendon Press, 1967), 31c–d.
[387] Xenpophon, "Memorabilia Socratis", ed. James Adam, trans. Edgar Marchant, *Xenophon. Memorabilia, Oeconomicus, Symposium, Apology* [Loeb Classical Library 168] (Cambridge, MA and London: Harvard University Press, 1997), I.1.3.1.

During the next seven centuries, until the decline of the pagan Roman empire, the distinction between the good and the evil demon was preserved, enriched, and, occasionally, rejected.[388] Intellectuals such as Plutarch (c. 45–120), who wrote a whole treatise *On the Demon of Socrates* (Περὶ τοῦ Σωκράτους δαιμονίου), were particularly interested in the *Daimonion* of Socrates. In the third century, the idea of a personal *genius* was common in Neoplatonism. In his *Life of Plotinus*, Porphyry tells the story of the encounter between the personal demons of Plotinus and those of an Egyptian priest. The meeting was to be held in the temple of Isis in Rome — the holiest place in the city. Surprisingly, when the genius of the philosopher was summoned, a *god* (θεός) came instead of a *being of the demonic order* (τοῦ δαιμόνων... γένους). [389] Around 180 A.D., the sophist Maximus of Tyrus even "calculated" that exactly 30,000 demons haunted the world.[390] Every demon was, in fact, the *eidos* of a particular human talent; he chose his protégé and endowed them with this talent.

Surprisingly, the guardian demon has no specific place in the elaborated demonological system of the leading figure of Neoplatonism in the late third and early fourth centuries, Iamblichus. According to his treatise *On the Egyptian Mysteries*, demons are creatures of an immortal nature. Their primary function is to fulfill the gods' orders and reveal their will to

---

[388] For example, the comic poet Menander tries to persuade his audience that everybody is accompanied by one good guardian demon alone. According to him, the widespread belief in evil demons comes from people who lead vicious lives and who prefer to blame their misfortunes on supernatural powers rather than on themselves (Menander, "Fragmenta longiora apud alios auctores servata", ed. Francis Sandbach *Menandri reliquiae selectae* [Oxford: Clarendon Press, 1972], fr. 714).

[389] Porphyry, "On the Life of Plotinus", ed. Hans-Rudolph Swyzer and Paul Henry, trans. Arthur Armstrong, *Plotinus*, vol. 1: *Porphyry on the Life of Plotinus and the order of his books, Enneads I. 1–9* [Loeb Classical Library 440] (Cambridge, MA: Harvard University Press, 1989), §10.21–25: *When the spirit was summoned to appear a god came and not a being of the demonic* [Armstrong: spirit] *order, and the Egyptian said: "Blessed are you who have a god for your demon* [Armstrong: spirit] *and not a companion of the subordinate order"* (κληθέντα δὲ εἰς αὐτοψίαν τὸν δαίμονα θεὸν ἐλθεῖν καὶ μὴ τοῦ δαιμόνων εἶναι γένους· ὅθεν τὸν Αἰγύπτιον εἰπεῖν· «μακάριος εἶ θεὸν ἔχων τὸν δαίμονα καὶ οὐ τοῦ ὑφειμένου γένους τὸν συνόντα).

[390] Maximus Tyrius, *Philosophoumena - ΔΙΑΛΕΞΕΙΣ*, ed. George Koniaris, [Texte und Kommentare 17] (Berlin and New York: De Gruyter, 1995), VIII.173–75.

mortals through divination. In other words, they are mediators between the intelligible world of *ideas* and the material world. Iamblichus asks rhetorically, "who is capable of performing any sacred ritual or of predicting the future without the participation of both a god and a demon?"[391]

The concept of the demon-mediator was dangerous for the Christian religion, as we will see in the story of St. Cyprian.

The guardian demon appears again in Proclus's demonological system, one of the last heads of the Academy (fifth century). In his *Commentaries on Plato's Alcibiades*, he distinguishes between "demons by substance" (δαίμονες κατ' οὐσίαν) and "demons by analogy" (δαίμονες κατ' ἀναλογίαν). The demons of the former kind have a divine nature and origin, whereas "demons by analogy" are spirits who choose a human being and take care of them.[392] Proclus does not explain why he calls this kind of demons "by analogy"; possibly, in his opinion, they were celestial creatures of a different nature that bore some resemblance to the "demons by substance".

2.3.2. St. Cyprian: the mage-philosopher who became a Christian

The most dangerous rivals of Christianity in the third and fourth centuries were various religious and philosophical doctrines, like Neoplatonism and Gnosticism, where theurgy and initiation in various mystery cults and rituals were considered the main path to the unification with the divine and the salvation of the soul.[393] The demonization of these pa-

---

[391] Jamblique, *Les mystères d'Égypte*, ed. Édouard des Places, [Collection Budé 174] (Paris: Les Belles Lettres, 1966), III.30.37-39 (§175.10-12).

[392] Proclus Diadochus, *Commentary on the first Alcibiades of Plato*, ed. Leendert Westerink (Amsterdam: North-Holland Publishing, 1954), 73-75.

[393] The bibliography on this subject is extensive. See, e.g., Walter Burkert, *Antike Mysterien. Funktionen und Gehalt* (Munich: C. H. Beck, 1990), 56-75; John Anton, "Theourgia - Demiourgia: A Controversial Issue in Hellenistic Thought and Religion", in *Neoplatonism and Gnosticism*, ed. Richard Wallis and Jay Bregman [Studies in Neoplatonism: Ancient and Modern, 4] (Albany: SUNY Press, 1992), 14ff, 21ff, and 25ff; Paulina Remes, *Neoplatonism* (London and New York: Routledge, 2014), 25; Polymnia Athanasiadi, "The Chaldean Oracles: Theology and Theurgy", in *Pagan Monotheism*

gan rituals and the condemnation of theurgy, in general, is evident in the legend of St. Cyprian of Antioch. The story is preserved in two versions. The first contains the *Confession of St. Cyprianus* (Μετάνοια τοῦ ἁγίου Κυπριανοῦ)[394] and was written by an anonymous author between 350 and 370.[395] The second version is the *Life of St. Cyprian and Justina* [BHG 452–452c], preserved in three sub-versions, edited and translated into German by Ludwig Radermacher.[396] From the Christian perspective, *The Confession of St. Cyprian* represents the path the heathen philosopher was to follow to achieve complete control over the higher powers. At the age of six, the future Saint was sent by his parents to be initiated into the mysteries of Mithra. When he was ten years old, he served as *dadouchos* (torch-bearer) in the Eleusinian mysteries. He then visited Mount Olympus, where he remained for forty days, dancing and fighting with deities and demons. At fifteen, he studied arcane arts under the guidance of seven different *hierophants*, was initiated in the mysteries of Artemis of Argos and Artemis of Lacedaemon, and was taught all the divination techniques by the Phrygians.[397] Afterward, Cyprian traveled to Memphis and observed all kinds of demons and evil powers, as well as the incarnated images of deceptions of Greek philosophers[398] — perhaps a distant echo of the Platonic *eidē*. His encounter with the Devil was the culmination of his education in the art of magic and theurgy. Cyprian is said to have met him in Chaldea at the age of thirty (Christ's age when He began His ministry). Having learned from the Chaldean wise men all the secrets of the stars, plants, and fire, and after seeing the so-called "mediator demons" (δαίμονες μεσῖται), he was ready to come face to face with their

---

in *Late Antiquity*, ed. Polymnia Athanasiadi and Michael Frede, (Oxford: Clarendon Press, 1999), 176.

[394] "The confession of Saint Cyprian", ed. Ryan Bailey, "The Confession of Cyprian of Antioch: Introduction, Text and Translation", PhD diss. (McGill University, 2009), 33–107.

[395] This dating is accepted by Richard Reitzenstein, Ludwig Radermacher, and Theodor Zahn (see Bailey, *The Confession of Cyprian*, 3–5).

[396] "Cyprianus und Justina", ed. Ludwig Radermacher, *Griechische Quellen zur Faustsage*, 76–113.

[397] "The Confession of Saint Cyprian", 34–38.

[398] Ibid., 38–44.

master. According to the text, Cyprian described the encounter: "Believe me, I saw this devil and placated him with sacrifices. Be sure, I gladly accepted him, and I talked with him, and I was granted the highest power among his servants. He turned his face to me and called me 'wise youth, a new Jambres, apt to serve him, worthy of communicating with him'".[399]

Cyprian was appointed chief of a "phalanx of demons" (φάλαγγα δαιμόνων) and, with their support, was able to accomplish all his plans. He settled in Antioch and gained huge influence with his magical skills,[400] which were much in demand by the local nobility. His life changed when a powerful and wealthy lawyer, Aglaides, asked the mage to grant him the love of a virtuous maiden called Justina. Cyprian tried everything, but his efforts were in vain. Even the most powerful demon summoned by the wizard was incapable of breaking her unwavering piety.[401] According to the *Life of St. Cyprian and Justina*, Cyprian asked the Devil to reveal the reason for this constant failure. Before answering, the Evil One demanded from his loyal servant that he swear an oath that he would never renounce him. Cyprian accepted and said: "I swear to all your might, I will never renounce you."[402] The Devil informed Cyprian that the source of Justina's strength against all temptations was Christ and that none was more powerful than Him. The mage then abandoned his pagan ways and became a Christian. To accomplish this task and to escape the power of the Devil, he was helped by a priest, who demanded from him a lengthy confession and repentance. In addition, Cyprian had to burn his devilish books and become a monk.[403]

Cyprian, it must be stressed, did not break the deal. As we have seen, he swore in the name of Satan's powers. If he renounced his master, all the might of the Evil One would supposedly be against him. Yet, if

---

[399] Ibid., 46.
[400] Ibid., 52: ὀνομαστὸς ἤμην μάγος φιλόσοφος.
[401] Ibid., 54–60; "Cyprianus und Justina", 84–100.
[402] "Cyprianus und Justina", 100ff. The content of the oath is identical in all versions of the text.
[403] "The Confession of Saint Cyprian", 62–104; "Cyprianus und Justina", 104–113.

Christ is more powerful than the Devil, Cyprian would *a fortiori* be fully protected, even if he did not keep his promise.

The image of the mage Cyprian, who obtained all conceivable knowledge only to find that ultimate power lies in the hands of the Christian God, mirrors the profound identity crisis in the late Roman empire. In addition, the story reveals the propagandistic use of demonization as a weapon against the widespread mystery cults and practices in the second half of the fourth century. The plot of the written contract with Satan has yet to take its final shape, but some of its essential elements are already present. Cyprian meets the Devil personally, makes sacrifices to him, speaks with him, obtains power over demons, and swears not to renounce the Devil. All these features will evolve in the following centuries.

2.3.3. The professional magician and his clients

Between the late fourth and the third decade of the seventh centuries, the struggle between Christianity and the pagan cults continued, but the enemy of the Church was now different. As a consolidated intellectual movement mixed with mysticism and based on specific sacred texts ("textual community"), Neoplatonism was gradually marginalized by the efforts of fanaticized Christian bishops. It waned and finally died out with the last pupils of Olympiodorus of Alexandria in the late sixth century. Nevertheless, the magical practices inherited by the cosmopolitan Hellenistic and Roman worlds continued to flourish. According to many hagiographical texts, professional magicians became significant figures in the megapolises of the empire. Among their clients were the noblest and wealthiest citizens. Reasonably enough, Church authorities felt threatened and inspired fierce polemics against these magicians, usually called "poisoners" (φαρμακοί). The "tragicall histories" of people who sold their souls to the Devil during this period ended happily — the misled victims were forgiven and welcomed back into the bosom of the Church.

One of the versions of the *Life of St. Basil the Great* [BHG 246y–260] is the first known text containing mention of a written contract with the Devil. This text was erroneously ascribed by its first editor, François

Combefis, to St. Basil's close associate, Bishop Amphilochius.[404] Radermacher prepared the critical edition of this particular version [BHG 253a] with the title *On the one who renounced Christ in written form* (Greek: Περὶ τοῦ ἀρνησαμένου τὸν Χριστὸν ἐγγράφως).[405] The author and the date are unknown but, based on circumstantial data, we are able to suppose that the *Life of St. Basil the Great* was compiled before the seventh century, most likely in the late fifth century.[406] The events took place during the reign of the heretic Emperor Valens (364–378), when a pious senator, Proterius, disgusted by the ruler's religious views and policies, went into self-exile and settled with his daughter in the Holy Land.[407] He wished her to become a nun, but this was not to the taste of the Evil One. Inspired by the Devil, a youth fell in love with her. When she resisted his lust, the man resorted to the services of an "enchanter" (ἐπαοιδός)[408] or a "poisoner"/"magician" (φαρμακός).[409] To his great disappointment, the magician declared that he was powerless against the girl's virtue and advised his client to renounce Christianity in written form and seek his master's help.[410] The enchanter gave the youth a letter addressed to the Devil, wherein he briefly described his client's passion and firm decision to abandon his faith. The young man had to take this letter to a particular graveyard at a certain hour of the night, sit upon a pagan grave, and wait.[411] Everything was precisely carried out. As soon as the lover-to-be

---

[404] Pseudo-Amphilochius, "On the life and the miracles of our father St. Basil, Bishop of Caesarea in Cappadocia" [Greek: Εἰς τὸν βίον καὶ τὰ θαύματα τοῦ ἐν ἁγίοις πατρὸς ἡμῶν Βασιλείου ἀρχιεπισκόπου Καισαρείας Καππαδοκίας], in *Amphilochii Opera Omnia*, ed. François Combefis (Paris: Piget, 1644), 155–225.

[405] "Die Erzählung des Helladius (Proterius)", in Radermacher, *Grieschiche Quellen*, 117–49.

[406] Radermacher, *Grieschiche Quellen*, 64.

[407] "Die Erzählung des Helladius (Proterius)", 122 and 123.

[408] "Die Erzählung des Helladius (Proterius)", 122 and 125.

[409] "Die Erzählung des Helladius (Proterius)", 124. The Greek word could have both meanings.

[410] "Die Erzählung des Helladius (Proterius)", 124.

[411] "Die Erzählung des Helladius (Proterius) ", 126.5–6 and 127.5. In hagiographical texts, such places are frequently inhabited by demonic powers and a standard place for meeting them. A good example in this instance is the *Life* of St. Theodore of Sykeotes, §43

raised his hand with the letter, he was surrounded by demons, who brought him triumphantly to their master's throne. The Devil accepted the document and demanded that the youth sign a contract in which he "renounced his baptism by his own will, passed to the side of the Evil One, and accepted to face, along with Satan, the eternal damnation prepared for him in the Last Judgement".[412] With the help of the demons, the man successfully seduced the girl. Ashamed, she convinced her father to agree to her marriage with the seducer. The couple lived happily afterward, but their neighbors noticed that the husband avoided church and did not take communion.[413] They told his wife that he was not Christian, and the apostate confessed everything to her. Together they visited St. Basil.[414] To take back his contract, the man had to be locked in a small room inside the church, where he bravely resisted a horde of demons who relentlessly threatened him with utter destruction. On the fortieth day, the evil spirits disappeared, and the bishop showed the repentant one to his fellow citizens, announcing his salvation.[415] At this point, Satan himself appeared with the contract, but St. Basil encouraged the throng to shout at the top of their lungs, "*Kyrie, Eleison*" ("Lord, have mercy"). A fierce wind then blew and tore the document from the Devil's grasp, laying it in the hands of the bishop instead. St. Basil tore it to pieces, and the young husband was accepted back into the Church.[416]

The meeting with the Devil and the selling of one's soul in the *Life of St. Basil the Great* are related to significant literary and social phenomena. Cyprian is simply called a "mage" and a "philosopher". By contrast, in this text, the man who urged the desperate youth to sign a contract with Satan is not just a "mage"; he is a "poisoner" or "magician", and this denotes a precise social function, well-documented in judicial texts. A

(the inhabitants of the village of Bouzaion use raw materials from ancient graveyards). On this point, see Part Four, Chapter 2, §2.1.

[412] "Die Erzählung des Helladius (Proterius)", 128 and 129.
[413] "Die Erzählung des Helladius (Proterius)", 132ff.
[414] "Die Erzählung des Helladius (Proterius)", 136–38.
[415] "Die Erzählung des Helladius (Proterius)", 142ff.
[416] "Die Erzählung des Helladius (Proterius)", 146 and 147. Cf. Greenfield, *Traditions of Belief*, 255; Vakaloudi, *Magic*, 217ff.

φαρμακός (*pharmakos*) is a professional sorcerer who performs magic rituals and frequently provides different herbs and poisonous potions for his clients.[417] As we will see, the magician's role in the ritual of signing contracts with the Devil is a constant.

The author and the exact date of the following text, the *Life of St. Mary of Antioch* [BHG 1045],[418] are unknown. The plot and the main characters suggest that this hagiographical work was written between the second half of the sixth century and the Arab conquest (in 637).[419] A poor and pious widow had a daughter named Maria, who was brought up according to Christian morals. The girl grew up and was so beautiful that even the wealthiest and most influential men in Antioch were drawn to her. Nevertheless, she did not succumb to temptations and only left her house only to accompany her mother to Church. Unfortunately, there she was spotted by a certain Anthemius — one of the wealthiest youths of the Syrian capital.[420] For the next two years, he constantly tried to seduce her, but all his efforts were fruitless. The man had almost abandoned all hope when by chance he witnessed a strange scene. An impressive and supercilious person approached his company, and his noble friends paid him enormous respect. He asked them who this man was, and they answered that he was Megas — an experienced professional "poisoner"/"sorcerer" (φαρμακός, γόης), for whom nothing was impossible.[421] The social status of Megas was very high. The wealthy and noble youth called him "sir" (κύριέ μου) and bowed to him. Anthemius implored his

---

[417] Cf. e.g., the laws against this profession in *Novellae*, ed. Rudolph Scholl and Wilhelm Kroll, *Corpus iuris civilis*, vol. 3 (Berlin: Weidman, 1895), 537.16 (Nov. CXV, ch. I-II.4.), where the term φαρμακός is used.

[418] "Anthemius", in Radermacher, *Griechiche Quellen*, 258–71 (older edition: "Vita Sanctae Mariae Antiochenae virginis", in *AASS*, Maii tomus 7 [1866], 49C–55D).

[419] According to the text, the city of Antioch was already mostly Christian. The Christianization process of this megalopolis was probably completed by the second half of the sixth century and, as a consequence, the text must have been written after that period. On the other hand, there is no mention of the Arab invasion of the city (637), so this seems like a probable *terminus ante quem*.

[420] "Anthemius", 261.

[421] "Anthemius", 262 (γόης); 262, 263, 266, 267 (φαρμακός). As we have seen, the latter word denotes a particular social role according to Justinian's *Novellae*.

help. The magician took the assignment and promised that the maiden would come to him that night, but the next day he disdainfully informed his client that he had forgotten about him.[422] Afterward, the magician assigned the mission to two of his demons. One of them took the shape of the girl and accompanied her mother back to their home. The other evil spirit disguised himself as the mother and brought Maria to Anthemius' house. The young aristocrat offered her money and expensive jewelry if she agreed to become his wife. Swayed by his insistence, she swore to fulfill his wish after fifteen days, having persuaded her mother to bless the marriage.[423] Anthemius agreed and let her go. Impressed by the immense power of the demons, he offered Megas as much gold as he wished if he made him a mage and gave him control over these spirits. Anthemius was even ready to give up his Christian faith.[424] The sorcerer wrote a note, gave it to the youth, and instructed him to go to a particular bridge in the evening (a common symbol of the transition between life and death)[425] and to wait there. At midnight he would hear a tumult and see some magnificent lord, Satan himself, riding in a chariot and accompanied by a vast retinue of followers. He said Anthemius would not be harmed if he held the magician's letter high. Afterward, he would have to greet the kingly personage respectfully, say that Megas had sent him, and give the note to the lord. In addition, if he wanted to achieve his goal, he was never to make the sign of the cross. The youth acted as he was told. The Devil read the letter and wrote an answer to Megas. Anthemius's wish would be fulfilled, it turned out, but under one condition, namely, that he renounce his Christian faith in written form. The client produced the following document: "I, Anthemius, deny Christ and my faith in Him; I renounce my baptism, and the name 'Christian,' and His cross, and I vow

---

[422] "Anthemius", 263.
[423] "Anthemius", 264ff.
[424] "Anthemius", 267. It is interesting that Anthemius does not want to be a professional *magician* (φαρμακός) like Megas himself, but only to acquire the skills of a mage and to control the demons.
[425] See, e.g., the struggle between St. George of Lesbos (eighth to ninth centuries) and I-meros, commander of a demonic army, which took place on a bridge (David, Symeon and George, §11). Cf. Vakaloudi, *Magic*, 218.

never to use or mention these symbols".[426] As soon as he pronounced these words, the apostate sweated from head to toe, which indicated that God's grace had been taken from him. Megas approved the text and warned Anthemius not to demand more than one or two demons as servants from the Devil — they would press him night and day to assign them tasks. The youth handed the document to Satan, who raised it to the sky, and shouted triumphantly to God, "I took a soul from you!" This cry sobered up the apostate. He tried to persuade the master of the demons to give him back the contract, but all his efforts were in vain. The Devil said he would use the document as evidence on the Day of Judgment.[427] The desperate youth turned for help to the local bishop, who declined his plea to be baptized again but advised him to repent. Anthemius sold all his property and distributed the money among the poor — three pounds of gold. In this way, his soul was saved.[428]

In 1903, in a short paper, Léon Clugnet and François Nau published the first paragraphs and the abstracts of some texts dedicated to the lives of early Christian saints and hermits. Among these, we find an anonymous and incomplete story, missing from Radermacher's collection, about the ritual that concerns us here.[429] It takes place in an entirely different environment from the eastern cities, where St. Cyprian, Aglaides, and Anthemius sold their souls. In this case, the events happen in the imperial capital, Constantinople. According to the text, during the reign of Emperor Mauricius, a man named Mesites lived in the city, surpassing in skill all the magicians who had lived before him. He hired as his *notarios* (secretary) a pious man who had just arrived in the capital. Deeply desiring to make him renounce his Christian faith, Mesites invited him to ride together. The two men arrived at a field where a group of demonic Ethiopians was gathered. A huge black man was their leader — the Devil himself. But their encounter was spoiled by the piety of the secretary. As

---

[426] "Anthemius", 268.
[427] "Anthemius", 267–69. Cf. Vakaloudi, *Magic*, 218ff.
[428] "Anthemius", 269ff.
[429] "Vies et récits d'anachorètes (IV-e – VII-e siècles)", ed. Léon Clugnet and François Nau, *Révue d'Orient Chrétien* 8 (1903): 91–100.

soon as he saw this godless throng, he fearfully crossed himself, and all vanished.

Anastasia Vakaloudi points out that this story resembles the ceremonies in which a contract with the Devil was made.[430] According to the text, Mesites took his secretary to the devilish gathering to coerce him to renounce Christ. The very name of the magician is somehow allegorical — Mesites (Μεσίτης) means "mediator" (between humans and the Devil). Even though, at the beginning of the text, a different etymology is ironically given by the anonymous author (Μεσίτις — Μεσίας/Messiah), it is possible that there was an urban legend behind this narrative, which preserved the memory of the Neoplatonic idea of the *mediator* between the earthly and the celestial world — a concept very threatening for Christians.

In medieval Western Europe, the most popular legend related to a contract with the Devil was the story of Theophilos, Church manager (*oeconomus*) in the Cilician city of Adana. This story is narrated in the anonymous *Confession of St. Theophilos*. Four Greek versions of the text have been preserved [BHG 1319-1322]. Only one of them is signed [BHG 1321][431] — the author's name was Eutychianos, reportedly a close friend of St. Theophilos.[432] Its original title was "The repentance and the departure for the realms of our Lord Christ, with the mediation of the saint and most glorious Virgin Mary, Mother of God, of one Theophilos, Church *oeconomus* of the city of Adana, in the eastern lands" ("Μετάνοια καὶ ἀνάκλησις πρὸς τὸν κύριον ἡμῶν Ἰησοῦν Χριστὸν γενομένη παρά τινος οἰκονόμου ὀνόματος Θεοφίλου ἐκκκλησίας τῆς ἀνατολικῆς χώρας τοὔνομ' Ἀδανῶν διὰ τῆς μεσιτείας τῆς ἁγίας καὶ ὑπερενδόξου Θεοτόκου καὶ ἀειπαρθένου Μαρίας"). The first Latin translation of this text [BHL 8121-8126], made in the ninth century by Paul, deacon of Neapolis, was

---

[430] Vakaloudi, *Magic*, 223.
[431] [Euthychianus], "Theophilus nach der Bearbeitung des Eutychianus mit daraus abgeleiteten Fassungen", ed. Ludwig Radermacher, *Griechische Quellen*, 182–218.
[432] "Theophilus nach der Bearbeitung des Eutychianus", 218.

probably based on this version. Paul's translation went through different redactions and elaborations in the centuries following.[433]

The question of the date of the described events has largely been solved. All the versions mention a "Persian invasion" (ἐπιδρομὴν Περσῶν, *incursio Persarum gentis*). The oldest [BHG 1322],[434] according to Radermacher,[435] refers to Emperor Heraclius (610–641).[436] If we accept this date, the described events must have happened between 612/613 (when the Persian invasion of the empire became almost unstoppable) and 628 (when the treaty with Shah Kavad II [628] was signed, and the Persian threat was eliminated forever).[437]

According to the texts, Theophilos was an extraordinarily pious person who held the position of *oeconomus* of the Church in Adana, Cilicia. Being humble, he refused to be ordained bishop after the previous hierarch's death, and the archbishop chose another priest for this post. A few days later, he was slandered and threatened unjustly with removal from his office.[438] The Devil "entered his heart" and inspired in him the idea to turn to "magicians" (φαρμακοί)[439] for help. Theophilos decided to visit a Jew who was a notorious servant of Satan. The sorcerer was afraid when he saw a high-ranking Christian priest knocking on his door — an

---

[433] "De Sancto Theophilo poenitente, vicedomino sive oeconomo ecclesiae Adane in Cilicia", in *AASS*, Februarii tomus 1 (1863), 486B–497E. For the Latin version of the text ("Miraculum Sanctae Mariae. De Theophilo poenitetente auctore Eutychiano"), see ibid., 489E–497E.

[434] "Theophilus. Älteste Fassung", ed. Ludwig Radermacher, *Griechische Quellen zur Faustsage* (Vienna and Leipzig: Hölder-Pichler-Tempsky in Komm, 1927), 164–77.

[435] "Theophilus. Älteste Fassung", 164–67 (Cod. Marcianus gr. cl. II 101).

[436] "Theophilus. Älteste Fassung", 164: Ἐν τοῖς χρόνοις Ἡρακλείου πρὸ τοῦ τοὺς Πέρσας κατὰ Ῥωμανίας ἐξελθεῖν; cf. Vakaloudi, *Magic*, 216.

[437] The pact between Shah Kavad II and Emperor Heraclius was signed in the last months of 628 (Christophilopoulou, *Byzantine History*, 2.1: 28). Despite the existence of the version that mentions Emperor Heraclius, the editors of *Bibliotheca Hagiographica Latina* date the story of Theophilos to the sixth century, after *AASS*, Februarii tomus 1, 486Bff (where the events are dated c. 538, before the great invasion of Shah Khosrow I Anushirvan in 540 (Christophilopoulou, *Byzantine History*, 1: 276).

[438] "Theophilus nach der Bearbeitung des Eutychianus", 182–86; "Theophilus. Älteste Fassung", 164.

[439] "Theophilus nach der Bearbeitung des Eutychianus", 186; "Theophilus. Älteste Fassung", 164.

indication of the steady marginalization of Jews in the later Roman Empire and their constant fear of repression, whose main instigator was the Church. Nevertheless, the magician agreed to hear the troubles of Theophilos and invited him the next night to an audience with his *patron* (πάτρων).[440] The priest agreed and, at midnight, was taken to the city's hippodrome. This location is closely related in Byzantine sources with the so-called *nekyodaimones* (νεκυοδαίμονες), i.e., the souls of people who suffered a violent death and who afterward haunted the place of their demise or the graveyard where they were buried.[441] In addition, the hippodrome is *le monde à l'envers* (to follow Gilbert Dagron), similar to the Roman *Saturnalia*, in which every ceremony bears the opposite of its usual meaning. Before the meeting, the Jew advised his client in the same way as Mesites did Anthemius in the *Life* of St. Mary of Antioch: no matter what he heard or saw, he had by no means to make the sign of the cross. Immediately afterward, he showed him a long procession of ghostly humanlike figures clad in white chamids and carrying lighted candelabras. In the midst of them their master was seated. These creatures were the Devil and his servants. The Jew took Theophilos by the hand to his mentor and explained the case. Satan promised to help the priest and to give him power over the bishop only if he renounced his faith and became his servant. Theophilos agreed, and the Devil kissed him several times on the mouth — in this way, the author says, the Evil One entered him. The priest quickly drew up the agreement and gave it to his new master.[442] The effect was immediate. The bishop apologized to him, and Theophilos suddenly became the most powerful cleric in the city. Despite his great success, the priest feared Hell and quickly changed his mind. He decided to save his immortal soul and begged the Virgin Mary to help him. After forty days and forty nights spent in prayer in one of her churches, she finally appeared, and, following her advice, he re-

---

[440] "Theophilus. Älteste Fassung", 164–66; "Theophilus nach der Bearbeitung des Eutychianus", 188.
[441] Vakaloudi, *Magic*, 117–22 and 217.
[442] "Theophilus. Älteste Fassung", 166–68; "Theophilus nach der Bearbeitung des Eutychianus", 188–90.

cited the Creed aloud. Three days later, St. Mary appeared to him anew in a dream, giving him back the contract.[443] In the morning, the document was lying on his chest. Repentant and grateful to his heavenly patron, Theophilos gave the contract to the bishop and asked him to read it publicly and burn it before the crowd. The priest's body gradually weakened three days later, and he finally died.[444]

According to the texts dating from the fourth to the seventh centuries, the absolution of the sinners who made a contract with the Devil was a compromise. The didactic message of such stories is clear: anyone could be accepted into the bosom of the Church, even the worst sinner. Nevertheless, Theophilos of Adana's was the last story wherein one who sold his soul was saved. In the age of Emperor Heraclius and the Arab invasion, another type of person emerged, utterly different from the cosmopolitan city-dweller of the eastern Roman empire. The ethical and religious values and the code of behavior of this new man are entirely determined by the Church and its ministers. Bishop Leo is the representative of this almighty institution, in a position not to compromise with the stray sheep of his flock. The conclusion of the Faustian narrative is taking shape — the sinner loses his soul forever.

2.3.4. The story of Bishop Leo of Catania and the mage Heliodorus

The next link in the tradition of the Faustian legend is the story of the mage Heliodorus and his punishment, incorporated in the abovementioned *Life* of Leo of Catania. This story influenced Western literature and culture since we have at least one Latin translation [BHG 4838–4839], and, in addition, the events take place in the far Byzantine west (in the Sicilian town of Catania). According to the text, the young Heliodorus belonged to Catania's high society. Despite his position, his arro-

---

[443] "Theophilus. Älteste Fassung", 170 and 172–74; "Theophilus nach der Bearbeitung des Eutychianus", 198 and 204–6. The confession of Theophilos is actually a paraphrase of the Nicene Creed.

[444] "Theophilus. Älteste Fassung", 176; "Theophilus nach der Bearbeitung des Eutychianus", 210 and 214–18.

gant temperament and behavior incited the local populace against him. His craving for power and glory inspired him to strive for the position of *eparch* (governor) of Catania using his innate slyness. Unable to fulfill this goal, he turned for help — like Theophilos of Adana — to a Jew. Unlike the texts that describe events that occurred in the period between the fourth and the seventh centuries, in the *Life* of Leo of Catania, the mediator between the young and ambitious Christian and the Devil was not called φαρμακός and did not practice in public.[445] Heliodorus invited this man to his home and took lessons from him. At the end of his training, the Jew gave him a written note, looking like a letter, and ordered him to take it at midnight to a place where ancient heroes (ἥρωες) were buried. Heliodorus was told to sit upon a gravestone and wait. Supposedly, he would see a "person, dreadful in appearance and stunning, flying in the air".[446] The youth had to stay calm. The creature would come to him and promise to fulfill his every wish. Heliodorus followed the instructions exactly. The very moment when he stood with the note in hand on the gravestone, he beheld, flying on a colossal deer, "the devilmaster of the air". The Devil promised Heliodorus one of his servants if he agreed to renounce Christ. The wicked youth gladly obeyed, fell in prostration before the Devil, kissed[447] his hand, and was awarded the demon Gaspar as his servant. The master of the air ordered this evil spirit to help Heliodorus in everything and vanished into the darkness.[448]

The detailed account of the mischief of the mage and his friends with the help of Gaspar is fascinating, and highly humorous in style. For example, the youths would walk the streets and instill into passing women the delusion that they were wading in deep water. By this cunning strategy, they made them lift their chitons to the thighs. Such scenes were not only delightful to the young men's lustful eyes but also pro-

---

[445] Leo of Catania, §10: Ἑβραῖόν τινα ἐπὶ μαγείᾳ καὶ γοητείᾳ ἐπίσημον (Some Jew, known for his profound knowledge of magic and sorcery).
[446] Leo of Catania, §10: κἀκεῖσε κατιδεῖν" μέλλεις ἐρχόμενον διὰ τοῦ ἀέρος φοβερὸν τῇ θέᾳ καὶ πάνυ κατάπληκτον.
[447] The verb ἀσπάζω in medieval Greek is liturgical and means *to kiss*.
[448] Leo of Catania, §12.

voked laughter in other spectators. But not all of their actions were so harmless. The young rascals inspired irresistible passion and "furious lust" in the hearts of the daughters of noble citizens. This madness "burned" the poor maidens and pushed them out of their homes right into the hands of Heliodorus' gang. The mage's activities also disrupted the town's economic life. He made the traders see common stones as gold and useless objects as necessary. Everyone in Catania was in utter despair. All trade ceased, and the inhabitants were condemned to starve.[449] In these circumstances, Lucius, the governor, was urged to ask the central government for help. The emperor sent his *strator* (military officer) Heraclides, but even his intervention could not save the world from the gang. Heliodorus managed to escape the executioners with the assistance of Gaspar. Only Bishop Leo was able to put an end to his outrages. After many attempts to save Heliodorus from his delusions, he dragged the mage out to the Achilion, where executions were usually carried out. There the priest ordered a furnace to be lit and entered into it with the mage. The latter burned but Leo remained unharmed.[450]

The legend of the Sicilian mage Heliodorus differs significantly from the previous stories. The *Confession of St. Cyprian* and the *Lives* of St. Basil the Great, St. Mary of Antioch, and St. Theophilos of Adana have clear didactic functions: to demonstrate the omnipotence of the Christian God and to diminish the popularity of other mystical practices and cults. The *Life* of Leo describes events in a wholly Christianized social and religious environment, with no rival to the dominating religion. The Jewish sorcerer in this narrative has almost nothing in common with influential figures like Megas from the legend of Anthemius of Antioch. They ventured to speak roughly and scornfully to a respectable member of local society. The marginalization of the professional magicians, who once grew wealthy from the populace's credulity, is evident in the *Life of Theophilos of Adana*. Here the Jew was terrified as soon as he saw the priest knocking on his door. We can only imagine what repressions he was

---

[449] Leo of Catania, §13–15.
[450] Leo of Catania, §34.

afraid of. In the *Life* of Bishop Leo, we observe the final stage of this marginalization. The magician was scared not only to practice his "profession" publicly, but was also unable to do so even in the comfort of his own house, instead being forced to settle in the home of the noble and ambitious youth. The struggle is no longer between mystery cults and Christianity, between Neoplatonism and the new popular religion, but between the Church authorities and the local populace. The image of Heliodorus is not as tragic as the one of Theophilos of Adana and his long monologues of public repentance. Before the audience stands a dissolute and ambitious young man who, along with his friends, makes fun of the bishop's authority, the serious businessmen of the town, and even the emperor himself. The anonymous author parodically uses the standard hagiographical thematic pattern and terms to describe the events. The gravestone where Heliodorus must wait for the arrival of Satan is designated by the word στήλη, which ironically refers to the στῦλος (the tall pillar of the stylites). The Devil himself flies riding a giant deer — a symbol of Christ, e.g., in the martyrology of Eustathios Placidas, where the animal appeared before the Roman commander and converted him to the true religion.[451] The only event narrated with any seriousness was Heliodorus' death in the furnace.

2.3.5. Emperor Constantine V: the contract with the Devil as a propaganda weapon

All of the above-mentioned hagiographical texts are related to semi-legendary personages and were written by anonymous authors. The contract with the Devil was never accepted as theological doctrine and did not become a widespread phenomenon in literature until the late eighth century. It was used by iconodule authors as early as the first decade of the ninth century. During this crucial period of the iconoclast crisis, hagiography became a powerful weapon of Orthodoxy against its rivals. According to the *Life* of St. Stephen the Younger, the heretic Emperor Constantine V (741–775) made his contracts (συνθήκας) with the de-

---

[451] Kazhdan, *History of Byzantine Literature*, 1: 300ff.

mons in the ruins of the St. Mavra Church, located in the suburbs of the capital, which he had himself demolished. Reportedly, he sacrificed young boys to them. One of these boys, says Stephen, was the son of a certain Sulphamios.[452] The same story can be found in the chronographic work of George Hamartolos:

> This wicked god-hater and new Julian renounced the Holy Virgin and all the saints. This new Julian worshipped Aphrodite and Dionysus, like the Greek, and used to make human sacrifices to them outside the city, where stood once the church of the Martyr Mavra. He demolished the temple and established a special place for murders, calling it "Mavra", sacrificing a boy during his demonic mysteries every night. A witness was the slaughtered son of Suphlamios, whom the demonic emperor secretly had sacrificed — this event was made widely known.[453]

Many authors mention this story during the whole of the tenth century. Constantine VII and his associates included it in their encyclopedic work *On Virtues and Vices* and the compilation known today as *Excerpta*.[454] An account of the son of Sulphamios can also be found in the Suda lexicon.[455]

2.3.6. Accounts of Byzantine legal documentation

All the accounts of the contract with the Devil mentioned above occur in literary texts and have a concrete political, social, or ethical function. We can only guess what actual magical practices stood behind such stories. Very few official documents and court judgments that mention the contract have been preserved. Nevertheless, secondary sources about such cases would allow us to look into the nether reaches of the capital and the

---

[452] Stephen the Younger, 165.14–21.
[453] *Georgii Monachi Chronicon*, ed. Carl de Boor, vol. 2 (Stuttgart: Teubner, 1978), 751.20–752.11.
[454] *Excerpta historica iussu imp. Constantini Porphyrogeniti confecta: Excerpta de virtutibus et vitiis*, ed. Antoon Roos, Theodor Büttner-Wobst, Ursul Boissevain, and Carl de Boor, vol. 2: *Excerpta de virtutibus et vitiis* (Berlin: Weidmann, 1906), 155.
[455] *Suidae lexicon*, ed. Ada Adler [Lexicographi Graeci, vol. 1], Part 3: *K-O* (Stuttgart: Teubner, 1967), s.v. K.2286. Cf. Ilse Rochow, *Kaiser Konstantin V (741–775). Materialen zu seinem Leben und Nachleben* (Frankfurt: Peter Lang, 1994), 137.

provincial cities of the late Roman and Byzantine world. Some criminals were known to be associated with evil spirits and demons.

A typical example is a lawsuit against two women charged with child murder under the influence of the demon Gello. The official authorities did not pay great attention to such accusations since the father of the future patriarch Tarasios (784–806), the imperial judge George, quickly found them innocent.[456] The *Life* of Patriarch Tarasios mentions neither a contract with the demon nor a renunciation of Christ.

More information can be obtained from Late Byzantine court protocols and judgments. Two synodal decisions by the Church of Constantinople on cases of voluntary desecration of Christ's name and making use of the "assistance" (συνεργία) of Satan have been preserved. The first dates from November 1338, and the name of the individual accused of these charges was George Tzerentzes. This man wrote the name of Christ and then covered it with ink. In addition, he ritually scrawled spells to summon demons. For these blasphemous acts, he was sentenced to stay outside the church during the psalmody and to beg everyone who entered or exited the building for forgiveness. His punishment included fasting and a hundred days of penitence.[457] Written renunciations of Christ and for the reward of satanic help were nothing but a contract with the Devil.[458]

An analogous story is described in a decision of the court of Thessalonica (fifteenth century).[459] A sorcerer called Cappadocos was notorious for his magical skills and books on the impure arts. His influence upon the souls of the citizens was incredibly destructive. Innumerable penances were imposed on him by the Church authorities. A monk began to visit him, pretending that he was trying to get him on the right path, but his true intention soon came to light, a scandal ensued, and, as a result, the Church's image was seriously damaged. The monk was a very

---

[456] Patriarch Tarasios, §5 (English translation, 172).
[457] *Acta et diplomata graeca medii aevi sacra et profana*, Franz Miklosich and Joseph Müller, vol. 1, (Athens: Spanos, 1996), 180.
[458] Greenfield, *Traditions of Belief*, 255.
[459] *Acta et diplomata graeca*, 342-344; Greenfield, *Traditions of Belief*, 255.

ambitious man who strived for a higher position and tried to make "an alliance" with the Devil. To achieve his goal, he had to write and recite a specific prayer (probably the Lord's Prayer) aloud backwards, along with the names of the persons responsible for his promotion. In addition, Cappadocos had to write an "impure and sinful letter" to be read by the monk all night under the starlight and then be worn under his cassock as an amulet.

This shameful episode forced the Church to put the monk on trial and to produce the decision edited by Franz Miklosich and Joseph Müller. Unfortunately, the final paragraphs are lost, and we have neither a date nor information about the imposed punishments. Even though there is no mention of a written contract with the Devil, there are many similarities with the stories in the above hagiographical texts. The monk "was asking for an alliance with the Devil". The letter, written by Cappadocus, resembles the correspondence between the magician and his evil master in the *Lives* of St. Basil the Great and St. Mary of Antioch.

* * *

The Faustian legend is rooted in the Greco-Roman world's long-lasting mythological and philosophical tradition. The concept of a hero's supernatural guardian, already found in Homer, was elaborated firstly by early poets — Theognis and Pindar –who used the term *daimon* to refer to the divine protector instead of the Homeric "god". This difference, though seemingly minor, gave rise to a new idea — the demon was anonymous, unintelligible, both a beneficent and a malevolent power. The belief in this unknown higher power was fatalistic and quite different from socially acceptable piety and the devotion to the Olympian gods. Demons were conceived as the very manifestation of chaos and disorder; they were thought to be innumerable and unnameable; it was believed that they acted of their own obscure will and that mortals had no power over them.

Plato brought a significant change to the concept of the guardian *daimon*, giving a philosophical elaboration of this ancient idea. The *Dai-*

monion of Socrates was not the chaotic and frequently destructive power of the early poets — the word *daimonion* was synonymous with "conscience" or even with "superego" (in Carl Jung's sense). According to the *Phaedo*, everybody ought to choose the way of virtue, despite the influence of their demon.

Neoplatonism entwined the philosophical concept of the protector demon with its typical mysticism. According to Porphyry, and his teacher Plotinus, exceptionally pious and holy persons had gods for guardians instead of *daimones*. According to Maximus of Tyros, the Platonic *ideas* of human talents had their manifestations, i.e., demons, who chose their protégé and gave them this talent. Along with this function of protecting humans, demons in the theogonies of the Neoplatonic philosophers were mediators between the human world and the celestial powers. From the philosophical and theological point of view, these functions of protection and mediation were crucial for the religious systems of the late pagan Roman world. Precisely for this reason, the Christian Church had to eradicate the very notion of the good *daimon* from the collective mind and demonize the professional mage at the very heart of pagan Hellenistic culture. One of the propagandistic tools used to this end was the Faustian legend.

As a rhetorical and literary topos, the concept of the pact with Satan probably originated in the eastern Roman provinces (Syria, Asia Minor). It appears for the first time as a story in a few hagiographical texts in the mid-fourth century. Stories such as this were undoubtedly one of the many instruments used to demonize the ancient pagan mysteries and practices of Neoplatonism.

From the late fourth to the early seventh centuries, in hagiographical texts, the contract was relatively common. The narrative pattern (the protagonists and the plot) is pretty standard. The story is laid in an eastern city or Constantinople. The ambition or carnal passion drives a Christian of high standing to ask the local magician — a well-respected man, at least until the late sixth century — for help. His assistance had a price. The client had to renounce Christianity, accept Satan, and sign a contract to sell his soul. The ceremony is held in places typically related to pagan cults or haunted by demons: a bridge, an ancient graveyard, or the hippodrome. During this period, only the sorcerer was damned to eternal torment in Hell. The client repents, and his immortal soul is saved. Although the authors condescend to their sinful heroes, the punishments gradually become more severe. While St. Cyprian and Anthemius of Antioch were entirely purified of their sins, Theophilos of Adana had a different fate. He was accepted back into the bosom of the Church but died immediately after his absolution. In addition, the image of the magician, who played the role of mediator between the pious priest and the Devil, differs from that of his earlier colleagues. He is simply a frightened and marginalized Jew, scared to death of the Church authorities.

After the Arab invasions and the decisive cultural, political, and religious changes in Byzantium, starting from approximately the middle of the seventh century, the narrative motive also changed. Heliodorus and Constantine V did not only die bodily but also lost their souls because of their agreements with the powers of the Evil One. The ceremony continued to be held in places traditionally haunted by demons: a grave of an ancient hero or a ruined church. In addition, in the *Life* of St. Stephen the Younger, the use of the topos is propagandistic — the damnation of the heretic emperor.

In these stories, distinguishing reality from merely literary phenomena is exceptionally complicated. Later judicial documents give only circumstantial evidence that practices similar to the ones described in hagiographical texts from the fourth to the seventh centuries existed throughout the empire — the written renunciation of Christ and the Devil's aid were well-established in the fourteenth century.

It is essential to emphasize the numerous Latin translations of Byzantine texts that provide accounts of the contract with the Devil. The stories of Theophilos of Adana and Bishop Leo of Catania were well-known to the Catholic world as early as the ninth century. *The Tragicall Story of the Life and Death of Doctor Faustus* was a literary, political, and cultural phenomenon with a long history. The works by Christopher Marlowe and Johann von Goethe were only stages in this phenomenon's development.

2.4. The Neoplatonic tradition: from the "bad" to the "evil" demon

In the English language, as in many others, there is a significant semantic difference between the adjectives "bad" and "evil" (from "Devil"). "Bad" means "of poor quality or a low standard; unpleasant" and, unlike "Evil", could never be an uncountable noun. This notion is not objective, transcendental, and abstract but must always be subjected to something or somebody. It has no concrete origin but denotes some defect, shortcoming, or insufficiency. The same is true of the meaning, at least primarily, of the Greek word κακός,[460]: *ugly; bodily, mentally, or morally imperfect; cowardly; unskillful*. In the Greco-Roman world before Christianity, "badness" originated in a person's imperfection and vices, not in some abstract Enemy who makes conscious and purposeful efforts to divert them from the right way of living. For this reason, approximately before the first century A.D., a demon is referred to as a harmful, destructive, and torturing force, but never as something "evil" in the Christian sense.

By contrast, "Evil" is a somewhat problematic term for everyday use. It has a definite source and origin, namely the primordial Enemy of Humankind, the absolute antithesis of God. As a notion, "Evil" is extremely difficult to define ontologically in traditional Platonic-Aristotelian philosophy. For Plato, the substantivized adjective *the bad* (τὸ κακόν) and the noun *badness* (κακία) denote the gradual loss of perfection, which leads everything in the world to decline and ultimately end (διαφθείρειν), a type of entropy. To be "bad", to lack some quality, to be insufficient in a given manner, is instead something incorporated into the natural order. By contrast, for Christians, Evil violates God's order, and is something external to the primordially perfect world. Thus, badness is usually associated with the privative prefix ἀ-, as the lack of morality is ἀ-

---

[460] On the meanings of the word κακός in Classical Greek, see *LSJ*, s.v. "κακός".

δικια ("in-justice"),[461] but, of course, could also be expressed as a complete noun, like disease, which is nothing but the absence of health. It neither has nor could have a beginning, end, or personification.[462] Transcendental "badness" is a logically impossible and unthinkable notion because everything that exists needs an *eidos*; since τὸ κακόν is a lack of good (τἀγαθόν), its *eidos* would be equal to the existence of that which does not exist, i.e., would lead to the sophistic paradox "non-being exists" (τὸ μὴ ὂν εἶναι).

On the other hand, for Plato, the demon has a relatively positive influence on humans. The Socratic *daimonion* is *a voice* (φωνή τις) that prevents the philosopher from doing something but never tells him what to do.[463] In the *Symposium*, Diotima speaks of Eros, one of the great *daimonia*, in the following way:

> He is a great spirit (daimon), and like all spirits he is intermediate between the divine and the mortal. ... He interprets between gods and men, conveying and taking across to the gods the prayers and sacrifices of men, and to men the commands and replies of the gods; he is the mediator who spans the chasm which divides them, and therefore in him all is bound together, and through him the arts of the prophet and the priest, their sacrifices and mysteries and charms, and all, prophecy and incantation, find their way.[464]

---

[461] The proto-Indo-European negative particle n̥, which could be used as a negative prefix, evolves in Greek as ἀ-/ἀν-, in Latin as in-/im-, and in English as im-/in- (through Latin and Old French) or as un- (of German origin).

[462] On the Platonic concept of "bad", see, e.g., Plato, "Respublica", 608d – 611d. On the Platonic "demon", see John Finamore, "Reason and Irrationality: The intersection between philosophy and magic in later Neoplatonism", in *Plato in the Third Sophistic*, ed. Ryan Fowler (Boston and Berlin: De Gruyter, 2014), 39ff.

[463] See, e.g., Plato, "Phaedrus", ed. John Burnet, *Platonis opera*, vol. 1 (Oxford: Clarendon Press, 1967), 242b8–c3.

[464] Plato, "Symposium", ed. John Burnet, *Platonis opera*, vol. 2 (Oxford: Clarendon Press, 1967), 202d–e: καὶ γὰρ πᾶν τὸ δαιμόνιον μεταξύ ἐστι θεοῦ τε καὶ θνητοῦ; Ἑρμηνεῦον καὶ διαπορθμεῦον θεοῖς τὰ παρ' ἀνθρώπων καὶ ἀνθρώποις τὰ παρὰ θεῶν, τῶν μὲν τὰς δεήσεις καὶ θυσίας, τῶν δὲ τὰς ἐπιτάξεις τε καὶ ἀμοιβὰς τῶν θυσιῶν, ἐν μέσῳ δὲ ὂν ἀμφοτέρων συμπληροῖ, ὥστε τὸ πᾶν αὐτὸ αὑτῷ συνδεδέσθαι. διὰ τούτου καὶ ἡ μαντικὴ πᾶσα χωρεῖ καὶ ἡ τῶν ἱερέων τέχνη τῶν τε περὶ τὰς θυσίας καὶ τελετὰς καὶ τὰς ἐπῳδὰς καὶ τὴν μαντείαν πᾶσαν καὶ γοητείαν (for a translation, see Plato, *Symposium*, in *Dia-*

However, by the late second and early third centuries A.D., various dualistic religions and teachings of Eastern origin were already widespread in the Greco-Roman world. In the New Testament, evil spirits and the Devil are often present. The traditional schools of philosophy could not ignore these trends and leave the concept of Evil without definition. Plotinus, one of the pioneers of Neoplatonism, was among the first intellectuals who undertook this task. Summarizing his conceptions, advocated in the First Ennead, we must emphasize an essential terminological feature. While in later Neoplatonic works and the Christian theological traditions, transcendental Evil is denoted by its term (τὸ πονηρόν), Plotinus uses the standard Greek word τὸ κακόν, which, as we have already mentioned, can be found in Plato as well. Plotinus often uses this substantivized adjective in the plural (τὰ κακά), which contributes to its vagueness. The "evils" in the world are many, and they can hardly be united in one transcendental idea, as Plato did with the concept of the "Good" (τἀγαθόν). In the cultural and philosophical context of the ancient world, this plural form makes absolute sense. It accords perfectly since, as we have already pointed out, Evil has no *eidos* of its own, nor could it possibly have one, because it is formless by nature; it can take any form but can neither be identified nor defined by any existing particular form[465] and, therefore, is entirely "a-logical" and "ir-rational". For Plotinus, Evil is *unmeasuredness, excess, and defect* (ἀμετρίαν καὶ ὑπερβολὴν καὶ ἔλλειψιν).[466] Its purest and clearest manifestation is the mortality of the material human body, the latter being defined by the philosopher as

---

logues *of Plato*, I, 4th ed., trans. Benjamin Jowett (Oxford: Oxford University Press, 1964), 534f.).

[465] Plotinus, *Enneads*, ed. Hans-Rudolph Swyzer and Paul Henry, trans. Arthur Armstrong, *Plotinus*, vol. 1: *Porphyry on the Life of Plotinus and the order of his books, Enneads I. 1-9* [Loeb Classical Library 440] (Cambridge, MA: Harvard University Press, 1989), I.8.1.11–13: *For intellect and soul, since they are forms, would produce knowledge of Forms and have a natural tendency towards them. But how could anyone imagine that evil is a form when it appears in the absence of every sort of good?* (Νοῦς μὲν γὰρ καὶ ψυχὴ εἴδη ὄντα εἰδῶν καὶ τὴν γνῶσιν ἂν ποιοῖντο, καὶ πρὸς αὐτὰ ἂν ἔχοιεν τὴν ὄρεξιν· εἶδος δὲ τὸ κακὸν πῶς ἄν τις φαντάζοιτο ἐν ἀπουσίᾳ παντὸς ἀγαθοῦ ἰνδαλλόμενον;).

[466] Plotinus, *Enneads*, I.8.4.9–10.

the "prison of the soul", and the soul is by nature perfect and clean (τελεία... ψυχὴ ἀεὶ καθαρά).[467] On this basis, Evil is the primordial chaos, the yet formless and lifeless matter, which Ovid calls a "rude and disordered mass" (rudis indigestaque moles) in his Metamorphoses.[468] Since Evil is related, on the one hand, to both deficiency and excess and, on the other, to matter as the lowest form of existence, according to Plotinus, ugliness is one of its main manifestations. This quality could be both corporeal, i.e., deformity and disease; and spiritual, i.e., the lack of virtue. This concept fits very well with the ancient Greek idea of the *kalokagathia*, that is, the combination of spiritual and bodily beauty. The material form of the Byzantine evil spirit, as we will see below, is always defined by excess or insufficiency. The human-like body of the demon is always asymmetrical, deformed, too tall or too short, excessively male or (more rarely) female; its clothing is too luxurious or utterly ragged; its physical strength is often immense, and it is frequently given to emotional outbursts. We are far from the idea that this link between physical ugliness and spiritual degradation is necessarily Platonic, for Plato himself casts some doubt on the concept of *kalokagathia* through the image of the old and ugly but divinely wise Socrates. This was a widely held view in the Greco-Roman world, incorporated subsequently into Christian theology. In addition, it seems unclear whether Plato used his teacher's image as a serious philosophical rebuttal to the shallow effort of the narrow-minded majority to establish a simple, short-circuit logical connection between the realms of matter and spirit, or whether he used it instead as a literary technique to attract his audience's interest. In the former case, we must accept that the great philosopher, who was himself an exemplary soldier and professional wrestler, *entirely* denied *any* connection between the body and the soul; on the other hand, he could have used Socrates as simply a one-time antithesis, as a way to remind the reader that *sometimes* the soul can be wrapped in a surprisingly unsuit-

---

[467] Plotinus, *Enneads*, I.8.5.25–26; cf. and I.8.4.6–7: *The soul is not in itself evil, nor is it all evil* (ψυχὴ δὲ καθ' ἑαυτὴν μὲν οὐ κακὴ οὐδ' αὖ πᾶσα κακή).

[468] *Publii Ovidii Nasonis Metamorphoses*, ed. William Anderson (Stuttgart and Leipzig: Teubner, 1981), I.7.

able material shape and that, on some occasions, even an ill-looking penniless dotard could defeat and ridicule the cream of Athenian intellectual and business society. However, the beautiful soul is always in love, "in Eros", with a beautiful body. Socrates always needs his Alcibiades.

Plotinus wrote his *Enneads* in the mid-third century A.D. This was when the concept of demons as evil spirits was, according to Origenes, *accepted by almost everybody*.[469] Nevertheless, classical schools of philosophy found it challenging to accept and substantiate, using the traditional methods of logic, the existence of evil creatures with their own will and eidos. In addition, the passage from the First Ennead does not at all use the term *demon* in its Christian meaning.

* * *

The Neoplatonic teaching developed by Porphyry, Iamblichus, Emperor Julian, and Proclus created a world model where demons play the role of the intermediaries between the highest deities and humans. For Iamblichus, they are neither the *pure demons* (ἁγνοί δαίμονες) of Hesiod nor the demonic souls of the dead of the Pythagoreans; they are creatures of divine origin and belong to the category of the so-called *higher powers* (οἱ κρείττονες). At the same time, for most people, this ancient harmful, anonymous, and fateful power gradually becomes the evil servant of the Devil, the eternal enemy of God and humankind. In the conceptual and linguistic struggle between the two notions, victory undoubtedly belonged to the Christians.

Despite his efforts to formulate and define the concept of Evil philosophically, Plotinus paid little attention to demonology as a system of beliefs. The same is true of his disciple, Porphyry (204–*c*. 305). They both focused predominantly on the idea of the personal *daimonion*. However, in Porphyry's treatises, we can already find certain theoretical "postu-

---

[469] Origène, *Contre Celse*, ed. Marcel Borret, vol. 4: *Livres VII et VIII* [Sources Chrétiennes 150] (Paris: Éditions de Cerf, 1969), VII.69.1–2: *Not only do we call the demons "evil", but almost all suppose that demons exist* (Φαύλους δὲ δαίμονας οὐ μόνοι λέγομεν ἡμεῖς ἀλλὰ καὶ σχεδὸν πάντες, ὅσοι δαίμονας τιθέασιν εἶναι).

lates" about the concrete forms that the various categories of demons assume. According to him, "evil demons" are subject to the power of the god Pluto; they dwell in the aerial regions just above the earth and usually possess humans or haunt them in the shape of animals;[470] in addition, these harmful spirits take pleasure in blood and filth — Porphyry even believes that contact with something dirty could "infect" a human with the demons that inhabit it.[471]

Later Neoplatonic philosophers created a whole demonological system, which can be very useful for studying Byzantine evil spirits. Iamblichus proposed a well-developed and explicit hierarchy of divine entities, called *The Better Ones* or *The Higher Ones* (οἱ κρείττονες).[472] The highest of these was the Demiurge, the Father of all (δημιουργός, πατὴρ τῶν ὅλων). The first and most perfect of his emanations were the Intelligible, Incorporeal gods (νοητοί, ἀφανεῖς θεοί), which inhabit the universe of the *eidē*, and the visible gods (ὁρατοί, ἐμφανεῖς θεοί), which have a stable material form and do not change, such as the Seven Planets, the Sun, and the Moon.[473] Below them were the lesser beings of divine nature, the Archangels, the Angels, the Demons, and the Archons or Cosmocrators. The Archangels and the Angels have universal power, their material forms are stable and unchangeable, and their image is described as *severe and merciless* (βλοσυροί)[474] — a term that will persist in Byzantine hagiography for both the angels and demons. By contrast, the Demons receive the higher deities' power only partially, serving them and fulfilling

---

[470] *Porphyrii de philosophia ex oraculis haurienda: librorum relinquiae*, ed. Gustav Wolff (Hildesheim: Georg Olms, 1962), 147.5–11 and 148.4–149.3.

[471] *Porphyrii de philosophia*, 149.6–7: *They enjoy most of all blood and filth and take pleasure in them, sneaking in [the bodies of] those who are in contact with such things* (μάλιστα δ' αἵματι χαίρουσι καὶ ταῖς ἀκαθαρσίαις, καὶ ἀπολαύουσι τούτων, εἰσδύνοντες τοῖς χρωμένοις.). Cf. Tambornino, *De antiquorum daemonismo*, 22.

[472] See, for this hierarchy, Jamblique, *Les mystères d'Égypte*, II.3 (§70.9–74.10) and II.7 (§83.9–86.4).

[473] Jamblique, *Les mystères d'Égypte*, I.19 (§55.10–62.4).

[474] Jamblique, *Les mystères d'Égypte*, II.3 (§71.10).

their commands.[475] They are responsible for particular regions,[476] and their appearance constantly varies. The latter is defined as *frightful* (φοβερά) and causes anxiety (ταραχή) and confusion (ἀταξία) in those who happen to see them.[477] These concepts — demonic power over particular places and the varying nature of the demons' material form — will remain almost intact in both the Christian theological system and in the folklore represented in hagiography. The Archons, or Cosmocrators, literally the "rulers of the world" (ἄρχοντες, κοσμοκράτορες), are the masters of the elements in the material world, which is located under the Moon. Their forms also vary but are less perfect than those of the Archangels, Angels, and Demons.[478] The term "Cosmocrator", which can also be found in the New Testament,[479] was ubiquitous in Late Antiquity and denoted various world powers,[480] to which we will return in Part IV.

The last category in the Iamblichean hierarchy includes Souls (ψυχαί) and heroes (ἥρωες) who differ from gods and demons by nature (κατ' οὐσίαν). While the demons oversee the course of events in the world and the fulfillment of the higher deities' will, heroes are devoted to life and reason, and control human souls.[481]

For Iamblichus, demons, in particular, fall into different subcategories. Those who are closer to the gods he calls "good demons" (ἀγαθοὶ

---

[475] Jamblique, *Les mystères d'Égypte*, I.20 (§63.4–64.6, esp. §64.2–5): ὅλως δὲ τὸ μὲν θεῖόν ἐστιν ἡγεμονικὸν καὶ προϊστάμενον τῆς ἐν τοῖς οὖσι διατάξεως, διακονικὸν δὲ τὸ δαιμόνιον καὶ παραδεχόμενον ἅπερ ἂν παραγγείλωσιν οἱ θεοὶ προθύμως.

[476] Jamblique, *Les mystères d'Égypte*, I.20 (§63.10–12 and §62.15ff) where the Neoplatonic philosopher stresses that both the intellectual and the visible deities have absolute power over the mighty aerial demons (τῶν ἀερίων βασιλεύει δαιμόνων).

[477] Jamblique, *Les mystères d'Égypte*, II.3 (§71.11ff). The terms ταραχή and ἀταξία are used in II.3 (§72.12–17), where demonic *anxiety* is opposed to divine *serenity* (ἠρεμία).

[478] Jamblique, *Les mystères d'Égypte*, II.3 (§71.3–8).

[479] Eph. 6:12.

[480] The exact phrase used by Iamblichus is: ... *if you really believe that the cosmocrators are those who rule the elements below the Moon* (Jamblique, *Les mystères d'Égypte*, II.3 [§71.4ff]: εἰ μέν σοι δοκοῦσιν οὗτοι οἱ κοσμοκράτορες οἱ ὑπὸ τὴν σελήνην στοιχεῖα διοικοῦντες). This conditional sentence indicates that the meaning of the word "cosmocrators" was rather unclear in his own time.

[481] Jamblique, *Les mystères d'Égypte*, II.1–2 (§67.1–§68.7). Cf. Luck, *Arcana Mundi*, 144 and 288.

δαίμονες), and their influence is beneficial. Below them are the "vengeful demons" (τιμωρητικοὶ δαίμονες) who punish sins. The lowest category is the "evil demons" (πονηροὶ δαίμονες). They are described as "harmful and blood-thirsty wild beasts" (θηρία τινὰ βλαβερὰ καὶ αἱμοβόρα καὶ ἄγρια).[482] While his predecessor Plotinus uses the common Greek word for "bad" (κακός), Iamblichus prefers the particular term "evil" (πονηρός), which is found in the Christian tradition as well.

In the demonological system of Iamblichus, demons are related to various elements. They can be *celestial* (οὐράνιοι), *aerial* (ἀέριοι), and *earthly* (χθόνιοι). The aerial demons are made of fire, and the earthly ones are reportedly *blacker* (μελάντερον) than the others.[483] The relationship between demons and the elements will be preserved in the intellectuals of Byzantium and is visible in the works of Michael Psellus (mid-eleventh century) and, above all, in thirteenth-century demonological treatises. The aerial demons are common in the hagiography of the sixth to the tenth centuries and play an essential role in the afterlife journey of the soul.

Another key feature of demons, according to the treatise *De mysteriis*, is the power of divination. Iamblichus distinguishes between the real *theurges*, who can summon the highest demons, and charlatans, who resort to lower and evil powers or take advantage of human credulity.[484]

In the second half of the third century, Iamblichus was influenced by the dualism of his epoch. He includes in his theological system the category of "evil demons" (πονηροί δαίμονες), an unthinkable concept for Plotinus a century before. In the treatises of the next generations of Neoplatonic philosophers, categorizations become even more specific, and the idea of Evil is much more defined. This tendency is evident in the works of Emperor Julian (361–363). According to the latter, Evil was banished from Heaven and scattered throughout the Earth by the will of

---

[482] Jamblique, *Les mystères d'Égypte*, II.7 (§83.16–§84.6).
[483] Jamblique, *Les mystères d'Égypte*, II.7 (§85.1–6).
[484] Jamblique, *Les mystères d'Égypte*, III.31 (§§176.13–177.6); cf. *Procli Diadochi in Platonis rem publicam commentarii*, ed. Wilhelm Kroll, vol. 1 (Amsterdam: Hakkert, 1965), 290. See Vakaloudi, *Magic*, 116.

the Demiurge. This supreme Creator ordered his highest creatures, the gods and demons, to judge the souls of mortals. Administering punishment, meted out to the sinful, are the *evil and mindless demons* (πονηροί, ἀνόητοι δαίμονες).[485] They also attack the *godless Christians* and inspire them to go willingly to their death or to live alone in the wilderness against their human nature as social beings (ζῷα πολιτικά), ostensibly to reach Heaven. Very rarely, Julian mentions a specific category of high demons who watch over mortals, bestowing peace and bliss on them.[486] For example, the demon who visited Rhea Silvia, the mother of Romulus and Remus, in the form of the god Mars/Ares, is "Ares-like and brave" (ἀρηϊκὸς καὶ γενναῖος).[487] It must be pointed out that Julian uses the term "demon" with extreme caution because his audience is already under the strong influence of its Christian meaning. Had he used the word in its entirely positive Pythagorean and Platonic sense, he would have risked his whole philosophical and religious system, which was the ideological foundation of his political reforms.[488] Maybe this is the reason why Julian does not include demons in his tripartite classification of divine powers (νοητοί, νοεροί, αἰσθητοί).[489] His views of these creatures are somewhat scattered in his works, and there is no particular tendency towards a well-defined demonology like the one in Iamblichus less than a century before.

---

[485] Julien, "Sur les actions de l'empereur ou Sur la royauté Second Éloge de Constance", ed. and trans. Joseph Bidez, *L'empereur Julien. Oeuvres complètes*, vol. 1.1 (Paris: Les Belles Lettres, 1932), §30.35–37.

[486] Julien, "A Thémistius", ed. and trans. Gabriel Rochefort, *L'empereur Julien. Oeuvres completes*, vol. 2.1 (Paris: Les Belles Lettres, 1963), §5.19–24.

[487] Julien, "Sur Hélios le Roi", ed. and trans. Christian Lacombrade, *L'empereur Julien. Oeuvres completes*, vol. 2.2 (Paris: Les Belles Lettres, 1964), §40.22–28.

[488] For more detail on the relation between the philosophical and the political views of Emperor Julian, see Polymnia Athanasiadi, *Julian: An Intellectual Biography* (London: Routledge, 2014).

[489] Demons are mentioned in the *Hymn to the King Sun* only once, along with the other "Higher ones" (κρείττονες) who accompany Helios (angels, demons, heroes, souls). The philosopher does not clarify their functions and appearance (see Julien, "Sur Hélios le Roi", §24.23–26).

Undoubtedly, the most developed and detailed Neoplatonic demonology is that of Proclus (412–487). One of the last great "Diadochoi" (Successors) of the Academy was the author of a treatise *On the Substance of Evils*. Yet, at the beginning of this work, the author tries to clarify the essence of Evil (τὸ ὄντως κακόν).[490] His demonology, however, is presented most exhaustively in his commentaries on Plato's *Republic*.[491] According to him, the highest heavenly powers (ὑπερκόσμιοι δυνάμεις), the source of cosmic laws, are the Monad or Necessity (Ἀνάγκη) and the Triad or the three Moirai (the goddesses of Fate — Lachesis, Clotho, and Atropos).[492] The Universe has a tripartite structure and consists of the Underworld or Tartarus beneath the Earth (ὑπόγειον), the Earth itself (χθών), and Heaven (οὐρανός). Between the Earth and the upper realms of Heaven, where the gods dwell, there lies an immense space for which the terms *air* (ἀήρ) and *ether* (αἰθήρ)[493] are used. Through these dangerous aerial regions, the so-called *demonic place* (δαιμόνιος τόπος),[494] the souls of the dead must pass to reach the realms of the gods. Its upper parts, the ether, are inhabited by the *archons*[495] or *divine demons*,[496] who rule over living creatures and do not allow them to violate the laws of

---

[490] See, e.g., Proclus Diadochus, "De malorum substinentia liber", ed. Helmut Boese, *Procli Diadochi tria opuscula* (Berlin: De Gruyter, 1960), §4.30–31: ἀνάγκη δήπου τὰς κακίας οὐ λόγῳ μόνον εἶναι κακίας, ἀλλ' ὄντως κακὸν.

[491] The demonological system that Proclus presents in his commentaries on Plato's *Republic* is much closer to Christian demonology than the one found in his commentaries on *Timaeus*.

[492] *Procli Diadochi in Platonis rem publicam commentarii*, vol. 2, 100 (cf. Plato, "Republica", 617b). See also Vakaloudi, *Magic*, 98, who erroneously presents Proclus' cosmology as valid for all Neoplatonic philosophers and even as the standard for the period of Late Antiquity as a whole. In fact, her almost only source is Proclus, who wrote at the very end of the ancient world.

[493] The term *ether* is extremely rare. See, for example, Basil the Younger, Part II, §41.18., where the *fearsome breadth of the ether* (τὰ φοβερὰ πλάτη τοῦ αἰθέρους) is mentioned.

[494] The *demonic space* is described in detail, with many references to Plato and arguments against various predecessors of Proclus - see *Procli Diadochi in Platonis rem publicam commentarii*, 2: 125–36.

[495] *Procli Diadochi in Platonis rem publicam commentarii*, 2: 100.16.

[496] *Procli Diadochi in Platonis Timaeum commentaria*, 1: 71.4: οἱ μὲν πρώτιστοι καὶ ἀκρότατοι θεῖοι δαίμονές εἰσι.

Providence and Justice.[497] Just below the ether is the air, where the *courts of justice* (δικαιωτήρια) are located; there, the *demons of punishment* (ποniαῖοι δαίμονες) judge the souls of the dead and decide which of them will be allowed to ascend to Heaven and which ought to be taken down to the Underworld, where they are to be subjected to various tortures and purifications by the demons of vengeance under the watchful eye of the demon-guards.[498] The demons of the latter three categories — namely, the punishers, the vengeful, and the guards — are described by Proclus as *frightful and terrible apparitions*. Some of them appear in animalistic or fantastic forms (bulls, dragons) and the very sight of them is torture for the sinful soul. Others, however, are rational beings (λογικοί); they look like *fiery men* (ἄνδρες διάπυροι)[499] and cleanse the sinners of evil (πονηρία) with fire.[500] After this purification, the souls reincarnate in a new body, but they remember both their journey in the aerial spaces and the ordeals in Tartarus.[501]

The demons that belong to the above categories, according to Proclus, are *demons by essence* (δαίμονες κατ'οὐσίαν), and they have no human origin. There are two other groups. The so-called *demon by analogy* (δαίμων κατ'ἀναλογίαν) is a divine entity (a god or a lesser spirit) that takes care of every single mortal, a demon guardian. The *demon by relation* (δαίμων κατὰ σχέσιν) is a human whose righteous life (εὐ βεβιωκώς) has earned him certain powers, which make him demon-like.[502]

The cosmological system of Proclus in general, and his demonology in particular, is pivotal to the study of some aspects of the Byzantine demon. Some of the most interesting traditions of belief, represented in the

---

[497] *Procli Diadochi in Platonis rem publicam commentarii*, 2: 100.19: οὐκ ἐῶνται παρεκβαίνειν τοὺς ὅρους τῆς προνοίας καὶ τῆς δίκης.

[498] See, e.g., *Procli Diadochi in Platonis rem publicam commentarii*, 2: 168.12–14, 180.8 and passim.

[499] The Greek word διάπυρος means both *ablaze* and *fiery*.

[500] *Procli Diadochi in Platonis rem publicam commentarii*, 2: 180ff. On the so-called διάπυροι δαίμονες, see 1: 118.27.

[501] *Procli Diadochi in Platonis rem publicam commentarii*, 2: 186ff.

[502] On these three categories, see Proclus Diadochus, *Commentary on the First Alcibiades*, §§73.18–75.1. Vakaloudii (*Magic*, 100) omits the category of *demons by analogy* (δαίμονες κατ'ἀναλογίαν).

hagiographical texts of the period between the sixth and the tenth centuries, could hardly be properly understood without these texts, written about half a century before the reign of the Emperor Justinian and the irrevocable transformation of the ancient empire into the medieval Byzantine state. They were preserved in the Middle Ages, and this shows that the interest that the intellectual circles had for them was very much alive until the end of the empire.

Olympiodorus the Younger (c. 495–570) was one of the last Neoplatonists in the Egyptian capital of Alexandria. In his works, primarily commentaries on Plato's dialogues, demonology was strongly influenced by astrology, and the demons themselves were identified exclusively with the "elements" or the "stoicheia" (στοιχεῖα).[503] According to Olympiodorus, the Universe is divided into two parts. The entirely incorporeal gods inhabit the regions above the air. The demons dwell in the earthly material world (ἐγκόσμιοι) and are divided into the following categories:[504]

1. Heavenly demons (οὐράνιοι);
2. Ethereal or fire demons (αἰθέριοι or πύριοι);
3. Aerial demons (ἀέριοι);
4. Aquatic demons (ἐνύδριοι)
5. Terrestrial demons (χθόνιοι), some of which are the overlords of the elements (the so-called *klimatarchai*), and others the guardians of cities and homes (the so-called *poliouchoi* and *katoikidioi*, respectively).[505] "Domestic demons" featured as a widespread folklore motif that was found in both ancient Greek and Roman mythology. In Rome, the altars of the so-called *lares* and *penates*, or the divine patrons of the house, were placed in the home's central and most frequented quarters, namely the atrium. During the early modern period (the fifteenth to the seventeenth centu-

---

[503] On the "elements" (στοιχεῖα), see Tim Crowley, "On the use of stoicheion in the sense of 'element'", *Oxford Studies in Ancient Philosophy* 29 (2005): 367–94.
[504] Olympiodorus, *Commentary on the First Alcibiades of Plato*, ed. Leendert Westerink, (Amsterdam: Hakkert, 1982), §19.11–§20.2.
[505] It is interesting that in modern Greek the word "katoikidio" (κατοικίδιο) is still in use and means "domestic animal".

ries), "domestic demons", called "familiars" in England, were considered servants of the Devil by the Church, and communion with them was a sign that a witch had made a pact with Evil;
6. Demons of the underworld, which inhabit Tartarus (ὑποτάρταροι).

The different categories of demons were primarily inventions of philosophers with a taste for mysticism. However, we have no reasons to doubt that these theories were based on actual folklore beliefs and traditions. In the *Lives* of the saints, we find unmistakable traces of these ideas reflected in Neoplatonic literature, although entirely devoid of their philosophical aspect and wholly adapted to Christian dogmatics. The demons of the elements ("cosmocrators"), which are part of the categories of Iamblichus and Olympiodorus, are relatively common in Byzantine hagiography, and the association of evil spirits with the aerial spaces is one of the most widespread beliefs. During the period under study, the demonic masters of the air were almost commonplace, especially in the sixth and seventh centuries.[506] One of the versions of the *martyrion* of the Martyrs of Amorion, executed by the Arabs after the city's capture in 838, mentions them without any further explanation; this is a clear sign that the text's audience in the mid-ninth century was well-acquainted with this particular image. The black demons, the incarnation of absolute materiality, were also frequently encountered topos during the period under study.

After a long interval, demonological categories became popular, even fashionable, among the Byzantine intellectuals only after the mid-eleventh century. Michael Psellus, the father of late Byzantine demonology, claims that such theories are typical predominantly for the *Hellenic* (i.e., pagan) *prating* (Ἑλληνικὴ ἀδολεσχία), not for Christian theology.[507]

---

[506] Symeon the Holy Fool, 101.9–11; John the Merciful, 396.30–36; Leo of Catania, §11; Anastasios of Persia, *Roman miracle*, §5.14ff; Martyrs of Amorion (v. 3), §17.

[507] Michael Psellus, "Greek Provisions on Demons", [Greek: "Ἑλληνικαὶ διατάξεις περὶ δαιμόνων"], ed. John Duffy and Dominic O'Meara, *Michaelis Pselli philosophica minora*, vol. 2 (Leipzig: Teubner, 1989), 126: ταῦτα μὲν οὖν τῆς ἑλληνικῆς ἀδολεσχίας εἰσίν· ἡμῖν δέ, οἷς λόγος τὸ προσκυνούμενον, λῆρος ἅπαν δοκεῖ τὸ παρὰ τὰς ἡμετέρας καὶ

His treatise, *Greek Provisions on Demons* (Ἑλληνικαὶ διατάξεις περὶ δαιμόνων) is little more than compilations copied from Proclus. They are of little use as sources for the actual beliefs of Psellus's contemporaries, let alone the hagiographical image of the demon in the previous four centuries. The Neoplatonic hierarchies, however, are clearly evident in another text written long after the period on which this study focuses. This is the anonymous dialogue *Timotheos or on the Operation of the Demons* (Τιμόθεος ἢ περὶ ἐνεργείας δαιμόνων). For a long time, this text was beleived an original work of Psellus. However, in the 1980s, the French scholar Paul Gautier proved that it was compiled in the mid-thirteenth century, 200 years after the great Byzantine philosopher.[508] The anonymous author surveys various theoretical and practical demonological issues; he discusses the demons' materiality, their corporeal forms, outer appearances, powers, and types. He frequently mentions well-known Neoplatonic concepts, e.g., the link between evil spirits and the elements (fire, earth, air, and water.) Even though the tone of the dialogue is ironic, *On the Operation of the Demons* indicates that beliefs and conceptual systems of Late Antiquity were still alive during the Late Byzantine period. The pamphlet is also key to many ideas presented in the hagiographical literature from the sixth until the tenth centuries.

θείας διατάξεις λεγόμενον. It must be noted that the words Ἕλλην and Ἑλληνικός in Middle Greek could mean "pagan" (both as a noun and as an adjective) and not *Greek*.
[508] See Gautier, "De Daemonibus", 131.

CHAPTER 2
THE DEMON AND THE CHRISTIAN TRADITIONS

Already between the first and the third centuryies, various cults of predominantly Eastern origin were infiltrating the Greco-Roman world on a large scale. They spread like wildfire and, in addition, gained political influence. In the previous chapter, we briefly summarized the main strategies by which the elitist Neoplatonic philosophy of this turbulent period struggled to objectivize and define the concept of transcendental "Evil", so alien to classical Platonism, even in its most mystical aspects. Furthermore, this idea is absurd in terms of the carefully developed system of Aristotelean logic, which is the very intellectual foundation of ancient philosophy. These efforts were mostly unsuccessful, and this may have been one of the reasons that pagan philosophy proved unable to provide the basis for a stable political ideology or adequately meet the needs of an empire trying desperately to find a way out of a severe political, economic, military, and, last but not least, religious crisis. By contrast, the relatively young and vigorous Christian religion had no problem with the concept of transcendental Evil and its logical unsoundness, being itself built in the first place upon the eerie foundation of Faith and only afterward on the solid basis of Reason. Even though you cannot prove the existence of the Devil's eidos, you can easily believe in it and use it to explain the many "evils" in the world. An emperor, a saint, a patriarch, or a popular leader could legitimize his right to rule by being a brave soldier of Good against Evil; being a determined guardian of the people against the Bad is just ridiculous.

Modern researchers like Steward and Greenfield are tempted to use the term "standard Orthodox tradition". As we mentioned in the Introduction, this term is probably more suitable for the Late Byzantine period (the eleventh to the fifteenth centuries), when a whole corpus of commonly accepted commentaries on Scripture, canons, theological treatises, and synodal decisions was available. Between the sixth and the tenth centuries, *"la lutte pour l'Orthodoxie"* (the war for Orthodoxy) was in full swing both against the heretics in the bosom of the Church and the remnants of pagan cults, religions, and philosophical systems. During that time, the only texts every Christian absolutely accepted as sacred were the Old and the New Testaments. In 565, the process of theological consolidation was far from complete. Three more Ecumenical Synods were to be convened, at least two major heresies, Monothelitism and Iconoclasm, had to be defeated, the wars against Zoroastrian Persia and the Caliphate were to be fought, and critical theological and dogmatic works were to be written. At the same time, during this period, the influence of Late Antique philosophy and its mysticism was still strong, something well-reflected in the hagiographical texts; a typical example of this influence is the revival of the concept of the journey of the soul in the ninth and the tenth centuries. Most of the ideas and images related to demons in the *Lives* of the saints could not be explained by any "standard Orthodox tradition" — they are just a variety of beliefs of different origins, loosely tied together by the conceptual system of Scripture. Authors refer to the works of the Church Fathers very rarely. They often do not bother to lay down theoretical concepts about demons' origins, functions, and goals as servants of transcendental Evil. Byzantine hagiography does not develop demonology, and the countless demonic stories described in the *Lives* are more reflections of folklore in the Eastern Mediterranean and inner Asia Minor than a representation of a consolidated theological system. For this reason, we ought to consider the postulates of the great theologians of the fourth and fifth centuries, but not study the hagiographical material exclusively from their perspective.

1. The origin and the nature of Evil

1.1. The Devil

In the Christian theological system, an important place is assigned to the Enemy, the incarnation and the prime source of Evil in the world. Byzantine theologians call him by different names, taken from the Bible: "Devil" (Διάβολος, or lit. "the Deceitful One"), Satan (Σατανᾶς), Belial/Beliar (Βελίαρ), Beelzebub (Βεελζεβούλ), the Light-bringer (Greek

Ἑωσφόρος, Latin *Lucifer*).[509] The idea of the Devil as the primary source of transcendental Evil and master of the demons needed a long time to take shape and is primarily the product of high theology. It is founded on a few passages of the Old and the New Testament, where the origin of Evil was not explained in detail.[510] In the official Orthodox Bible, the story of the giants, who were born of the communion between the *sons of God* (υἱοὶ τοῦ Θεοῦ) and the daughters of men, and subsequently caused innumerable evils, is very short. It does not even mention the name of Azazel, the leader of the armies of men and giants who rebelled against God.[511]

According to the official Orthodox version, the Devil was a mighty angel with his own servants, who rebelled against God, but lost the battle against His armies of angels and was cast down to earth and Hell. The prophet Isaiah refers to the fall of Lucifer, "the morning star" and "the son of the dawn", from Heaven to the very depths of Hell because of his wish to raise his throne above the stars and to become *like the Most High* (ὅμοιος τῷ ὑψίστῳ).[512] The prophet Ezekiel mentions the *ruler* (ἄρχων) of

---

[509] The bibliography on the Devil in Byzantium is enormous (see Greenfield, *Traditions of Belief*, 7–153). On the dogmatic postulates regarding the Devil and Demons, officially accepted by the Orthodox Church, see Androutsos, *Dogmatics of the Eastern Orthodox Church*, 127–29. The first part of Conybeare's study remains useful especially for the demonology of the New Testament (see Conybeare, "Christian Demonology", I, 576ff). Much less detailed is offered in the relatively brief summary of Stewart, *Demons and the Devil*, 141–47, who focuses on modern Greek folklore. On the image of the Devil in Byzantine and post-Byzantine art, see Provatakis, *The Devil*, 23–46, with bibliography. Provatakis summarizes the information provided by the Old and the New Testament. On the name "Satan" (Σατανᾶς), see Edward Langton, *Satan, a Portrait* (London: Skeffington & Son, 1945), 9–65; Edward Langton, *Essentials of Demonology: A Study of Jewish and Christian Doctrine, Its Origin and Development* (London: The Epworth Press, 1949), 52–59, 68–71, 128–29, 136–39; 164–71; On the name "Belial/Beliar" (Βελίαρ), see Langton, *Satan, a Portrait*, 16ff. On the name "Beelzebub" (Βεελζεβούλ), see Aitken, "Beelzebul", 34ff; Langton, *Satan, a Portrait*, 27ff; Langton, *Essentials of Demonology*, 165–67;

[510] Greenfield, *Traditions of Belief*, 9; Stewart, *Demons and the Devil*, 141; Mango, "Diabolus Byzantinus", 217.

[511] Gen. 6:1-4. The narration is much more detailed in the Book of Enoch and the later Rabbinic tradition, to which we will return below.

[512] Isa. 14:12–20.

Tyrus, who was *the seal of perfection, full of wisdom and perfect in beauty*; his *settings and mountings were made of gold*, and he was *anointed as a guardian cherub*, but because his heart had grown proud (ὑψώθη ἡ καρδία σου), God *threw* him *to the earth* and *made a spectacle* of him *before kings*.[513] The story of the King of Tyrus is probably an allusion to the Fallen Angel, the Devil.[514] In the New Testament, information about the rebellion of the Devil and his followers and their banishment from God's Kingdom is also scarce. Still, this event seems to be a well-known and commonly accepted idea.[515] In the Gospel of Luke, Christ says: *I saw Satan fall like lightning from heaven*.[516] In the Book of Revelations, St. John the Apostle speaks of the war fought by Michael and his angels against the dragon, also called "Devil" and "Satan". The latter was unable to defeat the armies of God, lost his place in Heaven, and was hurled along with his angels down to earth.[517] The Devil knows, however, that his time on earth is short and that *eternal fire* (πῦρ τὸ αἰώνιον)[518] was prepared for him — he was destined to be *driven out of this world*, which he had ruled before the advent of Christ.[519] According to St. Peter and St. Jude, God *did not spare angels when they sinned* (ἀγγέλων ἁμαρτησάντων) *but sent them to hell, putting them in chains of darkness to be held for judgment*.[520] Satan is God's creature, but this does not mean that God is the source of Evil as well.[521] According to St. Paul, the reason for his fall was pride,[522] and the different Greek terms for this sin (τῦφος, ἔπαρσις, ὑπερηφανία, ἀλαζονεία) remain critical notions in the theology of the following centuries. St. Basil the Great stresses that the Devil is not evil by nature (φύσις),

---

[513] Ezek. 28:2–19.
[514] Greenfield, *Traditions of Belief*, 9.
[515] Conybeare, "Christian Demonology", I, 577ff.
[516] Luke, 10:18.
[517] Rev. 12:7–9.
[518] Matt. 25:41.
[519] John 12:31 and 16:11.
[520] 2 Pet. 2:4; Jude, 6.
[521] See in detail, for example, Androutsos, *Dogmatics of the Eastern Orthodox Church*, 128 (especially on the term "pride", or ἀλαζονεία); Greenfield, *Traditions of Belief*, 10–13 and 23ff; Stewart, *Demons and the Devil*, 141.
[522] 1 Timothy, 3:6.

but of his own choice (ἐκ προαιρέσεως) embraced the *disease of the envy*.[523] Pseudo-Dionysius the Areopagite uses Platonic terminology and argumentation, borrowed from Plato's *Republic*, to prove that it is impossible and absurd to accept that demons are wholly evil by nature (*οὐ πάντη οὐδὲ ἐπὶ πάντων οὐδέ αὐτὰ καθ' αὐτὰ κακά*).[524] According to him, if the demons had been evil from the beginning, they would have destroyed themselves.[525]

1.2. The demons and the evil spirits

In the Old Testament, the concept that Satan is the supreme overlord of the demons is unclear and controversial.[526] The word "demon" or, in its diminutive form, "daimonion" (δαιμόνιον), is used almost entirely for all deities other than Yahweh.[527] The prophet Isaiah uses this term to denote the gods of the peoples *after* the will of God had destroyed their nations; these sinister remnants of old divine powers, deprived of their long-vanished worshippers, were condemned to *dance* in the depopulated ruins of Babylon after the inevitable destruction of this mighty city.[528] Some of these deities could even be identified, like the *evil daimonion* (πονηρὸν δαιμόνιον) Asmodeus, mentioned in the Book of Tobit (3:8 and 3:17). According to the Biblical text, Asmodeus fell in love with the young

---

[523] Basilius Magnus, "Homilia quod Deus non est auctor malorum", MPG, vol. 31 (Paris, 1857), 348A-B.

[524] Pseudo-Dionysius Areopagita, "De divinis nominibus", ed. Beate Regina Suhla, *Corpus Dionysiacum*, vol. 1 [Patristische Texte und Studien 33] (Berlin and New York: De Guyter, 1990), 171.18ff (IV.23).

[525] Pseudo-Dionysius Areopagita, "De divinis nominibus", 171.8-172.6 (IV.23). See Gerhardus Bartelink, "Μισόκαλος, épithéte du Diable", *Vigiliae Christianae* 12, no. 1 (May 1958): 37ff; Greenfield, *Traditions of Belief*, 2ff.

[526] Greenfield, *Traditions of Belief*, 17, who quotes Ezek. 28:2-19 (the story of the ruler of Tyrus) and Ps. 82:6-7, where Yahweh delivers a prediction to the "gods" (θεοί) of their death *like mortals* and their fall *like one of the princes* (probably, Prince Lucifer).

[527] Ps. 82:6-7: ἐγὼ εἶπα Θεοί ἐστε καὶ υἱοὶ ὑψίστου πάντες· ὑμεῖς δὲ ὡς ἄνθρωποι ἀποθνήσκετε καὶ ὡς εἷς τῶν ἀρχόντων πίπτετε.

[528] Isa. 13:21 (in the King James version of the text, the phrase is translated as "wild beasts of the desert" or "howling creatures", but, in Greek, the Septuagint uses the word "demons"; cf. Rev. 18:2. See Isa. 34:14; Isa. 65:11-12 (where God says that all who sacrifice to "daimonia" will be punished by the sword).

Sarah, from the Persian city of Ecbatana, and killed the seven young men who intended to marry her. In all likeliness, this evil deity is of Iranian origin and is identical to the Zoroastrian god of wrath, Aēšma.[529] In a few hagiographical texts of the period between 565 and 1000, the term "demon" is used with the meaning of a "foreign deity", an "idol".[530]

On only one occasion in the Septuagint does the word "daimonion" refer to an evil spirit not directly related to the deities of other peoples. This is the so-called "noon demon", mentioned in the Psalm 90. We will return to this spirit below.[531]

Evil spirits and *evil angels* are mentioned intermittently in the Old Testament, but they are not related to the Devil. God always sends them to punish sinners. A typical example is the demon that possessed King Saul after God abandoned him.[532] Another sent by God is the *lying spirit* (πνεῦμα ψευδές) who instigated the prophets of King Ahab to predict his victory over the Syrian armies and, in this way, led the sinful ruler to his destruction.[533] *Evil angels* (ἄγγελοι πονηροί) appear only once in the Old Testament; God sends them against Egypt.[534]

* * *

The Old Testament has relatively little influence on the image of the demon in Byzantine hagiography both because the word δαιμόνιον is rarely used in the Septuagint and because of its specific meaning, i.e., a *foreign god*. The hagiographers tend much more to use the New Testa-

---

[529] On the different theories of the origin of the name "Asmodeus", see Paul Haupt, "Asmodeus", *Journal of Biblical Litetature* 40 (1921): 175ff. In contrast, Barr rejects any relationship between this demon and the Iranian Aēšma, arguing that, most likely, the name "Asmodeus" has a Semitic origin (James Barr, "The Question of Religious Influence: The Case of Zoroastrianism, Judaism, and Christianity", *Journal of the American Academy of Religion*, 53, no. 2 (June 1985): 214–16.

[530] See George of Choziba, §9.42.1–14. Cf. Joannou, *Démonologie*, 11.

[531] Ps. 90:6.

[532] I Sam. 16:14–15; see also Judg. 9:23, where God sends the spirit of ill will (πνεῦμα πονηρόν) to *the men of Shechem* to bring destruction to King Abimelech.

[533] 3 Kings 22:21ff; 2 Chron. 18:20ff.

[534] Ps. 77:49. On the later tradition related to this passage, see Greenfield, *Traditions of Belief*, 8 and n. 6.

ment, where demons and evil spirits are common, and the hierarchy of Evil is much clearer.[535] The master of the demons (ἄρχων τῶν δαιμονίων) was called Beelzebub[536] or *the prince of the power of the air* (ἄρχων τῆς ἐξουσίας τοῦ ἀέρος).[537] The word *daimon* occurs in the New Testament only once, in the story of the demons whom Jesus allowed to pass into a herd of swine.[538] Everywhere else in the text, the diminutive *daimonion* is preferred.[539] This peculiarity is by no means accidental and is not only due to the peculiar penchant of the post-classical common Greek language (*koinē*) for diminutive nouns with the suffix –*ιον*. Demons are depicted everywhere in the Gospels not as the proud and mighty officers of the supreme angel Lucifer, who had rebelled against God, but as weak and wretched creatures who shudder in fear at the very mention of Christ's name. This almost grotesque fear before the absolute might of God is described in the following words of St. James the Great:

> In the same way, faith by itself, if it is not accompanied by action, is dead. But someone will say, "You have faith; I have deeds." Show me your faith without deeds, and I will show you my faith by my deeds. You believe that there is one God. Good! Even the demons believe that — and shudder.[540]

The word "daimonion" is rarely used in the New Testament with its Old Testament meaning of "foreign deity". For example, St. Paul probably makes an allusion to Deuteronomy 32:17 when he says:

> No, but the sacrifices of pagans are offered to demons, not to God, and I do not want you to be participants with demons. You cannot drink the cup of

---

[535] On the Devil as the overlord of the demons, see Conybeare, "Christian Demonology", I, 578ff; Francis Gokey, *The Terminology for the Devil and Evil Spirits in the Apostolic Fathers* (Washington DC.: Catholic University of America Press, 1961), s.v. "Archon"; Greenfield, *Traditions of Belief*, 18ff, with useful references to the Fathers of the Church and later Byzantine theologians.

[536] Matt. 12:24; Mark 3:22; Luke 11:15.

[537] Eph. 2:2.

[538] Matt. 8:32.

[539] See, e.g., Mat. 7:22 and 9:32 and passim.; Marc 1:34 and 39 and passim.; Luke 8:2 and 13:32 and passim; John, 10:20; 1 Timothy, 4:1.

[540] James 2:17–19.

the Lord and the cup of demons too; you cannot have a part in both the Lord's table and the table of demons.[541]

The most common synonym of "daimonion" is the word *spirit* (πνεῦμα), combined with the adjectives *unclean* (ἀκάθαρτον) or *evil* (πονηρόν).[542] While in the Old Testament such spirits are almost always sent by God as a punishment, in the New Testament they are the very personification of transcendental Evil and the servants of the Devil. However, without such adjectives, the word "spirit" is entirely neutral and not necessarily related to Good or Evil. In the Pauline epistles, it is used for the Holy Ghost (τὸ Ἅγιον Πνεῦμα). There are "spirits" of different human qualities, both positive and negative, like the spirit of faith,[543] the spirit of wisdom,[544] the spirit of gentleness,[545] the spirit of life,[546] and the spirit of prophecy.[547] *But the fruit of the Spirit is love, joy, peace, longsuffering, kindness, goodness, faithfulness*, says the Apostle Paul in one of his epistles.[548]

On the other hand, there is also the spirit of fear, opposed to the *spirit of power and of love and of a sound mind*,[549] and the spirit of error or the deceiving spirit, opposed to the spirit of truth.[550] The word "spirit" could denote the human spirit which inhabits the mortal body and, after

---

[541] 1 Cor. 10:20–21.

[542] The terms πνεῦμα πονηρόν/ἀκάθαρτον and δαιμόνιον are used in Mark, 6:7 and 13; Mark, 7:25–26 and 29–30; Luke, 4:33–36; Luke, 8:27–38. See and Mark 5:2, 15, 16 and 18, where the expressions *[possessed] by an unclean spirit* (ἐν πνεύματι ἀκαθάρτῳ) and *possessed by a demon* (δαιμονιζόμενος/δαιμονισθείς) are also synonymous. In Acts the term *unclean spirit* (πνεῦμα πονηρόν/ἀκάθαρτον) is obviously preferred. On this see Conybeare, "Christian Demonology", I, 579ff (especially 579, n. 3); Delatte and Josserand, "Contribution", 208; Greenfield, *Traditions of Belief*, 13, who refers to very few passages of the New Testament; Stewart, *Demons and the Devil*, 141.

[543] 2 Cor. 4:13.

[544] Eph. 1:17.

[545] Gal. 6:1.

[546] Rom. 8:2 and Rev. 11:11 (the Greek word πνεῦμα is correctly translated as *spirit* in the King James version, while in other English versions of the New Testament the original Greek term appears as *breath*.)

[547] Rev. 19:10.

[548] Gal. 5:22.

[549] 2 Tim. 1:7.

[550] 1 John 4:6, cf. and 1 Tim. 4:1.

death, leaves it; for example, according to St. Luke, after the crucifixion, Christ appeared to two of his disciples, and they took Him for the spirit of a dead man.[551] While humans have bodies (σῶμα) and spirits (πνεῦμα), a demon has only an evil/unclean spirit but not a stable material form. Because they are bodiless by nature, the servants of the Devil constantly struggle to find a host and possess them.[552] This is evident, for instance, in the Gospel of Luke, where the expression "a spirit of an unclean demon" (πνεῦμα δαιμονίου ἀκαθάρτου) is used.[553] In the New Testament, other than the Book of Revelation, demons are predominantly represented as incorporeal beings that exist only as spirits. This tendency probably evolved as a reaction on the part of the first Christians against the numerous various images of pagan deities.

As we already mentioned, in the New Testament, the noun "spirit" as a synonym of "demon" almost always needs some adjective, like *evil* (πονηρόν)[554] or, more often, *unclean* (ἀκάθαρτον).[555] These two epithets are also the most common in Byzantine hagiography.[556] However, spirit could be defined by some attribute that denotes a specific harmful influence: the mute spirit,[557] the spirit of infirmity,[558] or the deceitful spirit of divination (spirit Python in the Greek original).[559] According to the Acts

---

[551] Luke, 24:37.
[552] See for example Matt. 43–45 and Luke 11:24–26, where an *unclean spirit* (πνεῦμα πονηρόν) is expelled from its victim, wanders in the wilderness, and was not able to find peace.
[553] Luke 4:33.
[554] See, e.g., Matt. 12:45; Luke 7:21 and 8:2; Acts 19:13 and 15.
[555] See, e.g., Matt. 10:1, 12:43; Mark 1:23, 1:26–27, 3:11, 3:30, 5:2, 5:8, 5:13, 6:7, 7:25, 9:25; Luke 6:18, 8:29; Acts 8:7; Rev. 16:13.
[556] The adjectives πονηρός and ἀκάθαρτος are extremely common in sixth to tenth century Byzantine hagiography. On the adjective πονηρός, see, e.g., Anastasios of Persia, *Roman miracle*, §9.17; George of Choziba, §10.52.1; Stephen the Thaumaturge, §161; Theodore of Edessa, §15; Stephen the Younger, 123.6ff; Eustratios of Agauros, §60 and passim. On the adjective ἀκάθαρτος see, e.g., Symeon the Holy Fool, 69.12; Symeon Stylites the Younger, §40.27; David, Symeon and George, §24.9ff; Peter of Atroa, §61.6; Elias the Younger, §74 and passim.
[557] Πνεῦμα ἄλαλον is mentioned, e.g., in Mark 9:17 and 25. Luke 11:24 uses the expression δαιμόνιον κωφόν in the same sense.
[558] Luke 13:11.
[559] Acts 16:16.

of Apostles, the latter possessed a slave girl, and her masters made good business out of her false talent. The Apostle Paul successfully exorcized the young woman.[560] Even when, very rarely, the word is used without an attribute, the context does not allow any misunderstanding.[561]

A plesionym of the word "demon" is the mass noun πνευματικά τῆς πονηρίας which could roughly be translated as *the spiritual hosts of wickedness*.[562] Though it is used only once in the New Testament, in the Letter of St. Paul to the Ephesians, the expression is relatively common in the hagiographical texts of the period under study. It denotes, in particular, the evil spirits which inhabit the aerial spaces just above the earth (τὰ ἐπουράνια). One of the primary duties of the monk is to fight against them.[563]

In the New Testament, the Devil's servants (δαίμονες, δαιμόνια, πνεύματα πονηρά/ἀκάθαρτα, πνευματικά τῆς πονηρίας) are evil, wicked spirits which possess their victims and never have flesh and bones of their own.[564] The Evangelists do not clarify the question of their materiality, and epithets like *incorporeal, intellectual,* and *invisible* (ἄσαρκος, νοητός, ἀόρατος) are used chiefly by the theologians and hagiographers of later times.[565] Various fantastical or realistic forms are described only in the

---

[560] Acts 16:16–19. On this passage see Greenfield, *Traditions of Belief*, 129.

[561] See, e.g., Mat. 8:16, where the word πνεῦμα is used as a synonym of δαιμονιζόμενοι, κακῶς ἔχοντες. In Luke 9:39, the father of a possessed boy uses the noun without an adjective, but the symptoms of his son's condition clearly suggest possession by an evil spirit.

[562] Eph. 6:12 (New King James version).

[563] See for example Eustratios of Agauros, §5.

[564] See Luke 27:34–43, where the Apostles *supposed that they had seen a spirit,* when the Lord appeared before them after His crucifixion. He tells them that *a spirit hath not flesh and bones, as ye see me have.*

[565] On the usage of these terms in the works of the Church Fathers and among the later theologians see Greenfield, *Traditions of Belief*, 13ff; Stewart, *Demons and the Devil*, 144. They occur often in Byzantine hagiography. Of particular interest is the epithet νοητός because of its Neoplatonic origin (see, for example, George of Choziba, §10.50.3; Stephen the Thaumaturge, §161; Ioannikios (*Peter*) §47, Ioannikios (*Sabbas*), §12 et al.; Antony Kauleas, §23; Pancratius of Taormina, 352.4 et al.; Nikon Metanoeite, §55.3). The epithet ἀόρατος see, for example, in: Martyrs of Amorion, §2, §15 et al.; Eustratios of Agauros, §5; Gregory of Dekapolis, §1.2; John the Psichaites, §1. The epithet ἄσαρκος is relatively less common and is used in Antony Kauleas, §23. It must be

Book of Revelation, where the Devil gives spirit to the image of the beast,[566] the demons of false prophecy appear as frogs,[567] and the Devil's messenger is a *beast* with *seven heads and ten horns, and upon his horns ten crowns, and upon his heads the name of blasphemy.*[568] Such images are almost absent from the hagiographical texts between the sixth and the tenth centuries. This absence is only to be expected since their appearance is a sign that Doomsday is near — a terrifying event that the authors of these texts would hardly dare to herald very lightly. The only demonic form to any degree influenced by the Book of Revelation is the dragon, described by St. John as a *great red dragon, having seven heads and ten horns and seven crowns upon his heads.*[569] Such evil creatures are common, especially in the Byzantine hagiography of Palestine (eighth century) and Bithynia (ninth century). The descriptions, however, are not similar to the ones found in the New Testament and, as we will see below, were probably influenced by local folklore and ancient mythological images.[570]

As a consequence of their fall from grace, demons are associated with a pattern of qualities and emotional predispositions.[571] The primary cause for their rebellion against God is their **pride**, one of the gravest sins into which they could tempt humans.[572] As inventors and personifica-

---

noted that the hagiographers do not use the epithet "incorporeal" (ἄϋλος) for the demons but only for the heavenly powers and their beneficial influence upon the humans (see, for example, Patriarch Tarasios, §60.17; Patriarch Nikephoros, §1, §43 et al.; Pancratius of Taormina, 346.14, 358.11 et al.; Paul of Latros II, §30.10.

[566] Rev. 13:15.
[567] Rev. 16:13.
[568] Rev. 13:1-2.
[569] Rev. 12:3ff.
[570] On the origins of the demonic dragons in Byzantine hagiography of the period under study, see Part Three, Chapter 3, §2.
[571] On the standard pattern of epithets used both by theologians and hagiographers for the Devil and his servants, see, for example, Androutsos, *Dogmatics of the Eastern Orthodox Church*, 127ff; Greenfield, *Traditions of Belief*, 23–29.
[572] On the demon of Pride, see, e.g., Phantinos the Younger, §33.

tions of Evil, they are usually called *the source of Evil* (ἀρχέκακοι),[573] *creators of all Evil* (πάσης κακίας δημιουργοί), *evil-doers* (κακοῦργοι).[574] Because of their entirely lost communion with God, the demons and their prince feel **hatred** (*μῖσος*) and **bitterness** (*πικρία*) towards Him, towards His angels, and especially towards humans, who are blessed with His mercy. The epithets *haters of the Good* (μισόκαλος)[575] and *bitter* (πικρός)[576] remain among the most common both in theological and hagiographical works.

Under Neoplatonic influence, Origen (whose ideas were rejected by the Orthodox Church) and Pseudo-Dionysius the Areopagite argue that the Devil and demons are not evil by nature and, consequently, could be saved.[577] Such ideas were entirely alien to the hagiographers of the period under study. For them, unlike Adam and Eve, the fallen angels had not been subjected to temptation and therefore could not repent and take their previous place with God.[578] For example, according to Michael Psellus, St. Auxentios admonishes an evil spirit:

> Go away from this man, from this here God's likeness! Having abandoned the order to which you were appointed from the beginning, you can never again return because, as an angel, you are free from all corporeal nature.

---

[573] The epithet ἀρχέκακος is very common in hagiography. See, e.g., George of Choziba, §10.51.23; Anastasios of Persia, *Roman miracle*, §3.4 and §9.3; Niketas of Medikion, §18; Nikephoros of Medikion, §11.38; Peter of Atroa, §77.22ff.

[574] See Stephen the Thaumaturge, §33.

[575] The epithet μισόκαλος was probably introduced by one of the first Christian theologians, Philo of Alexandria (first century A.D.). See, e.g., Symeon Stylites the Younger, §60.1, §99.2, and §130.12; John the Merciful, 383.23, Stephen the Thaumaturge, §34; Peter of Atroa, §20.20, §63.11, and §79.5ff; Elias the Younger, §10. On its origin and evolution in the Christian tradition in general, see Bartelink, "Μισόκαλος, épithéte du Diable", 38ff; Greenfield, *Traditions of Belief*, 29.

[576] See, e.g., Stephen the Younger, 123.5-7, where the demon and the heretical iconoclasts bitterly besiege the Church; Peter of Atroa, §28.33: *there is much bitterness against you in the demons* (πολλὴ κατὰ σοῦ τοῖς δαίμοσί ἐστιν πικρία); Luke of Steiris, §95.3; Paul of Latros I, §14.2 and passim.

[577] On the ideas of Origen and Pseudo-Dionysius, see Bartelink, "Μισόκαλος, épithéte du Diable", 37ff; Greenfield, *Traditions of Belief*, 21ff.

[578] Bartelink, "Μισόκαλος, épithéte du Diable", 37ff; Joannou, *Démonologie*, 42; Greenfield, *Traditions of Belief*, 21ff, who refers predominantly to post-thirteenth century authors; Stewart, *Demons and the Devil*, 146.

Therefore, you are not liable to the passions and temptations of a material form. On the other hand, man is under the tyranny of bodily needs and is constantly drawn by his material existence to a sinful life but has not entirely rejected the seeds of the Good. Whenever his reason leads him to fulfill his fundamental duties, he returns to God and is never forgotten by his Creator.[579]

Michael Psellus wrote this text as late as the mid-eleventh century when the Orthodox world's theological and demonological conceptual system was already relatively well-developed. By contrast, Byzantine hagiography before the beginning of the eleventh century provides very little information about the nature, functions, and goals of demons. Still, the general ideas are identical to those found in the *Life* of St. Auxentios. Any details were usually obtained from the conversations between demons and exorcists, which were extremely rare. A typical example of such a "philosophical" dialogue is preserved in the *Roman Miracle of St. Anastasios of Persia*. During the exorcism, which occurred in 713, the king of the demons confessed that the fire of Hell was already prepared for him and that he would never kneel before Christ, but would eternally be the enemy of Humankind.[580] Another example is the *Life* of St. Irene of Chrysobalanton (late tenth or early eleventh century), where the demon reveals to the pious nun that he and his brothers are not capable of doing good and that only Hell awaits them and those humans they managed to win over.[581]

Both in the New Testament[582] and in hagiography demons are traditionally associated with **darkness** (σκότος) and with the so-called **"outer darkness"** (ἐξώτερον σκότος) in particular, into which they will be cast along with the sinners.[583] Yet, in the Gospels, there occurs the idea

---

[579] Auxentios, §20.31–37.
[580] Anastasios of Persia, *Roman Miracle*, §7.8-13.
[581] Irene of Chrysobalanton, §15.
[582] John 1:5 and 3:19–20; Eph. 6:12.
[583] Mat. 8:12, 22:13, 25:30. On the black demons in the works of the Church Fathers and among the later Byzantine theologians, see Greenfield, *Traditions of Belief*, 26ff. The black demons and the Ethiopian-demons in hagiographical texts will be discussed in more detail in Part Three, Chapter 2, §1.

that Evil and communion with its servants *darkens* the human body.[584] This "outer" darkness could be related to the aerial spaces beneath Heaven, inhabited by demons. This concept is supported by numerous passages in the Old and the New Testaments where "demons of the air" are mentioned.[585] The air (ὁ ἀήρ) as the dwelling place of the evil spirits could be found both in early apologetics and among the Fathers of the Church.[586] This relationship is of utmost importance for studying Byzantine hagiography and will be discussed in Part Four of this book.

* * *

According to the predominant theological ideas of the sixth to the tenth centuries, the fall of the Devil and the demons is an event not directly related to the history of Humankind, which happened not as a consequence of some external stimulus but due to the pride and envy of Sa-

---

[584] Mat. 6:23 (ἐὰν δὲ ὁ ὀφθαλμός σου πονηρὸς ᾖ, ὅλον τὸ σῶμά σου σκοτεινὸν ἔσται) and Luke 11:34 (ἐπὰν δὲ πονηρὸς ᾖ, καὶ τὸ σῶμά σου σκοτεινόν).

[585] Eph. 2:1–2: *You used to be dead because of your offenses and sins that you once practiced as you lived according to the ways of this present world and according to the ruler of the power of the air* (καὶ ὑμᾶς ὄντας νεκροὺς τοῖς παραπτώμασιν καὶ ταῖς ἁμαρτίαις ὑμῶν, ἐν αἷς ποτε περιεπατήσατε κατὰ τὸν αἰῶνα τοῦ κόσμου τούτου κατὰ τὸν ἄρχοντα τῆς ἐξουσίας τοῦ ἀέρος). In Eph. 6:12, the Apostle Paul speaks of *the evil spiritual forces in the heavenly realm* (τὰ πνευματικὰ τῆς πονηρίας ἐν τοῖς ἐπουρανίοις.)

[586] One of the earliest Christian apologists, Athenagoras of Athens (second century), says: *These angels, fallen from Heaven, dwell in the air and on the earth, being incapable of reaching the Heaven above* (Οὗτοι τοίνυν οἱ ἄγγελοι οἱ ἐκπεσόντες τῶν οὐρανῶν, περὶ τὸν ἀέρα ἔχοντες καὶ τὴν γῆν οὐκέτι εἰς τὰ ὑπερουράνια ὑπερκύψαι δυνάμενοι) (Athenagoras, "Legatio sive Supplicatio pro christianis", ed. William Schoedel, *Athenagoras. Legatio and De resurrection* [Oxford: Clarendon Press, 1972], §25.1.) According to the *Life* of St. Antony the Great, written by St. Athanasios the Great in the second half of the fourth century, demons cannot pass through the locked gates of Heaven and wander through the air (Antony, §28.13–16). For other mentions of aerial demons in the patristic tradition, see Greenfield, *Traditions of Belief*, 15ff and n. 45–50. On the depictions of these evil spirits, see Provatakis, *The Devil*, 27ff, and n. 37. For more details about the ideas of Philo of Alexandria, see Archie Wright, *The Origin of Evil Spirits. The Reception of Genesis 6:1-4 in Early Jewish Literature* (Tubingen: Mohr Siebec, 2005), 205–15

tan himself.[587] At the very moment that God created Adam and Eve, the seeds of Evil were already sown. Now, the Fallen Angels and their master were about to cross paths with the crown of God's creation, to lead humans into original sin, and to play their role in the history of Humankind.

2. Demons in the sacred history of humankind

The fall of the Devil and his angels and their consequent evil, impurity, pride, and bitterness affect people only indirectly. The Old and especially the New Testament show how evil spirits directly influence humanity and its "sacred history".[588] The first milestone in this sequence of events is the Expulsion of Adam and Eve from Eden, where, at least in the original text of the Scriptures, the role of the Devil is controversial. The Serpent (Hebrew *ha-Nachash*, Greek ὁ ὄφις) misled Eve[589] to eat from *the tree of the knowledge of good and evil*, which was forbidden to Adam.[590] Consequently, God expelled the first man and the first woman from Eden, took away the gift of immortality from them, and doomed them to a short life full of labor and trials.[591] Neither the original official Hebrew version of the Old Testament nor the Septuagint explicitly identifies the Serpent with the Devil. Still, this concept is relatively common in the apocryphal Jewish tradition, e.g., in the lost Greek translations of the Book of Enoch,[592] the Book of Revelations, and in Christian theological texts.[593]

---

[587] See Greenfield, *Traditions of Belief*, 9–11, with references to the most important theological texts; Stewart, *Demons and the Devil*, 141. For further information, see Greenfield, *Traditions of Belief*, 11–13, with bibliography. In the Byzantine hagiography of the period under study under study, the theoretical problem of the origin of Evil and the fall of the Devil is not discussed.

[588] For the critical events of the sacred history of Humankind, see Greenfield, *Traditions of Belief*, 34ff. Greenfield uses the term "mythical history". The much more suitable term "sacred history" is preferred by Nicolas Kiesling, "Antecendents of the Medieval Dragon in Sacred History", *Journal of Biblical Literature* 89, no. 2 (June 1970): 167.

[589] Gen. 3:13.

[590] Gen. 2:9,

[591] Gen. 3:16–19.

[592] The most complete preserved version of the Book of Enoch, the Ethiopian, was translated from Aramaic and, probably, from Greek in the fourth to the sixth centuries (see

The story of Original Sin and the Devil's deceitful influence gave birth to numerous fundamental notions which will persist intact in the hagiographical tradition:[594]

1. **Envy** (*φθόνος*) and **malice** (*βασκανία*).[595] The Devil was the primary cause for Adam and Eve's subjection to death through envy. The harmful influence of this sinful emotion is ambivalent. On the one hand, Satan himself is triggered by it because he envied the first humans for being in God's grace. On the other, Adam and Eve were affected by the envious wish to *become like God, knowing good and evil.*[596] The concept that the Devil is jealous (*φθονερός*) by nature and that this was the cause for his downfall is evident in the Scriptures.[597] It is an essential element of the Greek Orthodox theological tradition[598] and hagiogra-

---

Boryana Hristova, *The Book of Enoch. Ethiopian Version; Slavonic (Bulgarian) Version* [Bulgarian: Боряна Христова, *Книга на Енох. Етиопска версия; Славянска (Българска) версия)*] (Sofia, 2008), 11–13). Where the Hebrew original is concerned, only fragments are preserved in the Talmud and other Rabbinic writings (Hristova, *The Book of Enoch*, 13ff). The Greek version was translated from Aramaic in the second or the frist century B.C. and exists today in fragments and, partially, in the *Chronography* of George Synkellos of the early ninth century (Hristova, *The Book of Enoch*, 14ff). The Slavic translations of the text, which hugely influenced the formation of the Bogomil Heresy, are also of utmost importance for the reconstruction of the original (Hristova, *The Book of Enoch*, 16–18).

[593] See Greenfield, *Traditions of Belief*, 36 and n. 131; Henry Kelly, "The Metamorphoses of the Eden Serpent During the Middle Ages and the Renaissance", *Viator* 2 (1971): 302; Langton, *Essentials of Demonology*, 55 and 134ff; Langton, *Satan, a Portrait*, 20ff.

[594] On these terms in the Byzantine theological tradition, see Greenfield, *Traditions of Belief*, 29ff and 36ff. The author, however, does not refer to any hagiographical text at all.

[595] On the two meanings of the word *βασκανία* (*malign influence* and *envy*), see LSJ, s.v. "*βασκανία*".

[596] Gen. 3:5.

[597] Wisd. of Sol. 2:24 (Septuagint). The Book of Wisdom or the Wisdom of Solomon is not a part of the Protestant Bible but is included in the Septuagint and is officially accepted by the Orthodox Church.

[598] See Greenfield, *Traditions of Belief*, 36–37. Greenfield refers to St. John of Damascus, John Chrysostom, Gregory Palamas, et al.

phy.⁵⁹⁹ In the *Lives* of the saints in the period under study, the *envy* and the *malign influence* caused by it are reported to be the leading cause for the enmity of the Devil and the demons for righteous and pious persons, especially monks and nuns.⁶⁰⁰

2. **Enmity** against Humankind. The Devil and his demons are the eternal enemies of mortals. For this reason, some of the most frequent epithets used by the hagiographers to describe them are

---

⁵⁹⁹ See Symeon Stylites the Younger, §99.1ff, where the expression *the primordially envious and good-hating Devil* (ὁ ἐξ ἀρχῆς φθονερὸς καὶ μισόκαλος διάβολος) is used; Nikephoros of Medikion, §11.33–41, where, in a few sentences, the author lays down the standard concepts of the innocence of Adam and Eve before Original Sin, the envy of the *primordially evil Serpent* (ἀρχέκακος ὄφις) towards them, their being led astray, and their final expulsion from the Garden of Eden; George of Choziba, §§10.55–13.21, where the *malignant envy* (βασκανία) of the Adversary is referred to as the cause of such events as Original Sin, the murder of Abel by his brother Cain, and the crucifixion of Christ by the Jews. The expression *envious and murderous serpent* (βάσκανος καὶ βροτοκτόνος ὄφις) is used for the Devil, e.g., in Gregory of Dekapolis, §65.3.

⁶⁰⁰ The more frequent term is undoubtedly φθόνος (see for example Niketas of Medikion, §18, where a pious monk is attacked by a demon; Elias Speleotes, §43, where the envious Devil is mad (ἐμμανής) with envy because of the pious efforts of the Saint to build a monastery and does everything possible to stop him; Euthymios the Younger, §20, who could not escape the envy of the demons (ἀνεπίφθονος τοῖς δαιμόσιν) and was constantly assailed by them with feelings of loneliness during his hermitage in 858–59; Euthymios the Younger, §29, where the demons hinder the building of the church of St. Andrew because they envy the salvation of many human souls that the temple would bring about; Nikephoros of Sebaze, §5 where the envious demon uses Emperor Leo V (813–820) as his instrument in order to tempt his subjects to accept the sinful Iconoclast heresy; Elias the Younger, §10, where the *good-hating and envious Devil* is the one who always envies the faithful (ὁ δὲ μισόκαλος καὶ φθονερὸς διάβολος, ὁ ἀεὶ φθονῶν τοὺς πιστούς). The term *malice* (βασκανία) is rarer. It is used, e.g., in the following hagiographical texts: Symeon Stylites the Younger, §130.12–17, where the Devil kindles the malice of the Georgian priests against a monk, who was blessed by St. Symeon the Younger; Euthymios the Younger, §25.5ff, where the malice inspired by the Devil causes a group of Arabs to attack the Saint and his pupils and kidnap them; Paul of Latros I, §10.24, where a hermit was influenced by the *malice of the demon* (βασκανία δαίμονος) and as a consequence saw a ghostly procession of temptingly beautiful women; Sabbas the Younger, §39, where the Demon feels malice towards the piety of a nobleman named Dorotheos and assails him with seizures. The terms φθόνος and βασκανία could also be used as a pair. For example, Gregory of Dekapolis (§30.2) was overtaken by the *envy (φθονεῖται) of the malicious (τοῦ βασκαίνοντος) demon* because of his virtue.

enemy (ἐχθρός,⁶⁰¹ πολέμιος),⁶⁰² adversary (ἀντίδικος),⁶⁰³ hater of humankind (μισάνθρωπος).⁶⁰⁴ Also widespread was the term *the adversarial power* (ἡ ἀντικείμενος/ἀντικειμένη δύναμις), which is the Greek translation of the Hebrew word "Satan".⁶⁰⁵

3. **Lie (ψεῦδος), deceit (ἀπάτη), misleading (πλάνη), slander (διαβολή)**. The Devil *deceived* Eve and tempted her to eat from the tree of knowledge. In the following centuries, theologians made the deceitfulness of the Devil a key concept in Christian doctrine.⁶⁰⁶ According to the Byzantine hagiographical texts, this is the primary weapon used by Satan and the demons to separate humans from God. The terminology used in the biblical narrative of Original Sin to describe the Serpent/Devil includes the verb ἀπατῶ (*to cheat, to deceive*), the nouns ἀπάτη (*trick, fraud,*

---

[601] See Mat. 13:25 and 39; Luke 10:19. The noun *Enemy* (ἐχθρός) and others having the same root are widespread. See, for example, Symeon the Holy Fool, 62.7 and 71.25; George of Choziba, §3.13.3; Stephen the Younger, 123.22, 149.8 and passim.; John the Psichaites, §5 and §13; David, Symeon and George, §5.20; Peter of Atroa, §77.23 and §83.25; Eustratios of Agauros, §29; Martyrs of Amorion (v. 3), §2; Gregory of Dekapolis, §39.1 and §40.1; Euthymios the Younger, §32.5; Luke of Steiris, §45.2 and passim.

[602] See, e.g., Stephen the Younger, 109.13, where the whole chapter is full of military terminology related to the Church's struggle with the Iconoclast heresy; Stephen the Younger, 123.7; Martyrs of Amorion (v. 7), §41; Luke of Steiris, §95.29; Paul of Latros, §25.28. The words ἐχθρός and πολέμιος could be used together – see, e.g., Anastasios of Persia, *Roman Miracle*, §7.9: *the enemy and the foe of Humankind* (ἐχθρὸς καὶ πολέμιος τυγχάνων τοῦ ἀνθρωπίνου γένους).

[603] See 1 Peter 5:8. The Devil is called *The Opponent* (ἀντίδικος) in the following *Lives*: Symeon the Holy Fool, 61.4; Phantinos the Younger, §22.8; Euthymios the Younger, §33.5.

[604] Alypios Stylites, §14.21; Sabbas the Younger, §39.19.

[605] See Zech. 3:1; 2 Thess. 2:4. St. Basil the Great translates the Hebrew name "Satan" as *The Opponent* or *The Adversary* (ὁ ἀντικείμενος) (Basilius Magnus, "Homilia quod Deus non est auctor malorum", 351D–352A: *Satan bears this name because he opposed the Good; because this is the meaning of the word in the language of the Jews* (Σατανᾶς μὲν οὖν, διὰ τὸ ἀντικεῖσθαι τῷ ἀγαθῷ· οὕτω γὰρ σημαίνει ἡ φωνὴ τῶν Ἑβραίων). On the use of this term in works of the Church Fathers and the later Byzantine theological tradition, see Greenfield, *Traditions of Belief*, 30 and n. 113. It is used in the following hagiographical texts: Anastasios of Persia, §13.8; Anastasios of Persia, *Roman Miracle*, §9.3; Eustratios of Agauros, §9 and §26; John the Psichaites, §5; Paul of Latros I, §25.35, §38.11 and passim.; Luke of Steiris, §45.9.

[606] See Greenfield, *Traditions of Belief*, 30ff.

deceit) and ἀπατεών, and the adjective ἀπατηλός (*producing illusion*). These terms in Greek imply the idea of the gullibility, of the inadequate intelligence of the object of the deception — for this reason, in modern Greek, the verb απατώ/απατάω means *to cheat* (on one's husband or wife.) Since the noun *serpent* (ὁ ὄφις) in Greek is masculine, it is not surprising that demons that appear in this form are often tempters who lead women into sin. Probably because of the emerging sexual connotations, the words having this root are not among the most common in Byzantine hagiography of the period under study.[607] The authors show a preference for synonyms, usually borrowed from the Scriptures, like *lead astray/mislead* (πλανῶ),[608] *lie/liar* (ψεύδομαι/ψεῦδος, ψευδής),[609] *entice* or *bait* (δελεάζω),[610] *cunning contrivance to de-*

---

[607] In a slightly ironic sense, the anonymous author of the *Life* of Paul of Latros says that the demons made unsuccessful efforts to deceive the Saint, pretending to be angels (Paul of Latros I, §17.4–5). The verb ἀπατάω, the noun ἀπάτη and the adjective ἀπατηλός are used to describe the deceitful operations of the demons in the following hagiographical texts: George of Choziba, §10.55.16–17 (where the author refers to Cain, *deceived* by the Devil); Nikephoros of Medikion, §1.24; Paul of Latros I, §41.12; Antony Kauleas, §22 et al. The noun ἀπατεών as an epithet of the Devil see, for example, in Martyrs of Amorion (v. 7), §41.

[608] See 1 Tim. 4:1: *deceitful spirits and teachings of demons* (πνεύμασιν πλάνοις καὶ διδασκαλίαις δαιμονίων); Rev. 12:9: *the deceiver of the whole world* (ὁ πλανῶν τὴν οἰκουμένην ὅλην); Rev. 20:8: *to deceive all the nations* (πλανῆσαι τὰ ἔθνη πάντα). The words with the root πλαν- are prevalent. For example, the author of the *Life* of St. Stephen the Thaumaturge §33 says: *Deceitful villains are the demons, always misleading liars*. See also Symeon Stylites the Younger, §160.37 (ἡ πλάνη τοῦ διαβόλου), §221.44 (τῆς τῶν δαιμόνων πλάνης) et al.; Anastasios of Persia, §33.14; George of Choziba, §10.48.14 (σατανικὴ πλάνη καὶ χλεύη τοῦ ἐχθροῦ); Phantinos the Younger, §10.9, where the Devil is called *The Misleading One* (ὁ πλάνος); *demonic misleading* (πλάνη) are characterize magical practices (see Anastasios of Persia, §16.4; Theodore Graptos, §2.27–29), idols and, heresies (Symeon Stylites the Younger, §188.14, Anastasios of Persia, §7.17–18, §33.8 and passim; Patriarch Tarasios, §13.25; Patriarch Nikephoros, §47; Demetrianos of Cyprus, §1.

[609] See John, 8:44 (ψεύστης); Acts 5:3 (ψεύσασθαι). On the demons of Falsehood and their aerial tollhouse, see Basil the Younger, Part II, §15.

[610] Symeon Stylites the Younger, §18.15; Bakchos the Younger, §1.9; Sabbas the Younger, §5.14.

ceive/deceitful/deceit (δόλος/δολερός/δολιότης),⁶¹¹ crooked/to act as a crook (σκολιός, σκολιεύω),⁶¹² knavish/knavish trick/ knavery (πανοῦργος/πανούργευμα/πανουργία).⁶¹³

4. Interestingly, the hagiographers occasionally refer to the Devil also by epithet *resourceful, inventive* (πολυμήχανος),⁶¹⁴ applied by Homer in an entirely positive sense to Odysseus.⁶¹⁵

5. **Death**. The most critical consequence of Original Sin was the loss of immortality. After the expulsion of Adam and Eve from Eden, God ordered a cherub with a fiery sword to guard the tree of life; thus, all humankind was punished by death.⁶¹⁶ Since the

---

⁶¹¹ See, for example, Alypios Stylites, §12.18; Symeon Stylites the Younger, §223.14ff: *unclean and cunning spirit* (ἀκάθαρτον καὶ δόλιον πνεῦμα); George of Choziba, §10.52.20, where the Devil is called *the cunning polluter of our life* (ὁ δόλιος καὶ λυμεὼν τῆς ζωῆς ἡμῶν); Antony Kauleas, §12, where the *envy* (φθόνος) and the *cunning deceit* (δόλος) of the Devil led to the expulsion of the first humans from Eden and the loss of their immortality; Sabbas the Younger, §40.19, where the Devil is called *The Cunning One* (ὁ δόλιος); Anastasios of Persia, §3.1, where the Devil is called *the malicious and cunning Enemy of the pious people* (ὁ βάσκανός τε καὶ δόλιος τῶν εὐσεβῶν ἐχθρός; Anastasios of Persia, *Roman Miracle*, §10.1 and §11.12, where the demon which possessed the daughter of a wealthy Roman bishop is *cunning* (δόλιος) et al.

⁶¹² The adjective σκολιός means in Greek *crooked* in both senses (*curved, bent*, and, metaphorically, *unrighteous, dishonest*). In its non-metaphorical meaning, it is frequently used for rivers, their shape reminiscent of reptiles. The word stem σκολ- is usually associated with demonic dragons, most of which live in rivers or, more generally, in water basins, at least in hagiography. On this relationship, see Greenfield, *Traditions of Belief*, 31 and n. 121. Examples of the usage of these terms can be found in the following *Lives*: Peter of Atroa, §79.12ff, and §79.17ff: *after the dragon crooked* (σκολιευσαμένου τοῦ δράκοντος); Euthymios the Younger, §13.4ff: *the renegade dragon, the crooked adviser, the Artful One* (ὁ ἀποστάτης δράκων, ὁ σκολιόβουλος καὶ κακότεχνος); Nikephoros of Medikion, §13.19: *of the crooked and manifold serpent* (τοῦ σκολιοῦ καὶ πολυμόρφου ὄφεως); David, Symeon, and George, §10.25: *of the crooked dragon* (τοῦ σκολιοῦ δράκοντος). It must be noted that in modern Greek, the word *skouliki* (σκουλίκι) means *a worm* and is frequently used as an insult for people who act dishonestly.

⁶¹³ Anastasios of Persia, §5.8 and §13.5; Phantinos the Younger, §1.18.

⁶¹⁴ Euthymios the Younger, §32.14.

⁶¹⁵ See for example Homer, *Iliad*, IV.358, VIII.93 and passim; Homer, *Odyssey*, X.488, XI.405 and passim.

⁶¹⁶ Gen. 3:22 and 24. See and Wisd. of Sol. 2:24; Mat. 19:28; John, 8:44; Rom. 5:12; Heb. 2:14. On the Devil as an angel of the Death, see Langton, *Essentials of Demonology*, 56; Langton, *Satan, a Portrait*, 19ff; Greenfield, *Traditions of Belief*, 47ff; Stewart, *Demons*

Devil was the one who deceived Eve and brought destruction to her and her husband, he is frequently called *the Enemy of our life* (ὁ ἐχθρός τῆς ζωῆς ἡμῶν),[617] the *Murderous One* (μιαίφονος),[618] the *Murderer of the mortals* (βροτοκτόνος).[619] Different terms from the word stem φθειρ-/φθορ- (*to corrupt, to spoil*)[620] and φον- (*to murder*) are also common.[621]

Finally, the evil spirit could be described with some epithet that indicates that it is a particular harmful influence. A typical example is the *unclean demon of the visions* (θεωρητικὸν πνεῦμα ἀκάθαρτον). According to the author of the *Life* of St. George of Choziba, this creature *settled in the man's eyes and skull and opened his physical and spiritual eyes to misleading and harmful visions.*[622]

* * *

After committing Original Sin, a difficult period began for the offspring of Adam and Eve. Expelled from the Garden of Eden and separated from its Creator, Humankind was subject to the power of the Devil, who gathered the souls of the dead in his kingdom, Hell. The people who lived between Adam and Christ are frequently represented in theological and hagiographical works as slaves who have been sold to the Tyrant.[623]

---

and the Devil, 141. The concept that the Devil became the prime source of death through Original Sin is detailed in the *Life* of St. George of Choziba, §10.51.10ff.

[617] George of Choziba, §3.13.3.
[618] Stephen the Younger, 123.7.
[619] Gregory of Dekapolis, §65.3in.
[620] *To corrupt, to spoil* (φθείρω): Euthymios the Younger, §13.5; *corruptor, seducer* (φθορεύς): George of Choziba, §10.51.20; *soul-corrupter* (ψυχοφθόρος): Stephen the Younger, 111.4; Peter of Atroa, §31.8; Euthymios the Younger, §20.9; Paul of Latros II, §33.3; Phantinos the Younger, §9.18.
[621] *Murderous* (φονικός and φόνιος): George of Amastris, §5; Gregory of Dekapolis, §30.4.
[622] George of Choziba, §10.51.7-9: ἐκαθήται τῇ τε ὁράσει καὶ τῷ κρανίῳ τοῦ ἀνθρώπου καὶ τὴν βλεπτικὴν αὐτοῦ ὅρασιν τὴν σωματικήν τε καὶ τὴν ψυχικὴν διανοῖγον πρὸς θεωρίας πεπλανημένας καὶ βλαβεράς.
[623] See Rom. 5:14-15 and 21; Rom. 7:14; Gal. 4:3-11. On the Devil and the demons as *tyrants* (τύραννοι), see Greenfield, *Traditions of Belief*, 49ff (esp. n. 179-81); Stewart, *Demons and the Devil*, 141ff.

Satan, the demons, and their servants (pagan rulers, heresiarchs, heretical emperors, etc.) are also called *tyrants,* and the verb *to tyrannize* is frequently explicitly used for demonic possessions.[624] Before Christ, only a few prophets and righteous people knew God; all others lived in the spiritual darkness spread by false gods and idols, called, as we have already mentioned, *daimonia* (δαιμόνια).

The hagiographers made standard use of a few Biblical stories in which the Devil played a crucial role. The first of these narratives is the story of Job, who was deprived of his wealth, children, and health by Satan with the permission of God.[625] This motif is very popular in Byzantine art,[626] and many hagiographical texts refer to or make allusions to it. A case similar to Job, for example, is that of St. Symeon the Younger, when God allowed the Devil as a winged Ethiopian to spread the plague above Antioch in 541.[627] Even more typical is the *Life* of St. Philaretos the Merciful, the grandfather of Maria of Amnia, who married Emperor Constantine VI (780–797) in 788/9. According to the text, this Paphlagonian nobleman was wealthy and blessed with a good, though slightly shrewish, wife, and beautiful daughters and granddaughters. He showed much sympathy and compassion towards the poor and the needy and regularly gave them food and money. However, God decided to test him and permitted the Devil to impose trials, *like Job.*[628] Consequently, his estate was plundered by Arabs, and he was left with only one field, a horse, an apiary, and a vast, old, empty house. Despite all his misfortune, the pious man did not fail in spirit. He continued to give easily and generously to those in need from the little property he had left, and the reward finally

---

[624] See, e.g., Patriarch Germanos, §26; Stephen the Younger, 110.27, 106.4 and passim; Peter of Atroa, §15.14 and §60.21; Niketas of Medikion, §19; Empress Theodora, §5.5–8; Luke of Steiris, §89.21 and §94.40 and passim.

[625] Job 1:6–2:7.

[626] See Provatakis, *The Devil,* 54–56. The Devil in the story of Job is usually depicted in Byzantine art in three ways: a black, usually winged member of the heavenly hierarchy; a prosecutor in the trial against Job; and as a tempter in various animal forms.

[627] See Symeon Stylites the Younger, §124.13–34, where the Saint loudly reads the Book of Job to his flock; §124.69ff, where the Devil appears before God and He permits him to spread the plague; §125., where the Saint fights against the Devil.

[628] Philaretos the Merciful, 115.20–23ff.

came. Imperial envoys visited his home and took his granddaughter Maria to court; she won the bride show organized for the young Emperor Constantine VI and was chosen to marry him. The emperor restored her grandfather's family to its former wealth and position.[629]

Another viral Old Testament story about demonic temptation is the story of Joseph and the wife of his Egyptian master Potiphar. In the original biblical version, Joseph, son of Jacob, was sold as a slave by his brothers. His new master was the commander of the Pharaoh's guard, Potiphar. Soon, with God's help, the young Jew proved himself a capable and energetic servant and was appointed chief of the whole household by his master. But the wife of Potiphar was a lustful woman possessed by carnal desire and tried to seduce the handsome youth. When she saw that her *wily words* (τὸ ῥῆμα τὸ πονηρόν) would not persuade him to betray his master, she accused him of trying to rape her, and Potiphar unjustly threw him in jail.[630] There is no mention of the Devil or his servants in this story. According to the Byzantine hagiographers, Satan was the driving force of the temptation to which Joseph was subjected.[631] A good example can be found in the *Life* of St. Elias the Younger. In the 830s, the inhabitants of Sicily were constantly tormented by Arab raids. The Muslim armies mercilessly attacked and plundered the island's coastal areas. The misfortune fell upon the young John (whose secular name was Elias), who lived with his parents in the fortified town of St. Mary. The young boy was imprudent enough to go outside the town's wall alone. The Arabs captured and sold him as a slave to a Christian fur merchant in North Africa.[632] The reader has the impression that from this point on, the narration leaves the

---

[629] On the marriage of Maria of Amnia and Constantine VI, see Petrinski, *The Bride-Shows*, 37–72. For other mentions of the story of Job, see the following hagiographical texts: John the Merciful, 380.5ff; George of Amastris, §13; Patriarch Nikephoros, §84; Patriarch Tarasios, §47.17 and §58.22–23; Peter of Atroa, §79.17ff; Elias the Younger, §45; Demetrianos of Cyprus, §1; Nikon Metanoeite, §19.4–7.

[630] Gen. 39:1–20.

[631] See, e.g., Elias the Younger, §12 (ἡ ἀσελγὴς ἐκείνη τοῦ διαβόλου μαθήτρια (*that adulterous female student of the Devil*).

[632] The story is set in the second half of the 830s. On the date of the main events in the text and on the political and military developments in Sicily during this troubled period, see Vasiliev, *Byzance et les Arabes*, 1: 127–31.

ninth century, forgets about Arabs and Christians, and goes back to Biblical times. Like Joseph, John won his master's trust and was made the overseer of the whole household. But the *envious demon, who hates the Good*, attempted to destroy him. Satan planted an insatiable sexual desire for the youth in his master's wife, and she tried to seduce him while her husband was away. However, the young man, afraid for his soul, remained unflinching and was accused of attempted rape before his master. The denouement of this dramatic story, so similar to that of Joseph, differed from the Biblical original. The adulterous woman was caught in her own trap. Her husband soon discovered her with a lover, kicked her out of the house, and restored his faithful slave John to his previous position.[633] The story of John-Elias and the lustful wife is a typical example of the mechanism of Byzantine literary thinking. The line between truth and fiction, between the real world of the Arab invasions in Sicily and the mythical times of Joseph and Potiphar, is thin and often blurred. The point of fusion, the bridge that connects the centuries, is *the One, who always envies the faithful*, i.e., the master of the demons, the Devil. The adventures of John/Elias in North Africa are by no means an isolated example; many other stories about various temptations, especially sexual ones, are constructed on the model of Gen. 39:1–20.[634]

From the dark period between the expulsion of Adam and Eve and the advent of Christ, humankind inherits the ancient false gods, the "daimonia", but also pagan philosophy. The attitude of the Byzantine hagiographers towards the ancient literary and philosophical heritage is highly complex and multilayered, and we will not study it in detail. In

---

[633] Elias the Younger, §§9–14. In this text, the Devil is mentioned as the primary source of the trials to which John/Elias was subjected (§10); for the analogy with Joseph, see ibid., 14 (§9), 16 (§11), and §12. The anonymous hagiographer indirectly refers to Joseph's story, using the same terminology as the Book of Genesis. See, for example, the verb *to mock at* (ἐμπαίζω) both in Elias the Younger, §13 and in Gen. 39:14, and the adjective *evil* (πονηρός) in Elias the Younger, §12 and in Gen. 39:9.

[634] See Stephen the Younger, 101.17–27; Pancratius of Taormina, 360.32–361.1; Patriarch Nikephoros, §84, where the Iconoclast heresy, rejected by the Patriarch, is likened to the wife of Potiphar; Patriarch Tarasios, §21.4ff; Gregory of Dekapolis, §70.4–6; Antony Kauleas, §6; Demetrianos of Cyprus, §1; Elias Speleotes, §22.

some texts, however, the Devil and his demons are directly or indirectly linked to philosophy and rhetoric. One of the most naturalistic examples of the demonization of the ancient intellectual heritage is found in the *Life* of St. John the Psichaites. As a young monk, the future Saint was extremely studious, but he only paid attention to theological texts. According to the anonymous author, he considered such things as word order, the peculiarities of dialects, and Homer's silly talk about harnessing and unharnessing of chariots utterly useless subjects. In his opinion, especially the Homeric *epos* was full of *myths, and fictions, and worship of demons* (τῶν μύθων καὶ πλασμάτων καὶ δαιμονίων σεβασμάτων). Equally negative was the Saint's attitude toward the art of rhetoric; John's speech was naturally bedecked by the Truth and needed no stylistic embellishments. The hagiographer says that for this holy man, grammar, logic, and the other *sophisms* could conceal the lies of ancient philosophy, untouched by the light of the true God, *as a cobweb, which covers a heap of excrement, could save somebody from getting his feet dirty*.[635] Even well-educated hagiographers show this attitude. Nicethas the Philosopher, the author of the *Life* of Patriarch Antony Kauleas (893–901), despite his highly elaborate style, ironically compares the Saint's Christian virtues and great contributions to the Church with the philosophy, built on false foundations, of Socrates, Plato, Solon, and Epimenides.[636]

Adam and his offspring were subjected to the power of Satan and death, justly and deservedly, because of Original Sin. However, God never forgot the crown of his Creation and, as predicted,[637] sent His Son to Earth. To achieve the salvation of Humankind, the Devil himself must be deceived. Christ was born in a cave, and the Tyrant tried to find Him in vain. The next attempt to avert the fulfillment of Isaiah's prophecy was the Massacre of the Innocents,[638] and infanticide is a popular motif in the hagiography of the period under study. It was also a powerful propaganda weapon. A typical example is the legend of the iconoclast Emperor Con-

---

[635] John the Psichaites, §4.
[636] Antony Kauleas, §6.
[637] Isa. 7:14.
[638] Mat. 2:16–18; cf. and Jer. 31:15.

stantine V (741–775), who, according to the *Life* of St. Stephen the Younger, used to sacrifice small children to demons in the St. Mavra church that demolished near Constantinople.[639] The Devil's third attempt to remove the Son of God from his path involved the Temptations (πειρασμοί) in the desert, in the Temple, and on the Mountain, which is one of the most popular themes in Byzantine art.[640] There is almost no more widespread topos in hagiography. Satan and the demons are constantly tempting all the saints in every possible way, and the "desert"[641] is the usual place where demons appear.[642] One of the most typical allusions to Satan's attempt to tempt Christ is in the *Life* of St. Theodore Sykeotes. Already as a twelve-year-old boy, the future Saint was preparing himself to retire to the desert when by chance he encountered one of his classmates, Gerontios, who led Theodore to a rocky place at the edge of a bottomless precipice. There they started talking, and Gerontios turned the conversation to his friend's decision to dedicate his life to God. He slyly challenged him to test God's benevolence and to jump off the cliff. "It is deep, and I am scared!" exclaimed Theodore. Then Gerontios, who had never been very brave before, calmly stepped over the edge, smoothly landed on the bottom, and shouted to his friend to do the same — there was nothing to be afraid of. Horror-stricken and already full of suspicion, Theodore felt a firm hand grasp his shoulder and drag him away from the edge; this hand belonged to his guardian, St. George, who revealed to him the real identity of his false schoolmate. "Gerontios" was the Devil himself, who had

---

[639] Stephen the Younger, 165.18–21. See and *Georgii Monachi Chronicon*, 2: 751.20–752.11; *Excerpta historica*, 155.

[640] On the depiction of the Temptations, see Provatakis, *The Devil*, 56–58.

[641] The English word "desert" means "arid land with usually sparse vegetation". In Greek, however, the semantic field of the word ἔρημος is broader, and the noun means "wilderness", i.e., any uninhabited area (a desert, a forest, a mountain). The word *hermit* (from the Greek ἐρημίτης) denotes a man who retires from society and lives in solitude. This concept, as we have already mentioned, was largely inadmissible for ancient philosophical thinking since the abnormal state of reclusion deprived humans of their very essence as social beings (ζῷα πολιτικά). On the wilderness as a "demonic space" par excellence, see Part Four, Chapter 2, §1.1.

[642] See, for example "Vies et récits d'anachorètes", 93ff; Ioannikios (*Peter*), §20; Paul of Latros I, §11; Nikon Metanoeite, §17.27ff.

tempted him as he had Christ. If he had jumped from the precipice, he would have lost his soul since none is allowed to test God.[643] It must be stressed that this sinister story is strongly influenced by rhetorical narrative theory, a standard topic in Byzantine schools of this period. The text is full of implications that something was wrong with the whole chain of events — Theodore meets his schoolmate by chance (!), then, again by chance, this schoolmate initiates a conversation about the might of God, and finally, he jumps into the abyss, and nothing happens to him.

Between Original Sin and the redemption of the world through the death and the resurrection of Christ, Satan had temporary power over Earth; for this reason, the demons are often called "cosmocrators". The Temptations of Christ culminated when the Devil showed Him all the kingdoms on the earth and offered to subject them to Him.[644] In Byzantine hagiography, the image of the demon-king is relatively popular,[645] but the authors' attitude to this power is unmistakably ironic. For example, the demon who possessed the daughter of the bishop in the *Roman Miracle of St. Anastasios of Persia* claims that he is a crowned Emperor (βασιλεύς) who rules the air and the earth and commands innumerable armies. Nevertheless, a mere youth in love with some girl took him prisoner by magic, wrapped him in a fig leaf, and forced him to obey his orders. To the ironic comments of the monks, the demon replied angrily: *Don't you dare to mock me, because I'm a king and it's my right to rule!*[646]

Christ holds power over the Devil's servants, and the latter's position as King after the advent of the Son of God is an illusion. This is evident from numerous passages in the Scriptures, frequently referred to by the hagiographers. The authors directly quote the Miracle of the Swine[647] or allude to it to demonstrate the demons' pathetic weakness.[648] Accord-

---

[643] Theodore Sykeotes, §11.
[644] Mat. 4:1–10; Marc 1:13; Luke 4:1–13.
[645] See, e.g., Ioannikios (*Peter*), §53; Ioannikios (*Sabbas*), §32.
[646] Anastasios of Persia, *Roman Miracle*, §6.11–12.
[647] Mat. 4:1–10; Marc 1:13; Luke 4:1–13.
[648] On the pathetic impotence of the demons, *who failed to gain total power even over the herd of swine*, see, e.g.: Peter of Atroa I, §20.20 and §79.19.

ing to the Gospel texts, in the region of Gergesa, Christ met a man[649] possessed by a "Legion" of unclean spirits who lived in the tombs, and none could restrain him, even with a chain. Christ expelled them from their victim but permitted them to enter into a large herd of pigs; due to their malignant influence, the swine *rushed down a steep slope into the sea and drowned there*.[650] The hagiographers often mention tombs and graveyards as typical dwelling places of unclean spirits and their victims,[651] demons in the shape of pigs,[652] and legions of demons.[653] Though less frequently, they refer to another episode of the New Testament where the Pharisees accused Jesus of working with Beelzebub.[654] For example, St. Peter of Atroa had to defend himself against the same unjust accusations from the part of envious clerics.[655] The episode is also used by the authors as a metaphor. It was quoted by St. Ioannikios the Great to soothe the Patriarch Methodios (843–847), who was forced to bear and repel the attacks of the Zealot party.[656]

The passages of the New Testament, in which Jesus delegates His power over evil spirits to his twelve[657] or seventy-two[658] disciples, are of

---

[649] Two men, according to Mat. 8:28.
[650] Mark 5:1–12.
[651] See Part IV, Chapter 2, §2.1.
[652] See Part III, Chapter 3, §4.2.
[653] See Part II, Chapter 2, §3.
[654] Mat. 9:32–34 and 12:22–32; Marc 3:20–30; Luke 11:14–21.
[655] Peter of Atroa, §37.1–15 (the Biblical text is quoted in 37.8).
[656] Ioannikios (*Sabbas*), §47.
[657] Mat. 10:1: *Then Jesus called his twelve disciples to him and gave them authority over unclean spirits, so that they could drive them out and heal every disease and every illness* (καὶ προσκαλεσάμενος τοὺς δώδεκα μαθητὰς αὐτοῦ ἔδωκεν αὐτοῖς ἐξουσίαν πνευμάτων ἀκαθάρτων ὥστε ἐκβάλλειν αὐτά); Mark 3:15: *and to have the authority to drive out demons* (ἔχειν ἐξουσίαν ἐκβάλλειν τὰ δαιμόνια) and 6:7: *giving them authority over unclean spirits* (καὶ ἐδίδου αὐτοῖς ἐξουσίαν τῶν πνευμάτων τῶν ἀκαθάρτων); Luke 9:1 *and gave them power and authority over all the demons and to heal diseases* (ἔδωκεν αὐτοῖς δύναμιν καὶ ἐξουσίαν ἐπὶ πάντα τὰ δαιμόνια καὶ νόσους θεραπεύειν). In the hagiographical texts of the period under study, these Gospel passages are not frequently quoted as the basis of the saints' power over evil spirits (see, e.g., Phantinos the Younger §21.17ff; Niketas of Medikion §17). A possible explanation is that absolute authority over demons was bestowed exclusively on the Apostles, to whom the saints cannot be considered equal.

utmost importance for the image of the saints and their eternal enemies. According to the Gospel of Luke, He says to His disciples: *Look! I have given you the authority to trample on snakes and scorpions and to destroy all the enemy's power, and nothing will ever hurt you.*[659] This quote is one of the most frequent arguments for the power of holy persons over the forces of Evil.[660] For these forces, the Apostle Luke metaphorically uses the images of poisonous animals (snakes, scorpions) and, as we will see below, demons standardly appear in these forms in hagiography.

The Crucifixion of Christ is the final attempt of the Devil against the Son of God and His mission. In addition, with the Death and the Resurrection of Jesus, Satan was finally and ultimately deceived, and Humankind was redeemed. Evil was devoid of power over mortals, whose souls were doomed to Hell because of the Original Sin.[661] Since Christ was the sinless Son of God, he was unjustly taken to the Abyss. His descent into Hell and subsequent victory over the Devil reopened the gates of Heaven for the righteous. With the Advent of Christ, humans ceased to be the slaves and hostages of Satan.[662] The latter's power along with the pagan cults and religions, which he inspired, were brought down by the triumph of the Church. However, the impotence of the forces of Evil to gain ulti-

---

[658] Luke 10:17-19: *The 70 disciples came back and joyously reported, "Lord, even the demons are submitting to us in your name! He told them, "I watched Satan falling from heaven like lightning. ¹⁹ Look! I have given you the authority to trample on snakes and scorpions and to destroy all the enemy's power* (Ὑπέστρεψαν δὲ οἱ ἑβδομήκοντα [δύο] μετὰ χαρᾶς λέγοντες, Κύριε, καὶ τὰ δαιμόνια ὑποτάσσεται ἡμῖν ἐν τῷ ὀνόματί σου. εἶπεν δὲ αὐτοῖς, Ἐθεώρουν τὸν Σατανᾶν ὡς ἀστραπὴν ἐκ τοῦ οὐρανοῦ πεσόντα. ἰδοὺ δέδωκα ὑμῖν τὴν ἐξουσίαν τοῦ πατεῖν ἐπάνω ὄφεων καὶ σκορπίων, καὶ ἐπὶ πᾶσαν τὴν δύναμιν τοῦ ἐχθροῦ).

[659] Luke 10:19.

[660] See, e.g., Symeon Stylites the Younger, §41.30; Stephen the Younger, 149.7-8; Gregory of Dekapolis, §9.5; Ioannikios (*Peter*), §20.

[661] "Sheol" in Hebrew. On this point, see Gen. 37:35 and 42:38; Num. 16:30; Job 14:13; Ps. 15:10, 54:16, and 62:10; Isa. 38:10. For more detail on all souls being taken to Hell before the Advent of Christ and on Christ's victory over the powers of the Evil and Death, see Greenfield, *Traditions of Belief*, 56-67. Greenfield refers to the most important theological works; Provatakis, *The Devil*, 72ff (on iconography); Stewart, *Demons and the Devil*, 142.

[662] See Gal. 4:1-11.

mate victory increased the envy of the Devil and his servants towards Humankind, to which the gates of Eden were once again open. This is a common concept in hagiographical texts. For example, in the *Life* of St. Anastasios of Persia, the anonymous author says:

> The consubstantial Son of God pitied Humankind, which was subjected to the tyranny of death and destruction. He left the Heavens and descended from them, as it is written, became a slave through His Nativity, communed with the people, gave them everything needed for their Salvation, and with His own Death, destroyed the one who had power over Death.[663]

The Devil and his servants no longer have any real power, but this does not prevent them from ensnaring through deceit those who are weak and susceptible to earthly pleasures and sin. Emperor John VI Kantakouzenos (1347–1354) compares Satan to a convicted criminal, who sits locked in his cell and expecting his imminent execution, but is still alive for a little while.[664]

The Devil's malicious activities are directed not only against individuals but also against the Church and the Salvation of Humankind as a whole. According to the hagiographers of the period under study, their most deadly instruments were the various heresies supported by corrupt tyrants. In the period between the sixth and the tenth centuries, the most lethal danger to the Orthodox Church was undoubtedly Iconoclasm. The surviving *Lives* of the saints are powerful propaganda weapons in the struggle against this heresy, and the authors of the eighth and ninth centuries use standardized images of Evil to demonize the emperors Leo III, Constantine V, Leo V, and Theophilos, who actively persecuted Orthodox monks and priests.

According to New Testament eschatology,[665] Satan's complete and eternal downfall will come with the end of this world, Doomsday. Shortly

---

[663] Anastasios of Persia, §1.1–7.
[664] Joannes Cantacuzenus, "Pro Christiana religione contra sectam Mahometicam apologiae IV", in MPG, vol. 154 (Paris, 1866), 481A. On this passage, see also Greenfield, *Traditions of Belief*, 66 (with English translation), and Stewart, *Demons and the Devil*, 143.
[665] Mat. 24; Marc 13; Luke 21:7ff; Rev., passim.

before this event, the Devil will send one of his servants to tempt as many people as possible and rob them of their salvation. However, in the end, he will ultimately be defeated and thrown into Hell for eternity along with the sinners. According to Orthodox theologians, this will be the end of the "sacred history" of our world.[666]

---

[666] See also Greenfield, *Traditions of Belief*, 72–76; André Guillou, *Le Diable Byzantin* (Paris-Athènes: Daedalus, 1997), 27–31.

Part Three
FORMS, TRANSFORMATIONS, AND INFLUENCE OF THE DEMONS

INTRODUCTION
„POLARIZATION" AND PARODY IN THE IMAGE OF THE DEMON

The modern movie industry, both in the USA and in Europe, makes large-scale use of one particular image of Evil, which Norman Cohn calls the "inner demon".[667] The hidden demonic creature, the vampire, the werewolf, is often well-integrated into society, well-dressed, wealthy, even, sometimes, fabulously rich. It knows how to conceal its abilities and true nature and always acts with the utmost secrecy. Its distinctive characteristics are hardly recognizable to anyone other than the exorcist, its highly specialized eternal enemy. An ordinary person would scarcely notice anything abnormal beyond a random act of cruelty, a flash of a long canine gleaming in the bright moonlight, or some seemingly insignificant expression of weird behavior. This evil creature, whose roots can be traced back to the troubled and hysterical time of the wars of religion and the Great Witch Hunt (the fifteenth to the seventeenth centuries), is much more influenced by the Old Testament and, above all, by the "apocalyptic" Book of Revelation than by the Gospels. We are used to reading Anne Rice-like novels or watching movies where the Devil is the mighty and resourceful fallen Angel who has nothing to do with the pathetic and usually dumb evil spirit of the New Testament. To medieval man, this image would be unusual,[668] and for a good reason. As we mentioned in the preceding part, after the Advent of the Son of God, and especially after His Crucifixion and Resurrection, the Devil and his servants were stripped of their previous power, and all that remained of their might was a mere reflection, an apparition. This apparition is as harmless as the ghosts of the fallen soldiers in the battle of Marathon, but it can be deadly to those who are susceptible to sin or who are simply naïve. The Byzantine demon is rarely ca-

---

[667] Norman Cohn, *Europe's Inner Demons: An Enquiry Inspired by the Great Witch-Hunt* (Sussex and London: Sussex University Press and Heinemann Educational Books), 1975.
[668] Cf. Muchembled, *Une Histoire du Diable*, 51–66. On the Byzantine demon as a weak creature, see Mango, *Empire*, 163.

pable of hiding and always abides *inside* a person, never *among* people.⁶⁶⁹ His outer appearance is relatively easy to recognize by its abnormality — the *excess and shortcoming* of Plotinus.⁶⁷⁰ His eyes could be bloody or squinting; he is too tall or too short; his skin is often black; he smells terrible; his behavior is openly aggressive. The evil spirit is usually silly and weak and it is relatively easy to attract and expel it.

The pathetic and not very smart demon, able only to deceive the ignorant with heresies and temptations, is often a subject of parody, not only in the *Lives* of the saints, but also in the whole of medieval literature in both the East and the West.⁶⁷¹ One of the most typical examples of this trend is the *Life* of St. Leo of Catania. In this text, the *devil-master of the air* is reported to ride a doe (ἡ ἔλαφος), and the impious mage Heliodorus waits for him sitting upon a pagan tombstone (στήλη).⁶⁷² For the modern reader, these details may sound insignificant. For the medieval audience of the text, however, they are openly parodic. The doe is one of the symbols of Christ and Heliodorus perversely resembles a stylite sitting on his pillar (στῦλος). The world of Evil is a *monde à l'envers*, a parodic and distorted imitation of the world of the Good. Beyond the stylistic aspects of such descriptions, we can only speculate about the Platonic roots of this idea in post-Greco-Roman Byzantine culture. Good and the Evil share the same eidos, the same tree in the Garden of Eden, but the emanations (μιμήσεις) of this eidos are antithetical. After Christ, humans are free to recognize and

---

⁶⁶⁹ Probably the only story in the Byzantine hagiography of the seventh to the eleventh centuries in which demons hide in a crowd, without being recognized, comes from the *Life* of St. Paul of Latros (900–955). According to this text, during the ceremonial relocation ("*translatio*") of the Saint's holy relics, the Devil couldn't endure the piety of the gathered spectators and assumed the image of a monk. He then began to bang stones loudly together to disturb the ceremony, but the Saint himself appeared and chased him away. The demons of his venue, hidden in the crowd, asked the people who had scared away their master. *God's soldier* was the answer (see Paul of Latros I, §46).

⁶⁷⁰ Plotinus, *Enneads*, I.8.4.9–10.

⁶⁷¹ On parodies of the demon in the West, see Tsotscho Bojadschiew, *The Night in the Middle Ages* [Bulgarian: Цочо Бояджиев, *Нощта през средновековието*] (Sofia: Sofi-R, 2000), 284ff.

⁶⁷² See Kazhdan, *History of Byzantine Literature*, 1: 300ff. In Medieval Greek, the words στῦλος (pillar) and στήλη (tombstone) differ only in suffix and grammatical gender, while the pronunciation is almost identical.

accept Truth and the Good; some of us, though, choose the distorted imitation and subject ourselves to the perverse and false power of the Devil.

The story of Heliodorus is by no means the only example of spoofing Evil in the hagiography of the period under study. The monks in the *Roman Miracle of St. Anastasios of Persia* mock a demon bragging about his armies and royal power; in fact, he is an insignificant pipsqueak, so weak that a mere youth managed to wrap him in a fig leaf and blackmail him.[673] Shortly before his execution, St. Elias of Heliopolis laughs at the black demon who appears in his dream and threatens him with a giant sword, because he already sees the crown of martyrdom prepared for him.[674] The demon of adultery is tortured terribly by the prayers of St. Ioannikios the Great. The creature begs the Saint to allow it to leave, but the Saint mockingly invites it to stay a little longer.[675] In the *Life* of St. Irene of Chrysobalanton, demons use the grotesque as a weapon; in their attempts to disturb her prayer, they twist and contort their bodies to make her laugh, ape her gestures like mimes, and make various silly jokes.[676] St. Luke of Steiris disdainfully calls the Devil "Louse" (ὁ Κονιδάριος) when he appears to him in the shape of a filthy black imp.[677] In the hagiographic texts of the period under study, evil spirits take the form of a dwarf much more often than that of a giant or a sinister zoomorphic creature.

The Byzantine demon is not "supernatural" in the modern sense of the word. He has no real magical powers, and all his actions are mere tricks or optical illusions. This concept is in full accordance with one of the most important postulates of Christian theology –only God's power can perform miracles. In St. John of Damascus's opinion, to accept the ability of the *strigas*, i.e., the witches, to separate their souls from the bodies means to mock Jesus Himself, who did this only once in His earthly life.[678]

---

[673] Anastasios of Persia, *Roman Miracle*, §6.4–15.
[674] Elias of Heliopolis, §12.
[675] Ioannikios (*Peter*), §28.
[676] Irene of Chrysobalanton, §11.
[677] Luke of Steiris, §68.
[678] Joannes Damascenus, "De draconibus", 1604.

CHAPTER 1
THE ELEMENTS OF THE DEMONIC IMAGE

The hagiographic text presumably reflects Christian dualism, the exact distinction between Good (God and angels) and Evil (Devil and demons). However, how strictly an author adheres to theological postulates depends on their abilities and knowledge of theology. Many hagiographers, especially before the tenth century, were poorly educated people who covered folklore traditions with a thin veneer of learned canons. Commenting on the information that hagiography can give about the dogmatic views of icon-worshipers in the eighth and the first half of the ninth centuries, Ihor Ševčenko makes the following analogy: "we should no more expect doctrinal information from them than we expect information on Leninism from a biography of a Soviet partisan hero of World War II".[679]

The difference between Good and Evil, between the world of Light and the world of Darkness, between God and Satan, between angels and demons, is undoubtedly clear to hagiographers as an abstract idea. However, it fades out of recognition when a supernatural being must appear in a particular image, especially a human image. There is widespread uncertainty in determining whether some supernatural creature belongs to God's realm or the Devil's kingdom. When they reveal themselves in human form, the outer appearances of demons and angels are the opposite sides of the same literary-folkloric image.

Unlike angels, who are sexless and therefore presented only as eunuchs,[680] demons usually have emphatically male or, much more rarely, female features. Gender is also a *differentia specifica* of some categories of demons. Thus, Pseudo-Psellus argues that the two middle categories of evil spirits, the aquatic and the terrestrial, can take whatever im-

---

[679] Ševčenko, "Hagiography", 127.
[680] Angels often appear as white-clad eunuchs in the hagiographical texts (see, e.g., Symeon Stylites the Younger, §135.4–7ff). On the demon's clothing, see Part III, Chapter 1, §2.

age they want; however, they show certain proclivities.⁶⁸¹ According to this author, terrestrial demons (χθόνιοι δαίμονες) usually prefer to appear as males. They hate moisture and live in dry, waterless places.⁶⁸² Byzantine hagiography, however, makes almost no connection between male demons and arid areas. Although in most cases, they inhabit caves, this can by no means be accepted as a principle — for example, according to the *Life* of St. Eustratios of Agauros, in the early ninth century a frightful demon in the form of a giant black Ethiopian settled in a river called Gorgytes (Γοργύτης) north of the city of Prussa (Bithynia).⁶⁸³ The "philosophical" criteria provided by the demonological treatises do not allow for a correct typology of the hagiographic material.

As we will see, Byzantine hagiographers speak mostly of male demons. The few surviving images of evil spirits in Byzantine art confirm the thesis that both their sex and gender, according to Byzantine notions, are presumably male.⁶⁸⁴

1. Organismic: the demonic body

1.1. The metamorphoses of ugliness

We already outlined above the critical concept of *kalokagathia* (καλοκἀγαθία), the harmonious combination of physical beauty and spiritual virtue. It has often been claimed that Christianity, especially Orthodox Christianity, destroyed this principle or at least radically transformed it, putting in its place a peculiar "esthetics of the ugliness",⁶⁸⁵

---

[681] Pseudo-Psellos, "Timothée ou des demons", ed. Paul Gautier, "De daemonibus de Pseudo-Psellos", *Revue des Études Byzantines* 38 (1980): 169 (ll. 543-45): *The aquatic and the earthly* [demons] *can change their many forms* (Ὑδραῖοι δὲ καὶ χθόνιοι ... δύνανται μὲν μορφὰς ἐξαλλάττειν πλείους, πλὴν αἷς ποτε χαίρουσι, ταύτας ὡς ἐπίπαν ἐμμένουσιν.)

[682] Pseudo-Psellos, "Timothée ou des demons", 171 (ll. 548-50): Ὅσοι δὲ τόποις ἐνδιατρίβουσιν αὐχμηροῖς ὑπόξηρά τε τὰ σώματα ἔχουσιν..., εἰς ἄνδρας οὗτοι σχηματίζουσιν ἑαυτούς; see Vakaloudi, *Magic*, 112.

[683] Eustratios of Agauros, §29. On the demon-Ethiopians, see below.

[684] See Provatakis, *The Devil*, 112-23.

[685] Myrto Hatzaki, *Beauty and the Male Body in Byzantium: Perceptions and Representations in Art and Text* (New York: Palgrave Macmillan, 2009), 67-73.

where spiritual might and grandeur abide in the body of a pious monk, deformed by fasts and vigils, in the image of the bloodstained corpse of Christ, or even in the rotten flesh and the putrefying wounds of some old hermit.[686] This is true, but not entirely. In fact, except for some particular forms of ascesis, in Byzantine culture, beauty remains the emanation of the Good and God, and ugliness continues to be a distinctive feature of Evil and the Devil. In other words, the image of the vampire Lestat from the movie *Interview with a Vampire*, with his refined and exaggerated beauty, long blond hair, and soft white skin, would have been entirely incomprehensible to our medieval ancestors.

Today, maybe due to gender stereotypes, the expression "beautiful man" sounds somehow weird — we would prefer the adjective "handsome". "A man must be a little more beautiful than a monkey", an old Russian proverb says. By contrast, beauty in Byzantium, at least as a philosophical and theological concept, is almost utterly desexualized since it is essentially a virtue of the soul, and the soul has no gender or sex — it is a "neuter" quality. A person can be truly beautiful in body only when their soul is virtuous. The (male) beauty, so thoroughly studied by Myrto Hatzaki, is predominantly a matter of proportion and moderation. The beautiful body, male or female, must be neither too tall nor too short in stature; its parts must be symmetrical, and its skin must be snow white.[687]

On the other hand, physical ugliness is associated with spiritual degradation and, ultimately, with Evil. The deformed and foul-smelling black male giant or dwarf, dressed in clothes that are too shabby or too rich, is the perfect and standard image of Evil.[688] However, there is a significant terminological difference between the ugliness of a human being and that of materialized evil spirit and its victims. The "de-formity" of human ugliness is evident from the word stem associated with it in Byzantine and modern Greek. The adjective ἄ-σχημος (*ugly*, lit. *formless*) and the verb ἀ-σχημίζω (*to deface, to disfigure*, lit. *to deform*) denote and ac-

---

[686] Elias Speleotes, §20.
[687] For the elements of stereotyped male beauty in Byzantium, see Hatzaki, *Beauty*, 8–14.
[688] Hatzaki, *Beauty*, 34–37.

centuate the lack of natural harmony between the various parts of the human body as a **subject**. The characteristic qualities of the image of Evil are the same, but the terminology is different. The demon is not ἄσχημος, but ἀνείκαστος (*unattainable by conjecture, indescribable*) and δυσειδής (*shapeless, difficult to discern, torturous for the eye*). The demon is ugly, but his ugliness has no stable material form. It lies only in human perception, and the evil spirit remains an **object**. Describing the demons that had come to take her soul, Theodora, the pious servant of St. Basil the Younger, stresses precisely the impression they made on her:

> I saw clearly multitudes of Ethiopians ... contorting in mockery their black and gloomy and dark faces, the mere sight of which alone seemed to me most terrifying and more bitter than even the *Gehenna of fire*. For it would be better for a living person to fall into that *Gehenna of fire* than to hear and see such things.[689]

Because the adjective δυσειδής concerns perception, the authors usually do not clarify it. When the future Patriarch Antony Kauleas (893–901) lit by chance upon two *hideous* (δυσειδεῖς) figures near the pit where the decapitated bodies of executed criminals were usually being disposed of, the author of the text does not consider it necessary to further enrich his description of their hideousness — it is just "torturous for the eye".[690] The ugliness of the human is what it is. The ugliness of the demon is what we see and what we *want* to see because the feeling of horror is strictly subjective and depends wholly on one's own fears. This concept is not at all that far from the modern Western mentality. It is visible in the sinister "It" of Stephen King's novel of the same name, where the ancient alien

---

[689] Basil the Younger, Part II, §6.28–29 and §6.34–37: ἑώρων καθαρῶς πλήθη Αἰθιόπων... διαστρέφοντας χλευαστικῶς τὰ μέλανα ἑαυτῶν ζοφώδη τε καὶ σκοτεινὰ πρόσωπα, ὧν ἡ θεωρία καὶ μόνη φρικωδεστάτη καὶ πικροτέρα μοι ἐφαίνετο καὶ αὐτῆς τῆς Γεέννης τοῦ πυρός. Κρεῖσσον γὰρ ἦν ἵνα ζῶν τις εἰς αὐτὴν ἐμπέσῃ τὴν τοῦ πυρὸς Γέενναν, ἢ ἵνα τοιαῦτα ἀκούῃ καὶ ὁρᾷ. For other examples, see "La version longue de la vision du moine Cosmas", 84.82–83, where the adjective ἀνείκαστος is used; Cyrillus Alexandrinus. "De exitu animi, et de secondo adventu", in MPG, vol. 77 (Paris, 1864), 1073C, where the image of the demons that judge the human soul is *more tormenting than the whole of Hell*.

[690] Antony Kauleas, §20.

monster chooses different forms according to each child's individual terror, or in the tortures which take place in Room 101 in George Orwell's famous novel *Nineteen Eighty-Four*, adapted to the deepest fears of each victim.

On the other hand, the idea of the δυσειδής and ἀνείκαστος demon is relatively complex and complicated. To be suitable for the average reader or hearer, the image of the evil spirit cannot remain entirely formless. It must be adapted to the standard concepts of human ugliness. Even though they do not use terms like ἄσχημος for the evil spirits, the authors strictly adhere to the typical physical traits of the ugly male body and hyperbolize these features to the point of the grotesque.

1.2. Disproportions: excess and deficiency

One of the essential elements of the stereotypical image of the ugly demon is the absence of proportion and measure in his height. In its material form, the evil spirit is almost always either too tall and heavily built or too short and thin. However, the demon-giant and the demon-imp are parts of complex mythological and folklore traditions that cannot really be explained in esthetic terms. The Biblical, and hence the theological, prototype of the demon-giant is undoubtedly Goliath, the mighty enemy of David, who reportedly was six feet and one span tall.[691] In the Old Testament, the battle between the future king of Israel against the Philistine warrior is presented as a struggle undertaken in the name of Jehovah.[692] This inspired the Byzantine hagiographers to use Goliath as a symbol and allegory of warlike demonic power. A typical example of the frightful giant as a personification of evil passions can be found in the *Life* of St. George of Amastris. According to this text, the future Saint constantly struggled against the assaults of demonic temptations, whose symbol was Goliath.[693] Like King David, Patriarch Antony Kauleas (893–902) is also

---

[691] I Sam. 17:4–51.
[692] I Sam. 17:45: *Then David told the Philistine, "You come at me with a sword, a spear, and a javelin, but I come to you in the name of the Lord of the Heavenly Armies, the God of the armies of Israel whom you have defied".*
[693] George of Amastris, §38.

said to have defeated not the material Goliath but *that Goliath, visible only with the spiritual eye, the wicked and incorporeal demon*.[694] In the *Life* of St. Theodore of Stoudios, the eminent abbot is like a new David, who fights against the demonic iconoclasts, represented allegorically as the Philistine warrior.[695]

Goliath is a part of the text of the Scriptures officially accepted by the Church. However, behind the image of the demon giant, we can also discern the apocryphal tradition, well-studied by Archie T. Wright in his book on the origin of evil spirits in early Jewish literature.[696] In one of the most controversial passages of the Book of Genesis, the story of the ancient giants is briefly told. According to this text, they were born of the intercourse between angels and the daughters of the men.[697] but no other information on the subject is provided. The whole story is described in much more detail in the already-mentioned apocryphal Book of Enoch, part of which is preserved in Greek under the title The Watchers. As specified by this text, two hundred angels, the so-called "Watchers",[698] led by Azazel and Shemhazai, defiled themselves (ἤρξαντο μιαίνεσθαι) by sexual intercourse with the daughters of men. Terrible giants (γίγαντας μεγάλους)[699] were born of this impure and unnatural communion.[700] They ate every bit of the food the humans were producing, but it was still impossible for them to be sated. As a result, these frightful creatures began to eat men, women, and children alike.[701] The world was filled with

---

[694] Antony Kauleas, §23: *against the intellectual Goliath, the evil and incorporeal spirit* (κατὰ τοῦ νοητοῦ Γολιάθ, τοῦ πονηροῦ καὶ ἀσάρκου δαίμονος).

[695] Theodore Studites, §24.

[696] On the rebelion of the angels in the Book of Enoch, see Wright, *Origin of Evil Spirits*, 11–50. Cf. Conybeare, "Christian Demonology", II, 75ff.

[697] Gen. 6:1–4.

[698] In the Greek text, the term is ἐγρήγοροι (*wakeful*). On the question of terminology in general, see Wright, *Origin of Evil Spirits*, 16. On the three possible interpretations of the Hebrew expression *Bene-Elohim*, see ibid., 97–104.

[699] *Apocalypsis Henochi Graece*, ed. Matthew Black [Pseudepigrapha veteris testamenti Graece 3] (Leiden: Brill, 1970), 7:1 and 8:3, 9:8-9.

[700] On the impurity of this act and the four possible explanations, see Wright, *Origin of Evil Spirits*, 130ff. According to Wright, the most plausible explanation is that the angels polluted themselves with menstrual blood.

[701] *Apocalypsis Henochi*, 8:3ff.

violence, terrible crimes, and bloody wars. God, along with His archangels, decided to end this horror. The Archangel Raphael was ordered to put Azazel and Shemhazai in chains and to play the other giants off against each other.[702] After their violent deaths, these scions of the angels and mortal women became invisible evil spirits (πνεύματα πονηρά) who bring humans all kinds of sorrows, injustices, and ordeals.[703] The giants are also mentioned on other occasions in the Old Testament. According to Deuteronomy 3:11, the last of them was King Og of Bashan, whose iron bed was *nine cubits long and four cubits wide*. The story of the wicked giants and their origin attracted the interest of Origen, among others. The early Christian theologian claims that *some evil demons exist, the so-called "titanic" or "gigantic" demons*.[704]

The Byzantine hagiographers of the period under study were undoubtedly well-acquainted with the passages from the Book of Genesis and the fascinating story of the giants. The apocryphal Book of Enoch was also a relatively well-known text in the Middle Byzantine period. The Greek version, edited by Matthew Black, is preserved in two manuscripts, one from the sixth and the other from the eleventh century, and was also incorporated in the highly popular chronography of George Synkellos, written in the late eighth or early ninth century.[705] The story of the giants and their evil ghosts significantly influenced the development of the demonic images in the *Lives* of the saints from the sixth to the tenth centuries.

Since the demon in Byzantine hagiography is chiefly considered a weak and low creature, demonic giants are relatively rare. One full description of such a frightful monster is preserved in the *Strange and useful vision of the monk Cosmas* (tenth century). According to this text, in a dream the elderly monk Cosmas traveled to Hell. There he saw a *giant*

---

[702] *Apocalypsis Henochi*, 10:4–9.
[703] *Apocalypsis Henochi*, 15:8–12.
[704] Origen, *The Philocalia*, ed. Joseph Robinson (Cambridge: Cambridge University Press, 1893), §20.19.1–3: δαίμονές τινες φαῦλοι (ἵν᾽ οὕτως ὀνομάσω) τιτανικοὶ ἢ γιγάντιοι.
[705] *Georgii Syncelli Ecloga chronographica*, ed. Alden Mosshammer (Leipzig: Teubner, 1984), 11.20– 17.27. Cf. Hristova, *The Book of Enoch*, 14.

man, black in appearance, with a weird face. His right hand was stunted, but the left was as thick as a column, bare, and exceptionally long. With this hand, he clutched the sinners and flung them into a bottomless pit.[706] Such monstrous demons could be found not only in descriptions of Hell but also occasionally in the earthly world. For example, a story of this kind is told in the *Life* of St. David, Symeon, and George. While reading the Scriptures, St. Symeon (*c*. 764/5–844) suddenly heard the roof creaking. When he looked up, he saw a human-like giant with an iron rod in his hand. With a threatening voice, the monster told Symeon that, despite his well-known victories over Evil, the holy monk would not be able to defeat him. Symeon answered that he was a humble man, but God's might was with him. That holy power would help him expel every evil spirit. Symeon then made the sign of the Cross, blew against the demon, and the latter immediately disappeared.[707] Much more detailed is the description of the *lord of the demons* (ἄρχων δαιμόνων), who was chased away from his "property" by St. Ioannikios the Great between 825 and 829.[708] The author describes him as a giant with legs like columns who angrily strode towards the holy monk and was about to assault him.[709] Here the material body of the demon is obviously a sign of its high standing as a *lord*. The giant stature is also an element in the image of the black demon-Ethiopian[710] and demon-warrior. For example, St. Michael Maleinos, the uncle of Emperor Nikephoros II (963–969), reportedly saw a great battle between the Byzantine and the Bulgarian armies in his dream. Suddenly, two huge men emerged from the two fighting forces, and their duel decided the battle's outcome.[711] In this case, the Bulgarian warrior was black and his Byzantine opponent was white. The vision was a

---

[706] "La version longue de la vision du moine Cosmas", §§83.112–84.119.
[707] David, Symeon and George, §11. See Abrahamse and Domingo-Forasté, "Life of David, Symeon, and George", 169 and note 132.
[708] On the dating of the events in the *Life* of St. Ioannikios the Great see above, Part One, Chapter 2, §4.
[709] Ioannikios (*Peter*), §53; Ioannikios (*Sabbas*), §32.
[710] See, e.g., Eustratios of Agauros, §29; Elias Speleotes, §44; Theodora of Thessalonica, §50.
[711] Michael Maleinos, §20.

prophecy about one of the Tzar Symeon's campaigns between 914 and 923.

More often, though, the distinctive physical trait of an evil spirit's material form is its excessively short stature. Short demons and demons in the shape of children are common in the hagiography of the period under study. This stereotype is undoubtedly a part of the ironic attitude towards the pathetic and deformed spirit, wholly subjected to the holy power of God and the saints. As we have already mentioned, Christ defeated Satan decisively, humiliated him, and enslaved him, making him a prisoner who awaited Doomsday and his punishment. In consequence of this idea, demons are often depicted as slaves on ancient stelae, and their height is about half that of the angels and the saints.[712] This peculiarity could be explained theoretically by the First Epistle of St. John, which says, *You belong to God and have overcome them because the one who is in you is greater than the one who is in the world.*[713] According to the words of the Apostle, God and his servants are *greater* and *bigger* than the Devil since the Greek comparative adjective μείζων means both. As early as the sixth century, in the *Life* of St. Symeon Stylites, the holy man was attacked on his pillar by a sinister demon; the winged creature had a small child's face.[714] The image of the demon-child remains in later hagiography, but its functions become clearer; it is usually associated with various illnesses, especially death. In the *Life* of St. Peter of Atroa (†837), an evil spirit, who had infected a sinful monk with leprosy, appears in the form of an ugly and foul-smelling little boy clad in shabby rags.[715] According to the *Strange and useful vision of the monk Cosmas*, most of the demons

---

[712] On the short stature of the demon in Byzantine art, see Provatakis, *The Devil*, 273–80; for a brief theoretical survey of this concept in the biblical tradition, see ibid., 273–75.

[713] 1 John, 4:4: ὑμεῖς ἐκ τοῦ θεοῦ ἐστε, τεκνία, καὶ νενικήκατε αὐτούς, ὅτι μείζων ὁ ἐν ἡμῖν ἢ ὁ ἐν τῷ κόσμῳ.

[714] Symeon Stylites the Younger, §39.4ff. For the dating, see Van den Ven, *La Vie ancienne*, 1: 113*ff.

[715] Peter of Atroa, §70.19–22. Cf. the black dwarf (ἐν σχήματι μέλανος ἀνθρωπίσκου) who entered the cell of St. Luke of Steiris according to his *Life*, threatened the future Saint, and left (Luke of Steiris, §68).

surrounding the deathbed of the ill abbot are also black dwarfs and represent the Death itself[716]

A short or gigantic stature is but one element of the stereotyped ugliness of the Byzantine demon. The evil spirit belongs to a different world, a distorted antipode of the Earth, where horror, death, and sin reign. Given this, the parts of its material body — the limbs, the eyes, the face, the voice, and the clothing — are entirely devoid of harmony, out of proportion, and weirdly distorted. The key word here is indeed the adjective "weird". In English, "weird" denotes everything both strange, inexplicable, and unnatural. In general, this "otherness"[717] of the demonic image and the supernatural is discernible in modern literature and the film industry. It is sufficient to recall the inhabitants of the Red Room in *Twin Peaks*, written by the famous David Lynch. Their speech is a weird and slow drawling, there is always some minor but annoyingly out-of-place element, and their actions obey only their own distorted and incomprehensible logic. The descriptions of demons and evil spirits in Byzantine literature are by no means so polished and refined as Lynch's screenplays, and the weird "otherness" is always evident and exposed, even parodic and grotesque. One of the best examples is the *black headless and formless demon*[718] who infected a boy with fever or plague in the *Life* of St. Symeon the Younger.[719]

The bodies of the demon and his victims are deformed and mutilated as a consequence of sins committed, and, in response, every sin or crime leaves an imprint on the perpetrator's body in the form of some deformity or illness. Today this idea is mainly about sexually transmitted diseases like syphilis and AIDS, which are primarily considered to be the

---

[716] "La version longue de la vision du moine Cosmas", §84.82–83.
[717] The term *otherness* comes from Byron, *Symbolic Blackness*, 51. See Bojadschiew, *The Night in the Middle Ages*, 266ff.
[718] Symeon Stylites the Younger, §231.75ff: *some demon, black and formless, who happened to be also headless* (δαίμων τις μέλας καὶ ἀειδής, ἀκέφαλος τυγχάνων). On the image of the headless black demon, see Part Three, Chapter 2, §1.
[719] On this personification of the demon of the plague, see Theodor Dimitrov, "Fever-Demon or Plague-Demon? Toward a new interpretation of v. Sym. Styl. J. 231", *Etudes Balkaniques* 4 (2015): 15–22.

logical result of immorality and promiscuity. Apart from the numerous examples of this concept in ancient times, maybe the most typical case in hagiography is the venereal disease which slowly killed Emperor Alexander (912–913) due to his sinful life.[720] However, in Byzantium, the so-called "mirror punishments" [721] were not reserved for sexual vice alone. The *Ecloga*, the primary law code of the Middle Byzantine period (edited in 726), is based on the principle that the punishment must reflect the committed crime. For example, for perjury under oath, the tongue must be cut off,[722] theft is often punished by severing the hand,[723] the penalty for bestiality is castration,[724] and the face of the adulterer must be mutilated by cutting off the nose.[725] Today, this postulate is applied in the Muslim *Shariah*.

The concept of "mirror punishments" is also related to the material forms of evil spirits. The demons are fallen angels, and their downfall is reflected in their bodies. One of the best examples of this concept can be found in the *Life* of St. Basil the Younger, in which the outer appearance of the demons corresponds to the particular vice or sin they personify. For example, the demon of Heartlessness and Cruelty appears to be *ossified by a most grievous disease, and as if wailing on account of his wicked-*

---

[720] Patriarch Euthymios, §21.
[721] On the "mirror punishments" ("ποινές-κάτοπτρα"), see Konstantinos Pitsakis, "Some thoughts on the 'mirror punishments' in the Medieval Greek space", in *Tolerance and Repression in the Mid-Byzantine Period*, ed. Katerina Nikolaou [Greek: Κωνσταντίνος Πιτσάκης, "Μερικές σκέψεις για τις «ποινές-κάτοπτρο» στον Ελληνικό μεσαιωνικό χώρο", in *Ανοχή και καταστολή στους μέσους Βυζαντινούς χρόνους*, ed. Κατερίνα Νικολάου] (Athens: Institute of Byzantine Research, 2002), 285–312. On the idea that the sycophants are liable to the same punishment that would be imposed on their victims, see Giorgos Kaouras, *Byzantium: Sexual crimes and Their Punishments* [Greek: Γιώργος Καούρας, *Βυζάντιο. Τα ερωτικά εγκλήματα και οι τιμωρίες τους*] (Athens: Periplous, 2003), 217ff. On the penalties which the demons impose on the sinners in Hell, see Lambakis, "The Descents into Hell", 43ff; Lambakis quotes the apocryphal texts, Revelation of Peter and Revelation of Thomas.
[722] *Ecloga. Das Gesetzbuch Leons III. und Konstantinos' V*, ed. Ludwig Burgmann, [*Forschungen zur Byzantinischen Rechtsgeschichte* Band 10] (Frankfurt: Löwenklau Gesellschaft, 1983), §17.2.
[723] *Ecloga*, §17.10–14, §16, §18.
[724] *Ecloga*, §17.39.
[725] *Ecloga*, §17.27–28, §30-31, §34 and passim.

ness, with contorted face and grin countenance, clearly carrying around himself the forms and characteristics of the passions he ruled over;[726] the chief demon of Homosexuality and Pederasty appears as a savage pig, surrounded by foul odor.[727] In the *Strange and useful vision of the monk Cosmas*, the right hand of the evil giant who casts the souls of the sinners into the river of fire, is stunted and useless, which is an allusion to the Right side of God, where the righteous will stand on Doomsday.[728] Very rarely, the demon could take the grotesque form of a single body part. For example, a Devil's servant in the image of a human hand tried to disturb the prayers and the solitude of St. Symeon Stylites the Younger on his column between 533 and 541/2.[729] The evil spirits often possess not the whole body and mind of humans, but their limbs or organs, paralyzing and deforming them.[730] In the *Life* of St. Symeon Stylites the Younger, a demon entered and wrenched the tooth of an old man, and it had to be extracted.[731] In the same text, another old man was overtaken by a great misfortune caused by an evil spirit. While working in his orchard, he heard his wife calling him. Thinking that the voice belonged to her, the man turned and responded, but the demon, who had taken her shape, was already gone. However, the very contact with the evil creature caused a terrible bodily deformation; he found that his penis and testicles hung down to the level of his knees. In great pain, the old man managed somehow to reach the monastery of St. Symeon on the Admirable Mount. The future Saint miraculously cured him, and his groin returned to normal.[732] The painful experience of the old man is probably a typical example of "mirror punishment" since the whole story alludes that by answering his

---

[726] Basil the Younger, Part II, §40.3-7: ὡς ἀπὸ τῆς ἄγαν ἀσπλαγχνίας αὐτοῦ φαίνεσθαι αὐτὸν ὑπὸ βαρυτάτης νόσου κατεσκληκότα καὶ ὥσπερ ἀποκλαιόμενον ὑπὸ τῆς ἐνοικούσης αὐτῷ κακίας, τζιγραίνοντά τε καὶ δριμυσσόμενον, καὶ τῶν ὧν ἐξῆρχε τὰ σχήματα καὶ τὰ ἰδιώματα ἐν ἑαυτῷ περιφέροντα.
[727] Basil the Younger, Part II, 32.5-9.
[728] "La version longue de la vision du moine Cosmas", §84.116-117.
[729] Symeon Stylites the Younger, §39.14-16.
[730] Pseudo-Psellos, "Timothée ou des demons", 157-59 (ll. 360-74).
[731] Symeon Stylites the Younger, §120.11-14.
[732] Symeon Stylites the Younger, §167.1-34.

wife's call, he responds to sexual desire, something unsuitable for one his age and therefore constitutes a sin. Consequently, the demon injures the "guilty" part of the body.

1.3. Impurity and filth

As we mentioned above, one of the most common epithets for the evil spirit is *impure* (πνεῦμα ἀκάθαρτον). Theoretically, this impurity of the Devil and his servants is not material but spiritual and is caused by Satan's downfall and his rejection of the divine light.[733] In Late Antiquity, however, this idea fused with Neoplatonic concepts of matter as the lowest level of existence and with the ancient ideal of *kalokagathia*. In this way, material filth reflected spiritual impurity in the Christian conceptual system. This is evident, for example, in the works of Origen, according to whom, *after their fall from Heaven, the demons wallow in the dirt of the earth, among the thickest material bodies*.[734] In the Byzantine hagiography of the period under study, the corruption and the spiritual uncleanness of the demons are directly related to the physical filth of their material form.

For this reason, the evil spirit is often defined as αἰσχρός, which means spiritually, morally, and physically *unclean*; this adjective could be used, for example, for unlawful sexual intercourse,[735] impure thoughts,[736] or filthy lucre.[737] The same word could also denote that ugliness caused by a lack of care for the body and is associated with dirt, stench, and unkempt clothing.[738] Foul odor (δυσώδεια, δυσώδης) especially is one of the most common elements of the demonic image. According to the *Life* of St. Basil the Younger, bad smell is associated with sexual vices in particu-

---

[733] See Hesychius Hierosolymitanus Presbyterus, "Ad Theodumum sermo compendiosus animae perutilis, de temperantia et virtute", in *MPG*, vol. 93 (Paris, 1865), 1500–1501A. Cf. Gokey, *Terminology*, 152–70; Greenflied, *Traditions of Belief*, 27ff.

[734] Origen, *The Philocalia*, §20.19.

[735] See, e.g., Symeon Stylites the Younger, §169.10 (αἰσχρὰ μῖξις γυναικός); Nikon Metanoeite, §59 (ἀκάθαρτοι ἡδοναί).

[736] See, e.g., Paul of Latros II, §25.12; Phantinos the Younger, §33.16.

[737] Antony Kauleas, §12. In modern Greek, αισχροκέρδεια is a legal term and means *profiteering*.

[738] Peter of Atroa, §70.19–22.

lar. In this text, the tollhouse of Homosexuality and Pederasty is full of a *foul odor, extensive and bitter and painful*,[739] and that of Adultery is *abominable and foul-smelling*.[740] In the latter case, the author uses a specific stylistic device parodically, in a way typical of Byzantine mentality and literature in general. The perfect participle ῥεραντισμένον (sprinkled) is an allusion to Psalm 50 of the Septuagint (51 in the Protestant Bible), where the same verb (ῥαντίζω) is used.[741] The same verb is used both for the filthy clothing of the repulsive demon of adultery, sprinkled with froth and blood, which symbolizes the abominable sin, and for the sinner, who has been sprinkled with the sacred *hyssop* and thus made clean from vice.

A foul odor and rotting flesh give away the presence of an evil spirit in the body of one possessed, and the demon himself could also come out of his victim in the form of *foul-smelling, rotten* blood or entrails. An interesting source of this superstition is the *Life* of St. Symeon Stylites the Younger. The anonymous author tells the story of a leprous soldier living in the small town of Suros on the Euphrates. Despite his illness, he decided to visit the local *thermae*, and one of his fellow troopers loudly urged their comrades in the bathing chamber to forbid him the use of the same water as them and to chase him away from the premises. Divine punishment for this sober lack of sympathy was quick and merciless. The healthy soldier soon fell ill with the same terrible disease but with even more severe and painful symptoms. His flesh rapidly fell off his bones, his face became unrecognizable, and his nose rotted to such a degree that he was about to die of asphyxiation.[742] Stricken with this terrible misfortune, he understood his sin and sincerely repented. Salvation came fast. God sent a man who advised him to ask Symeon Stylites for help, and the holy

---

[739] Basil the Younger, Part II, §32.8–9: περὶ δὲ κύκλῳ αὐτοῦ δυσωδία πολλὴ καὶ πικρὰ καὶ ἐπώδυνος.

[740] Basil the Younger, Part II, §33.5: μυσαροῦ ἐκείνου καὶ δυσώδους τελωνείου.

[741] Psalm 50:9 (Septuagint): *Cleanse/Sprinkle* (ῥαντιεῖς) *me with hyssop, and I will be clean; wash me, and I will be whiter than snow* (ῥαντιεῖς με ὑσσώπῳ, καὶ καθαρισθήσομαι· πλυνεῖς με, καὶ ὑπὲρ χιόνα λευκανθήσομαι).

[742] Symeon Stylites the Younger, §219.14–19.

man agreed to expel the demon who had infected him with the disease. During the ritual, the anonymous author says, every vein in the poor sinner's body looked as if it had been cut open by the invisible hand of some physician, as in the medical procedure of phlebotomy, and rotten, foul-smelling blood gushed out of his palate. In this way, his body was healed and cleansed from demonic influence, and the illness disappeared.[743]

There are other descriptions of the same type in this text: the foul-smelling water gushing out of some possessed man's stomach,[744] for example, or the exceptionally foul odor emanating from the body of some sinner threatened by demons.[745] Such stories continue to be present in the hagiographic tradition of the following four centuries. The demon of voluptuousness, who tormented St. Gregory of Dekapolis in the caves of Isauria (southeastern Asia Minor) in the second quarter of the ninth century, left his body through a deep gash in his stomach in the shape of rotten and stinky entrails.[746] The dwellings of evil spirits, like wells[747] or graves,[748] are usually associated with a foul smell caused by the Devil's presence. Hell is fetid as well.[749]

According to the hagiographical texts, demons are particularly attracted by feces as the ultimate form and symbol of death. For example, an evil spirit appears as excrement in the *Life* of St. Theodora of Thessalonica (812–August 29, 892). According to this text, shortly after her death, the Saint saved a possessed youth named Gregory from an evil spirit by pulling something which resembled human excrement out of his

---

[743] Symeon Stylites the Younger, §219.39–54. It must be observed that leprosy is traditionally attributed to demonic influence only when it strikes a sinner as a punishment. In the next paragraph, the author refers to the story of a leprous citizen of Antioch named Theodoros, whose illness is not caused by an evil spirit.

[744] Symeon Stylites the Younger, §245.

[745] Symeon Stylites the Younger, §222. For other such stories, see Symeon Stylites the Younger, §212 (a foul-smelling ulcer on a small boy's leg); §227.4–9 (the leg of an inhabitant of Isauria, utterly devoid of flesh, whose bone was black and foul-smelling).

[746] Gregory of Dekapolis, §10.3–12.

[747] See, e.g., Nikon Metanoeite, §27.5.

[748] George of Choziba, §3.13.48ff; David, Symeon, and George, §22.22ff.

[749] Phantinos the Younger, §31.5 (χῶρος καπνοῦ δυσώδους πεπλησμένος).

mouth.[750] An especially unpleasant and crude joke was played on St. Antony the Younger (785–865) during his hermitage on Mount Olympus (southwestern Bithynia). One night the pious monk was startled by someone loudly knocking on his cell door and asking him for a lighted candle. Antony thought that the nocturnal visitor was one of the monks of the nearby monastery and reached for a candle to give to him, but he found his hand full of excrement. He instantly understood it was a demonic trick and suppressed his sinful anger.[751] The hagiographical texts of the period under study also describe two cases of eating feces under the influence of a demon.[752]

* * *

Filth is not exclusively related to evil spirits in Byzantium. It could also signify exceptional holiness and complete ascesis. According to his *Life*, St. Gregory of Choziba (†625) used to eat only the leftovers of other monks' meals in his monastery. This scant and not very tasty food was brought to his remote cell in a foul pot full of worms, which was never washed.[753] In addition, George used to rummage in rubbish dumps and even lavatories and gathered all sorts of rags for his clothing.[754] Another example of the same concept is the dirty cassocks of St. Euthymios the Younger and his friend Joseph, who lived as hermits on Mount Athos between 859 and 863. Contact with filth was a trial of endurance and piety; Euthymios stayed, but his fellow was unable to endure the terrible conditions and left.[755]

---

[750] Theodora of Thessalonica, §51.
[751] Antony the Younger, §29. The event could be dated between 824 (the death of the rebel Thomas the Slav), when Antony was still a layman and an official of Emperor Michael II (Antony the Younger, §13), and 830, when, already a monk, he was prosecuted by Emperor Theophilos for embezzlement (Antony the Younger, §33).
[752] Stephen the Thaumaturge, §24; Elias the Younger, §73.
[753] George of Choziba, §2.6.
[754] George of Choziba, §3.12.6–8.
[755] Euthymios the Younger, §20.

2. Clothing and jewelry

Of the elements of nonverbal communication, clothing and accessories constitute the most crucial display of social status and cultural affiliation. Byzantine society inherited the complex social system of the later Roman Empire. The foundations of this system were solidified by the reforms of the emperors Diocletian and Constantine I in the late third and first half of the fourth centuries. The officials' hierarchy was strict, and every rank and title had its own "uniform". The fabrics, colors, and insignia are described in detail in the numerous "Kletorologia" (*Κλητορολόγια*), or lists of offices, and in the voluminous *Ceremonial Book*, compiled in the tenth century. This distinctive feature of Byzantine society influenced the images of angels and demons alike. Since the angels and the saints are the "officials" of God, the Emperor of emperors,[756] their clothes usually resemble the uniforms of the imperial court. Chitons are typically white and bear the so-called *tablion*.[757] This concept is clearly illustrated in mosaics and frescoes.[758] Since angels are sexless, they usually appear to mortals with the insignia of the offices reserved for eunuchs, like *praepositus* (provost of the sacred bedchamber)[759] and *cubicularius* (chamberlain).[760] A typical example is the *Life* of St. Patriarch Ignatios, where the regent

---

[756] See Mango, *Empire*, 151–55.

[757] The *tablion* was a rectangular or trapezoidal panel embroidered on Byzantine officials' ceremonial mantle (chlamys). It had a different color for every specific official rank.

[758] See, e.g., the image of the Archangel Gabriel on the mosaic in the apsis of the Panagia Angeloktisti church in Cyprus, dating from the sixth century (Nano Chatzidakis, *Greek Art – Byzantine Mosaics* [Athens: Ekdotike Athenon, 1994], 231 and fig. 22), where the Archangel wears a white chiton with gold embroidered stripes; see also the image of St. Demetrios in the St. Demetrios Church in Thessalonica, dating from the mid-seventh century, in which the Saint wears a snow-white chlamys with gold embroidered trimming and a blue-and-purple *tablion* (Chatzidakis, *Greek Art*, 230 and fig. 14).

[759] On the development of the title *praepositus sacri cubiculi*/*πραιπόσιτος* and its insignia, see Rodolphe Guilland, *Recherches sur les institutions Byzantines*, vol. 1 [Berliner Byzantinische Arbeiten, 35] (Berlin: Akademie-Verlag, 1967), 333–80 (for the period after the sixth century, see ibid., 338–65).

[760] On the development of the title *cubicularius*/*κουβικουλάριος* and its insignia, see Guilland, *Recherches sur les institutions*, 1: 269–82 (for the period after the sixth century, see ibid. 277–82).

Bardas sees in his dream two frightful angel-chamberlains, who led the young Emperor Michael III in chains before the throne of St. Peter to be judged.[761] More rarely, angels could appear in the outfit of clerics,[762] and saints could wear the uniform of some profession.[763]

Plain white[764] or (much more rarely) purple[765] clothes, usually shimmering and spreading light,[766] are also one of the most common distinctive features of the image of both saints and angels in hagiography. We have some clues that this concept also existed in the urban legends of the capital. According to the anonymous, semi-legendary *Narration of the construction of Holy God's Church named after Holy Wisdom* (ninth century),[767] one day the workers went to the official lunch organized by Emperor Justinian instead of eating at the construction site as usual. The

---

[761] Patriarch Ignatios, §28. Another example of a eunuch-chamberlain can be found in the *Life* of St. John the Merciful, 379.23–39.

[762] Theodora of Thessalonica, §51.

[763] See, e.g., Peter of Atroa, §36. According to this text, St. Cosmas and Damianos appeared as physicians in the dream of the possessed nephew of St. Peter of Atroa. The young man joined, c. 823, the army of the rebel Thomas the Slav against the lawful Emperor Michael II, and two "doctors" ordered him to leave the troops of the usurper immediately, go to Constantinople, and rejoin the army of the emperor.

[764] See, e.g., Symeon Stylites the Younger, §10.1–10, where a white-clad angel leads the six-year-old Symeon to his first hermitage in the Syrian desert; Symeon himself appears in a white mantle to the abbot John in a dream and announces his arrival at John's monastery (Symeon Stylites the Younger, §11.6); the three men who descended from Heaven according to the same text are dressed in snow-white clothes and their hair is like gold (Symeon Stylites the Younger, §129.97). See also John the Merciful, 368.6–369.10, where the angels who placed the good deeds on the scales after somebody's death are clad in white; John the Merciful, 352.14ff (a white-clad angel gives a purse with a hundred gold coins to John, the future Patriarch of Alexandria); Elias the Younger, §7 (St. Ananias appears as a horseman in white to Elias in his boyhood and promises to rescue him from the hands of the Arabs).

[765] Purple is the mantle worn by the two angels who visited St. Symeon Stylites the Younger during the devastating Persian raid in 540 (Symeon Stylites the Younger, §57.30).

[766] See, e.g., John the Merciful, 376.5–9B (a Christian is released from a Persian prison by an *angel in white, shining like the Sun*); Anastasios of Persia, §26.2–5 and Anastasios of Persia, Encomion by George Pisides, §28.11–12 (two white-clad, shining persons enter the cell of St. Anastasios, and he immediately recognizes them as angels).

[767] See the detailed analysis of Gilbert Dagron, *Constantinolpe imaginaire. Étude sur le recueil des «patria»* [Bibliothèque byzantine: études, 8.] (Paris: Presses Universitaires de France, 1985), 193ff (on the dating).

chief overseer Ignatios left his fourteen-year-old son to watch the tools. Shortly afterward, a beautiful eunuch with cheeks glowing with fire, clad in a snow-white shining mantle, appeared before the boy and ordered him to go immediately to his father and tell him to come back quickly with his crew and resume construction of the temple without further delay. He promised to remain on guard until the boy came back. When Ignatios heard the story, he was so impressed that he took his son to the table where the emperor was having lunch. Justinian showed him all the eunuchs of the court, but none looked like the one who had approached the child. When the ruler heard the detailed description of the alleged court messenger, he immediately understood that the visitor was, in fact, an angel. He showered the boy with precious gifts but sent him in exile in the remote Cycladic islands; in this way, the emperor made certain that the overseer's son would never again be near the Church and the angel would forever guard the building.[768]

White clothing is often the distinctive feature of the angels and distinguishes them from disguised demons. When St. Germanos of Kosinitza was visited in his homeland by a frightful person and was ordered to leave Palestine and to found a monastery in the remote region of Macedonia, the white clothing he wore was proof, and convinced the pious monk that he had an angel before him.[769] In another example, in the dream of St. Michael Maleinos, two fearful male figures, one white and one black, fight a duel to decide the outcome of a battle between the Byzantines and the Bulgarians.[770] However, in this case, the author does not specify whether the "whiteness" and "blackness" are related to the skin color of the two supernatural warriors or to their clothes.

Like the angels and the saints, demons also appear in distinguishable clothing, but they never wear any official insignia. Their garments are always either too lavish or utterly shabby and ragged, typical of the

---

[768] "Anonymi narratio de aedificatione templi S. Sophiae", ed. Theodor Preger, *Scriptores originum Constantinopolitanarum*, vol. 1 (Leipzig: Teubner, 1975), §10.36–40.
[769] Germanos of Kosinitza, §8.
[770] Michael Maleinos, §20. The battle was probably part of one of the campaigns waged by the Bulgarian tsar Symeon between 914 and 923.

"polarized" image of the Byzantine evil spirit. Since holy monks are usually dressed in rags as a sign of their striving for ultimate ascesis and humility, such attire could even create confusion. In the 820s, St. Ioannikios the Great was traveling to St. John Church near the city of Ephesus. When he got tired, he decided to rest in a small chapel by the road. Once inside, the holy monk came upon two men who were there to pray. On seeing the heavily-built former soldier with huge, glowing eyes, barefoot and attired in a shabby old cassock, they leaped back in fear. Ioannikios smiled kindly and explained that he was neither an *evil spirit* nor a *ghost* (πνεῦμα, φάντασμα) but just a man like them.[771] Relatively more common is the image of the lavishly dressed demon. The biblical archetype of this idea is probably the description of the Whore of Babylon in the Book of Revelation,[772] but resentment and suspicion of luxury and riches are based obviously on essential principles of the Christian religion, in which ascesis and abstinence play a crucial role. In addition, lavishness is closely associated with pride, and pride is the primary cause of the Devil's downfall. There are numerous examples of demons dressed in rich clothes and wearing precious jewels scattered throughout the Byzantine hagiography of the period under study. As a young boy in the late 520s, St. Symeon Stylites the Younger sees much gold and precious stones adorning carnal pleasures as a clay effigy covered with expensive jewels.[773] The elderly Arsenios, the spiritual father of St. Elias Speleotes (860/870–September 11, 960), says in this regard:

> The ones who externally decorate their bodies with red and white garments are internally full of hatred, and greed, and fleshly decay; they

---

[771] Ioannikios, (*Sabbas*), §11. According to the *Sabbas* version (see Ioannikios [*Sabbas*], §13), this event occurred during St. Ioannikios's journey from Ephesus to the Kundurian mountains (c. 800). The *Peter* version dates this event much later, to the reign of Emperor Michael II (820–829), when the Saint traveled to the same region again.

[772] Rev. 17:4: καὶ ἡ γυνὴ ἦν περιβεβλημένη πορφυροῦν καὶ κόκκινον, καὶ κεχρυσωμένη χρυσίῳ καὶ λίθῳ τιμίῳ καὶ μαργαρίταις.

[773] Symeon Stylites the Younger, §18.11–13: εἶδε... χρυσόν τε καὶ μαργαρίτην καὶ λίθον τίμιον ὡς πηλὸν τεθησαυρισμένον πρὸς τὴν τῶν ἡδονῶν κολακείαν. See Symeon Stylites the Younger, §27.41ff, where the future Saint advises monks against demonic temptations.

blacken their soul's face and undeservedly take God's bread in Holy Communion.⁷⁷⁴

Another "theoretical" explanation of the conceptual relationship between lavishness and demons can be found in Michael Psellus's *Life* of St. Auxentios (mid-eleventh century). According to this text, the so-called "flesh-loving" (φιλόσαρκοι) demons were particularly attracted to showily dressed women. However, the reason for this attraction was not sexual desire for such externally beautiful ladies. According to the great Byzantine humanist and philosopher, they felt great pleasure in making themselves comfortable in the deep folds of their opulent gowns and living there in the shape of snakes, driving them mad. In addition, says Psellus, these evil spirits were very fond of elegant hairstyles because they could settle in the curls in the same way.⁷⁷⁵ These childish superstitions are not mentioned by any other hagiographical source between the sixth and the tenth centuries, but, judging from works of art, they do not seem to stem from Psellus's imagination alone. For example, snakelike demons twine around the bodies of female sinners with curly hair in a fresco in the Panagia Church, located in Mesa Mani, in the Peloponnese.⁷⁷⁶ According to Nikolaos Drandakis, the image dates to the late twelfth century.

Gregory, the author of St. Basil the Younger's *Life* describes the demon of Fornication as clad in a particularly exotic garment:

> The official in charge of this tollhouse was quite wicked and bitter, presiding over it like an untamed lion, wearing a short tunic spattered with putrid foam and blood, in which he delighted as if it were imperial purple, preening himself and putting on airs. Images in the shape of conjoined demons, engaged, it would seem, in intercourse, could be seen worked upon this tunic and woven from the shameful and vile act of those who, like pigs, fearlessly and insatiably, or better to say with reckless abandon,

---

⁷⁷⁴ Elias Speleotes, §17: οἱ δέ γε τῇ ἔξωθεν μορφῇ τοῦ σώματος λευκαῖς καὶ ἐρυθραῖς στολαῖς καλλωπιζόμενοι, ἔσωθεν γέμουσι μίσους καὶ ἁρπαγῆς, καὶ μολυσμοῦ σαρκικοῦ, οὗτοι μελαίνονται τὸ τῆς ψυχῆς πρόσωπον, ὡς ἀναξίως τοῦ θείου ἄρτου μεταλαμβάνοντες.

⁷⁷⁵ Auxentios, §16.42-46.

⁷⁷⁶ Nikolaos Drandakis, *Byzantine Frescoes of Mesa* [Greek: Νικόλαος Δρανδάκης, Βυζαντινές τοιχογραφίες τῆς Μέσα Μάνης] (Athens: Archeological Society of Athens, 1995), 208ff and fig. 56.

wallow in the intercourse of fornication, the images fashioned noetically and appropriately for the exarch of this form of pleasure.[777]

Demons are occasionally clothed in rich garments as an element of parody. Gregory, a disciple of St. Luke of Steiris (897–February 7, 953), had severe stomach pains during fast days and asked his mentor to heal him. Luke tried everything, but his efforts were in vain. Finally, he had a dream in which the demon, who had possessed the young monk and had caused the illness, attempted to deceive him about his pupil's spiritual integrity. The old monk saw *a frightening man clothed in golden and precious garments* (ἄνδρα τινά... φοβερὸν ἐδόκουν ὁρᾶν... χρυσοῖς δὲ καὶ φιλοτίμοις τοῖς ἐσθήμασιν ἐκεκόσμητο) near to Gregory. Luke asked the evil spirit to leave the young man immediately and spare him the usual tedious and humiliating begging that he be left in his body. The demon surprisingly replied that it would be better for Gregory to stay possessed for the time being because he wanted to become a monk. Puzzled, Luke pointed to his pupil's cassock and told the evil spirit that Gregory was already a monk. The demon answered that the habit does not make the monk, but the path to true monastic perfection was paved with bodily pain. Gregory made no reply — he only began to chant the thirty-ninth psalm softly. Luke then awoke and shortly afterward took pity on his young pupil. He appeared to Gregory in a dream as a doctor and applied something like a medical dressing on his stomach. Later the pain vanished miraculously.[778] In this case, the contrast (real and metaphorical) between the rich garments of the demon, a symbol of pride, and the

---

[777] Basil the Younger, Part II, §36.2–11: Ὁ οὖν ἄρχων τοῦ τοιούτου τελωνείου πονηρὸς καὶ πικρὸς ἦν λίαν, προκαθεζόμενος ὥσπερ λέων ἀνήμερος, περιβεβλημένος χιτώνιον κονοηποδῆ (sic) ἄφρῳ καὶ αἵματι ῥεραντισμένον, ἐφ' ᾧ ὡς ἐν πορφύρᾳ βασιλικῇ τερπόμενος ἐγαυριᾶτο καὶ ὡραΐζετο. ἐν τούτῳ δὲ τῷ χιτωνίῳ ἐφαίνοντο εἰκονίσματά τινα δαιμονιόμορφα κεκολλημένα πρὸς ἄλληλα δῆθεν διαλεγόμενα, εἰργασμένα ἐν αὐτῷ καὶ ἐξυφασμένα ἀπὸ τῆς αἰσχρᾶς καὶ βεβήλῳ ἐργασίας τῶν δίκην χοίρων τῇ μίξει τῆς πορνείας ἀδεῶς καὶ ἀκορέστως, ἢ μᾶλλον εἰπεῖν ἀσώτως ἐγκυλινδομένων, νοητῶς καὶ καταλλήλως κατεσκευασμένα τῷ τῆς ἡδονῆς ταύτης ἐξάρχοντι.

[778] Luke of Steiris, §69. The event occurred during the last hermitage of the Saint in Phocis between 946 and 953 (see Part One, Chapter 2, §10).

humble cassock of Gregory, a symbol of spiritual perfection and ascesis, is intentional.

Demonic possession could sometimes leave a mark on the body even after the evil spirit had been expelled. A servant of the Devil attacked St. George of Amastris, when he was three years old, out of envy for his future glory. The demon could not harm the child, but his impure presence left George's legs with burn scars. However, shortly after this unpleasant experience, the future Saint recovered completely.[779]

The demon's ugly and deformed physical image is the material embodiment of sin and incurable spiritual corruption. There is no repentance and no salvation for the Devil and his servants. On the other hand, the illness and the injuries inflicted by evil spirits on humans are caused either by envy or by the victim's susceptibility to sin. They could be deadly both for the mortal body and the soul, but the repentant sinner could successfully be cured and saved, especially with the help of a holy monk. The permanence of the demon's corrupted material image is clearly, if not explicitly, opposed to the transience of demonic possession and its consequences in humans. But ugliness and deformity remain the most typical features of the demon and his victims, ossifying the ancient concept of "kalokagathia". In the medieval Orthodox world, physical beauty remains the very incarnation of the Good.

3. Kinesics

3.1. Facial expression and gestures

The lack of symmetry, the deformity, and the ultimate ugliness of the evil spirit's physical body are closely related to its facial expressions and gestures (kinesics). The conduct of the demon and those possessed by him is the ultimate and absolute antithesis of the ethical principles and rules of socially accepted behavior. To successfully grasp the real meaning behind the descriptions of this behavior, we have to look at the philosophical and rhetorical origins of the concepts related to "demonic" behavior.

---

[779] George of Amastris, §7.

The main principle of Aristotelean ethics is *moderation* (τὸ μέτριον). Every display of excessive emotion is considered barbaric and even beastly. According to Aristotle, behavior is the mirror of the character.[780] He often mentions the *mean* (τὸ μέσον)[781] and forbearance (ἐγκράτεια)[782] as a function of the reasonable part of the soul (τὸ λογικόν). Yet in the first chapters of the Nicomachean Ethics, he affirms that "good" is a complex notion since it is predicated in all of the ten categories; in quantity, it is that which is moderate.[783] From this point of view, the immoderate and the excessive must necessarily be the quantitative predicates of the "not-good". *Excess and defect*, says Aristotle, *are characteristic of vice and the mean of virtue*.[784] As we already pointed out, both for the Platonists and for the Aristotelians, the notion opposed to the "Good" was not "Evil", but "Bad", i.e., the "lack of good". Ugliness is

---

[780] See, e.g., Aristotle, Nicomachean Ethics, ed. Harris Racham [Loeb Classical Library 73] (Cambridge, MA: Harvard University Press, 1926), 1128a (IV.8.3): *as bodies are discriminated by their movements, so too are characters* (τοῦ γὰρ ἤθους αἱ τοιαῦται δοκοῦσι κινήσεις εἶναι, ὥσπερ δὲ τὰ σώματα ἐκ τῶν κινήσεων κρίνεται, οὕτω καὶ τὰ ἤθη). In this passage, Aristotle establishes a clear relation between the kinesics of the *well-bred* and the *vulgar* man and their characters.

[781] See, e.g., Aristotle, Nicomachean Ethics, 1106b (II.6.8): *Thus, a master of any art avoids excess and defect, but seeks the intermediate and chooses this* (οὕτω δὴ πᾶς ἐπιστήμων τὴν ὑπερβολὴν μὲν καὶ τὴν ἔλλειψιν φεύγει, τὸ δὲ μέσον ζητεῖ καὶ τοῦθ' αἱρεῖται).

[782] See, e.g., Aristotle, Nicomachean Ethics, 1145b (VII.1.6): *Now both continence and endurance are thought to be included among things good and praiseworthy, and both incontinence and soft, ness among things bad and blameworthy; and the same man is thought to be continent and ready to abide by the result of his calculations, or incontinent and ready to abandon them.* (Δοκεῖ δὴ ἥ τε ἐγκράτεια καὶ καρτερία τῶν σπουδαίων καὶ [τῶν] ἐπαινετῶν εἶναι, ἡ δ' ἀκρασία τε καὶ μαλακία τῶν φαύλων καὶ ψεκτῶν, καὶ ὁ αὐτὸς ἐγκρατὴς καὶ ἐμμενετικὸς τῷ λογισμῷ, καὶ ἀκρατὴς καὶ ἐκστατικὸς τοῦ λογισμοῦ).

[783] Aristotle, Nicomachean Ethics, 1096a (I.6.3): *Further, since 'good' has as many senses as 'being' (for it is predicated both in the category of substance, as of God and of reason, and in quality, i.e., of the virtues, and in quantity, i.e., of that which is moderate, and in relation, i.e., of the useful, and in time, i.e., of the right opportunity, and in place, i.e., of the right locality and the like)* (ἔτι δ' ἐπεὶ τἀγαθὸν ἰσαχῶς λέγεται τῷ ὄντι (καὶ γὰρ ἐν τῷ τί λέγεται, οἷον ὁ θεὸς καὶ ὁ νοῦς, καὶ ἐν τῷ ποιῷ αἱ ἀρεταί, καὶ ἐν τῷ ποσῷ τὸ μέτριον, καὶ ἐν τῷ πρός τι τὸ, καὶ ἐν χρόνῳ καιρός, καὶ ἐν τόπῳ δίαιτα καὶ ἕτερα τοιαῦτα).

[784] Aristotle, Nicomachean Ethics, 1106b (II.6).: *for these reasons also, then, excess and defect are characteristic of vice, and the mean of virtue* (καὶ διὰ ταῦτ' οὖν τῆς μὲν κακίας ἡ ὑπερβολὴ καὶ ἡ ἔλλειψις, τῆς δ' ἀρετῆς ἡ μεσότης·)

not neutral; it is the ultimate manifestation of moral decay, irrational behavior, and everything that causes irretrievable damage to the spirit. In this regard, ignorance is considered repulsive precisely because it prevents the right choice of pleasures and pains.[785]

For the Christian, though, Evil has an eidos of its own; therefore, if the Good/God is that which is moderate, then Evil/the Devil is that which is immoderate and excessive. As a consequence, in hagiography, *ecstatic* (ἔκστασις) or *Bacchic* behavior[786] becomes one of the typical symptoms of demonic possession, clearly opposed to temperance, the calm, and the forbearance of the pious man. The impact of these ideas, somewhat abstract but deeply typical of Greek culture, is enormous. A public figure's spiritual virtues and nonverbal behavior are strictly determined by Aristotelian "temperance" in rhetorical and philosophical treatises and handbooks throughout Antiquity. This is evident in the strict code of rules regarding the *orator's* socially acceptable conduct set out by the anonymous author of the *Rhetorica ad Herennium*, with its three (and only three) tones of voice (*vocis figurae*)[787] and the three sets of gestures (*corporis motus*) corresponding to them.[788] Some of these rules may sound ridiculous to the modern PR or communications specialist. The basic position of the orator's body is specified, along with his conversational tone (*sermo*), when he lays down his point of view or tells a story, remaining calm and almost unmoving, allowed to gesture only slightly with his right hand; in this case, the sole purveyor of emotion is his facial expression.[789] When arguing with an oppo-

---

[785] Petar Plamenov, *Ecstasy of the text* [Bulgarian: Петър Пламенов, *Екстазът от текста*], Sofia: Sofia University Press, 2023, 99.

[786] See, e.g., Nicholas of Stoudios, §9, where attacks on the icons are described as *Bacchic frenzy* (βακχευόμενος).

[787] [Cicero,] *Ad C. Herennium de ratione dicendi (Rhetorica ad Herennium)*, ed. and trans. Harry Caplan [Loeb Classical Library] (London: William Heinemann, 1954), I-II.XI.19-20. The three basic tones of the voice are the conversational (*sermo*), that of debate (*contentio*), and the tone of amplification (*amplification*), each with its subdivisions.

[788] [Cicero,] *Ad C. Herennium*, III.XV.26-27.

[789] [Cicero,] *Ad C. Herennium*, III.XV.26: *Nam si erit sermo cum dignitate, stantis in vestigio, levi dextrae motu, loqui opportebit hilaritati, tristitia, mediocritate vultus ad sermonis sententias adcommodata.*

nent, a decent public figure can behave a little more freely and *shall use a quick gesture of the arm, a mobile countenance, and a keen glance*. He *must extend the arm very quickly, walk up and down, occasionally stamp the right foot, and adopt a keen and fixed look*.[790] And finally, with the so-called "Pathetic Tone of Amplification" (*amplificatio per conquestionem*), the orator may become really free; he is allowed *to slap* his *thigh and beat his head and sometimes to use a calm and uniform gesticulation and a sad and disturbed expression*.[791] These precepts are significant for the present study because they represent a wholly developed and systematic code of socially acceptable conduct aimed at everyone who claims to be an *orator*, i.e., a person actively involved in public life. Every type of behavior outside these strict rules, every display of excessive emotion, is socially unacceptable and, therefore, stigmatized — at least in theory.

Almost two centuries after Pseudo-Cicero, Quintilian made his own significant contribution to the nonverbal behavior of a public figure. His recommendations are more practical than those of the anonymous author of the *Rhetorica ad Herennium* but less systematic. The great Roman rhetorician similarly stressed the importance of *temperantia* but also gave a few guidelines and advice for expressing seemingly excessive emotion at some points in the speech. In his opinion, in the epilogue, the good orator must look emotionally and physically exhausted but content with his well-performed work. His toga should be slipping from his body; his hair should be tousled and sweaty. However, Quintilian emphasizes that such behavior is acceptable and recommended only at the end of the speech when the audience has already been persuaded and convinced by the speaker's sober and logical argumentation. At any other moment, the impact of such conduct would be highly unfavorable.[792] In this manner,

---

[790] [Cicero,] *Ad C. Herennium*, III.XV.27: *bracchio eleri, mobile vultu, acri aspect utemur; porrectione perceleri bracchii, inambulatione, pedis dexteri rara supplausione, acri et defixo aspect uti opportet.*

[791] [Cicero,] *Ad C. Herennium*, III.XV.27: *Sin utemur amplificationem per conquestionem, feminis plangore et capitis ictu, nonnumquam sedato et constanti gestu, maesto et conturbato vultu uti opportebat.*

[792] Quintilian, *The Institutio Oratoria*, XI.3.147–49.

even excessive behavior is strictly confined within the theoretical framework of an elaborate code of social rules.

Since the most important guiding principle for the free citizen as a socially and politically active figure in the ancient Greco-Roman world, at least in theory, is self-restraint and self-control in emotion and behavior, every other conduct is considered uncivilized, barbarous, and beastly. There are many examples of kings and emperors who deliberately violated these rules to demonstrate their power and position above the law, which the ordinary rank and file must strictly obey. Marc Antony, Caesar's general and successor in the East, married a barbarian queen and adopted Egyptian customs; Caligula tried to marry his sister and made his horse a senator; Nero reportedly slept with his mother and frequently demonstrated his artistic abilities on the theatrical stage; Justinian married a frivolous actress of common origin who likely sometimes made a living as a prostitute. Apart from these displays of excessive behavior, which had disastrous consequences for the self-assured leaders, temperance remained one of the public figure's four essential virtues (the other three being practical wisdom, justice, and bravery) in Byzantium as well. On the other hand, lack of self-control and emotional excess are among the most typical traits of the demon and clear symptoms of demonic possession. When only a part of the human body, usually a hand or a leg, has been affected by the evil spirit, it stirs, twitches, or moves uncontrollably, while the rest of the body stays still.[793] A typical example of this condition is vividly described by the author of the *Life* of St. Sabbas the Younger, where a possessed woman from Calabria was *flapping her hands uncontrollably and was continuously stamping her feet on the ground, becoming in this way a pitiful spectacle for the onlookers.* She was rescued by Sabbas, who afterward ordained her a nun.[794] In addition, according to the *Life* of St. Theodore Sykeotes (the sixth to the seventh centuries), a demon tries

---

[793] Theodore Sykeotes, §106; Peter of Atroa, §31.5–8: ἐκ δαιμονικῆς ἐνεργείας ἔπασχε τὴν χεῖρα, τοῦ λοιποῦ σώματος σωφρονοῦντος; John the Psichaites, §9; Luke of Steiris, §83.

[794] Sabbas the Younger, §40: χεῖρας στροβοῦσα καὶ τοῖς ποσὶν ἀτάκτως τὸ ἔδαφος παίουσα, ἐλεεινὸν θέαμα τοῖς ὁρῶσιν ἐτύγχανεν.

to escape physical contact with the exorcist by such uncontrollable movements.[795]

Another body part often possessed by evil spirits is the face or the head. Here a demon's malicious influence does not cause uncontrollable movements and twitches but, rather, rigid and unnatural grimaces. For example, in the *Life* of St. Theodore Sykeotes, the innkeeper Pherentinos was attacked by an evil spirit in the shape of an enraged ghostly dog. Consequently, a doglike sneer froze on his face, and the poor man could not move his muscles.[796] According to the *Life* of St. Elias Speleotes (860/870–September 11, 960), the peasant Christophoros of the village of Skiron (near Regium in Calabria) was struck by the harmful influence of the "noonday demon", whereupon his facial expression became particularly exotic. His eyes continuously blinked, while the rest of the face and the head remained motionless; the only salvation from this condition came from the healing properties of the Saint's miraculous tomb.[797]

The emotions of the demons and their victims are always uncontrollable, and the most important of them is indubitably anger. The demonic origin of this violent and frantic affect is the Devil. In his *Life* of Patriarch Ignatios, Niketas-David of Paphlagonia calls anger the *sidegrowth of frenzy* and *mother of every obscene conduct*.[798]

It is not surprising that demonic fury appears exclusively in the eyes. They are usually swollen, bloodshot (καθημαγμένοι) or pale (πελιδνοί), fierce (βλοσυροί), murderously glaring (φονίως βλέποντες), popping out of their sockets (τὸ τοὺς ὀφθαλμοὺς ἐξωθεῖν), wide open (παμμεγέθεις), full of venomous bile and bitterness (μετὰ χολῆς καὶ πικρίας ὁρῶντες), and (surprisingly enough) squinting (διάστροφοι).[799]

---

[795] Theodore Sykeotes, §91.2–5 and §91.10–11.
[796] Theodore Sykeotes, §106.
[797] Elias Speleotes, §88.
[798] Patriarch Ignatios, §39: ὀργὴν δέ, ὡς ἐκστάσεως οὖσαν παράφυσιν, ὡς ἀσχημοσύνης μητέρα καὶ ὡς τοῦ πονηροῦ τυγχάνουσαν ἔξαλμα, φυγῇ φύγωμεν, μήποτε τῇ ταύτης ἐξαναλωθῶμεν φλογα.
[799] Symeon Stylites the Younger, §74.1–3 (eyes popping out of the sockets); Basil the Younger, Part II, §16.10ff, where the faces of the demons of anger are contorted and their eyes are fierce and full of venomous bile and bitterness; "La version longue de la

The whole face can be distorted by mad anger (διεστραμμένη ὄψις).[800] One of the most vivid descriptions can be found in the *Life* of St. Basil the Younger, which portrays the demons of Wrath and Anger:

> As the offspring of anger and wrath, they were biting one another with their teeth like dogs, uttering unintelligible words full of mad frenzy. When therefore we arrived before those pestilential Ethiopians, who were observing us with contorted face and grim eyes amid bile and bitterness, they interrogated me in a bloodthirsty manner.[801]

A similar description is provided by the anonymous author of the *Strange and useful vision of the monk Cosmas*, where the demonic giant is cross-eyed:

> The faces of some of them were twisted, the eyes of others were pale and bloodless, others glared murderously and like beasts with their bloodshot eyes.[802]
> He was cross-eyed, enormous, and bloodshot; his eyes cast huge flames.[803]

The eyes are an essential element of the demonic image in revealing dreams and visions as well. In a dream, a group of frightful men with murderous glares appeared to the elders of Amastris a few months before the birth of the future St. George of Amastris. They threatened the venerable officials with terrible punishments and only afterward revealed the cause of their visit — the aldermen had not paid sufficient respect to George's mother, who was then pregnant with her illustrious offspring.

---

vision du moine Cosmas", §82.84–87 (pale or bloodshot eyes; murderous and beastly glare); Auxentios, §18 and §19 (bloodshot eyes); "La version longue de la vision du moine Cosmas", §83.114–84.2.

[800] "La version longue de la vision du moine Cosmas", §82.84–85.

[801] Basil the Younger, Part II, §16.7–11: κἀκεῖνοι τῆς ὀργῆς καὶ τοῦ θυμοῦ γεννήματα ὄντες, ἀλλήλους ὡς κύνες τοῖς ὀδοῦσι κατήσθιον, ἄσημά τινα καὶ μανίας πλήρη ῥήματα φωνοῦντες. Ὡς οὖν κατήχθημεν πρὸς τοὺς λοιμοὺς τούτους, διεστραμμένῳ προσώπῳ καὶ βλοσυρῷ ὄμματι μετὰ χολῆς καὶ πικρίας ὁρῶντες ἡμᾶς, ἐξήταζον φονικῶς...

[802] "La version longue de la vision du moine Cosmas", §82.84–87: οἱ μὲν διεστραμμένας τὰς ὄψεις εἶχον, οἱ δὲ τοὺς ὀφθαλμοὺς πελιδνούς, ἄλλοι καθημαγμένους φόνιως καὶ θηριώδες βλέποντας.

[803] "La version longue de la vision du moine Cosmas", §83.114–84.2: οὗ ὀφθαλμοὶ μὲν διάστροφοι καὶ λίαν παμμεγέθεις καὶ ὕφαιμοι, καὶ φλόγα πυρὸς πολλὴν ἐναπέπεμπον.

On the morrow, the elders visited her, bowed with profound respect, and asked her forgiveness.[804]

Bloodshot eyes and eyes popping out of the sockets are typical symptoms of demonic possession. According to the *Life* of St. Symeon Stylites the Younger, *a young man, about nineteen years old, was continuously tortured by a demon, and the violence of the evil spirit was so powerful that his eyes were about to pop out of their sockets.*[805] Michael Psellus describes as *bloodshot* the eyes of a baby that was possessed as a consequence of the sins of the inhabitants of a village in western Bithynia.[806] Demonic influence could also force victims to roll their eyes uncontrollably, as happened to the noble Dorotheos of southern Italy, according to the *Life* of St. Sabbas the Younger.[807]

According to the Byzantine texts of the period under study, demonic possession and its symptoms could pass from the healed victim to another person or persons. This idea is prevalent in sixth- and seventh-century hagiography. For example, a certain deacon, Dometianos by name, was very skeptical about St. Theodore Sykeotes' skills as an exorcist; in his opinion, the "miracles" were staged. Meanwhile, a mute child was delivered by its father to Theodore to be exorcized and cured. The bishop performed the ritual, and at the end of the prayer, the boy opened his mouth and said, "Amen!", regaining speech. At that very moment, the faithless deacon fell to the ground, shaking uncontrollably with panic. According to Dometianos's own account, when the child spoke for the first time, a great blaze came out of its mouth, and this blaze was the *Devil's energy* (ἐνέργεια διαβολική). The deacon's sinful disbelief had made him susceptible to demonic influence, and the evil power had passed into him (ἐκ τοῦ παιδίου χωρήσῃ ἐν αὐτῷ), causing the seizure. Immediately after his "panic attack", Dometianos visited Theodore, knelt

---

[804] George of Amastris, §5.
[805] Symeon Stylites the Younger, §74.1–3 (ὥστε δοκεῖν καὶ αὐτοὺς τοὺς ὀφθαλμοὺς αὐτοῦ ἐξωθεῖσθαι τῇ πολλῇ βίᾳ τῆς οἰκείας τάξεως).
[806] Auxentios, §19.
[807] See, e.g., Sabbas the Younger, §39.

before him, repented, and was healed by the pious bishop.[808] Another interesting story, which demonstrates the nature of superstitions in Early Byzantium, is found in the *Life* of St. Symeon Stylites the Younger. According to the text, around 578,[809] a demon possessed a four-year-old boy, afflicting him with a painful leg ulcer. His mother immediately killed a chicken and brought it as a gift to Symeon, asking him to help her son. The holy man cured the child and sent them home. Meanwhile, the father discovered the bird's loss and got angry. As a result, when his wife and son returned home, they found him with the same ulcer on his own leg. The man repented before Symeon, and the holy hermit granted him forgiveness. The demon and the ulcer disappeared.[810]

3.2. Levitation

The term "levitation" refers to the ability to rise a little above the earth without visible aid (wings, mechanical means). In Middle Greek, a terminological distinction is usually (but certainly not always) made between verbs and compound expressions such as hang/circle/rise above the earth (κρέμαμαι/φοιτῶ/ὑψοῦμαι ἐν τῷ ἀέρι) and fly (πέτομαι). While levitation is a relatively common element of the demonic image, the ability to fly with wings in the Byzantine hagiography of the period under study is associated exclusively with the Devil and appears mostly in visions.[811]

Descriptions of saints able to soar above the earth, usually under specific circumstances, are relatively rare in the Byzantine hagiography of the period under study. In a prophetic vision, *c.* 527, John, abbot of a

---

[808] Theodore Sykeotes, §61.
[809] The episode is described immediately after the account of the coronation of Tiberius II as co-emperor with his dying predecessor Justin II (565–578) in 578. See Van den Ven, *La Vie ancienne*, 1: 122*ff.
[810] Symeon Stylites the Younger, §212.
[811] Symeon Stylites the Younger, §124.69-72. On the ability of the evil spirit Gelo and the older women possessed by it to fly, sneak into infants, drink their bodily fluids, and kill them, see Chapter 2, §4.1; see also Michael Psellus, "De Gillo", ed. John Duffy and Dan O'Meara, *Michaelis Pselli philosophica minora*, vol. 2 (Leipzig: Teubner, 1989), 164.17.

small monastery southwest of Antioch,[812] saw a small boy walking towards him through the air surrounded by a pillar of light, and shortly afterward, the six-year-old Symeon Stylites the Younger actually visited him.[813] Levitation during prayer occurs in the *Lives* of some Bithynian saints in the eighth to the ninth centuries, but is not uncommon in other texts as well. In the *Life* of St. Ioannikios the Great, the holy hermit is described at prayer, hovering two cubits above the ground, enveloped by a light brighter than the sun.[814] Hanging in the air (ἐν τῷ ἀέρι κρεμάμενον), St. Eustratios of Agaurous stretches out his hand to a burning nunnery and prays to God to extinguish the fire.[815] According to the brief *Life* of St. John, bishop of Gotia (Crimea) in the late seventh century, the Saint levitates one cubit above the ground while praying for the salvation of some captives condemned to death by the Khazar ruler.[816] In the late 960s, a peasant saw St. Nikon Metanoeite, traveling on the road to Argos, suddenly rising above the ground in a circle of bright light. The man watched him levitate (ἀεροβατῶν) until the Saint disappeared in the distance.[817]

Inanimate objects also could rise above the earth by the will of God. In the *Life* of St. Ioannikios the Great, as the Saint climbed a rocky cliff to return to his cell, a diabolical force intervened, and his iron cross dropped from his hand. In despair, St. John began to pray to God with tears in his eyes. The cross then rose into the air and returned to his palm.[818]

The ability of saints to levitate is a relatively rare motif. After the seventh century, it occurs in the Bithynian hagiography, the *Life* of St. John of Gotthia, who lived in the late eighth century, and the *Life* of St.

---

[812] For the location of this monastery in the mountains southwest of Antioch, on the western bank of the Orontes River, see Van den Ven, *La Vie ancienne*, 1: 191*ff.

[813] Symeon Stylites the Younger, §11. 8ff: ἄλλοτε δὲ τὸ αὐτὸ παιδίον ἅμα στύλῳ φωτεινῷ περιπατοῦν ἐν τῷ ἀέρι.

[814] Ioannikios (*Peter*), §25; Ioannikios (*Sabbas*), §21.

[815] Eustratios of Agauros, §31.

[816] John of Gotthia, §7.

[817] Nikon Metanoeite, §29.

[818] Ioannikios (*Peter*), §32.

Nikon Metanoeite, probably composed as late as the twelfth century but relating events of the late tenth century. Levitation is more commonly a characteristic of demons, traditionally associated with the dangerous aerial spaces.[819] Descriptions of levitating demons are not restricted to any particular literary school or geographical region. In the early *Life* of St. Theodore Sykeotes (†613), a helpless demon hangs in the air, screaming profanities and cursing during the exorcism of a young novice named Arsinos.[820] St. Stephen the Thaumaturge (725–794) observes demons floating through the air (ἐν τῷ ἀέρι φοιτῶντας), encouraging each other in joyful dancing; they had succeeded in inspiring disobedience in the young monks of the monastery, causing them to rise in revolt against their mentors and the old abbot Strategios.[821] In the *Life* of St. Elias Speleotes, a multitude of evil spirits appears to the villagers of Seminara in Calabria in the form of a giant Ethiopian hovering above the ground.[822]

Flying high in the air is also a metaphor for the deadly sin of pride, used as a propaganda tool to discredit religious and political opponents. In his *Life* of Patriarch Nikephoros (806–815), Ignatios Deacon addresses the Iconoclastic Emperor Leo V, murdered on Christmas Day 820:

> What happened to you who had risen so high, who flew in the lofty heights and hurled storms against us, who breathed draconian fire against the Church? Did your soul, which plotted fearful persecutions and smote thunderously the righteous, really fly away?[823]

Demons could transmit their ability to levitate to the possessed, usually when the exorcist threatened their power over the victim. This concept appears in the early Byzantine hagiography of the period under study, but is almost entirely absent from saints' *Lives* after the eighth century. The author of St. Theodore Sykeotes's *Life* includes two vivid descriptions of such public spectacles, often aimed to strengthen and increase the authority of leading religious figures. According to him, Theo-

---

[819] On demons in the air, see Part Four, Chapter 1, §2.
[820] Theodore Sykeotes, §46.
[821] Stephen the Thaumaturge, §33.
[822] Elias Speleotes, §44.
[823] Patriarch Nikephoros, §79.

dore and the bishops of Germia and Eudoxiada decided to visit the feast dedicated to the Holy Mother of God, held annually in a Galatian village called Mousgi.[824] When the procession reached the temple, they saw a local woman named Irene, *who had spirits hidden inside her for a long time*, standing near the church entrance and watching. When Bishop Theodore passed by her to enter the church, she suddenly threw the veil (*maphorion*) off her head, rushed in, and stirred up the crowd, her demons screaming, barking, and cursing the holy man through her mouth as if his very presence humiliated them. Frightened, the crowd began to scream *Lord, have mercy*. Then Irene rose above the ground as if something in the air was lifting her violently by the hands and flew from the pulpit (which in this period was placed in the middle of the central nave of the basilica)[825] to the altar partition. After the priest read the Gospel, she prostrated herself on the ground before the altar and licked the floor. This indecency was too much for Theodore to bear, so he took drastic measures, grabbing her by the hair and cursing the demons. The evil spirits left her body with screams, and Irine immediately calmed down. Later, after the deaths of her husband and children, the bishop ordered that she be isolated from the community and detained in a monastery, where he successfully helped her save her soul.[826]

The second story is set in Constantinople and takes place during the patriarchate of Cyriacus II (596–606). Three possessed men came to the Saint's cell for help, but he received an invitation from the Patriarch to visit him immediately. Theodore then commanded the demons to flee from their victims. Two of them escaped in a flash, leaving the men lying on the ground like corpses. The third evil spirit, however, proved stubborn and refused to obey. The exorcist decided to punish it severely and ordered it to stand motionless, suffer, and wait for him to return from the emergency visit. When Theodore came back to his cell after a long absence, he saw that the demon had complied with the restrictions imposed

---

[824] On this village, see *TIB*, vol. 4, 208.
[825] Nikolaos Gioles, *Early Christian Church Architecture (200–600)* [Greek: Νικόλαος Γκιολές, *Παλαιοχριστιανική ναοδομία (π. 200 – 600)*] (Athens, 1998), 76-78.
[826] Theodore Sykeotes, §71.

upon him but had suspended the victim in the air. In addition, it turned out that this evil spirit was an old acquaintance of the holy man; long ago, it had promised him not to possess humans but failed to keep the promise. It had to beg for a long time to be allowed to leave; finally, Theodore performed the necessary ritual, painful for both the victim and the demon, and allowed the Devil's servant to disappear.[827]

One of the miracles of Anastasios of Persia, which supposedly describes events of the early or mid-seventh century, also involves demonic levitation. A monk performed an exorcism on a possessed inhabitant of Abydos, using a small bone from the Saint's relics. The ritual took place in a church, and as soon as he stepped across the threshold with the holy object, the demon's victim, *as if flying* (ὥσπερ πετασθείς), fell heavily onto the pulpit and broke three candlesticks.[828] In the *Roman Miracle of Anastasios of Persia* (November 713), the possessed girl also floats over the floor, but the Saint turns her upside down and tortures the evil spirit severely.[829]

Levitation in the midst of exorcism reappears briefly in the second half of the eighth century, probably as a part of the iconodule propaganda war against the iconoclasts. During his exile on the island of Proconnesus (in the Sea of Marmara), St. Stephen the Younger spectacularly demonstrated the Orthodox faith's power when a wealthy woman from Cyzicus asked him to expel the demon who had possessed her nine-year-old son. During the ritual, the evil spirit repeatedly lifted the boy in the air and let him fall to the ground, screaming insults and profanities at the holy man.[830]

4. Vocalization, speech, and divination

During his wanderings in the mountains of Lydia shortly before the death of Emperor Leo V (December 25, 820), St. Ioannikios the Great

---

[827] Theodore Sykeotes, §93.
[828] Anastasios of Persia, Miracles, 149 (XVI (=ιϛ). 19ff.).
[829] Anastasios of Persia, *Roman Miracle*, §10.1–7.
[830] Stephen the Younger, 151.6–152.7.

took on the struggle against the demon of lust torturing a young girl. One night, as the holy man was falling asleep, the evil spirit attacked him in the shape of a bear. Ioannikios grabbed the demonic animal by the fur, and the contact with his saintly hand made the evil spirit *regain* its human speech.[831] This story is deeply typical of the Byzantine concept of the demon. In the *Lives* of the saints, human speech, combined with characteristic vocalization, is one of the most distinctive features of a materialized evil spirit, regardless of its particular form. As early as the third century, when the *Testament of Solomon* was probably written, the demon Phonos (Murder) was said to be headless, but despite the utter lack of vocal organs, could speak because he had stolen the voice of all mute persons in the world.[832] One of the most typical characteristics of the "polarized" image of the evil spirit is the notorious *mouth to utter proud words and blasphemies* of the Antichrist, mentioned by St. John the Apostle in the Book of Revelation.[833]

4.1. Languages and stereotypical phrases

In Late Antiquity's philosophical and literary traditions, the idea that demons speak the language of the region they come from was evidently widespread.[834] According to Proclus (fifth century), the so-called *climatarch demons* (κλιματάρχαι δαίμονες), the masters and protectors of the cities, were pleased when people spoke to them in the language of their native country;[835] this passage is quoted in the eleventh century by

---

[831] Ioannikios (*Peter*), §27; Ioannikios (*Sabbas*), §23. See Sullivan, "Life of St. Ioannikios", 284 and n. 230.

[832] *The Testament of Solomon*, 36. See Greenfield, *Traditions of Belief*, 180–81.

[833] Rev. 13:5: στόμα λαλοῦν μεγάλα καὶ βλασφημίας.

[834] See for example Lucian, "The Lover of Lies, or the Doubter (Philopseudes sive Incredulus)", ed. Austin Harmon, *Lucian*, vol. 3 [Loeb Classical Library 130] (London: Heinemann, 1960), §16: *and the demon responds in Greek or in some barbarian language, according to the region he comes from* (ὁ δαίμων δὲ ἀποκρίνεται, ἑλληνίζων ἢ βαρβαρίζων ὁπόθεν ἂν αὐτὸς ᾖ). For more on this concept and its development before the seventh century, see Vakaloudi, *Magic*, 114ff.

[835] *Procli Diadochi in Platonis Cratylum commentaria*, ed. Georgius Pasquali (Leipzig: Teubner, 1994), §57.7–9: χαίρουσι γὰρ οἱ κλιματάρχαι ταῖς τῶν οἰκείων χωρῶν διαλέκτοις ὀνομαζόμενοι.

Michael Psellus as well.[836] The same concept can be seen in the Eastern Orthodox tradition.[837] According to the anonymous demonological treatise *Timotheos* (thirteenth century), demons live among different peoples and adopt their languages. They usually speak, says the author, Greek or some eastern language, like "Chaldean" (i.e., Aramaic), Egyptian, Armenian, and Syrian. As an example, Timotheos, the main speaker, tells the story of a woman who had never learned a language other than her native Greek, but her speech suddenly became utterly incomprehensible. Her worried friends brought an old Armenian doctor, who recognized the language as Armenian. The demon who had possessed her obviously originated from that country.[838]

The story mentioned above, however, is an isolated example. The image of the demon speaking exotic languages remains a relatively rare phenomenon in hagiography before the seventh century. Between the seventh and the tenth centuries, it vanishes entirely. The strange and incomprehensible words and phrases so abundant in the *Testament of Solomon* and the magical papyri of Late Antiquity are replaced by a relatively standard repertoire of expressions in Greek. Demons use them when communicating with humans and among themselves. For example, in the *Life* of St. Peter of Atroa, the evil spirits encourage each other to hurry and possess a young novice. Meanwhile, one advises the others to touch his head to find out if he has a monastic tonsure. When they discover that he has already become a monk, the demons leave him.[839] In the *Life* of St. Stephen the Thaumaturge, demons inspire the monks of the Great Lavra of *St. Sabbas* near Jerusalem to organize a revolt against their abbot Strategios and afterward bolster each other in joyful dances to cele-

---

[836] Michael Psellus, "Greek provisions on demons", 125.13–14.
[837] See, e.g., Théodoret de Cyr, *L'histoire des moines de Syrie*, ed. Pierre Canivet and Alice Leroy-Molinghen, vol. 1 [*Sources chrétiennes* 234] (Paris: Éditions du Cerf, 1977), XXI.15.13–15, where the famous Christian theologian gives an account of the demon who came to torture the heretic Markion: *And an avenging demon came in the middle of the night yelling in the Syrian language* (Καί ποτε νύκτωρ ἦκέ τις βοῶν ἀλιτήριος δαίμων καὶ τῇ σύρᾳ κεχρημένος φωνῇ).
[838] Pseudo-Psellos, "Timothée ou des démons", 163 (ll. 435–59).
[839] Peter of Atroa, §79.25–28.

brate their success.[840] The two ugly humanlike figures (demons or ghosts) who appear in a graveyard to St. Patriarch Antony Kauleas encourage each other to escape the holy monk quickly.[841]

The strong emotions, so typical of the Byzantine demon, can be expressed in stereotypical phrases. The most common are *Oh, violence* (ὦ βία, ὦ τῆς βίας),[842] sometimes used along with pleas for mercy[843] or accusations,[844] and *Woe to me/us!* (Οὐαί μοι/ἡμῖν).[845] The hagiographers also borrow standard expressions from the New Testament, the most common being *What do you want with us* (Τί ἡμῖν καί σοι).[846] This phrase could express a threat, a plea, or fear.[847] Often, the demon cries the exorcist's name to scare him or as a display of fear. In the background, we can discern real propaganda strategies. This was probably the case with the ordination of St. Peter of Atroa, who became a presbyter between 803 and 805.[848] During the official ceremony, a demon screamed Peter's name

---

[840] Stephen the Thaumaturge, §33.
[841] Antony Kauleas, §20.
[842] Symeon Stylites the Younger, §118.14: Ὦ βία κατά σου; Theodore Sykeotes, §18.20, §35.4, §43.25 and §43.45, §84.17, §108.8, §156.39, and §161.151; Ioannikios (*Peter*), §27; Ioannikios (*Sabbas*), §23; Niketas Patrikios, §2.10.3; Elias Speleotes, §94; Phantinos the Younger, §10.10ff (Ὦ βία ἀπό σοῦ, Φαντῖνε!); Sabbas the Younger, §19.24–31; Auxentios, §7.
[843] Symeon the Holy Fool, 96.12–17; Ioannikios (*Peter*), §27; Ioannikios (*Sabbas*), §23; Elias Speleotes, §94.
[844] Sabbas the Younger, §19.24–31.
[845] Symeon Stylites the Younger, §118.25; Anastasios of Persia, *Roman Miracle*, §9.31, §10.5, and §11.9; Peter of Atroa, §13.
[846] Mat. 8:29; Mark 5:7; Luke 8:28 (Jesus Christ casts a legion of demons into a large herd of pigs). See also Mark 1:24; Luke 4:34 (Jesus drives an impure spirit out of the synagogue).
[847] Peter of Atroa, §36.6 (a demon possesses the nephew of the Saint's high-ranking patron during the revolt of Thomas the Slav); Peter of Atroa, §70.20 (a demon in the form of a small boy infects a monk with leprosy); Basil the Younger, Part III, §12.17–28 (a demon talks through a possessed Paphlagonian army officer); Auxentios, §15.4; Alypios Stylites, §14.21 (St. Alypios expels demons from his hermitage upon a column, probably in the second half of the sixth century).
[848] The episode can be dated relatively easily. According to Canon №14 of the Quinisext Council (*Constitution of the Godly and Holy Canons of the Saintly and All-Praiseworthy Apostles and of the Ecumentical and Local Synods and of the Holy Fathers*, ed. Georgios Rhalles and Michael Potles [Greek: Σύνταγμα τῶν θείων καί ἱερῶν κανόνων τῶν τε ἁγίων καί πανευφήμων ἀποστόλων καί τῶν οἰκουμενικῶν καί

through the mouth of a possessed woman, and the audience accepted this as a sign that the evil spirits feared Peter's power to expel them.[849] In the *Life* of St. Ioannikios the Great, the holy monk visited the Kunis monastery in Bithynia.[850] Not recognizing him at first, the monks put him at the very end of the table. Immediately afterward, a nun, who had a concealed demon, started screaming his name; in this way, the others identified him and asked his forgiveness.[851]

Frequently, the authors refer to the emotional patterns of the demons rather than to any concrete phrases they utter. The words of the evil spirits and their victims are usually *sorrowful* (γοερός), *mourning* (θρηνητικός), or *very scared* (σύντρομος). The exorcized evil spirit often comes out of the possessed person *crying loudly*.[852] Demons which appear only as voices — threatening, cursing, desperate, or full of sorrow — are also common. Intense emotion is the element that characterizes all of these voices.

One of the most common demonic emotions, according to the hagiographical texts, is **anger**, usually expressed in obscene and blasphemous speech. Since the demon is believed to use his victim as an *instrument* (ὄργανον, ἐργαστήριον), he often forces the possessed person to curse and swear. Hagiographers usually construct these stereotypical

---

τοπικῶν συνόδων καὶ τῶν κατὰ μέρος ἁγίων πατέρων, ed. Γεώργιος Ράλλης and Μιχαὴλ Ποτλῆς], 6 vols. (Athens, 1852), vol. 2, 337), the position of presbyter could not lawfully be obtained before the age of thirty. Paul, St. Peter's mentor, was very keen on the Church rules (§6.10), and we have no reason to doubt that he stuck to them rigorously when he ordained his pupil. The ordination of St. Peter (born in 773) could therefore not have happened before the year 803, the *terminus post quem*. On the other hand, when the future Saint became the abbot of the St. Zacharias monastery (805), he was already a presbyter. Hence, the ceremony must have been held between 803 and 805. For the main events of St. Peter of Atroa's life, see Part One, Chapter 2, §4.

[849] Peter of Atroa, §6.56. See also Peter of Atroa, §34.8–9, where the wife of a noble senator possessed by an evil spirit screams the name of Peter the moment that she sees him.

[850] On this monastery, see Janin, *Les églises et les monastères*, 164.

[851] Ioannikios (Peter), §44.

[852] This motif runs through the *Life* of Symeon Stylites the Younger. See §48.5; §50.3ff; §55.8.

phrases and sentences in accordance with the standard rhetorical schoolbook of Hermogenes of Tarsus, the famous rhetorician of the third century A.D. Hermogenes suggests several stylistic devices to the orator who wants to insult his opponent: frequent rhetorical questions, apostrophe, metaphor, allegory, and, above all, newly invented offensive compound words.[853] This motif runs through the *Roman Miracle of St. Anastasios of Persia*.[854] For example, the demon frequently calls the exorcist a "dog-eater" (κυνοφάγε).[855] However, when defeat was near, the evil spirit changed his tactic, addressing him as "Saint Anastasios".[856] In the *Life* of St. Stephen the Sabbaite, Leontios of Damascus describes in great detail the influence of the demon of blasphemy, who used to attack him during his first years as a monk in the Great Lavra of St. Sabbas near Jerusalem. As a novice, the youth was tormented by this evil spirit for almost two years, instilling him with an irresistible urge to swear at God; this unbearable situation and his inability to resist the demon's influence led Leontius to think about suicide. A short conversation with Stephen freed him from suffering for a while, but, despite the abbot's efforts, his salvation was temporary. The demon soon attacked again, inspiring Leontios to curse the Holy Virgin. Stephen then took decisive measures and acted immediately. The old abbot took the battle against the evil spirit upon himself. He explained to the young novice that at the Last Judgment, he would not be held responsible for his blasphemies since he had not made them of his own free will but under the influence of the Devil. In addition, said Stephen, the demon's real goal was not to afflict the soul of Le-

---

[853] Hermogenes, Περὶ ἰδεῶν λόγου ["On Types of Style"], ed. Hugo Rabe, *Hermogenis opera* [Rhetores Graeci 6] (Stuttgart: Teubner, 1969), I.7ff (on "invented words", see I.8.42–44); Hermogenes, *On Types of Style*, trans. Cecil Wooten (Chapel Hill: The University of North Carolina Press, 1987), 26–32.

[854] Anastasios of Persia, *Roman Miracle*, §5.8: διὰ τοῦ στόματος τῆς αὐτῆς νεάνιδος λαλεῖν ῥήματα βλάσφημα εἴς τε τοὺς ἁγίους μάρτυρας καὶ εἰς τοὺς δούλους τοῦ Θεοῦ. For other examples, see ibid., §5.21 and §7.3ff.

[855] Anastasios of Persia, *Roman Miracle*, §5.8 and §5.21.

[856] Anastasios of Persia, *Roman Miracle*, §11.9 and §15ff.

ontios through blasphemy but to lead him to utter despair and, ultimately, to incite him to commit the deadly sin of suicide.[857]

The curses and offences of the demons could contain justified but rather insignificant accusations. An evil spirit called St. Theodore Sykeotes a "son of a whore", which was true since his mother was an innkeeper and occasionally earned her money as a prostitute.[858] St. Anastasios of Persia was often accused of being a pagan and a mage before his conversion.[859] St. Nikon Metanoeite was constantly harassed c. 943-951[860] in the mountains of Asia Minor with accusations that he left his homeland and family to become a monk and a preacher.[861]

Even more widespread is the concept that a possessed person utters obscenities under the influence of the evil spirit. According to his *Life*, St. Stephen the Sabbaite expelled the demon from a nine-year-old boy whose mother was a wealthy inhabitant of Cyzicus. Using the child as its *instrument* and *changing* his voice, the evil creature bawled all sorts of obscenities at the exorcist during the ritual.[862] A noble girl, possessed by the demon of lust, became hysterical and swore at her mother in the rudest, most vilifying manner; only an accidental encounter with St. Ioannikios the Great saved her from harmful influence and restored her sanity.[863] A demonic "Ethiopian" (i.e., black man) forced the young son of a poor woman to yell shameless words (ἄσεμνα) at St. Theodora of Thessalonica; the holy nun took pity on the boy and cured him.[864] This motif is preva-

---

[857] The story is related over more than ten pages in the *Acta Sanctorum* edition. See Stephen the Thaumaturge, §116-26.
[858] Theodore Sykeotes, §84.18-24. On the mother of the Saint and her position and occupation, see Carolyn Connor, *Women of Byzantium* (New Haven: Yale University Press, 2004), 148ff. On the female characters in the same text, see ibid., 146-57.
[859] Anastasios of Persia, Miracles, 149 (XVI (=ιϛ).18ff); Anastasios of Persia, *Roman miracle*, §5.
[860] St. Nikon was born between 930 and 935. At eleven years of age, he entered a monastery and spent twelve years there. This means that he left the monastery to become a hermit as early as 943 and dedicated himself to preaching in western Asia Minor as late as 951. See Sullivan, *The Life of Saint Nikon*, 18; see Part One, Chapter 2, §10.
[861] Nikon Metanoeite, §17.38.
[862] Stephen the Younger, 151.12-14.
[863] Ioannikios, (Peter), §46: ἐβόα ἄσεμνα πρὸς τὴν ἑαυτῆς μητέρα.
[864] Theodora of Thessalonica, §50.

lent in the hagiography of southern Italy. For example, in the mid-tenth century, the son of one George of the village of Geanon in Calabria threw himself on the ground and screamed obscenities.[865] According to the *Life* of St. Elias Speleotes, the same "symptoms" appeared in a Calabrian shepherd during the exorcism, and the holy monk Sabbas only managed to heal him by putting the wooden shoe of St. Elias on his chest.[866]

Obscenities can be loosed against a saint by an unclean spirit which has taken material form. For example, St. Ioannikios the Great undertakes the task of exorcizing a haunted cave near his cell on Mount Olympus, whose demons greet him with *screams and vulgar words*.[867] Peter of Atroa expels the evil spirits from a bathhouse in the village of Pigadia,[868] and they *screech with pain and shout curses at him*.[869] The demon snake that possesses a beautiful woman in the *Life* of St. Auxentios hisses blasphemies and curses the Saint's mother during the exorcism.[870]

The obscenities are such a common "symptom" of demonic possession and so typical an element of the image and the influence of the evil spirit that they often lead to logical incoherencies. For example, *c.* 829, an inhabitant of Mount Kalon Oros in Lydia visited St. Ioannikios with his

---

[865] Elias Speleotes, §84. In this text, the expression used for *obscenities* is φωναὶ ἄσημοι (*words that must not be put into writing*). The adjective ἄσημος means *not imprinted, unmarked*, from which derives the Modern Greek word for *silver* (ασήμι – the raw material for silver coins).

[866] Elias Speleotes, §94. See another story in the *Life* of St. Sabbas the Younger, §40.

[867] Ioannikios (Peter), §33: *they shouted and uttered many indecent words. For some of them were cursing the holy man, others threatened him, and others were just in a hurry to get out of there; in addition, sometimes they were urging each other to undermine the cave itself* (κραυγαί τε πολλαὶ καὶ ἀπρεπεῖς φωναὶ ἐπέμποντο. Οἱ μὲν γὰρ αὐτῶν ὕβρεσι τὸν ὅσιον ἔβαλλον, οἱ δὲ ἠπείλουν καὶ ἕτεροι τῶν ἐκεῖσε ἀναχωρεῖν ἔσπευδον· ἔστι δ' ὅτε καὶ αὐτὸ τὸ σπήλαιον ἐκ τῶν θεμελίων κατασκάπτειν ἀλλήλοις διεκελεύοντο.)

[868] According to the text, this village was located near the St. Porphyry monastery in Western Bithynia. On it, see Janin, *Les églises et les monastères*, 209 (see also ibid., 151 and 162).

[869] Peter of Atroa, §61.13ff.: ἀνακραζόντων καὶ πολλὰ δυσφημούντων.

[870] See Auxentios, §16 (τῇ μητρὶ καταρώμενος). In Modern Greek, insults, which affect the offended person's mother, are highly uncommon. Today the rudest curses (for example, γαμώ τη Παναγία σου) are related to the victim's "Holy Mother of God," i.e., their guardian angel. By contrast, judging from the *Life* of St. Auxentios, in Byzantium existed obscene insults, which are more common today in the Slavic languages.

son because the boy was possessed by a *deaf-mute spirit* (πνεῦμα κωφὸν καὶ ἄλαλον). However, according to the text, this specific influence of the evil spirit did not impede the child from screaming obscenities.[871]

Other typical emotions attributed by the hagiographers to the evil spirit are **despondency, desolation**, and **gloom**. Demons are often described as wallowing in self-pity and making efforts, usually through stereotyped expressions and vocal patterns,[872] to provoke compassion in the exorcist. Since they are the very essence of Evil, this literary motif frequently has a comical effect, sprinkling the narratives with parody. A deal is often offered by demons, like the one who asks St. Symeon Stylites the Younger to let him depart his victim immediately and save him from the painful ritual of exorcism.[873] In such cases, the imploring usually begins with the expression *Let me go* (Ἄνες μοι). Sometimes the evil spirit will deliver a whole speech, full of apparently reasonable arguments, to be set free or even to be allowed to stay in the victim, like the demon in the *Life* of St. Symeon Stylites, who possesses a young woman and makes her barren. Symeon approaches her intending to expel the Devil's servant, and the demon greets him with a lengthy speech in which he claims that he has never offended the holy man himself; therefore, Symeon has no reason *to separate him from his 'wife'*.[874] The distorted concept of the "marriage" between the demon and the woman, which prevents her from having children, adds to the comical effect of the whole story, since the primary function of the typical marital relationship is to produce offspring. The evil spirits in Patermouthios, the iconoclast abbot of the Chareus monastery in Lydia, implore St. Peter of Atroa to leave the heretic to them because they have taken considerable efforts to possess him.[875]

---

[871] Peter of Atroa, §60.10. The event could be dated immediately before the accession of Emperor Theophilos (829–842).
[872] See, e.g., Ioannikios (*Peter*), §26, and Ioannikios (*Sabbas*), §22. The demons are described as screaming mournfully (θρηνητικῶς, γοερῶς).
[873] Symeon Stylites the Younger, §73.9–11; and §74.12-16, where the Saint's holiness and grace makes the demon suffer so much that he implores Symeon to let him go.
[874] Symeon Stylites the Younger, §118.14–19.
[875] Peter of Atroa, §28.

The demons who have been expelled from their victims could also try to provoke compassion among themselves or in others. In the *Life* of St. Alypios Stylites, the evil spirits, after their unsuccessful attempt to break down the holy man's resistance during his hermitage on a column, indulge in complaints and moaning on a deserted road. A group of travelers hear their words: they mournfully say that Alypios has banished them from their home, and now they have no dwelling.[876] When St. Gregory of Dekapolis approached a dangerous cave in the mountains of Isauria *c.* 829–830, intending to purify it from evil spirits, he immediately heard their piteous voices: *We are being expelled from our dwelling! In what foreign country are we going to settle now?*[877] A similar episode can be found in the *Life* of St. Elias Speleotes. When he decided to found a monastery in a cave near the village of Seminara in southern Italy, he discovered a terrible demon in the form of a giant black "Ethiopian" already dwelling there. It was no great challenge for the holy man to expel the evil creature. However, shortly afterward, a group of local villagers ran by chance across the Ethiopian, who explained to them *with a coarse voice, full of anger (τραχείᾳ καὶ ὀργίλῳ φωνῇ)*, that Elias has banished him from his home.[878]

The demon could also **threaten** the exorcist and boast about his power. A typical example of this concept occurs in the *Roman Miracle of St. Anastasios of Persia*. According to the text, in the autumn of 713, an evil spirit possessed the daughter of a noble Roman bishop. The creature threatened the monks, who were trying to help the girl, that they could never expel it because it was a crowned king with armies and courtiers.[879] The giant demon, who visited St. Symeon of Lesbos in the first half of the ninth century to disturb his prayers, boasted that the exploits of the monk against the Devil and all his holiness would not help him this time.[880] *With trembling voice and cowardly cry (συντρόμῳ φωνῇ καὶ*

---

[876] Alypios Stylites, §14.34–38.
[877] Gregory of Dekapolis, §8.5ff.
[878] Elias Speleotes, §44.
[879] Anastasios of Persia, *Roman Miracle*, §5.10.
[880] David, Symeon and George, §11.19ff.

δειλιώσῃ βοῇ), the evil spirits tried to drive St. Gregory of Dekapolis out of his cave in Isauria between 829 and 830.[881] The above-mentioned giant Ethiopian of the *Life* of St. Elias Speleotes warned the villagers of Seminara that he would come back soon with reinforcements and would take revenge on Elias.[882] These threats could also have a comic effect, like the small and foul-smelling Ethiopian, who boasted that he would *burn* St. Luke of Steiris just as he had burned demons many times.[883]

Since God permits the existence of Evil as a punishment for human sin, according to the official Orthodox doctrine, demons often reveal verbally why they have possessed their victim and how they can be expelled. When St. Peter of Atroa unsuccessfully tried to heal a monk who suffered from leprosy through prayer, the evil spirit of the sickness told him of own accord that the victim harbored an unconfessed sin.[884] The terrible men with murderous eyes who threatened the elders of Amastris, disclosed the identity of Megetho, who was pregnant with the future St. George of Amastris and forced them to pay reverence to her.[885] The hagiographical tradition around St. Anastasios of Persia provides typical examples of a demon revealing the means of his own expulsion. In his *Roman Miracle*, a demon possesses a young nun of noble origin. The evil spirit told the exorcist that the ex-fiancé of the girl, frustrated by her decision to break the engagement and become a nun, used magic to force the spirit to enter her body and torture her.[886]

On rare occasions, the demon could answer theoretical questions about his goals and deeds. Such conversations between the evil spirit and the exorcist are the forerunner of Byzantine demonology of the eleventh to the thirteenth century, but still do not form a coherent and complex

---

[881] Gregory of Dekapolis, §6.2.
[882] Elias Speleotes, §44.
[883] Luke of Steiris, §68.
[884] Peter of Atroa, §70.
[885] George of Amastris, §5.
[886] Anastasios of Persia, *Roman Miracle*, §6.4–18. See also Anastasios of Persia, Miracles, 149 (XVI (=ις).8–22), where the anonymous author tells the story of a possessed citizen of Abydos. In this text, the demon discloses to a ship-owner that only the holy relics of St. Anastasios could save his victim.

system of ideas. The basic concept is that God allows the Devil to send demons to possess and torture humans for their sins and to make them better.[887] However, sometimes their goal is to mislead their victims and, ultimately, to murder them.[888] The idea that they could be controlled through magic or ritual is very rare.

* * *

Demons were generally considered pathetic creatures and frequently became an object of ridicule. However, sometimes they could also demonstrate a sense of humor and mock the exorcist or the victim. According to the hagiographical texts, sarcasm and irony were typical rhetorical devices used by them.[889] For example, in the *Roman Miracle of St. Anastasios of Persia*, the demon says with feigned regret: *Ah! Ah! What did I achieve all day?! I managed to commit only three murders!* Immediately afterward, he adds: *I am pleased about my deeds!*[890] In the *Life* of St. Elias Speleotes, an evil spirit calls, with a combination of irony and sarcasm, the Saint's wooden shoe *a turtle*.[891] St. Paul of Latros (900–December 15, 955) was continuously threatened and mocked by demons during one of his early hermitages in western Asia Minor. At the funeral of the same Saint, a possessed man began to parody the Psalms under evil influence.[892]

One of the most detailed descriptions of the evil spirits' macabre sense of humor is found in the *Life* of St. Irene of Chrysobalanton. She used to pray all night without the slightest movement. Her piety was torture to the Devil's servants, and a phalanx of demons constantly tried to disturb her composure with silly shouts and make her move. Their most cunning trick, says the anonymous author, was to mock her, like mimes

---

[887] Luke of Steiris, §69.21–27; Irene of Chrysobalanton, §15.
[888] Symeon Stylites the Younger, §147.21–24.
[889] See Mango, *Empire*, 163.
[890] Anastasios of Persia, *Roman Miracle*, §7.5ff.
[891] Elias Speleotes, §94.
[892] Paul of Latros I, §45.9–10.

(*μυκτηρίζειν καὶ τὰ μίμων φθέγγεσθαι*), childishly laughing at her that she was *wooden* and *stood on wooden legs*.[893]

Finally, a typical display of the perverted demonic sense of humor was the ironic repetition of the sacred formulas uttered by exorcists to expel them. When St. Theodore Sykeotes was thirteen years old and already a highly esteemed religious figure in his region, the father of a possessed boy asked him to drive out an evil spirit from his son. The young hermit was still inexperienced, and the ritual took two days. One of the demon's sinister tricks was to repeat the incantation *Go away, go away, unclean spirit!* On the third day, Theodore's efforts were crowned with success, and the demon was finally expelled.[894]

4.2. Ventriloquism and divination

According to Byzantine hagiography, one of the most common methods used by demons to deceive humans was false prophecies.[895] This concept and the stories related to it provide the modern scholar with valuable information not only about the supernatural as an element of folklore and as a literary motif, but also about the professional "mediums" in the cities in Late Antiquity and the early medieval period. In his *Life* of St. Symeon the Fool, Leontios of Neapolis mentions *people possessed by demons who earned their living speaking and predicting the future* in Emesa, Syria. Such false prophets, says the hagiographer, used certain tricks to persuade their audience. Most typically, they used to change abruptly the timbre and the pitch of their voices to give the impression that some supernatural force had taken control of their vocal cords.[896] False predictions could be especially sinister, like the demon who portended the death of his victim three days after the exorcism performed by St. Theodore Sykeotes.[897]

---

[893] Irene of Chrysobalanton, §11; see also §15.
[894] Theodore Sykeotes, §18.
[895] For Byzantine beliefs in deceitful prophecies, see Greenfield, *Traditions of Belief*, 128ff and 291–97.
[896] Symeon the Holy Fool, 90.3ff.
[897] Theodore Sykeotes, §84.28ff.

Byzantine hagiography in the period under study almost entirely lacks information about concrete rituals for summoning demons to predict the future. This is not surprising. Such malicious practices and stories would have no place in religious texts that spread an edifying and soul-saving message. Late Byzantine demonological treatises and the *History* of Niketas Choniates provide much more information about procedures like lecanomancy (dish-divination) and katoptromancy (mirror-divination).[898] However, hagiographers occasionally mention **ventriloquism or gastromancy** (ἐγγραστριμυθία),[899] namely, a practice in which a person (a ventriloquist) creates the illusion that their voice is coming from the stomach in which some spirit has taken up residence.[900] This method of predicting the future was well-known both in Classical Greece and in the Jewish tradition. Aristophanes[901] and Plato[902] mention a famous ventriloquist named Eurycles, who was very influential in Athens in the second half of the fifth century. According to Plutarch, it was a widespread belief that a divine power possesses the body of the ventriloquist, also called *the python*,[903] and whispers prophesies through their mouth.[904] These examples, separated by

---

[898] On the λεκανομαντεία and κατοπτρομαντεία in Late Byzantine demonological treatises, see Armand Delatte, *La catoptromancie grecque et les dérivés* (Liège-Paris, 1932), 13–122; Greenfield, *Traditions of Belief*, 291–97. One of the most detailed descriptions of such magical practices is given by the anonymous treatise, ascribed to Michael Psellus, *What do the Greeks think about demons?* (Τίνα περὶ δαιμόνων δοξάζουσιν Ἕλληνες) (see [Pseudo-]Michael Psellus, "Quaenam sunt Graecorum opiniones de daemonibus", in MPG, vol. 122 (Paris, 1889), 880C–881C).

[899] On the meaning of the Greek word, see *Greek Lexicon of the Roman and Byzantine Periods*, ed. Evangelinos Sophocles, (Hildesheim – Zürich – New York, 1992), s.v. "ἐγγαστρίμυθος" (*speaking from the belly, ventriloquist*). See also Greenfield, *Traditions of Belief*, 128ff; Vakaloudi, *Magic*, 51, 62, 147 and 521.

[900] Philochorus, "Fragmenta", ed. Felix Jacoby, *Die Fragmente der griechischen Historiker*, vol. 3B (Leiden: Brill, 1954), fr. 78.4–5: *The ventriloquist* (ἐγγαστρίμυθος) *is a person who foretells through their stomach*.

[901] "Aristophanis Vespae", ed. Nigel Wilson, *Aristophanis Fabulae* (Oxford: Oxford University Press, 2007), ll. 1019–20.

[902] Plato, "Sophista", ed. John Burnet, *Platonis opera*, vol. 1 (Oxford: Clarendon Press, 1968), 952c.

[903] On the so-called *python spirit* (πνεῦμα πύθωνα), see also Acts 16:16.

[904] Plutarchus, "De defectu oraculorum", ed. Wilhelm Sieveking, *Plutarchi moralia*, vol. 3 (Leipzig: Teubner, 1972), 414e.

more than five centuries, show that this magical practice was widespread in the Greco-Roman world. The Septuagint provided the theoretical and conceptual basis for its demonization by Christianity. One of the best examples is the story about the Witch of Endor. According to the biblical text, King Saul banished the ventriloquists and the oracles from his kingdom after the prophet Samuel's death. However, the Philistines soon attacked him, and the King begged God to give him a revelation.[905] When his prayers remained unanswered, he consulted a woman from Endor, a renowned ventriloquist (γυναῖκα ἐγγαστρίμυθον).[906] With her help, the King summoned the spirit of the prophet Samuel.[907] This story does not mention evil spirits or the Devil, and the soothsayer is not burdened with negative connotations. She managed to summon the dead prophet's soul, not some deceitful spirit. Despite this, the official Hebrew tradition of the Old Testament usually treats ventriloquism with the utmost severity.[908] This is evident in the story of the abominable King Manasseh. Along with his other vices, this Jewish ruler paid great attention to various magical practices and frequently summoned the souls of the dead with the help of ventriloquists.[909]

---

[905] I Kings 28:3–6.
[906] I Kings 28:7.
[907] I Kings 28:11–19; I Chron., 10:13.
[908] Isa. 8:19: *mediums and spiritists, who whisper and mutter through their bellies* (τοὺς ἐγγαστριμύθους, τοὺς κενολογοῦντας οἳ ἐκ τῆς κοιλίας φωνοῦσιν); Lev., 19:31: *Do not turn to mediums or seek out spiritists* (Greek: *ventriloquists*), *for you will be defiled by them. I am the Lord your God* (Οὐκ ἐπακολουθήσετε ἐγγαστριμύθοις καὶ ἐπαοιδοῖς οὐ προσκολληθήσεσθε ἐκμιανθῆναι ἐν αὐτοῖς. Ἐγὼ εἰμὶ κύριος ὁ θεὸς ὑμῶν); Lev., 20:6: *I will set my face against anyone who turns to mediums and spiritists* (Greek: *ventriloquists*) *to prostitute themselves by following them, and I will cut them off from their people* (καὶ ἡ ψυχή, ἣ ἐὰν ἐπακολουθήσῃ ἐγγαστριμύθοις ἢ ἐπαοιδοῖς ὥστε ἐκπορνεῦσαι ὀπίσω αὐτῶν, ἐπιστήσω τὸ πρόσωπόν μου ἐπὶ τὴν ψυχὴν ἐκείνην καὶ ἀπολῶ αὐτὴν ἐκ τοῦ λαοῦ αὐτῆς). According to Lev., 20:27, *A man or woman who is a medium or spiritist* (Greek: *ventriloquists*) *among you must be put to death* (Καὶ ἀνὴρ ἢ γυνή, ὃς ἂν γένηται αὐτῶν ἐγγαστρίμυθος ἢ ἐπαοιδός, θανάτῳ θανατούσθωσαν ἀμφότεροι).
[909] II Chron., 33:6: *[he] practiced divination and witchcraft, sought omens, and consulted mediums and spiritists* (Greek: *ventriloquists*). *He did much evil in the eyes of the Lord, arousing his anger* (καὶ ἐκληδονίζετο καὶ οἰωνίζετο καὶ ἐφαρμακεύετο καὶ ἐποίησεν ἐγγαστριμύθους καὶ ἐπαοιδούς: ἐπλήθυνεν τοῦ ποιῆσαι τὸ πονηρὸν καὶ ἐναντίον κυρίου τοῦ παροργίσαι αὐτόν).

Despite the biblical text's not unfavorable attitude to the Witch of Endor, Byzantine hagiographers' interpretation was different. For example, the author of the *Life* of St. George od Choziba explains that the unclean spirit acting through the ventriloquist could not summon the real soul of the prophet Samuel and Saul talked to a demon.[910] However, the most interesting account of ventriloquism is mentioned by the anonymous author of the *Life* of St. Symeon Stylites. Even though the story was probably compiled under the influence of the Witch of Endor, this episode gives valuable information about the superstitions that dominated the imperial court in the late sixth century. According to the hagiographer, Emperor Justinus II (565–578) fell seriously ill, and Empress Sophia found a Jewish doctor named Timotheos to help him. The physician was a well-known *servant of the demons and was engaged in magical practices*,[911] but, despite the admonitions of Patriarch John III (565–577) and St. Symeon Stylites, the imperial couple refused to stop using his services. When the doctor's efforts to discover the reason for the emperor's illness proved unsuccessful, the Jew decided to take even more drastic matters and called a ventriloquist into the palace.[912] Justinus was punished for his behavior with fits of madness.[913]

It is extremely difficult for the modern scholar to discern the historical reality behind the episode of Emperor Justin and his soothsayer, since the influence of the biblical story of King Saul and the Witch of Endor is obvious. Nevertheless, there are other accounts on Byzantine rulers who consulted ventriloquists on various political matters. For example, the so-called *Synodal Letter to Emperor Theophilos*[914] claims that two Jew-

---

[910] George of Choziba, §10.52.1–3: *And Saul, tricked by the ventriloquist to see the evil spirit he had sighted as Samuel, approached him as he emerged from the earth, and greeted him respectfully* (Καὶ Σαοὺλ ὑπὸ τῆς ἐγγαστριμύθου παιχθεὶς πνεῦμα πονηρὸν θεωρήσας ὡς τὸν Σαμουὴλ βλέπων ἀναβαίνοντα ἐκ τῆς γῆς προσεγγίσας προσεκύνησεν).

[911] Symeon Stylites the Younger, §208.17ff.

[912] Symeon Stylites the Younger, §209.15–18.

[913] Symeon Stylites the Younger, §211.

[914] BHG [1387]. The text was compiled after the final restoration of the icons in 843, but was erroneously attributed to John of Damascus.

ish ventriloquists, banished by Caliph "Yezi", predicted to Leo, a young man of low origin, that he was destined to ascend the Byzantine throne.[915] Years later, the prophecy was fulfilled, and Leo III (717–741) became the first Iconoclast emperor. According to the same text, *the air demon Python*, using an ugly female ventriloquist, *predicted* the coronation of Emperor Leo V (815–820), who restored Iconoclasm as the official dogma.[916] The first story is inaccurate chronologically, since Yazid II (720–724) became Caliph almost three years after the beginning of Leo III's own reign in Constantinople. However, this is not a sound reason to reject the text as a source for such practices, both in the Caliphate and Byzantium.

---

[915] Joannes Damscenus, "Epistola ad Theophilum imperatorem de sanctis et venerandis imaginibus", in MPG, vol. 95, (Paris, 1864), 357A.
[916] Joannes Damscenus, "Epistola ad Theophilum", 368A. George Hamarolos copies the story almost verbatim (*Georgii Monachi Chronicon*, vol. 2, 736).

CHAPTER 2
COMPLEX ANTHROPOMORPHIC IMAGES

In the previous chapter we outlined the particular features that characterize the image of the demon and the bodies of its victims. A gigantic or dwarfish stature, disproportion and deformity, bloodshot eyes, a hoarse and threatening voice, rags or too sumptuous clothing, all constitute the stereotypical model of Evil's innate ugliness. Some of these elements can be found in ancient Greek and Roman literature and in biblical texts. However, it is a matter of great controversy whether Byzantine hagiographers consciously borrowed these features from ancient sources or, rather, inherited them as a part of various cultural traditions whose roots could be traced back to the most ancient mythological narratives of Europe and the Near East — and thence to the *Maleus Maleficarum* and modern horror novels and movies. We have no reason to accept as a proven fact that the deformed body of the Byzantine evil spirit necessarily belongs to a particular literary tradition or traditions. The ugliness of the demon is a reflection of the malicious supernatural creatures' image, one belonging, perhaps, to all times, cultures, and literatures. However, Byzantine hagiographers sift out some of the heterogeneous folklore elements and beliefs, shaping in this manner a simplified pattern of traits that resemble, if only remotely, standard biblical prototypes.

In this chapter, we will deal with the origins and characteristics of several more complex images. The standard traits of demonic ugliness outlined above continue to be invariably present. The demon can never fully attain the innocent and innate human beauty, the living image of our own divine creation. The demon spoils the perfect beauty of his human host and can be recognized by its ugliness, because: "...for us as human beings, no beauty resonates with our own essence, with our deep nature, like the grace and perfection of our own bodies. In its presence, we react instantly....".⁹¹⁷ However, with evil creatures like the "Ethiopian", the soldier, the Jew, the Arab, and the witch, the researcher finds himself on much more solid and familiar ground, able to discern with relative certainty borrowings from ancient literature and the biblical tradition. In addition, these images provide valuable information about the attitude towards distinct marginalized minorities and social groups. Racism and discrimination against women are by no means exclusively Western and modern phenomena. They can be effectively traced back to the origins of European culture both in the East and the West.

1. The black man: symbolism and transformations of darkness

1.1. Origins

It is hard to find a more common personification of Evil in Byzantine hagiography than the ugly black *Ethiopian* (Αἰθίοψ).⁹¹⁸ The evolution of this image before Christianity is highly complex, like the term *daimon* itself. Greek authors of the Archaic and Classical periods show a clear tendency to idealize the mythical inhabitants of Ethiopia, whose name could be translated as *the ones with the burned face* (from the verb αἴθω and the suffix -οψ) and is used for Africa's native tribes in general. Homer considers them *the farthermost of men*,⁹¹⁹ the very incarnation of the exotic

---

[917] Petar Plamenov, *The Promises of the Interesting* [Bulgarian: Петър Пламенов, *Обещанията на интересното*], Sofia: Sofia University Press, 2019, 180.

[918] On the meaning of the word denoting the black man in general, see *LSJ*, s.v. "Αἰθίοψ". See also Frank Snowden, "The Negro in Classical Italy", *American Journal of Philology* 68, no. 3 (1947): 268; Apostolos Karpozilos, "The position of blacks in Byzantine society", in *Marginal People in Byzantium*, ed. Chryssa Maltezou [Greek: Απόστολος Καρποζήλος, "Η θέση των μαύρων στη Βυζαντινή κοινωνία", in *Οι περιθωριακοί στο Βυζάντιο*, ed. Χρύσα Μαλτέζου], (Athens, 1999), 69. On the descriptions of black Ethiopians in ancient literature, see Byron, *Symbolic Blackness*, 39–41 (with bibliography).

[919] See Homer, *Odyssey*, I.22–24 who calls them ἔσχατοι ἀνδρῶν. On the Ethiopians as a distant, isolated people, see also *Strabonis geographica*, ed. Karl Müller (Cambridge: Cambridge University Press, 2015), I.2.27–28, which quotes numerous other authors. See also Byron, *Symbolic Blackness*, 31.

unknown; for Herodotus, they live *at the end of the world*.[920] However, the specific "otherness"[921] associated with the black man (female images are scarce) is controversial for the pagan and Christian weltanschauung. Reading the *Iliad*'s First Rhapsody, we have the feeling that the *blameless, excellent* (ἀμύμονες) Ethiopians are strange and mysterious, but also a semi-divine people, noble enough to organize a twelve-day banquet for Zeus and his wife Hera.[922] Herodotus adds other elements to their image: physical beauty, exceptional tallness[923], and running ability.[924] The color of their skin has no negative connotations, and the account of their black sperm just adds to their exotic image.[925]

The Ethiopian's black skin as a symbol of spiritual and corporeal vice appears in the poems of Pindar[926] and especially in the works of Aristotle. The latter is skeptical about their black semen[927] but replaces this peculiar legend with another: in his opinion, black people are cowardly by nature.[928] The contempt for black skin is also apparent in other Greek and Roman authors' works.[929] For example, in Pseudo-Callisthenes's *Alexander Romance*, the Ethiopian queen (Kandake) sends a letter to the Macedonian king where she advises him not to *look down on the color* of

---

[920] Hérodote, *Histoires*, ed. Philippe-Ernest Legrand, vol. 3: *Livre III: Thalie* [Collection Budé 92.2] (Paris: Les Belles Lettres, 1967), III.25–5, claims that the Ethiopians live at the end of the world (τὰ ἔσχατα τῆς γῆς).

[921] Byron, *Symbolic Blackness*, 51.

[922] Homer, *Iliad*, I.423ff.

[923] Hérodote, *Histoires*, vol. 3, III.20.5–7: Οἱ δὲ Αἰθίοπες... λέγονται εἶναι μέγιστοι καὶ κάλλιστοι ἀνθρώπων πάντων.

[924] Hérodote, *Histoires*, ed. Philippe-Ernest Legrand, vol. 4: *Livre IV: Melpomène* [Collection Budé 100.1] (Paris: Les Belles Lettres, 1945), IV.183.15.

[925] Hérodote, *Histoires*, 3: III.101.4–6.

[926] Pindar, "Fragmenta incerta", ed. Herwig Maehler and Bruno Snell, *Pindari carmina cum fragmentis*, vol. 2 (Leipzig: Teubner, 1975), fr. 225.1–226.1.

[927] Aristote, *Histoire des animaux*, ed. Pierre Louis, vol. 1: *Livres I–IV* (Paris: Les Belles Lettres, 1964), 523a.17ff.

[928] Aristoteles "Physiognomonica", ed. Immanuel Bekker, *Aristotelis opera*, vol. 2 (Berlin: De Gruyter, 1960), 812a.12ff. On this passage, see also Byron, *Symbolic Blackness*, 35.

[929] For a detailed list of the Greek and Roman authors who mention the αἰθίοπες/Aethiopes, see Snowden, "The Negro", 268–71.

her people's skin, because their souls are *brighter than the souls of the whitest* of his subjects.[930]

In ancient Roman literature, both the admiration for the black man's impressive stature and the contempt for his skin color is clearly preserved.[931] For example, this ambivalence can be found in Juvenal's *Satires*, where the Ethiopian symbolizes uncontrollable sexual potency, a great temptation for the noble Roman matron. The poet advises his reader to give his wife the abortion potion himself unless he is willing to become *[an] Ethiopian's father*.[932]

As early as the first century A.D., when major dualistic religions of eastern origin emerged in the Greco-Roman world, the Ethiopians proved to be a suitable image that could easily be charged with demonic functions and, above all, be associated with death and the Hereafter. According to Suetonius, the *Aethiopes* personified the world of the dead (*argumenta inferiorum*) in the nocturnal performances organized by Emperor Gaius Caligula.[933] A few decades later, Emperor Domitian frightened his distinguished guests in a similar way. He invited them into a black-painted hall and forced them to watch the creepy dances of boys with faces covered with black ink, who symbolized the dead.[934] About a

---

[930] "Historia Alexandri Magni. Recensio α sive Recensio vetusta", ed. Wilhelm Kroll, *Historia Alexandri Magni*, vol. 1 (Berlin: Weidmann, 1926), III.18.5: μὴ καταγνῷς δὲ τοῦ χρώματος ἡμῶν· ἐσμὲν γὰρ λευκότεροι καὶ λαμπρότεροι ταῖς ψυχαῖς τῶν παρὰ σοῦ λευκοτάτων.

[931] On the two meanings of the name *Aethiopes* in Roman literature, see Snowden, "The Negro", 268–71; Byron, *Symbolic Blackness*, 32–41.

[932] "Juvenalis Saturae", ed. and trans. Susanna Braund, *Juvenal and Persius* [Loeb Classical Library, 91] (Cambridge, MA: Harvard University Press, 2004), §6.600ff.: *esses Aethiopis fortasse pater, mox decolor heres impleret tabulas numquam tibi mane videndus*. On this passage and the attitude of Juvenal and his contemporaries to the Ethiopians, see the detailed study by David Wiesen, "Juvenal and the Blacks", *Classica et Mediaevalia* 31 (1970): 132-150, with bibliography.

[933] Suetonius, "Caligula", ed. and trans. John Rolfe, *De vita Caesarum*, vol. 1 [Loeb Classical Library 31] (Cambridge, MA: Harvard University Press, 1913), §57.4: *parabatur et in noctem spectaculum, quo argumenta inferiorum per Aegyptios et Aethiopas explicarentur*.

[934] *Cassii Dionis Cocceiani historiarum Romanarum quae supersunt*, ed. Ursul Boissevain, vol. 3, (Berlin: Weidmann, 1898), LXVII.9.1–5.

century later, Lucian described in his *Lover of Lies* (*Philopseudes*) a *black, smoke-like demon* who emerged from his victim.[935]

Little by little, at the beginning of our era, the man with a dark or swarthy skin (the "negro" and the Indian) gradually becomes the most persistent personification of death in European literature and culture. On a social level, this tendency will create enduring contempt for and fear of the black "race". It will also fertilize the soil for the discrimination and racism that dominated the Western world during the early modern period, with the arrival of the first ships carrying enslaved Africans on the shores of present-day Brazil.

Before we turn our attention to the main subject of this chapter, the black demon in hagiography, we must make a short survey of the other component of this complex image, namely the biblical tradition. In the Old Testament, Ethiopians are extremely rare and are by no means associated with the Devil. Sometimes they appear as enemies of the Chosen People[936] and are used in idioms with pejorative connotations.[937] An Ethiopian woman (αἰθιόπισσα) appears in the Book of Numbers, where Moses takes her as his wife, and his brother Aaron scorns him for this choice.[938] The African origin of the Queen of Sheba,[939] King Solomon's beloved girl, so beautifully exalted at the beginning of the Song of Songs,[940] is mere speculation.

---

[935] Lucian, "The Lover of Lies", §16.
[936] See, e.g., 2 Chron., 14:9–12, where God helps the Jewish king Asa to defeat the Ethiopian king Zerah (in the Greek text: Ζαρὲ ὁ Αἰθίοψ).
[937] See Jer., 13:23: *Can an Ethiopian change his skin or a leopard its spots? Neither can you do good who are accustomed to doing evil* (εἰ ἀλλάξεται Αἰθίοψ τὸ δέρμα αὐτοῦ καὶ πάρδαλις τὰ ποικίλματα αὐτῆς, καὶ ὑμεῖς δυνήσεσθε εὖ ποιῆσαι μεμαθηκότες τὰ κακά). On this passage, see Karpozilos, "The Position of the Blacks", 70.
[938] Num., 12:1–2.
[939] 1 Kings 10:1–12; 2 Chron. 9:1–13. The text says nothing about her appearance.
[940] Song, 1:4–5: *Dark am I, yet lovely, daughters of Jerusalem, dark like the tents of Kedar, like the tent curtains of Solomon. Do not stare at me because I am dark, because I am darkened by the sun. My mother's sons were angry with me and made me take care of the vineyards* (Μέλαινά εἰμι καὶ καλή, θυγατέρες Ιερουσαλημ, ὡς σκηνώματα Κηδαρ, ὡς δέρρεις Σαλωμων. μὴ βλέψητέ με, ὅτι ἐγώ εἰμι μεμελανωμένη, ὅτι παρέβλεψέν με ὁ ἥλιος· υἱοὶ μητρός μου ἐμαχέσαντο ἐν ἐμοί, ἔθεντό με φυλάκισσαν ἐν ἀμπελῶσιν·

In the New Testament, Ethiopians are also relatively positive characters. In the Acts of the Apostles, the apostle Philip meets a eunuch of the Ethiopian queen,[941] who had come to Jerusalem on pilgrimage. Inspired by God, he explains to him a passage from the prophet Isaiah and, at his request, baptizes him in a roadside spring.[942] In this story, St. Philip fulfills the mission assigned by Christ to His twelve disciples to spread His message *to the ends of the earth* (ἕως ἐσχάτου τῆς γῆς).[943] The high-ranking Ethiopian represents the most distant people in the world.[944]

The above few passages of the Old and the New Testament present the black African mainly in a positive light. This idea was useful to the first apologists in their struggle against paganism. In the early stages of its development, the Church tried to draw as many adepts as possible. Ethnic, racial, and even linguistic differences were unimportant in this effort. Characteristically, the word ἐθνικός (*a pagan, a non-Christian*) comes from the Greek word for *nation* or *tribe* (ἔθνος). Christians are united by their belief in the message of Christ, while other people are separated by their different customs, cults, languages, and outer appearance. In addition, the native inhabitants of North Africa, and especially Egypt, were among the first adepts of the new global religion, and many of them had a dark or swarthy complexion. In this context, ancient prejudices regarding black skin, expressed by authors like Juvenal, Suetonius, and Dio Cassius, were mortally dangerous to the global dominance of the Church.[945] Intellectuals like Origen were fully aware of this fact. In his interpretation, King Solomon's "black" lover (1 Kings 10:1–12) symbolizes the non-Jewish Church whose members are not descendants of *bright and enlightened ancestors* but nevertheless embrace the true God.[946] In addi-

---

ἀμπελῶνα ἐμὸν οὐκ ἐφύλαξα). The biblical text is more than clear that she was forced to work outside, unlike more affluent women. Her skin was tanned, not black.

[941] The title of the Ethiopian queen (κανδάκη) has been erroneously perceived as her given name.
[942] Acts 8:27–39.
[943] Acts 1:8.
[944] This interpretation belongs to Byron, *Symbolic Blackness*, 49, 109–15.
[945] This is the opinion of Karpozilos, "The Position of the Blacks", 70.
[946] Byron, *Symbolic Blackness*, 43 and 72–75; Karpozilos, "The Position of the Blacks", 70.

tion, this non-discriminatory attitude towards people with dark or black skin was politically helpful in the fourth to the seventh centuries, when the interests of the empire south of Egypt and on the western and eastern coast of the Red Sea required good relationships with the rulers of Ethiopia and Sudan.[947]

However, Origen's positive attitude toward the "Ethiopians" does not seem to have had much effect on popular prejudices against dark- or black-skinned people. Proverbs and idioms like *An Ethiopian does not turn white* (Αἰθίοψ οὐ λευκαίνεται), *to wash an Ethiopian* (Αἰθίοπα σμήχειν, meaning *to do pointless work*), *an Ethiopian always remains an Ethiopian* (Αἰθίοψ Αἰθίοψ μένει)[948] give us a clue about the level of discrimination in the Byzantine world. According to the so-called *Sayings of the Desert Fathers* (fifth century), a group of church priests insulted Father Moses the Ethiopian's black skin and kicked him off the altar. The humble old man asked himself rhetorically: *You are not human yourself — why do you come among people?*[949] In addition, if we believe Theodore Studite, the Byzantines, like Juvenal's contemporary Romans, still feared black men's sexual attractiveness. The learned eighth-century theologian mentions the obviously widespread superstition that *if a woman fantasizes about an Ethiopian during conception, she will give birth to an Ethiopian*.[950] As evident from Karpozelos's research,[951] such stories and sayings are by no means small in number in Byzantine literature.

---

[947] For more detail on the empire's relationships with Ethiopia and Sudan, see Karpozilos, "The Position of the Blacks", 70–73. Although information about these matters is scarce, the sources reveal an active diplomatic game led by the imperial envoys in the region, especially during the reigns of Constantine I (307–337), Constantius II (337–361), Anastasios I (491–518) and Justinian I (527–565).

[948] For more detail on these sayings, see Karpozilos, "The Position of the Blacks", 74 and n. 23, with bibliography.

[949] Palladius Hellenopolitanus episcopus, "Apophthegmata Patrum", in MPG, vol. 65 (Paris, 1864), 284B: Μὴ ὢν ἄνθρωπος, τί ἔρχῃ μετὰ ἀνθρώπων.

[950] *Theodori Studitae Epistulae*, ed. Georgios Fatouros, vol. 2 [*Corpus Fontium Historiae Byzantinae. Series Berolinensis* 31.2] (Berlin: De Gruyter, 1992), esp. 380.175–77: ἐγὼ δὲ καὶ ἄλλως ἄγαμαι τὴν φαντασίαν· φασὶ γάρ τινες γυναῖκα κατὰ τὸν τῆς συλλήψεως καιρὸν Αἰθίοπα φαντασθεῖσαν Αἰθίοπα ἀποτεκεῖν.

[951] Karpozilos, "The Position of the Blacks", 76–80.

The above prejudices towards the Ethiopian combine on a theoretical level with the biblical tradition related to darkness[952] as one of the most typical and powerful symbols of sin and death. Two passages from the Gospels probably played important role for the demonization of black color in particular:

> But if your eyes are unhealthy, your whole body will be full of darkness [Greek: σκοτεινόν]. If then the light within you is darkness, how great is that darkness![953]

In the Gospel of Luke, the idea that sin darkens the body is even more explicit:

> When your eyes are healthy, your whole body also is full of light. But when they are unhealthy, your body also is full of darkness. See to it, then, that the light within you is not darkness. Therefore, if your whole body is full of light, and no part of it dark, it will be just as full of light as when a lamp shines its light on you.[954]

In these passages of the New Testament, the darkness of the sinner's body is used rather metaphorically. The image of the *Black One* ('Ο Μέλας), an alias of the Devil, appears very early, in the works of the Apostolic Fathers about the end of the first century.[955] One of the most common human forms in Christian literature becomes that of the black man, for whom the authors use adjectives such as *dusky/darkish* (ζοφερός), *pale* (φαιός), and *black* (μέλας). As early as the mid-second century, this idea fused with the ancient literary image of the Ethiopian and popular prejudices towards black skin. The demonic negro, a giant or an imp, appears as the personification of sins or heresies in the earliest proto-hagiographical texts intended for the general public, usually as the main character of standardized storylines. Probably the most common of

---

[952] See, e.g., John, 1:4ff; John, 3:19ff; Eph. 6:12.
[953] Mat. 6:23: ἐὰν δὲ ὁ ὀφθαλμός σου πονηρὸς ᾖ, ὅλον τὸ σῶμά σου σκοτεινὸν ἔσται.
[954] Luke 11:34: ὁ λύχνος τοῦ σώματός ἐστιν ὁ ὀφθαλμός σου. ὅταν ὁ ὀφθαλμός σου ἁπλοῦς ᾖ, καὶ ὅλον τὸ σῶμά σου φωτεινόν ἐστιν· ἐπὰν δὲ πονηρὸς ᾖ, καὶ τὸ σῶμά σου σκοτεινόν.
[955] For the anonymous *Letter of Barnabas* and other early Christian texts in which "The Black One" appears, see Greenfield, *Traditions of Belief*, 24–27; Byron, *Symbolic Blackness*, 58–75.

the latter is the battle of a righteous, holy man against the forces of Evil. One of the earliest Christian examples of this story is the Latin version of the apocryphal Acts of Peter and Paul, written in the second half of the second century. In this text, the noble senator Marcellus sees a vast crowd in a dream. The people were watching *a repulsive woman, Ethiopian in appearance, wholly black*.[956] She was dancing deliriously, though in chains. At this moment, St. Peter, who was also watching, ordered Marcellus to cut off her head — she was the personification of Symeon the Mage's heresy. John Moschus (c. 550–619) tells a similar story in his *Spiritual Meadow*. An angel led a distinguished abbot in his dream to an overcrowded amphitheater. Half of the audience was clad in white, and the other half consisted of ugly Ethiopians. The monk had to fight with a giant black man. He overcame his fear, defeated his frightful enemy, and took the crown of victory. The Ethiopians immediately disappeared from the audience.[957] The black demon remains a symbol of the heresies in hagiography as well. In the *Life* of St. Melania the Younger (c. 383–439), the Devil spreads *the impure Nestorian heresy*. He appears before the Saint as a *black youngster (μετασχηματισθεὶς εἰς μέλανα νεανίσκον)* and inflicts unbearable pain to restrain her benevolent influence upon the people's souls.[958] The Ethiopian is also frequently associated with particular sins — pride, for example.[959]

1.2. Visions and dreams

Beginning in the early seventh century, the empire gradually lost control over the old Roman provinces in Africa, and its black population lost its importance for the Church. The Arabs conquered Egypt in 645, and the

---

[956] Acta Petri, 22: *mulierem quendam turpissimam, in expectu Aethiopissimam... totam nigram.*

[957] Joannes Moschus, "Beatis Joannis Eucratae liber, qui inscribitur pratum, quod floridam proferat vitarum narrationem coelestis roseti", in MPG, vol. 87.3 (Paris, 1863), 2917A–B.

[958] Melania, §2.54. On the relationship between heresies and black demons, see Byron, *Symbolic Blackness*, 46.

[959] See *Historia monachorum in Aegypto*, ed. André-Jean Festugière (Brussels: Société des Bollandistes, 1971), §8.30–33.

exarchate of Africa, along with its capital Carthage, followed fast in 697. Most of the hagiographers of the period under study very reasonably chose to adapt to the attitudes of their predominantly European audience and the popular prejudices toward the distant "Ethiopians". Although the black demon is by no means a rare phenomenon in the first centuries A.D., the image became stereotypical after the mid-sixth century, when it was enriched with standard demonic features like gigantic or dwarfish size, deformity, bloodshot eyes, and a hoarse voice.

In Byzantine hagiography, the ugly and evil Ethiopian appears as a dangerous creature, predominantly male. The only text that mentions a black female demon is the *Life* of St. Theodore Sykeotes.[960] Detailed accounts of his outer appearance are rare and usually appear in stories about visions and dreams. In one of his sermons before the despairing citizens of Antioch, devastated by the Persian invasions and natural disasters of the 540s, St. Symeon Stylites describes the Devil as *a shameless tall Ethiopian with a frightful gaze, standing in the air with no support* before God and His angels.[961] The Dark Lord wants to cover the whole earth with his black wings, but the power of the Holy Ghost cuts them off.[962]

Black demons are typically associated with the fate of human souls after death. They swarm around the dying person's bed, search their souls for unconfessed sins, and weigh their good and evil deeds on a scale, but they can also be deceived and defeated with a saint's help in a deadly dangerous dice game. Anthropomorphic evil spirits, called "Ethiopians" or "Indians",[963] typically appear in visions of the Underworld or the dangerous aerial regions between Earth and Heaven.[964] These terrible creatures put the souls of the dead to various trials and punish them for un-

---

[960] Theodore Sykeotes, §86.19–21.
[961] Symeon Stylites the Younger, §124.69–72: ἐνώπιον τοῦ Θεοῦ παρέστηκεν ὁ διάβολος αἰθίωψ ἀναιδής, μακρόν, βλοσυρὸν βλέπων, τοὺς ὀφθαλμοὺς αἱματώδεις ἔχων, καὶ ἵστατο ἐν τῷ ἀέρι οὐκ ἐπί τινος ἐστηριγμένος. The description is partially borrowed from Job 1:6-2:7.
[962] Symeon Stylites the Younger, §125.5: ἐξέκοψεν αὐτοῦ τὰς δύο πτέρυγας.
[963] George of Choziba, §7.30.9–15 (people of India).
[964] Symeon the Holy Fool, 75.7–11 and 101.9–11; Golinduch, 173.6–10; John the Merciful, 396.1–8 and 396.30–36; Basil the Younger, Part II, §§6–40.

confessed and unforgiven sins. The same image often occurs in association with the last few moments of life and the struggle with Death. The dice game with the Devil is a particularly interesting concept, with origins in Ancient Egypt.[965] According to the *Life* of St. Symeon the Fool, a high-ranking official, who was unfaithful to his wife, fell ill. When death was near, he had a horrible dream. He was sitting at a table, playing dice against a black Ethiopian, the personification of Death. The game was not going well for the man, and, at one point, his only hope to win was to throw three sixes. In this critical situation, he saw Symeon the Fool standing beside him, saying:

> What happened, dummy? This blackamoor is really going to win. But give me your word that you will never again defile your wife's bed, and I will throw the dice for you. He will not win![966]

The official solemnly vowed that he would never betray his wife again, and Symeon threw three sixes. When the man awoke, there was no trace of the illness, but the whole house was full of noise and bustle. Symeon was shuffling around the official's home and crying:

> Nice sixes you threw, fool! Believe me, if you break your oath, that blackamoor will do away with you![967]

---

[965] On the ancient Egyptian game *senet* (from the root *sn.t* – *passing, passage*), see Peter Piccione, "The Egyptian Game of Senet and the Migration of the Soul", in *Ancient Board Games in Perspective*, ed. Irving Finkel (London: British Museum Press, 2007), 54-63. Its exact rules remain unknown. Archeological evidence and depictions show that each player had to move five pawns across thirty fields called *homes*. Scenes with the diseased playing against an invisible opponent, symbolizing the Death, were widespread funeral decorations in the Ramesside period (1298-1077 B.C.). A reminiscence of the ancient Egyptian concept of the game against Death occurs in the story told by Herodotus: the dead King "Rhampsinit" (Rameses II) won a game of bones against the goddess Demetra/Hathor in the Underworld from which he returned alive (Hérodote, *Histoires*, ed. Philippe-Ernest Legrand, vol. 2: *Livre II: Euterpe* [Collection Budé 57.2] (Paris: Les Belles Lettres, 1944), II.122).

[966] Symeon the Holy Fool, 99.20-22: τί ἔν, ἔξηχε; ὄντως ἄρτι νικᾷ σε οὗτος ὁ μαῦρος. ἀλλὰ δός μοι λόγον, ὅτι οὐκέτι μιαίνεις τὴν κοίτην τῆς γυναικός σου, καὶ ἐγὼ καταρρίπτω ἀντὶ σοῦ καὶ οὐχ ἥττᾷ σε.

[967] Symeon the Holy Fool, 100.2-3: καλὰ τρίεκτα ἔβαλες, μάταιε. πίστευσον, ἐὰν παραβῇς τὸν ὅρκον σου, ὁ μαῦρος ἐκεῖνος πνίγει σε.

The dice game with the Death disappeared from the saints"*Lives* after the early seventh century, but black Ethiopians were still closely associated with the last moments of human life and with deadly danger. Seriously ill, the thirteen-year-old St. Theodor Sykeotes saw a *black, unclean demon* (ἀκάθαρτον δαιμόνιον μελανοειδές) near his bed, and only St. George was able to save the boy's life.[968] A multitude of Ethiopians (πλήθη αἰθιόπων) surrounded the bed of the venerable Theodora in the *Life* of St. Basil the Younger during her death struggle.[969] They swarmed like bees around the righteous woman's deathbed, trying to accuse her of real and false sins, and seeking to take her soul from the angels to Hell.[970] Theodora describes their faces as *black, gloomy, and dark,* and their appearance as *most terrifying and more bitter than even the Gehenna of fire.*[971] The monk Cosmas says that during a severe illness, he suddenly saw himself surrounded by *indescribable* small creatures with blackened faces.[972] All of them were physically deformed, with distorted faces, inflamed or bloodshot eyes, sore and swollen lips.[973] In the *Life* of St. Elias of Heliopolis (759–779/795), a frightful Ethiopian personifies physical and spiritual death. In 779, Elias was mercilessly scourged and tortured on the orders of the emir of Damascus but heroically refused to renounce

---

[968] Theodore Sykeotes, §17.
[969] Basil the Younger, Part II, §6.28ff. Cf. ibid., §9.40ff: *that dark Ethiopian demons* (οἱ αἰθίοπες ἐκεῖνοι καὶ σκοτεινοὶ δαίμονες).
[970] Basil the Younger, Part II, §9.10ff (ὥσπερ σμῆνος μελισσῶν, οἱ ζοφώδεις καὶ ἀπηγριωμένοι ἐκεῖνοι αἰθίοπες). Cf. also Phantinos the Younger, §30.9ff (ὑπὲρ μελιττῶν σμήνη τάγμασι φαιῶν τινων ἀγρίων).
[971] Basil the Younger, Part II, §6.34-36: τὰ μελανὰ ἑαυτῶν ζοφώδη τε καὶ σκοτεινὰ πρόσωπα, ὧν ἡ θεωρία καὶ μόνη φρικωδεστάτη καὶ πικροτέρα μοι ἐφαίνετο καὶ αὐτῆς τῆς γεέννης τοῦ πυρός. Cf. ibid., Part II, 10.13: *those dark and shadowy demons* (οἱ γοῦν ἀμαυροὶ ἐκεῖνοι καὶ ζωφωμένοι δαίμονες), where the adjective ἀμαυρός means *dark, having no light.*
[972] "La version longue de la vision du moine Cosmas", 84.82-83: πλῆθος ἀνθρωπαρίων ἀνεικάστων, πάντων μὲν ἐχόντων μεμελανωμένα τὰ μιαρὰ αὐτῶν πρόσωπα. See Mango, *Empire*, 152.
[973] "La version longue de la vision du moine Cosmas", 82.84-89.

Christianity.⁹⁷⁴ He had to spend his last night chained in a dungeon and had a prophetic dream. The young martyr was in some majestic place, sitting in a beautiful *pastophorium* (curtained shrine),⁹⁷⁵ a magnificent pavilion woven of flowers in front of him. When he turned his head, he saw behind him a black Ethiopian (τινα μαῦρον Αἰθίοπα) who threatened him with swords, fire, and other terrible deadly weapons. Elias only laughed at the creature, and it disappeared in shame.⁹⁷⁶

The black Ethiopian is also associated with the scales weighing the soul's good and evil deeds after death. This concept, which probably originates in ancient Egyptian mythology, appears only once in the Byzantine hagiography of the period under study, in the *Life* of Patriarch John the Merciful (†619). According to Leontius of Cyprus, the story begins with a group of beggars in an unknown city in North Africa. Idling and enjoying the warmth of the southern sun, they engaged in a vivid discussion about their fellow citizens' habits and characters. Somebody mentioned a certain tax-collector, a well-known miser, who never gave alms to anyone. Another beggar, an extremely pious man with a strong belief in human goodness, bet that he could get charity from the stingy official, and the others accepted. He took his place in front of the miser's home and waited for him. Soon, the master of the house returned from the local bakery. Seeing the beggar, he seethed with anger and, not having a stone, threw a piece of bread at him. The poor man took it and told his companions that the miser gave him the loaf. A few days later, the tax collector fell seriously ill and had an ominous dream. He saw before him a pair of scales. Black, ugly Ethiopians (τινες μαῦροι κακοειδεῖς... Αἰθίοπες) were busily piling up his evil deeds in one of its bowls, while some fearful white-clad figures (ἄλλων τινῶν ... λευχειμονούντων καὶ φοβερῶν τῷ εἴδει) bustled anxiously around the other one, having noth-

---

⁹⁷⁴ Elias of Heliopolis was tortured and sentenced to death by the emir of Damascus Muhammad ibn-Ibrahim (739/40–801). On the *Life* and the biography of St. Elias of Heliopolis, see Part One, Chapter 2, §2.
⁹⁷⁵ The so-called *pastophoria* (παστοφόρια) were special chambers with liturgical functions to the left and right of a church's apse. See *ODB*, vol. 3, s.v. "Pastophoria", 1594.
⁹⁷⁶ Elias of Heliopolis, §15.

ing to balance the scales. Suddenly one of the latter remembered the piece of bread the sinner had thrown at the beggar and put it in the other bowl. The scales leveled immediately, and the publican woke up healthy and vigorous. He made up his mind to spend the rest of his life full of goodness and charity.[977]

1.3. The black demon in the human world

The black demon — defined as "Ethiopian" or, much more rarely, "Indian" — often occurs in descriptions of visions and dreams related to the afterlife. However, this is one of the most common incarnations of evil spirits in the human world as well.[978] Here, the ugly Ethiopian retains the main characteristics: he is typically associated with deadly danger, death, diseases, and sin. One of the best sources for this image is the *Life* of Symeon Stylites the Younger. Since the Saint lived during the first outbreaks of the so-called "Justinianic Plague" (541–549), this is not surprising. This event, along with the military expeditions of Shah Khusraw I and other natural disasters, created an apocalyptic atmosphere in the Byzantine East and paved the way for an interesting mixture of mythological beliefs and ideas, until then scattered among the peoples living in these territories. The anonymous author of the *Life* of St. Symeon tells the story of a boy who caught the plague. His relatives lost all hope that he would recover, but the seemingly doomed patient suddenly had a vision. He saw St. Symeon dragging a chained headless black demon to a blazing oven.[979] The boy screamed loudly, his eyes popping out of the sockets, but when the Saint forced the terrible creature into the flames, he abruptly calmed down, and the fever suddenly disappeared. It must be noted that the *Life* of St. Symeon Stylites the Younger is by no means the only text that mentions the headless black demon as a personification of fever and

---

[977] John the Merciful, 368.6–369.10.
[978] See, e.g., Luke of Steiris, §68.14.
[979] Symeon Stylites the Younger, §231.75ff: *and he held some black, formless demon bound by him* (καὶ δαίμων τις μέλας καὶ ἀειδής, ἀκέφαλος τυγχάνων, κεκράτηται δεσμευόμενος παρ' αὐτοῦ). Cf. also Matthew Dickie, "Bonds and Headless Demons in Graeco-roman Magic", *Greek Roman and Byzantine Studies* 40, no. 1 (1999): 100ff.

plague. In the *Chronicle* of John of Ephesus, preserved in the Syrian *Chronicle* of Pseudo-Dionysios of Tel-Mahre, headless black figures wander about the Palestinian ports in bronze boats and spread the deadly illness.[980]

The anonymous author of the *Life* of St. Symeon combines three discrete elements to produce the complex image of the demon who infected the boy with fever: black color, headlessness, and shackles. Rituals involving chains and binding (κατάδεσις, κατάδεσμος, φιλτροκατάδεσμον) were widespread in love magic as early as the fourth century B.C.[981] During Late Antiquity, these practices required particular spells preserved in the so-called "magical papyri".[982] There are three other stories in the *Life* of St. Symeon that recall these ancient rites. In the first, two evil spirits hung a villager named Jacob on a tree by his legs, and the Saint sent them to Hell in chains.[983] In the second, a demon *bound* his victim, a noble official (*silentiarius*), in such a way that he was unable to have sexual intercourse with his wife.[984] Only the Saint was able to *free the man from the Devilish chains* and restore his potency.[985] In the third case, a village priest swore at St. Symeon, and many demons punished him for this profanity, binding his hands behind his back. In this way, the sinful clergyman was utterly unable to read the liturgy and perform his godly duties.[986]

---

[980] Pseudo-Dionysios of Tel-Mahre, *Chronicle, Part III*, ed. and trans. Witold Witakowski [Translated texts for historians 22] (Liverpool: Liverpool University Press, 1996), 77. See Dionysios Stathakopoulos, *Famine and Pestilence in the Late Roman and Early Byzantine Empire: A systematic survey of subsistence crises and epidemics* [Birmingham Byzantine and Ottoman Monographs 9] (Aldershot: Ashgate, 2004), 77.

[981] See Phaidon Koukoules, *Life and Culture of the Byzantines* [Greek: Φαίδων Κουκουλες, Βυζαντινῶν Βίος καὶ πολιτισμός], vol. 6, (Athens: Collection de l'Institut Français d'Athènes, 1955), 207–29; Dickie, "Bonds and Headless Demons", 102ff.

[982] See *PGM*, vol. 1, IV.296ff (φιλτροκατάδεσμος θαυμαστός). See also Dickie, "Bonds and Headless Demons", 99–104, who analyzes the archeological material related to the headless demon.

[983] Symeon Stylites the Younger, §91.14–16.

[984] Symeon Stylites the Younger, §151.2ff.

[985] Symeon Stylites the Younger, §151.10.

[986] Symeon Stylites the Younger, §239.6–9.

The second element of the image of the fever demon in St. Symeon's *Life* is his headlessness. The so-called *Kyrannides* mention a headless evil spirit who attacked both men and women with violent bouts of fever every four days (δαίμων τεταρταῖος... ἀκέφαλος).[987] Since he lacked eyes and ears to hear the healing spells, this sinister creature was tough to deal with.[988] About the same period, the *Testament of Solomon* refers to a demon called Phonos (Murder), who was *humanlike in every way but had no head*.[989] In his fierce desire to obtain one of his own, he used to eat the heads of men and women; being unable to fulfill his goal, he could never satisfy his hunger. Despite the absence of vocal cords, he had a lovely sweet voice. Phonos informed King Solomon that he had stolen it from his mute victims, mainly from newborn children. Like the *Kyrannides* and the *Life* of St. Symeon Stylites, this evil spirit is associated with fever. He *burns* the body with *fire* and, in addition, inflicts ulcers.[990]

The sinister black headless fever demon is a complex image that appears in Byzantine literature for only a relatively short period of time. A few decades after the *Life* of St. Symeon Stylites the Younger, the evil spirit that struck the thirteen-year-old St. Theodore Sykeotes with fever was described as *an unclean black demon* (ἀκάθαρτον δαιμόνιον μελανοειδές).[991] As early as the mid-seventh century, when the text was probably compiled, the headless fever demon had disappeared from the literary tradition.

* * *

---

[987] The so-called τεταρταῖος [πυρετός] or τεταρταίη means *quartan fever* or *quartan malaria*.

[988] *Die Kyraniden*, ed. Dimitris Kaimakis, [Beitrage zur Klassischen Philologie, 76] (Meisenheim: Anton Hain, 1976), I.1.152–55.

[989] *The Testament of Solomon*, ˙35.4ff.: δαιμόνιον, ἄνθρωπος μὲν πάντα τὰ μέλη αὐτοῦ, ἀκέφαλος δέ.

[990] *The Testament of Solomon*, ˙36.11–12: ἐγὼ εἰμὶ ὁ πυρῶν τὰ μέλη καὶ τοῖς ποσὶν ἐπιπέμπω καὶ ἕλκη ἐμποιῶ.

[991] Theodore Sykeotes, §17.6.

The black Ethiopian is typically associated with heresies, especially in the works of Leontios of Neapolis (the sixth to the seventh centuries). According to his *Life*, shortly after 588,[992] St. Symeon the Fool exorcized an evil spirit of this kind haunting a small side street in Emesa (modern-day Homs in Syria) using a lute.[993] The demon left the alley, but later appeared as an Ethiopian in the well-known heretic's drink shop[994] where Symeon himself lived. The evil creature smashed all the pottery inside, leaving the lady of the house in utter despair. When Symeon returned, she sadly told him about the *black villain* who had destroyed her property. The holy man burst into laughter and asked the woman if the Ethiopian was short and small. She confirmed that he was, and Symeon informed her that he had sent the demon to vandalize the shop. As her relatives and servants beat him mercilessly, he admonished them to go to the nearest Orthodox church and repent their heretical views. Otherwise, he would send the *blackamoor* the next day to destroy her merchandise again. Since the shopkeeper's family refused to do so, the evil spirit's attacks continued.[995]

After the seventh century, the black or dark demon's image retains its connection with death to some extent, remaining the personification of physical suffering and mortal danger in hagiography. For example, according to the *Lives* of St. Ioannikios the Great, a boy was sent by his parents to bring water. The spring was far from his home, and soon the child felt exhausted. At that moment, a group of *shadowy* men (ζοφερούς τῷ εἴδει) appeared before him. They promised to show the boy a shortcut to the spring but instead took him to the verge of a steep and bottomless

---

[992] On the main events of St. Symeon the Holy Fool's biography and his arrival in Emesa, see Part One, Chapter Two, §1.

[993] The so-called πανδοῦρα (Lat. *pandora, pandorium*) was a three-string lute (see Féstugiere, *Léontios de Néapolis*, 202). The *bandura* is still a Ukrainian traditional musical instrument.

[994] The "*phouskarion*" (φουσκάριον) was a shop where the so-called *phouska* (φοῦσκα) or *pusca* (in Latin) was sold. The *pusca* was the common drink of the poor and consisted of water mixed with sour wine or vinegar. In Greek, the same drink is called *oxykraton* (ὀξύκρατον).

[995] Symeon the Holy Fool, 87.18–88.8.

precipice hidden behind greenery and rocks. He was about to step over the edge when the demons suddenly felt the holy presence of St. Ioannikios nearby and threw themselves into the abyss with a pitiful cry. Thus was the boy saved from mortal danger.[996]

From the mid-ninth century, the black demon became the standard image taken by the Devil's servants in the real world, gradually losing its special relationship with illness, heresies, and deadly danger. "[The evil spirit appeared] as a little humanlike Ethiopian', says the author of the *Life* of St. Luke of Steiris, and continues: "he likes to take this image and is very unskillful in his choice [of form]". [997] However, it is not the Devil who should be blamed for lack of imagination, but rather the hagiographers themselves. Compared to interesting and sinister images like the headless Ethiopian of the sixth and seventh centuries, the black dwarf or giant of ninth-century hagiography sometimes seems too standardized, even banal. This doesn't mean, however, that the stories themselves are not fascinating.

One generation after St. Ioannikios, the black giant appears in the *Lives* of St. Eustratios of Agauros (†between 867 and 887)[998] and St. Niketas of Medikion.[999] In both texts, the image has no direct connection to death, sins, or heresy. In the *Life* of St. Eustratios, the abbot of the Agauros monastery[1000] ordered twenty monks to load carts with wheat and other supplies for a nearby marketplace. They had to cross a river to reach their destination, and the oxen got stuck in the muddy water, refusing to move further. The reverend brothers had lost all hope of accomplishing their task when they saw a giant Ethiopian emerge from the river. The terrible creature moaned and whined in pain. It told the startled monks that all his limbs were broken and Eustratios was to blame.

---

[996] Ioannikios (*Peter*), §26; Ioannikios (*Sabbas*), §22. According to the text, the event occurred during the reign of Emperor Leo V (815–820).

[997] Luke of Steiris, §68.5–7: ἐν σχήματι μέλανος ἀνθρωπόσκου – τοιοῦτος γὰρ φιλεῖ φαίνεσθαι, οἷος δὴ καὶ ἀτεχνῶς ἐστι τὴν προαίρεσιν.

[998] Eustratios of Agauros, §29.

[999] Niketas of Medikion, §20.

[1000] The Agauros monastery (Μονὴ Ἀγαύρου or Αὐγάρων) was located southwest of Prousa (Janin, *Les églises et les monastères*, 132–34).

After his encounter with the holy abbot, the Ethiopian was utterly harmless, and his only wish was to share its sad story. When it disappeared back into the water, the monks were able to pull the carts out of the mire easily.[1001]

In the tenth and early eleventh centuries, the demon-Ethiopian became a widespread image in Byzantine hagiography in southern Italy, Greece, and Constantinople. Many of these stories are fascinating descriptions of everyday life and provide the modern scholar with information about the prejudices against black people and about their position in Byzantine society. According to the *Life* of St. Theodora of Thessalonica (812–August 29, 892), in the late ninth century, a poor woman's son called Theodore bustled around Thessalonica, catching birds with traps on a hot September day. Suddenly he saw before him a tall and bulky Ethiopian (εἶδέ τινα μακρὸν καὶ ὑψηλὸν φαινόμενον αἰθίοπα). Frightened, Theodore tried to escape, but the creature grabbed him, knocked him down, hit him, and disappeared. Regaining consciousness, the boy returned home. His face expressed clear signs of despair and fear, and his mind was confused. Seeing her son in such a miserable condition, the mother immediately went to St. Theodora's grave for help. The demon announced his presence in this holy place, clouding the poor child's mind again. The Devil's servant forced the boy to jump around like mad, curse, scream uncontrollably, and avoid the slightest physical contact with the Saint's tomb. Mother and son spent three days in the holy place until, at last, St. Theodora appeared to the boy in a dream and asked him about his sickness. Theodore pointed to his head, indicating that he was mentally ill. The Saint told him to stand up — and he was healed. When he woke up, he anointed his head with holy oil from the tomb, and the demon was gone.[1002]

A keen reader of the above story can almost visualize the naughty boy getting involved in a street fight or even nagging a local black man,

---

[1001] This event can be dated between 843 (the final restoration of the icons described about five paragraphs before the story with the giant Ethiopian; Eustratios of Agauros, §22) and the Saint's death in the late 860s or the early 870s.
[1002] Theodora of Thessalonica, §50.

then hurrying to his mother and explaining that a giant black demon had possessed him. We could also speculate that little Theodore was startled by the "Ethiopian" for some reason and thought him an ominous black evil spirit. Both speculations are probable, and we cannot know what happened on that hot summer day. Either way, the prejudices against black skin, deeply rooted in Byzantine society, seem obvious.

The *Life* of St. Elias Speleotes (864–960) provides us with another interesting piece of information, both about the demon-Ethiopian and about the black population in southern Italy. The Saint himself was one of the prominent figures of the monastic movement in Calabria during the great Arab invasions in this region. According to the text's author, Kyriakos, Elias decided to found a cave monastery near the village Seminarion.[1003] A horde of evil spirits inhabited the place, and the monk put much effort into expelling them. Shortly after his battle with the Devil's servants, pious villagers met a horrible, giant Ethiopian with a gloomy face near the village. They took him for Photios, an acquaintance of theirs, and asked him politely where he was going. With an angry and hoarse voice, he answered that Elias had chased him away from his old dwelling, and he was now going to find his fellows and prepare for a new battle. With this threat, the evil black creature suddenly rose in the air and departed with a limp, cursing Elias. The peasants then understood that he was a demon and went home, glad the monk had rescued them from such a powerful evil spirit.[1004]

The image of the Ethiopian above is neither unusual nor especially interesting. It is the story's social and historical context that mainly attracts attention. For the Greek-speaking populace of Byzantine Calabria, the black man is no foreigner, and they treat him like an ordinary person. On the other hand, we can only speculate as to how Photios got his Greek name or if he found himself on Byzantine soil by chance during some Arab raid in the region.

[1003] The small town of Seminara is today located about 40 kilometers north of Reggio di Calabria.

[1004] Elias Speleotes, §44.

* * *

The product of a long and heterogeneous tradition, and smeared by purely social prejudices, the image of the black (dark, shadowy) demon is associated with some special influences upon humans. Both in visions and the world of the living, he is the personification of Death and the soul's keen inquisitor on its way to Heaven. He inflicts illnesses, especially fever and pain, on humans. The 'Ethiopian" usually appears either as a powerful, heavily armed man or else as a small, foul-smelly, and pathetic humanlike figure.

2. Arabs

Theoretically, the demonization of the "Ethiopian" is based on black being the color absolute opposed to God's light. Mixed with popular prejudices deeply rooted in ancient and medieval societies, this was probably the most common demonic image in Byzantine hagiography.

The elements of the evil spirit's outer appearance, outlined in Chapter 1, could be used subtly and indirectly to describe people and ethnic groups that seriously threatened both everyday life and the political stability of the empire. Arabs, Bulgarians, Jews, and Germans were demonized in this way, their image represented as somehow abnormal and inhuman. Major Muslim campaigns against Byzantine cities were sometimes attributed to demonic possession, like the terrifying siege of Collesano, Sicily, between 940 and 948. According to the *Life* of St. Sabbas the Younger, the *envious demon* could not bear the piety of the Saint's monastery, *possessed the Ishmaelite marauders* (τοὺς μιαιφόνους Ἰσμαηλίτας εἰσέδυ), and made them attack the Christian town forcing the citizens to the extreme of cannibalism.[1005] However, Byzantine hagiography of the

---

[1005] Sabbas the Younger, §5ff. Despite the absence of information in the text itself, circumstantial evidence allows dating the event between November 940 and 948. According to Patriarch Orestes, Euthymios's mother could not bear the sight of Muslim atrocities. She implored her son to lead the whole family out of Collesano and move to the Byzantine province of Calabria. Since the author notes that Euthymios wore the same chiton in the winter and the summer, we can assume that they spent at least one

period under study only mentions a demon taking the image of an Arab on one occasion. Surprisingly enough, the story is not set in one of the flashpoints of the conflict between the empire and the Muslims, like Asia Minor or southern Italy, but on the northern shores of the Aegean. St. Euthymios the Younger (823/4–898) became a hermit *c.* 870 and retired to a cave near the place where the Peristera monastery was to be built.[1006] One day, a demon that looked like a barbarian visited the holy man at noon and ordered him to leave the cave immediately. Euthymios replied that even if he had to die at the hands of the Arabs, he would never obey. Then a group of evil spirits disguised as Arabs approached, tied him up, and dragged him to a high precipice. At that moment, however, God came to the hermit's aid, spread fear among them, and they disap-

---

year there, when their new home was also invaded by the enemy (Sabbas the Younger, §8). According to the *Life*, troops led by a high-ranking official, patrikios *Malakinos*, were sent by the central government in Constantinople to defend the province. Other sources mention the same person (Μαλακηνός or Μαλακεινός) as the head of the Byzantine forces that tried to drive the Muslim invaders back to Sicily in 951–52 (see Alexander Vasiliev, *Byzance et les Arabes*, ed. Marius Canard and Henri Grégoire, vol. 2.1: *La dynastie Macedonienne (867 – 959)* [Brussels, 1968], 367; da Costa-Louillet, "Saints de Sicile et d'Italie", 154; Gay, *L'Italie méridionale*, 213ff) – in all likelihood, the same raid as described in the *Life*.

On the other hand, the Sunni of Sicily rebelled against the Fatimid dynasty of Egypt in 934–48. In 939–40, Emperor Romanos I Lekapenos (920–944) attempted to take advantage of this internal conflict and sent an armed force to the island. From their headquarters in Agrigento, these forces inspired the Christian population to rebel against the occupiers. The Muslim atrocities in Collesano were probably revenge on the part of the Fatimid Governor Abū'l-Qāsim al-Qā'im (934–945), who cleansed the region after the Byzantine armies' withdrawal in November 940 (see Vasiliev, *Byzance et les Arabes*, 2: 310ff). If this supposition is accurate, we have to date the raid of the *Ishmaelites* against the native town of St. Sabbas the Younger between November 940 and 948, when the Fatimid dynasty finally crushed the Sunni rebellion.

[1006] Papachryssanthou, "La vie de Saint Euthyme le Jeune", 234. For the church and the monastery, see Anastasios Orlandos, "The Catholicon of the Peristera Monastery near Thessaloniki" [Greek: Ἀναστάσιος Ὀρλάνδος, "Τὸ καθολικὸ τῆς παρὰ τὴν Θεσσαλονίκην μονῆς Περιστερῶν"], *Archeion ton Byzantinon Mnemeion tes Hellados* [Greek: Ἀρχεῖον τῶν Βυζαντινῶν Μνημείων τῆς Ἑλλάδος] 7 (1951): 146–67; Chrysanthi Mavropoulou-Tsioumi and A. Kountouras, "The Church of St. Andrew at Peristera, reconstructed in the 9th century" [Greek: Χρυσάνθη Μαυροπούλου-Τσιούμη and Ἀ. Κούντουρας, "Ὁ ναὸς τοῦ Ἁγίου Ἀνδρέα στὴν Περιστερὰ μετασκευασμένος τὸν 9° αἰ."], *Klironomia* 13, no. 2 (1981): 488ff.

peared.[1007] The appearance of demon-Arabs in the *Life* of Euthymios the Younger is not accidental. First of all, there was the undoubtedly real threat that the Saracens posed to the coasts and islands of the Aegean Sea between 824 and 961, when Crete was under Arab rule. Only about thirty years after the event described in the biography, in 904, the troops of Leo of Tripoli and his Arab pirates captured Thessalonica. The second reason for the presence of Saracen demons in this text is perhaps the Saint's origin. Euthymios was born in the Galatian village of Opso, where Muslim raids were frequent in the ninth century. For a person who spent his childhood and youth under the threat of Muslim emirs, evil spirits disguised as Arab soldiers would be more than expected. We can speculate that Basil, the author of the *Life*, obtained the information about the demonic horde of Saracens from the Saint himself or from somebody close to him.

3. The general and his soldiers

Demonic armies are a well-known but relatively rare phenomenon in ancient Greek and Latin literature. In his *Histories*, Herodotus describes an unconventional military strategy proposed by a diviner to the Phocians, who were at war with the Thessalians. The man advised the commander to paint the soldiers' bodies white and send them to the enemy camp. When the Thessalian garrison saw a sinister multitude marching with full military accoutrements, they took it for a *supernatural monstrosity* (τέρας).[1008] Pausanias mentions the *demons* of the soldiers fallen at Marathon who continued to fight their fierce battle, again and again, night after night. If somebody went to watch them, they would turn their wrath against him.[1009] Evil armies coming from Hell are mentioned in the New Testament as well, and their most famous description is undoubtedly in St. John's Book of Revelation:

[1007] Euthymios the Younger, §21.
[1008] Hérodote, *Histoires*, ed. Philippe-Ernest Legrand, *Livre VIII: Uranie* [Collection Budé 118] (Paris: Les Belles Lettres, 1964), VIII.27.10–17. See also Bojadschiew, *The Night in the Middle Ages*, 327ff and n. 659.
[1009] *Pausaniae Graeciae descriptio*, 1: I.32.3.4–8.

I looked, and there before me was a pale horse! Its rider was named Death, and Hades was following close behind him. They were given power over a fourth of the earth to kill by sword, famine and plague, and by the wild beasts of the earth.[1010]

In the same text, demonic armies invade the Earth to decimate one-fourth of humanity. The first to come are the hellish locusts with human faces, looking like horses prepared for battle; their commander is the angel Abaddon or Apollyon (Ἀπολύων — the Destroyer).[1011] Four angels with two hundred thousand mounted troops follow them to kill another one-third of humankind.[1012]

In the Western literary tradition, especially after the twelfth century, the demonic army, known from antiquity and the Bible, fused with elements of local folklore. This osmosis created a particularly influential concept, namely the so-called *Wild Hunt* (German: *Wilde Jagd*), where demonic souls of the dead and other supernatural creatures ride their ghostly horses in full armor during stormy nights. They are led by different mythical personages — the ancient goddess Diana, King Arthur, or the owl demon.[1013] In the sixteenth century, the Dutch physician, occultist, and demonologist Johann Weyer "calculated" the exact number of these sinister warriors in his work "De praestigiis daemonum" (1564). According to him, 7,409,127 evil soldiers made up the army of the demons' Emperor under the command of seventy-nine princes.[1014]

Byzantine hagiography mentions demonic armies relatively often, but their descriptions do not approach the horror inspired by the sinister Wild Hunt. In the East, the demon warrior is certainly a dangerous creature, but he utterly lacks the sense of impending doom and the ominous spell cast by the Western demonic souls. His image is frequently flavored

---

[1010] Rev. 6:8.
[1011] Rev. 9:7–11.
[1012] Rev. 9:15–17.
[1013] On the Wild Hunt in Western literature, see Carlo Ginzburg, *Ecstasies: Deciphering the Witches' Sabbath*, trans. Raymond Rosenthal (New York: Pantheon Books, 1991), 101–5; Bojadschiew, *The Night in the Middle Ages*, 138 and 325–49.
[1014] Jean Delumeau, *La peur en Occident (XVIe - XVIIIe cièc1es). Une cite assiégeé* (Paris: Fayard, 1978), 251.

with a tinge of humor and reminds us of the pathetic Legion quickly cast out by Jesus in the Gospels.[1015] The authors describe massive but powerless armies and weapons whose goal is to frighten a single man or woman or launch a ridiculous attack against them without success. The evil troops in the saints' *Lives* are scarcely an organized force led by the Devil against humankind as a whole. Their might is only imaginary, and their threats and bragging could only deceive the spiritually weak, who lack faith.

It must be noted that the hagiographers in the period under study only occasionally used the Biblical term *legion* (λεγεών) for the demonic armies. They prefer the Greek words παράταξις (*line of battle*)[1016] and, even more, φάλαγξ (*phalanx*).[1017] The latter term was certainly obsolete and essentially meaningless in the Middle Byzantine period. It was used almost exclusively for the Devil's armies; only occasionally could it be applied to an actual army, and always pejoratively.[1018] The angelic army, on the other hand, is called στρατιά,[1019] a well-organized military force properly arranged in *divisions* (τάγματα).[1020] In addition, the term *tagma* also denotes the emperor's elite guard assigned to Constantinople, like the *tagma* of the excubitors. The phalanx symbolizes chaos and the unknown, irrational and ancient Evil. The angelic troops, with their elite divisions, are the emanation of God's order into the world. The projection of this order is the empire with its sacred hierarchy and eternal mission to protect Christendom from the attacks of the barbarians and the Devil's servants.

[1015] Mat. 8:28–34; Mark 5:1–20; Luke 8:26–39.
[1016] Symeon the Holy Fool, 61.21.
[1017] The term has a generally negative sense. For example, the author of the *Life* of Patriarch Sophronios I (634–638) calls the Monothelites a *phalanx* (Sophronios of Jerusalem, 148.31.)
[1018] See, e.g., Nikon Metanoeite §43.16ff, where the author uses the word *phalanx* for the dangerous and *innumerable* army of the Bulgarian tsar Samuel: ἅπαν τὸ ἔθνος τῆς Βουλγαρικῆς ἀναριθμήτου φάλαγγος.
[1019] See, for example, Symeon Stylites the Younger, §65.16ff, §66.20, §73.15, and §74.4ff.
[1020] Symeon Stylites the Younger, §47.4, §129.46–49, and §135.4ff.

In the mid-ninth century, Michael Psellus expounded a theoretical explanation of the demon soldier. According to him, some of the unclean spirits attacked in groups similar to the infantry and cavalry units of the Byzantine army (ὥσπερ παρὰ τοῖς ἡμετέροις στρατεύμασιν ἡ φάλαγξ καὶ ἡ ἰλαρχία). Like any other military unit, the demonic phalanxes had leaders called *hegemons* (ἡγεμόνες) and *archons* (ἄρχοντες). When the demon commander attacked a susceptible soul, his subordinates immediately rushed after him. The outstanding achievement of St. Auxentios, according to his biographer, was his ability to put not only single demons to flight, but also these dangerous bands.[1021] However, theoretical explanations are scarce between the sixth and tenth centuries. The Biblical story of the Third Temptation of Christ, when the Devil showed the Son of God all the kingdoms of the world and offered them to Him, had some influence upon the hagiographical texts.[1022] Satan displayed his vast realm and innumerable phalanxes of demons to impress the young Symeon Stylites the Younger and win him over.[1023] The evil spirit who possessed the noble nun in the *Life* of St. Anastasios of Persia bragged about his kingship and royal crown; he proudly informed the monks that he commanded many phalanxes and had many courtiers.[1024]

Demonic soldiers in full battle array are typical of the hagiography produced in the Mount Olympus monasteries. Phalanxes of demons are often described as attacking hermits in lonely places, especially caves. For example, one such battle is mentioned in the *Life* of St. Gregory of Dekapolis. Evil spirits visited him in various guises, the most dangerous attacking him as a squad of soldiers armed to the teeth with spears, arrows, and swords.[1025] Even more vivid is the description of a demonic assault in

---

[1021] Auxentios, §15. See also Guillou, *Le Diable Byzantin*, 20.
[1022] Mat. 4:8–10; Luke 4:5–7. See also Rev. 16:10 and 17:17, where St. John the Apostle mentions the *throne* and the *kingdom* of the Beast sent by the Devil.
[1023] Symeon Stylites the Younger, §18.10ff.
[1024] Anastasios of Persia, Roman Miracle, §5.9–11: *I am King, and I have a crown, and I have obtained phalanxes and courtiers* (βασιλεύς εἰμι καὶ στέμμα ἔχω καὶ φάλαγγας κέκτημαι καὶ μεγιστάνους); ibid., §6.12: *I am King, and I have the power to rule* (βασιλεὺς εἰμὶ καὶ βασιλεῦσαι ἔχω).
[1025] Gregory of Dekapolis, §8.

the *Lives* of St. Ioannikios the Great. During one of his hermitages in Lydia (815–c. 820), the Iconoclasts secretly sent a man named Gourias to become the holy man's pupil and win his confidence. The unsuspecting monk accepted him, but Gourias soon revealed his true face, using various magical tricks to harm Ioannikios. On one occasion, he left his cell and went to a desolate place to summon his *demonic phalanxes* (τὰς συνυπουργούσας αὐτῷ δαιμονικὰς φάλαγγας). The evil army consisted of heavily armed horsemen and archers on foot who looked *as if* (φανταστικῶς) they had bows and quivers.[1026] The *disgusting magician* led them in battle against Ioannikios, and their tactics are described in a military manner; before they launch an attack, the demons pelted the cave's entrance with arrows and then skillfully used flanking maneuvers. Encouraged by what he thought their irresistible power, Gourias loudly ordered the holy monk to leave the place immediately and never return. But Ioannikios was not a person who could be easily intimidated. He simply started to sing a psalm, made the sign of the cross, and the demonic horde disappeared.[1027] Peter and Sabbas describe the commander of another evil *phalanx* in the caves of the island of Thasios, located in Apoloniada Lake (western Bithynia). This frightful demon was a giant with legs like columns,[1028] and the authors refer to him as *archon* [1029] or *toparch*.[1030] Both titles were the names of actual officer ranks in the Byzantine military in the eighth and ninth centuries.

[1026] Ioannikios (*Peter*), §21.
[1027] Ioannikios (*Peter*), §21.
[1028] Ioannikios (*Peter*), §53; Ioannikios (*Sabbas*), §32.
[1029] On the *archon*, see Guilland, *Recherches sur les institutions*, 1: 393; ODB, vol. 1, s.v. "Archon", 160. This rank was usually given to governors of relatively small (military) districts. The word is also used for the Devil's servants in the New Testament (see, e.g., the *archons of darkness*, Eph. 6:12). On the biblical meaning of the term, see also Sullivan, "Life of St. Ioannikios", 311 and n. 369.
[1030] *Toparch* (τοπάρχης) was the official title of a district governor. He was granted relative autonomy in his territory (χῶρα). See *ODB*, vol. 3, s.v. "Toparches", 2095; Jean-Claude Cheynet, "Toparque et topotèrétès à la fin du XIe siècle", *Revue des études byzantines* 42 (1984): 215–24.

The word *phalanx* could also be used in hagiography broadly in the sense of *multitude* or *horde*, without direct military connotations,[1031] or metaphorically.[1032] This was the case with Irene, the abbess of the Chrysobalanton monastery. The phalanx of demons who mock and maliciously laugh at her is not described as an army. However, their attacks on the Saint are organized and deadly; the evil spirits manage to set fire to her garment with the wick of a candle, taking advantage of her complete devotion to prayer.[1033]

4. The female demon

Demons who appear as women are a relatively rare phenomenon in the Byzantine hagiography of the period under study. The modern researcher is able to find much more information in various demonological treatises, Apocrypha, and texts containing magical rituals and exorcisms. As we will see, especially during the Iconoclast crisis, the hagiographers purposefully avoided female images typical of contemporary folklore in order to homogenize the material embodiment of Evil.

The image of the female evil spirit is highly complex. Its obscure origins can be traced to various mythological traditions in the Greco-Roman world and the Eastern Mediterranean.[1034] Unlike her male coun-

---

[1031] See, e.g., Theodore Sykeotes, §26a.15 and §116.7ff (hordes of demons haunting various regions in Galatia); Athanasia of Aegina, §6 (the Saint's grave expels hordes of demons).

[1032] See, e.g., Ioannikios (*Peter*), §2, where the holy man defeats the phalanxes of invisible enemies; Nikephoros of Medikion, §12.14–19, where Nikephoros calls on everyone to fight the Enemy's *phalanxes*; Stephen the Younger, 123.25, where the Devil sends his *phalanxes* (i.e., the Jews and heretics) to battle against the Orthodox Church; Empress Theodora, §6.15, where the author calls the heretics *phalanxes*; Demetrianos of Cyprus, §4, where the demonic passions cannot penetrate the holy man's soul, and their *phalanxes* disappear.

[1033] Irene of Chrysobalanton, §11.

[1034] See Sarah Jonston, "Defining the Dreadful: Remarks on the Child-Killing Demon", in *Ancient Magic and Ritual Power*, ed. Marvin Meyer and Paul Mirecki, [Religions in the Greco-Roman World, 129] (Leiden: Brill, 2001), 361–87; Walter Burkert, *The Near-Eastern Influence Orientalizing On Greek Culture Revolution In The Early Archaic Age*, trans. Margaret Pinder and Walter Burkert (Cambridge, MA and London: Harvard University Press, 1992), 82–87; Greenfield, *Traditions of Belief*, 184–90; Barb, "Antau-

terpart, the female demon is often explicitly mentioned by name. In the anonymous text *Expelling the Dirty and Unclean Gyllou*, the author lists thirteen ("twelve and a half") names of this evil spirit. The hagiographers usually describe her outer appearance in a way that omits the physical abnormalities and ugliness of male images. The main characteristics of the female demon are unkempt black hair, sometimes covering the whole body like a coat of feathers, and burning eyes. Her close connection with water and birds is well attested in both the saints' *Lives* and in the works of Michael Psellus.[1035] The actions and influences of the female demon are also stereotypical. She attempts to seduce men, never satisfying them sexually in the end, kills newborn babies, drinks women's bodily fluids after childbirth, and injures livestock. This homogeneous stereotype allows modern scholars like Alfons Barb, Richard Greenfield, and Anastasia Vakaloudi to make reasonable and well-founded parallels with various mythological personages.[1036] Barb and Greenfield, however, focus primarily on Late Antiquity and the Late Byzantine period, while Vakaloudi outlines some philosophical concepts and does not attempt to situate the female demon in a broader folklore and mythological perspective.

4.1. Gello[1037]: the Child-killer

The *Testament of Solomon* (c. third to fourth centuries)[1038] mentions the female demon *Obizouth* (Ὀβιζούθ). This sinister creature informed King Solomon that, in the middle of the night, she visited women in childbirth and strangled their babies. If at first she was unsuccessful, she would try again to kill them, injure their eyes, wound their mouths and brains, and cause them pain. Solomon could not see her body well because it was

---

ra", passim; Paul Perdrizet, *Negotium perambulans in tenebris. Études de démonologie gréco-orientale* (Strasbourg, 1922), 13ff. Greenfield's research focuses on the Late Byzantine period and does not refer to any hagiographical material.

[1035] Pseudo-Psellos, "Timothée ou des demons", ll. 545–48.
[1036] Vakaloudi, *Magic*, 112.
[1037] The name of the female demon has various spellings in Greek. We will use its standard Ancient Greek form "Gello".
[1038] McCown dates the text to the third or fourth century (*The Testament of Solomon*, 105–8).

black and covered with thick hair. The King ordered her hanged by the hair at the entrance of his Temple in Jerusalem.[1039] Another female demon who strangled people in the same text was *Onoskelis* (*the Donkey-legged*); she was reported to be very beautiful, but her physical attractiveness was somewhat spoiled by her horns and donkey legs.[1040] The discourse between an angel or person with authority over demons and an impure female spirit proved to be an enduring literary motif. In a fifteenth-century manuscript published by Émile Legrand (Bibliothèque Nationale de France, Ms. Gr. 2316, ff. 432a — 433a), which includes various exorcisms and incantations, the archangel Michael descends from heaven and sees a female demon with feather-like hair and burning eyes. When asked where she was going, the creature said she intended to visit some house where she would enter as a reptile and kill the cattle. She would also harm the women giving them heartache, drinking their breast milk, and killing their babies.[1041]

In the dialogue *Timotheus* (thirteenth century), Pseudo-Psellus repeats the main characteristics of the female demon outlined in the *Testament of Solomon*. He claims that the so-called water demons (ὑδραῖοι δαίμονες), who liked damp places and could also appear as birds, usually took female form.[1042] Further on, the anonymous author gives more characteristics of this evil spirit, probably attempting to "explain" postpartum depression by demonic possession.[1043] According to him, the ancients knew them as Naiads, Nereids, and Dryads. One of the participants in the

---

[1039] *The Testament of Solomon*, *43–*44; Greenfield, *Traditions of Belief*, 183.
[1040] *The Testament of Solomon*, *18 – *22; Greenfield, *Traditions of Belief*, 186–88.
[1041] "[Exorcism] of Gyllou" [Greek: Τῆς Γυλλοῦς], ed. Émile Legrand, *Bibliothèque grecque vulgaire*, vol. 2 (Paris: Maisonneuve, 1881), XVIII.
[1042] Pseudo-Psellos, "Timothée ou des demons", ll. 545–49: Ὅσοι μὲν γὰρ ἐν ὑγροῖς βιοῦσι καὶ τὴν μαλθακωτέραν στέργουσιν ἀγωγὴν ὄρνισί τε καὶ γυναιξὶν ἀμφερεῖς ἑαυτοὺς ποιοῦσι· διὸ δὲ καὶ Ναϊάδας τούτους καὶ Νηρηΐδας καὶ Δρυάδας θηλυκῶς καλοῦσιν Ἑλλήνων παῖδες.
[1043] Pseudo-Psellos, "Timothée ou des demons", ll. 552ff: *It is not a paradox that the demon who possesses the women after childbirth appears as in female form, since she is lustful and takes great pleasure in impure bodily fluids* (Οὐδὲν οὖν ἄπορον εἰ καὶ τὸ ταῖς λεχοῖς ἐνσκῆπτον δαιμόνιον θηλύμορφον ὁρᾶται, μάχλον ὂν καὶ ὑγρότησιν ἀκαθάρτοις χαῖρον). See Greenfield, *Traditions of Belief*, 185; Vakaloudi, *Magic*, 112.

dialogue, Timothy, "supports" these theoretical concepts with the story of a woman who, shortly after giving birth, saw a ghostly female walking toward her. The sinister spirit's hair rose as if blown by the wind, and she looked threatening.[1044]

The most common name for this child-killing, bloodthirsty demon in antiquity and Byzantium, however, is not of Jewish origin. According to Michael Psellus, the sinister witch Gillo (Γιλλώ) is mentioned neither in the *juggling books of Porphyry* nor in any other work written by Greek intellectuals.[1045] He says that this *well-known name* (πολυθρύλητον ὄνομα) appears only in an apocryphal demonological treatise ascribed to King Solomon. In fact, the *Laughing woman*, or Gello (Γελλώ),[1046] occurs in ancient literature more than once, but the great Byzantine scholar was obviously unaware of this fact or else, for whatever reason, chose to keep it to himself.

The name *Gello* comes from the Greek verb γελλώ/γελλάω (*to laugh*). Given the ominous nature of this demon, this sounds like a sinister joke or, at least, a euphemism. However, it could be a real given name. The mythological personage itself appears for the first time in a poem by Sappho, of which only a tiny fragment has survived, saying only *fonder of children than Gello*.[1047] The scholiast Zenobius explains this mysterious expression and tells the story of a Lesbian girl of this name. She died prematurely, her sad ghost wandering around the island, killing babies

---

[1044] Pseudo-Psellos, "Timothée ou des demons", ll. 456ff: δαιμόνιον ἔφη φάσμα σκιοειδὲς καὶ γυναικὶ προσεμφερὲς ἠνεμωμένας ἔχον τὰς κόμας.

[1045] Michael Psellus, "De Gillo", 164.7–8: οὔτε παρὰ τοῖς λογίοις, οὔτε παρὰ ταῖς ἀγυρτικαῖς βίβλοις τοῦ Πορφυρίου τῇ Γιλλῷ ἐντετύχηκα.

[1046] See Oikonomides, "Gello", 255–58. Oikonomides studies the development of Gello's image (Γιλλώ, Γελλώ, Γιλλού, Γελλού, Γιαλού, Ιαλλού, Γιαλλούδα) from Sappho until the Late Byzantine period. See also Perdrizet, *Negotium perambulans*, 13ff; Delatte and Josserand, "Contribution", 230–32; Greenfield, *Traditions of Belief*, 185–87; Burkert, *The Near-Eastern Influence*, 82–87; Jonston, "Child-Killing Demon", 365ff.

[1047] "Carminum Sapphicorum Fragmenta", ed. Edgar Lobel and Dennis Page, *Poetarum Lesbiorum fragmenta* (Oxford: Clarendon Press, 1963), fr. 178 (Γέλλως παιδοφιλωτέρα).

and small children.[1048] The lexicographer Hesychius[1049] associates her with Empusa, the shape-shifting one-footed demonic phantom controlled by the chthonic goddess Hecate, who took the form of a beautiful young girl, seduced travelers, sucked their blood, and ate their flesh.

During the Middle Byzantine period, the sources continued to reflect popular beliefs associated with Gello. Contemporary theologians maintained a highly skeptical attitude towards such superstitions. Reading St. John of Damascus, the *Life* of Patriarch Tarasios, and the "demonologist" Michael Psellus, we are left with the impression that the Byzantine intellectual and theological elite intended to eradicate the very idea of the female demon through the sinister Gello. Around the same time, in Western Europe, intellectuals and jurists displayed a similar attitude towards the so-called *strigae*, or witches. They perceived them as a mere delusion sent by Satan to confuse the minds of gullible and superficial people.[1050]

The spurious work of St. John of Damascus *On the Strigas* (Περὶ Στρυγγῶν) refers to these evil female spirits as *Gelloudes*, a derivative of the name of the ancient Gello, or as stri(n)xes (στρίξ/στρύ(γ)ξ). The latter term is of Latin origin (*strix*) and initially meant *owl*, but in medieval Latin, *striga* means *witch*.[1051] In the eighth century, when the treatise was

---

[1048] Zenobius, "Epitome collectionum Lucilli Tarrhaei et Didymi", ed. Friedrich Schneidewin and Ernst von Leutsch, *Corpus paroemiographorum Graecorum*. vol. 1 (Hildesheim: Olms, 1965), 58 (III.3).

[1049] *Hesychii Alexandrini lexicon*, ed. Kurt Latte and Ian Cunningham, vol. 1: Α-Δ [Sammlung griechischer und lateinischer Grammatiker 11] (Berlin and Boston: De Gruyter, 2018), gamma 307 and 308.

[1050] On the so-called *strigae* and *lamiae* in the Western medieval tradition – e.g., the *Canon Episcopi* by Regino of Prüm [906]), see Bojadschiew, *The Night in the Middle Ages*, 204–29 (esp. 209–11).

[1051] On the *strigae*, see Jonston, "Child-Killing Demon", 365ff and n. 11. Jonston considers this child-killing demon a part of the Roman mythology. In her opinion, in the first century B.C. the figure was already a part of Greek folklore. The word *strix* is obviously Latin, but it seems impossible to determine when it passed into the Greek language. It appears in the works of Aelius Herodianus (*c.* 180–250 A.D.), but he explains στρίξ as only *a kind of bird* (Herodianus, "De prosodia catholica", ed. August Lentz, *Grammatici Graeci* vol. 3.1: *Herodiani Technici reliquiae* [Hildesheim: Olms, 1965], 396.26). According to the lexicographer Hesychius (fifth to the sixth century), στρίγγλος means *owl*.

supposedly written, the Greek word had already acquired its modern meaning — *a female demon, a witch* (modern Greek: στρίγγλα, στρίγκλα). According to Pseudo-John of Damascus, people believed these creatures appeared at night and passed through locked doors to strangle babies, eat their livers, or suck their bodily fluids. The author refutes these heretical superstitions with the argument that even Christ's soul left His body only once in His mortal life. Were we to accept the idea that some mischievous witches could send their spirits to roam while their bodies lay still in bed, he argues, we would then have to conclude that the Son of God did not achieve anything extraordinary.

The relationship between the *Gelloudes* and the *strinxes* can also be found in an anonymous exorcism text ascribed to St. John Chrysostom, in which *gilou, and stringos, and striga* are cursed. In this text, the old word *strix* developed a masculine and a feminine form (στρίγγος and στρίγγα).[1052]

Gello was neither a demon nor a real person transformed into a beast because of her cruelty, says Psellus, but rather a *power* (δύναμις). She was an enemy of childbearing and used to kill babies in the womb. Mostly older women possessed this malicious power, and Gello gave them the ability to fly and visit newborn children unnoticed. The old witches sucked their bodily liquids and sucked the life out of them. For this reason, the midwives usually described the babies who died of sepsis (σύντηξις) as *eaten by Gello* (Γιλλόβρωτα). Psellus mocks such superstitions and proudly demonstrates his medical knowledge; he claims that such children died, in fact, for purely rational physical reasons.[1053]

The hagiographer Ignatios the Deacon affirms the popularity of Gello in the late eighth and early ninth centuries. According to his *Life* of Patriarch Tarasios of Constantinople, the *Hellenes* (i.e., the pagan authors) thought that she was a woman struck by premature death who visited newborn babies with various *ghosts* (φαντάσμασί τισιν), and killed

---

[1052] [Pseudo-]Joannes Chrysostomus, "In infirmos", ed. Alexander Vasiliev, *Anecdota Graeco-Byzantina*, vol. 1 (Moscow, 1893), 326.23: γυλοῦ ἢ στρίγγος ἢ στρίγγα.
[1053] Michael Psellus, "De Gillo", 164.15–25.

them. Some people, says the hagiographer, took advantage of this legend and accused women of being possessed by Gello:

> Fascinated by the evil spirit of this legend, some people, using false arguments, make attempts to attribute to women this unclean influence, as if real, and to charge them with the accusation that, being spiritually changed, they caused the death of those who died prematurely.[1054]

Ignatios notes that the father of Tarasios, an imperial judge of the mid-eighth century, saved two women who were unjustly accused of infanticide under Gello's influence.[1055]

The *Lives* of saints written by less learned authors do not share Psellus and Ignatios the Deacon's skeptical attitude towards Gello and the folklore beliefs related to her. In his *Life* of St. Peter of Atroa, the monk Sabbas mentions the son of the Phrygian nobleman Markianos, who suffered from *dehydration* (ἀποξηραμμένον). That demonic possession was the cause of this condition was so evident for the contemporary reader that the author only mentions the evil spirit at the very end of the story.[1056]

Another interesting source for Gello is the already mentioned *Expelling the Abominable and Unclean Gyllou*. This text of an unknown date was published by K. Sathas and is full of anachronisms. The anonymous author tells the story of a woman named Melitene who lived during the reign of Emperor Trajan (98–117). She gave birth to six children, but the *abominable and unclean Gyllou* (ἡ μιαρὰ καὶ ἀκάθαρτος Γυλλοῦ) took them all. When she found she was with child again, Melitene decided to depart for Constantinople (*sic!*). In this great city, which took its name from Emperor Constantine the Great more than two centuries after the reign of Trajan, she ordered a tall and strong tower to be built for her where she could bear and raise her baby. One day, her brothers came to

---

[1054] Patriarch Tarasios, §5.12–16: τούτῳ τῷ πονηρῷ τοῦ μύθου κλεπτόμενοι πνεύματι οἱ ταῦτα πιθανευόμενοι πειρῶνταί πως καὶ ἐπὶ γυναίων ὡς ἀληθῆ διαβιβάζειν τὴν τοιαύτην τοῦ μύσους ἐνέργειαν καὶ ταύταις ἀνατιθέναι, ἀλλοιουμέναις εἰς πνεῦμα, τῶν πρὸ ὥρας θανόντων τὸ αἴτιον.
[1055] Patriarch Tarasios, §5.1–31.
[1056] Peter of Atroa, §20.

visit her. One of them was St. Sisinnius. At first, Melitene refused to allow them inside, but they finally persuaded her and were permitted to enter the tower. Gello managed to sneak in on the horses, taking the form of a fly, and killed the child. Touched by his sister's grief, St. Sisinnius prayed to God, and an angel informed him that the evil spirit was in Lebanon. The brothers caught Gello and forced her to drink milk. Consequently, she vomited Melitene's children out whole and alive — a remote reminiscence of the story of Kronos and his offspring. Finally, Sisinnius set the demon on fire. He ordered her to speak her twelve and a half names:[1057] *Gyllou (Γυλλου),*[1058] *Amorphous (Ἀμορφους, the Formless), Abyzou/Avizou (Αβυζου),*[1059] *Karchous (Καρχους), Briane/Vriani (Βριανη), Bardellous/Vardellous (Βαρδελλους), Aigyptiane/Egyptiani (Αἰγυπτιανή, the Egyptian), Barna/Varna (Βαρνα),*[1060] *Charchanistrea (Χαρχανιστρέα, the Cackling One), Adikia (Ἀδικία, Injustice), Myia (Μυῖα, Fly).* One of the names is illegible, and the "half-name" is *Petomene/Petomeni (Πετομένη, the Flier).*[1061] According to the text, anyone who knows these names would have the power to control the evil spirit.

During the Late Byzantine period, Gello remains a standard literary character, especially in works written in Demotic Greek, like the *Rooster's Wedding* (*O Poulologos*, late thirteenth century).[1062] Her name occurs in modern Greek folklore, in which the demon herself has a wide variety of functions. The so-called *Gelloudes (Γελλοῦδες)* on the island of Naxos are water creatures who drown swimmers. Among the inhabitants of Lesbos, Rhodes, Cyprus, and Santorini (Thera), Gello has preserved her functions as a child-killer, and in Mytilene there still exists the expression *May*

[1057] For the twelve and a half names of Gello, and for other texts where the same expression is used, see Perdrizet, *Negotium perambulans,* 19. Here we will transliterate the names both with the Erasmian and the Reuchlinian pronunciation.

[1058] Some of the names in the text are unaccented.

[1059] *Abyzou (Ἀβυζού)* is in fact the ancient Sumerian goddess Abzu, whose name in Greek is rendered as *Abyssos (Ἄβυσσος).*

[1060] The name probably derives from Old Bulgarian/Old Slavonic ВРАНЪ (*vran, black*) with metathesis.

[1061] "Escape from the Abominable and Unclean Gyllou", 573.

[1062] *O Poulologos,* ed. Stamatia Krawczynski, [*Berliner Byzantinische Arbeiten* 22] (Berlin: Akademie Verlag, 1960), 106, 126, 128.

Gello eat you (νὰ σὲ φάῃ ἡ Γ(ι)λλού), which angry mothers use to curse their naughty children.[1063]

* * *

Byzantine hagiographers obviously avoid the image of the female evil spirit who kills children. She is mentioned only in the *Life* of Patriarch Tarasios where Ignatios the Deacon treats the popular superstitions with open contempt. In the *Life* of St. Peter of Atroa, Sabbas does not even mention that the demon who sucked the little boy's bodily fluids is female. Apparently, the Christian authors did not consider witches, unlike other pagan images, to be suitable incarnations of the Devil. Both theologians like St. John of Damascus and widely popular hagiographers like Ignatios the Deacon are unanimous in their concept of superstition (δεισιδαιμονία). The only connection between the horrible witch Gello, inherited from antiquity, and "real" Evil is the evil spirit in the false story about her (τὸ πονηρὸν τοῦ μύθου πνεῦμα), who possessed the slanderers in the court of the father of Patriarch Tarasios.

4.2. The Temptress

When he was fifteen years old and lived in his father's house on the island of Cyprus, the future Patriarch of Alexandria, St. John the Merciful (†619), had an odd dream; it was as if a young girl was standing by his side and poking him lightly in the ribs. Her face glowed more brightly than the sun, her jewelry was magnificent beyond imagination, and she wore a laurel wreath on her head. John woke up and saw her standing by his bed. *On seeing her,* says the holy man, *I thought: This is not a woman!* He continues with his story:

> I made the sign of the cross and told her: "Who are you, and how did you dare to break into my room when I was asleep?" Then, with a cheerful face

---

[1063] Oikonomides, "Gello", 250.

and a smile, she said: "I am the first of the Emperor's daughters". Hearing this, I prostrated myself before her.[1064]

The beautiful girl was neither an angel nor a demon. Of course, she was not the emperor's daughter either, but the personification of Mercy. This episode reveals a hugely important feature of the Byzantine demon: excessive female beauty is inevitably associated with sinfulness and temptation. The young John's first assumption was that a demonic ghost was sent to tempt him and he was ready to expel her with the sign of the cross.

Unlike the Child-killer, who occurs only occasionally in hagiography, the Temptress is a very common demonic character, primarily because of the moral message she purveys. Her image was hugely influenced by the *Life* of St. Antony, where many such evil spirits frequently visit the Egyptian hermit. In the *Life* of St. Auxentios, Michael Psellus attempts to explain the concept theoretically. In his opinion, if somebody decides to live in chastity, demons attack him with images (σχήματα) of adultery, such as female figures (εἴδωλα) adorned with jewelry.[1065] However, these descriptions could easily cross the line and become almost pornographic rather than instructive. Therefore, the authors approach the subject tactfully and avoid too much detail. They prefer to describe not the appearance of the Temptress herself but rather her corrupting influence upon men, a relatively common procedure in the personifications of sins, especially in the ninth century. Even in the two versions of St. Ioannikios the Great's *Life*, so rich in folklore beliefs, the demon of carnal temptation, who attacks a girl before her mother's eyes, is described as simply an influence upon the poor young woman.[1066]

[1064] John the Merciful, 351.25-35: τῷ τύπῳ οὖν τοῦ σταυροῦ κατασφραγισάμενος εἶπον αὐτῇ. "Τίς εἶ σὺ καὶ πῶς ἐτόλμησας εἰσελθεῖν ἐπάνω μου ὡς κοιμῶμαι;" τότε ἐκείνη ἱλαρῷ τῷ προσώπῳ καὶ μειδιῶσα τοῖς χείλεσι λέγει μοι· "Ἐγώ εἰμι ἡ πρώτη τῶν θυγατέρων τοῦ βασιλέως." ὡς δὲ ταῦτα ἤκουσα, εὐθέως προσεκύνησα αὐτήν. Cf. ibid., 408.10, where the maiden is likened to the sun.

[1065] Auxentios, §31.

[1066] Ioannikios, (Peter) §46.

Female demons in material form occur in the *Lives* of St. Antony the Younger and St. Paul of Latros. According to the anonymous author, St. Antony, who lived in a cell on Mount Olympus in Asia Minor, decided to get rid of the annoying lice in his monastic habit and wash the garment in the river. While he was waiting for it to dry, he suddenly saw a beautiful woman with loose hair (λυσίτριχος) coming to him. Startled, he hurried back to his cell and asked for advice from Bishop Jacob. The respected cleric answered that Antony had not seen a real woman but a *demonic apparition* (φαντασία δαιμονική). He told him to have no fear of such visions because *they come and go quickly* (γίνονται καὶ ἀπογίνονται ταχύ).[1067] We must note that the evil spirit's hair is long and loose, which is also a characteristic typical of the Child-killer.

The other text where the Temptress (or, rather, Temptresses) play a role is the *Life* of St. Paul of Latros. The story is somewhat humorous. In the mid-tenth century, the hermit Matthew, an acquaintance of St. Paul, lived on Mount Mycale (modern-day Samsun Dağı or Dilek Dağı) in western Asia Minor. The holy man used to visit the nearby church of St. John the Evangelist on its Patron's Day every year. On one of his visits, either because of *demonic envy* (βασκανία δαίμονος) or due to his own spiritual sluggishness (ῥαθυμία), a vision disturbed his religious fervor. An endless procession of female figures strode before his eyes, and the women were so numerous that they looked like a swarm of flies. Psychically tormented by this temptation, Matthew vowed never again to set foot in this church. According to Sabbas, the text's author, the hermit acted rashly and unjustly; he had to explore his soul thoroughly and ruthlessly eradicate carnal desire rather than blame the place where he had seen the disturbing vision. When Patron's Day came the following year, the hermit sank into depression. He lost his reason, and the desire to visit the temple tormented him unbearably. In his efforts to save himself from this condition and to excuse his disrespect to St. John, Matthew stood on a high cliff and cursed the demons all night. Suddenly, he heard a clap of thunder, a flash of lightning came from the East, and the outlines of a

---

[1067] Antony the Younger, §29.

male figure emerged in the transient gleam. It was St. John himself who told the disturbed monk to have no fear because he was with him. The Saint vanished, and Matthew could revisit the church.[1068]

The female demons of this story are nothing but a consequence of the monk's spiritual weakness and cannot harm him. They are merely apparitions and not materialized evil creatures, but they take advantage of their victim's internal instability. In this way, they fulfill Satan's sinister and cunning plan to divert the holy man from his piety and draw him into sin.

4.3. The Child-killer and the Temptress: a reconstruction of the image and its origins

Based on the sources mentioned above, we can reconstruct the main characteristics of the female demon in Byzantine hagiography as follows:

1. **Outer appearance:** loose hair, burning eyes; avian elements (hair like bird's feathers, wings) and a connection with owls.
2. Connection with dampness and the bodily fluids of women in childbirth and of newborn children.
3. **Activity and influence:** sucking the bodily fluids of babies and their mothers (blood and milk), harming the eyes, ears, and brain in babies and children; killing cattle (only in the *Testament of Solomon*); tempting men without sexual satisfaction.

What is the origin of this sinister demon's image, and is it possible to trace the traditions related to her?

According to Greenfield, Barb, and Burkert,[1069] many of the Byzantine female demon's sometimes apparently incompatible features can be successfully explained through a thorough analysis of Middle Eastern mythologies and the Jewish tradition. The two main aspects of this evil creature, namely child-killing and sexual seduction, are typical of the

---

[1068] Paul of Latros I, §10.22–36.
[1069] See Barb, "Antaura"; Greenfield, *Traditions of Belief*, 184–87; Burkert, *The Near-Eastern Influence*, 82–87. Jonston ("Child-Killing Demon", 365ff) rejects the Eastern origin of the female child-killing demon in the Greek mythological tradition.

demon Lilith. *Lilith* or *Lilîtu* is a plural form of the Sumerian *Lili*, which means *evil wind*.[1070] She appears in Sumerian mythology as early as the second millennium B.C. as a beautiful vampire maiden who could neither sexually satisfy a mortal man nor give birth. She selected and seduced her lover and never allowed him to leave.[1071] Her depictions often include avian elements, like wings or owl's talons.[1072] Archeological evidence shows that, around the seventh century B.C., she was believed to be an evil creature that brought death to women in childbirth.[1073]

The Hebrews borrowed this deity and erroneously associated her with night (from Hebrew *layil, night*).[1074] Though appearing only once in the Hebrew Bible,[1075] Lilith is a popular character in the Talmudic tradition and the Apocrypha between the second and the third century A.D.[1076] She was Adam's first wife, who demanded to be his equal, leaving him when he refused to comply with her request. When God banished Adam and Eve from the Garden of Eden, and they decided to practice sexual abstinence for 130 years, Lilith visited the first man at night and gave birth to innumerable demons. One of these was their son Lilin, who seduced Eve.[1077] Lilith's depiction as loose-haired and naked[1078] can also

---

[1070] Barb, "Antaura", 6; Greenfield, *Traditions of Belief*, 185; Patai, *The Hebrew Goddess*, 222.
[1071] On Sumerian beliefs of the influence of Lilith, see Barb, "Antaura", 4ff; Patai, *The Hebrew Goddess*, 221–22.
[1072] On the avian elements in the image of Lilith, see Barb, "Antaura", 7ff. Barb refers to similar features in various Greek deities (the Sirens, the Stymphalian birds, and Athena's owl). See also Patai, *The Hebrew Goddess*, 222, who refers to an Assyrian relief depicting a beautiful naked owl-woman.
[1073] See Patai, *The Hebrew Goddess*, 222, who refers to a magical spell written on a clay tablet used for expelling Lilith from women in childbirth.
[1074] Barb, "Antaura", 6; Patai, *The Hebrew Goddess*, 222.
[1075] Lilith is mentioned only in the original text of Isa. 34:14 (see Barb, "Antaura", 7; Patai, *The Hebrew Goddess*, 222ff; Bojadschiew, *The Night in the Middle Ages*, 205). In the Septuagint, her name is erroneously translated as *onokentauros* (ὀνοκένταυρος) – a kind of demon haunting wild places (καὶ συναντήσουσιν δαιμόνια ὀνοκενταύροις καὶ βοήσουσιν ἕτερος πρὸς ἕτερον...).
[1076] On the development of her image in the Hebrew traditions, see Patai, *The Hebrew Goddess*, 221–55. On the two functions of Lilith as child-killer and temptress, see ibid., 233ff.
[1077] Barb, "Antaura", 4; Patai, *The Hebrew Goddess*, 232.

be seen on the mugs (from the sixth to the seventh centuries) found during the excavations of a Hebrew colony near Nippur. The first element of her image, the loose hair, reminds us especially of the Temptress in Byzantine hagiography, where adjectives and expressions like λυσίτριχος[1079] and δαιμόνιον ἠνεμωμένας ἔχον τὰς κόμας[1080] are used.

Her harmful influence on women in childbirth and on newborn children is also a popular element in the image of Lilith. She has power over small boys until their circumcision ritual and over baby girls until the twentieth day after birth; the evil goddess chases them all over the world and murders them as retaliation for Original Sin.[1081] Due to aural similarity, she was associated with another female deity, the Assyrian Lamashtu, who was a cruel enemy of pregnant women and their babies.[1082]

According to one of the Talmudic traditions, Lilith was born as an aquatic creature on the fifth day of Creation.[1083] The Sumerian goddess Abzu whose name appears as one of Gello's twelve and a half names was also closely related to water.[1084] She was the primordial Ocean from which the whole world was made. She was related to the Babylonian Tiamat and the Hebrew Tehom, the evil mother of demons.[1085]

The Middle Eastern female deities we mentioned above and their specific characteristics and functions take various forms in ancient Greek mythology as early as the second millennium B.C. This unique fusion produced beautiful and mostly benevolent creatures, like the Nymphs, the Nereids, and the Muses, but also their dangerous counterparts — the

---

[1078] Patai, *The Hebrew Goddess*, 224ff.
[1079] Antony the Younger, §29.
[1080] Pseudo-Psellos, "Timothée ou des demons", l. 457.
[1081] Patai, *The Hebrew Goddess*, 223ff, 236–41.
[1082] Greenfield, *Traditions of Belief*, 186.
[1083] Patai, *The Hebrew Goddess*, 230.
[1084] "Escape from the Abominable and Unclean Gyllou", 573; Perdrizet, *Negotium perambulans*, 17 (Greek original) and 18 (French translation).
[1085] On the four mothers of the demons in Hebrew mythology (Lilith, Na'amah, Agrat, and Mahalath), see Gershom Scholem, "Demons, Demonology in Kabbalah", in *Encyclopaedia Judaica*, vol. 5, s.v. "Demons. Demonology" (Jerusalem, 2007), 576.

Sirens, the Harpies, and the Gorgons.[1086] Many of these supernatural beings retained both their connection with water and their destructive, seductive power over men. In Greek, the name *Abzu* was transliterated as *Abyss* (Ἄβυσσος). There were other variations of the same name in the Palaeologian period (1261–1453), like *Abyza* (Ἀβυζά), *Amizou* (Ἀμιζού), and *Amidazou* (Ἀμιδαζού).[1087] Burkert emphasizes that the most persistent of these images were Gello and Lamia, mentioned by Sappho and Stesichorus. In his opinion, the name *Gelo* is connected with Gallu, a Sumerian evil demon, and not with the verb γελῶ (*to laugh*).[1088]

Last but not least, the long, loose hair of the Middle Eastern female demon also occurs in various myths and popular beliefs. As already mentioned, in the *Testament of Solomon*, the Hebrew King ordered the monstrous Obizou to be hanged by the hair at the entrance of his Temple in Jerusalem. This story probably echoes rites and customs widespread throughout the Eastern Mediterranean. The so-called *Gorgoneia* (Γοργόνεια), or Medusa's heads, were depicted in reliefs above the gates of temples and synagogues during Late Antiquity and possessed apotropaic functions.[1089] According to the early Christian apologist Justinus Martyr (c. 100–c. 165), one of the Sibyls was hanged in a jar in the temple of Apollo at Cumae.[1090] This concept also became a literary motif in Byzantium. In the novel *Callimachus and Chrysorrhoea* (twelfth

---

[1086] Barb, "Antaura", 6ff; Greenfield, *Traditions of Belief*, 185. On the details of the relationship between these Middle Eastern deities and Greek mythological characters, see Martin Ninck, *Die Bedeutung des Wassers im Kult und Leben der Alten* [Philologus Supplementband XIV, II] (Darmstadt, 1960), 5, 15ff, 47ff, 8991, 143. On the demons who control human sexuality, see Otto Böcher, *Dämonenfurcht und Dämonenabwehr. Ein Beitrag zur Vorgeschichte der Christlichen Taufe* [Beiträge zur Wissenschaft vom Alten und Neuen Testament, 90] (Stuttgart: Kohlhammer, 1970), 33–40 and 124–36. The word *gorgona* (γοργόνα, Ancient Greek Γοργών/Γοργώ) means *mermaid* in modern Greek.
[1087] See Greenfield, *Traditions of Belief*, 186 and n. 561 (with bibliography); Perdrizet, *Negotium perambulans*, 20.
[1088] See Burkert, *The Near-Eastern Influence*, 82ff.
[1089] Barb, "Antaura", 9.
[1090] Justinus Martyr, "Cohortatio ad Graecos", in MPG, vol. 6 (Paris, 1857), 308ff.

century), young Callimachus finds his beloved Chrysorrhoea hanged by the hair at the dragon's castle.[1091]

4.4. Why did Byzantine writers avoid female demons?

The sources for the Byzantine female demon clearly show the prevalence of the evil spirits of the Gello tradition in folklore. St. John of Damascus dedicated a fiercely polemical work to them, whose purpose was to prove that such beliefs were utterly groundless and even ridiculous. Michael Psellus calls Gello *well-known*, and the story of Patriarch Tarasios's father shows the vitality of the tradition associated with the child-killing female demon in the imperial capital itself.

Nevertheless, the hagiographical literature of the ninth and tenth centuries shows a clear preference for male demons. Female images are extremely rare and scarcely move beyond the stereotype of the nameless temptress with loose hair who *comes and goes quickly* (in the words of Bishop Jacob of the *Life* of St. Antony the Younger quoted above). When a child-killing demon appears, the evil spirit is often genderless, and its external characteristics are not described, as in the case of the infant son of the Phrygian nobleman Markianos in the *Life* of St. Peter of Atroa. What is the reason for this silence of the hagiographers, which contrasts with the abundance of other accounts of female demons in folklore?

The polemical works of the iconoclasts against their opponents in the eighth and ninth centuries are almost entirely lost. Often only tiny fragments or titles survive. However, we know that a crucial element of the Iconoclast movement was the rejection of the Holy Virgin Mary and her veneration.[1092] Misogyny was an integral part of the overall attempt to

---

[1091] "The Romance of Callimachos and Chrysorrhoe", ed. Emmanuel Kriaras, *Byzantine Chivalric Romances* [Greek: "Τὸ μυθιστόρημα τοῦ Καλλιμάχου καὶ τῆς Χρυσορρόης", ed. Εμμανουὴλ Κριαράς, *Βυζαντινὰ ιπποτικὰ μυθιστορήματα*], (Athens, 1955), 38ff.

[1092] *Theophanis chronographia*, 415, 435, 442. On the iconodule movement and the role of women and the Virgin Mary, see Connor, *Women of Byzantium*, 160–65; Katerina Nikolaou, *Woman in the Middle Byzantine Period: Social Prototypes and Everyday Life in Hagiographical Texts* [Greek: Κατερίνα Νικολάου, *Η Γυναίκα στη Μέση Βυζαντινή Εποχή. Κοινωνικά πρότυπα και καθημερινός βίος στα αγιολογικά κείμενα*] (Athens:

create a masculine society in which the man, farmer and soldier (*stratiotes*), played a leading role in both economic life and the defense of the empire against the still vigorous Caliphate. In the militarized world of Leo III and his son, there was no place for theological and intellectual subtlety regarding the two natures of Jesus Christ, and, hence, no place for the Virgin Mary as the source of His human substance. For the "orthodox" iconoclast, she was just St. Mary — the pious woman who performed the simple task of giving birth to the Son of God, a mere womb.

This attitude was probably exaggerated by the iconodules. They accused their opponents of equating the Holy Mother of God with female demons. The anonymous author of the *Life* of St. Michael Synkellos (761–January 4, 846) says sadly that the emperors Constantine V and Theophilos looked upon the icon of the Virgin as some idol of Artemis.[1093] St. Stephen the Younger makes a similar accusation against Constantine V during his debate (*agon*) with the emperor just before his execution.[1094] This alleged outrageous blasphemy against the Mother of God was an efficient tool in the overall Iconodule propaganda in the late eight and the first half of the ninth centuries. Probably for this very reason, the hagiographers avoided female demons and the tradition related to Gello. Such images would have reminded their audience of the Iconoclast crusade both against the Virgin Mary and the female saints, undermining the Iconodule message. It must be noted that leading figures in the Orthodox movement were women — politicians like the empresses Irene and Theodora, intellectuals like Kasia the Hymnographer, and martyrs like St. Athanasia of Aegina. By avoiding mention of the evil witch Gello and of harmful female evil spirits in general, and by showing a clear preference for male or genderless demons, the iconodule hagiographers were in fact acting to save the image of the Virgin Mary and of women in general.

The National Hellenic Research Foundation, 2005), 229–35; Jenkins, *Byzantium. The Imperial Centuries*, 85ff.

[1093] Michael the Synkellos, §18.
[1094] Stephen the Younger, 156.9–12.

5. Demons disguised as saints and angels

The ontological difference between the "natural" and the "supernatural" in the Greco-Roman world is clear. The creatures that do not belong to the human world share the same pattern of outer characteristics that betray their otherness. Even the line between the gods of Olympus and the chthonic deities is sometimes thin, like the one between the earthly and the heavenly Aphrodite in Plato's *Phaedrus*, each responsible for a different kind of love. Good and Bad are relative categories. There could be no apparent difference between the material images of ever-changing supernatural forces, sometimes harmful and sometimes benevolent, but only between the outer appearances of the human and non-human. Despite the efforts of Christian theologians to draw a clear boundary between Good and Evil, sometimes Byzantine hagiographers did not take the trouble to make clear whether some creature belonged to the armies of God or the hordes of Satan. Such is the case with the awful men with murderous eyes who appear in a collective dream before the elders of Amastris and threaten to beat them for their disrespect to St. George's pregnant mother, Megetho.[1095] The reader cannot judge from their description whether they are angels or demons, but they obviously do not belong to the human world.

Nevertheless, the demonic images we analyzed above are relatively clearly defined and easily discerned. They confirm the basic concept that the evil spirit in Byzantium is foolish and unable to conceal its true identity and innate characteristics. Physical deformity, a black color, evil eyes, and a foul stench are not simply the embodiment of sin. They are sin itself, inseparable from the very nature of the demon as the objectivization of absolute Evil, both the signifier and the signified.

Sporadically, the demons could use their deformed angelic features to take the form of a saint or an angel. *And no marvel; for Satan himself is transformed into an angel of light,* says St. Apostle Paul in one of his epis-

---

[1095] George of Amastris, §5: θεωρεῖ ἕκαστος αὐτῶν ἄνδρας φοβεροὺς ταῖς χερσὶ κατέχοντας ῥόπαλον καὶ φονίῳ βλέποντας βλέμματι.

tles.¹⁰⁹⁶ Their devilish cunning could hardly mislead the true believer, like the evil spirits disguised as the Holy Forty Martyrs who tried to deceive St. Gregory of Dekapolis *c.* 829–830. They begged for permission to enter his cave, but the wise hermit recognized their true nature immediately and cast them out.¹⁰⁹⁷ The author does not clarify how exactly Gregory identified the demons. We must conduct a more thorough research of the hagiographical corpus to find the marks that distinguish an angel from a fallen angel.

5.1. Demonic fire and angelic light

The Orthodox theological tradition distinguishes between two essential functions of fire, to burn (καυστική) and to illuminate (φωτιστική). The Devil and his servants torture sinners in burning flames, entirely devoid of light.¹⁰⁹⁸ On the other hand, a fire that does not burn will shine upon the righteous in Heaven:

> Moreover, I think that the fire prepared in Hell for the Devil and his angels is separated through the Voice of God: since fire has two powers, burning and illuminating, the piercing and punitive part will be bestowed upon those who deserve to be burned, while the illuminating and shining part will be allotted to the brightness of those who rejoice. Since He separated the flame from the fire and distributed them, His voice ordered that the fire of Hell be devoid of light and the flame of the eternal rest remain unburning.¹⁰⁹⁹

---

¹⁰⁹⁶ 2 Cor. 11:14: Αὐτὸς γὰρ ὁ Σατανᾶς μετασχηματίζεται εἰς ἄγγελον φωτός.
¹⁰⁹⁷ Gregory of Dekapolis, §9.
¹⁰⁹⁸ See, e.g., the *vast fire..., entirely devoid of light* in the vision of St. Phantinos the Younger, §31.6ff (καὶ ὁρῶ πῦρ ἐκεῖ μέγα..., φωτὸς δὲ πάμπαν ὑπάρχον ἄμοιρον).
¹⁰⁹⁹ Basilius Magnus, "Homiliae super Psalmos", MPG, vol. 29 (Paris, 1857), 297B–C: Οἶμαι δέ, ὅτι τὸ πῦρ τὸ ἡτοιμασμένον εἰς κόλασιν τῷ διαβόλῳ καὶ τοῖς ἀγγέλοις αὐτοῦ διακόπτεται τῇ φωνῇ τοῦ Κυρίου· ἵνα, ἐπειδὴ δύο εἰσὶν ἐν τῷ πυρὶ δυνάμεις, ἥ τε καυστικὴ καὶ φωτιστική, τὸ μὲν δριμὺ καὶ κολαστικὸν τοῦ πυρὸς τοῖς ἀξίοις τῆς καύσεως προσαπομείνῃ, τὸ δὲ φωτιστικὸν αὐτοῦ καὶ λαμπρὸν τῇ φαιδρότητι τῶν εὐφραινομένων ἀποκληρωθῇ. Φωνὴ οὖν Κυρίου διακόπτοντος φλόγα πυρὸς καὶ μερίζοντος, ὡς ἀλαμπὲς μὲν εἶναι τὸ πῦρ τῆς κολάσεως, ἄκαυστον δὲ τὸ πῦρ τῆς ἀναπαύσεως ἀπομεῖναι. For the same idea, related to the fallen angels, see ibid., 372A: Εἶτα βάραθρον βαθύ, καὶ σκότος ἀδιεξόδευτον, καὶ πῦρ ἀλαμπές· ἐν τῷ σκότει τὴν μὲν καυστικὴν δύναμιν ἔχον, τὸ δὲ φέγγος ἀφῃρημένον. In his poem "On Demonic Battles", St. Gregory of Nazianzus says that the Devil sometimes appeared before him *like night*

Byzantine hagiographers of the period under study confirm the theoretical concept that angels and saints radiate pure, serene, and sun-like light.[1100] For example, in the late sixth or the early seventh century, the monks of the Choziba monastery reported frequently seeing their dead abbot Leontios standing before the church's altar as if made of bright and warm fire.[1101] According to Michael Psellus, demons were connected to darkness by nature, but one of them attempted to fake the brightness of the servants of God and deceive St. Auxentios the Great shortly after his return from the Council of Chalcedon (451) to Mount Scopa in Asia Minor.[1102] The evil spirit materialized in a blinding flash of light, but his magical tricks proved no match for the holy monk. A man of great inner power and introspection, Auxentios immediately sensed that the blaze was making him feel uneasy and disturbed (ἐθορυβεῖτο). Since divine light was characterized by absolute serenity (γαλήνη), this qualm was a clear sign that the creature before him was a demon and that the glow emerging from it was more somber and more evil than the most profound darkness.[1103]

Mortal eyes can perceive the divine light during prayer and in complete isolation. St. Paul of Latros (†December 15, 955) explained to his pupil, the monk Symeon that his joy and tranquility were absolute only when he was alone; on such occasions, he used to see himself surrounded by a circle of beautiful luminescence. This kind of light was pleasant and pure; it illuminated everything around, brought happiness and joy, and filled the human soul with serenity and love, but evil thoughts and unim-

---

(νυκτὶ ἐοικώς), and sometimes took the image of a *creature of light* (φωτὸς αὖθις ἐν... πλάσματι) – see Gregorius Nazianzenus, "De daemonum pugnis", 1429. See also Greenfield, *Traditions of Belief*, 73–75 on the punishment that will be given to the Devil and his servants after Doomsday. On Hellfire in Byzantine *Apocrypha*, see Lambakis, "The Descents into Hell", 46ff.

[1100] See, e.g., Anastasios of Persia, *Encomion by George Pisides*, §28.13ff. According to this text, a horde of demons gathered in St. Anastasios's cell shortly before his execution; they were shrouded in a light *resembling the fire from a torch*.

[1101] George of Choziba, §3.11.14–16.

[1102] The Scopa Mountain (modern-day Kayışdağı) is located about 45 kilometers northwest of ancient Chalcedon (see Joannou, *Démonologie*, 77, n. 47ff).

[1103] Auxentios, §26.

portant conversations chased it away. Whenever somebody violated his privacy and forced him to communicate, the state of happiness immediately disappeared, the divine light faded, and a demonic, flame-like, and repulsive blaze took its place, covering everything around with smoke.[1104]

Only the righteous possessed the ability to distinguish between the two kinds of light, however. Ordinary laypeople could hardly distinguish between pure angelic brightness and the fearsome fire emanating from evil creatures. The tall figure of St. Ioannikios, illuminated by a blinding radiance, fills its spectators only with the feeling of θάμβος, a mixture of astonishment and awe. For them, he is neither an angel nor a demon, but only a supernatural being, a *ghost* or a *phantom* (πνεῦμα, φάντασμα), and only his ability to speak like a human alleviates their fears.[1105]

5.2. Lack of persistence

Divine light and evil fire are abstract theological concepts, and the ability to distinguish between them is a privilege of the righteous few, holy men and women. There are other, more practical ways to judge whether some vision or being comes from God or the Devil. A popular legend tells the story of the poor peasant Basil who arrived in the vast empire's capital clad in shabby clothes. Night was approaching, and the man sat on the steps of St. Diomedes Church to rest. At that moment, Nicholas, the temple's *prosmonarios* (custodian), heard in his dream a voice ordering him to open the door and welcome the emperor. He obeyed but saw nobody outside but the ragged stranger, covered in dust. Nicholas cursed the Devil and his servants and went back to bed. The same voice repeated the order a second time, but the custodian knew better and paid no attention. Finally, a humanlike figure appeared by his bed and gave him a few violent blows with a wooden cudgel, urging him angrily to bring the man sitting outside into the church — he was the emperor. Shortly afterward, the prophecy was fulfilled, and Basil ascended the imperial throne.[1106] In

---

[1104] Paul of Latros I, §38.12-17.
[1105] Ioannikios (*Sabbas*), §11; Ioannikios (*Peter*), §42: ἄνθρωπός εἰμι ὁμοιοπαθὴς ὑμῖν; Ioannikios (Metaphr.), 48B.
[1106] Georgius Monachus, "Chronicon Breve", MPG, vol. 110 (Paris, 1863), 1041.

this story, widespread among the authors of the late ninth and the tenth centuries, one of the main differences between demonic visions and the prophecies sent by God becomes evident. When the naïve caretaker failed to grasp the meaning of the angelic message and thought at first that some evil force was fooling with him, the godly voice forgave him. It merely repeated the order, knowing full well that Basil did not look at all like an emperor. When Nicholas stubbornly stuck to his wrong judgment and refused to obey the command for a second time, there was no excuse, and the angel angrily threatened to punish him physically. In contrast, like a fake facial expression, a deceitful, demonic vision cannot last long and quickly fades away.

Byzantine hagiographers of the period under study confirm the concept of demonic volatility and inconsistency as opposed to angelic steadfastness. Like the beautiful apparition, resembling a woman with loose hair, that tempted St. Antony the Younger, evil visions *come and go quickly* (γίνονται καὶ ἀπογίνονται ταχύ).[1107] When St. Germanos of Kosinitza was thirty years old, a voice commanded him to depart from Palestine for Macedonia and build a monastery there. Still, he paid no attention, thinking the order a devilish temptation.[1108] As soon as the order was repeated by a frightful white-clad man, who whipped him for his disobedience, the monk understood his mistake, repented, and fulfilled his duty faithfully.[1109] In the mid-tenth century, St. Elias Speleotes and his mentor, Arsenios, reprimanded a local slave trader and warned him to give up his hateful business. Still, he refused to obey and shortly after died. His widow brought a coin to Arsenios, implored him to offer a liturgy for the deceased, and the holy man mercifully agreed. As soon as he began to chant, however, an angel stood behind him and stopped his mouth. Astonished, Arsenios thought at first that the vision was sent by the *opposite force* (μή πως ἐξ ἐναντίας ἐνεργείας ἐστὶν ὁ κωλύων) and attempted to resume the ritual, but the angel held him back again. When

---

[1107] Antony the Younger, §29.
[1108] Germanos of Kosinitza, §8.
[1109] Germanos of Kosinitza, §9.

this happened for a third time, the priest realized that the slave trader's soul was irretrievably lost and condemned. He returned the widow her money and advised her to visit another priest — he could not finish the prayer for her late husband's soul.[1110] When Emperor Theophilos (829–842) threw St. Antony the Younger in jail for embezzlement, the chains fell off miraculously. Assuming that a *demonic power* (δαιμονικὴ ἐνέργεια) had set him free as a temptation, he put the shackles on again. The pious man needed to be released two more times in the same manner to be persuaded that this, indeed, was the will of God.[1111]

[1110] Elias Speleotes, §18.
[1111] Antony the Younger, §33.

CHAPTER 3
ANIMALS AND PLANTS

> Death's cunning inventor transforms himself into anything he wants,
> A true Proteus he becomes, stealing shapes
> To conquer man through ambush or in open combat[1112]

These words of St. Gregory of Nazianzus from his short work "On Demonic Battles" concisely express the Byzantine conception of the demon's ability to deceive and mislead people through the mutability of his image. Like ancient Proteus, the evil spirit can assume all forms and, above all, take the shape of animals and fantastic monsters, through which it can inspire fear and awe in people, deceive them, or, on rare occasions, physically harm them.

In the Byzantine hagiography of the period under study, zoomorphic demons are less common than anthropomorphic ones, and evil spirits that appear in human form seldom transform into beasts. However, the animal forms themselves, fantastic or real, are quite numerous and varied. We can trace the origins of some of them — serpents, scorpions, and dragons to the Old and New Testaments. Hagiographers and theologians constantly try to find a biblical explanation, at least in part, for other zoomorphic images, like the bat, the owl, and the mouse. However, much more ancient substrates are often blended into their vivid descriptions. Many of them were inherited from the ancient Greek and Roman mythological and literary traditions. Others give the modern scholar precious insight into the evolution of real folklore, even if through the lens of a Christian intellectual writer, as well as information about the influences of myths and legends of southern Italian, Arabic, or Slavic origin. In other words, when analyzing the zoomorphic demon, we

---

[1112] Gregorius Nazianzenus, "De daemonum pugnis", in MPG, vol. 37 (Paris, 1862), 1429A:
Πάντα γάρ, ὅσσ'ἐθέλῃσι, πέλει θανάτοιο σοφιστής,
Γεγὼς Πρωτεὺς εἰς κλοπὰς μορφωμάτων,
Ὡς κέ τιν'ἢ λόχων, ἢ ἀμφαδόν, ἄνδρα δαμάσσῃ.

must apply two types of analysis. We will try to trace the images that belong to the ancient or biblical tradition back to their textual sources; they will be treated as pure literary phenomena incorporated for various reasons into the Christian conceptual system. On the other hand, the mythological adstrata require a comparative analysis to reveal the fusion of local beliefs and the legends of various newcomers. A typical example of the latter category appears in the Byzantine province of Bithynia, where ancient, even primordial, local myths about dragons and serpents probably merged with Slavic tales to produce the fascinating stories told by the authors of the two versions of St. Ioannikios the Great's *Life*.

In the Old and the New Testaments, zoomorphic demons appear only occasionally and are often mere allegories. The New Testament, in particular, clearly avoids them, probably to enhance the idea of the evil spirit as a weak and miserable creature. Only in the Book of Revelation do evil, mostly fantastic[1113] beasts, play a significant role. Since these creatures are supposed to announce Doomsday and the end of the world, Byzantine hagiographers carefully avoid such images. Surprisingly enough, demons in the shape of lions are also absent from the saints' *Lives* in the period under study,[1114] and the lion occurs only as a metaphorical wordplay on the names of the Iconoclast emperors Leo III (717–741) and Leo V (813–820). The most popular demonic incarnation is the serpent, through which the Devil played such a crucial and fateful role in the sacred history of Humankind. However, the origins of this widespread image by no means lie only in the Old and the New Testaments; they are a complex blend of many traditions of belief.

In the literature of Late Antiquity, the zoomorphic evil spirit also appears as a part of various theoretical categories and conceptualizations. It is often related to the so-called Noplatonic *chthonic demons* (χθόνιοι

[1113] Rev. 16:13 (*I saw three unclean spirits like frogs come out of the mouth of the dragon, and out of the mouth of the beast, and out of the mouth of the false prophet.*); Rev. 13:1-2 (*...and saw a beast rise up out of the sea, having seven heads and ten horns, and upon his horns ten crowns, and upon his heads the name of blasphemy*).

[1114] The so-called *lion-faced demons* (λεοντοπρόσωποι δαίμονες) are mentioned, for example, by Michael Psellus, "Greek provisions on demons", 125.3-5. According to the text, they were not made of *flesh and bone*, but of *some aerial and fiery matter*.

ANIMALS AND PLANTS   337

δαίμονες).[1115] In his treatise *Concerning Philosophy from Oracles*, Porphyry claims that some *evil* (πονηροί) demons controlled by Pluto have the power to take the shape of *various animals* in which they approach mortals.[1116] According to the commentaries of Proclus on Plato's *Cratylus*, demons, like nymphs, prefer to materialize as snakes and does.[1117] In Lucian's "The Lover of Lies", a spirit haunting a house in Corinth appears before the exorcist as a hound, a bull, and a lion.[1118] Origen tries to explain the existence of zoomorphic demons in his *Philocalia*. According to him, *they conceal themselves in the most rapacious and savage beasts* because *they desire to seduce the human race from their allegiance to the real God*,[1119] and each has his favorite animal.[1120] According to Pseudo-Psellus (thirteenth century), no matter what category they belong to, demons attack humans like wild beasts.[1121]

Some clues for the proper understanding of the zoomorphic demon's image can also be found in the so-called *Physiologus*. This treatise, dating from the second or the third century, didactically describes various animals and plants. The anonymous author tells interesting short stories that reveal the qualities of each species and, in addition, the superstitions and beliefs related to them.[1122] The many Greek versions of this treatise and its numerous translations into Latin and Old Slavonic show its great popularity and wide distribution in medieval Europe.

[1115] Vakaloudi, *Magic*, 112; Tambornino, *De antiquorum daemonismo*, 22; Joannou, *Démonologie*, 12.
[1116] *Porphyrii de philosophia*, 147.11: πᾶσι ζῴοις ὁμοιούμενοι προσίασι τοῖς ἀνθρώποις.
[1117] *Procli Diadochi in Platonis Cratylum commentaria*, §118.24–27.
[1118] Lucian, "The Lover of Lies", §31.21ff.
[1119] Origen, *The Philocalia*, §20.19.7-9: βουλόμενοι ἀπάγειν τοῦ ἀληθινοῦ θεοῦ τὸ τῶν ἀνθρώπων γένος, ὑποδύονται τῶν ζῴων τὰ ἁρπακτικότερα καὶ ἀγριώτερα (*The Philocalia of Origen*, trans. George Lewis [Edinburgh: T. & T. Clark, 1911], 130).
[1120] Origen, *The Philocalia*, §20.20.14ff: ἔοικεν οὖν τις εἶναι ἑκάστῳ δαιμόνων εἴδει κοινωνία πρὸς ἕκαστον εἶδος ζῴων (*The Philocalia of Origen*, 130).
[1121] Pseudo-Psellos, "Timothée ou des demons", ll. 550–54.
[1122] On the dating of the *Physiologus*, see Alan Scott, "The Date of the *Physiologus*", *Vigiliae Christianae* 52, no. 4 (November 1998): 430–41.

1. Snakes and scorpions

1.1. Origins

In the second part of the present study, we paid attention to the biblical accounts and theological interpretations of the most important event in the "sacred history" of humanity, the triumph of Christ over Satan, the personification and inventor of death and sin. A fundamental theoretical postulate of the Christian theological system, as it developed among the Fathers of the Church and the hagiographers in the first six centuries of our era, is the authority (ἐξουσία) of God over the Devil, demons, and evil spirits. According to the Apostle Luke, Christ delegates this power to His disciples,[1123] and this passage of the Gospel becomes the "backbone" of Christian demonology.[1124] In this case, two animals are chosen as personifications for the demonic threat to the righteous, namely, the scorpion and the serpent. Scorpions occur only occasionally in Byzantine demonology. They are not directly associated with the Devil or his servants in the Old and New Testament, but symbolize the danger hovering over the prophets[1125] and wickedness in general.[1126] These animals also personify the punishment meted out to the sinner.[1127] These biblical accounts make the poisonous scorpion a common but not particularly interesting demonic image in hagiography as early as the times of St. Athanasios of Alexandria.[1128] According to the saints' *Lives* between the sixth and the tenth centuries, it attacks hermits and monks in the caves where they try to find refuge from the world. Nothing in these narratives re-

---

[1123] Luke 10:19: *Behold, I give unto you power to tread on serpents and scorpions, and over all the power of the enemy: and nothing shall by any means hurt you.* (Ἰδοὺ δέδωκα ὑμῖν τὴν ἐξουσίαν τοῦ πατεῖν ἐπάνω ὄφεων καὶ σκορπίων καὶ ἐπὶ πᾶσαν τὴν δύναμιν τοῦ ἐχθροῦ, καὶ οὐδὲν ὑμᾶς οὐ μὴ ἀδικήσῃ).

[1124] Quotes of Luke 10:19; see, e.g.: Symeon Stylites the Younger, §41.30; Stephen the Younger, 149.7–9; Gregory of Dekapolis, §9.5; Ioannikios (*Peter*), §20.

[1125] Ezek., 2:6

[1126] Sir., 26:9 (the wicked and sly [πονηρά] woman is like a scorpion in the hands of the man who marries her); Luke 11:11ff.

[1127] Sir., 39.37; Rev. 9:3–5 and 9:10.

[1128] Antony, §9.23 and §24.29.

mains of the rich Mithraic astrological symbolism related to this image.[1129]

While the scorpion is a relatively rare and not very complex incarnation of Evil in hagiography, the snake is probably the most common demonic image in Byzantine iconography[1130] and literature[1131] until the very end of the empire in 1453. The noun ὄφις (serpent) in Greek is masculine, and the grammatical gender determines its particular features and functions: snakes do not appear as the personification of dangerous and wicked female attractiveness. On the contrary — as we will see, women in rich clothes, make-up, and, especially, luxurious hairstyles appeal to the snake-like evil spirits. By contrast, in Slavic languages, the serpent has both a feminine[1132] and a masculine[1133] gender form, the latter being a purely fantastical monster akin to the dragon (δράκων).

The theological turning point for the concept that the snake is the primordial incarnation of Satan is undoubtedly the biblical narrative of Adam and Eve's banishment from the Garden of Eden. In Genesis 3, the serpent persuades the first woman to disobey God's commandment not to touch the tree that grows in the middle of the Garden. She eats some of its fruit and tempts her husband to do the same. As a result, both their eyes were opened to the knowledge of good and evil, and the Lord expelled them from Eden and condemned them to spend their lives in toil and labor. The Old Testament does not explicitly connect the snake with the Devil — he was just craftier than any of the wild animals the Lord

---

[1129] On the symbolism of the scorpion in Mithraism, see Giovanni Casadio, "The Failing Male God: Emasculation, Death and Other Accidents in the Ancient Mediterranean World", *Numen* 50, no. 3 (2003): 231–68.

[1130] On the iconography of snake-like demons, see Provatakis, *The Devil*, 131–67; Panayotis Vocotopoulos, "Demons, Reptiles and the Devil in Representations of Baptism", in *Eukosmia. Studi miscellanei per il 74-o di Vincenzo Poggi S. J.*, ed. Vincenzo Ruggieri and Luca Pieralli (Rubbettino, 2003), 617–24.

[1131] Joannou, *Démonologie*, 12; Greenfield, *Traditions of Belief*, 86.

[1132] Old Slavonic/Old Bulgarian **ЗМЬЯ**, Bulgarian змия, Russian змея, Serbian змеја, Polish z̓mija, etc.

[1133] Old Slavonic/Old Bulgarian **ЗМЬН**, Bulgarian змей, Russian змей, Serbian змâj, Polish z̓mij, etc.

God had made.[1134] Some canonical texts[1135] and numerous Hebraic apocrypha identify this animal as the incarnation of Satan.[1136] Still, later theologians met obvious difficulties commenting on the famous passage of Genesis 3:1. Though they[1137] did not call into question the fact that the Devil was the one who deceived Eve, they claimed that he did not himself take the shape of a snake but rather possessed the body of an actual reptile. This concept is evident in John Chrysostom's *Homilies on Genesis*, where the Church Father claims that the Devil made use of this creature as an instrument and through it ensnared that naïve and weaker vessel, namely, woman, in his deception by means of conversation.[1138] One of Chrysostom's spurious sermons on the same subject is even more explicit. The author describes Satan as wearing the snake as a garment (ἔνδυμα) and claims that Eve would have run away from him had he appeared before her in his actual form.[1139] Much later, Gregory Palamas

---

[1134] Gen. 3:1: ὁ δὲ ὄφις ἦν φρονιμώτατος πάντων τῶν θηρίων τῶν ἐπὶ τῆς γῆς, ὧν ἐποίησεν κύριος ὁ θεός.

[1135] See Isa., 27:1; Rev. 12:9; Rev. 20:2.

[1136] On the Devil in the Hebraic tradition, see Greenfield, *Traditions of Belief*, 36 and n. 131. Greenfield refers to various apocrypha, like chapter 69 of the Book of Enoch whose Greek translation is now lost; Kelly, "The Metamorphoses of the Eden Serpent", 302, with a reference to the works of Rabbi Eliezer (ninth century); Langton, *Essentials of Demonology*, 55, 134ff; Langton, *Satan, a Portrait*, 20ff. For more detail on the Late Byzantine tradition related to the role of the Devil in Original Sin, see Greenfield, *Traditions of Belief*, 36–41.

[1137] See, e.g., Justinus Martyr, "Dialogus cum Tryphone Judaeo", in MPG, vol. 6 (Paris, 1857), 573A; Basilius Magnus, "De ieiunio homilia I", MPG, vol. 31 (Paris, 1857), 168B; Epiphanius Constantiensis, "Panarium, sive Arcula adversus octoginta haereses", MPG, vol. 41 (Paris, 1863), 641B-C, 644D–645A, with a reference to the sect of the so-called *ophites*, who worshipped the snake.

[1138] Joannes Chrysostomus, *Homiliae in Genesim*, in MPG, vol. 53 (Paris, 1862), 127.1-4: τούτῳ ὥσπερ ὀργάνῳ τινὶ χρώμενος, δι'αὐτοῦ τὸ ἄπλαστον καὶ ἀσθενέστερον σκεῦος, τὴν γυναῖκα λέγω, διὰ τῆς ὁμιλίας εἰς τὴν ἑαυτοῦ ἀπάτην ἐκκαλεῖται (John Chrysostom, *Homilies on Genesis 1-17*, trans. Robert Hill [The Fathers of the Church. St. John Chrysostom. A New Translation 74], (Washington: The Catholic University of America Press, 1986), 208ff: *He made use of this creature like some instrument and through it inveigled that naive and weaker vessel, namely, woman, into his deception by means of conversation.*)

[1139] [Pseudo-]Joannes Chrysostomus, "Homiliae in Genesim", in MPG, vol. 56 (Paris, 1862), 531.46: *And the Crafty One does not approach Eve naked... but speaks to the woman wearing the snake as a garment to deceive her* (Καὶ οὐ γυμνὸς προσέρχεται τῇ

uses the same metaphor, insisting that the serpent could not have talked itself, being a speechless animal.[1140] One of the versions of the Physiologus also maintains the idea that the Devil spoke to Eve through the body of the crafty reptile[1141] and draws the etymology of the Greek word ὄφις (snake) from the verb φημί (*to speak*) and its participle ὁ φής (the one who spoke [to Eve]).[1142]

The story of Original Sin is probably the most famous biblical reference to the snake. Yet it is by no means the only one, and Byzantine hagiographers do not mention it very often when they use the serpent, directly or metaphorically, as an incarnation of the Devil, demons, sins, and passions. Holy monks and hermits often use the words of Psalm 90 as a spell during the ritual of exorcism: *You will tread on the lion and the cobra; you will trample the great lion and the serpent.*[1143] The Prophet Isaiah also refers to God's victory over *Leviathan the gliding serpent, Leviathan the coiling serpent.*[1144] The New Testament refers to the snake as the incarnation of the Devil even more clearly. In the Book of Revelation, St. John the Apostle mentions twice *that ancient serpent called the Devil, or Satan.*[1145]

Εὔᾳ ὁ δόλιος, ἀλλ' ἐν ἐνδύματι τοῦ ὄφεως προσομιλεῖ τῇ γυναικὶ πρὸς τὸ δελεάσαι αὐτήν). Ibid, 531.50. Clad in the form of the snake (Ἀλλὰ τὴν τοῦ ὄφεως μορφὴν ἐνδυσάμενος.)

[1140] Greenfield, *Traditions of Belief*, 37ff, with a reference to Gregory Palamas.

[1141] See "Physiologus (diversarum versionum capita disiecta in vulgare lingua)", ed. Francesco Sbordone, *Physiologus*, (Milan: Società Anonima Editrice 'Dante Alighieri', 1936), §5.22–24.

[1142] "Physiologus (redactio prima)", §30.18: ὄφις, ὁ φής, ἤγουν ὁ λαλήσας τῇ Εὔᾳ ποτέ.

[1143] Ps. 90:13 (Septuag.)/91:13 (NIV): ἐπ' ἀσπίδα καὶ βασιλίσκον ἐπιβήσῃ καὶ καταπατήσεις λέοντα καὶ δράκοντα. For the usage of this passage as a spell, see, for example, Paul of Latros I, §25.

[1144] Isa. 27:1: Τῇ ἡμέρᾳ ἐκείνῃ ἐπάξει ὁ θεὸς τὴν μάχαιραν τὴν ἁγίαν καὶ τὴν μεγάλην καὶ τὴν ἰσχυρὰν ἐπὶ τὸν δράκοντα ὄφιν φεύγοντα.

[1145] Rev. 12:9: *The great dragon was hurled down – that ancient serpent called the devil, or Satan, who leads the whole world astray. He was hurled to the earth, and his angels with him* (καὶ ἐβλήθη ὁ δράκων ὁ μέγας, ὁ ὄφις ὁ ἀρχαῖος, ὁ καλούμενος Διάβολος καὶ ὁ Σατανᾶς, ὁ πλανῶν τὴν οἰκουμένην ὅλην – ἐβλήθη εἰς τὴν γῆν καὶ οἱ ἄγγελοι αὐτοῦ μετ'αὐτοῦ ἐβλήθησαν); Rev. 20:2: *He seized the dragon, that ancient serpent, who is the devil, or Satan, and bound him for a thousand years* (καὶ ἐκράτησεν τὸν δράκοντα, ὁ ὄφις ὁ ἀρχαῖος, ὅς ἐστιν Διάβολος καὶ ὁ Σατανᾶς, καὶ ἔδησεν αὐτὸν χίλια ἔτη).

Theological interpretations and elaborations of biblical references to snakes and scorpions as personifications of the Devil and his servants are numerous, and we cannot exhaustively survey them here. A typical example of this rich tradition is a passage from St. Theophylact of Ohrid's commentary of the Gospel of Luke:

> The snakes and the scorpions are the phalanxes of demons dragged down [to Earth]; snakes are those who attack openly. By contrast, the ones who appear in the shape of scorpions strike in secret. For example, the demons of adultery and murder are snakes — for they cause apparent harm. Scorpion, on the other hand, could be the demon who persuades a man to use baths, aromas, and other such stupidities, supposedly to heal illnesses. Because his sting does not strike openly but in secret urges people to take great care of their bodies does he throw the ones who obey him into severe sin.[1146]

The biblical tradition was by no means the only reason for the snake-like demon's great popularity. The vitality of this image in the Orthodox world would not have been possible without an exceptionally complex folklore and mythological substrate underlying the stories of demonic possessions and attacks in Byzantine hagiography. These relics of the past needed to be homogenized, elaborated, and included in the theological system of the Christian religion. The *Lives* of the saints, however, fall into different categories. Some of the texts are written by learned theologians, like Leontios of Neapolis and Michael Psellus — in these, the snake is just a dangerous reptile easily used by the Devil as a *garment*. Holy men and women, monks and nuns, dodge its attacks, repel them and ... that's the end of the story. We will find many such not-very-exciting descriptions inspired directly by St. Athanasios the Great and his

---

[1146] Theophylactus, "Enarratio in evangelium Lucae", in MPG, vol. 123 (Paris, 1864), 840C–D: Ὄφεις γὰρ καὶ σκορπίοι αἱ τῶν δαιμόνων φάλαγγες κάτω συρόμεναι· καὶ ὅσοι μὲν ἐμφανέστερον πλήττουσι, οὗτοι ὄφεις. Ὅσοι δὲ ἀφανέστερον, οὗτοι σκορπίοι, οἷον ὁ μὲν τῆς πορνείας καὶ τοῦ φόνου δαίμων, ὄφις. Εἰς προφανῆ γὰρ κακὰ συνωθεῖ. Ὁ δὲ διὰ νόσον δῆθεν πείθων τὸν ἄνθρωπον λουτροῖς χρᾶσθαι καὶ μυρίσμασι καὶ ταῖς ἄλλαις βλακείαις, ὁ τοιοῦτος δαίμων σκορπιὸς ἂν κληθείη. Μὴ γὰρ ἐμφανὲς ἔχων τὸ κέντρον, ἀλλὰ λεληθότως τὴν σάρκα περιποιεῖσθαι σπεύδων, ἵνα ῥίψῃ τὸν πειθόμενον εἰς πτῶμα μέγα.

Life of St. Antony[1147] in the hagiographical texts, especially from the Iconoclast period (726–843). The young god or hero who struggles fiercely with a snake or other giant reptile, real or fantastic, is very common in Greco-Roman mythological traditions — suffice it to recall the triumph of the celestial god Apollo over the chthonic monster Python or the exploits of Heracles. There is, however, hardly a hint of such literary narratives or folklore substrates among the Byzantine hagiographers in the period under study. Only the story of the three-year-old Gregory of Amastris, who defeats the Devil in the shape of a snake,[1148] vaguely resembles the ancient myth of the infant Heracles, who, in his cradle, killed the snakes sent by Hera.

Yet some hagiographers allow a certain number of folklore motifs inherited from the ancient world to pass through the sieve of theological doctrines. Biblical texts can only explain some of the serpent-like demon's influences and functions. Wrapping itself around its victim or entering its mouth, this evil spirit causes insanity and disease, especially paralysis, and arouses uncontrollable sexual desire. Very rarely, it appears as a symbol of false predictions and divination, like the ancient Python, and is also said to haunt houses and towers. These facets of its image undoubtedly reflect myths and beliefs that Christianity only partially succeeded in erasing.

As a venomous creature (ἰοβόλον θηρίον) par excellence, the snake is closely associated both with healing and inflicting diseases and with the eternal cycle of life, with the continuous renewal and resurrection achieved by shedding the old skin. This idea is attested in many sources, including the *Physiologus*. According to this text, the snake retires for forty days, during which it fasts and, after this period, sloughs off its old skin.[1149] As a symbol of renewal and resurrection, the serpent is associated with healing and its patron god Asclepius. The myth that formally

---

[1147] Antony, §9.20–26.
[1148] George of Amastris, §7.
[1149] "Physiologus (redactio prima)", §11.12. Cf. Eusebius Caesariensis, *Die Praeparatio Evangelica*, ed. Karl Mras, *Eusebius Werke*, vol. 8.1: *Einleitung. Die Bücher I bis X* (Berlin: De Guyter, 1982), I.10.47ff.

justifies this connection is told in the Latin work *Astronomica*, attributed to the Roman fabulist Gaius Julius Hyginus (first century AD). According to this text, the celebrated healer lost his dear friend Glaucus, son of King Minos. He retired to an isolated cell to mourn and to try to find a way to restore his friend's life. One day, he saw a serpent coiled around his staff and killed it. Not long after, another snake came holding a herb in its mouth. As soon as it deposited it by the slain snake, it immediately came back to life, and Apollo's son used the same plant to resurrect Glaucus.[1150]

As early as the first centuries A.D., Christianity had to grapple with this ambivalence in the image of the serpent as a symbol of both death and immortality, of poison and medicine — an ambivalence reflected in the very meanings of the Greek word φάρμακον. In its view, the serpent was to remain exclusively the absolute incarnation of Evil that led to Original Sin and the banishment of Adam and Eve from Eden. In Byzantine hagiography of the period under study, no venom is ever mentioned. Demons who take the form of snakes usually bring madness and disease to their victims, entering their bodies through the mouth or wrapping themselves around them.

Another essential feature of the snake-like demon is its relation to madness. The so-called Agathodemon, or the "Good Demon", was venerated as a serpent during the Classical period.[1151] He was honored with libations of unmixed wine in the temple of Dionysus.[1152] According to Diodorus of Sicily, he was made the same offering at the beginning of private feasts when the participants summoned him to bring them pleasant inebriation. At the end of the symposium, when the drunkenness was over, a libation was made again, with mixed wine now dedicated to an

---

[1150] Hyginus, *De Astronomica*, ed. Ghislaine Viré, (Stuttgart and Leipzig: Teubner, 1992), II.14.588–98.

[1151] On Agathodemon, see *Dictionnaire des antiquités Grecques et Romaines*, vol. 1 (Paris: Librairie de L. Hachette, 1873), s.v. "Agathodaemon"; Burkert, *Greek Religion*, 180 n. 9.

[1152] "Aristophanis Equites", ed. Nigel Wilson, *Aristophanis Fabulae* (Oxford: Oxford University Press, 2007), l. 85.

Olympian deity, Zeus Soter.[1153] The orgiastic, raging Bacchic frenzy[1154] and the incessant thirst for wine[1155] is a literary, mythological, and folkloric topos that we will encounter as part of the palette of harmful influences exerted by the snake-like demon on its victims, according to Byzantine hagiography as well.

Ancient mythological tradition associates the chthonic serpent with death. Various demonic deities, predominantly female, appear under this zoomorphic form — like Medusa, whose locks were writhing serpents, or the Erinyes, the sinister goddesses of vengeance, who sometimes take the form of poisonous reptiles.[1156] According to Plutarch, snakes were also associated with violent and heroic death. In his biography of Cleomenes, he says that a snake was wrapped around the dead King's head, completely covering his face and preventing birds from pecking at him.[1157] Origen is even more explicit. According to him, the bone marrow of the dead was transformed (μεταπλάσσεται) into a serpent after death.[1158]

In the Byzantine literature of the period under study, we will often encounter the serpent as a demon inhabiting homes from which it must be exorcised through prayers and rituals. This motif undoubtedly reflects the ancient notion of the serpent as a *genius loci*, or guardian of the home, the domestic hearth, and the domestic storehouse of provisions.[1159]

[1153] *Diodori bibliotheca historica*, ed. Immanuel Bekker, Ludwig Dindorf, and Friedrich Vogel, vol. 1 (Stuttgart, 1985), IV.3.4.8–14.

[1154] See, e.g., Auxentios, §16, where a woman is possessed by a snake-like demon who strikes her with *bacchic madness* (ἀνεβακχεύετο).

[1155] See, e.g., Elias Speleotes, §91, where a peasant is tormented by a terrible thirst for wine under the influence of a snake-like demon.

[1156] For more detail on the relationship between the Gorgons and especially the Erinyes with the serpents, see Jane Harrison, *Prolegomena to the Study of Greek Religion* (Cambridge: Cambridge University Press, 1922), 232–36.

[1157] Plutarchus, "Agis et Cleomenes", ed. Konrad Ziegler, *Plutarchi vitae parallelae*, vol. 3.1 (Leipzig: Teubner, 1971), §60.

[1158] Origène, *Contre Celse*, ed. Marcel Borret, vol. 2: *Livres III et IV* [Sources chrétiennes, 136, 2] (Paris: Éditions du Cerf, 1968), IV.57.23–26. In the same text, Origen claims that the marrows of various mammals are also transformed after death (IV.57.26ff).

[1159] On the snake as a *genius loci*, see Harrison, *Prolegomena to the Study*, 306ff; Burkert, *Greek Religion*, 29ff and 130; Thalia Howe, "Zeus Herkeios: Thematic Unity in the He-

As Francis Lazenby's research shows, it was a common pet in the ancient world.[1160]

1.2. Appearance and influence

Above, we drew attention to the power *to tread on serpents and scorpions*, which Christ ceded to the apostles and holy people according to the New Testament. Based on these passages, the Byzantine hagiographers often characterized the demonic power attacking saints during their hermitage as having the image of a serpent or scorpion. In these cases, the demon is usually not trying to thwart the monk's spiritual power by suggesting sinful thoughts or temptations. It is merely an external threat, arising not so much from certain mythological, folkloric, or theological notions as from the purely real danger posed by a poisonous reptile. The motif of the hermit's struggle against such assaults is not limited either temporally or geographically: it is characteristic of the whole hagiography of the period under study. The saints never fight a single, mighty scorpion — the mythological motif of the battle of the giant Orion with such a monster, born of the goddess Gaia, is completely forgotten[1161] — and the venomous arthropods always appear in large swarms. They are mentioned only in the *Lives* of Gregory of Dekapolis and Euthymios the Younger, where, in the company of other zoomorphic evil spirits, they attacked the caves in which the saints dwelled.[1162] Serpent-like demons occur in similar con-

---

katompedon Sculptures", *American Journal of Archaeology* 59, no. 4 (October 1955): 295.

[1160] On the snake as a common household pet in antiquity, which rid the house of mice and other unclean animals, see Francis Lazenby, "Greek and Roman Household Pets", I, *The Classical Journal* 4 (January 1945): 248ff.

[1161] According to the myth, the giant Orion had become such a good hunter that he began to boast to the goddesses Diana and Leto that he could kill any creature born on earth. Angered by his arrogance, they sent a fearsome chthonic monster against him, the giant Scorpion, who killed him. The two adversaries were subsequently transformed by Zeus into the constellations Scorpio and Orion. See, e.g., Hyginus, *De Astronomica*, II.26.1037-50.

[1162] Gregory of Dekapolis, §6ff; Euthymios the Younger, §21.

texts. They were usually described as being larger than ordinary reptiles[1163] or as attacking in great numbers.[1164]

Hagiographical texts often speak of snake-like demons that enter a person's body and are removed through the mouth by exorcism rituals.[1165] An evil spirit tormented the female slave of a Constantinopolitan noble for twenty-eight years. Her master finally asked St. Theodore Sykeotes for help. The demon, however, was aggressive and difficult to overcome; through the girl's mouth, he spewed a barrage of profanities at the Saint and made ominous and false predictions about her death, but finally failed to resist the sign of the cross, with which Theodore exorcized him. The material form of the evil spirit, in this case, is visible only to the victim — only when she comes to herself does she tell those present of the foul (μυσαρόν) serpent that came out of her mouth.[1166]

A demon coming out of the victim's mouth in the form of a serpent is absent from the hagiography of the seventh until the ninth century, but is relatively widespread in the saints' *Lives* of southern Italy and the Peloponnese. The author of the biography of St. Elias Speleotes mentions two such exorcisms, both performed in a dream. The first case involved a fascinating account of the gender roles and the gender-based social restrictions among the Greek-speaking population in the region. According to the text, a monk named Jacob had a niece who was mentally injured (τὸν νοῦν καὶ τὰς φρένας βεβλαμμένην) by a demon. Because she was a woman, she did not have free access to the Saint's tomb in the male mon-

---

[1163] See Symeon Stylites the Younger, §39.13ff, where the Saint is attacked by demonic serpents; Ioannikios (*Peter*), §37, where the Saint casts out hordes of demonic snakes from the island of Thasios (in Lake Apollonias, Central Bithynia); Gregory of Dekapolis, §40.1ff, where the Saint finds a demonic snake in his bed; Phantinos the Younger, §10, where the Saint was attacked during his hermitage by giant snake-like demons.

[1164] See Paul of Latros, I, §25. In this text, a vast swarm of demonic serpents slithers up the stairs to the Saint's cave on Samos Island, preventing the residents from listening to his sermons and asking him for deliverance from sickness and evil influence.

[1165] On this concept in medieval Western Europe, see Ginzburg, *Ecstasies*, 138ff. Ginzburg refers to the legend of the Burgundian King Guntram. In this case, however, the small serpent that comes out of the King's mouth and shows him a hidden treasure is not a demon.

[1166] Theodore Sykeotes, §84.32–36.

astery near the village Seminara in western Calabria. For this reason, her uncle dressed her in men's clothes and covered her head modestly. She kissed the grave with awe and stayed up all night praying. When she dozed for a while, St. Elias appeared to her in a dream. He smiled good-humoredly and told her she had stolen her salvation through her illicit intrusion into the temple. Then he commanded her to open her mouth from which he pulled out a wriggling snake. The Saint trampled it, pronounced her healed, and sent her home. In the morning, she felt that *the demonic scourge* was really gone. She sang psalms with the monks, unrecognized, and happily departed.[1167] In the second story, the serpent struck his victim with an unslakable thirst, which reminds us of the influence of the ancient Agathodemon. According to the text, an evil spirit seemed to burn the peasant Glaucaeus from within and he could not quench his thirst, no matter how much water and wine he drank. After medical science proved powerless to help, he resorted to a *spiritual physician*. He stayed up for two nights without sleep by the Saint's tomb, and St. Elias finally appeared to him in a dream. The Saint made him open his mouth, fumbled inside, and drew from his stomach a coiled serpent, which he killed before his very eyes.[1168] At the beginning of the eleventh century, an inhabitant of the Peloponnesian village of Elos (near Sparta) was struck by a similar misfortune. Provoked by the envy of the *spiritual serpent* (i.e., the Devil), a real snake came to eat his entrails. The man immediately went to the tomb of St. Nikon Metanoeite, where he begged the Saint for salvation. It came in an unexpected way. One of the side effects of the evil reptile was a burning, insatiable thirst. The suffering man could not control himself and, by mistake, instead of water, drank the holy ointment from a vessel that hung over the sarcophagus. Quite logically, this caused him to vomit, and the snake was successfully cast out of his body.[1169]

[1167] Elias Speleotes, §82.
[1168] Elias Speleotes, §91.
[1169] Nikon Metanoeite, §55.

A familiar iconographical[1170] and literary image in Byzantium is the demon serpent that wraps itself around the body of its victim and causes **insanity or paralysis**, usually as a punishment for sin. In his *Life* of St. Auxentios the Great, Michael Psellus tells the story of a *body-loving demon* (φιλοσώματος δαίμων) who possessed a coquette and *wrapped himself around her body in the form of a serpent* (ὄφεως ὑπεδύετο θέαν καὶ τῷ σώματι τῆς παραφόρου περιεπλέκετο). He caused her *bacchic madness* and forced her to utter inarticulate cries like a dog barking.[1171] Another story told in the *Life* of St. Peter of Atroa refers to such a spirit as a punishment for sin. The relatives of a long-paralyzed iconoclast delivered him to the Lydian monastery where St. Peter of Atroa was a monk around 817–819.[1172] Peter convinced the sick man to confess all his sins, but he remained silent about his heretical convictions, and consequently, the Saint's prayers failed to help him. God, however, was merciful. Peter saw the cause of the illness in a vision where a terrible serpent had wrapped itself around the heretic's body, squeezing his joints and preventing his limbs from freeing themselves from the paralysis. On hearing of the vision, the heretic immediately confessed, worshipped the icon of Christ, accepted Orthodox dogma, and walked home on his own two feet.[1173]

[1170] Snake-like demons entwined around the bodies of sinners and tormenting them are common in depictions of the Last Judgment. See Provatakis, *The Devil*, 80–84, 154–63, and 182–89; Greenfield, *Traditions of Belief*, 75 and n. 250.

[1171] Auxentios, §16.

[1172] The monastery was located near the fortress Plataia Petra in Lydia. This place is mentioned on three occasions in Byzantine sources. According to Theophanes Continuatus (*Theophanis Continuati liber V. Vita Basilii imperatiris*, ed. Ihor Ševčenko [*Corpus fontium historiae Byzantinae* 42] [Berlin: De Gruyter, 2011], §19.17ff), and John Scylitzes (*Ioannis Scylitzae Synopsis Historiarum*, §13.76–78), in 867, the usurper Symbatios fled there from the forces of the triumphant Emperor Basil I. In 933 another claimant to the throne, Constantine Doukas, confiscated supplies for his army from the region (*Ioannis Scylitzae Synopsis Historiarum*, §27.70–73). And finally, the stronghold was captured by the supporters of Bardas Skleros after his unsuccessful attempt to seize the throne (*Ioannis Scylitzae Synopsis Historiarum*, §10.54). See also Peter of Atroa, 121, note 1.

[1173] Peter of Atroa, §24.

The serpent is associated with **licentiousness and bodily adornment** relatively often. Theophylact of Ohrid discusses this concept from a theological point of view in the passage of his commentary on the Gospel of Luke that we quoted above.[1174] According to Michael Psellus, these evil spirits often attacked women who liked to wear rich clothes and fashionable hairstyles; the demons entangled themselves in their elaborate curls and the folds of their garments, constantly twining around their bodies and "suffocating" their good reason. No sexual desire enticed them to possess their beautiful victims, however. They were drawn only by the female penchant for fine clothes and accessories.[1175] Demons entangling themselves in the hair or wrapped around the bodies of naked female sinners are also quite common in Byzantine iconography, one of the oldest examples of this persistent motif being the images in the narthex of the church of Yilanli Kilisé in Cappadocia (ninth century).[1176]

Probably influenced by the Old Testament story of the temptation to which the Devil, in the guise of a serpent, subjected Eve, the demon serpent very often attacks and possesses women. Michael Psellus's theoretical postulate makes it clear that women's usual penchant for expensive clothing, elaborate hairstyles, and bodily care attracts the so-called *body-loving demons*. In most of the cases analyzed above, the evil spirits inflict mental illness precisely on women.

Snake-like demons frequently haunt **houses and dwellings**, the appearance of a reptile in the home being a clear sign of an evil presence. Such a story is vividly described in the mid-seventh century in the *Life* of St. Theodore Sykeotes. An officer named Theodore, recently cured of a mental illness inflicted by an evil spirit, asked the Saint to come to his home in the marketplace of Pylai (Πύλαι). His family and cattle were exposed to the harmful influence of the unclean spirits (ἐνεργούμενα ἐκ τῶν ἀκαθάρτων πνευμάτων) that haunted the house in various forms. The

---

[1174] Theophylactus, "Enarratio in evangelium Lucae", 810D: ὁ μὲν τῆς πορνείας... δαίμων ὄφις. See Joannou, *Démonologie*, 12.
[1175] Auxentios, §16.
[1176] Provatakis, *The Devil*, 155ff and fig. 123. For other examples, see Provatakis, *The Devil*, 155ff.

malicious demons pelted the family with stones during lunch and supper, smashed the crockery, and broke the women's looms. In addition, they made access to the house almost impossible, as it was filled with mice and snakes. Theodore easily cleansed the house with prayers and holy water.[1177] A snake-like demon also tried to block the path to salvation of a young monk in the monastery of Medikion. Even as a novice, the young man had an unclean spirit, but he tried with all his might to hide this from Niketas, the monastery's austere abbot. His condition, however, was exposed the night after his ordination as a monk when *the Deceiver* began to torment and frighten him with all sorts of visions. Realizing that the situation was getting serious, the young man immediately went to Niketas's cell to seek salvation. To his astonishment, he found the entrance blocked by a giant snake writhing and hissing menacingly. The monk overcame his fear, leaped over the creature, and entered the cell. Niketas calmed him down and, not long afterward, delivered him entirely from the plague with prayers and the sign of the cross.[1178]

Python, the ancient snake-like chthonic deity of divination, and the general association of the serpent with divination and magical rituals, are almost completely absent from the hagiography of the period under study. One of the rare mentions of this ancient concept comes from the *Life* of St. Basil the Younger, where the demons of Magic and Divination appear as *snakes, serpents, vipers, similar to horned asps and myriad other loathsome and wicked reptiles*.[1179]

The serpent in the hagiographic literature of the period under study is a symbol of Evil and the Devil. What has entirely disappeared is the ancient philosophical symbolism associated with the eternal cycle of life and this animal's wisdom. The authors also avoid mentioning the serpent's venom (φάρμακον) because of its ambivalence as a symbol of both death and healing. However, analysis of the image reveals the relatively strong

---

[1177] Theodore Sykeotes, §131.
[1178] Niketas of Medikion, §19.
[1179] Basil the Younger, Part II, §26.4–6: πνεύματα ἀκάθαρτα πλεῖστα ὀφεόσχημα, δρακοντόσχημα, ἐχιδνόσχημα, κεράσταις καὶ ἄλλοις βδελυροῖς μυρίοις ἑρπετοῖς πονηροῖς.

influence of other aspects of Greco-Roman mythology that were well-known to audiences in the sixth to the tenth centuries and were probably part of folklore. The texts contain references to the traditional functions of the ancient Agathodemon, which caused insatiable thirst and Bacchic madness. The serpent-protector of the home became an evil spirit that possessed houses and living spaces, or else blocked access to them.

2. Dragons

In Greek, the word "dragon" (δράκων) is etymologically derived from the verb δέρκομαι (*to have a particular look in one's eyes*). According to Bruno Snell, the snake owes this designation to the uncanny glint in its eye and because its stare commands attention.[1180] In the Old Testament, it sometimes occurs as a synonym of "serpent" (ὄφις).[1181] Especially in the Psalms,[1182] a standard source of incantations against demons, the dragon is usually a monster associated with the abyss of the sea, lakes, and rivers. No direct connection is made with the demons or Satan in these cases. In the New Testament, however, the dragon appears as a natural incarnation of evil spirits and the Devil. The Apostle John describes the Fallen Angel as a *great red dragon with seven heads and ten horns, and on his*

[1180] Bruno Snell, *The Discovery of the Mind in Greek Philosophy and Thought* (New York: Dover Publications, 2011), 17ff.

[1181] Ex., 7:9–10, 7:12 (δράκων) and 7:15 (ὄφις), where the two words are synonymous; Deut. 32:33.

[1182] Ps. 73:13: τῶν δρακόντων ἐπὶ τοῦ ὕδατος; 103:26: δράκων οὗτος, ὃν ἔπλασας ἐμπαίζειν αὐτῷ; 148:7: δράκοντες καὶ πᾶσαι ἄβυσσοι. See also Job 7:12: πότερον θάλασσά εἰμι ἢ δράκων; Amos, 9:3: ἐὰν καταδύσωσιν ἐξ ὀφθαλμῶν μου εἰς τὰ βάθη τῆς θαλάσσης, ἐκεῖ ἐντελοῦμαι τῷ δράκοντι; Ezek., 29:3: Φαραω τὸν δράκοντα τὸν μέγαν τὸν ἐγκαθήμενον ἐν μέσῳ ποταμῶν; Ezek., 32:2: ὡς δράκων ὁ ἐν τῇ θαλάσσῃ (where the Pharaoh is compared to a river and sea dragon). On the relationship between dragons and water, see Laskarina Bouras, "Dragon Representations on Byzantine Phialae and their Conduits", *Gesta* 16, no. 2 (1977): 65ff. On the Hebrew word for *water dragon* and its meanings, see Kiessling, "Antecendents of the Medieval Dragon", 167.

heads seven crowns,[1183] and then explains that he is speaking of the *great dragon, that old serpent which is called the Devil and Satan*.[1184]

In Byzantine iconography, the dragon was typically associated with rivers, lakes, and springs.[1185] On the more than five-foot-high late antique phiale,[1186] in the outer narthex of the church of St. Sophia in Constantinople, the intertwined bodies of two giant reptiles resembling dragons or snakes are still visible today.[1187] This architectural element did not disappear later and can be seen in a bronze figural composition in the Great Laura of Mount Athos, probably dating from 1060, part of which represents a dragon.[1188]

In Byzantine literature, the dragon retains its symbolic significance as a fantastic monster directly related to the Devil. However, his image seems to have caused much controversy between the theologians, on the one hand, and popular literature reflecting various folk beliefs, on the other. Probably in the second quarter of the seventh century, St. John of Damascus dedicated a small work to dragons called Περὶ δρακόντων. This mini-treatise focuses on their two main characteristics, their large dimensions and peculiar eyes. The great theologian's contemporaries imagined the dragon as a fantastic beast that could assume human form, abduct women, and have sexual intercourse with them.[1189] One of his sources was Cassius Dio. According to Dio, a popular urban legend in Rome said that Octavian's mother Attia conceived the future Emperor in the temple of Apollo, where the god appeared before her as a great

---

[1183] Rev. 12:3: δράκων πυρρὸς μέγας, ἔχων κεφαλὰς ἑπτὰ καὶ κέρατα δέκα καὶ ἐπὶ τὰς κεφαλὰς αὐτοῦ ἑπτὰ διαδήματα.

[1184] Rev. 12:9: ὁ δράκων ὁ μέγας, ὁ ὄφις ὁ ἀρχαῖος, ὁ καλούμενος Διάβολος καὶ ὁ Σατανᾶς; 20:2: ἐκράτησεν τὸν δράκοντα, ὁ ὄφις ὁ ἀρχαῖος, ὅς ἐστιν Διάβολος καὶ ὁ Σατανᾶς, καὶ ἔδησεν αὐτὸν χίλια ἔτη. See also 12:7: καὶ ὁ δράκων ἐπολέμησεν καὶ οἱ ἄγγελοι αὐτοῦ.

[1185] See Bouras, "Dragon Representations", passim.

[1186] The phiale was a large stone vessel or fountain, usually enclosed in a special building. It was placed at the entrance to the church and used for washing hands before entering the temple.

[1187] Bouras, "Dragon Representations", 65 and fig. 1.

[1188] See Bouras, "Dragon Representations", 65 and n. 10, with bibliography.

[1189] Joannes Damascenus, "De draconibus", 1600A.

dragon.[1190] St. John quotes the same author's accounts of a giant reptile, 120 feet long, killed by the soldiers of the Roman consul Marcus Atilius Regulus shortly after their arrival on the shores of Africa in 256 B.C.,[1191] and of the two-headed monster that appeared in Etruria, causing a lot of damage before it was finally burned to death by lightning.[1192] In these cases, the great theologian's attitude is similar to his opinion of the female demon Gello. He ridicules popular superstitions related to these monsters, considering them common serpents.[1193] Some had unusually large heads, glittering golden eyes, and a beard. In addition, according to St. John, *dragons* were the only non-poisonous snakes.[1194]

In light of the vehemence with which John of Damascus tried to convince his readers that the dragon was neither a demon nor something supernatural, we can judge that such beliefs were common among his contemporaries. The hagiographic corpus shows clearly that this fantastic beast was not perceived as a mere serpent, as the theologian claims.[1195] The descriptions provided in the saints' *Lives* emphasize the same two main external characteristics as the short treatise *On Dragons*, namely their large size and their eyes. The monsters, however, do not abduct women or take human form. They are either evil creatures that torment the population of a particular region or (much more commonly) the personifications of sins in visions and dreams.

Only rarely does the dragon appear as an evil creature made of blood and bones in the Byzantine hagiography of the period under study. It is relatively common only in the hagiographical literature produced in

---

[1190] *Cassii Dionis Cocceiani historiarum Romanarum quae supersunt*, ed. Ursul Boissevain, vol. 2 (Berlin: Weidmann, 1898), XLV.1.2.

[1191] Cf. *Cassii Dionis Cocceiani historiarum Romanarum quae supersunt*, ed. Ursul Boissevain, vol. 1 (Berlin: Weidmann, 1895), 160. On this legend, see Edward Bassett, "Regulus and the Serpent in the *Punica*", *Classical Philology* 50, no. 1 (January 1955): 1–20.

[1192] *Cassii Dionis Cocceiani historiarum Romanarum quae supersunt*, 2: L.8.5.

[1193] Joannes Damascenus, "De draconibus", 1600B.

[1194] Joannes Damascenus, "De draconibus", 1600B.

[1195] See Joannou, *Démonologie*, 12. Joannou claims that *the dragon is nothing but a kind of snake* ("*le dragon n'est qu'un variant du serpent*"). The French researcher does not support this highly controversial thesis with any evidence nor does she even refer to St. John of Damascus.

the monasteries in western Asia Minor, especially Bithynia and Lydia. The information provided by these vernacular texts is highly interesting and sheds light not only on the remnants of ancient myths and legends in ancient Troas, but also gives precious information about the folklore traditions of the Slavic populations that settled in this region in the eighth century.

There are numerous examples in Greco-Roman mythology of dragon-slayers who save a community from a giant monster, such as the tales of King Cychreus, who liberated the island of Salamis;[1196] the second labor of Heracles, who liberated the vicinity of Lerna from the fearsome many-headed hydra;[1197] the hero Phorbas, who slew the giant serpents tormenting the inhabitants of the island of Rhodes;[1198] and the hero Menestratus, who saved the city of Thespia in Boeotia from a dragon.[1199] Many such legends have been associated since prehistoric times with the northwestern parts of Asia Minor (Lydia, Phrygia, and Bithynia). In Lydia there lived the terrible Meonian dragon, which tortured the subjects of Queen Omphala and was slain by the hero Heracles by the river Sangarius.[1200] This myth is preserved in another version, where a local hero, the dragon slayer Damascene destroyed the monster.[1201] According to Claudius Aelianus, giant dragons as long as ten *orgyai* (more than fifty feet)[1202] lived near the river Rhyndacus (Ρύνδακος), which flowed through the western parts of Phrygia and passed by the northern border

---

[1196] "Apollodori bibliotheca", ed. Richard Wagner, *Pediasimi libellus de duodecim Herculis laboribus* [*Mythographi Graeci* 1] (Leipzig: Teubner, 1996), III.161; *Diodori bibliotheca historica*, ed. Immanuel Bekker, Ludwig Dindorf, and Friedrich Vogel, vol. 1 (Stuttgart, 1985), IV.72.4–5.

[1197] "Apollodori bibliotheca", II.77–80 (see esp. II.77.3ff: ἐξέβαινεν εἰς τὸ πεδίον καὶ τά τε βοσκήματα καὶ τὴν χώραν διέφθειρεν); *Diodori bibliotheca historica*, 1: IV.11.5ff.

[1198] *Diodori bibliotheca historica*, 2: V.58.4-5; Hyginus, *De Astronomica*, II.14.563–76.

[1199] *Pausaniae Graeciae descriptio*, ed. Maria Helena Rocha-Pereira, vol. 3: *Libri VIII-XI* (Leipzig: Teubner, 1989), IX.26.7ff.

[1200] Hyginus, *De Astronomica*, II.14 548–53.

[1201] See *Nonni Panopolitani Dionysiaca*, ed. Rudolph Keydell, vol. 2 (Berlin: Weidmann, 1959), XXV.452ff.

[1202] Ὀργυά or ἁπλὴ ὀργυά was a measure of length amounting to 6 πόδες or 73.8 in (Erich Schilbach, *Byzanntinische Metrologie* [München, 1970], 22ff).

of Mysia. They stood on their tails, and attracted birds with their song, which flew into their open mouths. The same dragons threatened flocks and often tore even the shepherds apart.[1203] According to Homer, Trojan dragons emerged from the sea near Ilion and killed the seer Laocoön, who was trying to warn his fellow citizens of the danger of bringing the wooden horse inside the city.[1204]

Most hagiographical accounts of battles with demonic dragons originate from the same region. According to the *Life* of St. Ioannikios the Great, shortly before the death of Emperor Leo V (December 24, 820),[1205] God allowed a demonic dragon to settle in a cave near Prusa in southern Bithynia and torment the villagers for their sins. The beast devoured their cattle, and none could defeat it. During one of his journeys in the region, St. Ioannikios saw the plight of the people and slayed the dragon with the words of Psalm 90 and the sign of the cross.[1206] God sent another *fearsome dragon* (δράκων φοβερώτατος) to punish the inhabitants of the islet of Thassios in Lake Apollonias (western Bithynia).[1207] The dragon took up residence in a cave and harassed the whole surrounding area horribly. Between 825 and 829,[1208] Daniel, the abbot of a local monastery, persuaded Ioannikios to rid the island of the plague. The Saint imposed a vigil on the monks and went out against the beast. Sensing the presence of a man of God, the dragon writhed even more vio-

---

[1203] *Claudii Aeliani de natura animalium libri xvii, varia historia, epistolae, fragmenta*, ed. Rudolph Hercher, vol. 1 (Leipzig: Teubner, 1971), II.21.9–24.

[1204] On the widespread legend of Laocoön, see, e.g., "Apollodori epitoma", ed. Richard Wagner, *Pediasimi libellus de duodecim Herculis laboribus* [*Mythographi Graeci* 1] (Leipzig: Teubner, 1996), V.17a–18a; and Hyginus, *Fabulae*, ed. Peter Marshall (Munich and Leipzig: Saur [Bibliotheca Teubneriana], 2002), CXXXV. The two authors call the monsters *dragons* (δράκοντες, dracones).

[1205] For the main events of St. Ioannikios's life, see Part One, Chapter 2, §4.

[1206] Ioannikios (*Peter*), §29; Ioannikios (*Sabbas*), §24. After the battle with the dragon, a maiden with pure faith in her heart washed the Saint's feet. As Sullivan notes ("Life of St. Ioannikios", 285 and n. 237), Homer uses the verb ἐξαπονίζω (*to wash thoroughly*) in *Odyssey*, XIX.387, where Eurycleia washes the feet of Odysseus.

[1207] For the island of Thassios, located in the northern part of Lake Apollonias in Western Bithynia, see Janin, *Les églises et les monastères*, 153ff.

[1208] That is, between the fifth year of the rule of Emperor Michael II (820–829) and his death. Cf. Ioannikios (*Sabbas*), §29.

lently, hissing and shaking everything around. At sunrise, it finally fled as if chased by fire and disappeared into the sea.[1209] A third dragon settled in the middle of a local river, stopping it from flowing normally and severely hampering the locals. The Saint decided again to help. He returned to his cell and immersed himself in fasting, vigils, and prayers to God, then went to battle. He found the dragon leisurely basking in the sun. When the wretched beast spotted the man of God, it opened its mouth to devour him, but St. Ioannikios turned his eyes heavenward, drew strength from thence, and pierced the head of the monster with his iron cross.[1210] In other examples, the demonic beast inhabited a desolate area and did not directly harm the population. One such creature, sixty cubits long, was slain by St. Ioannikios with a prayer between 815 and 820 in Lydia.[1211] In the deserted rocky area of Potamia in the vicinity of the town Prusias (in northeastern Bithynia),[1212] another *fearsome dragon* appeared to frighten and punish Antony the Younger for his disobedience. The humble monk had declined the bishop's invitation for lunch, fearing that he would overeat.[1213]

In their two versions of St. Ioannikios's *Life*, Peter and Sabbas pay special attention to the evil dragon's peculiar eyes. During one of his journeys in the Kundurian mountains in southern Lycia,[1214] the Saint took shelter from a storm in a cave. From the entrance, he saw something like burning coals deep inside. Not knowing that these were the eyes of a dragon, Ioannikios gathered damp leaves to cover the fire. When he tried to do so, the beast was not very happy. It immediately jumped up, ready to attack the Saint, but God's grace saved him, and he managed to with-

---

[1209] Ioannikios (*Peter*), §37; Ioannikios (*Sabbas*), §31.
[1210] Ioannikios (*Peter*), §40, where the event is dated between 820 and 838; Ioannikios (*Sabbas*), §14, where it is dated c. 810; in this case, the author does not give any details. On this chronological inconsistency, see Part One, Chapter 2, §4.
[1211] Ioannikios (*Peter*), §46; Ioannikios (*Sabbas*), §20.
[1212] The town of Prusias/Plusias has been identified with the ancient Prusias ad Hypium in the Boukellarion district (Janin, *Les églises et les monastères*, 176ff).
[1213] Antony the Younger, §42.
[1214] *TIB*, vol. 8: *Lykien und Pamphylien*, ed. Friedrich Hild and Hansgerd Hellenkemper (Vienna: Austrian Academy of Sciences Press, 2004), 669ff; Sullivan, "Life of St. Ioannikios", 304 and n. 334.

draw into the opposite corner of the cave. The Saint cohabited with the monster until the storm passed, and afterward, headed intact to his cell.[1215]

The information provided by the *Lives* of St. Ioannikios the Great and St. Antony the Younger can hardly be explained in terms of the Dragon-Slayer Horseman St. George, as Denis Sullivan proposes.[1216] In both texts, the holy men fight their heroic battles on foot. Much more convincing is the hypothesis that behind the numerous stories told by their authors lay various legends of the local communities of Bithynia, Phrygia, and Lydia.

In the *Life* of the Isaurian Saint Gregory of Dekapolis, we meet the dragon as a creature that inhabits not dark caves and watery depths but a tower in the Sicilian city of Syracuse. According to the text, while living as a hermit in this abandoned building, the Saint provoked the envy of a demon. The evil spirit incited the fearsome dragon that inhabited the tower to frighten Gregory. However, Gregory did not flinch before the gaping maw of the beast and invited the dragon to attack him if it had the strength — if not, it should go away. Gregory's words struck the monster like a whip, and the dragon hurried back to its lair.[1217] In this story, we can probably discern a distant echo of the concept of the ancient domestic serpent, the protector of the house. In a Christian setting, it has become its supernatural counterpart, a great and dangerous dragon, and no longer a part of a human-occupied space — like a ghost in modern horror movies, it haunts an abandoned building.

* * *

As we already pointed out, heroic battles with "real" dragons are almost absent from hagiography outside western Asia Minor. However,

---

[1215] Ioannikios (*Sabbas*), §12; Ioannikios (*Peter*), §47.

[1216] See Sullivan, "Life of St. Ioannikios", 244 and n. 9. On the dragon-slayer saints in general, see Perdrizet, *Negotium perambulans*, 5–16. Perdrizet argues in favor of their Egyptian origin. See also Christopher Walter, "The Thracian Horseman: Ancestor of the Warrior Saints?", *Byzantinische Forschungen* 14 (1989): 657–73 (Thracian origin).

[1217] Gregory of Dekapolis, §30ff.

these demonic beasts often appear in the saints' *Lives* as the imaginary form taken by evil spirits. A man asked, *c.* 836-7, St. Peter of Atroa (773–837) to accept him in his monastery as a novice, and the abbot gladly agreed. Shortly before his ordination as a monk, a *deceitful demon* attacked him with false visions, forcing him to deviate from the holy life he had chosen. One of the deceptive images used by the Devil was that of a hissing dragon.[1218] In the same disguise, an evil spirit attempted to drive St. Euthymios the Younger (823/4–898) away from his cave on Mount Athos. The holy hermit expelled the *demonic phantom* (φάσμα δαιμόνιον) using only threatening words.[1219]

The dragon also appears in visions and dreams as a personification of the sinful passions instilled by the Devil and evil spirits. One example is a detailed story from the *Life* of the Palestinian Saint Stephen the Thaumaturge (725-794). According to the text, in a dream the holy man saw a monk of his acquaintance who seemed to be pursued by a giant black dragon with terrible, crimson and blood-filled eyes (μέγαν δράκοντα καὶ ἐρεμνόν, φρικώδεις ἔχοντα καὶ φοινικοέντας καὶ δαφοινοὺς ὀφθαλμούς). The monk at first refused Stephen's help, but when the danger became mortal, he held out his hand imploringly. The Saint took the first object he encountered and struck the beast but only succeeded in driving it away.[1220] Stephen immediately understood the dream's meaning: the monster symbolized the sinful temptations to which his friend was about to succumb. Soon the vision proved true, and the same monk came to Stephen for help. At first, he was ashamed of his sinful thoughts, but finally confessed them all. With prayers and spiritual advice, the abbot temporarily cured him. Shortly afterward, however, the monk departed for Jerusalem, away from his help, and the Saint saw him again in a dream pursued by the dark dragon, which caught up with him and bit him savagely.[1221]

[1218] Peter of Atroa, §79.9-21.
[1219] Euthymios the Younger, §21.
[1220] Stephen the Thaumaturge, §153.
[1221] Stephen the Thaumaturge, §154.

The hagiographers of the period under study frequently refer to the image of the dragon as purely a metaphor for the Devil, his servants, and death.[1222] A virtuous life was the only way to avoid its harmful influence,[1223] according to the *Life* of St. Ioannikios the Great. Such concepts paved the path for using the image as a powerful instrument in the ideological and political struggles in Byzantium, especially during the Iconoclast crisis. The "Dragon Emperor" par excellence was, undoubtedly, the heretic Constantine V,[1224] but hagiographers and historians also apply the same insulting metaphor to other rulers and political figures.[1225]

3. Birds

In the Byzantine hagiographical literature of the period under study, demons taking the form of birds are seldom mentioned. Naturally, the most common images are those associated with darkness and death, i.e., the raven and the owl. The fact that these animals are considered unclean in the books of Leviticus and Deuteronomy[1226] facilitates their demonization in a Christian cultural context. Sporadically, the authors also give interesting information about other winged creatures, like the bat and the sparrow. In the following pages, we will shed some light on the complex folklore-mythological tradition behind them.

3.1. Ravens

Strictly speaking, the Old and the New Testament provide almost no basis for demonizing the raven (κόραξ), even though the books of Leviticus

---

[1222] See, e.g., Golinduch, 159.5-6, 159.22, and 160.21-22: ἀποστάτης καὶ νοητὸς δράκων. See also Ioannikios (*Peter*), §54, where Death is called *the mouth of the fearful dragon*. On Hell being called metaphorically *the dragon from the depths* in the apocryphal Apocalypse of Baruch, see Lambakis, "The Descents into Hell", 41. On the dragon in depictions of the Last Judgement, see Provatakis, *The Devil*, 182-89.

[1223] See Ioannikios (*Sabbas*), §30.

[1224] See, e.g., Plato of Sakkoudion, §17.

[1225] See, e.g., Ioannikios (*Sabbas*), §46 (Emperor Theophilos); Stephen the Younger, 161.14 (Michael Lachanodrakon).

[1226] The unclean birds are listed in Lev., 11:13-19, and in Deut., 14:12-18.

and Deuteronomy consider it an unclean (i.e., non-edible) animal.[1227] According to the Book of Kings, these birds deliver food by God's will to the Prophet Elijah on the shores of the River Jordan,[1228] and in the Psalms and the Gospel of Luke, God Himself feeds the crow and its offspring.[1229] In Proverbs, the ravens that inhabit shadowy ravines (φάραγγες) punish those who disrespect their parents.[1230]

In Byzantine hagiography, ravens often inhabit dark caves and mountain ravines. This demonic image, however, appears very rarely, only in the ninth and tenth centuries, and always in texts written and set outside of the imperial capital — in Bithynia, southern Italy, and Greece. Among the texts belonging to the hagiographic school of Mount Olympus in Asia Minor, this evil spirit appears in the *Lives* of St. Ioannikios the Great and St. Peter of Atroa. In the former, the raven-like demons are simply personifications of the external threat to Ioannikios, who settled as a hermit in a cave between 820 and 825.[1231] They were easily cast out in just a few days through fervent prayers to God.[1232] In the *Life* of St. Peter of Atroa, the story is more interesting since the function of the demons is to punish heresy. Persecuted between 817 and 819 by the iconoclastic authorities, St. Peter left Bithynia, departed for Lydia, and faced terrible misfortune. The demons that inhabited the mountain caves left their refuge as ravens, flew through the surrounding villages and possessed numerous iconoclasts. Unable to bear their influence and stricken with madness, the repentant heretics visited the Saint, renounced their false views, and Peter expelled the evil spirits.[1233]

[1227] Lev., 11:15; Deut., 14:14.
[1228] III Kings 17:6.
[1229] Luke 23:24; cf. Ps. 146:9.
[1230] Prov., 30:17: ὀφθαλμὸν καταγελῶντα πατρὸς καὶ ἀτιμάζοντα γῆρας μητρός, ἐκκόψαισαν αὐτὸν κόρακες ἐκ τῶν φαράγγων. The Greek word φάραγξ does not mean *valley* (as translated in the New International Version of the Bible), but *ravine*.
[1231] According to the text, the event occurred between the first and the fifth year of Emperor Michael II's rule (820–829); cf. Ioannikios (*Sabbas*), §29.
[1232] Ioannikios (*Peter*), §33; Ioannikios (*Sabbas*), §26.
[1233] Peter of Atroa, §22.7ff.

Biblical texts can offer us little help in interpreting several other hagiographical stories that involve raven-like demons. To understand some of their functions and manifestations, and their influence over their victims, we have to resort to the symbolism of this black bird in Greco-Roman mythological traditions. The raven is the sacred animal of the oracle-god Apollo, but the ominous predictions of this herald of death are not ordinary, just as the color of its black wings is not accidental. According to the myth,[1234] the wealthy and god-fearing Clinis who lived near Babylon decided to worship Apollo like the Hyperboreans and, rather than the usual goats and sheep, began to sacrifice donkeys to him. The god warned him that he did not like this innovation, and Clinis told his sons to stop the ritual. However, one of them, Lycius, disobeyed his father's order, untied the donkeys, and led them to the altar. The enraged Apollo struck the animals with madness, and they attacked Clinis's entire family, threatening both the culprit and innocents with death. However, Poseidon, Artemis, and Leto interceded in their favor, and Apollo commuted the punishment, turning the whole family into birds instead of killing them. Lycius himself became a white raven, the sacred animal of the god. The second part of the myth connects the raven, the color black, and death. The white raven informed Apollo of the infidelity of his beloved Thessalian princess Coronis (from κορώνη, crow). Pregnant with the god's son Asclepius, she cheated on her godly lover with the handsome youth Ischius. The enraged Apollo persuaded his sister Artemis to kill her but later regretted his decision. He took the baby from the dead woman's womb and, as a sign of mourning, changed the wings of the herald of misfortune and death from white to black.[1235]

The raven in Byzantine literature is generally associated with divination and ancient magic rituals. Pseudo-Psellus attests to this concept in the demonological dialogue *Timothy*, in which the professional exorcist

---

[1234] Antoninus Liberalis, *Metamorphoseon synagogue*, ed. Ignatius Cazzaniga (Milan: Istituto Editoriale Cisalpino, 1962), §20.

[1235] "Apollodori bibliotheca", III.118–19; *Publii Ovidii Nasonis Metamorphoses*, II.536 and II.596ff; Hyginus, *Fabulae*, CCII; Antoninus Liberalis, *Metamorphoseon synagogue*, §20.7.

ANIMALS AND PLANTS 363

Thrax describes his attempt to expel the demon who had possessed a man from the town of Elasson in Thessaly. This person had been kidnapped by a Libyan charlatan who took him to an unknown mountain at night and gave him some herbal potion to drink. He then spat in his mouth and smeared his eyes with ointment, after which the man began seeing demons. Suddenly a raven-like evil spirit entered his mouth. From that moment, he began to disclose to others the mysteries that *the moving power* (τὸ κινοῦν) wished to reveal. However, he could not predict the future during Holy Week and on the feast of St. Anastasia. Thrax says that this man told the inhabitants of Elasson of his coming to the town before he had even left the suburbs of Constantinople and warned him about the great dangers to which the angry demons would subject him on his way back.[1236]

The black raven is associated with divination in the *Life* of St. Elias Speleotes. As in the story told by Pseudo-Psellus, the raven-like demon enters through the victim's mouth, but, in this case, appears as a punishment for magic and divination. According to the text, at the beginning of the tenth century, the priest Epiphanius lived in the Calabrian village of Asfaldeus. He undertook various strange rituals which he performed on humans and animals. He mumbled incantations, foretold the future, and dealt with things that should not be described. In order to re-educate him, God gave him over to a powerful evil spirit. The demon dragged the wretch by the right hand, lifted him into the air, and then dropped him on the ground. Worrying that he should lose his priestly office[1237] if the demonic possession became known to his congregation, Epiphanius asked Elias for help. The saint smiled, laid his hand on the head of this village "shaman", and promised him salvation if he would promise to do no more such *wicked and unlawful deeds* (πονηρὰ καὶ ἀθέμιτα ἔργα).

[1236] Pseudo-Psellos, "Timothée ou des demons", ll. 391–29.
[1237] According to Orthodox canon law, a person who is possessed by a demon is considered sinful and, in the words of John Zonaras, *devoid of reason and capacity* (ἐστέρηται λογισμοῦ καὶ διαθέσεως), since he has attracted the evil power to dwell in him. He has no right to be ordained a priest or to perform priestly duties until he is purified (see *Constitution of the Godly and Holy Canons*, 2: 101–3).

When Epiphanius sincerely promised to do so, Elias made the sign of the cross, read him a prayer, and left him to rest. Throughout the night, the holy man implored God for help, and finally, he saw a raven coming out of the wicked priest's mouth. In the morning, Epiphanius was healed. He never again engaged in divination or magical practices.[1238]

In the previous chapter, we analyzed the elements of the female demon's image: her connection with birds, water, and filthy liquids.[1239] Many female deities in the Greco-Roman mythological tradition, mostly malignant, appear as feathered humanlike creatures living in lakes or the sea.[1240] We can discern a distant echo of these concepts and beliefs in the *Life* of St. Nikon Metanoeite. A girl lived in the town of Chalcis on the island of Euboea. Once, as she was grinding barley, her mother needed water and sent her daughter to fetch it from a clear spring at some distance from the house. The girl was lazy and wanted to skip the long walk and instead bring water from the nearest long-abandoned well. As soon as she lowered her jug into the sludge, a raven-like demon fluttered out of the dirty pit and entered her body. Angry at her tardiness, her mother looked for her and found her lying on the ground, frothing at the mouth. She took her daughter to St. Nikon Metanoeite, who traveled through central Greece in 968–70,[1241] and asked him for help. The preacher at first refused, saying that the request was beyond his abilities, but then fell to his knees and prayed. He then bound the girl with a chain and, accompanied by a vast crowd, led her back to the well. The holy man prayed again, and finally, the demon flew out, leaving her convulsing on the ground. Then

---

[1238] Elias Speleotes, §57.
[1239] Pseudo-Psellos, "Timothée ou des demons", ll. 545-549; Greenfield, *Traditions of Belief*, 185; Vakaloudi, *Magic*, 112.
[1240] A typical example is the Styphalian birds with female faces who lived in a swamp in Arcadia and destroyed crops, cattle, and people ("Apollodori bibliotheca", II.92; *Strabonis geographica*, VIII.6.8.2-9; *Pausaniae Graeciae descriptio*, 3: VIII.22.4; *Diodori bibliotheca historica*, 1: IV.13.2; *Publii Ovidii Nasonis Metamorphoses*, IX.187ff).
[1241] Sullivan, *The Life of Saint Nikon*, 1 and 19. On the date of the main events in the *Life* of St. Nikon, see Part One, Chapter 2, §10.

Nikon cursed the evil spirit, and it returned to the stinking well, which was immediately covered with earth by the locals[1242].

3.2. "Birds" of the night: bats and owls

The raven is an ominous harbinger of death and is associated with Evil by one outward sign: its black feathers. By contrast, the bat and the owl are demonized on the basis of their connection with night. The Greek word for bat (νυκτερίς) means literally "a creature of the night", and the term for owl (νυκτικόραξ) means "night raven". Despite this symbolism and the various ancient mythological and folklore traditions associated with them, they are not among the usual forms taken by the demons in the *Lives* of the saints in the period under study.

According to modern zoology, the bat is the only flying mammal. Late antique and Byzantine authors sometimes refer to it as a bird, sometimes as a *winged creature*.[1243] It appears as an incarnation of a demon only once in the Byzantine hagiography from 565 to 1000, in the *Life* of the southern Italian Saint Elias Speleotes. In the middle of the tenth century, the Saint settled in a small cave, but soon many monks began to flock to him. They decided to expand their living space, and God sent them a sign where a new monastery was to be built: a swarm of bats came out of a small hole in a nearby hill. The monks lit candles and entered through the same opening, behind which they found a large cave. However, Elias feared that no sunlight would enter through the small gap, sending the monk Cosmas with a team of builders inside to solve this problem. They explored the cave and made a new entrance to the south, through which daylight would illuminate the new dwelling and chase away *the birds and the dark designs of evil and unclean spirits* (τά τε... πετεινὰ τά τε νοήματα τῶν πονηρῶν καὶ ἀκαθάρτων πνευμάτων).[1244]

[1242] Nikon Metanoeite, §27.

[1243] The bat is considered a *bird* (ὄρνεον) in the famous *Oneirocritica* (*The Interpretation of Dreams*) of Artemidorus of Daldis (*Artemidori Daldiani onirocriticon libri V*, ed. Roger Pack (Leipzig: Teubner, 1963), III.65.1–2). The *Cyrannides* call it simply a *winged animal* (πτερωτόν ζῷον) (*Die Kyraniden*, II.28.2).

[1244] Elias Speleotes, §42.

These measures soon proved necessary, for the cave was the abode of bat-like demons. Elias sensed their presence and quickly expelled them with God's help.[1245]

The long-eared owl (Greek νυκτικόραξ, Lat. *Asio otus*) is the nocturnal equivalent of the raven (from νῦξ and κόραξ). In the Old Testament, it is numbered among the unclean and inedible animals,[1246] symbolizing, in addition, the sinner who has lost God.[1247] Because of its nocturnal nature, hunting at night, Christian theologians consider it an enemy of the Creator's light and a wretched creature that belongs to the world of Evil.[1248] According to Patriarch Sophronios of Jerusalem, urged by the demons, this bird nested on the roofs of churches in whose precincts the possessed and sick slept in search of deliverance, polluting them and their beds with droppings. In this way, the evil spirits tried to make their victims leave the holy places and remain under their power.[1249]

In addition to its nocturnal lifestyle, the owl is associated with the demonic world by the eerie sounds it produces. Its hooting portends death and indicates the presence of Evil.[1250] According to the *Life* of St. Stephen the Younger, after subjecting the Saint to numerous tortures,

---

[1245] Elias Speleotes, §43.

[1246] Lev., 11:17.

[1247] Ps. 101:7 (Septuag.): *I have become like an owl in a ruined house* (ἐγεννήθην ὡσεὶ νυκτικόραξ ἐν οἰκοπέδῳ); Ps. 102:7 (NIV): *I have become like a bird alone on a roof*. This passage is quoted by Eusebius of Caesarea in his *Commentary on the Psalms* (Eusebius Caesariensis, "Commentaria in Psalmos", in MPG, vol. 23 (Paris, 1857), 1256B) and by St. Athanasios the Great in his *Expositions on the Psalms* (Athanasius Alexandrinus, "Expositiones in Psalmos", MPG, vol. 27 (Paris, 1837), 427A). Cf. Bojadschiew, *The Night in the Middle Ages*, 137; Bojadschiew surveys the tradition related to the owl in Western medieval literature.

[1248] Théodoret de Cyr, *Thérapeutique des maladies helléniques*, ed. and trans. Pierre Canivet [*Sources chrétiennes* 57.1] (Paris: Éditions du Cerf, 1958), II.2.5–II.3.2; see "Physiologus (redactio prima)", §5, where the Old Testament is quoted. On the demonic nature of the owl in the Western tradition, see Bojadschiew, *The Night in the Middle Ages*, 136ff.

[1249] Cyr and John, §67.4–6.

[1250] See, e.g., *Hori Apollinis hieroglyphica*, ed. Francesco Sbordone (Naples: Loffredo, 1940), II.25: νυκτικόραξ θάνατον σημαίνει.

ANIMALS AND PLANTS   367

Emperor Constantine V gave him the opportunity to renounce the icons and thus save his life. Stephen solemnly refused, and an owl-like demon informed the tyrant of his decision to sacrifice himself and become a martyr of Orthodoxy.[1251]

3.3. Other images

The **eagle** (ἀετός) is rarely present in depictions of demons. One of the few examples is a miniature from a manuscript dated 1180,[1252] displaying the Gospel story of Jesus Christ expelling the Legion of evil spirits into a herd of swine.[1253] In this miniature, one of the demons emerges from its victim in the form of a black eagle,[1254] In the Byzantine hagiography of the period under study, the eagle occurs only once. The Devil visited the monk St. George of Choziba in this form in the late sixth or early seventh century[1255] during a hot, sultry night. The bird, as tall as a man, landed on the roof of his cell and began flapping its wings to create a strong breeze and disturb the hermit's prayer. George immediately relized that this was a diabolical attack and stroke the eagle, which immediately disappeared like smoke.[1256]

A **goose-like demon** (χήν) is mentioned only once during the period under study, in the *Life* of St. Theodore Sykeotes. According to this text, a high-ranking courtier (*silentiarius*) named Manas suffered from a severe internal illness due to the influence of the Devil. He often visited

---

[1251] Stephen the Younger, 168.23ff.
[1252] Provatakis, *The Devil*, 246.
[1253] Matt. 8:28-32; Luke, 8:26-39; Mark, 5:1-20.
[1254] Provatakis, *The Devil*, 246 and fig. 217. Provatakis notes that birds rarely appear as evil spirits in Byzantine iconography.
[1255] The *terminus post quem* is the Persian invasion (ἐπιδρομὴ Περσῶν) that occurred before the departure of St. George from Mount Choziba (George of Choziba, §3.12.16-20). It is difficult to determine whether the author is talking about one of the military expeditions between 572 and 591, or the ones launched during the reign of Emperor Phocas (602-610). The *terminus ante quem* is the capture of Jerusalem by the forces of Shah Khusraw II in 614 (George of Choziba, §4.15-20). For more detail about these events, see Christophilopoulou, *Byzantine History*, 1: 306-10 (the expeditions between 572 and 591), and 328ff (on the campaigns during the reign of Phocas); Christophilopoulou, *Byzantine History*, 2.1: 16-18 (on the capture of Jerusalem in 614).
[1256] George of Choziba, §3.13.2-10.

the Saint but was ashamed to reveal the nature of his condition. Theodore himself asked him why he was hiding his problem. Manas then fell on his knees and asked him to pray before God for his deliverance and to come to his house and bless the household. Two days later, Theodore visited his home and prayed the whole night for the man, in the grip of the usual crisis. The following day the holy monk's disciple Julian told his mentor about a strange dream he had. It was as if Theodore was standing on the beach. Manas approached him, holding in his arms a *giant, three-headed wild goose* (ἀγριόχηνον μέγα τρικέφαλον), and gave the animal to the exorcist. When he took it, it immediately turned into a cat, and then quickly disappeared into the sea. After the morning service, Theodore went to the sick man and told him that the illness would trouble him no more.[1257]

The last bird-like demon occurs only once in Byzantine hagiography but involves an amusing allusion to ancient poetry. What remained in the medieval saints' *Lives* of the ancient symbol of Aphrodite, **the sparrow**, which Roman girls kept in their homes so often as a pet?[1258] In two of his most famous poems, the poet Catullus describes the games of his beloved Lesbia with her *passer* and the girl's grief at its death.[1259] We have no information about pet sparrows in Byzantium, but a demonic story from the *Life* of St. Athanasia of Aegina sounds like a deformed parody of Catullus' verses. According to the anonymous author, a little girl about eight years old was playing outside when suddenly a *black sparrow* (στρουθίον μέλαν) flew by. She played with the bird for a while, but soon the bitter truth came out. The playful sparrow was a demon and injured the girl's arm, which began to twitch uncontrollably, causing her

---

[1257] Theodore Sykeotes, §89.
[1258] On the sparrow as a house pet for Roman girls, see Lazenby, "Greek and Roman Household Pets", 247 and 250; Francis Lazenby, "Greek and Roman Household Pets", II, *Classical Journal* 5 (February 1949): 299.
[1259] "Gai Valeri Catulli Veronensis Liber", ed. Francis Cornish, John Postgate, and John Mackail, *Catullus. Tibullus. Privilegium Veneris* [Loeb Classical Library 6] (Cambridge, MA: Harvard University Press, 1921), II and III.15–18.

great pain. It took seven days of praying on the tomb of St. Anastasia to remove the harmful influence with the help of the Holy Spirit.[1260]

4. Mammals

4.1. Mice: plague, filth, and death

The mouse (μῦς) is one of the most interesting images connecting Semitic Near East mythologies and the Greco-Roman world. Little remains in the Byzantine hagiography of its functions and influences. However, even in a heavily reworked Christian context, this small rodent, the symbol of deadly epidemics and famine, preserves and transmits through the centuries a distant echo of a centuries-old mythological tradition.

At the beginning of his *Iliad*, Homer describes a terrible scene: the plague sent by Apollo Smyntheus to decimate the Achaean armies.[1261] The eponym of this ominous deity derives from the word σμίνθος (*mouse*),[1262] and a coastal town near Ilion, whose exact location is unclear, bore this name.[1263] In the following centuries, Apollo, whose sacred animal was the small rodent and whose name is sometimes associated etymologically with the verb *to destroy* (ἀπόλλυμι), occurs elsewhere in Greek literature as the god of epidemic diseases and pestilence. During the Peloponnesian War, when the "plague" (λοιμός) scourged the population of Attica, the Athenians believed that he had sided with their enemies, the Spartans.[1264] Apollo is merely a syncretic image, only occasion-

---

[1260] Athanasia of Aegina, §28.
[1261] Homer, *Iliad*, I.39.
[1262] See George Hill, "Apollo and St. Michael: Some Analogies", *Journal of Hellenic Studies* 36 (1916): 135–37; Alexander Krappe, "ΑΠΟΛΛΩΝ ΣΜΙΝΘΕΥΣ", *Classical Philology* 36, no. 2 (April 1941): 134, according to whom the word is of Mysian origin.
[1263] On the coastal towns bearing the name Smynthos, see Frederick Bernheim and Ann Zener, "The Sminthian Apollo and the Epidemic among the Achaeans at Troy", *Transactions of the American Philological Association* 108 (1978): 12, where the authors speculate that in antiquity (as during the Middle Ages) epidemics were transmitted mainly by ship, explaining why the cult of Apollo Smyntheus was widespread in seaports.
[1264] Thucydides, *History of the Peloponnesian War*, ed. and trans. Charles Smith, vol. 1: *Books I and III*, [Loeb Classical Library 108] (London: Heinemann, 1956), II.54; see

ally associated with the harmful mice and rats that spread disease and eat the crops, sowing death among human populations. In Greco-Roman literature (and Western European and Slavic folklore), mice and the "mouse king" are images associated with disease, graves, and the world of the dead.[1265] The same animal and its god-master can also stop an army in other ways — by gnawing the bowstrings and leather straps of shields.[1266]

In the Old Testament, the mouse is considered as unclean as swine, and the prophet Isaiah threatens utter destruction to all who taste its flesh.[1267] However, this animal also appears in an episode that reflects the mythological tradition associated with Apollo Smyntheus. Around 1060 BC, over a hundred years after the plague among the Achaean army,[1268] a terrible calamity befell Palestine. Swarms of mice invaded one of its harbors, and a terrible epidemic began,[1269] which some researchers identify as bubonic plague.[1270] As in the *Iliad*, the priests quickly discovered the cause of this calamity. The Philistines had appropriated a great relic, the Hebrew Ark of the Covenant, and now they had to return it to the Chosen People along with five gold rats and five gold *tumors* (probably buboes)[1271] to stop the wrath of Sabaoth. The similarities between the epidemic caused by Apollo Smyntheus (the "Mouse" Apollo) in the Achaean army and the one spread among the Philistines by the God-sent mice

---

other examples in John Geyer, "Mice and Rites in 1 Samuel V-VI", *Vetus Testamentum* 31, no. 3 (July 1981): 300; Bernheim and Zener, "Sminthian Apollo", 12ff.

[1265] Cf., e.g., *Strabonis geographica*, III.4.18, where the author describes a λοιμική νόσος, spread by mice in Spain. For details on the connection between mice, epidemics, and death, see Krappe, "ΑΠΟΛΛΩΝ ΣΜΙΝΘΕΥΣ", 135ff; Bernheim and Zener, "Sminthian Apollo", 12ff; Hill, "Apollo and St. Michael", 135–38.

[1266] See, e.g., Hérodote, *Histoires*, 2: II.141, where the mice stop the armies of Sennacherib during his campaign against Egypt in this manner. See also Bernheim and Zener, "Sminthian Apollo", 12ff.

[1267] Isa., 66:17; see Lev., 11:29.

[1268] On the date of this event, see Bernheim and Zener, "Sminthian Apollo", 12.

[1269] 1 Sam. 5:6 and 6:1.

[1270] See Othniel Margalith, "The Meaning of *plym* in 1 Samuel V-VI", *Vetus Testamentum* 33, no. 3 (1983): 39ff. Margalith analyzes in detail the terminology of the Hebrew original.

[1271] 1 Sam. 6:4.

have long been noted by modern researchers.[1272] In all likelihood, the cult of the disease- and vengeance-bringing "master of mice" was adopted by the Philistines under Hittite (i.e., Indo-European) influence and was widespread throughout Asia Minor.[1273]

Nevertheless, the rodent is not only the symbol of disease and death in the Greco-Roman world and the Middle Eastern mythological traditions. The jumping mouse was a standard image found on various protective amulets in the Chaldean and Babylonian cultures[1274] and continued to be part of numerous magical practices well into Late Antiquity.[1275] In his *Myriobiblos*, Patriarch Photius speaks at length of the Neoplatonist Iamblich, who was of "Babylonian" descent and had a profound knowledge of Chaldean magical teachings. According to the learned patriarch, Iamblich categorized the types of magic according to the animals in whose forms the demons participated in the rituals. The rites associated with mice played an important role.[1276]

In Byzantine hagiography, the mouse retains its association with dead bodies, mortality, and decay. This animal appears as a demonic creature sent by Satan in the *Life* of the Lesbian saints David, Symeon, and George, where the author includes them in a story full of allegories and biblical allusions. During the last period of persecution against the iconodules in the 830s, the iconoclast Emperor Theophilos (829–842) ordered the future Patriarch Methodius flogged and thrown into a *tomb-like prison* (ὑπόγαιον τάφος) along with two criminals. As in Hell, stench

---

[1272] See James Moulton and A. T. C. Cree, "ΣΜΙΝΘΕΥΣ, Pestilence and Mice", *Classical Review* 15, no. 5 (June 1901): 284; Geyer, "Mice and Rites", 300; Margalith, "The Meaning of *plym*", 340.

[1273] See Geyer, "Mice and Rites", 300–304, with many examples of the close cultural and linguistic connections between the Philistines and the Hitites; Margalith, "The Meaning of *plym*", 340ff.

[1274] On mice and the magical rituals related to them, see Joseph Bidez and Franz Cumont, *Les Mages hellénistés*, vol. 1 (Paris, 1938), 148ff; Felix von Oefele, "A Babylonian Representation of a Jumping Mouse", *Journal of the American Oriental Society* 38 (1918): 140.

[1275] Vakaloudi, *Magic*, 113.

[1276] Photius, *Bibliothèque*, ed. René Henry, vol. 2: *Codices 84-185* [Collection Budé 142] (Paris: Les Belles Lettres, 1977), 148ff (cod. 94).

and darkness (δυσωδία καὶ ζόφωσις) reigned, and the robbers soon died as a consequence of the unhealthy conditions. *Preserved by the almighty right hand of the Lord*,[1277] Methodius himself survived. However, his life in the pit became unbearable as nobody removed the dead bodies from the cell, and swarms of mice, attracted by the stench of decaying flesh, settled in the darkness.[1278] The future patriarch spent five long years in this place but was finally set free. This terrible scene alludes to the crucifixion of Christ, who was crucified along with two thieves, descended into Hell, defeated death, overcame its master, the Devil, and rose from his grave. The author of the text uses terminology that makes this allusion clear to a medieval audience. The narrow cell is located, like Hell, under the earth; it is full of death and foul smells; and only the hand of God can save the righteous man from physical and mental destruction. The swarms of mice attracted by the smell of death play the role of instruments and messengers of the Evil One, and their vivid description illustrates the metamorphosis undergone by the mighty and revered ancient deity of famine and epidemics, Apollo Smyntheus. In a Christian world, his functions were naturally taken over by the lord of death, the Devil.

The Byzantine hagiographers associated the mouse with impurity and the desecration of a human-inhabited space. In the 930s, St. Gregory of Decapolis settled as a hermit in an abandoned tower in Syracuse. Immersed in prayers and vigils, the holy man forgot to clean his sheepskin bedding for a long time, and when he finally lifted it, he discovered a swarm of hideous mouse-like demons. It cost Gregory much effort to drive them out with the sign of the cross.[1279] According to the *Life* of

---

[1277] David, Symeon and George, §22.17ff: ὑπὸ τῆς παγκρατίστης δεξιᾶς τοῦ Ὑψήστου περιφρουρούμενος.

[1278] David, Symeon and George, §22.21: τά τε τῶν μυῶν πλήθη διὰ τὴν τῶν νεκρῶν ἐν αὐτῷ σωμάτων δυσωδίαν ἐμφιλοχωροῦντα.

[1279] Gregory of Dekapolis, §27.

Irene of Chrysobalanton, the entry of a mouse into a church disrupts the liturgy and is considered a sinister demonic influence.[1280]

Along with the snake, the mouse is one of the standard forms in which demons enter the human body, causing various physical afflictions and illnesses. In the *Life* of Theodore Sykeotes, the unclean spirit that possessed the hand of the wealthy shipowner Theodoulos of Pontus was like a mouse, shuffling under the skin of its victim and avoiding the touch of the holy man. During the exorcism, St. Theodore had first to restrict its influence to the forearm of Theodoulos. Then he recited a healing prayer and concluded the procedure with the sign of the cross.[1281] Much more painful were the methods that the same Saint applied to another possessed person who, under the demon's influence, assailed him fiercely with curses and profanities. Theodore forced the evil spirit out of the poor man's body with blows, curses, and, again, the sign of the cross. The growling and screaming creature came out through the victim's mouth like a mouse.[1282]

4.2. Pigs, swine, and boars: aggression and homosexuality

In the Old Testament, pigs, swine, and wild boars (χοῖροι, ὕες/σύες, μονιοί, σύαγροι) appear as a symbol of aggressiveness. Like the *Demons* of Dostoevsky, they represent the uncontrollable, irrational force that attacks an inhabited space and destroys it as God's punishment or for no reason.[1283] The same concept could also be found in the Greco-Roman mythological tradition, where Heracles delivered the inhabitants of western Arcadia from the dreaded Erymanthian boar. In hagiography, pig-

---

[1280] Irene of Chrysobalanton, §17. See also Abrahamse and Domingo-Forasté, "Life of David, Symeon, and George", 178, n. 183; Joannou, *Démonologie*, 12.
[1281] Theodore Sykeotes, §123.
[1282] Theodore Sykeotes, §132.
[1283] See for example 2 Kings 17:8 (2 Sam. 17:8 in NIV): ὡς ὗς τραχεῖα ἐν τῷ πεδίῳ (the bravery and wrathfulness of Solomon's army are compared to a *ferocious boar in a field*); Ps. 79:13 (Ps. 80:13 in NIV): *Swines from the forest ravaged it* (i.e., the vine that symbolizes the Chosen People), *and wild boars destroyed it* (ἐλυμήνατο αὐτὴν σῦς ἐκ δρυμοῦ, καὶ μονιὸς ἄγριος κατενεμήσατο αὐτήν).

like demons are the symbol,[1284] the instrument,[1285] or the physical incarnation[1286] of Evil. They attack with terrifying aggressiveness both hermits and entire human communities. The image is also frequently used as a metaphor for the outer appearance of demons' victims, with frothing mouths, in fits of rage.[1287]

Another essential element of the pig's hagiographical image is its filthiness: eating its unclean (ἀκάθαρτον) flesh is explicitly forbidden by the books of Leviticus and Deuteronomy.[1288] This feature, mentioned in the New Testament, makes this animal a suitable incarnation of the demon in general but also associates it with a particular set of sins.[1289] In one of his epistles, the Apostle Peter draws attention to *those who follow the corrupt desire of the flesh* and lead God's flock into sin.[1290] He compares those who indulge in sexual pleasures to a washed sow who *returns to her wallowing in the mud*.[1291] In hagiographical literature, however, the wallowing pig is not a symbol of all sins of the flesh, but specifically of male and female homosexuality.[1292] The Old and the New Testaments

---

[1284] See Symeon Stylites the Younger, §40.10ff, where the anonymous author exclaims: *And look, the demons on the earth are like wild boars!*

[1285] See for example Phantinos the Younger, §12, where the forces of the Evil urge the wild boars to attack the holy man in the mountains of Lucania.

[1286] See for example Peter of Atroa, §79, where pig-like demons scatter the belongings of a young monk with their snouts all night and disturb his sleeping.

[1287] Sabbas the Younger, §19, where a possessed man froths *like a swine*; Ioannikios (Peter), §27, where a woman, possessed by the spirit of fornication, wanders *like wild swine* in the mountains of Lydia.

[1288] Lev., 11:7 – 8: *And the pig, though it has a divided hoof, does not chew the cud; it is unclean for you. You must not eat their meat or touch their carcasses; they are unclean for you.* (καὶ τὸν ὗν, ὅτι διχηλεῖ ὁπλὴν τοῦτο καὶ ὀνυχίζει ὄνυχας ὁπλῆς, καὶ τοῦτο οὐκ ἀνάγει μηρυκισμόν, ἀκάθαρτον τοῦτο ὑμῖν· ἀπὸ τῶν κρεῶν αὐτῶν οὐ φάγεσθε καὶ τῶν θνησιμαίων αὐτῶν οὐχ ἄψεσθε, ἀκάθαρτα ταῦτα ὑμῖν); cf. and Deut., 14:8.

[1289] Mat. 8:32; Mark 5:12 – 13; Luke 8:33.

[1290] 2 Pet. 2:10: *τοὺς ὀπίσω σαρκὸς ἐν ἐπιθυμίᾳ μιασμοῦ πορευομένους.*

[1291] 2 Pet. 2:22: *A sow that is washed returns to her wallowing in the mud* (ὗς λουσαμένη εἰς κυλισμὸν βορβόρου).

[1292] Lev. 18:22 and 20:13, where homosexual intercourse between men is punishable by death. In Rom. 1:26ff, 1 Cor. 6:9, and 1 Tim. 1:10, the Apostle Paul refers to both male and female homosexuality. For more detail on the Church and secular penalties for homosexuality, see Kaouras, *Byzantium: The Sexual Crimes*, 98–115. On Rom. 1:26ff, see also Mark Smith, "Ancient Bisexuality and the Interpretation of Romans 1:26 –

ANIMALS AND PLANTS   375

forbid this sexual behavior on many occasions, and, specifically, men who indulge in such practices are subject to the death penalty according to Byzantine law codes.[1293] From this point of view, its demonization in hagiography is perfectly logical. According to the *Life* of St. Basil the Younger, the demon of Homosexuality and Pederasty constantly changes his appearance, but usually takes the form of a pig *happily wallowing in the mire*.[1294] In this case, the expression ὥσπερ χοῖρος ἡδέως τῷ βορβόρῳ... κυλιόμενος is borrowed directly from the Apostle Peter's epistle cited above.

The pig-like demon of homosexuality in St. Basil the Younger's *Life* represents, from a Christian point of view, a distorted deviation from the masculine norm, in the first place the active participant in the sexual act who "violates" his partner and, consequently, deserves spiritual damnation and legal punishment.[1295] This image is very far from the early modern and Victorian concept of the effeminate gay man who accepts, of his own volition and by his uncontrollable lust, the traditional female gender role. Comparing the two images, we are faced with two political and social propaganda strategies that use homosexuals as a scapegoat in different ideological struggles and for different political, social, and religious purposes. Christian theologians chose to demonize the "pig wallowing in the mire", who demonstrates his excessive masculinity by raping another male body and depriving his victim of its own virility through unnatural sexual intercourse. The propaganda machine of the Catholic League and, afterward, that of the French King Henry IV (1589–1610), the founder of the Bourbon royal dynasty in the late sixteenth century, adopted a differ-

---

27", *Journal of American Academy of Religion* 64, no. 2 (Summer 1996): 225, where the author puts the passage in the conceptional framework of St. Paul's dogmatics.

[1293] *Ecloga*, §17.38, where both the active and the passive participant are punishable by death: Οἱ ἀσελγεῖς, ὅ τε ποιῶν καὶ ὁ ὑπομένων, ξίφει τιμωρείσθωσαν. When the passive participant is less than twelve years old, the crime is considered *child abuse* (παιδοφθορία) – another sin under the "jurisdiction" of the pig-like demon in the *Life* of St. Basil the Younger. On capital punishment for homosexuality in Justinian's law code, see Kaouras, *Byzantium: The Sexual Crimes*, 102ff.

[1294] Basil the Younger, Part II, §32.8ff: ὥσπερ χοῖρος ἡδέως τῷ βορβόρῳ ἐπηυφραίνετο κυλιόμενος.

[1295] Kaouras, *Byzantium: The Sexual Crimes*, 101.

ent approach to defile the reputation of the last Valois King Henry III (1574–1589), representing him as an effeminate and self-indulgent sodomite who occasionally dressed like a woman and, supposedly, wrote love letters to his *mignons*.[1296] Both strategies led to terrible outbursts of aggression towards homosexuals throughout the centuries and are equally despicable.

Pigs and boars also symbolize the reversal of the established world order, and their image is often parodic and absurd. Diodorus of Sicily describes Heracles' heroic struggle with the Erymanthian boar amidst deep winter snowdrifts; the denouement of this epic story is a comic scene in which the hero carries the dead animal's corpse to King Eurystheus, and the chicken-hearted Mycenaean ruler hides in a huge jar.[1297] The *golden ring in a pig's snout* is the Biblical counterpart of the English idiomatic expression "to put lipstick (*or* a silk hat) on a pig", meaning "to superficially alter something in the hope of making it seem more appealing than it is in actuality".[1298] Due to his sinful disrespect and disobedience to his father, the Prodigal Son in the New Testament is dehumanized by eating food for swine.[1299] The image of the pig, both a sinister and parodic incarnation of irrationality and absurdity, appears in the *Life* of St. David, Symeon, and George: a pig with cut ears,[1300] enters a church in Mytilene and settles on the episcopal throne, grotesquely portending the return of the Iconoclast heresy and the installation of a heretic as bishop of Lesbos.[1301]

A possible reminiscence of the ancient Eleusinian Mysteries occurs in the *Life* of St. Elias Speleotes. Its author, the monk Kyriakos, tells the

---

[1296] Robert Jean Knecht, *Hero or Tyrant? Henry III, King of France, 1574–89* (Burlington: Ashgate, 2014), 136ff, with extensive bibliography.

[1297] *Diodori bibliotheca historica*, 1: IV.12.1ff.

[1298] Prov. 11:22: *Like a gold ring in a pig's snout is a beautiful woman who shows no discretion* (ὥσπερ ἐνώτιον ἐν ῥινὶ ὑός, οὕτως γυναικὶ κακόφρονι κάλλος).

[1299] Luke 15:16: ἐπεθύμει χορτασθῆναι ἐκ τῶν κερατίων ὧν ἤσθιον οἱ χοῖροι.

[1300] Cutting the pig's ears was the usual punishment for trespassing, and the custom continued to exist in modern Greece in the 1950s and 1960s (Abrahamse and Domingo-Forasté, "Life of David, Symeon, and George", 178 n. 182, with bibliography).

[1301] David, Symeon and George, §14.

story of the high-ranking Calabrian archon Gaudius, who was possessed by an evil spirit in the 920s.[1302] Unable to find salvation from the demon's harmful influence in any of the nearby monasteries, he asked Elias for help. The holy man advised him not to resort to secular physicians but to endure to the end of his God-sent punishment. Gaudius refused to obey and headed by sea for the city of Panormum, which was famous for its qualified Arab physicians. The Saint continued to pray for him, and the nobleman saw Elias in a dream removing a piglet from his stomach and throwing it into the sea. When he awoke, Gaudius was already cured and ordered the sailors to return his ship to the Christian shore.[1303] This episode reminds us of the Legion of demons that Christ allowed to enter a herd of swine, forcing the animals to throw themselves into the sea.[1304] However, the story of Gaudius may reflect a much earlier cultural substrate. Late antique Christian writers blamed the pagans for innumerable superstitions and sought to make public as much information as possible about the rituals associated with the various mystery practices.[1305] According to late antique sources, on the second day of the Eleusinian mysteries, the initiates had to wash in the sea with a piglet, then sacrifice it, thus purifying and preparing themselves for the initiation rituals.[1306] There is no way of proving with any certainty that an echo of the literary or folkloric tradition associated with the famous Eleusinian mysteries reached the monk Kyriakos in the tenth century. However, the parallels between the story of the archon Gaudius and the ritual called ἄλαδε μύσται allow such a supposition.

[1302] According to the text, Gaudius was possessed by the demon shortly after the rebellion of John Mouzalon (or Byzalon), *strategos* of Calabria, in 921/922 (see *Ioannis Scylitzae Synopsis Historiarum*, §5.50–54; Vasiliev, *Byzance et les Arabes*, 2: 247ff; Giovanni Musolino, *Santi eremiti Italogreci: grotte e chiese rupestri in Calabria* [Soveria Mannelli: Rubbettino, 2002,] 42–44).

[1303] Elias Speleotes, §59ff.

[1304] Mat. 8:28–34; Mark 5:1–20; Luke 8:26–39.

[1305] Clément d'Alexandrie, *Le protreptique*, ed. Claude Mondéser [*Sources chrétiennes* 2] (Paris: Éditions du Cerf, 1949), II.21.2.

[1306] Gilbert Murray, *Five Stages of Greek Religion* (Oxford: Clarendon Press, 1925), 15; Burkert, *Greek Religion*, 285ff.

4.3. Dogs and wolves

Like most of the demonic animals mentioned above, the dog in the Old and New Testaments is considered unclean[1307] and shameless,[1308] and its way of life is humiliating.[1309] It appears as a metaphor for the sinner who has lost God, *snarls like a dog, wanders about for food, and howls if not satisfied*.[1310] It also symbolized foolishness, and the expression "I am not a dog head!" meant "I am no fool".[1311] These concepts formalize the demonization of the dog in Christian literature in general, and hagiography in particular, but the thin biblical layer is nothing but a veneer over a rich and multilayered mythological tradition. The image of the sinister doglike demon in the saints' *Lives* during the sixth and seventh centuries is part of the standard strategy of Christian writers to use the sacred texts to create yet another objectified image of Evil, one that would sound familiar to their Late Antique audience. Greco-Roman mythological traditions and cults persistently associated the black dog with the underworld, the dead, and black magic. One of the most famous such images is the guardian of the Kingdom of Hades, the three-headed dog Cerberus. The retinue of the patron goddess of black magic, Hecate, consisted of demons in the form of black dogs, and she was often depicted as dog-headed.[1312] This tradition was well known to the famous Byzantine lexicographer Hesychius of Alexandria.[1313]

Doglike demons were relatively common in the *Lives* of saints who lived in the second half of the sixth and the early seventh centuries.

[1307] Ex. 22:31; Prov. 26:11; 2 Pet. 2:22.
[1308] See Isa. 56:11 (Septuag): *and the dogs are shameless in their soul, and they know no satiety* (καὶ οἱ κύνες ἀναιδεῖς τῇ ψυχῇ, οὐκ εἰδότες πλησμονήν) (my translation).
[1309] See, e.g., Job 30:1.
[1310] Ps. 58:15 (Septuag.); Ps. 59:15 (NIV).
[1311] 2 Kings 3:8 (Septuag.); 2 Sam. 3:8 (NIV): *Am I a dog's head...?* (μὴ κεφαλὴ κυνὸς ἐγὼ εἰμί).
[1312] See Vakaloudi, *Magic*, 74, 110ff, who refers to numerous Late Antique papyri related to the cult of Hecate and her retinue of black dogs.
[1313] *Hesychii Alexandrini lexicon*, vol. 1, s.v. alpha.252; *Hesychii Alexandrini lexicon*, ed. Kurt Latte and Ian Cunningham, vol. 2: E–X (Hauniae: Munksgaard, 1966), s.v. epsilon.1267.

Around 551 or 588,[1314] St. Symeon the Fool rescued a resident of Emesa in Syria from a demon that had possessed him as punishment for adultery with a married woman.[1315] Symeon, pretending to be mad, came near the man who was prostrate on the ground in terrible agony, struck him on the chin, and said: *Do not commit adultery, you wretch, and the demon shall not touch you anymore!* Immediately afterward, the Saint expelled the demon and he came out of his victim as a black dog (κῦνα μαῦρον).[1316]

In the early seventh century, black wolflike and doglike demons appear as incarnations of the spiritual danger sent by the Devil to frustrate the efforts of the young Theodore Sykeotes to devote himself to God. At the age of twelve, his protector St. George took him to a chapel shortly after the boy recovered from the bubonic plague. On the way there, demons began pouncing on him like wolves[1317] and other wild beasts, but St. George drove them away with his staff and cleared the way to the holy place.[1318] Later in his life, Theodore traveled to the chapel of the Holy Mother of God in Sozopolis (in central Asia Minor, near Amorion). During the trip, the innkeeper Ferentinus invited him to spend the night in his roadhouse and bless the household. When the holy man arrived, he found the landlord lying half-dead on a bed, his face stretched unnaturally like a dog's snout. With great difficulty, Ferentinus told him that, as he stood outside the inn, a black dog came to him, curled its lips back, and bared its teeth menacingly. Against his will, Ferentinus made the same facial expression. The creature disappeared, but he ran a fever, and his face remained stretched back and deformed. Theodore immediately

---

[1314] For the main events in the *Life* of St. Symeon the Holy Fool, see Part One, Chapter 2, §1.
[1315] Symeon the Holy Fool, 83.19–23.
[1316] Symeon the Holy Fool, 83.27–85.
[1317] Though a complex mythological and folkloric image, this animal appears as a demonic image in the Byzantine hagiography of the period under study only very rarely. See Patriarch Nikephoros, §71, where Ignatios the Deacon emphasizes that the wolf is not among Christ's creatures (οὐ γὰρ τῶν Χριστοῦ θρεμμάτων); Gregory of Dekapolis, §41.2ff, where the Devil visits Gregory in Thessalonica as a wolf.
[1318] Theodore Sykeotes, §8.10–27.

felt the demonic presence, performed the necessary rituals, and successfully rid his host of the influence of the evil spirit.[1319]

No hagiographical text mentions a doglike demon from the early seventh to the late tenth century. However, possessed persons, especially victims of the demon of fornication, are often described as barking like a dog. This literary motif is relatively common in the *Lives* of St. Anastasios of Persia (seventh century), St. Ioannikios the Great (ninth century), St. Sabbas the Younger (tenth century), and St. Auxentios the Great (eleventh century).[1320]

Without directly mentioning a demon, the black dog appears in the *Life* of St. Michael Maleinos. Probably in 914, during the preparations for a military campaign against the Bulgarian tsar Symeon, pious people went to the holy man and asked him to foretell the outcome of the impending war. The man of God suddenly burst into tears and moaned bitterly, then described to them his vision. He had seen a vast field where two armies faced each other, one clad in white, the other entirely in black. Suddenly, two giant dogs emerged from each side. The black dog tore the white one to pieces and devoured it. After finishing his story, Michael warned his visitors that the terrible wrath of God would quickly come upon the Romans, and the Bulgarians would win the decisive battle. The ominous prophecy proved true.[1321]

5. Insects

Insect-like demons are extremely rare in Byzantine hagiography; and, of these, only the **wasp** appears more than once. As is evident from the *Life* of St. Eustratius of Agauros, its function is to punish the sinners. According to this text, in the first half of the ninth century, the abbot of the

---

[1319] Theodore Sykeotes, §§106 and 109.
[1320] Anastasios of Persia, *Encomion by George Pisides*, §47.10–15; Ioannikios (*Peter*), §27 and Ioannikios (*Sabbas*), §22, where a young girl is possessed by the demon of Fornication; Sabbas the Younger, §19.18ff, where the demon yells obscenities through his victim, as if barking; Auxentios, §16.10, where a body-loving demon possesses a woman, and she barks instead of talking.
[1321] Michael Maleinos, §20.

monastery of Agauros in southern Bithynia sent the monk Timothy to pick grapes in the vineyard. One night the young man heard banging on the fence. Supposing a thief was trying to rob the garden, he went to check but was fiercely attacked by a swarm of wasp-like demons. Unable to withstand their furious onslaught, the monk rushed back to the monastery, begging Eustratius for help. The abbot worriedly asked him if the wasps had entered his mouth. When Timothy answered that only his head and face were affected, the Saint grabbed him by the hair, knocked him down, and read him a long prayer. Finally, he struck him in the stomach, chest, and shins with his heel. After performing this operation, he told the monk that he was free from the harmful influence of the wasp-like demons that had attacked him so unexpectedly.[1322]

The story of the unfortunate monk Timothy is interesting not only for the rare form chosen by the demons but also for the cruel ritual of exorcism performed on him. Eustratius does not use the usual means of expelling evil spirits. He does not anoint the victim with consecrated oil or bless him. In his view, the wasps did not attack the monk by accident. They punished him for his sins, and the exorcism had to be a punishment that would deliver Timothy from what drove him to sin.

Around 970, another swarm of wasp-like demons attacked the workers hired by St. Nikon Metanoeite to build a church in Sparta. When they lifted a large stone, the evil spirits emerged from underneath and began to sting them mercilessly. St. Nikon managed to heal the victims quickly with a prayer and the sign of the cross, cursing the sinister creatures and sending them screaming to hell.[1323]

Mosquito-like demons are mentioned only in the short Synaxarion *Life* of St. Thomas Dephourkinos, who lived in the late ninth and early tenth centuries. While praying, the holy man had to endure the attacks of the Devil and his servants. The Evil One sent swarms of gnats (τούτῳ

[1322] Eustratios of Agauros, §27.
[1323] Nikon Metanoeite, §36.

πλῆθος ἐπιρρίπτει κωνώπων) against him. The insects entered his mouth and caused him unbearable pain, yet he did not stop praying.[1324]

As mentioned above, according to the anonymous text "Escape from the Abominable and Unclean Gyllou" (Ἀποστροφὴ τῆς μιαρᾶς καὶ ἀκαθάρτου Γυλλοῦς),[1325] the sinister witch Gello could take the form of a fly. In the hagiography of the period under study, however, fly-like demons occur only in the early *Life* of St. Theodore Sykeotes as personifications of death and decay. According to the text, a swarm of demons emerged from an ancient pagan tomb and attacked the population around the village of Bouzaion in the province of Gordiana in Asia Minor.[1326] When St. Theodore delivered the people from this plague, the evil spirits took the form of flies and returned to their former abode of ancient bones. The Saint instructed the villagers to bury the grave along with the demons, and then he sealed it with prayer.[1327]

The **beetle** is only mentioned as a demonic incarnation in the *Life* of St. Luke of Steiris (late tenth century). A *most bitter demon* (δαίμονι ἁλοὺς πικροτάτῳ) tormented a poor native of Euboea, and the man went to the tomb of the Saint for help. In the meantime, the *kommerkiarios*[1328] Christopher arrived at the monastery to sleep near the holy relics. Abhorred by the prospect of sharing lodgings during the night with the villager, he insisted that the monks move him to another place. They obeyed, and the high-ranking official was left alone at the tomb. The Euboean felt forgotten by the Saint's mercy, but Luke appeared to him in a dream displaying a bright and benevolent face. Calling him by his name, he ordered him to open his mouth, poked inside, and pulled out a

---

[1324] Thomas Dephourkinos, 295ff.
[1325] "Escape from the Abominable and Unclean Gyllou", 574.
[1326] For its location, see Festugière, *Vie de Théodore de Sykéôn*, 199; William Ramsay, *The Historical Geography of Asia Minor* [Royal Geographical Society. Supplementary Papers, vol. 4] (London, 1890), 246.
[1327] Theodore Sykeotes, §43.53–61.
[1328] In the eighth and ninth centuries, the *kommerkiarios* (Lat. *commerciarius*) was a senior official in charge of the state food warehouses. On this figure, see Nikolas Oikonomides, "Silk Trade and Production in Byzantium from the Sixth to the Ninth Century: The Seals of Kommerkiarioi", *Dumbarton Oaks Papers* 40 (1986): 33–53.

single black hair with a beetle hanging from it. At the end of the story, the Saint explained to the villager that the insect symbolized the abomination of the Devil, and the hair was the disease itself.[1329]

6. Plants

In Late Antiquity, Christian authors inherited and reflected the animism and superstitions of the pre-Christian period and believed that demons, like the ancient nymphs, could possess both living creatures and inanimate objects.[1330] In the fourth century, Eusebius of Caesarea mentioned trees speaking with female voices,[1331] and in the *Life* of St. Nicholas of Sion, written around the same period, a powerful evil spirit possessed a giant cypress tree and murdered all who came near. When the Saint cut down the tree, the demon pushed it over the gathered crowd, and only God's mercy saved the people.[1332] The situation changed drastically after the sixth century and the relative homogenization of the Orthodox conceptual and dogmatic system. Demons that took the form of plants were extremely rare in hagiography. The earliest mention of such an evil spirit during the period under study comes from the *Roman Miracle of St. Anastasios of Persia*. The demon who possessed the noble Roman nun in the autumn of 713 explains to the assembled monks that the girl's former fiancé had captured and bound him by magic in a fig leaf.[1333] More than a century later, a friend of St. Eustratios of Agauros bought an estate around Prousa and had to build additional facilities there. He hired a

---

[1329] Luke of Steiris, §95.
[1330] Vakaloudi, *Magic*, 83
[1331] Eusebius Caesariensis, "Contra Hieroclem", ed. Carl Kayser, *Flavii Philostrati opera*, vol. 1 (Hildesheim: Olms, 1964), §34.4ff.
[1332] Nicholas of Sion, §§16–18; Eleonora Kountoura-Galaki", "Two-way Relationships of an Obscure and Prominent Saint: The Case of Saint Nicholas", in *Heroes and the Nameless, Obscure and Famous on the Fringes of the History of Art* [Greek: Ελεονώρα Κουνδούρα-Γαλάκη, "Αμφίδρομες σχέσεις αφανούς και επιφανούς αγίου: η περίπτωση του αγίου Νικολάου", in *Ήρωες και ανώνυμοι, αφανείς και επώνυμοι στις παρυφές της ιστορίας και της τέχνης*] (Athens: The National Hellenic Research Foundation, 2006), 76.
[1333] Anastasios of Persia, *Roman Miracle*, §6.4–8.

team of workers and seventy oxen to carry a massive tree from a port called "Katabolai"[1334] to his property, but they were blocked by demonic influence (ἐκ διαβολικῆς ἐνεργείας) during the trip and could not move the tree for seven days. The man visited the holy abbot and asked him for help. Eustratius made the sign of the cross over the tree, and suddenly the oxen were set free from the evil power.[1335]

Demon-possessed plants occur twice in the *Life* of St. Michael Maleinos (894–July 12, 961). At noon on a summer day, the Saint had stopped to rest under a tree during one of his trips. A poor peasant approached him and offered three delicious pears. The holy man ate them gladly and asked where they came from. The man replied that the fruits were from his orchard, which gave him his livelihood. However, a terrible misfortune then befell him: out of envy, a demon had possessed the pear tree, and it had stopped bearing fruit. Michael managed to drive away the evil spirit through prayer.[1336] In the second story, the evil spirit used a tree to punish sinful behavior. Michael, then abbot of a monastery in Bithynia,[1337] sent a novice named Luke to bring timber for the construction of a new church. The young man was obviously unhappy with the task, and Michael warned him of the spiritual and practical harm that discontent could bring. The novice ignored the admonition, and a powerful demon came to punish his annoyance and disobedience along the way. A great log fell upon him from the carriage, threatening him with a violent and painful death. Michael miraculously became aware of what had happened and sent a servant to free Luke.[1338]

7. Conclusion

The hagiographical image of the anthropomorphic demon includes certain typical and standard elements that sharply distinguish it from the

---

[1334] On "Katabolai" or "Katabolos", see Part Four, Chapter 2, §1.3.
[1335] Eustratios of Agauros, §19.
[1336] Michael Maleinos, §19.
[1337] The Lavra, founded by Michael Maleinos, was located on Mount Kyminas in Bithynia. Michael remained its abbot from *c.* 925 until his death on July 12, 961.
[1338] Michael Maleinos, §22.

normal human body and norms of behavior. Some of these features also affect the descriptions of possessed persons. The evil spirit's material body is always "polarized", grotesquely deformed, dark or black, shaggy, giant or dwarfish, with bloodshot eyes and puffy lips, a voice heavy with anger and other emotions, foul-smelling, dressed in rags or else in gold and silk. Unlike its "colleague" in modern novels and movies, it seldom hides behind beautiful forms to seduce people susceptible to sin and mislead them. Excessive emotion and irrationality define the demon's behavior, making it the exact opposite of the philosophical and rhetorical concept of moderation and temperance that defined socially acceptable conduct. The overall polarization of Evil's appearance paved the way for propaganda using the features mentioned above as tools in ideological, political, and religious struggles.

The most typical demonic image, whose roots can be traced to various literary and mythological traditions, is undoubtedly that of the "Ethiopian". Unfortunately, the black African man's dark skin and the prejudices inherited from the Greco-Roman world make him a convenient personification of death, disease, and violence. The discriminatory attitudes associated with the "Ethiopian" find considerably more fertile ground in popular hagiographical literature than in theological treatises directed at more educated audiences.

Some other demonic images are relatively less common. Demonic armies, their leaders and kings, often parodied and ridiculed, usually frighten rather than inflict actual physical harm. While the authors use actual military terms to describe the angelic armies, the Devil's troops are usually defined by the archaic term *phalanxes* (φάλαγγες), which reinforces the idea of their dangerous "otherness".

Despite the rich literary and mythological tradition behind the image of the female demon, Byzantine hagiographers rarely mention it. The wicked witch Gello, the descendant of various Near Eastern deities (the Hebrew Lilith, the Sumerian Abzu), is perceived by theologians and hagiographers alike as a diabolical superstition rather than an actual evil spirit. Demons that seduce their victims are almost absent from the saints' *Lives* of the period under study, and there is no mention of sexual intercourse with an evil spirit. The female demon-temptress has no material body: she is only a vision meant to arouse wicked thoughts.

The hagiographers of the period under study predominantly exploit zoomorphic images occurring both in the Greco-Roman mythological and literary tradition and in biblical texts. Authors of the iconoclastic and post-iconoclastic periods avoid referring to a wide variety of evil spirits in animal form, giving little information about actual popular beliefs during this period. The tendency towards unification and standardization of storylines and motifs is evident both in the Constantinopolitan anti-iconoclastic texts dedicated to the martyrs of Orthodoxy, and in provincial hagiography, especially the hagiographical school of Mount Olympus in Bithynia. The *Lives* of St. Ioannikios the Great, St. Eustratios of Agauros, and St. Peter of Atroa provide relatively more information about the folklore of the period. However, this information (with few exceptions) mainly concerns one particular demonic image, the dragon.

Byzantine southern Italy and Greece show significant generic differences compared to the hagiographic schools of the ninth century. *Lives* of the saints who lived in the late ninth and tenth centuries, such as St. Elias Speleotes, St. Sabbas the Younger, St. Phantinos the Younger, St. Luke of Steiris, and St. Nikon Metanoeite, exploit a variety of zoomorphic images like bats and ravens.

In the Late Antique hierarchies of demons, and according to the treatises of Michael Psellus (eleventh century) and Pseudo-Psellus (thirteenth century), spirits of air and fire constitute the two highest categories of divine demons, able to assume all sorts of fantastic forms. The Greco-Roman and Near Eastern mythological traditions are also full of strange zoomorphic, anthropomorphic, and mixed creatures. However, Byzantine hagiographers of the seventh to the tenth centuries are surprisingly laconic about such images and tend to avoid them as mere superstitions or else identify them as ordinary animals.

Part Four
THE DEMONIC SPACE

CHAPTER 1
THE INVISIBLE WORLD

1. Humankind besieged

In the first part of the present study, we presented and analyzed the Pythagorean (or Neo-Pythagorean)[1339] and Neoplatonic[1340] concepts of the dangerous aerial regions inhabited by various immortal demons or demonic souls. This idea, however controversial from a theological point of view, remains within the conceptual frame of Orthodox Christianity as an element of the world's quadripartite structure.[1341] God's kingdom, Heaven (οὐρανός, οὐρανοί), or the Ether, is spread on top of the universe — glorious and perfect, like the realm of Plato's transcendental *eidē*. Only the righteous souls are admitted there to unite with God and live eternally in absolute peace and harmony. Below it is the air (ἀήρ), or the sky, where the demons of various mortal sins scrutinize the souls of the dead for crimes committed during their earthly existence and block the access of the impure to God's Kingdom on their path either through the so-called "aerial tollhouses" (τελώνια) or to climb the "Ladder to Heaven". The visible world of the living is enclosed between two dangerous demonic spaces, the sky above and the kingdom of Satan in the depths of the Earth. In the latter terrible place, also called "Hell" (Κόλασις), "Hades" (Ἅιδης) or, less often, "Tartaros" (Τάρταρος), demons place sinners in "temporary custody" to be punished for their offences and await the Creator's ultimate decision on Judgment Day.

The quadripartite structure, apparently inherited from Neoplatonism and other philosophical and religious teachings and relatively widespread both in theological works and hagiographical texts of the

---

[1339] See *Diogenis Laertii vitae philosophorum*, VIII.32.1-4.
[1340] See *Porphyrii de philosophia*, 147.5-11 and 148.4-149.3; Jamblique, *Les mystères d'Égypte*, II.7. (§85.4); *Procli Diadochi in Platonis rem publicam commentarii*, 2: 168.12-14 and 180.8.
[1341] See, e.g., Eph. 2:1ff and 6:12; Athenagoras, "Legatio sive Supplicatio", §25.1; Antony, §28.13-16.

period under study, is by no means elevated to the status of official Orthodox doctrine. It coexists peacefully with the idea of the "River of Fire", which reminds us of the ancient River Styx. A narrow bridge or some more complex device allows the few righteous souls to pass over to the other bank and enter the Kingdom of God, but the sinners who fail to cross are doomed to burn in eternal flames, utterly devoid of light. These two seemingly controversial descriptions occur in the hagiographers of the ninth and tenth centuries, and every author seems free to choose between them. This peculiar "overlap" is explicable if we perceive them not as theological concepts but as mere metaphors designed to represent the trials and punishment of the human soul after death.

2. Trial: the demons of the air

In Byzantine hagiography, the aerial regions appear as dangerous places inhabited by the evil spirits of various deadly sins, who rigorously examine the human soul after death and prohibit its admission to Heaven. In his *Life* of St. John the Merciful (†619), Leontios of Neapolis describes the *aerial sea* in the following manner:

> There are many winds in this place, demonic storms, waves, rocks, pirates, great darkness, and terrible cold. Many beasts pursue [the passerby], and many torrents pour upon him, threatening to throw him into the abysses of the earth's depths. Great fear and great terror reign in this sea of air, and great are the dangers in it.[1342]

The author envisions the air as a place continually buffeted by storms where terrible pirates roam — the demons that test and torment the human soul that has left its material body. Should it not pass the examination, the winds and torrents cast it into Hell.

[1342] John the Merciful, 396.30–36: πολλοὶ γὰρ ἄνεμοι ἐν αὐτοῖς, πολλαὶ σπιλάδες δαιμονικαί, πολλὰ κύματα, πολλὰ βράχη, πολλοὶ πειραταί, πολὺς γνόφος, πολὺς ὁ χείμων, πολλὰ τὰ παρακολουθοῦντα θηρία, πολλοὶ οἱ καταποντίζοντες σίφωνες καὶ κατασπῶντες εἰς τὰ κατώτατα τῆς γῆς, πολὺς ὁ φόβος, πολὺς ὁ τρόμος, πολὺς ὁ κίνδυνος τοῦ πελάγους τοῦ ἀέρος τούτου.

The space of the air appears as the demons' realm in several hagiographical texts. In the *Roman Miracle of St. Anastasios of Persia*, which refers to the events of October–November 713, the demon vehemently denies that the *Nazarene* (i.e., Christ) has any authority over the air and earth and claims that they are entirely under his control.[1343] This concept of the complete dominion of the demons over the air provokes a reaction from more theologically educated hagiographers. In the *Life* of St. Symeon Stylites the Younger, the anonymous author claims that the power of the evil spirits and their master over the world below Heaven is deceptive and imaginary. Describing one of his visions, the Saint says that he *saw the ineffable power of God in every part of the air and of the earth, and no place was abandoned by His fearsome might*.[1344] The same author refutes the common perceptions of God's withdrawal from the space between Heaven and Earth and elsewhere. He stresses that the heavenly powers[1345] and the throne of God[1346] stand *in the air* (ἐν τῷ ἀέρι). In one of his visions, the Saint sees a ship with two angels hovering over the sea near Seleucia's harbor;[1347] in another, innumerable angels appear in the sky.[1348] The Holy Spirit descends together with the angels as if from the air (ὥσπερ ἐκ τοῦ ἀέρος) to deliver Symeon's home district in Antioch from the plague in the late 550s or early 560s.[1349]

By God's will, a few holy people can separate their souls from their material bodies while alive and travel through the fearsome domains above and below the Earth. The so-called *ecstasis* (ἔκστασις) is a relatively rare literary motif and appears mainly in tenth-century texts, like the *Vision of the monk Cosmas* and the *Life* of St. Phantinus the Younger. Eve-

---

[1343] Anastasios of Persia, *Roman Miracle*, §5.14ff: ἐμοῦ δέ εἰσιν ὅ τε ἀὴρ καὶ ἡ γῆ.
[1344] Symeon Stylites the Younger, §104.20–26. The event took place on Mount Admirable in the early 550s.
[1345] Symeon Stylites the Younger, §104.32ff.
[1346] Symeon Stylites the Younger, §104.35.
[1347] Symeon Stylites the Younger, §104.56–58.
[1348] Symeon Stylites the Younger, §129.123ff.
[1349] Symeon Stylites the Younger, §126.19ff. Van den Ven (*La Vie ancienne*, 1: 119*ff) dates the event to 555, 558 or 560.

ryone's soul must make a fearful journey through the air to reach the Kingdom of Heaven, where various demons scrutinize it for deadly sins. The concept of the so-called "tollhouses", where this examination takes place, is one of the most interesting and complex phenomena in the Byzantine hagiography of the period under study. The most detailed and vivid description comes from the *Life* of St. Basil the Younger, parts of which were highly popular in the medieval Slavic world. This text, however, is nothing but a single link in a long chain gathering various literary, mythological, and philosophical traditions. The journey of the soul appears, vanishes, and reappears in different epochs where it fulfills many discursive functions in particular political and social contexts.

2.1. The "tollhouses"

The term "tollhouse" (τελώνιον) originally meant a customs post where fees were collected from passing merchants and travelers.[1350] Such stations were scattered throughout the empire and especially in the "economic region" of Constantinople.[1351] The assiduous tax collector, or *telonarches* (τελωνάρχαι), who scrutinized each passer-by and only let him pass if he was able to pay the fee, became a fearsome figure and a suitable incarnation and metaphor for the demons responsible for the examination of the human soul before being granted permission to enter the Heavenly Kingdom. This explanation of the gradual semantic conversion of the word τελώνιον from a mere administrative term to a complex religious notion over the centuries is clear but not particularly exhaustive. In the New Testament, Jesus Christ commands the tax collector Matthew to follow Him and saves him from a sinful life.[1352] This well-known biblical story created the conditions for a Christian reworking of various ideas and literary motifs circulating in the Late Antique

---

[1350] See for example *Strabonis geographica*, XVI.1.27.25; cf. *LSJ*, s.v. "τελώνιον".
[1351] On the tollhouses in Constantinople and Abydos from the eighth to the ninth centuries, and the *kommerkiarioi* who were responsible for them, see Nikolaos Oikonomides, "The Role of the Byzantine State in the Economy", in *The Economic History of Byzantium: From the Seventh through the Fifteenth Century*, ed. Angeliki Laiou [Dumbarton Oaks Research Library and Collection 39], vol. 3 (Washington, D.C.: Dumbarton Oaks, 2002), 986ff.
[1352] Mat., 9:9.

world. In the following centuries, the word τελώνιον gradually lost its original meaning and came to signify only the sinister tollhouses in the air. By contrast, the new term τελωνεῖον appeared to denote the customs houses of the earthly world.[1353]

2.1.1. Origins

The concept of the dangerous aerial tollhouses can be traced to two different literary, mythological, and philosophical traditions, namely the afterlife journey of the soul and "mortal sins".[1354] The combination of these two elements does not seem to have taken place earlier than the second century A.D., when the idea of the voyage through the realms (κλίματα) of the seven gods-planets became part of numerous systematized religious and philosophical systems.[1355] In the following pages, we will propose a reconstruction of both traditions and analyze how they blended in the *Life* of St. Basil the Younger.

We can only speculate about the origin of the millennia-old concept of transgressions that bring doom to the human soul. In the famous chapter 125 of the Egyptian Book of the Dead, the soul must stand the trial of the forty-two gods, each responsible for a particular sin. The diseased person has to exonerate themselves before each of these supreme judges by pronouncing a particular formula:

> O Usekh-nemmit, comer forth from Anu, I have not committed sin.
> O Fenti, comer forth from Khemenu, I have not robbed.
> O Neha-hau, comer forth from Re-stau, I have not killed men.

[1353] *Suidae lexicon*, ed. Ada Adler [Lexicographi Graeci, vol. 1], Part. 4: Π-Ψ (Munich and Leipzig: Saur, 2001), s.v. T.291. In modern Greek, there is a sharp distinction between the words τελώνιο and τελωνείο.

[1354] For general information on mortal sins in the Christian tradition, see Morton Bloomfield, "The Origin of the Concept of the Seven Cardinal Sins", *Harvard Theological Review* 34, no. 2 (April 1941): 127ff; Stewart, *Demons and the Devil*, 143ff; Guillou, *Le Diable Byzantin*, 15ff.

[1355] Bloomfield, "The Origin of the Concept", 121-25; Murray, *Five Stages*, 146. On the *klimatarch* demons, see Vakaloudi, *Magic*, 109. On astrological influences on ancient philosophy in general, see John Burnet, *Early Greek Philosophy* (London: A & C. Black, 1920), 12ff, 34, 43-45, 82ff, 169ff.

O Set-qesu, comer forth from Hensu, I have not lied.
O Uammti, comer forth from Khebt, I have not defiled any man's wife. etc.[1356]

The Book of the Dead took its final form between 663 and 525 BC, and we still require concrete proof that the text directly influenced the Hebrew and Greco-Roman concept of the deadly sins. However, it suggests that the idea itself has accompanied humankind for a long time.

Before Evagrius of Pontus, considered the first Christian author to compile a comprehensive list of mortal sins, various other texts of this kind circulated in the Hellenistic and especially the late Roman world. The Testament of Reuben (*c.* 109–106 B.C.) mentions the seven spirits of Evil, namely Fornication, Gluttony, Belligerence, Vanity, Pride, Falsehood, and Injustice, each of them associated with a particular human sense (sight, hearing, smell, taste, sexual pleasure).[1357] Almost the whole text deals with the spirit of Fornication, advising men not to succumb to female charm and beauty, since women were considered more prone to sin than men.[1358]

Less than eighty years later, in the early 30s B.C., the Roman poet Horace mentions the eight diseases (*morbi*) of the human soul, i.e., Greed (*avaritia*), Lust (*cupido*), Love of Glory (*laudis amor*), Envy (being *invidus*), Anger (being *iracundus*), Sloth (being *iners*), Inebriation (being *vinosus*), and Debauchery (being *amator*).[1359] Of course, for Horace, these are vices and not religious sins. The poet emphasizes the importance of the "social diseases" of Greed and Sloth, which lead to one's social destruction.

[1356] *The Ancient Egyptian Book of the Dead*, ed. and trans. by Wallis Budge and Epiphanius Wilson (New York: Quarto Publishing Group, 2016), 26.

[1357] "The Testament of Reuben, the First-Born Son of Jacob and Leah", ed. Robert Charles, *The Apocrypha and Pseudepigrapha of the Old Testament in English*, vol. 2 (Oxford, Clarendon Press, 1913), §2.1 and §3.2–9; see Bloomfield, "The Origin of the Concept", 123. The Testament of Reuben is part of the collection of Hebrew *pseudepigrapha* called *The Testament of the Twelve Patriarchs*.

[1358] "The Testament of Reuben", §5.

[1359] *The Epistles of Horace*, ed. Augustus Wilkins (London and New York: Macmillan, 1888), I.1.33–40. Cf. Bloomfield, "The Origin of the Concept", 123.

THE INVISIBLE WORLD 395

In the first two centuries A.D., in the cosmopolitan world of the vast Roman Empire, the interest of various religious and philosophical movements in both astrology and the afterlife journey of the soul grew enormously. Proclus Diadochus (412–485) says that after separation from the body, the soul must pass through the *demonic space* (δαιμόνιος τόπος), the dreaded and dangerous *air* (ἀήρ), to reach the realm of the gods in Heaven. Nevertheless, the Neoplatonic philosopher, with his magnificent classical education, shows contempt for astrology and especially the *ridiculous beliefs* of the Neopythagorean Numenius (second century A.D.), who capriciously twisted Plato's words with his *monstrous tales* (τερατολογίαι):

> He told many other wondrous tales of souls leaping from the tropics to the equator and then moving [back] to the tropics. In recounting these things, he himself jumps from one to the other and stitches together Plato's words indiscriminately...[1360]

This fragment of Proclus' commentaries on Plato's *Republic* provides valuable insights into the beliefs associated with the soul's afterlife journey in Late Antiquity, greatly influenced by contemporary astrology. The anonymous author of *Poimandres*, the first book of the *Corpus Hermeticum* (first century), describes the soul's passage through the realms of the seven heavenly bodies in more detail. On this journey, one is gradually purified of all passions and affections; if the purification is successful, one reaches the so-called *ogdoad nature* (ογδοατική φύση), the Demiurge himself.[1361]

The journey of the soul through the realms of the seven "planets" (πλανῆτες) was also typical in Mithraism. Origen (c. 185–254) reports that, according to Celsus, the symbol of this journey in the Mithraic mysteries was the so-called "ladder with seven gates" (κλῖμαξ ἑπτάπυλος). Each gate was made of a different metal (lead, tin, copper/bronze, iron, alloy, silver, gold), and behind each lay the dominions of a planet-god

---

[1360] *Procli Diadochi in Platonis rem publicam commentarii*, 2: 129.8–13.
[1361] "Poimandres", ed. Arthur Nock and André-Jean Festugière, *Corpus Hermeticum* (Paris, 1972), §24–26. Cf. Bloomfield, "The Origin of the Concept", 125.

(Cronus, Aphrodite, Zeus, Hermes, Ares, Moon, Sun). After the successful ascent of the ladder and passage through these ominous realms, the soul reached the Eighth Gate (the so-called Ὀγδόη),[1362] where it ceased to be in the control of the Seven and of Ananke (Necessity) and was free to unite with the Demiurge.[1363]

Despite his contempt for Mithraic superstitions, Origen attempted to adapt this idea of the afterlife journey to the Christian theological system. His own version of the concept is strongly dualistic, and the planet-archons, familiar from *Poimandres*, became the evil demon-personifications of sins in his *Homilies*. He describes them as follows:

> The moment the soul separates from the body, it is encountered by the demon-sins, the hostile forces, the spirits of the air. If they detect any of their own deeds and acts in it, these spirits seek to draw it to themselves. Thus, to every soul, as it passes out of this world, comes one of the rulers of this world,[1364] of the powers of the air, and they seek to find something of their own in it. Whoever finds greed, the soul is his. He who finds desire for riches, envy, or any other quality peculiar to himself, is also entitled to take it away.[1365]

Origen is the first Christian author known to combine the concept of mortal sins and the soul's afterlife journey. Notably, the Christian Origen shows the same contempt for astrology as the Neoplatonist Proclus did a few centuries later. While accepting the hitherto pagan idea of the soul's wanderings and trials in the air and enriching it with Christian

---

[1362] Origéne, *Contre Celse*, ed. Marcel Borret, vol. 3: *Livres V et VI* [Sources Chrétiennes 147] (Paris: Éditions de Cerf, 1969), VI.22.1-20; Cosmas Hierosolymitanus, "Collectio et Interpretatio Historiarum quarum meminit divus Gregorius in carminibus suis, tum ex Scriptura tum ex profanes Poetis atque Scriptoribus", MPG, vol. 38 (Paris, 1862), 461ff; Eusebius Caesariensis, *Die Praeparatio Evangelica*, XI.24.9-10. See also Arthur Nock, "Studies in the Graeco-Roman Beliefs of the Empire", *Journal of Hellenic Studies* 45, no. 1 (1925): 98ff., and n. 103 on the symbolism of the ladder in Mithraism and early Christianity; Burkert, *Antike Mysterien*, 70ff.

[1363] Murray, *Five Stages*, 147.

[1364] Cf. Eph. 6:12.

[1365] Origenes, "Commentaria in Psalmos", in MPG, vol. 12 (Paris, 1862), 1366B-C.

demonological elements,[1366] he apparently avoided the astrological beliefs typical of Hermeticism and Mithraism.

The afterlife journey appears in Judaic literature as well. Unlike Origen, the *Testament of Solomon* (second to fourth centuries) emphasizes the astrological element in the concept. According to its anonymous author, seven beautiful female demons present themselves before the throne of King Solomon. They are the seven Elements or Mistresses of darkness: Deceit (Ἀπάτη), Enmity (Ἔρις), Klotho (Κλωθώ), Inebriation (Ζάλη), Delusion (Πλάνη), Might (Δύναμις), and The Most Evil (Κακίστη). Each has her star in the sky, influencing human life differently.[1367]

In the fourth century AD, the afterlife journey in the demonic realms was already widespread in almost all of the most influential philosophical and religious movements: Hermeticism, Neopythagoreanism, Neoplatonism, Mithraism, and, through Origen, Christianity.[1368] Though the latter was later condemned as a heretic, the ground was already prepared for the orthodox Christian version of the concept to develop.

2.1.2. St. Athanasios the Great, St. Ephraem Syrus, and St. Cyril of Alexandria

In the fourth and early fifth centuries, mortal sins were a common idea among Christian writers. However, it was one rarely associated with the afterlife journey of the soul and was entirely devoid of astrological elements. In other words, Evagrius of Pontus and Bishop John Cassian were trying to create a Christian version of these beliefs, stripped of all pagan religious and philosophical concepts. The lists of deadly sins in this period are almost identical. Evagrius of Pontus (345/346–399), who wrote the extensive and popular treatise *On the Eight Spirits of Evil* (Περί

[1366] Origen is considered one of the fathers of Christian demonology. Since he was later condemned as a heretic, some of his views were considered incompatible with Nicene Orthodoxy. On this point, see Guillou, *Le Diable Byzantin*, 8–14.

[1367] *The Testament of Solomon*, 32–34 and 51.

[1368] Cf. *Ioannis Lydi liber de mensibus*, ed. Richard Wünsch (Leipzig: Teubner, 1898), IV.25.12–18.

τῶν ὀκτὼ πνευμάτων τῆς πονηρίας) in the third quarter of the fourth century, refers to Gluttony (γαστριμαργία), Fornication (πορνεία), Avarice (φιλαργυρία), Anger (ὀργή), Despair (λύπη), Sloth (ἀκηδία), Vainglory (κενοδοξία), and Pride (ὑπερηφανεία).[1369] The list drawn up by St. John Cassian (c. 360-425) includes six sins (*gastrimargia, fornicatio, phylargyria, ira, tristitia*, and *acedia*), which were connected with each other (*inter se cognatione, et ut ita dixerim, concateatione connexa sunt*), while another two sins, Vainglory (*cenodoxia*) and Pride (*superbia*), were described separately since, according to him, they usually occurred when one had already overcome the other six.[1370]

Evagrius of Pontus and John Cassian chose not to follow Origen's path and mentioned neither the afterlife journey nor the role of demons as judges of human souls. However, other Christian authors proved bolder in borrowing pagan concepts and including them in the Christian conceptual framework. Two texts, one theological and one hagiographical, attest to this.

The *Life* of St. Anthony the Great, written by St. Athanasios of Alexandria, was one of the most influential hagiographical texts of all time. Generations of young Christians followed the example of the Egyptian hermit, and their biographers used the same rhetorical and literary devices (motifs, images, plots) as the great Patriarch of Alexandria to describe their struggles with demons and passions, including the soul's journeys and trials in the air. Once, Athanasios reports, shortly before noon, Antonius felt his soul separate from his body and rise into the air, following some vague figures: his guardian angels. On his way through the air, various bitter and terrible beings tried to stop the Saint. They called him to account for all the sins he had committed, and his companions argued fiercely with them. At last, the demons agreed that Antony was cleansed of all his sins by taking the monastic vows and let him pass

---

[1369] Evagrius Ponticus, "De octo spiritibus malitiae", in MPG, vol. 79 (Paris, 1865), 1045-64. See also Bloomfield, "The Origin of the Concept", 127ff; Stewart, *Demons and the Devil*, 143ff; Guillou, *Le Diable Byzantin*, 15ff; Angelidi, "The Life of St. Basil", 184.

[1370] Joannes Cassianus, "Collationum XXIV collectio in tres partes divisa", in MPL, vol. 49.1 (Paris, 1846), 621ff.

THE INVISIBLE WORLD   399

through their realms unharmed.¹³⁷¹ There is no hint of astrology and planets in this comparatively brief description, free of any details. Unlike in Origen, the human soul is not alone on its dangerous and fateful journey. Guardian angels appear to protect it.

Around the middle of the fourth century, about the same time that St. Athanasios the Great wrote his *Life* of St. Antony, another prominent theologian described the afterlife journey and the demons of the air. In two of his works, namely *On the Departed in Christ* and *On the Second Coming and the Last Judgment*, St. Ephraem Syrus (c. 306–373) called these sinister evil spirits *tax collectors* (τελώνης) for the first time and described the so-called *death struggle* (ψυχομάχημα).¹³⁷² According to him, when the soul separates from the body for the last time, it observes the corporeal form with disgust as something decayed and foul. The description is approximately the same as that found in St. Athanasios of Alexandria:

> Then the angels take up the soul and pass along with it through the air where the Powers stand, the world-rulers of Evil, our bitter accusers, the dreadful tax collectors, the registrars, and the tax officers. They meet it, rummage through the papers, investigate, and expose the diseased person's sins, committed in youth and old age, willingly or unwillingly, in deeds, words, or thoughts. Great fear comes over the unhappy soul, and great trembling seizes it.¹³⁷³

---

¹³⁷¹ Antony, 934C–936A. Cf. Angelidi, "The Life of St. Basil", 184; Mango, *Empire*, 164; Mango, "Diabolus Byzantinus", 215.

¹³⁷² On the "death struggle" in Byzantine literature and Greek folkore, see Georgios Spyridakis, "The Death Rituals of the Byzantines According to Archeological Sources" [Greek: Γεώργιος Σπυριδάκης, "Τὰ κατὰ τὴν τελευτὴν ἔθιμα τῶν Βυζαντινῶν ἐκ τῶν ἁγιολογικῶν πηγῶν"], *Annuaire de l'association d'études byzantines* [= Ἐπετηρὶς τῆς Ἑταιρίας Βυζαντινῶν Σπουδῶν] 20 (1950): 93–101.

¹³⁷³ Ephraem Syrus, "Sermo de secundo aduentu et iudicio", ed. Kontantinos Frantzolas, *The Works of St. Ephraem Syrus* [Greek: Κωνσταντίνος Φραντζόλας, Ὁσίου Ἐφραίμ τοῦ Σύρου ἔργα], vol. 4 (Thessalonica, 1995), 228.7–229.1: Τότε παραλαμβάνοντες οἱ Ἄγγελοι [καὶ] τὴν ψυχὴν διὰ τοῦ ἀέρος ἀπέρχονται, ἐν ᾧ ἵστανται ἀρχαί, ἐξουσίαι καὶ οἱ κοσμοκράτορες τῶν ἐναντίων δυνάμεων, οἱ πικροὶ ἡμῶν κατήγοροι, οἱ δεινοὶ τελῶναι καὶ λογοθέται καὶ φορολόγοι, ἐν τῷ ἀέρι συναντῶντες, λογοθετοῦντες, ἐξερευνῶντες, προσφέροντες τὰ τοῦ ἀνθρώπου ἁμαρτήματα, τὰ ἐν νεότητι, τὰ ἐν τῷ γήρει, τὰ ἑκούσια, τὰ ἀκούσια, τὰ δι' ἔργων, τὰ διὰ λόγων, τὰ δι' ἐνθυμήσεων. Πολὺς ὁ φόβος ἐκεῖ· πολὺς ὁ τρόμος τῆς ἀθλίας ψυχῆς. There is a similar description in Ephraem Syrus, "Sermo in

Until the fourth century, the afterlife journey among the demons of the air was a relatively rare concept. None of the writers referred to the fate of those who fail the trial, nor did they mention how the soul could escape the ominous judges and what exactly were the mortal transgressions personified by the sinister *tax collectors*. The person who took up the task of elaborating the idea theologically was none other than the great and revered theologian St. Cyril of Alexandria (c. 378–444). The elements of his description would be enriched in the following centuries but were preserved almost with no essential change.

According to St. Cyril, when death approaches, the forces of Good, represented by the angelic armies, and those of Evil, personified by the rulers of darkness, the customs officials, and the registrars of the air, gather around the deathbed. The Saint describes these demons as shadowy (ζοφώδεις) Ethiopians, *the sight of whom alone is more terrible than Hell* (ὧν καὶ αὐτὴ ἡ ἰδέα μόνη χαλεπωτέρα ὑπάρχει πάσης τῆς κολάσεως).[1374] The angels thereupon accompany the soul on its journey to Heaven. In its passage through the air, it is detained for questioning at the tollhouses (τελώνια), each in charge of a particular sin. In the tollhouse of Slander (καταλαλία), the evil officials conduct an investigation for crimes committed with the mouth and the tongue, namely, Falsehood (ψεῦδος), Perjury (ἐπιορκία), Idle Chatter (ἀργολογία, φλυαρία), Food Abuse (γαστριμαργικαὶ παραχρήσεις), Wine Abuse (ἀσωτοποσία οἴνου), Excessive and Indecent Laughter (ἄμετροι καὶ ἀπρεπεῖς γέλωτες), Indecent Kisses (ἄσεμνα καὶ ἀπρεπῆ φιλήματα), and Lewd Songs (ᾄσματα πορνικά). In the second tollhouse, the soul is examined for the crimes performed with the sense of sight, especially Curiosity (τὸ περίεργον) and watching obscene scenes and gestures (ἀπρεπεῖς θέαι, δόλια νεύματα). The third, fourth, and fifth tollhouses are responsible for the offenses

---

eos, qui in Christo obdormierunt", ed. Kontantinos Frantzolas, *The Works of St. Ephraem Syrus* [Greek: Κωνσταντῖνος Φραντζόλας, Ὁσίου Ἐφραὶμ τοῦ Σύρου ἔργα], vol. 6 (Thessalonica, 1995), 105ff.

[1374] On the guardian angels who gather around the deathbed to fight for the salvation of the soul, see Spyridakis, "The Death Rituals", 99ff.

performed by the ears, the nose, and the sense of touch.[1375] The author also mentions the checkpoints of Envy and Jealousy (φθόνος καὶ ζῆλος), Vainglory and Pride (κενοδοξία καὶ ὑπερηφανία), Bitterness and Anger (πικρία καὶ ὀργή), Fornication (πορνεία), Adultery (μοιχεία), Moral Weakness (μαλακία), and Murder and Poisoning (φόνος καὶ φαρμακεία).[1376] The angels, for their part, present the corresponding good deeds, like prayers and singing of the psalms[1377]. If these counter-evidences do not outweigh the sins, the soul hears the words *Let the wicked be removed from here, lest he see the glory of God!* At that moment, the evil Ethiopians are allowed to seize the soul and drag it to its doom and eternal suffering in the dungeons of Hell.[1378]

St. Cyril of Alexandria describes a much larger number of mortal sins than St. Ephraem Syrus, St. Evagrius of Pontus, and St. John Cassian. However, he seldom mentions specific transgressions; instead, as in the *Testament of Reuben*, he groups them into various categories corresponding to the basic human senses and faculties (speech, vision, audition, smell, and so on). The famous theologian also introduces the concept that every sin's "good' counterpart acts to cancel it from the demons' sinister registers.

2.1.3. The early hagiography and St. Anastasios Sinaita

Despite the enormous influence of St. Cyril of Alexandria, the learned theologians of the following centuries preferred to omit the aerial tollhouses, for various reasons. The image of the frightful demons of the air had deep roots in pagan religious and philosophical movements and folklore. Consequently, they were probably considered dangerous and unsuitable for inclusion in official Orthodox dogma — all the more so in a period of intense struggles with all sorts of heresies that weakened the Church. Thus, the Devil and his evil officials in the sky were tacitly condemned by Church authorities to lose all judicial power over the

---

[1375] Cyrillus Alexandrinus. "De exitu animi", 1073–1076.
[1376] Cyrillus Alexandrinus. "De exitu animi", 1076A.
[1377] Cyrillus Alexandrinus. "De exitu animi", 1073C-D, 1075B.
[1378] Cyrillus Alexandrinus. "De exitu animi", 1076C-1077A.

souls of the dead. As mentioned above, the anonymous author of the *Life* of St. Symeon Stylites the Younger even rejects the demons' power over the air itself.

However, the biography of Symeon Stylites the Younger is rather an exception as far as the tollhouses are concerned. Unlike the learned theologians, many other hagiographers in the sixth and seventh centuries, probably influenced by St. Athanasios the Great and St. Cyril of Alexandria, used this widespread idea to make their texts more appealing to a broader audience. However, the descriptions are usually not very detailed.[1379] According to the *Life* of St. John the Merciful, written by Bishop Leontios of Neapolis in the mid-seventh century, at the moment when the soul leaves the body and ascends into the air, squads (τάγματα) of demons meet it:

> When the soul leaves the body, it is met on its ascent from earth to heaven by numerous choirs of demons, each in his division. The chorus of the demons of Pride encounters it and examines whether it has performed any of their deeds. The choir of the spirits of Slander meets it and examines whether it has slandered and not repented. The demons of Fornication meet it higher up and examine it for their habits.[1380]

Like St. Cyril of Alexandria, Leontios does not provide a complete list of deadly sins, giving only a few examples of such transgressions (Pride, Slander, and Fornication) and hinting that there are many others. In addition, he stresses that the angels would not help the soul on its last

---

[1379] See Golinduch, 173.6–10, where the Persian martyr Golinduch-Maria (†July 13, 591) leaves her mortal body, defeats the world-rulers of darkness, passes unhindered through the sky where the master of the air is unable to stop her, and reaches the kingdom of God; George of Choziba, §9.39.27–30.

[1380] John the Merciful, 396.1–8: Ἐξερχομένης τῆς ψυχῆς ἐκ τοῦ σώματος ἀπαντῶσιν αὐτῇ ὡς ἀνέρχεται ἀπὸ τῆς γῆς εἰς τὸν οὐρανὸν χοροὶ χοροὶ δαιμόνων ἕκαστος ἐν τῷ ἰδίῳ τάγματι. ἀπαντᾷ αὐτῇ ὁ χορὸς τῶν δαιμόνων τῆς ὑπερηφανίας, ψηλαφῶσιν αὐτὴν ἐὰν ἔχει τὰ ἔργα αὐτῶν. ἀπαντᾷ ὁ χορὸς τῶν πνευμάτων τῆς καταλαλίας, θεωροῦσιν ἐὰν ποτε κατελάλησεν καὶ οὐ μετενόησεν. ἀπαντῶσιν πάλιν παράνω οἱ δαίμονες τῆς πορνείας, ἐρευνῶσιν ἐὰν εὕρωσιν ἐν αὐτῇ τὰ ἐπιτηδεύματα αὐτῶν.

journey through the air; only its virtues could save it from the *cruel and merciless toll collectors* (ὠμοὶ... καὶ ἄσπλαγχνοι τελῶναι).[1381]

Leontios is less comprehensive in his *Life* of St. Symeon the Fool. According to the text, the Saint prays to God when he senses his mother's death:

> Grant her angels to save[1382] her soul from the evil and merciless spirits and beasts of this air that strive to devour all who pass through them. Send her, O Lord, O Lord, strong guardians to damn every unclean power she meets ...[1383]

Later in the text, the Saint admonishes a high-ranking official who had cheated on his wife:

> Your strength and power are great, but take care of your soul so that you may pass untroubled through the world rulers of this air's darkness.[1384]

The sinister tollhouses are described even more vividly in a hagiographical text of uncertain date, published in 1902 by François Nau. Its Latin title is "De taxeota seu de milite redivivo" ("On the Officer, or the Risen Soldier" — BHG [1318]), and its author is probably Anastasios Sinaita (fl. Between 640 and 700).[1385] The story is set in Carthage and takes place when its Byzantine governor was a patrician named Niketas.

[1381] John the Merciful, 396.9ff; 396.19-22. See Bloomfield, "The Origin of the Concept", 126.

[1382] The verb διασῴζω has two meanings in medieval Greek: *to save* and *to see somebody through*. In this case, both translations are suitable.

[1383] Symeon the Holy Fool, 75.7–11: δὸς αὐτῇ ἀγγέλους διασῴζοντας αὐτῆς τὴν ψυχὴν ἐκ τῶν πνευμάτων καὶ θηρίων τοῦ ἀέρος τούτου τῶν πονηρῶν καὶ ἀνελεημόνων τῶν ἐπιχειρούντων καταπιεῖν πάντας τοὺς δι' αὐτῶν παρερχομένους. ἐξαπόστειλον αὐτῇ, κύριε, κύριε, φύλακας ἰσχυροὺς ἐπιτιμῶντας πάσῃ ἀκαθάρτῳ δυνάμει συναντώσῃ αὐτῇ....

[1384] Symeon the Holy Fool, 101.9–11: ἀλλ' ὅση σοι ἰσχὺς καὶ δύναμις, φρόντισον τῆς οἰκείας σου ψυχῆς, ἵνα ἀχειμάστως τοὺς κοσμοκράτορας τοῦ σκότους τοῦ ἀέρος τούτου διαπεράσαι δυνηθῇς.

[1385] On the authorship of this collection, see François Nau, "Le text grec sur les récits du moine Anastase sur les saints pères du Sinai", *Oriens Christianus* 2 (1902): 59. See Stergios Sakkos, *On the Anastasioses of Sinai* [Greek: Στέργιος Σάκκος, Περὶ Ἀναστασίων Σιναϊτῶν] (Thessalonica, 1964), 174–85; Lambakis, "The Descents into Hell", 50. On St. Anastasios Sinaita, see Krumbacher, *Geschichte der byzantinischen Literatur*, 64–66.

Because of an outbreak of bubonic plague in the city, an anonymous army officer moved with his wife to the suburbs, where he began an adulterous affair with a peasant's wife. Soon, he caught the deadly plague and died, not having enough time to confess his sin. He was given a proper burial in a nearby monastery, but suddenly, while chanting a funeral prayer, the monks heard a voice from the depths of the grave asking them to have mercy on him. They immediately opened the sarcophagus and discovered the soldier sitting inside screaming. At his request, they took him to *the servant of God, Thalassias*.[1386] Four days later, the resurrected man managed to pull himself together and told those present of his death and the subsequent journey of his soul through the air. The story begins as usual: ugly Ethiopians surround the dying man, and *their outer appearance alone is more horrible and tormenting than Hell*.[1387] At this dangerous and frightening moment, his guardian angels approach his deathbed as young men dressed in white. They take his soul into the sky, where it has to pass through the tollhouses (τελονεία [sic!], τελωνεῖα, τελώνια)[1388] run by their evil officials, or "telonarchs", each responsible for a particular sin: Falsehood, Envy, Blasphemy, and so on.[1389] The telonarchs accurately present each of the criminal deeds of the deceased, and the angels counter each accusation with a relevant good deed, which they produce from a bag (βαλάντιον). The good deeds in the bag run out when the gates to the Kingdom of Heaven are already in sight. At that point the party arrives at the tollhouse of Fornication and Adultery, the most difficult trial. The demons charge the soldier with every act he performed since the age of twelve. The angels manage to exonerate him from almost all, arguing that he had confessed his sin and repented. However, because of his sudden death, the deceased was unable to confess his rela-

---

[1386] Anastasios Sinaita, "De taxeota, seu de milite redivivo", ed. François Nau, "Le text grec", 84.11ff: πρὸς τὸν δοῦλον τοῦ θεοῦ Θαλασσιον, τὸν πᾶσαν τὴν Ἀφρικὴν κοσμήσαντα.
[1387] Anastasios Sinaita, "De taxeota", 84.21ff: ὧν καὶ αὕτη μόνη ἡ ἰδέα πάσης κολάσεως χαλεπωτέρα ὑπάρχει.
[1388] Anastasios Sinaita, "De taxeota", 84.27 (τελονεία), 85.1 (τελωνεῖα), 85.10 (τελώνιον).
[1389] Anastasios Sinaita, "De taxeota", 85.3ff: ἁπλῶς ἕκαστον πάθος καθεξῆς ἰδίους τελωνάρχας καὶ φορολόγους ἔχει ἐν τῷ ἀέρι.

tionship with the peasant's wife. The angels have nothing to help his soul and leave him in the hands of the demons. The Ethiopians gladly snatch the wretched soldier and carry him down some dark, narrow, and stinking corridors into the depths of the earth to torment his soul until Judgment Day.[1390] Fortunately, he sees the two angels at this point, and with tears in his eyes, begs them for mercy. They take his soul, like a radiant pearl, and carry it back to his former body, which looks like dark, stinking mud.[1391] The deceased initially refuses to re-enter this abominable abode, but the angels threaten to return him to the realm of the demons. The soldier returns to his bodily shell and lives in fasting and penance for another forty days, during which he becomes an example of piety to his family and friends.

It is not easy to date the story of the resurrected soldier accurately. It undoubtedly refers to events of the seventh century, since Carthage fell into the hands of the Arabs in 695.[1392] St. Anastasios Sinaita flourished as a hagiographer in the second half of the seventh century and was a younger contemporary and associate of Maximus the Confessor in the common struggle against Monothelitism.[1393] To this same circle also belonged Thalassios, mentioned in the text, an Orthodox monk and abbot of a monastery in Libya, with whom Maximus corresponded frequently.[1394] The mention of bubonic plague as the cause of the soldier's death is not of much help. The only local plague epidemic in the region of Carthage in the sixth to the seventh centuries, listed by Dionysios Statakopoulos, occurred between 599 and 600,[1395] when Thalassios could not have been abbot, and the exarch of Carthage was not Niketas but Hera-

---

[1390] Anastasios Sinaita, "De taxeota", 85.21–86.7; cf. 86.16.
[1391] Anastasios Sinaita, "De taxeota", 86.25ff: ὥσπερ βόρβορον καὶ πηλὸν δυσώδη καὶ ζωφεράν.
[1392] Charles Diehl, L'Afrique byzantine. Histoire de la domination byzantine en Afrique (533 – 709) (Paris: Ernest Leroux, 1896), 582ff.
[1393] Krumbacher, Geschichte der byzantinischen Literatur, 64ff.
[1394] On Thalassios, see Krumbacher, Geschichte der byzantinischen Literatur, 147; Nau, "Le text grec", 84 and n. 6.
[1395] Stathakopoulos, Famine and Pestilence, 332–33.

clius the Elder, the father of the future Emperor.[1396] Identifying the Patrician Niketas himself would perhaps shed more light on the problem.[1397] Charles Diehl claims that St. Anastasios Sinaita is referring to the famous Niketas, a cousin of Emperor Heraclius, who occupied the post of exarch of Africa between 619 and 629,[1398] and Alexander Kazhdan accepts this hypothesis.[1399] Therefore, we must date the story of the resurrected soldier between 619 and 629. In addition, the list drawn up by Stathakopoulos should be supplemented with the local epidemic of bubonic plague in North Africa during this period.

2.1.4. George Hamartolos and the Life of St. Basil the Younger: Demon-sins in Byzantine hagiography

The texts of the period between the first half of the seventh and the second half of the ninth centuries rarely mention the afterlife journey and trials of the soul. Shortly before their martyrdom in Samara on March 6, 845, the Forty-Two Martyrs of Amorion invoked their faith as their companion (συνέκδημος) on their impending journey through the spirits of Evil and the Lord of the Air.[1400] Ignatios the Deacon described St. Patriarch Tarasios fighting frantically with some invisible enemies shortly before his death in February 806. The holy man seemed to defend himself before some accusers and argued fiercely with them. When his tongue could no longer answer, he angrily chased them away with gestures. At last, he achieved victory and was allowed to join the angels in Heaven.[1401] Neither author uses the term "tollhouses".

Both in theological treatises and hagiographical texts, the tollhouses were mentioned by ardent supporters of the Orthodox Church against the various heresies. After the restoration of the icons, and two centuries of silence, the story of the resurrected soldier reappeared in the *Chronicle*

[1396] Diehl, *L'Afrique byzantine*, 597
[1397] Anastasios Sinaita, "De taxeota", 84.17.
[1398] Diehl, *L'Afrique byzantine*, 524ff and 597 n. 40. On Niketas, see *PLRE*, vol. IIIB, s.v. "Niketas 7", 940-43; *ODB*, vol. 3, s.v. "Niketas David Paphlagon", 1480.
[1399] *ODB*, vol. 3, s.v. "Niketas", 1480. Cf. *PLRE*, vol. IIIB, s.v. "Niketas 7", 943.
[1400] Martyrs of Amorion (v. 3), §17.
[1401] Patriarch Tarasios, §60.4-32.

of the fanatical iconodule George Hamartolos.[1402] He adopted the text of St. Anastasios Sinaita almost word for word, only omitting the Patrician Niketas and referring to Thalassios as a bishop instead of an abbot. The tollhouses are also generally the same.

The *Chronicle* of George Hamartolos was a widely known text with a huge manuscript tradition. It was written in the second half of the ninth century, and, in all likelihood, the tale of the Carthaginian soldier was a directly influence on the much more detailed description in the *Life* of St. Basil the Younger. His biographer Gregory developed an elaborate conceptual system related to the aerial dwellings of the demons and to human destiny after death.[1403] Even though he borrowed the main idea from earlier sources, he completed and enriched this account with numerous intriguing details and compiled the most detailed list of deadly sins in Byzantine literature up to the end of the tenth century. According to the text, the aerial tollhouses were not only the checkpoints where souls were interrogated for their crimes. There were also the *workshops* (ἐργαστήρια) where sins were produced.[1404]

According to the *Life* of Basil the Younger, a good and an evil angel were allotted to each person at their baptism, each leading him or her to good and evil deeds respectively. The evil angel records the bad deeds, classifies them, and sends the records with the perpetrator's name to the appropriate tollhouse office, where the demonic officials carefully keep them. Based on these documents, they have the right to detain the soul after death, cast it down into Hell, and keep it in custody until the Day of Judgment, when God will decide its fate.[1405] In earlier theological and hagiographical texts, the soul is either alone during its faithful journey or accompanied only by guardian angels, whose role is limited. By contrast, in the *Life* of St. Basil, the demons rarely acquit Theodora on the basis of her righteousness alone, and her salvation usually comes from the guard-

---

[1402] *Georgii Monachi Chronicon*, 2: 678–83.
[1403] See the brief references to this journey, as described in the *Life* of Basil the Younger, in Mango, *Empire*, 164ff; Lambakis, "The Descents into Hell", 55–58.
[1404] Basil the Younger, Part II, §24.4.
[1405] Basil the Younger, Part II, §38.11–13.

ian angels and her protector, the holy Basil. He is not the usual humble monk we encounter in hagiographical literature,[1406] but the personification of perfection and a mediator between humans and God.[1407] Still living, he possesses a vast, splendid heavenly palace where the souls saved through his intervention abide.[1408] In addition, Theodora is not a holy woman or a saint but an ordinary person who has humbly followed the instructions of her spiritual mentor and, despite her sins, reaches Heaven through his benevolence.

According to the *Life*, the soul can be saved in three ways. Firstly, only a few people, like Basil himself, can rely on their own spiritual strength to resist temptations and achieve salvation by full infallibility. Others usually make mistakes, often unconsciously, and these transgressions can be crucial during their souls' examination, and lead to their ultimate doom. For this reason, the other two options are considered safer for a layperson. One can confess and repent; after a due period of penance, the sins are stricken from the demons' registers.[1409] Finally, if the sinner wins the benevolence of a holy man who has achieved the right *to speak freely* with God (παρρησία), he or she can be redeemed from certain wrongdoings even without having repented. In the case of Theodora, the means of this redemption is *a scarlet bag full of pure gold*, which Basil gives to the angels before her afterlife journey.[1410]

[1406] Angelidi, "The Life of St. Basil", 58-60. In the *Life* of St. Basil, the author omits the standard elements of the hagiographical *encomion* (see above, Part One, Chapter 1). There is no mention of the holy man's origins, family, birthplace, or life before becoming a monk. His social position is obscure, and there is no hint of a particular monastic community to which he eventually belonged.

[1407] On the three levels of holiness in the *Life*, see Angelidi, "The Life of St. Basil", 69ff. The first includes virtues such as patience (ὑπομονή), humility (ἄκρα ταπείνωσις), and prayer (προσευχαί); every good Christian can and must achieve it. The second is attained chiefly by monks and includes the prophetic gift, silence, and wisdom. The third level, perfection, represents ultimate holiness.

[1408] Basil the Younger, Part II, §4.1-11.

[1409] Basil the Younger, Part II, §27.22-25. See and Part II, §37.5-14, where the demons examine Theodora for Fornication; it turns out that she had concealed various youthful transgressions from Basil, which impeded her journey.

[1410] Basil the Younger, Part II, §10.6ff: βαλάντιον κόκκινον χρυσίου καθαροῦ μεστόν. See and Angelidi, "The Life of St. Basil", 180.

According to Christine Angelidi, the story of Theodora is set between 928 and 941.[1411] When the pious servant died in Constantinople, the monk Gregory went to her master Basil to ask him what happened to the soul of such a righteous woman. With a small smile, Basil promised to show him. The next evening, when Gregory was already dozing off after prayer, two young men invited him to visit the holy man at once. They instructed him to follow the path to the church of Theotokos of Blachernai, located in the city's northwestern corner.[1412] At one point, he thought he caught a glimpse of the figure of Basil from afar and followed him. As he walked, Gregory realized that the street had become a narrow and steep pathway. Ultimately, he reached the holy man's magnificent heavenly palace, where all his spiritual children lived, and knocked on the door. Theodora herself opened and hesitantly let the visitor in, though puzzled to see him come into this place while still living.[1413] He asked about her passage through *all the spirits of evil in the air*,[1414] and the dead woman agreed to recall the memories of that terrible journey. Her description resembles those of Cyril of Alexandria, Anastasios Sinaita, and George Hamartolos. It began with the agonizing physical pain of the last moments of life. Worst of all, the demon-Ethiopians gathered around her deathbed, *creating disturbance and commotion, howling like dogs and wolves, jeering, foaming rapidly*. They examined her actions, *producing false settlements* and *carrying around in their hands* to prove her guilt.[1415]

Already in utter despair, Theodora saw her two guardian angels approach, looking like *exceedingly beautiful young men* with golden hair and snow-white skin, clad in *dazzling garments*.[1416] While they argued fiercely with the demons, a fearful apparition of Death arrived, constantly

---

[1411] Angelidi, "The Life of St. Basil", 46–49 and 146–64.
[1412] On this church (Θεοτόκος τῶν Βλαχερνῶν), see Raymond Janin, *La géographie ecclésiastique de l'émpire Byzantin. Les églises et monastères de Constantinople* (Paris, 1953), 169–79.
[1413] Basil the Younger, Part II, §2–5.
[1414] Basil the Younger, Part II, §5.17: πάντα τῆς πονηρίας ἐν τῷ ἀέρι πνεύματα.
[1415] Basil the Younger, Part II, §6.29–35. Cf. and Cyrillus Alexandrinus. "De exitu animi", 1073, where the terminology is almost the same.
[1416] Basil the Younger, Part II, §7.6–9.

changing his[1417] image: now a roaring lion, now a young barbarian brandishing *all types of knives, scythes, saws, stone-cutting tools, spits, adzes, and many other fearful tools of torture.*[1418] The angels commanded him to free Theodora from her bonds, and the frightful creature dismembered her corpse completely. Ultimately, Death slit her throat and gave her a cup of an extremely bitter drink. Her soul was separated from its body, and the angels took her up into the dreaded air to be examined by the demons and safely admitted to the Kingdom of God.[1419]

According to the text, Theodora had to pass through twenty-one *tollhouses* (τελώνια) or *workshops* (ἐργαστήρια) where each group of evil spirits manufactured a particular sin for which it examined the soul: [1] Slander (καταλαλιά); [2] Verbal Abuse (λοιδορία); [3] Envy (φθόνος); [4] Falsehood (ψεῦδος); [5] Wrath and Anger (θυμὸς καὶ ὀργή); [6] Pride (ὑπερηφανία); [7] Idle Chatter and Obscene Language (μωρολογία, αἰσχρολογία); [8] Usury and Deceit (τόκος καὶ δόλος); [9] Ennui and Vainglory (ἀκηδία καὶ κενοδοξία); [10] Avarice (φιλαργυρία); [11] Excessive Wine Drinking and Inebriation (πολυποσία καὶ μέθη); [12] Malice (μνησικακία); [13] Incantations, Poisoning, Magic, Divination, and Summoning of evil spirits (τῶν ἐπαοιδῶν, φαρμακῶν, μάγων, μάντεων, κληδονιστῶν); [14] Gluttony; [15] Idolatry and Heresy (εἰδωλολατρεία); [16] Homosexuality and Pederasty (ἀνδρομανία καὶ παιδοφθορία); [17] Adultery (μοιχεία); [18] Murder (φόνος); [19] Theft (κλοπή); [20] Fornication (πορνεία); [21] Heartlessness and Cruelty (ἀσπλαγχνία καὶ σκληροκαρδία). Judging from his descriptions, Gregory imagined the tollhouses as platforms or "islands" hanging in the air, one above the

---

[1417] It must be noted that the Greek word for *death* (θάνατος) is masculine, and therefore "his" personifications are also male.

[1418] Basil the Younger, Part II, §8.4–6.

[1419] Cf. Cyrillus Alexandrinus. "De exitu animi", 1073, where the angels "carry" the soul on its journey.

other. The soul struggled along a *pathway* (ὁδός)¹⁴²⁰ under imminent threat of being pushed off it by the demons.¹⁴²¹

Six of the seven accusations against Theodora were gender-related and reflect the stereotypical prejudices towards women. Her offenses were either verbal (Slander, Verbal Abuse, Idle Chatter and Obscene Language) or carnal (Excessive Wine Drinking and Inebriation, Gluttony, and Fornication), but none major crimes against society, like Murder, Theft, or Usury. Gregory explicitly defines Falsehood as a female sin.¹⁴²² Only her seventh sin, Wrath and Anger, was typically associated with men, but it could be considered a general human vice.

Most forms taken by the evil spirits resembled the particular sin they were responsible for. The demons of Gluttony were *swollen, stout, and fat*.¹⁴²³ The personification of Homosexuality and Pederasty changed its shape constantly but usually appeared as a *savage pig*, relaxing in the *foul odor, extensive and bitter and painful*.¹⁴²⁴ The evil spirits of Incantations, Magic, and Divination appeared as various reptiles, probably a reminiscence of ancient deities associated with divination, like Apollo-Python.¹⁴²⁵ The demons of Inebriation looked *blind drunk and besotted with much wine*, which did not prevent them from pointing out exactly how many cups and glasses of wine Theodora had drained, when, with whom, and with what consequences.¹⁴²⁶ Much like the High Court of Chancery, the heart of the allegorical fog shrouding London in Dickens's *Bleak House*,¹⁴²⁷ a *dark cloud of mist* surrounds the tollhouse of Avarice,

---

¹⁴²⁰ Basil the Younger, Part II, §23.26 and §26.2.
¹⁴²¹ Basil the Younger, Part II, §23.28ff: *in order not to be buffeted by them and forcefully led down to the gloomy dungeons of Hades in the darkness and shadow of death* (ἵνα μὴ ὑπ'αὐτῶν κολαφιζόμενος βίᾳ καταχθῇ εἰς τὰ ζοφερὰ ταμεῖα τοῦ ᾅδου ἐν σκοτεινοῖς καὶ σκιᾷ θανάτου).
¹⁴²² Basil the Younger, Part II, §15.10ff.
¹⁴²³ Basil the Younger, Part II, §30.4.
¹⁴²⁴ Basil the Younger, Part II, §32.5–8.
¹⁴²⁵ Basil the Younger, Part II, §26.4–6.
¹⁴²⁶ Basil the Younger, Part II, §22.8–9.
¹⁴²⁷ Charles Dickens, *The Bleak House*, ed. Michael Slater (New York: Signet Classics, 2011), 10.

so thick and heavy that the evil Ethiopians form their booths from it.[1428] Probably the most detailed and vivid description is that of the chief demon of Fornication; he was clad in a *short tunic spattered with putrid foam and blood* and adorned with depictions of conjoined demon-like figures (εἰκονίσματά τινα δαιμονιόμορφα).[1429]

Material personification of demon-sins appeared rarely in the Byzantine hagiography of the period under study. The hagiographers usually described only their influence upon victims, and the accounts are rather stereotypical.[1430] A few interesting stories are related to the demons of Avarice, Idolatry, and, above all, Fornication.

Demons of Paganism and Idolatry appear in the *Life* of St. Symeon Stylites the Younger (sixth century), who lived during the reign of Emperor Justinian when the central government struggled to erase the last remnants of the old religions and cults. The author tells the story of a young stonemason from Isauria who lived and worked near Antioch. He was a Christian but, secretly, continued to worship the old gods of his native country. Once, the master mason sent him to bring timber from a pagan village called Poulion. When he attempted to lift a massive log, he was possessed by a demon, became paralyzed, and asked for help from the holy Symeon. The monk touched him and made the sign of the cross, but the ritual failed since the worker had not confessed his sin. Symeon was aware of his patient's dubious religious affiliation and instructed him to go home and reconsider his views. He had to wait three years until Symeon sent another pious man to heal him. The former pagan broke or

---

[1428] Basil the Younger, Part II, §21.1-5. The translation of the Greek word σκηνή as *tent, a booth* is my own.
[1429] Basil the Younger, Part II, §36.4-11.
[1430] On the demon of Jealousy and Envy, see Peter of Atroa, §3.10ff. On the demon of Sloth, see Stephen the Thaumaturge, §64, where the author describes the monk Cosmas, who fought this evil spirit by making baskets; Ioannikios (*Sabbas*), §21; Elias Speleotes, §37; Antony the Younger, §27; Patriarch Ignatios, §39. On the demon of Pride, see Phantinos the Younger, §33. On the demon of Gluttony, see Antony the Younger, §42.

burned the idols hidden in his home in disgust and became a convinced Christian.[1431].

Demons of Paganism appear in the *Lives* of the two famous Persian saints, Golindukh-Maria (†July 13, 591) and Anastasios (†January 22, 628), who lived during the last great political, military, and religious conflict between the empire and Sassanian Persia. Anastasios' path to martyrdom was continuous war against *the demons and beasts* that his countrymen worshipped with sacrifices and spells, namely, the sun, the moon, fire, the horse, and the mountains.[1432]

Byzantine hagiography of the period under study seldom mentions the **demon of Avarice**. This evil spirit appeared before Symeon Stylites the Younger in his youth, opening wide his jaws to devour the world, but the text gives no further information, and the description is somewhat allegorical.[1433] The spirit is the driving force behind the sinful actions of a pirate crew in one of the adventures of St. Nikon Metanoieite. The story is fascinating mainly from a literary point of view since it demonstrates how Christian literature treats, re-elaborates, and uses well-known ancient motifs for its own purposes. In 968, after seven years of preaching on Crete,[1434] the holy man arranged to leave the island and boarded a ship. However, Nikon sensed that the demon of Avarice had possessed the sailors and decided to give them a lesson and save them from its malign influence. He filled his purse with salt, making them think it was gold. All the members of the crew, except one, decided to drown the man of God in the sea and steal his money. One day, Nikon produced the purse during lunch and ostentatiously poured some salt on his meal. Pointing out the salt, he asked them if they had lost their minds because

---

[1431] Symeon Stylites the Younger, §188ff.
[1432] Anastasios of Persia, §23. Cf. Anastasios of Persia, §33 and Anastasios of Persia, Encomion by George Pisides, §36.5ff and §9.11.
[1433] Symeon Stylites the Younger, §18.16ff: πνεῦμα φιλαργυρίας χαῖνον τοῦ καταπιεῖν τὸν κόσμον.
[1434] On St. Nikon's mission to Crete, see Sullivan, *The Life of Saint Nikon*, 19.

of *this*. Frightened and ashamed, they immediately knelt before the Saint, begging forgiveness.[1435]

This pious and highly instructive story is borrowed, directly or indirectly, from the *Histories* of Herodotus. Once upon a time, in Corinth, there lived the gifted musician Arion. His native city did not provide many opportunities for his exceptional talent, so he went to southern Italy to make some money. Taking a ship back home, the sailors found out that he carried a purse full of gold and hatched a devious plan to steal his money. They caught poor Arion and presented him with two options: to be murdered by them or else jump overboard and, most likely, drown in the sea. Considering there to be a slight possibility of his surviving long enough to be rescued by a passing ship, he chose the second option but implored the captain to honor his last wish and allow him to wear his best clothes and sing a wonderful song before jumping into the tides. This was granted. In his best outfit, Arion sang his swan song, threw himself into the sea, and the ship slowly faded into the distance. At that moment, a real miracle happened. A dolphin approached the despairing musician and carried him safely to the shore of the Peloponnese.[1436] This story was well-known in the Greek world, not only due to Herodotus's popularity but also because it was a part of the school program. In his treatise *Progymnasmata* (*Rhetorical Exercises*), Hermogenes of Tarsus uses it to illustrate his narrative theory,[1437] so every educated person in the empire was acquainted with it.

The **demon or spirit of Fornication** (δαίμων/πνεῦμα τῆς πορνείας, πνεύματα πορνικά) often occurs in Byzantine hagiography, though mainly as an abstract notion.[1438] In theological literature and, occasionally, in saints' *Lives*, it sometimes appears as a serpent that wraps itself around the body of those who have fallen into the sin of concupiscence. As mentioned above, the author of the *Life* of St. Elias Speleotes associ-

---

[1435] Nikon Metanoeite, §22.
[1436] Hérodote, *Histoires*, vol. I, I.23–24.
[1437] Hermogène, "Exercices préparatoires", V.2.
[1438] See, e.g., Stephen the Thaumaturge, §87 and §168; Niketas of Medikion, §15; Elias the Younger, §§11–14; Elias Speleotes, §63.

THE INVISIBLE WORLD 415

ates it with wealth and rich clothes and accessories,[1439] and Michael Psellus argues that body-loving demons (φιλόσαρκοι δαίμονες) are attracted to the beautiful and richly frilled garments of women.[1440] In most cases, however, the hagiographers describe only the influence of this malevolent spirit. In his version of St. Ioannikios the Great's *Life*, the monk Peter vividly describes two such cases.[1441] The first occurred somewhere between Ephesus and the Koundurian mountains (near Myra in Lycia) during the reign of Emperor Theophilos (829–842). With God's permission, the spirit of Fornication possessed the daughter of a noble nun. The girl yielded and began to scream obscenities at her mother. The latter, devastated, tried to bring the maiden to her senses, reminding her of the excellent upbringing she had been given, the hellfire prepared for those who defile the temple of their bodies, and suggesting that they stop for prayer. Nothing helped. The daughter hysterically begged her mother simply to let her go and satisfy her unbearable sexual desire, threatening to kill herself otherwise. In utter despair and tears, the elderly nun begged God to send an angel or a holy man to help her and quench the terrible fire in her daughter's body. At that moment, she saw St. Ioannikios approaching and, like Mary Magdalene, threw herself at his feet, asking him to pity her daughter. When he heard the story, he took the girl's hand and laid it on his neck, saying: *Child, let your struggle come upon me! Be healed of the demon that scourges you by the grace of God.* The girl immediately recovered and the demon went away.[1442]

Another similar story occurred on Mount Alsos in Lydia between 815 and 820, during the pursuits of Emperor Leo V (813–820). The body of a woman possessed by the demon of Fornication seemed wholly to burn with agonizing bursts of voluptuousness. She strived with all her wits to preserve her innocence, but, in the end, the cruel and already lost

---

[1439] Elias Speleotes, §17.
[1440] Auxentios, §16.
[1441] On these, see also the analysis of Alexander Kazhdan, "Byzantine Hagiography and Sex in the Fifth to Twelfth Centuries", *Dumbarton Oaks Papers* 44 (1990): 141.
[1442] Ioannikios (*Peter*), §46. On the demon of Fornication, see, e.g., Elias the Younger, §§11–14; Elias Speleotes, §63, where the evil spirit is called φιλόσαρκος.

struggle drove her to madness and frenzied passion. She wandered like a wild boar through the wilderness with torn clothes and loose, indecently disheveled hair. She refused to eat human food but tore her own flesh with her teeth. Her face was beast-like, her eyes looked fearful, her teeth gnashed, and her blood flooded the ground. She barked like a dog, snorted like a bull, brayed like an ass, and hissed like a snake.[1443]

The demon of Fornication made even monks submit to him. According to the *Life* of Symeon Stylites the New (521–592), the evil spirit drove a hermit to leave his cell and indulge in shameful cohabitation with a woman. St. Gregory of Dekapolis was shot with *flaming arrows* (πεπυρωμένοις βέλεσιν) by demonic lust during his hermitage in the mountains and caves of the Isaurian Decapolis in 829–830, and (Pseudo-) Ignatios Deacon described the holy man's spectacular deliverance. Gregory dreamed of a very modest-looking woman, resembling his mother, who compassionately pointed her finger at his navel. *What is this pain that torments you, child?*, she asked, immediately cutting his abdomen open with a sword. Rotten entrails spilled out, and he was delivered forever from the demon's influence.[1444]

Demons punish not only the dead for their sins but also the living. Possession by an evil spirit due to wickedness or disobedience to a spiritual mentor is widespread. According to the *Life* of St. John the Merciful, the pious Alexandrian monk Vitalius tasked himself with re-educating the city's prostitutes. During the day, he collected alms, and at night he hired a harlot and watched over her all night, praying for her soul. Once, on his way out of the brothel, one of his fellow citizens reprimanded him for his supposedly unchristian behavior and slapped him in the face. Soon after, the elderly monk died in his cell, and a demon in the form of an ugly Ethiopian appeared to the man, hit him, and told him that Father Vitalius had sent him this whack. The demon tormented him so terribly that all the people of Alexandria gathered around his house. Then the

---

[1443] Ioannikios (*Peter*), §27. Sabbas tells the same story in his version of the *Life* in less detail (Ioannikios (*Sabbas*), §22).
[1444] Gregory of Dekapolis, §10.3–12.

man understood his sin, ran to the monk's cell, and bitterly repented. Vitalius, however, was already dead in the posture of prayer. A note lay on the floor beside his body: *Alexandrians, judge not prematurely until the Lord comes to earth*. The repentance saved the possessed, and he was finally healed.[1445] A similar story is told in the *Life* of St. Luke of Steiris (897–953). In 918,[1446] a famous stylite monk in Achaea invited Luke to serve him, and he responded willingly. However, a local priest disliked the newcomer and, moved by envy, assailed him with slanders and curses. When Luke refused to fight back, he even struck him on the chin. Shortly afterward, the jealous priest was possessed by a demon for the rest of his life, shaming his priestly office.[1447]

Avenging demons (τιμωρητικοὶ δαίμονες) also punish heresy. The problem of iconoclast priests became particularly delicate and ticklish after the first restoration of the icons in 787, when Theodore Studites and the Zealot party generally refused to accept them back into the Orthodox Church even if they repented. Most of the hagiographical accounts of such cases, however, obviously adopt the position of the Moderates. According to the biography of the distinguished defender of the icons, Makarios of Pelekete (†July 18, 840), one of his subordinate priests became an iconoclast but shortly afterward changed his mind and repented. The holy monk received him kindly and granted him absolution but forbade him to perform priestly duties. The man disobeyed, held service, and gave those present Holy Communion. A group of nuns who had supported him in his disobedience also tasted the Eucharistic bread and wine and were immediately punished by avenging demons. Scourged by the evil spirits, they went to Makarios and told him of the disobedience of the defrocked priest. Despite his shock and indignation, the holy man pitied them all; he exorcized the demons, healed the women, and wel-

---

[1445] John the Merciful, 387.25–390.30.
[1446] On the datation, see da Costa-Louillet, "Saints de Grèce", 337ff and 343; Sofianos, *The Life of St. Luke*, 35ff and 38. On the main events of St. Luke's *Life*, see Part One, Chapter 2, §3.
[1447] Luke of Steiris, §44. For other cases of demonic possession as a punishment for sins, see Elias Speleotes, §50 and §57; George of Amastris, §5; Gregory of Dekapolis, §54; Peter of Atroa, §21 and §70.

comed the former priest back into the bosom of Holy Mother Church.[1448] In the *Life* of St. Peter of Atroa, Father Patermouthios, abbot of the monastery of Hareus in Lydia, officially renounced the icons and was possessed by demons. Peter saved him in the last years of the reign of Emperor Leo V (813–820).[1449]

If not stopped in time, the influence exerted by the demons of the sins could escalate and lead to the death of the possessed. According to the *Life* of St. Michael Maleinos (864–July 12, 961), a monk named Kyriakos neglected the care of his soul and gradually fell into greater and greater sins. One night, a demon urged him to take a knife and attack Michael himself. However, when he entered the abbot's cell, he saw him praying as if wrapped in flames. He trembled, and the weapon fell from his hand. Michael then turned to him calmly and invited him to come in. Kyriakos stepped into the cell and began to repeat monotonously: *I have sinned*. When he finally pulled himself together, the abbot sent him to pray, for his end was near. Indeed, forty days later, the monk died.[1450]

2.2. The Ladder to Heaven

The aerial tollhouses, a fairly common idea in the hagiography of the sixth to the seventh and then the tenth centuries, were associated with another theological concept formulated by John Climacus (before 579–c. 650),[1451] namely, the so-called "Ladder to Heaven" (οὐράνιος κλῖμαξ) located in the aerial regions. The theory is based on Jacob's Dream in Bethel:

> He had a dream in which he saw a stairway resting on the earth, with its top reaching to heaven, and the angels of God were ascending and descending on it. There above it stood the Lord, and he said: "I am the Lord, the God of your father Abraham and the God of Isaac. I will give you and your descendants the land on which you are lying.[1452]

[1448] Makarios of Pelekete, §12.
[1449] For other such cases, see Peter of Atroa, §22 and §24ff.
[1450] Michael Maleinos, §17.
[1451] Ioannes Climacus, "Scala paradisi", in *MPG*, vol. 88 (Paris, 1864), 631–1161.
[1452] Gen. 28:12–13.

In Late Antiquity, the idea of the ladder to heaven seems to have been relatively widespread, paving the way for its detailed development in John Climacus. As mentioned above, according to Origen, the ladder leading to the seven gates (κλῖμαξ ἑπτάπυλος) was also part of Mithraic symbolism.[1453] The Martyrdom of St. Perpetua (early third century) described a vision in which a copper ladder connected the Earth and heaven. It was narrow and surrounded by blades, and at its base lay a giant dragon ready to tear apart all who failed to climb to the top.[1454] However, Byzantine hagiographers mentioned this concept only rarely. The only text to mention it before the second half of the ninth century is the *Life* of St. Symeon Stylites the Younger.[1455] It occurs in a few hagiographical texts written in a highly rhetorical Attic Greek and influenced by John Climacus. In one of the late eulogies of St. Anastasios of Persia, composed according to Bernard Flusin in the second half of the ninth or in the early tenth century,[1456] the Saint had the following vision shortly after his conversion to Christianity in 620:

> Not even the great Jacob saw so high a ladder as that which appeared to Anastasios; when he saw it, he immediately began ascending it and came to the top.[1457]

In the early tenth century, Niketas-David of Paphlagonia uses the Ladder as a metaphor:

> For just as those who ascend in the way of virtue climb up to God by their good deeds as by a ladder, so also those who forsake the right way, by their evil deeds, associate themselves with the father of evil and do not cease to entangle evil in evil until they fall into the pit of their deeds.[1458]

The anonymous author of the *Life* of St. Paul of Latros (900–December 15, 955) also mentions the work of John Climacus[1459] and uses

---

[1453] Origène, *Contre Celse*, 3: VI.22.
[1454] Lambakis, "The Descents into Hell", 49.
[1455] Symeon Stylites the Younger, §124.66ff.
[1456] Flusin, *Saint Anastase*, 2: 264ff.
[1457] Anastasios of Persia, Encomion, §10.1ff.
[1458] Patriarch Ignatios, §17.
[1459] Paul of Latros I, §8.25.

a witty metaphor based on the Ladder and the demonic obstacles that surround it. According to him, the steps to the holy man's cell were built so that people would have easy access to Paul and he could descend them quickly, but the Evil One did not want his sermons to contribute to the salvation of human souls and used to send evil spirits in the form of serpents to cover the stairs from top to bottom, and so block people's way to the spiritual virtues and God's grace.[1460]

The work of John Climacus had almost no influence on the afterlife journey of the soul in the hagiography of the period under study. The idea of the Ladder to Heaven occurs only as an abstract notion in a few texts written by well-educated authors with deep theological knowledge.

3. Punishment: the demons of Hell

The Christian concept of Hell, whose origins can be traced back to various Greco-Roman and Middle Eastern mythological and philosophical traditions, emerged as early as the first and second centuries A.D. Visions of the gloomy depths of Earth where terrible demons torture the sinners' souls occur in various "Books of Revelation", of which only the work of St. John the Apostle was included in the official Nicene New Testament, as well as in the apocryphal Gospels, like the Gospel of Nicodemus. In Byzantium, the tradition continued with texts like the *Revelation of the Theotokos*, probably composed in the fifth century, and the *Revelation of Anastasia*.[1461] In Byzantine hagiography, descriptions of Hell are relatively rare and, at least before the tenth century, were not usually associated with the presence of demons but mostly with darkness and fire. For example, in the vision of the Persian Saint Golindukh-Maria (†July 13, 591), an angel takes the future martyr to an extremely dark and gloomy place, where he points out some wandering human figures. He explains to her that these are her fire-worshipping Persian ancestors and then,

---

[1460] Paul of Latros I, §15 and §25.
[1461] For more detail on the apocryphal texts describing Hell, see Lambakis, "The Descents into Hell", 40–82.

THE INVISIBLE WORLD   421

through a small doorway, shows her the vast and bright heavenly settlements.[1462]

The apocryphal *Revelation of Theotokos*, dated by Lambakis to the mid-fifth century, is the first to mention the so-called "River of Fire". According to this text, every human soul has to pass over a narrow bridge[1463] — an alternative to the tollhouses and the Ladder — to reach Heaven. If a soul fails to do so, it falls into the River, and the stream of flames carries it away to suffer until Judgment Day. There is no salvation for those who killed their children, unjustly accused another person, and made false oaths.[1464] In Byzantine hagiography between the sixth and the late ninth centuries, the River occurs only intermittently, with little detail and no mention of demons. At the age of seven, shortly after the death of his grandfather St. Philaretos the Merciful, Niketas of Paphlagonia had a vision of *the other world* (τὸν ἐκεῖθεν κόσμον). The little boy found himself on the bank of a *deep, bubbling river of fire* (τὸν ποταμὸν τὸν πύρινον βαθὺν πάνυ κοχλάζοντα), in which many naked men and women suffered. Beyond this horrible place lay the beautiful, flowering Paradise, where Philaretos sat on a golden throne. A bridge as thin as a hair connected the two banks. Terrified, Niketas refused to set foot on it, but his grandfather encouraged him, held out his hand invitingly, and the boy finally crossed the River.[1465]

There is no mention of demons in the vision of Niketas of Paphlagonia, where the sinners are tormented only by the flames of the burning river. The *Life* of St. Philaretos the Merciful was written in 820. A century or so later, Byzantine literature had already used and enriched the concept of the descent into Hell in various apocryphal[1466] and hagiographical texts. According to *The Fearful and Useful Vision of the*

[1462] Golinduch, 153.7–15.
[1463] On the haunted bridges in Byzantine hagiography, see also Part Four, Chapter 2, §4.
[1464] See Lambakis, "The Descents into Hell", 46ff.
[1465] Philaretos the Merciful, 161–65. On this story, see Lambakis, "The Descents into Hell", 51ff.
[1466] On these, see Lambakis, "The Descents into Hell", 45–82.

Monk Cosmas, in 933,[1467] the severely ill abbot Cosmas suddenly sat up in his bed and remained stiff and unconscious for three whole hours, only briefly regaining consciousness to ask for two crusts of bread. Cosmas finally awoke at noon, and, at dusk, all the monks gathered, imploring him to describe his vision. He told them that impish black demons with various bodily deformities had come to his bedside, taken him away, and pushed him to the edge of some terrible chasm, which was not very wide, but as deep as Tartarus. The wicked *Ethiopians* then forced him to cross over an extremely narrow stone bridge with them. On the other side stood a fearsome giant who hurled the souls of sinners into the abyss with his strong left arm. The creature looked at Cosmas and said *This one is my friend*, reaching out to grab him. At that exact moment, however, the Apostles Andrew and John appeared, rescued him, and took him to see the blessed Paradise. On his way back to the world of the living, they led him again through the domain of the terrible giant, who vowed not to cease in his attempts to cast him into the abyss.[1468]

The image of the fearsome giant who throws the souls of sinners into a lake of fire with his huge hands far predates the Vision of Cosmas. It occurs in the first quarter of the fifth century, in the Lausiac History (Ἡ πρὸς Λαῦσον ἱστορία or Λαυσιακὴ ἱστορία) of Palladius. This text, dedicated to the exploits of the Desert Fathers, describes the human destiny after death as follows:

> Furthermore, I saw a tall black giant rising to the clouds, stretching out his arms to the sky. And under him was a lake the size of the sea, and I saw souls flying like birds. And the angels saved those who flew over his hands and head. And those who were crushed by his hands fell into the lake.[1469]

[1467] In the thirteenth year of Emperor Romanos I Lekapenos (920–944).
[1468] "La version longue de la vision du moine Cosmas", 82.71–84.123.
[1469] Palladius Helenopolitanus, "Historia Lausiaca", in MPG, vol. 34 (Paris, 1860), "Historia Lausiaca", 1076B–C: Καὶ ἐθεασάμην μακρὸν γίγαντα μέλανα ὑψούμενον μέχρι τῶν νεφελῶν τὰς χεῖρας ἐκτεταμένας ἔχοντα εἰς τὸν οὐρανόν. Καὶ ἦν ὑποκάτω αὐτοῦ λίμνη θαλάσσης ἔχουσα μέτρον, καὶ ἑώρων ψυχὰς ἀνιπταμένας ὡς ὄρνεα. Καὶ ὅσαι μὲν ὑπερίπταντο αὐτοῦ τῶν χειρῶν καὶ τῆς κεφαλῆς, διεσώζοντο ὑπὸ ἀγγέλων. Ὅσαι δὲ ὑπὸ τῶν χειρῶν αὐτοῦ ἐκοσσίζοντο, ἐνέπιπτον εἰς τὴν λίμνην. On this passage, cf. Lambakis, "The Descents into Hell", 49.

THE INVISIBLE WORLD   423

The narrow stone bridge over the abyss of hellfire was not the only "device" that allowed the souls of the righteous to reach Paradise. Around 958,[1470] the Calabrian Saint Phantinos the Younger (902-974) fell into an ecstatic trance and spent almost twenty-four hours in the same posture of prayer. When he finally awoke, the elderly abbot ignored the monks' questions, threw off all his clothes, and wandered in the nearby mountains for a long time. On his return, Phantinos agreed to share the terrible vision that had shocked and disturbed him so much with a close friend. According to his narration, prayer filled his soul with a burning love for God that day. He raised his hands to Heaven, his eyes and mind fixed only on the Lord's might. At that moment, two glittering figures stood before him amid bright and radiant light. The angels took him up in the air, among the swarms of black demons,[1471] allowed him to glimpse God's Kingdom, and initiated him into some *unspeakable mysteries* (*ἀρρήτων τινῶν μεμύημαι*). Then Phantinos heard a thunderous voice calling upon the angels to show him what awaits the sinners after death. He describes the Underworld as follows:

> As soon as they heard this voice, my guides, who had brought me there, grabbed me again, calmly drew me with them, and placed me in a place full of stinking smoke. And I saw an enormous fire of incomparable breadth and length, but utterly devoid of light. Above it hung something like a horn illuminated by lamps. To some souls it showed its back so they could pass along it [over the flames]. Others, however, the horn greeted with its gaping maw and poured them down into the fire [...] And I, beholding these terrible and fearful things, was ready to faint. However, at that very moment, my good companions took me up and led me over the above-mentioned horn-like object, which swayed on all sides amid the endless expanse of fire, and brought me back to a shining and ineffably pleasant place, incomparable and eternal.[1472]

[1470] On this date, see Follieri, *La vita di San Fantino*, 77-79.
[1471] Phantinos the Younger, §30.2-10.
[1472] Phantinos the Younger, §§31.3-32.5: Ὡς δὲ τῷ λόγῳ πάλιν ἀπάραντες οἱ τοῖς ἐκεῖ με πρώην ἐνέγκαντες, καὶ τοῖν χεροῖν ἑκάτεροι πρὸς ἑαυτοὺς ἠρέμα με συνυφέλκοντες, εἴς τινα χῶρον καπνοῦ δυσώδους πεπλησμένον παρέστησαν. Καὶ ὁρῶ πῦρ μὲν ἐκεῖ μέγα, πλάτει καὶ μήκει ἀσύγκριτον, φωτὸς δὲ πάμπαν ὑπάρχον ἄμοιρον· μέσον δ' αὐτοῦ ὥσπερ κεραία τις λαμπαδηφόρος ἐκρέματο, καὶ τὰς ἐξ αὐτοῦ διερχομένας ψυχάς, ἃς μέν, νῶτα δεικνύουσα, διαπερᾶσθαι ἐβράβευεν, ἃς δέ, κατὰ στόμα προσυπαντῶσα, ἐν τῷ πυρὶ

The main difficulty posed by the above description is the meaning of the noun κεραία. The Greek word is a derivative of κέρας (*horn*) and denotes any horn-like object. Follieri assumes that it refers to a ship's rail. The beam of ancient ships was loosely fastened to the top of the mast so that the sail suspended from it could move and turn freely according to the direction of the wind.[1473] Its unsteadiness somewhat suits the description in the *Life* of St. Phantinos the Younger, where the soul's journey to Heaven above hellfire is highly precarious. In addition, beams with stone or lead weights (κεραῖα λιθοφόρος and κεραῖα δελφινοφόρος) were often used on warships in Late Antiquity to damage nearby enemy ships during battle by breaking their masts and sweeping the crew out to sea.[1474] The Greek adjectives λιθοφόρος and δελφινοφόρος resemble the epithet λαμπαδηφόρος in the *Life* of St. Phantinos, where the sinners' souls *were shot down* (κατηκοντίζοντο) into hellfire like sailors swept away from their ship's deck into the sea during battle.

Follieri's supposition is reasonable enough, but it seems overcomplicated and insufficiently supported by the data in the description itself. Nor does it explain the strange terms *back* (νῶτα) and *mouth/maw* (στόμα), which lead us instead to the original meaning of the word κεραία, namely, something horn-like, a funnel. According to the text, this "horn" turns its pointy, narrow end to the righteous souls, allowing them to pass along its back (i.e., along its curved outer side). To the sinners, however, it displays its open end, vividly described as a *maw*. They enter

---

κατηκόντιζε... Ἐγὼ δὲ ἐξ ὧν ἑώρων δεινῶν καὶ φοβερῶν μέλλων λιποθυμεῖν, οἱ προσφιλεῖς με δῆθεν λαβόντες, καὶ ἣν προέφην φλογίνην κεραίαν μέσον πυρὸς ἀπλέτου ἐνστρεφομένην περάσαντες, εἰς χῶρον φαιδρὸν καὶ λίαν ἡδύτατον, ἀσύγκριτον καὶ ἀίδιον, θᾶττον πάλιν ἀπήγαγον.

[1473] Follieri, *La vita di San Fantino*, 56. For the beams on ancient and medieval ships, see John Morrison and Roderick Williams, *Greek Oared Ships (900 - 322 B.C.)* (Cambridge: Cambridge University Press, 1968), 273–78 and 294; Lionel Casson, *Ships and Seamanship in the Ancient World* (Princeton: Princeton University Press, 1971), 231–33 and 273ff; Phaidon Koukoules, *Life and Culture of the Byzantines*, [Φαίδων Κουκουλες, Βυζαντινῶν Βίος καὶ πολιτισμός], vol. 5 (Athens: Collection de l'Institut Francais d'Athenes, 1952), 354ff.

[1474] Follieri, *La vita di San Fantino*, 56ff; Morrison and Williams, *Greek Oared Ships*, 273–78; Casson, *Ships*, 239.

the opening, pass through the inside of the horn, and pour down into the infernal flames. In addition, many Byzantine depictions of Hell represent the wicked souls conveyed from the foot of the throne of God to the fiery Gehenna along a sort of narrow funnel.[1475]

The sparse hagiographical descriptions of Hell, especially from the ninth and tenth centuries, are relatively homogeneous and differ primarily in detail. The place where sinners' souls have to suffer their punishment is an abysmal river of fire; a narrow bridge, *as thin as a hair*, stretches over it, allowing the chosen few to pass over the flames to the other bank and live eternally in Paradise. The black demonic giant, who throws his *friends* in the River, only appears as an alternative to the bridge in the Vision of Cosmas. By contrast, in the story of the Carthaginian officer (see Chapter 1), Hell is described more like an ordinary dungeon with its stinking dark corridors. In this way, the anonymous author emphasized that the Devil's kingdom, in the depths of the earth, serves as a temporary "detention center" where "criminals" await their trial and the Supreme Judge's ultimate decision on their destiny.

[1475] Provatakis, *The Devil*, figs. 60, 62, and 64.

CHAPTER 2
THE VISIBLE WORLD

The visible world of the living is the battlefield, encircled by the demons of the air and those of Hell, where the Devil desperately struggles to restore his power, lost with the victory of Christ. As we saw in Part Two, the Fallen Angel cannot win this war, but he and his demons are still able to mislead people and lead them to sin and damnation. Since the evil spirits prowl to catch human souls as their valuable prey, they are rarely attached to a particular place and can appear anywhere. No place in the visible world can be considered safe, and the only protection from malicious attacks is the presence and activity of a holy person.

However, some places provide the Devil's servants with more opportunities to divert their victims from the ways of God. Monasteries and monastic cells attract them because monasticism is *a struggle against the powers of this dark world and against the spiritual forces of evil*.[1476] According to the *Life* of St. Ioannikios the Great, before devoting himself to asceticism in the wilderness, a monk must undergo appropriate training in a monastery, mastering the art of fighting and resisting his passions.[1477] As mentioned above, demons tempt the monks or attack them in their cells out of envy, taking the form of dangerous or unclean animals — snakes,[1478] scorpions,[1479] poisonous insects,[1480] wild beasts,[1481] birds,[1482]

[1476] Eph. 6:12. This passage from the New Testament is used as a definition of monasticism, e.g., in Antony, §§28.42–45 and §21.9–13; Stephen the Younger, 103.25–104.2; Theodora of Thessalonica, §21; Nikon Metanoeite, §12; Peter of Atroa, §5. See also David Brakke, *Demons and the Making of the Monk: Spiritual Combat in Early Christianity* (Cambridge, MA and London: Harvard University Press, 2006), 3–23.

[1477] Ioannikios (*Sabbas*), §8.

[1478] Gregory of Dekapolis, §40.1ff; Paul of Latros I, §14 and §25; Phantinos the Younger, §10; Niketas of Medikion, §19.

[1479] Gregory of Dekapolis, §7.5; Euthymios the Younger, §21.

[1480] Eustratios of Agauros, §27; Thomas Dephourkinos, 295ff.

[1481] Theodore Sykeotes, §8.10–27; Gregory of Dekapolis, §41.2ff.

[1482] Ioannikios (*Peter*), §33; Ioannikios (*Sabbas*), §26; Elias Speleotes, §42; George of Choziba, §3.13.2–10

and mice[1483] — or attractive women,[1484] soldiers and black Ethiopians,[1485] and even excrement.[1486] The demon that tempted a novice in the Medikion monastery appeared in the form of a serpent at the door of the cell of Abbot Niketas, thus blocking the young man's communion with his mentor.[1487] The monk Sabbas describes St. Peter of Atroa suddenly bursting into his cell and fiercely dealing blows with his staff to the invisible evil spirits in the room.[1488] The demon often caused its victim to fall into a fit of rage in the vicinity of a monastery due to the beneficent presence of a holy person[1489] or during a ceremony in a church.[1490]

Not unlike humans, demons were considered to inhabit particular geographical areas and speak their languages.[1491] In the *Life* of St. Theodore Sykeotes, evil spirits complain that the holy man has left the borders of his province of Galatia and has come to Gordiana. In a burst of local pride, they warn him they are braver than their "colleagues" in his homeland.[1492] The author of the *Life* of St. Peter of Atroa mentions evil spirits permanently residing in the city of Chonai (old Colossae in Phrygia)[1493] and Mount Kalon Oros in Lydia (near the city of Apollonia, about fifty kilometers east of Pergamum).[1494] Hagiographers of the sixth and seventh centuries also mention pagan cities, villages, and rural areas that attract the Devil's servants to settle permanently and harm crops, cattle, and people. During that period, this concept was harnessed as a propaganda tool in the political, religious, and ideological struggle between Byzan-

---

[1483] Gregory of Dekapolis, §27.
[1484] Antony the Younger, §29; Paul of Latros I, §10.22–36. Cf. and Auxentios, §31.22–26.
[1485] Theodore Sykeotes, §17; Ioannikios (*Peter*), §21; Eustratios of Agauros, §29; Gregory of Dekapolis, §8; Niketas of Medikion, §20; Euthymios the Younger, §21; Irene of Chrysobalanton, §6; Luke of Steiris, §68.5–7. Cf. and Auxentios, §15.
[1486] Antony the Younger, §29.
[1487] Niketas of Medikion, §19.
[1488] Peter of Atroa, §72.
[1489] See, e.g., Stephen the Younger, 151.9–15; Sabbas the Younger, §29.
[1490] See, e.g., Theodore Sykeotes, §71 and §93; Anastasios of Persia, Miracles, 149 (XVI (=ις).19ff); Anastasios of Persia, *Roman miracle*, §10.1.4–7; Sabbas the Younger, §12.
[1491] Mango, *Empire*, 162; Vakaloudi, *Magic*, 112–14.
[1492] Theodore Sykeotes, §43.25–29.
[1493] Peter of Atroa, §13.
[1494] Peter of Atroa, §22. On Mount Kalon Oros, see Janin, *Les églises et les monastères*, 162.

THE VISIBLE WORLD   429

tium and Sassanian Persia. For example, according to the *Life* of St. George of Choziba, the region around the Raitho monastery suffered from a demonic "invasion" after the Persian occupation of Sinai; under their evil influence, the caper bushes (Capparis spinosa) bore only one third of the buds they produced when the province was under Christian control.[1495]

However, demons did indeed show a preference for particular places as long-term dwellings, such as the wilderness, caves, desecrated churches, ancient pagan shrines and graveyards, houses, or even inanimate objects. References to evil spirits *haunting*[1496] a specific area are crucial for the study of Byzantine culture because they shed light on surviving ancient mythological traditions and display local beliefs that sometimes survived for centuries.

The hagiographers of the period under study use six verbs to denote the permanent presence of evil spirits in a particular area. Four of them are relatively common, everyday words that could be applied to humans and animals as well: κατοικέω (*to settle, to dwell*), ἐπιχωριάζω (*to visit frequently*), ἐμφωλεύω (*to lurk*), and περιέχομαι (*to be shut in*). The fifth and sixth, στοιχειόω and στοιχειάζω, meaning *to haunt*, are products of a centuries-old philosophical tradition. They both derive from the noun στοιχεῖον. Initially a measure of time, it means *an elementary principle* or *an element* of speech, matter, or logical proof in rhetoric and philosophy. As early as the third century B.C., it became an astronomical and astrological term,[1497] and the great philosopher, theologian, and astronomer at the court of the first Ptolemies, Manetho, uses στοιχεῖα to denote the stars by which time is measured.[1498] In the New Testament, astral bodies and,

---

[1495] George of Choziba, §9.42.1–14. Cf. Joannou, *Démonologie*, 11.
[1496] The most common verbs used in Greek are στοιχειόω/στοιχειάζω, κατοικῶ, ἐμφιλοχωρῶ, and ἐγχωριάζω.
[1497] Delatte and Josserand, "Contribution", 209; Greenfield, *Traditions of Belief*, 190–92; Claes Blum, "The meaning of στοιχεῖον and its Derivatives in the Byzantine Age", *Eranos Jahrbuch*, XLIV (1946): 315–25.
[1498] Manetho, "Apotelesmatica", ed. Arminius Koechly, *Poetae bucolici et didactici* (Paris: Didot, 1862), §4.624.

especially, their evil rulers are also called στοιχεῖα on many occasions.[1499] According to the Epistle of St. Paul to the Galatians, before the coming of the Savior, humankind was *in slavery under the elemental spiritual forces* (τὰ στοιχεῖα τοῦ κόσμου) who *by nature are not gods*.[1500] In his Second Epistle, St. Peter prophesies the Advent of Christ, when the *elements will be destroyed by fire* and *melt in the heat*.[1501] The term is not absent from the Hebrew tradition either. In the *Testament of Solomon*, the στοιχεῖα are the seven evil deities, each associated with its star or planet.[1502]

In Middle Greek and Byzantine literature, the term στοιχεῖον undergoes an apparent transformation. While in the New Testament and the *Testament of Solomon*, it is used to designate the all-powerful world-rulers and deities of the astral bodies, as early as the sixth or seventh century, it was associated with inferior spirits haunting a particular area and spreading their harmful influence over it. For example, the monk George mentions in the *Life* of St. Theodore Sykeotes a haunted (στοιχειαζόμενον) fishing boat[1503] and notes that the open country around Hellenopolis and Pylai in Bithynia suffered from the permanent evil presence there.[1504] In the epic poem *Digenes Akrites* (tenth to the eleventh century), the enemies of the hero consider him *a local demon* (στοιχεῖον τοῦ τόπου).[1505] Later Byzantine authors used the term in the same sense.[1506]

[1499] On the two meanings of στοιχεῖον, *evil spirit* and *astral body*, see Greenfield, *Traditions of Belief*, 191; Peter O'Brien, "Principalities and Powers and Their Relationship to Structures in Ephesians and Colossians", *Reformed Theological Review* XL (1981): 1-10.

[1500] Gal. 4:3 and 4:8. Cf. Col. 2:8.

[1501] 2 Pet. 3:10 and 12.

[1502] *The Testament of Solomon*, 45, ˊ32–ˊ34, and ˊ51. See also Greenfield, *Traditions of Belief*, 191ff.

[1503] Theodore Sykeotes, §158.35–37.

[1504] Theodore Sykeotes, §158.7.

[1505] *Digenes Akrites*, ed. John Mavrogordato (Oxford: Clarendon Press, 1956), VI.320 and 326. Cf. Greenfield, *Traditions of Belief*, 192.

[1506] See Greenfield, *Traditions of Belief*, 193–95.

1. The uncivilized space

1.1. The open wilderness

The exclusive demonic domain is in the air and the depths of the earth. Mortal humans can only visit these frightening and dangerous realms stripped of their bodily shells after death or in a vision. After the resurrection of Christ, the Devil lost his power over the visible world, but his phalanxes were still able to invade and pollute it. The process of cultivating and civilizing a particular area by a Christian community, its enclosure within walls, gradually filling with churches and monasteries, administrative buildings, and homes, was a process of expelling Evil through certain consecration rituals. Civilized space needs constant care and a joint effort to resist and repel demonic attacks, but it provides the only possible shelter for laypeople. By contrast, the wilderness around these safe islands, where the forces of evil hover undisturbed and latent, harbored innumerable dangers known to everyone — like the young maid Photo after sunset, overtaken by darkness by the River Jordan, awaiting with terror the imminent attacks of wild animals and demons.[1507] According to the saints' *Lives*, it is not uncommon for people already possessed by evil spirits to have fits and seizures when wandering in the open country.[1508] Sometimes the wilderness was associated with the so-called "Noonday demon" mentioned in the Old Testament.[1509] The monk George associates this unclean spirit with the ancient goddess Artemis,[1510] one of the most typical personifications of Evil not only in the medieval Orthodox world but also in Western Europe.[1511] According to the hagiographical texts, it possessed unfortunate victims in open areas,

---

[1507] Anastasios of Persia, Miracles, 143 (XII (=ιβ).10ff).
[1508] See, e.g., Ioannikios (*Peter*), §46; Ioannikios (*Peter*), §27.
[1509] Ps. 90:6 (Septuag.); Ps. 91:6 (NIV). On the Noonday demon, see also *ODB*, vol. I, s.v. "Demons", 609.
[1510] Theodore Sykeotes, §16.4.
[1511] See Martin Nilsson, *A History of Greek Religion* (Oxford: Clarendon Press), 1949, 13ff; *ODB*, vol. I, s.v. "Demons", 609; Vakaloudi, *Magic*, 83ff. On Artemis/Diana and her demonization, see Ginzburg, *Ecstasies*, 89–122; on the same ancient goddess in fifth-century hagiography, see Mango, "Diabolus Byzantinus", 216.

under the scorching sun, and, not surprisingly, its harmful influence often resembled sunstroke.

The only one who dared live far from villages and cities and endure these dangers, was the holy monk or hermit. In these cases, the demons guarded their wild and desolate dwellings with fervor and zeal, just as human communities protected their own cities, villages, and farms. However, their efforts to expel the God's servants were usually in vain. In the 950s,[1512] St. Nikon Metanoeite traveled in Asia Minor as a missionary urging the local populace to repent their sins. During his voyage, the demons that haunted *the wooded and impassible spots* in the mountains[1513] subjected him to innumerable dangers, but his whoop "Repent!" was sufficient to drive them away in terror. Seeing their own impotence, they went into a complete frenzy, attacking the Saint with more and more daring in various strange forms and insulting him in the most vulgar way. The demons even tried to persuade him to leave their "dominions" by appealing to tradition, arguing that they had dwelled in these mountains for a very long time and, therefore, have become their masters (κυρίους τοῦ τόπου).[1514] Nikon, however, stood steadfast and successfully resisted their assaults, protected by God's grace, and struggled through the woods, singing the words of the Psalm 29.[1515] The anonymous author of the *Life* of St. Paul of Latros describes a similar situation even more vividly. Paul's presence in their dwellings aroused the *envy* of the local demons, and they tried to drive him away in every possible way:

[1512] On the date of the main events in St. Nikon's *Life*, see Part One, Chapter 2, §9.
[1513] Nikon Metanoeite, §17.27ff.
[1514] Nikon Metanoeite, §17.41–43.
[1515] Ps. 26:1ff (Septuag.): Κύριος φωτισμός μου καὶ σωτήρ μου, τίνα φοβηθήσομαι κύριος ὑπερασπιστὴς τῆς ζωῆς μου, ἀπὸ τίνος δειλιάσω ἐὰν παρατάξηται ἐπ'ἐμὲ παρεμβολή, οὐ φοβηθήσεται ἡ καρδία μου (Ps. 27:1ff (NIV): *The Lord is my light and my salvation—whom shall I fear? The Lord is the stronghold of my life—of whom shall I be afraid? When the wicked advance against me to devour me, it is my enemies and my foes who will stumble and fall. Though an army besiege me, my heart will not fear*). St. Ioannikios uses the same sacred formula to repel the attacks of the mage Gourias (Ioannikios [Peter], §21).

What disorders and noises did they not create around him? Sometimes they appeared as visions of various beasts, hissing, clattering, and knocking; on other occasions, they turned into human figures, gnashing their teeth, speaking nonsense, hurling taunts and threats, giving the impression of tumbling rocks and earthquakes, dragging trees and skins along the ground, and causing all sorts of visions. What did the demons want to achieve through these fierce and vigorous attacks, and why did they launch them? To no other end but to frighten the Saint by such acts and to banish him from the desert because his love and longing for the desert, his affection for virtue, kindled great envy in them.[1516]

The summoning of demons and the Devil also often occurs in the wilderness. A typical example is the *Life* of St. Ioannikios the Great, where the mage Gurias gathers his phalanx of evil warrior spirits in a deserted area near the elderly monk's cell.[1517] According to a short text partly translated into French by Léon Clugnet and François Nau and published in 1903, during the reign of Emperor Maurice (582–602), the skilled magician Messites invited his young secretary to ride with him outside the city. Suddenly they arrived at a field where a giant black man, the Devil, awaited them with his retinue of black Ethiopians. The secretary, however, made the sign of the cross and the demonic horde disappeared immediately.[1518]

In the ancient world, misfortunes were considered natural consequences of provoking some deity's wrath, and to eliminate a plague, famine, or military setback, the human community had to discover and remove the cause of that wrath. Thus, religious crime was not a personal matter but a "pollution" (Greek ἄγος) that befell the community through the principle of collective responsibility. By contrast, in the Christian

---

[1516] Paul of Latros I, §11: ποῖον γὰρ εἶδος ταραχῶν καὶ θορύβων αὐτῷ μὴ ἐπήγαγον·; τοῦτο μὲν εἰς θηρίων ἰδέας διαμορφούμενοι, συριγμοὺς τε καὶ πατάγους καὶ κτύπους ἀποτελοῦντες, τοῦτο δὲ καὶ εἰς ἀνθρώπων μορφὰς μεταβάλλοντες, ὑποτρίζοντες τοὺς ὀδόντας, φωνὰς ἀσήμους ἀφιέντες, χλευάζοντες, ἀπειλοῦντες, κλόνους πετρῶν καὶ γῆς σεισμοὺς σχεδιάζοντες, ξύλα καὶ βύρσας κατὰ γῆς ἕλκοντες καὶ ἄλλα δὴ μυρία δείματα ποιοῦντες. ὅτου χάριν ταῦτα καὶ τί βουλομένοις τοῖς δαίμοσι τὸ ἄγριον τοῦτο καὶ συντεταμένον τῆς ἐπιθέσεως; οὐδὲν ἕτερον ἢ ἵνα τὸν ἅγιον τοῖς τοιούτοις ἐκδειματώσαντες, ἄποικον θῶσι τῆς ἐρημίας· πολὺν γὰρ αὐτοῖς ἀνῆπτε τὸν φθόνον τὸ φιλέρημον αὐτοῦ καὶ φιλάρετον καὶ ἡ πολλὴ πρὸς ταύτην ὁρμή.
[1517] Ioannikios (*Peter*), §20.
[1518] "Vies et récits d'anachorètes", 93ff.

world, God does not punish or harm humans, but His wrath manifests itself by granting permission to the forces of Evil to invade and destroy, partially or entirely, the otherwise perfect human body and space. Thus, one of the primary social functions of the holy person was to provide assistance, advice, and support to local communities when such a calamity befell them. Typical examples of this concept occur in the *Lives* of St. Theodore Sykeotes (†614) and St. Ioannikios the Great (754/5 or 762–846). In the late sixth and early seventh centuries, when St. Theodore was active in Asia Minor, evil spirits were often described as emerging from ancient pagan graveyards dug up by careless and greedy persons from which they invaded villages as illnesses. By contrast, in the *Life* of St. Ioannikios, demons often came from the wilderness as dragons and serpents.

* * *

Descriptions of haunted open areas are relatively rare in the Byzantine hagiography of the period under study. They are focused on small regions of central Asia Minor, along the lower Sangarius River (the sixth to the seventh centuries), Bithynia and the island of Aphousia in the Sea of Marmara (ninth century), the regions of Sparta and Achaea in the Peloponnese (tenth century), and the region of Regium in Calabria (tenth century). However, it is not easy to judge whether this concentration was due to local lore or simply to the generic features of the hagiographical texts that provided information about them, namely the *Life* of St. Theodore Sykeotes, Bithynian hagiography, and the texts produced in Greece, Sicily and Calabria.

The earliest hagiographical records of concrete haunted areas during the period under study come from the *Life* of Theodore Sykeotes (†613). As soon as he began to prepare for the monastic life by fasting, the thirteen-year-old Theodore heard of the so-called "Arkea", about 12 kilometers from his native village of Sykeon in the province of Galatia

Prima,[1519] haunted by the so-called Artemis and her demons. The evil presence tortured the people who happened to be there to death, making the place inaccessible, especially at midday. Theodore frequented the spot all through the summer but, due to Christ's protection, saw no hint of the Devil's influence.[1520]

Another haunted place in the *Life* of St. Theodore of Sykeon was "Zounboulios" in Galatia Prima, near the village of Ergobrotos.[1521] Neither men nor horses could approach this *harmful* (ἐπιβλαβής) place, especially at midday and after sunset, because they became dangerously disoriented (ἐπικίνδυνος πλάνη). The locals asked Theodore to expel the demons; he remained there from Christmas to Palm Sunday, in fasting and vigils, and chased away the evil phalanx. According to the text, the exorcism was quite noisy, and the inhabitants heard the cries and moans of the unclean spirits for days.[1522] The story supports Michael Psellus's account that the activity of evil forces increased between Christmas and New Year's Eve[1523] (the so-called "Dirty Days" of Bulgarian folklore tradition).[1524]

Two hagiographical accounts from the eighth and ninth centuries refer to haunted open areas in western Asia Minor. One of them comes from the *Life* of St. Antony the Younger and refers to a desolate area called "Potamia" ("Riverland") near Plousias in eastern Bithynia.[1525] According to the *Life*, a demonic dragon lurked there and frightened Antony during one of his travels in the mid-ninth century,[1526] but no other information is available about this place. The other haunted locality, Aphousia, is one of the small islands in the sea of Marmara, called

---

[1519] Theodore Sykeotes, §16.1ff. The village of Sykeon was twenty kilometers from Athanasioupolis (Theodore Sykeotes, §3.1–4; *TIB*, vol. 4, 228ff).
[1520] Theodore Sykeotes, §16.
[1521] For its location, see Ramsay, *The Historical Geography*, 246; Festugière, *Vie de Théodore de Sykéôn*, 186ff; *TIB*, vol. 4, 217.
[1522] Theodore Sykeotes, §26a.
[1523] Michael Psellus, "De Babutzicario", ed. John Duffy and Dan O'Meara, *Michaelis Pselli philosophica minora*, vol. 2 (Leipzig: Teubner, 1989), 163.22ff.
[1524] Theodore Sykeotes, §62.
[1525] On Plousias/Prousias and its region, see Janin, *Les églises et les monastères*, 17ff.
[1526] Antony the Younger, §42.

"Ophiousa" ("Snake Island") or "Physia" ("Windy Island") in the first centuries A.D.[1527] In that period, it was probably inhabited, but, for a long period afterward, it was almost deserted.[1528] The island reappeared in the sources in the late eighth century under the name "Aphousia" when Emperor Constantine VI and his mother Irene visited it.[1529] In 811, the sons of Emperor Constantine V were sent there after an unsuccessful attempt to usurp the throne, and the last iconoclast rulers used the island to exile iconodules like St. Makarios, abbot of the Pelekete monastery.[1530] The *Life* of St. Symeon, David, and George of Lesbos mentions a location near the eastern shore, utterly inaccessible at noon due to the evil influence of the demons haunting the place. Shortly before the restoration of the icons in 843, St. Symeon expelled the spirits, consecrated the area, and built a monastery and church dedicated to the Holy Mother of God.[1531] There is no archeological evidence of the exact location of these buildings.[1532]

The only hagiographical account of a haunted open area in southern Italy refers to the vicinity of the village of Skiron near Regium in Calabria. According to the *Life* of St. Elias Speleotes, shortly after the Saint died in 960, a farmer named Christopher set out for the sea to buy corn. He had to pass through a desolate area under the broiling sun to reach his destination, and the Noonday demon harmed him badly. Under its malign influence, the peasant could neither eat nor sleep for twenty days. He followed the advice of a relative, spent a night near the tomb of St. Elias, and the Saint healed him.[1533]

[1527] On Aphousia, see Manuel Gedeon, *Proconnesus: Church Community, Temples and Monasteries, and Bishoprics* [Greek: Μανουήλ Γεδεών, Προικόννησος: ἐκκλησιαστική παροικία, ναοί καί μοναί, μητροπολίαι καί ἐπισκοπαί] (Istanbul, 1895), 69–74; Frederick Hasluck, "The Marmara Islands", *Journal of Hellenic Studies* 29 (1909): 17.

[1528] Gedeon, *Proconnesus*, 74.

[1529] Gedeon, *Proconnesus*, 69ff.

[1530] On other iconodule exiles in Aphousia, see Gedeon, *Proconnesus*, 71–73; Cyril Mango and Ihor Ševčenko, "Some Churches and Monasteries on the Southern Shore of the Sea of Marmara", *Dumbarton Oaks Papers* 27 (1973): 245. On the *Life* of St. Makarios of Pelekete, see Part One, Chapter 2, §4.

[1531] David, Symeon and George, §24.

[1532] Janin, *Les églises et les monastères*, 200ff.

[1533] Elias Speleotes, §88.

1.2. Caves

In antiquity, caves were considered the dwellings of gods and supernatural beings and were used for cult practices as early as the Minoan period.[1534] Homer associates them mainly with sea goddesses, like the Nereids,[1535] and, less often, with male monsters, like the Cyclopes.[1536] The demigoddess and sorceress Calypso also lived in a *deep dark cave* (*σπέος γλαφυρόν*), where Odysseus spent some years before journeying to the island of the Phaeacians[1537] The fearsome Scylla, the terrible female monster with twelve legs and six necks, lurked half-hidden in her cave, her mouth with three rows of sharp teeth protruding and devouring sea animals and passing ships.[1538] According to the *Testament of Solomon*, the sinister female demon Onoskelis also lived in caverns, harming in various ways passersby and especially sailors.[1539]

As we will see, the concept that caves are the complete opposite of human dwellings inhabited by alien, tempting, and often dangerous supernatural beings remains almost intact in the medieval Orthodox world. Still, in Byzantine hagiography, the occupants have changed their nature and master, if not their functions, and become Satan's servants. As in the wilderness, only demons haunt the caves, and only holy monks and hermits endowed with God's grace can fight them.[1540] In addition, there is no indication in the sources that these places were connected to unclean female spirits. Their occupants are neither temptresses like Calypso nor sinister monsters like Scylla, but wild animals and dragons or cruel and bloodthirsty male creatures reminiscent of the ancient Polyphemus. They often appear only as sounds and voices or invisibly harm travelers and local inhabitants.

[1534] See Burkert, *Greek Religion*, 24–26.
[1535] Homer, *Iliad*, XVIII.50.
[1536] Homer, *Odyssey*, IX.114 and 476
[1537] Homer, *Odyssey*, V.155, 194, and 226; XXIII.335.
[1538] Homer, *Odyssey*, XI.80–101.
[1539] *The Testament of Solomon*, ˉ18ff. See also Delatte and Josserand, "Contribution", 223; Greenfield, *Traditions of Belief*, 187ff and 231ff.
[1540] Delatte and Jossrand, "Contribution", 223; Joannou, *Démonologie*, 11; Greenfield, *Traditions of Belief*, 231ff and 260; Mango, "Diabolus Byzantinus", 220.

According to both versions of the *Life* of St. Ioannikios the Great, the famous dragons of northwestern Asia Minor dwelled in caves in the mountainous regions of Bithynia, Phrygia, and Lydia. One of these areas, where cave-dwelling dragons attacked cattle, was Mount Olympus in Bithynia,[1541] especially its southern slopes near Prusa, called "Mount Trichalix".[1542] The second was Mount Alsos in Lydia,[1543] east of Ephesus and southwest of Mount Olympus, where a "Marsalinon" cave was located.[1544] The third region included the Kundurian Mountains near Myra in southern Lycia,[1545] where Ioannikios had two unpleasant encounters with demonic dragons; he killed one with his iron cross[1546] and shared a cave with the other during a fierce storm.[1547] Such accounts are essential for the study of Byzantine culture, as they indicate the places where local mythological traditions of ancient origin continued to exist in the ninth century. The *Life* of St. Ioannikios also mentions numerous haunted caves on the small island of Thassios in the northern part of Lake Apollonias in central Bithynia,[1548] where, probably in 825–29,[1549] the Saint traveled. When he arrived, Abbot Daniel asked him to free the island from a sinister dragon and his malicious serpents.[1550] Subsequently, St. Ioannikios also cleansed an area full of terrible caves where a demonic lord (ἄρχων δαιμόνων) and his army of evil spirits dwelled. This place was so dangerous that nobody dared to set foot there, but after the ritual

---

[1541] Ioannikios (*Peter*), §29 and Ioannikios (*Sabbas*), §24.

[1542] Only the *Sabbas* version mentions "Mount Trichalix" (Ioannikios [*Sabbas*], §24). It was probably identical to "Mount Agaurinos" in Ioannikios (*Peter*), §10 and §11. See Sullivan, "Life of St. Ioannikios", 264; Janin, *Les églises et les monastères*, 188ff.

[1543] On Mount Alsos or Lisos, see Janin, *Les églises et les monastères*, 150; Sullivan, "Life of St. Ioannikios", 274 and n. 167).

[1544] Ioannikios (*Peter*), §46; Ioannikios (*Sabbas*), §20. See Sullivan, "Life of St. Ioannikios" n. 331; Janin, *Les églises et les monastères*, 150 n. 292.

[1545] On the Kundurian Mountains, see *TIB*, vol. 8.2, 669ff; Sullivan, "Life of St. Ioannikios", 304 and n. 334.

[1546] Ioannikios (*Sabbas*), §12.

[1547] Ioannikios (*Peter*), §47; Ioannikios (*Sabbas*), §12.

[1548] Sullivan, "Life of St. Ioannikios", 294; Janin, *Les églises et les monastères*, 153ff.

[1549] St. Ioannikios traveled there between the fifth year of Emperor Michael II's rule (820–829) and the heretic ruler's death (cf. Ioannikios [*Sabbas*], §29).

[1550] Ioannikios (*Peter*), §37; Ioannikios (*Sabbas*), §31.

performed by the holy man, the local inhabitants were able to resettle in it.[1551]

A haunted cave in Dekapolis, in southwestern Asia Minor,[1552] appears in the *Life* of St. Gregory of Dekapolis. The holy man spent a year in this region as a hermit between 829 and 830 and expelled the shape-shifting demons who inhabited the deep and terrible cavern.[1553] Unfortunately, the text does not provide enough information to localize the place more accurately.

The only haunted cave in the Peloponnese in the period under study appears in the *Life* of St. Elias the Younger. In 879–880, during a notorious Arab military campaign against Regium in Calabria, organized by Husayn ibn Riyah, the governor of Sicily,[1554] St. Elias the Younger and his disciple Daniel emigrated to the Peloponnese, untouched by the Arab forces, and settled in monastic cells near the church of St. Cosmas and Damian, in the vicinity of Sparta. Daniel retired to a deep and dark cave one night to pray, but the demons hidden in its depths could not bear his piety and beat him almost to death out of envy. The following day, Elias found and quickly healed his novice.[1555]

Demons, appearing in various forms, possessed the large cave near the village of Seminara, forty kilometers from the Calabrian capital of Regium, where Elias Speleotes founded a monastery in the early tenth century. Fearing that the place was haunted, the holy man sent the monk Kyriakos to cut a tunnel in the dark cave through which the sun's rays could penetrate and chase away the evil. After the consecration of the altar, he prayed and chanted Psalms all night, imploring God to drive the demons out. Enraged, Satan unleashed all his destructive power against him, trying to frighten him with visions and loud noises, but Elias fought fiercely and expelled the demons. Later, they appeared before a group of

---

[1551] Ioannikios (*Peter*), §53; Ioannikios (*Sabbas*), §32.
[1552] *TIB*, vol. 5.1, 235ff.
[1553] Gregory of Dekapolis, §6.9ff.
[1554] Gay, *L'Italie méridionale*, 111–14 and 257; da Costa-Louillet, "Saints de Sicile et d'Italie", 100ff. See Vasiliev, *Byzance et les Arabes*, 2: 95ff and 96–99.
[1555] Elias the Younger, §27.

local villagers in the form of a giant black man, who informed them that he planned to ask for help from other local demons that haunted the caves in the nearby area of Mesobianon.[1556]

1.3. Rivers

Perhaps the sinuous, meandering shape of rivers inspired Greco-Roman mythological traditions and art, in which rivers were often inhabited by dragons and river gods that usually had a serpent-like body.[1557] The myth of the god Achelous, whom Heracles fought for the hand of Deanira, inspired both literature and visual arts for centuries.[1558] In Byzantine literature and folklore this ancient tradition was preserved. Procopius of Caesarea describes the Dragon River in Bithynia as follows:

> Close to this city flows a river which the natives call Dragon from the course which it follows. For it twists about and winds from side to side, reversing its whirling course and advancing with crooked stream, now to the right and now to the left.[1559]

Procopius is not the only Byzantine author to attest to the connection between the shape of rivers and the curved body of mythical drag-

---

[1556] Elias Speleotes, §§42–44.
[1557] For more general information on the ancient river gods and their depictions, see Harry Brewster, *The River Gods of Greece* (London and New York, 1997). In addition to reptiles with human heads and arms, rivers (most notably the Acheron) were also depicted as bulls (Ruth Gais, "Some Problems of River-God Iconography", *American Journal of Archaeology* 82, no. 3 [1978]: 355–79).
[1558] One of the most famous depictions of the battle between Heracles and Achelous, which shows the river god with a serpent-like body and a horn on his head, is on the Attic red-figure stamnos dated *c*. 520 B.C., now in the British Museum (London E437). Sophocles describes Achelous as a *curved dragon* (δράκων ἑλικτός) during the same battle (Sophocles, "Trachinae", ed. Alphonse Dain, trans. Paul Mazon, *Sophocle*, vol. 1 [Paris: Les Belles Lettres, 1967], l. 12). Strabo explains that the god was perceived as a dragon because of the meandering curves of his river (*Strabonis geographica*, X.2.19.23 and 30ff).
[1559] Procopius, *On Buildings*, ed. and trans. Henry Dewing and Glanville Downey [Loeb Classical Library 343] (Cambridge, MA: Harvard University Press, 1940), V.2.6–V.2.7.3: Ταύτης δὲ ῥεῖ τῆς πόλεως ἄγχιστα ποταμός, ὅνπερ ὁμώνυμον τῷ σχήματι Δράκοντα καλοῦσιν οἱ ἐπιχώριοι. περιστρέφεται γὰρ ἑλισσόμενος ἐφ' ἑκάτερα καὶ ἀπ' ἐναντίας αὐτῷ ἀντιπεριάγων τὰς δίνας, σκολιῷ τε τῷ ῥοθίῳ, πῇ μὲν ἐν δεξιᾷ, πῇ δὲ ἐν ἀριστερᾷ προσιών.

ons.[1560] According to urban legends, by the late fifth century, there was an image of a dragon on the bridge above a small river near the church of St. Mammas on the Golden Horn's north shore to which the inhabitants of Constantinople offered sacrifices. This practice was stopped by the order of Emperor Zeno (475–491), who destroyed the image.[1561]

As mentioned above,[1562] most demonic dragons appear in the *Lives* of the Bithynian saints of the late eighth and ninth centuries. Three traditions probably influenced this complex image in western Asia Minor: the loose conceptual framework of the Greco-Roman mythology as a whole; the local folklore tradition in the region; and, hypothetically, Slavic lore. Though most of these fantastical creatures are reported to inhabit caves, two hagiographical accounts mention the Gorgytes River (Γοργύτης). Janin and Sullivan identify it with Ainessi Dere, a tributary of the Nilüfer River[1563] in southwest Bithynia. According to the *Life* of St. Ioannikios the Great, a dragon blocked navigation, thus hampering economic activity in the region. The holy man killed the dragon and thus saved the livelihood of the inhabitants.[1564] The other account comes from the *Life* of Eustratios of Agarous. According to this text, between 843 and the 870s, the Saint chased away the giant Ethiopian demon that prevented his friend's carts from crossing the river and delivering a load of timber from the port of Katabolos (Κατάβολος)[1565] to his estate. Katabolion (Καταβόλιον), also called Katabolai (Καταβολαί) or Katabolion (Καταβόλιον) was located a few kilometers south of the city of Kyos and was an important commercial center.[1566]

[1560] Bouras, "Dragon Representations", 66.
[1561] *Michaelis Glycae Annales*, ed. Immanuel Bekker [*Corpus scriptorum historiae Byzantinae* 16] (Bonn: Weber, 1836), 492.15–20. See Bouras, "Dragon Representations", 66.
[1562] On the image of the demonic dragon, see Part Three, Chapter 3, §2.
[1563] Sullivan, "Life of St. Ioannikios", 297 and n. 293; Janin, *Les églises et les monastères*, 149ff.
[1564] Ioannikios (*Peter*), §40; Ioannikios (*Sabbas*), §14.
[1565] Eustratios of Agauros, §29.
[1566] On *Katabolos* as an important trade center, see Maria Gérolymatou, "Les échanges commerciaux à Byzance du VIIIe Siècle à 1204", PhD diss. (Université Paris I – Panthéon – Sorbonne, 1994), 67.

2. Decivilized space

2.1. Graves, relics, and hidden treasures

In the second part of this book, we touched on the problem of the first objectivization of the notion of "daimon". For Hesiod, demons were the immortal souls of the great men who lived in the Golden Age, the pure guardians of mortals who were the mediators between them and the gods. For Plato, they were the souls of those who had led a virtuous life.[1567] In parallel, however, much like today, the ancient Greeks and Romans were also superstitious about the souls of those who died violently or remained unburied and sought revenge for their unhappy fate, wandering around their tombs and harming the living. A good illustration of this concept is the famous scene in the *Odyssey* in which Odysseus meets the souls of the dead,[1568] and his young friend Elpenor, who had died prematurely on the island of Circe, begs him to go back and give his body a tomb.[1569]

The connection between the souls of the dead and the places of their death and burial is well-attested in sources as early as the dawn of the Classical period in ancient Greece. In his tragedy *The Persians*, Aeschylus describes the ghost (εἴδωλον) of Darius appearing on the tomb of the dead king.[1570] Plato dwells at length on the fate of those souls who are too bound to their earthly bodies and refuse to leave them even after death. According to the philosopher, they wander eternally around their graves and can be seen as shadow-like ghosts (σκιοειδῆ φάσματα).[1571] In Late Antiquity, many writers attested to the widespread belief that the souls of sinners and persons who had lost their lives violently and prematurely usually did not want to leave their bodies, and hovered around

---

[1567] See Part Two, Chapter 1, §2.
[1568] Homer, *Odyssey*, IX.38–41.
[1569] Homer, *Odyssey*, IX.51–54; 71–0.
[1570] Aeschylus, "Persae", ll. 681–42.
[1571] Plato, "Phaedo", 81c–d. See Burkert, *Greek Religion*, 195; Luck, *Arcana Mundi*, 212.

where their bones rested.¹⁵⁷² If these people were virtuous and brave when alive, like the soldiers who died at Marathon,¹⁵⁷³ their wrath does not fall on the occasional passersby. However, if they had been evil and sinful, they could harm those imprudent or ignorant enough to visit their dwellings. Places of executions and pits where the severed heads of criminals were disposed of were also considered dwellings of evil spirits and ghostly apparitions.¹⁵⁷⁴ St. John Chrysostom reproachfully observed that many of his contemporaries believed that the evil dead became not mere ghosts but demons who dwelled upon their graves¹⁵⁷⁵ The concept of the so-called *nekyodaimones* (νεκυοδαίμονες or νέκυες καὶ δαίμονες), common in Roman Egypt, is well-attested both in the magical papyri¹⁵⁷⁶ and in the so-called "tabulae defixionum",¹⁵⁷⁷ used to summon and control these spirits to gain power or predict the future. Since Byzantine hagiography between 565 and the tenth century hardly describe such divination practices, the question of necromancy remains beyond the scope of the present study.¹⁵⁷⁸

As early as the fourth century, the veneration of Christ, the crucified Son of God, and the tortured and executed martyrs, their tombs, graves, and relics gave rise to a logical but superficial contradiction. In

---

[1572] See, e.g., Porphyrius, "De abstinentia", ed. Johann Nauck, in *Porphyrii philosophi Plutonici opuscula selecta* (Leipzig: Teubner; Hildesheim: Olms, 1963), II.47; Lucian, "The Lover of Lies", §30ff (the home of Eubatides in Corinth); Joannes Chrysostomus, "In Matthaeum Homiliae", in MPG, vol. 57 (Paris, 1862), 353.

[1573] *Pausaniae Graeciae descriptio*, 1: I.32.3.4–8. Cf. Luck, *Arcana Mundi*, 238–40.

[1574] Sozomenus. *Kirchengeschichte (Historia Ecclesiastica)*, ed. Joseph Bidez and Günther Hansen [Die griechischen christlichen Schriftsteller 50] (Berlin: Akademie-Verlag, 1960), IV.3.

[1575] Joannes Chrysostomus, "In Matthaeum Homiliae", 353.

[1576] PGM, vol. 1, IV.1454ff. On the term *nekyodaimon* and its use, see Emmanuel Voutiras, "Euphemistic names for the powers of the neither world", in *The World of Ancient Magic: Papers from the First International Samson Eitrem Seminar at the Norwegian Institute at Athens, 4 – 8 May 1997*, ed. David Jordan, Hugo Montgomery, and Einar Thomassen (Bergen: The Norwegian Institute at Athens, 1999), 75; Vakaloudi (*Magic*, 117ff) claims that "the belief in *nekyodaimones* has Babylonian origins", but does not provide any source to support her hypothesis.

[1577] P. Collard, "Une nouvelle *Tabula defixionis* d'Égypte", *Révue de Philologie de Littérature et Histoire Anciennes* 4 (1930): 249.

[1578] On necromancy in early Byzantium, see Vakaloudi, *Magic*, 117–24, with bibliography.

the conceptual system of the Greco-Roman philosophical, mythological, and religious traditions, their violent deaths should have turned them into demons, eternally seeking revenge and roaming around their bodily remains. In its usual manner, the Christian religion reversed this idea, well-known to its audiences around the late Roman Empire, and used it for its own purposes. Christ suffered and died, but His humiliating death on the cross was unjust and unholy since He had no sin and was not subject to the Devil's power like ordinary mortal humans. Though tried, tortured, and executed like criminals, the martyrs had given their lives for God, and their faith and deaths became the triumph over Death itself.[1579] This fundamental theological concept combined with the crusade of the early Church Fathers against pagan superstitions. According to St. John Chrysostom, the demonic ghosts of those who died violently, mentioned in *childish old women's tales*, had no human origin and were, in fact, evil spirits, since the human soul must depart immediately from the world of the living.[1580] The martyrs are the only ones who retain their vital power by God's will, and Satan tries to desecrate their glory by subjecting them to a humiliating, violent death, which would equate them with the executed criminals demonized in popular belief.[1581] A few decades later, the ecclesiastical historian Sozomen (*c.* 400–*c.* 450) describes the purification of a place of execution near Constantinople which had become *inaccessible* (ἄβατον) because of demonic presence. This cleansing was not carried out by an exorcist or with a particular ritual but through the unjust and unholy execution of two martyrs, St. Martyrius and St. Marcian, after which the spot not only became safe but also began to expel evil spirits.

According to the hagiography of the period under study, the holy graves of saints and martyrs were familiar places of exorcism.[1582] The evil

---

[1579] On this theological concept, see Part Two, Chapter 2, §1.

[1580] Joannes Chrysostomus, "In Matthaeum Homiliae", 353ff; Joannes Chrysostomus, "In memoriam martyrum", in MPG, vol. 52 (Paris, 1862), 833; Joannes Chrysostomus, "Contiones VII de Lazaro", in MPG, vol. 48 (Paris, 1862), 984.

[1581] Joannes Chrysostomus, "Contiones VII de Lazaro", 983.

[1582] See, for example, Anastasios of Persia, Miracles, 125ff (IV (=δ).1-10) and passim; Niketas of Medikion, §48; Ioannikios (*Peter*), §71 and Ioannikios (*Sabbas*), §54; Eustratios of Agauros, §40 and §52; Patriarch Tarasios, §66.33–42; George of Amastris, §41;

spirit often caused fits and seizures in its victim near such consecrated places or appeared there in various forms. The idea that saints visited their graves and often resided there is vividly exemplified in the *Roman miracle of St. Anastasios of Persia*. According to this text, a Roman bishop arranged to have the relics of the martyr brought to his possessed daughter from a nearby male monastery so that she could wear one of Athanasios's teeth around her neck. However, the demon had taken measures. He caused a great admirer of Anastasios to break his leg crossing a river. The martyr, having gone to help his friend, was not near his relics. The demon remained in his victim's body until Anastasios's return.[1583]

The rituals of exorcism that use sacred relics are usually complex, even exotic, and highly dubious from a hygienic point of view. For example, in *The Miracles of St. Anastasios of Persia*, a physician treated his patients with the miraculous balm that flowed from the Saint's relics and had various recipes for mixing the liquid with drinks and making ointments.[1584] In the *Life* of St. Elias Speleotes, the body of a little Calabrian slave, possessed by an evil spirit, was rubbed with the sponge used to wash the dead body of the Saint.[1585] The miraculous powers of holy graves and tombs attracted the faithful, who flocked around these places in huge crowds, disturbing monastic life. After the death of Abbot Paul of Latros, his successor Symeon even sat by the Saint's grave and rebuked him, saying that because of the too-obvious exorcism performed by his relics, the monastery would fill up with laypeople. In order to prevent further turmoil, the Abbot decided to rebury the remains of his predecessor else-

---

Elias the Younger, §74; Elias Speleotes, §82, §83, §84, §85, §88 and passim; Phantinos the Younger, §58; Sabbas the Younger, §50; Demetrianos of Cyprus, §14; John the Psichaites, §12; Luke of Steiris, §83, §88, §89, §94, and §95; Naum of Ohrid, §9 and §14; Nikon Metanoeite, §51, §52, §53 and passim; Philaretos the Merciful, 161; Theodora of Thessalonica, §50, §51 and §55. The concept is so common that it appears even in *Lives* of saints whose authors avoid mentioning demons – e.g., in the *Life* of St. Patriarch Ignatios, where the saint's relics heal the possessed after his death (Patriarch Ignatios, §42 and §50).

[1583] Anastasios of Persia, *Roman Miracle*, §6.20–27.
[1584] Anastasios of Persia, Miracles, 123 (II (=β).64.7).
[1585] Elias Speleotes, §92.

where; from then on, St. Paul ceased to expel demons openly.[1586] Paradoxically, the demons themselves sometimes drove the possessed to the relics of a saint to be healed.[1587]

The ancient concept that sinners and executed criminals became evil and demonic beings who lurked by their graves and tombs did not disappear in Byzantium. Hagiography gives some insight into such beliefs. Theophanes Confessor mentions the so-called "Ta Pelagiou" (τὰ Πελαγίου), a place near the church of St. Andrew in the western part of Constantinople, where the bodies of the executed were disposed of.[1588] According to his *Life*, Patriarch Antony Kauleas (893–901) went there as a youth and observed two ugly human figures. When they saw him, one told his companion it was time for them to go because they could not bear the pious young man's presence. Immediately afterward, they ran away and disappeared.[1589]

Not only mass graves for executed criminals but also common cemeteries were considered haunted places. Demons often drew their victims there, like the possessed young man who roved about the burial places near Regium in Calabria shortly after St. Elias the Younger's death in 903,[1590] or the inhabitant of the village of Plagia near Corinth in central Greece who entered tombs and covered his head with the ashes and bones of the dead not long after St. Nikon Metanoeite passed away in the late tenth or early eleventh century.[1591] This concept, relatively rare in hagiography, stems from the general idea that Satan is the master of

---

[1586] Paul of Latros I, §45.
[1587] Eustratios of Agauros, §54.
[1588] See *Theophanis chronographia*, 420 (the story of Patrikios Bakangios, an associate of the usurper Arabasdos, whose wife was forced by Emperor Constantine V to exhumate her late husband's remains and dump them in the pit for the bodies of executed criminals); *Theophanis chronographia*, 437 (the story of St. Stephen the Younger, thrown in the same pit); *Theophanis chronographia*, 442 (the story of the former patriarch Constantine II, decapitated as a criminal in 766). On "Ta Pelagiou", see Cyril Mango, Roger Scott, and Geoffrey Greatrex, *The Chronicle of Theophanes Confessor: Byzantine and Near East History AD 284 – 813* (Oxford: Clarendon Press, 1997), 582.
[1589] Antony Kauleas, §20.
[1590] Elias the Younger, §73.
[1591] Nikon Metanoeite, §52.

Death, and consequently, an evil presence in places where Death reigns is permanent and not necessarily related to the sinfulness and vice of the deceased. Only holy men and women could visit potentially dangerous graveyards and other uninhabited areas, like the open wilderness and caves. The obscure St. John, Bishop of Gotthia in the second half of the eighth century, was reported to frequent a graveyard in his parish by night and to communicate with the dead as with the living.[1592]

Pre-Christian Greek literature associated graves not only with the ghosts of those buried there but also with the presence of other demons of immortal origin.[1593] Pausanias mentions the demon Eurynome, who ate the flesh of corpses and left only their bones. The painter Polygnotus (fl. c. 475–450 B.C.) depicted him as blue-black like the flies flying around the dead, with long sharp teeth, sitting on the feathers of a vulture.[1594] Evil spirits could also appear in the guise of deceased persons by their graves and thus deceive the relatives who came to honor them.[1595] The anonymous author of the *Testament of Solomon* mentions such a fearsome demon, the ghost of a slain giant, who would sit at night by someone's grave, assume the image of the one buried, and kill with his sword anyone who came near the spot.[1596] In the *Life* of St. Theodore Sykeotes, the product of a religiously and culturally transitional epoch, the ancient belief that demons crowded burial places combined with the Christian demonization of the ancient idolatrous world, with its buildings and monuments scattered around the Mediterranean.[1597] The evil spirits in this text often emerge from pagan graves dug up by greedy treasure hunters. Most of these ancient haunted cemeteries are located in a relatively small area on the banks of River Sangarius between the provinces of Galatia Prima and Gordiana, and the vicinity of the village Sykeon some thirty kilometers from Athanasoupolis in central Asia Mi-

---

[1592] John of Gotthia, §8.
[1593] Greenfield, *Traditions of Belief*, 231 and 259 (referring to the *Life* of St. Theodore Sykeotes); Guillou, *Le Diable Byzantin*, 19.
[1594] *Pausaniae Graeciae descriptio*, 3: X.28.7.
[1595] Joannes Chrysostomus, "In memoriam martyrum", 833.
[1596] *The Testament of Solomon*, 17.
[1597] Joannou, *Démonologie*, 11.

nor. Since these burial places can be localized relatively accurately, we will pay closer attention to them.

One of the haunted pagan graveyards described in the *Life* of St. Theodore Sykeote was located near the village of Bouzaion (Βουζαῖον) near a city called Gratianopolis (ὑπὸ τὴν Κρατιανῶν πόλιν) somewhere along the lower Sangarius River, not far from the city of Juliopolis.[1598] The residents decided to build a bridge across a mountain precipice and hired a team of masons. Influenced by the Devil, members of the working party went to a nearby hill to get construction materials and dug up some pagan gravestones on the pretext that they needed them for the project. As the author explains, they were actually driven by a desire to get their hands on the grave offerings to the dead, which they would distribute among themselves in private, without the villagers suspecting anything. Immediately afterward, a swarm of unclean spirits emerged from the desecrated graves and began to spread diseases among the local populace, the travelers, and the horses. The villagers threatened the demons with the name of the great exorcist Theodore Sykeotes, and they were scared away for a while. However, the people wanted a permanent solution to the problem and asked Theodore to come in person and deliver them from the evil presence. As soon as he arrived, the demons complained that the exorcist had left the confines of his own province of Galatia and come to Gordiana. In a burst of local pride, they warned him they were braver than their fellows in his province. Their big words were of no avail, and with the very first prayer, the Saint temporarily banished them. However, the situation was so severe that an entire exorcism ceremony on the field was required. The next day all the infected gathered, and Theodore blessed them and led a procession around the village. After purifying the settlement, he visited the excavated graves on the hill. For a long time, he tormented the demons through God's grace, making the sign of the cross, striking the possessed on the chest, and praying. Finally, the spirits obeyed his orders, tore their victims' garments from the inside,

---

[1598] Theodore Sykeotes, §43.1ff. On the location, see Festugière, *Vie de Théodore de Sykéôn*, 199; Ramsay, *The Historical Geography*, 246.

and came out of their bodies screaming. However, one of the demons, who had possessed a local woman, refused to leave and tried to negotiate. The exorcist did not dignify that with an answer but immediately started pulling the woman's hair, beating her with the cross, and cursing. The exorcism ended with another litany around the village, after which the surrounding area became safe.[1599]

The relationship between a disastrous evil influence upon a local community and the greed for ancient treasures hidden in pagan graves is evident in three other stories of St. Theodore's *Life*, set in the villages of Sandos, Permataia, and Eukraon. These episodes vividly describe Byzantine rural communities' life and social climate on the eve of the Arab conquest, and the strategies for social stigmatization and marginalization. Guilt for various misfortunes was laid on particular members of the community, their supposed greed, sinfulness, and sacrilege. However, the position of the Church and the imperial authorities in such situations differed fundamentally from the role played by royal judges and professional exorcists during the Great Witch Hunt of the early modern period. As the Church's representative, Theodore did not support public castigation. Unlike the Catholic and Protestant exorcists of a millennium later, he never blamed the evil influence on individuals, supposedly susceptible to devilish temptations, because the most dangerous enemy of the Church in the peaceful central Asia Minor of the late sixth century were the spiritual and material remnants of the pagan past. On the other hand, the central authorities did not need to establish, legitimize, demonstrate, or increase their control over the local communities like the royal government in France in the sixteenth and seventeenth centuries, but only to keep order. Euphranthios, the governor of Ancyra, showed blatant indifference to particular local conflicts and their social impact, and was even somewhat disinterested in the Church's crusade against paganism; he always tended to take radical, but rational measures, not bothering to approach justice with kangaroo courts. The villagers, appalled at the pros-

---

[1599] Theodore Sykeotes, §43. On this episode, see also Mango, *Empire*, 161.

pect of his intervention, looked to Theodore and the Church to resolve their problems.

According to the text, the farmer Eutolmios from the village of Sandos in the region of Protomeria, western Galatia, decided to build a new barn and began leveling the ground for the construction, but he accidentally dislodged an ancient stone while digging. A swarm of evil spirits emerged from the hole, possessing the animals and many villagers. The demons tormented their victims and turned the local community against Eutolmios, claiming he had been digging for treasure out of greed. As grave robbing (τυμβωρυχία) was a serious criminal offense, and since the law dictated that a share of any treasure found had to be given to the state, the governor of Galatia Prima, Euphranthios, prepared to come from Ancyra and personally investigate the matter. Frightened by both the demons and the prospect of being visited by a government representative, the villagers set out to burn Eutolmius and his house, holding him responsible for the misfortunes that had befallen the community. However, the village elders foiled this plan, and a delegation was sent to the monastery to ask Theodore to come and deliver them from the misfortune. He inspected the ditch and assured the villagers that Eutolmios had not done anything wrong, nor had he found any treasure; he just had dug too deep, and the evil spirits lurking in the depths of the earth had emerged. The next day, the holy man performed a litany around the village and stood atop the hill where Eutolmius had been digging. He bowed his head, prayed, cursed the demons, and cast them out of their victims with Christ's help. Under the supervision of the Holy Spirit, he then closed up the hole, pushed the stone back in place, and made the sign of the cross over it. From then on, the village and its vicinity were safe.[1600]

Immediately after the exorcism in Sandos, when the Saint was about to return to his monastery, a delegation from the village of Permetaia asked him to deliver eight women and six men tormented by many demons. The spirits had come out from under a *stone slab* (πλακίον, πλάξ), probably a gravestone, dug out from the earth. Theo-

---

[1600] Theodore Sykeotes, §114.

dore agreed, but the evil spirits caused his mule to slip on the way there. The holy man fell, and two pieces of wood from the saddle pierced his hairshirt and cut into his flesh. Despite the severity of the injury, Theodore simply bandaged the wound with a linen rag and continued his trip. When he finally arrived at Permataia, everyone thought he would lose consciousness from exhaustion and blood loss, but God's grace helped him, and he, sturdy as an iron statue, stayed awake all night to praise God. The purification ritual was similar to the one in the village of Sandos.[1601]

The most detailed description of the action of demons on an entire settlement is the case of the village of Eukraon, located in the district of Lagatine in western Galatia, north of Sykeon.[1602] The farmer Timothy excavated a hill rumored to contain rich ancient graves. The biographer claims not to know the man's real intentions; he might not have been pleased by the prospect of finding hidden treasure but simply wanted to improve the soil and sow it. Be that as it may, it turned out that a malicious phalanx of unclean spirits haunted the hill, and they began *to cling* (ἐκολλήθη) to local inhabitants and cattle. Under their evil influence, the possessed created all sorts of disorder and property damage. The enraged governor Euphranthios ordered Timothy's arrest and severe punishment as a grave robber, and some of the possessed were also detained for their misconduct and sentenced to be brutally flogged with ox sinews. However, they reacted to the punishment with crazy laughter instead of begging for their release, and even encouraged the floggers to beat them some more. Set free at last, the possessed invaded Timothy's farm, from which he had escaped, and burned his haystacks. They then scattered around the village and began destroying the food supplies, breaking into houses, smashing the furniture, stealing, and beating anyone who attempted to stop them.

[1601] Theodore Sykeotes, §115.

[1602] According to the text itself, Eucraon was located in the diocese of Athanasioupolis, about 50 kilometers west of Ancyra; on this village, see also Ramsay, *The Historical Geography*, 246; Festugière, *Vie de Théodore de Sykéôn*, 242; *TIB*, vol. 4, 197.

The situation in Eukraon got entirely out of control, and the few sane villagers and the clergy implored Theodore to help them. When he arrived, he could barely struggle through the crowd of the possessed to get to the local church of Archangel Michael, where he spent the night in prayer. In the morning, Theodore cursed the demons and commanded them to return to the hill, then remained in the temple to pray and charged his pupil Julian and the local priests with the litany around the village and the reading of the Gospel on the hill. During the exorcism ceremonies, the demons tried in vain to repel Theodore's prayers, as if an angelic army was attacking them, but in the end, God's might prevailed. Screaming, they left the bodies of their victims and returned to the ditch, which the villagers refilled with earth. At the closing ceremony, Theodore celebrated Mass and placed a cross on the spot where the evil spirits had come out.[1603]

However, this was not the end of Eukraon's misfortunes. A marble sarcophagus near the village contained the remains of ancient *Hellenes* (i.e., pagans) guarded by demons. The demons suggested to some farmers that they remove the lid and use the sarcophagus for storing water. The demons crawled everywhere and tormented the villagers and their domestic animals. The villagers again sent for Theodore, and he delivered them through prayer. He returned the evil spirits to the place whence they had come but refused their request to let them live in the sarcophagus, which remained as a sign of the Saint's miracles.[1604]

Though the most informative, the *Life* of St. Theodore Sykeotes is by no means the only hagiographical text of the sixth and seventh centuries to describe the close relationship between demons and ancient graveyards, both as an element of the folklore of the epoch and as a propaganda tool in the Orthodox Church's struggle against pagan remnants. Probably in the mid-sixth century, St. Alypios Stylites lived as a hermit in the mountains south of Euchaita in Pontus, Asia Minor.[1605] He

---

[1603] Theodore Sykeotes, §116ff.
[1604] Theodore Sykeotes, §118.
[1605] The *Life* gives almost no indications of its date other than the death of Alypius at the age of 99 during the reign of Emperor Heraclius (610–640). The purification of the an-

searched for a place near the city with a water source where he could retreat, and found a frightening ancient cemetery full of demons. Nobody dared to set foot there, and the residents tried in vain to dissuade Alypios, who had decided to purify the place, build a chapel, and live there in peace. He was not a man who could be frightened by the Devil's forces and investigated the area thoroughly to find the source of the evil influence. Behind one of the graves, he finally found an ancient column with a statue of a fantastic creature, half lion and half bull. Alypios destroyed it with an iron bar and replaced it with a cross as a sign of Christ's victory over Satan's forces.[1606]

Despite the similarities with the *Life* of St. Theodore Sykeotes half a century later, this story displays a somewhat different picture of the social and religious climate in the rural communities of northern Asia Minor. Unlike the evil spirits of Sandos, Permataia, and Eukraon, demonic influence in this case was limited to the boundaries of the ancient graveyard and did not harm the inhabited area. Though Christian, the populace does not seek the holy man's assistance to exorcize the place — quite the opposite. Alypios is the one who insists on expelling the demons and settling in the formerly haunted area to display his holy power as a man of God and a representative of the Church. Bishop Theodore Sykeotes lived in an entirely different environment. By the early seventh century, the Church's authority was already undisputed, and the local populace turned to him to counter the governor's radical measures. We can only make hypotheses about the real motives behind the outrageous behavior of the tumultuous gang that ravaged Eukraon; nevertheless, by finding a demonic explanation for them, Theodore saved the community from the intervention of Euphranthios at least partially.

Lastly, ancient graveyards are the most common places for concluding a contract with Satan, whose outlines we gave above.[1607] In one of

---

cient cemetery near Euchaita is described in paragraph 9, and we can therefore place it some time early in the Saint's life, probably in the mid-sixth century (see Delehaye, *Les Saints Stylites*, lxxix).

[1606] Alypios Stylites, §9.4ff and §9.18–26.
[1607] See Part Two, Chapter 1, §2.3.

the versions of the *Life* of St. Basil the Great, written in the late fifth century, a young man, Helladius, fell in love with a noble Roman senator's daughter, who had decided to become a nun. Disheartened by the girl's persistent refusal to yield to his passion, he resorted to a local sorcerer and poisoner in Caesarea, who arranged a meeting with his master, the Devil, near a pagan grave.[1608] The youth had to bring a "recommendation letter" to the Evil One and sign a pact with him there. Helladius sold his immortal soul in exchange for marriage with the girl, and only the fervent prayers of his new wife and those of St. Basil the Great saved him in the end. The other story comes from the *Life* of the obscure bishop of Catania in Sicily, Leo, set in the late seventh century. A Jewish magician introduced the young and ambitious aristocrat Heliodorus to the art of magic; his training concluded with the young man renouncing his Christian faith and a pact with a demon, the master of the air. The contract was signed at midnight near a tomb of *ancient heroes*, and the evil spirit put the demon Gaspar in Heliodorus's service. Unlike the story of Helladius, in this case, the wicked man's soul was not saved in the end.[1609]

2.2. Desecrated churches

As noted, Byzantine hagiographers frequently mention evil spirits tempting and tormenting monks in monasteries and desolate hermitages. Such cases, however, do not concern the demon's connection to a particular place: the Devil's servants do not permanently haunt such places but only appear there to undermine the piety of those devoted to God. The saints' *Lives* of the period under study also mention churches and monasteries built on ground, previously haunted by demons and evil spirits who attempted to prevent their construction. For example, St. Theodore Sykeotes exorcized a horde of Satan's servants that emerged from the earth during the construction of a chapel dedicated to the Holy Mother of God near Heraclea Pontica (modern Ergeli in Turkey),[1610] and St. Symeon

---

[1608] Die Erzählung des Helladius (Proterius), 126.5ff and 127.5.
[1609] Leo of Catania, §34.
[1610] Theodore Sykeotes, §44.

Stylites the Younger expelled the Devil who had entered the foundations of his monastery and shook the whole building.[1611]

By contrast, destroyed and desecrated holy places were considered to be under the control of evil spirits.[1612] According to Stephen the Deacon, the iconoclastic emperor Constantine V (741–775) concluded contracts with demons (τὰς πρὸς τοὺς δαίμονες συνθήκας ἐποιεῖτο) in the ruins of St. Mavra Church near Constantinople, which he had destroyed himself. The rituals included human sacrifices, and the most notorious of his victims was the little son of one Suphlamios.[1613]

After the reintegration of the Peloponnese, central Greece, and the territories around Thessalonica into the administrative and political system of the empire in the first half of the ninth century, and after the final restoration of the icons in 843, the reconsolidated Orthodox Church took special measures to increase its influence in these territories, some largely populated by Slavs. These measures included the building of churches and monasteries on a large scale. Influential figures like St. Luke of Steiris in Boeothia, St. Euthymios the Younger in Athos, the obscure St. Germanos of Kosinitza in Macedonia, and the famous St. Nikon Metanoeite in Crete and the Peloponnese led the movement. Judging from the *Lives* of St. Euthymios and St. Nikon, they often established new religious centers where the ruins of old, desecrated churches still existed, urging the local populace and the authorities to fund their enterprise and performing spectacular exorcisms of the ancient monuments.

One of the most interesting stories of this kind concerns the old haunted temple of St. Andrew near Thessalonica and the foundation of the Peristera monastery. During his stay on Mount Athos, the Lord commanded St. Euthymios to go to the mountains east of Thessalonica and find an old church that had been turned into a fold, so as to consecrate and restore it. He obeyed, but the demons that inhabited the desecrated place hindered its purification and rebuilding. Jealous that a tem-

---

[1611] Symeon Stylites the Younger, §99ff. Van den Ven (*La Vie ancienne*, 1: 116*), dates the event shortly after the great Antioch earthquake of 551.
[1612] See Joannou, *Démonologie*, 11. Joannou refers only to a few early hagiographical texts.
[1613] Stephen the Younger, 165.20ff. On this story, see Part Two, Chapter 1, §2.3.5.

ple was being constructed for the salvation of souls, the evil spirits not only harmed the builders spiritually but also shouted and threw stones at them. Once, in the middle of the day, they began to shake the scaffolding violently, trying to knock the master builder off it. However, he managed to hold on, and this strengthened the determination of Euthymios and the others to continue the work. Shortly afterward, there was an even more terrible attack. At midnight, when everyone was asleep from fatigue, the evil spirits shook the already completed left aisle of the church so violently that they managed to collapse it. Rebuilding the ruined section became a war of the pious against the demons. Their attacks were incessant and extremely exhausting: they tried to ambush Euthymios and attacked him even as he watered the garden, but he always managed to drive them away with a torch and a cross. Finally, the holy man lost his patience and shouted that they were powerless cowards. He dared them to do what they could — he was not afraid to fight. If they did nothing, then they should stop getting on his nerves (ἐκνευρώσαντες) and get out. Frightened, the unclean spirits disappeared, and the dedication of the four-domed church of St. Andrew took place in 6379 (871).[1614] Later, the great monastery of Peristera, also founded by the Saint, grew around this temple.

We can only speculate who the aggressive demons in the story of the rebuilding of St. Andrew were. As the hagiographer informs us, the property with the fold had owners, and they were not very pleased about the discovery of the old temple of God: the case would have been analogous to the discovery of an archaeological site in an expensive plot of land in Greece today. The demons do not behave in the standard way of Byzantine hagiography: they do not possess anyone or anything nor do they appear in any form. They attack mainly at night. "Getting on somebody's nerves" is not usually part of the repertoire of unclean spirits. This is probably a picturesque description of how the Byzantines defended

---

[1614] Euthymios the Younger, §29; Papachryssanthou, "La vie de Saint Euthyme le Jeune", 235ff.

their property in such cases. Except that the monk Euthymios proved to be courageous.

The *Life* of St. Nikon Metanoite also provides information about a possessed ancient church consecrated by a holy man and restored by him. During his stay in Sparta, probably in the early 970s, Nikon decided to build a temple in the town, and Bishop Theopompos and the local clergy supported his decision. During the construction, the workers came across a huge stone. As they were struggling to move it, the demons inhabiting the place came out as wasps and began to sting and harass the people. In the author's opinion, it was because of these evil spirits that God wanted the temple built.[1615] The exact location of the church dedicated to Jesus Christ, the Virgin Mary, and St. Paraskeva is controversial. Adamantdios Adamandiou[1616] identifies a tenth-century church on the Acropolis of Sparta with the one built by Nikon, but this is not considered proven.

2.3. Wells

The so-called "water demons" (ὑδραῖοι δαίμονες) are part of both the Late Antique and Late Byzantine classifications of supernatural beings, which we examined in more detail in the second part of this study.[1617] The characteristics they were given by Neoplatonic and Christian writers are not particularly helpful in explaining the few accounts of haunted water sources in Byzantine hagiographers. An interesting observation comes from Pseudo-Psellus in the middle of the thirteenth century, who says that water demons usually take female forms or appear as birds and possess women.[1618] According to the anonymous author of this text, the

---

[1615] Nikon Metanoeite, §36.
[1616] See Sullivan, *The Life of Saint Nikon*, 286, with bibliography.
[1617] See Part Two, Chapter 1, §2.
[1618] Pseudo-Psellos, "Timothée ou des demons", ll. 545–48 and 552ff. See Greenfield, *Traditions of Belief*, 189ff; Vakaloudi, *Magic*, 112.

"Hellenes" called these evil spirits "naiads", "nereids", and, surprisingly enough, "dryads".[1619]

The association between the female sex, birds, and water agrees somewhat with the information about the demon-possessed well in the *Life* of St. Nikon Metanoeite, where bringing water from a polluted well is a symbol of sexual desire and fornication. According to the text, a woman from the city of Chalcis in Euboea[1620] sent her daughter for water between 968 and 970.[1621] The maiden unwisely decided to go to the nearest foul-smelling and abandoned well. As she leaned over it, an evil spirit emerged from the water source as a raven and entered her. St. Nikon forced the demon to return to its abode and ordered the inhabitants to cover the well.[1622] In this case, there is both possession of a woman and the demon bird flying out of a water source.

A similar allusion can be found four centuries earlier, though without mentioning a bird, in the *Life* of St. Symeon Stylites the Younger, in which a demon has tortured a young woman since she was a little girl. Due to its evil influence, she was unable to conceive. Her husband banished her, but despite the solid legal basis for annulling the marriage, he remained faithful to her. Symeon forced the demon to bring water from a well, treating him as a servant, and afterward allowed him to leave its victim's body. From then on, the woman was able to deliver children.[1623]

The above story is full of allusions that must have been recognizable to the text's contemporary audience. Supposedly, the demon aimed to torture the young woman but also to force her husband to commit the deadly sin of adultery, symbolized by the standard motif of bringing water from a well. When he refused to yield to the temptation, Symeon forced the evil spirit to undertake the menial chore as a symbol of his

---

[1619] The dryads (from δρῦς, *oak*) are not water deities, like the naiads and the nereids, but tree nymphs.

[1620] Nikon Metanoeite, §26. On Chalcis, see Sullivan, *The Life of Saint Nikon*, 281; *TIB*, vol. 1: *Hellas und Thessalia*, ed. Johannes Koder and Friedrich Hild (1976), 156–58.

[1621] On the dates of the main events of St. Nikon's life, see Part One, Chapter 2, §10. For more about this case and the raven-like demons, see Part Three, Chapter 1, §3.1.

[1622] Nikon Metanoeite, §27. See Mango, "Diabolus Byzantinus", 220.

[1623] Symeon Stylites the Younger, §118.21–25.

humiliation and the failed attempt to break the couple's sexual purity. The wife, in this case, is not the real object of the diabolical plan but a mere instrument.

3. Civilized space

3.1. Streets and buildings

Only a few texts during the period under study describe events that take place in cities, and only Leontius of Neapolis gives information about demon-possessed streets. According to the *Life* of St. Symeon the Fool, shortly after the Saint arrived in the Syrian city of Emesa,[1624] he expelled a demon from a side alley, sent him to destroy the business of a heretic shopkeeper and his family, and punished him in this way for his deadly sin. Later, Symeon came to a crossroads in the same town, saw a demon lurking to prey on passers-by, and began to throw stones at people for them to avoid danger.[1625] He continued to do this until the evil spirit possessed a stray dog and thus saved the people from danger.[1626]

The Late Antique and Byzantine stories of haunted buildings sound quite familiar to the modern reader. In the second century A.D., Lucian told the story of the notorious house of Eubatides in Corinth, in which no one could set foot because of the evil demonic influence spread over the place. The Pythagorean Arignotus, a self-proclaimed Egyptian magic expert, ignored the neighbors' warnings and decided to spend a night in the building. Calm and confident, he made himself comfortable in one of the rooms and began to read quietly. The demon soon appeared, naively believing Arignotus to be an ordinary man. The evil creature rose up blacker than the deepest darkness and began to attack the uninvited visitor in various forms, now appearing as a dog, now as a bull or a lion. Its attempts to scare the magician were in vain, and when Arignotus began

---

[1624] St. Symeon the Fool arrived in Emesa probably after the earthquake in 588 (Festugière, *Léontios de Néapolis*, 8ff; Symeon the Holy Fool, 84.21 (where Emperor Maurice is mentioned).
[1625] Symeon the Holy Fool, 87.18–88. 8.
[1626] Symeon the Holy Fool, 91.5–11.

to hum something in Egyptian, the ghost withdrew to a corner and disappeared. In the morning, the exorcist and his friends dug up the spot and found human bones underneath. After their interment, Eubatides's home became habitable again.[1627]

In the Byzantine hagiography of the period under study, evil spirits haunt houses and towers, appearing either as a formless malicious force or in a material form. Some of the stories are no less vivid than the tale in Lucian, like the account of the home of the high official (*strategos*) Theodore in the *Life* of St. Theodore Sykeotes. This haunted mansion was located in the marketplace of Pylai in Bithynia, on the southern shore of the Sea of Marmara.[1628] The unclean spirits pelted the family with stones during lunch and dinner, frightened them, and broke the crockery and the women's looms. After the building became full of mice and snakes, the situation was so severe that finally nobody could enter the house. At the request of the dignitary, Theodore Sykeotes spent a night inside, praying to God. On the morrow, he cleansed the premises with holy water, and the house was free from the harmful influence of the demons.[1629]

The haunted house of *strategos* Theodore in Pylai remains an isolated phenomenon in the Byzantine hagiography of the period under study, and, after a gap of about two centuries, the only other buildings mentioned in the saints' *Lives* are not private homes but towers. The earliest of these accounts concerns the dragon that inhabited the tower in Syracuse where St. Gregory of Dekapolis settled the 830s,[1630] but the most vivid description, which is reminiscent of both Eubaties's house in Lucian and a modern horror story, comes from the *Life* of St. Elias Speleotes about half a century later. During the troubled years that followed the capture of Syracuse by the Sicilian Arabs in 878, the Byzantine theme of Calabria was under constant threat from Muslim raids. One of the worst of these raids was mounted against Regium in 888. According to the text,

---

[1627] Lucian, "The Lover of Lies", §30ff.
[1628] Ramsay, *The Historical Geography*, 187; Festugière, *Vie de Théodore de Sykéôn*, 250; Janin, *Les églises et les monastères*, 82, 87, and 96.
[1629] Theodore Sykeotes, §131.
[1630] Gregory of Dekapolis, §30ff.

Elias Speleotes and his mentor Arsenios learned of the impending event by God's wish and left for Patras in the Peloponnese. There, they approached the bishop and the clergy, asking to be shown a suitable place to pursue their prayers in safety. The local priests replied that there was a tower in a suburb where the monks could lead a quiet life, but so far, no one had been able to resist the spirit that haunted the place, created apparitions (φάσματα) and tumult, and frightened everybody who dared to set foot inside. Old Arsenios remarked with a slight amount of irony that he had never seen a demon with his own eyes in his long monastic life and set out with Elias to investigate the matter. On the first night, the demon appeared and began to make noise in one of the tower's corners but failed to frighten the holy men, and they prayed with fervor to counter its attacks. The next night the spirit emerged again, but this time it did not confine its influence to the corner but produced numerous apparitions (φαντασιοκοπῶν) throughout the tower. On the third, the demon's noise, blows, and pitiful groans were already on the outside of the building, and thereafter it vanished forever. Arsenios and Elias lived there undisturbed for another eight years, until 896.[1631]

One of the towers in the stories above was located, according to the *Life* of St. Gregory of Dekapolis, in Sicily, and the other concerned the Italian St. Elias Speleotes. These are the only accounts of such haunted buildings in the Byzantine hagiography of the period under study. They provide a unique insight into the local folklore that probably inspired, a millennium later, the classical Gothic literary tradition, beginning with *The Castle of Otranto* by Horace Walpole (1764).

3.2. Baths

In contrast to the wells possessed by evil spirits, which remain an isolated phenomenon in the Byzantine hagiography of the period 565–1000, the saints' *Lives* provide numerous accounts of demons haunting baths

---

[1631] Elias Speleotes, §21.

(λουτρά, βαλανεῖα).[1632] As is evident from the story of the philosopher Porphyry, who chased away a demon called "Causatha" (Καυσάθα) from a bathhouse in Rome,[1633] this concept was probably a part of the urban legends of Late Antiquity, but it gained significance in Christian literature in particular, since nudity and sex were closely associated with places where people gathered together to relax and take care of their bodies. Gregory of Nyssa composed one of the most vivid descriptions of a bathhouse possessed by an evil spirit at the end of the fourth century. He recounts the story of a deacon, a disciple of St. Gregory the Theologian, who went on a pilgrimage, when night overtook him in some town. He stayed there overnight and decided to take refresh himself from the road in the local bath. However, after sunset, the place was frequented by a killer demon (δαίμων τις ἀνθρωποκτόνος), whose doom-bringing power (φθοροποιὸς δύναμις) had made the place inaccessible after dark. The deacon persuaded the custodian to give him the key and entered. While he was still in the anteroom, the demon sent humanlike and beastlike apparitions made of fire and smoke. They whispered to him in hoarse, rasping voices, rage around and tried to frighten him. He managed to get out of that room by continually crossing himself. Inside, even greater horrors awaited the priest. It was as if an earthquake shook the building, cracking the floor, exposing the thick fumes of the heating system below (as is well known, in the so-called hypocaust, the floors of antique baths are double and hot air circulates between the two layers). In this room, the deacon crossed himself and took a soothing bath. In the end, it turned out that the malevolent supernatural being had closed the door, and the servant of God had difficulty getting out. This did not scare him either: the sign of the cross solved the problem again, and he walked out undisturbed.[1634]

[1632] On haunted baths in general, see Campbell Bonner, "Demons of the Bath", in *Studies Presented to F. L. Griffith* (London, 1932), 204–8; Greenfield, *Traditions of Belief*, 216; Vakaloudi, *Magic*, 113, who claims, without referring to any source, that the concept originated in Egypt and Syria.

[1633] *Eunapii vitae sophistarum*, ed. Giuseppe Giangrande (Rome: Polygraphica, 1956), IV.1.12.4ff.

[1634] Gregorius Nussenus, "De vita Gregorii Thaumaturgi", in MPG, vol. 46 (Paris, 1863), 949D–952D.

The hagiography of the period under study also contains graphic descriptions of demon-possessed baths and their workings. Around 829, Peter of Atroa traveled to the monastery of St. Porphyry.[1635] When he passed through the village of Pigadia (literally, "Wells"), the Saint stayed as usual at the home of one Constantine. However, his hospitable friend had serious difficulties at the time. He had built himself a house near a ruined old bath, where many unclean demons had taken up residence. They would not let anyone live peacefully in Constantine's new home, and whoever stayed long developed twisted mouths, withered limbs, and madness. Peter stayed in the house and cast out the demons with prayer.[1636]

According to the hagiography of Elias Speleotes, baths need cleansing of demonic presence by default. According to this text, between 888 and 896, the bishop of Patras invited Elias for a bathe during his stay in the Peloponnese. The young man agreed, and the bishop asked him to consecrate the water before they entered the pool. As soon as Elias performed the ritual, the place filled with a divine fragrance. The author pointed out that no one bathed there since. For many years, people only visited the closed building to smell the incense through the door.[1637]

The bath is associated with magical practices in the *Life* of Leo of Catania. According to the text, Emperor Constantine IV (667–685) received a complaint from the governor (*eparch*) of Catania, Loukios, that the life of the city was being disturbed by the sorcerer Heliodorus's impure enchantments and his corruption of the noble maidens. Constantine sent the senior officer (*strator*) Heraclides to Sicily with his soldiers, giving him thirty-two days to arrest Heliodorus. Upon his arrival in Catania, the magician graciously received the commander and persuaded him to rest in his house for the remaining days of his mission. On the last day, Heliodorus invited Heraclides and his men to a bath, warning them not to mention the name of Christ. The men bent down to wash their heads,

---

[1635] On the St. Porphyry monastery on the outskirts of Mount Olympus in Bithynia, see Janin, *Les églises et les monastères*, 209 (cf. 151 and 162).
[1636] Peter of Atroa, §61.
[1637] Elias Speleotes, §26.

and when they raised them, they found themselves in a bathing house in Constantinople, their clothes standing in the dressing room untouched. Heraclides himself was magically transported into the vast imperial thermae.[1638]

4. The bridge between worlds

In Byzantine literature, the bridge is a highly complex symbol of the passage between worlds.[1639] Metaphorically, it appears as a metaphor for the Virgin Mary, the mediator between the human world and Heaven,[1640] and for baptism as the initiation into the Christian community.[1641] The bridge also symbolizes the passage into the Underworld, and Proclus of Constantinople (fourth century) calls Christ's descent into Hell *the bridge of the dead to the resurrection*.[1642] The souls of the dead cross a bridge over the River of Fire to reach Paradise, as is evident from texts like the Revelation of St. Anastasia.[1643] The same concept is common in medieval Western European literature[1644] and modern Greek folklore.[1645] As we

---

[1638] Leo of Catania, §21.
[1639] *ODB*, vol. 1, s.v. "Bridges", 325; Vakaloudi, *Magic*, 218 and n. 336.
[1640] Gregorius Pisides, "Hymnus Acathistus", in *MPG*, vol. 92, 1337C; Ephraem Syrus, "Precationes ad Dei matrem", ed. Kontantinos Frantzolas, *The Works of St. Ephraem Syrus* [Greek: Κωνσταντίνος Φραντζόλας, Ὁσίου Ἐφραίμ τοῦ Σύρου ἔργα, ed.], vol. 6 (Thessalonica, 1995), 363; [Pseudo-]Sophronius Hierosolymitanus, "Triodium", in *MPG*, vol. 87.3 (Paris, 1863), 3968C.
[1641] Joannes Chrysostomus, "De Baptismo Christi et de Epiphania", in *MPG*, vol. 49 (Paris, 1862), 366C.
[1642] Proclus Constantinopolis archiepiscopus, "Orationes", in *MPG*, vol. 65 (Paris, 1864), 785C.
[1643] Lambakis, *The Descents into Hell*, 58–60.
[1644] See, e.g., Grégoire le Grand, *Dialogues*, vol. 3, ed. Adalbert de Vogüé, trans. Paul Antin (Paris: Éditions de Cerf, 1980), §8, where Pope Gregory the Great describes a stinking river with murky black water under the bridge (*pons erat, sub quo niger atque caligosus foetoris intolerabilis nebulam exhalans fluvius decurrebat*); on its far bank lies a beautiful meadow, full of fragrant flowers. For other mentions of the bridge in medieval Western literature, see Lambakis, *The Descents into Hell*, 116 (on the *Visio Alberici*, written in the Monte Cassino Monastery c. 1130), 118 (on the *Visio Tnugdali*, written by the Irish monk Mark between 1148 and 1149), and 120 (on the *Tractatus de purgatorio Sancti Patricii*, written in Saltrey, England, between 1185 and 1190).
[1645] Lambakis, *The Descents into Hell*, 198ff and 203.

have seen above, however, the bridge appears only rarely in hagiographical descriptions of Hell, and probably the only such mention in the period under study is the narrow bridge, as thin as a hair, over the River of Fire which little Niketas of Paphlagonia fears to cross, according to the *Life* of St. Philaretos the Merciful.[1646] In the *Life* of Basil the Younger, the ambiguous *path* (ὁδός) between the tollhouses appears instead of a bridge.[1647] Although the hagiographical texts between the sixth and the tenth centuries do not often mention bridges as haunted places, two particular accounts provide insight into the Byzantine East's folklore of this period.

According to the *Life* of Mary of Antioch, written probably in the sixth century, a magician named Megas sent the noble Antiochene Anthemius to a bridge near Antioch with instructions to wait and not to make the sign of the cross. At midnight the youth heard a commotion and saw the master of the demons riding in a chariot and accompanied by a large retinue. The Antiochene produced a letter of recommendation which the wicked magician had given him, and made the contract whereby he renounced his soul.[1648] In this case, the bridge served as an intersection where two different realities meet: the world of mortals and the world of evil forces.

A battle with a demon on a bridge in the Byzantine hagiography of the period under study occurs in the *Life* of the Lesbian saints David, Symeon, and George. According to the text, George had the custom of going into the woods at night to cut wood to leave at the doors of infirm inhabitants. Once, as he was returning with his load, he felt a horde of demons (στῖφος δαιμόνων) walking behind him, pelting him with stones, and shouting in a disorderly way. When they reached the so-called Great Bridge, the cries of the evil ghosts (φάσματα) became even louder, and George overheard articulate speech: they were summoning a certain Himeres (Ἱμερῆς) to come out and meet the Saint. Himeres was an excep-

---

[1646] Philaretos the Merciful, 163–65. See also Part Four, Chapter 1, §3.
[1647] See Part Four, Chapter 1, §2.
[1648] Anthemius, 267.5–269.4.

tionally evil demon (πονηρότατόν τι δαιμόνιον) who had dominion over the bridge, shaking it day and night, throwing passers-by into the river, and drowning them. The Saint found himself between a rock and a hard place, with the demons behind him and the lurking Himeres in front. When one of the evil spirits started to push him into the water, George made up his mind. He threw down the log he was carrying and ran down to the bridge, where he engaged in a fierce battle with the evil guardian spirit of the place. The battle was terrible and lasted until morning. At last, Himeres felt that his strength was failing him, and in a last desperate attempt, he struck the Saint on the jaw. With God's help, George stood his ground and countered with a blow from the left, which caused his opponent to collapse into the abyss. From that moment, the bridge became completely passable. When one of the nuns in the monastery, Sister Hilaria, saw his nose broken by the demon's blow, she immediately sent him to his brother Symeon, who praised and healed him with the sign of the cross.[1649]

It is difficult to locate the "Great Bridge" of the text. The fortress of Mytilene on Lesbos was built on an islet and separated from the city by a narrow strait, and it is possible that the bridge connected these two places. Even more problematic is the question of the demon Himeres, whose name is obviously a euphemism and can be translated as "The Desired One" (from the verb ἱμείρω). He does not occur elsewhere in ancient or Byzantine literature and was probably part of local folklore.[1650]

5. Confining and controlling the demon

A few accounts of the saints' *Lives* of the period under study attest that the Byzantines believed demons could be confined to a particular place or in an inanimate object. Though Pseudo-Psellus does not mention pentagrams and pentalphas in his treatise (thirteenth century), he advises the magician to encircle the place where the summoned demon was sup-

---

[1649] David, Symeon and George, §11ff.
[1650] Abrahamse and Domingo-Forasté, "Life of David, Symeon, and George", 171 and n. 147.

posed to appear with burning fires.[1651] Almost six centuries earlier, St. Theodore Sykeotes used a circle to confine an evil spirit as well. According to his biography, a wealthy woman brought him one of her slaves, terribly tortured by a demon. Since the evil creature refused to leave the victim voluntarily, the exorcist walked around the possessed, encircling him, not allowing the man or the demon to move, then left them to suffer excruciating pain in this position and went to pray. He refused to free the Devil's servant for hours.[1652] Later, Theodore treated another possessed person in a similar manner, ordering the demon to wait for his return from an urgent visit to Patriarch Kyriakos. The spirit remained enclosed in its victim's body for more than three hours, suffering terribly.[1653]

Inanimate objects could be used for black magic and for confinement, like the fig leaf in which the young man from the *Roman Miracle of St. Anastasios of Persia* wrapped a demon to control him and with his help win the love of a girl devoted to God.[1654] According to the *Life* of St. Basil the Younger, the enemies of Theodore, the favorite slave of a rich Constantinopolitan, asked a witch to harm him with a magic spell. She gave them some nails with demons attached to their points, and they hammered them into the wall in a dark room in Theodore's master's house. Thereupon, the slave lost control of his limbs and fell into a severe condition. St. Basil discovered and removed the possessed nails from the wall and thus saved the man.[1655] The demon who had possessed one John of Phocis shortly after the death of St. Luke of Steiris (February 7, 953) was strung on a fishhook during the exorcism.[1656]

* * *

We will conclude the survey of demonic space with two stories from the *Life* of the semi-legendary Constantinopolitan St. Irene, the ab-

---

[1651] Psellus, "Quaenam sunt Graecorum opinions", 880D.
[1652] Theodore Sykeotes, §92.
[1653] Theodore Sykeotes, §93.1–37.
[1654] Anastasios of Persia, *Roman Miracle*, §6.4–15.
[1655] Basil the Younger, Part III, §3ff.
[1656] Luke of Steiris, §90.

bess of the Chrysobalanton monastery, which can serve as an epilogue to this book. They are imbued with an innovative philosophical spirit and strive for a theoretical conceptualization of the image, purposes, and actions of the Devil and his servants. The driving force behind the first is a deep and uncontrollable affection, the unbridled love and passion that Satan instilled in a nun's ex-fiancé. The young man resorted to the services of a magician, but St. Anastasia and St. Basil the Great appeared to Irene and showed her the various clever devices (σοφίσματα τῆς πονηρίας) used to bring the girl back to him: lead statuettes of the two former fiancés and other objects tied with hair and with paper strips on which were written the names of the Devil and various demons. Praying, the nuns untied these objects, and the following day the priest from the St. Anastasia Church burned them; with each magic item burnt, the nun was freed partially from the demon's influence and restored to her sanity. When all the objects were reduced to ashes, a cry rose from the charred pile like the scream of pigs at slaughter, the demons crying out that Irene's power was too great to fight. The evil spells were broken, and the young nun was free of the youth's passion.[1657]

However, this was not the last occasion on which the abbess of the Chrysobalanton monastery struggled with amorous passion caused by the Wicked One. A few paragraphs later, we meet the unfortunate youth Nicholas, employed to pick the monastery grapes, who yielded to an unholy passion for another nun. One night the Devil cast a cloud of darkness over his eyes, causing him to imagine that he had entered through the convent door and found himself in the cell of his beloved. When he was supposedly about to jump into her bed, he slumped to the ground in the garden and began to roll in the dust, foaming at the mouth. When she found out what happened, Irene immediately sent him chained to the church and began praying by his side. Soon, during Mass, Nicholas suddenly jumped up, broke his chains, and attacked the priest, meaning to bite him. A terrible struggle began then between Irene and the unclean spirit, in which the prayers of the holy woman prevailed. The demon was

---

[1657] Irene of Chrysobalanton, §13.

bound with invisible chains within a circle around the possessed, guarded by an angel. After Mass, Irene did not let the creature go but began questioning him about the demons' purposes and the means they used to tempt their victims and bring them to doom. In this conversation, unique in the Byzantine hagiography of the period under study, the evil spirit explained that Nicholas had long neglected his Christian duties. When he fell passionately in love with the nun, this was immediately reported to the Devil. The demon said that his master had charged him with fulfilling Nicholas's desire but soon realized the great power of the abbess and the impossibility of this undertaking. For this reason, he abandoned all attempts to instill passion in the young woman and took up permanent residence in the youth's body. Gradually the demon's speech developed into a eulogy of Satan's achievements. The only thing that frustrated the evil spirits was the power of Jesus Christ, which tormented them constantly. Unable to do good, they had directed their efforts to causing people to apostatize from God, turning those who had already apostatized into their instruments, and possessing those who had lost all communion with the Almighty. For doing this they received one, and only one, reward — they thus gained companions in the inevitable hellish torments awaiting them.[1658]

The vivid stories of the two young lovers from the *Life* of St. Irene of Chrysobalanton, composed at the very end of the period under study, represent a new epoch in Byzantine history and culture, when the scattered and heterogeneous images of the saints' *Lives* between the sixth and the tenth centuries were conceptualized and arranged in coherent systems. The speech of the demon possessing the unfortunate youth Nicholas before the abbess of Chrysobalanton constitutes the bridge between the age of folk demonology, to which the present study was devoted, and the age of critical demonology, which Michael Psellus, Pseudo-Michael Psellus, and the authors of the Palaeologian Period will develop and spice up with a touch of irony in the following centuries.

[1658] Irene of Chrysobalanton, §15.

CONCLUSION

The image and functions of the Byzantine demon combine, in specific ways and for particular purposes, various theoretical concepts, motifs, images, and plots inherited and extracted from Greco-Roman and Middle Eastern mythology, literature, and philosophy. We must be cautious, however, in analyzing phenomena that belong to the field of the history of human thought in terms of evolution. Medieval concepts of the world of Evil are segments of a web rather than links in a chain. The elements of the demonic image as represented in the hagiographical literature between the mid-sixth and the late tenth centuries, drawn from various sources, are only loosely modeled on and incorporated into an Orthodox Christian theological system that still has a long way to go before reaching a relatively conclusive and stable form. Some of the most interesting demonic images and narratives come from texts written before the last ecumenical council in 787, like the *Lives* of St. Symeon Stylites the Younger, St. Symeon the Fool, and St. Theodore Sykeotes. Though committed to the Scriptures, the sacred history of humankind, and the Christian concept of Evil, the hagiographers felt free to select, omit, or combine these elements to create the always-polarized but ever-changing image of their demons, to adjust it to their audience's knowledge and needs, and use it for specific religious, ideological and political purposes. It would be an oversimplification to think of the Byzantine evil spirit, material or metaphorical, as exclusively a historical, cultural, mythological, or theological phenomenon. It belongs to all of these fields.

Before Christianity, two distinct conceptual trends, the "Homeric" and the "Hesiodic", intersected each other and coexisted for millennia to define the demon. In Homer, "daimones" were the unknown and irrational forces that embodied a disastrous, fatal, and dramatic turn in human life, whose source was obscure and whose consequences were fateful. Homer's demons symbolized the chaotic force opposed to the Olympian gods with their concrete and strictly assigned functions. For this reason, they had neither a fixed outer appearance nor a cult nor names of their own to distinguish them from one another. Disastrous and incomprehensible phenomena like storms and epidemics were their principal domain.

Unlike the wholly formless Homeric demons, Hesiod was the first Greek thinker to create a "demonology", defining the demon in a new conceptual framework that philosophers and theologians would complement, enrich, and reconsider in the following centuries, adapting their views to the ever-changing spiritual and political needs of their own epochs. He defined and objectified "pure" demons as the souls of idealized virtuous people who lived during the Golden Age, the guardians of Humankind.

Judging from Late Antique authors like Alexander Polyhistor and Iamblichus, the Pythagoreans believed that demons were not the good and virtuous guardian spirits of the Golden Age but the souls of the dead in general. According to Marcel Detienne, their views reflected the local folklore of southern Italy, having little in common with Hesiod. The Pythagorean "ghosts" or "specters" (εἴδωλα) were incorporeal but assumed the appearance they had in life. Their influence is ambivalent: they can bring illness and death, but also send various omens, which help if interpreted correctly. The abode of the demon souls is the air immediately above the earth, which mortals can also visit in dreams and visions. The idea of demons as ghostly souls of the dead is evident not only in the consolidated doctrine of (neo)Pythagoreanism. Beyond a strictly philosophical context, this idea is seen in various authors throughout antiquity and reflects a widespread belief. After their deaths, some great men became demons, such as King Darius in Aeschylus, King Admetus and Queen Alcestis in Euripides, and the Athenian warriors who died at Marathon, who eternally fought their ghostly battle with the Persians according to Pausanias.

The association of demons with the spirits of the dead represents only one of the various objectivizations of this notion. The concept of the so-called *paredros* (πάρεδρος), the personal guardian spirit that can influence one's life positively or negatively, leading one to virtue and happiness or dishonor and misfortune, was already present in the poems of

Pindar and Phocilides of Miletus (sixth century B.C.) and was further developed by Plato, who made Socrates' *daimonion* one of the most famous images in ancient literature and philosophy. We discern it in the comedies of Menander, the biographies of Plutarch, the magical papyri of Late Antique Egypt, and many other texts that influenced, directly or indirectly, the hagiographical tradition. The image of the mighty spirit of the air, which grants the wishes of whoever manages to summon and control it, not only stood as the basis of the Faust legend; it also became a part of the same conceptual milieu as the Western European idea of the pact with Satan that led to the Great Witch hunt.

The transition from the malevolent to the evil demon occurred in various religious and philosophical movements, probably around the second century A.D. when Eastern dualistic doctrines infiltrated the cosmopolitical Greco-Roman world on a large scale. One of the first Neoplatonic philosophers, Porphyry, created a detailed classification of immortal beings, part of which included the category of "evil demons" (πονηροὶ δαίμονες) who inhabited the air, possessed humans and cattle, and harmed them. In Iamblichus, Proclus Diadochus, and Olympiodorus of Alexandria, demons played a crucial role in the afterlife trial, purification, and punishment of human souls in the sinister and frightening spaces between the visible world and the realm of the Demiurge. Though the aerial tollhouses, where evil spirits examine and investigate the souls of the dead for various sins, occur exclusively in the works of Cyril of Alexandria among the early theologians, this concept appears in the detailed accounts of hagiographical literature, especially in the ninth and tenth centuries. Even more common, both in Byzantine philosophy and in the saints' *Lives* of the period under study, are the demons who punish the souls of those found guilty and subject them to various tortures in Hell, where the condemned await Judgment Day and the Lord's final decision on their fate.

Some Neoplatonists, mainly Iamblichus and Olympiodorus, classify demons on the basis of their relationship to the four elements of matter, namely air, fire, earth, and water. Such typologies were extremely popular in the demonological treatises of Michael Psellus (eleventh century),

Pseudo-Michael Psellus (early thirteenth century), and the authors of the Paleologian period. In the period under study, fire, air, and water demons appear in various theological works and, occasionally, in hagiographical texts, like the *Life* of Bishop Leo of Catania and the Martyria of the Forty-Two Martyrs of Amorion.

The Christian idea of the demon appeared and developed in the profoundly syncretic cultural, mythological, religious, and philosophical milieu of the late Roman empire, primarily the eastern Mediterranean. The early Christian apologists and theologians inherited, carefully sifted, and adjusted the images of the sinister avenging spirits, *paredroi*, elements, and many others in their sacred texts. However, before the tenth century, this process was far from complete, and there was still no integrated and commonly accepted "orthodox tradition" to unite the amorphous mass of conceptions, poorly homogenized through passages from the Old and New Testaments and moments in the "sacred history" of humanity. This "sacred history", in which the Fallen Angel plays a central role, forms the only comprehensive framework in which the various folk beliefs and remnants of ancient philosophical ideas find a place. The rebellion of the Devil (Beelzebub, Belial, Satan) against God, Eve's deception, the subjugation of humanity to Death, and the victory of Christ give the hagiographers, above all, a specific terminological apparatus and a particular set of qualities to define and describe the Evil, like hatred, bitterness, pride, envy, and deceitfulness. The creatures of Evil are persistently associated with darkness and blackness, with the sinister aerial regions below God's Kingdom and Hell beneath the Earth, with destruction and death. In addition, since the Devil and his servants were defeated through the sacrifice and the sinless death of Christ, demons are only capable of deceiving and misleading, and for that reason, hagiographers frequently describe them as miserable and powerless creatures with no real ability to harm people. Evil spirits are the object of open ridicule in quite a few texts, like the *Lives* of St. Anastasios of Persia, St. Leo of Catania, St. Luke of Steiris, and St. Irene of Chrysobalanton.

* * *

Evil spirits can appear in any material form and have various harmful influences, especially illness. From this point of view, hagiographical literature inherits the Homeric concept of the demon as an unknown and unpredictable force causing unexpected and usually fatal twists in human life. However, some common stereotypical characteristics can be identified, the most important of which is ugliness. The hagiographers distinguish it from human ugliness by specific terms such as ἀνείκαστος (indescribable, ineffable), δυσειδής (painful to behold), ἀειδής (formless), which do not refer to a stable corporeal form, but rather to the observer's perception, grotesquely reflecting everybody's fears. The concrete elements constructing the anomalous demonic body, both the material image of the demon and that of the possessed, belong to a relatively consolidated and standardized pattern. They include excessively large or excessively small stature, deformity and disproportion, association with impurities (stench, decay, blood, and excrement), utterly shabby or extremely rich clothing, extreme emotions, and vulgar speech. These elements function as a symbol of the corrupt and sinful nature of the Devil's servants and reflect the judicial concept of the so-called "mirror punishments". The evil spirit seeks to inflict sickness and physical torment on its victims but also suffers from them; it tempts humans into sin, but sins deform and twist it.

The common stereotypical elements that form the image of the demon can hardly be attributed to a particular cultural or literary tradition. They substantiate the "otherness" that marks the supernatural in general, some remaining almost unchanged even today. On the other hand, Byzantine hagiographers also describe complex demonic images that we can effectively trace back to various literary, mythological, and philosophical traditions. The most common of these is undoubtedly the black Ethiopian. An embodiment of otherness, idealized or burdened with negative qualities in Greco-Roman literature as early as the age of Pindar, the black African man was by no means absent from the cosmopolitan Roman society of the first century A.D. Due to his physical strength and qualities, he became a symbol of virility and sexual prowess, but his dark skin made him also a suitable personification of Death and the Underworld. However, the early Christian theologians avoided demonizing the black "race", whose representatives were potential objects for Christianization for the churches in North Africa. In the Acts of the Apostles and the works of Origen and Gregory of Elvira, the "Ethiopian" symbolizes Christian triumph in the world's remotest corners. In hagiographical literature from as early as the second century, the widespread prejudices against the menacing, dark-skinned Black found much more fertile ground. They blended with the negative connotations of the color black, creating a complex image — evil, beastly, and uncivilized — that infected Western civilization and underpinned racism, discrimination, and slavery.

In the Byzantine hagiography of the period under study, the evil Ethiopians remain the most common personifications of Death, sin, and mortal danger both in the visible world and in descriptions of the aerial regions and Hell. Giant or dwarfish, clad in rich garments or disgusting rags, menacing or deceitful, monstrously deformed or mutilated, they are the most convenient image and metaphor for the Devil's servants. We find them playing a deadly game of dice with a fatally sinful adulterer, weighing a greedy tax collector's good and bad deeds on scales, crowding around somebody's deathbed, or testing the human soul in the aerial tollhouses and greedy to take the deceased with them to their infernal abodes. In the world of the living, the image of the black or dark demon, sometimes shadow-like, gradually expands its functions during the period under study. At first, it symbolized diseases and heresies, like the black headless demon, which first occurs in the *Testament of Solomon* and the *Cyranides* and during the initial stage of the Justinianic plague and personifies the spread of the disease which mercilessly decimated the population of the empire in the middle of the sixth century. A generation later, this complex image had already lost one of its elements, and the evil spirit that infected the young Theodore Sykeotes with the plague was described only as "black" and "unclean". The sinister and somehow comical Ethiopian, sent by St. Symeon the Fool to punish a stubborn shopkeeper in Emesa for his heretical views during the last struggles of the central government with the Monophysites and other powerful heresies in the

East, leaves the political and ideological arena. The leading figures of the iconodule movement two centuries later prefer to use other images to discredit their enemies. From the mid-ninth century, the black demon becomes the standard, even banal image of the Devil's servants in the real world, gradually losing its special relationship with illness, heresies, and deadly danger, but retaining the other standard elements of the demonic image, namely, physical anomalies and ugliness.

The anthropomorphic demon in hagiographic literature reflects the fear of the empire's real enemies rather poorly. Although Persians, Arabs, and Bulgarians posed a constant threat to the very existence of the Empire and to the lives and property of its subjects, evil spirits are seldom described as appearing in their guise. This seemingly surprising absence of formidable foreign soldiers from the corporeal forms that an evil spirit might assume demonstrates the limits of the objectifying "Hesiodic" trend. Despite the many outward appearances it can assume, the demon remains a syncretic, abstract concept that belongs to the domain of the supernatural, which embodies equally abstract physical and corporeal diseases, like illness and sin, or misfortunes and dangers in general. He may visit the visible world but does not belong to it. The fearful enemy soldier is an object of demonization as a tool of Satan but not a suitable outward appearance for the demon himself. On the other hand, hordes of demonic soldiers and their leaders are relatively common in the saints' *Lives*, but only as an abstract notion. The hagiographers avoid describing them in contemporary military terms but use the archaic word "phalanx", which connoted sinister and primordial danger. By contrast, like the imperial army that protected the civilized Christian realm from barbarians and infidels, angels are usually organized in armies (στρατιαί) and brigades or divisions (τάγματα). Early hagiographers call the leaders of the demonic troops "kings", but the texts after the seventh century, like the *Life* of St. Ioannikios the Great, show a clear preference for the titles of "archon" (ruler) and "toparch" (local governor).

The anthropomorphic evil spirit appears in hagiography almost exclusively as a man. The much rarer female demon, behind which lies a long and relatively homogeneous mythological and literary tradition, has distinguishable features. Her set of functions is also limited and produces two relatively separate images, namely, the sinister witch who drinks newborns' blood and their mothers' milk, devours babies' livers, and kills them; and the Temptress who seduces and murders her male victims without giving them sexual satisfaction. The connection of both images to various eastern deities, such as the Semitic Lilith and the Sumerian Abzu, has been long established and can be considered proven. Under the name of Gello, which appears for the first time in Sappho, or the more general term of Striga/Strigla (witch), the Child-killer is one of the most enduring mythological and folklore characters of the Eastern Mediterranean, alive even in modern Greek folklore. Despite her popularity, however, hagiographers avoid this image, and Byzantine intellectuals treat it with profound and flagrant contempt as mere superstition (δεισιδαιμονία). Surprisingly enough, the Temptress also proves unpopular in the saints' *Lives* of the period under study. In the *Life* of St. Antony the Younger, the nameless figure with loose hair who approaches the Saint is characterized not as an actual material incarnation of Evil but as a demonic apparition that comes and goes quickly. Equally semi-abstract and ghostly are the endless rows of female visions that appear in the comic story of the monk Matthew in the *Life* of St. Paul of Latros; they are devoid of any materiality, a mind game played upon the holy man by the Devil.

Angels and demons, which have a common origin, represent the two poles of the same supernatural stereotype in hagiographic literature. Their images are usually based on the contrast between blackness and whiteness, ugliness and beauty, disproportion and harmony, stench and fragrance. The Apostle Paul's idea that Satan disguises himself as a bright angel is undoubtedly present in the hagiographical texts as a theoretical notion. Still, the authors generally avoid describing demons that hide behind angelic forms, and when they do, they usually focus on the ability of the evil spirits to imitate the heavenly glow emitted by the angels. While the divine light brings peace and happiness to the beholder, the demonic blaze burns and repulses anyone who senses it. However, the distinction between the two types of light is considered perceptible only to holy monks.

The clash between the desire to create a homogeneous and stereotypical demonic image and the need adequately to portray the diverse characters of popular belief is evident in the various descriptions of zoomorphic demons. There is no doubt that the serpent, by default, dominates over the other forms that Evil can take, both in literature and in iconography. Other fantastic and real creatures, like dragons, birds, mammals, and insects, are numerous but much less common and scattered throughout the hagiographic corpus. In addition, an essential feature of the evil spirit is the lack of mixed zoomorphic and anthropomorphic images that could revive the memory of the ancient deities and negatively influence the audience.

The most common features of zoomorphic demons are also stereotyped. Evil spirits in animal form pose a common physical threat to monks and hermits, and fighting them is part of the hermit's exploits against Evil. Since reptiles, ravens, owls, mice, and pigs are considered unclean animals in the Old Testament, in hagiography they generally symbolize impurity and spiritual decay, but can also acquire more specific functions. The serpent, which deceived Eve and became the cause of Original Sin, personifies deceit, temptation, and lust. Because of its uncleanness and stench, in the *Life* of St. Basil the Younger, the pig is the incarnation of Homosexuality and Pederasty. As a symbol of the Antichrist in St. John's Book of Revelation, the dragon is associated with heresies, blasphemy, idolatry, and sinful thoughts, also becoming a metaphor for the iconoclastic emperors. Influenced by the Proverbs of Solomon, the raven appears as an avenging demon.

Beyond the stereotypical features directly influenced by the Old and New Testaments, zoomorphic demons reflect ancient mythological beliefs that were probably still a part of folklore between the sixth and the tenth centuries. Such images and tales, well known to the hagiographers' audience, are sometimes only vaguely suggested by the authors. Still, their presence is determined by the fact that the saints' *Lives* of the period under study are designed to be popular "bestsellers". The serpent of Asclepius, the god of healing, is transformed on Christian grounds into an evil spirit that takes up residence in the body of its victim and causes illness and physical torment or else wraps itself around him and brings paralysis. The demon who brings Bacchic madness and unquenchable thirst reminds us of the "Agathodemon", the ancient patron of wine and inebriation. The old protector of the home now haunts houses and towers. The dragon, the mighty enemy of various mythological heroes and part of the folklore of northwestern Asia Minor from the earliest times, becomes the demonic adversary of St. Ioannikios the Great and St. Antony the Younger. The black raven, a sacred animal of the diviner god Apollo, punishes those who practice pagan divination rituals. The mouse, whose ancient master is the sinister plague god, Apollo Smyntheus, retains its connection with disease, dead bodies, and decay. The piglet, thrown in the sea by the Italian nobleman Gaudios in a dream, may represent a rare remnant of one of the rituals practiced in the Eleusinian Mysteries.

* * *

As it appears steadily in Byzantine hagiography, Christian cosmology is quadripartite. At the top are the Heavens and the Kingdom of God, to which only the angels and the souls of the righteous have access. The visible world inhabited by humans is enclosed between the air and Hell, where terrible demons put the dead to perilous trials and punish them if they fail to prove their innocence. Several persistent narratives illustrate this connection. Theologians and hagiographers represent the Journey of the Soul to Heaven in various ways. One of the most controversial concepts includes the so-called "aerial tollhouses" (τελώνια), the checkpoints where demons who resemble state officials test and investigate the soul for specific sins. The roots of this concept can be traced to various consolidated Late Antique philosophical and religious doctrines, like Mithraism, Neoplatonism, Hermeticism, and Jewish demonology, which influenced Christianity in the first centuries of its development. The philosophical-religious idea of the soul's afterlife journey to the world of the intellectual deities was combined with the concept of mortal sins and adapted to Christianity in one of the works of Cyril of Alexandria in the first half of the fifth century. While the concept of the aerial tollhouses did not find popularity with later theologians and remained only on the periphery of Christian doctrine, it was present quite steadily in Byzantine hagiography since the age of St. Antony the Great (fourth century). It appears in the *Lives* of St. Simeon the Fool, St. John the Merciful, St. Golinduch-Maria, and other early works during the period under study, but the most detailed description before the tenth century comes from the story "On the Officer, or the Risen Soldier", attributed to Anastasios Sinaita. This text includes images and motifs like the black Ethiopians, personifying death and various sins, the two guardian angels who help the soul through the air, and the bag containing good deeds to compensate for the crimes committed in life. After the seventh century, the tollhouses were virtually absent from hagiography: such a semi-apocryphal plot was problematic in the already dogmatically complex era of the iconoclast crisis. However, only twenty years after the final restoration of the icons in 843, it reappears in the *Short Chronicle* of George Hamartolos, who enriches and re-elaborates Anastasios Sinaita's account of the resurrected soldier. In the middle of the tenth century, the monk Gregory provided a highly detailed and fascinating description of the twenty-one tollhouses, each responsible for a particular sin, where the souls of the dead were investigated and tried for their evil deeds.

The literary motif of the descent into Hell, though relatively common in early Christian apocrypha, was not particularly popular in Byzantine hagiography before the tenth century. A place of torture and suffering, the Underworld is not associated with the presence of demons but with darkness and the "River of Fire" in the early *Lives* of St. Golinduch-Maria and St. Philaret the Merciful. In the tenth-century *Life* of St. Phantinos the Younger and the *Vision* of Cosmas, however, the depths of the earth are already crowded with various evil spirits who punish sinners mercilessly. The highly detailed, spectacular, and even dramatic descriptions of these texts remind the modern reader of the great masterpieces of early Western European literature.

The significance of the particular interest of the tenth-century hagiographers in the human soul's fate in the air and Hell, the sinners' torments, and the role of demons as investigators and punishers of human actions can hardly be overestimated. This revival of Christianized Late Antique ideas, such as the journey of the soul and the descent into Hell, coincided with the period when the Byzantine intellectual elite was preoccupied with collecting and classifying the ancient literary heritage. The return to this heritage, led by the encyclopedists around the learned emperor Constantine VII, was not only expressed in the copying and commentary on classical works of the rank of Plato and Homer. It was a multifaceted process that affected popular hagiographic literature, reining the authors into the new cultural mainstream and engaging them in a search for previously little-exploited semi-apocryphal ancient concepts and literary motifs.

Demons are represented in hagiographic literature as outsiders rushing into the visible world from their habitual abodes in the depths of the earth or the air, drawn by the human susceptibility to sin, or haunting particular areas in the wilderness, in abandoned and desecrated churches, or in places associated with paganism and sin, like ancient graveyards, pits used for disposing of the corpses of executed criminals, or bathhouses. After the triumph of Christ, they have no real power over the living unless people succumb to their lies and deceptions. However, this concept is only theoretical and abstract since ordinary people are susceptible to sin, and only holy monks and hermits are beyond the reach of Satan and his cunning temptations, protected by their absolute piety.

The Byzantine concept of space in the visible world differed significantly from ours. Modern Western civilization has inherited from early nineteenth-century Romanticism the idea of "Nature", that is, the totality of plants, animals, mountains, oceans, seas, and rivers, as the highest and most perfect embodiment of order and beauty, whose contemplation brings harmony, serenity, and reunion with the divine fount of life. Not unlike the Parisian bourgeois and his "serious need" to "see the sea and to roll in the grass", so sarcastically described by Fyodor Dostoevski in his "Winter Notes on Summer Impressions", modern, sophisticated metropolitans seek refuge from their busy and stressful lives in the cities by exploring underground caves, climbing mountains, or just taking a walk or having a picnic in the park. This concept would be entirely absurd to the medieval mentality, where the very idea of the material world was founded on the contrast between wilderness and civilization. In this regard, the ἔρημος (lit. *the void, the deserted*) was the place where the unknown and demonic forces of the Devil roamed undisturbed in all sorts of dangerous forms, along with the wild animals and the elements of nature. To ward them off, humans create a network of relatively protected and consecrated spaces, like cities, homes, churches, and monasteries. These shelters are not entirely secure, but the Evil One penetrates less easily into them, and it is no coincidence that descriptions of possessed houses in the saints' *Lives* of the period under study are so rare. Leaving these relatively safe places was not a romantic adventure but a dangerous experience that no one undertook for pleasure or in search of harmony. Only the holy hermit, with the power of God at his side, dared to step out of the human community of his own free will and confront Satan's unknowable and nameless forces. The hermit's life in the wilderness, in the solitary cell or the dark cave, was a constant struggle *against the principalities, against the powers, against the world rulers of this present darkness* (in the famous words of the Apostle Paul), which required long preparation. It is no coincidence that, in Late Antiquity, this arbitrary separation from the protection and laws of human society and civilized space was considered a paradoxical and antisocial phenomenon that turned the established order upside down. Emperor Julian, with astonishment and a touch of disgust, regarded the monastic life as madness through which the demons themselves attracted gullible Christians to their abodes. More than three centuries later, a similar suspicion and hostility against monks became one of the cornerstones of Iconoclasm.

Although the wilderness is considered a space where demonic forces roam relatively unmolested, according to the hagiographical texts, their power is not absolute, and they often inhabit and control a particular zone. Haunted open areas, often associated with the Noonday demon, are attested along the lower reaches of the river Sangarius in western Asia

Minor (the sixth to the seventh centuries), in southern Bithynia, on the sparsely populated island of Aphousia in the Sea of Marmara (ninth century), around Sparta and Patra in the Peloponnese (late ninth century), and around Regium in Calabria (tenth century). Haunted caves are relatively common in hagiography after the seventh century, and the records refer to various mountainous areas in southern Bithynia, Lycia, Lydia, the islet of Thasios in Lake Apollonias (west of the city of Prusa in Bithynia), Decapolis in Isauria, around Sparta in southern Greece, and Calabria in southern Italy. Rivers and lakes are usually associated with evil dragons, mainly in the *Lives* of the Bithynian saints.

Not only uncivilized but also decivilized space is persistently associated with a demonic presence. Demons roaming by the graves of deceased pagans usually appear in texts from the sixth and the early seventh centuries, mainly from the *Life* of St. Theodore Syceotes (†613), and concern the border region between Gordiana and Bithynia. Haunted baths occur in pagan and Christian authors of Late Antiquity, like Porphyry and Gregory of Nyssa, and in the saints' *Lives* of the period under study.

Despite human efforts, civilized space still does not provide absolute protection from the forces of evil. Though rarely, hagiographical texts describe haunted streets, homes, and fortresses. Such cases are mostly characteristic of the hagiographies of the sixth to the seventh centuries and the tenth century. The descriptions are spectacular, their vividness recalling Lucian's story of Eubatides' house in Corinth. As a common symbol for the transition from life to death, haunted bridges occur only in the semi-apocryphal story of the young Anthemius and his pact with the Devil (the sixth to the seventh centuries), set in Antioch, and the *Life* of St. David, Simeon, and George of Lesbos (the eighth to the ninth centuries), set in Mytilene.

Byzantine hagiography is highly syncretic and draws its demonic repertoire from folklore, mythology, various consolidated Late Antique doctrines such as Neopythagoreanism and Neoplatonism, and the canonical and apocryphal biblical traditions. The saints' *Lives* undoubtedly reflect "folk demonology" with its numerous supernatural beings, and with the zoomorphic and anthropomorphic images inherited over centuries and millennia. However, they show a clear tendency towards stereotyping and the consolidation of the concept of the evil spirit, which is evident in the uneven use of anthropomorphic and zoomorphic images. Some of them, like the black Ethiopian, the warrior, the serpent, and the dragon, appear en masse. Others, like mice and rats, pigs, dogs and wolves, ravens, bats, owls, eagles, sparrows, and geese occur persistently but intermittently. The functions and influences of demons are also unified, their spheres of action being death, disease, physical torment, and a portent of evil. In this regard, the hagiographical texts written between the sixth and the tenth centuries link the amorphous mass of various demonological concepts, inherited from Greco-Roman mythology and Late Antique philosophical-religious traditions, with the era of the well-studied late Byzantine "critical demonology", advocated in the treatises of Michael Psellus, Pseudo-Michael Psellus, and the intellectuals and theologians of the Palaeologian period.

BIBLIOGRAPHY

I. Primary sources

HAGIOGRAPHICAL

Auxentios:
Author: Michael Psellus
BHG: [203]
Edition: Joannou, Périclès-Pierre, *La démonologie populaire à Byzance au XIe siècle. La vie inédite de S. Auxence par M. Psellos*, Wiesbaden, 1971, 64-132.
DOHD: n/a

Alypios Stylites:
Author: Anonymous
BHG: [65]
Edition: Delehaye, Hippolyte, *Les Saints Stylites*, Brussels and Paris, 1923, 148-69.
DOHD: n/a

Anastasios of Persia:
Author: Anonymous
BHG: [84]
Edition: Flusin, Bernard, *Saint Anastase le Perse et l'histoire de la Palestine au début du viie siècle*, vol. 1, Paris: Centre National de la Recherche Scientifique, 1992, 41-91.
DOHD: n/a

Anastasios of Persia, *Encomion*:
Author: Anonymous
BHG: [87]
Edition: Flusin, Bernard, *Saint Anastase le Perse et l'histoire de la Palestine au début du viie siècle*, vol. 1, Paris: Centre National de la Recherche Scientifique, 1992, 261-66.
DOHD: n/a

Anastasios of Persia, *Roman miracle*:
Author: Anonymous
BHG: [89]

Edition: Flusin, Bernard, *Saint Anastase le Perse et l'histoire de la Palestine au début du viie siècle*, vol. 1, Paris: Centre National de la Recherche Scientifique, 1992, 165–87.

DOHD: n/a

Anastasios of Persia, *Encomion by George Pisides*:

Author: George Pisides

BHG: [86]

Edition: Flusin, Bernard, *Saint Anastase le Perse et l'histoire de la Palestine au début du viie siècle*, vol. 1, Paris: Centre National de la Recherche Scientifique, 1992, 203–59.

DOHD: n/a

Anastasios of Persia, Miracles:

Author: Anonymous

BHG: [89]

Edition: Flusin, Bernard, *Saint Anastase le Perse et l'histoire de la Palestine au début du viie siècle*, vol. 1, Paris: Centre National de la Recherche Scientifique, 1992, 117–53.

DOHD: n/a

Antony:

Author: Athanasius, Patriarch of Alexandria

BHG: [140]

Edition: Bartelink, Gerhardus, *Athanase d'Alexandrie, Vie d'Antoine*. [*Sources chrétiennes* 400], Paris: Éditions du Cerf, 2004, 124–376.

DOHD: n/a

Antony Kauleas:

Author: Nikephoros the Philosopher

BHG: [139]

Edition: Leone, Pietro and François Leroy, "L' "Encomium in patriarcham Antonium II Cauleam" del filosofo e retore Niceforo", *Orpheus* 10 (1989): 404–29 (412–29).

DOHD:
https://www.doaks.org/research/byzantine/resources/hagiography/database/dohp.asp?cmd=SShow&key=84

Antony the Younger:

Author: Anonymous

BHG: [139]

Edition: Papadopoulos-Kerameus, Athanasios, *Collection of Palestinian and Syriac hagiology*, [Greek: Παπαδόπουλος-Κεραμεύς, Αθανάσιος, Συλλογὴ Παλαιστινῆς καὶ Συριακῆς ἀγιολογίας] [Pravoslavnyj Palestinskij Sbornik 19.3], vol. 1, St. Petersburg, 1907, 186–216.

DOHD:
https://www.doaks.org/research/byzantine/resources/hagiography/database/dohp.asp?cmd=SShow&key=2

Athanasia of Aegina:

Author: Anonymous

BHG: [180]

Edition: Carras, Lydia, "The Life of St. Athanasia of Aegina: a critical edition with introduction", in *Maistor: Classical, Byzantine, and Renaissance Studies for Robert Browning*, ed. Ann Moffatt, [*Byzantina Australiensia* 5.], Canberra: The Australian Association for Byzantine Studies, 1984, 199–224 (212–24).

DOHD:
https://www.doaks.org/research/byzantine/resources/hagiography/database/dohp.asp?cmd=SShow&key=1

Bakchos the Younger:

Author: Anonymous

BHG: [209B]

Edition: Demetrakopoulos, Photios, "St. Bakchos the Younger" [Greek: Δημητρακόπουλος, Φώτιος, Ἅγιος Βάκχος ὁ Νέος], *Epistemonike Epeteris tes Philosophikes Scholes tou Panepistemiou Athenon* 26 (1979): 331–63 (344–50).

DOHD:
https://www.doaks.org/research/byzantine/resources/hagiography/database/dohp.asp?cmd=SShow&key=107

Basil the Younger:

Author: Gregorius

BHG: [263-264]

Edition: *The Life of St. Basil the Younger. Critical Edition and Annotated Translation of the Moscow Version*, ed. and trans. Denis F. Sullivan, Alice-Mary Talbot, and Stamatina McGrath [Dumbarton Oaks Studies XLV.], Washington, DC: Dumbarton Oaks Research Library and Collection, 2014.

DOHD: n/a

Cyr and John:

Author: Sophronios Monk and Sophist

BHG: [477]

Edition: Fernández Marcos, Natalio, *Los Thaumata de Sofronio: contribución al estudio de la incubatio Cristiana* [Manuales y anejos de "Emérita" 31], Madrid: Instituto "Antonio de Nebrija", 1975, 243–400.
DOHD: n/a

David, Symeon and George:
Author: Anonymous
BHG: [494]
Edition: van den Gheyn, Ioseph, "Acta graeca ss. Davidis, Symeonis, et Georgii Mitylenae in insula Lesbo", *Analecta Bollandiana*, 18 (1899): 209–59 (211–59).
DOHD:
https://www.doaks.org/research/byzantine/resources/hagiography/database/dohp.asp?cmd=SShow&key=4

Demetrianos of Cyprus:
Author: Anonymous
BHG: [495]
Edition: Grégoire, Henri, "Saint Démétrianos, évêque de Chytri (île de Chypre)", *Byzantinische Zeitschrift* 16 (1907): 217–37.
DOHD:
https://www.doaks.org/research/byzantine/resources/hagiography/database/dohp.asp?cmd=SShow&key=56

Elias of Heliopolis:
Author: Anonymous
BHG: [578-79]
Edition: Papadopoulos-Kerameus, Athanasios, *Collection of Palestinian and Syriac hagiology* [Greek: Παπαδόπουλος-Κεραμεύς, Ἀθανάσιος, Συλλογὴ Παλαιστινῆς καὶ Συριακῆς ἁγιολογίας] [Pravoslavnyj Palestinskij Sbornik 57/19.3], vol. 1, St. Petersburg, 1907, 42–59.
DOHD:
https://www.doaks.org/research/byzantine/resources/hagiography/database/dohp.asp?cmd=SShow&key=110

Elias Speleotes:
Author: Anonymous
BHG: [581]
Edition: *AASS*, Septembris tomus III, Paris & Rome, 1868 (repr.), 848–88.
DOHD:
https://www.doaks.org/research/byzantine/resources/hagiography/database/dohp.asp?cmd=SShow&key=58

Elias the Younger:

Author: Anonymous

BHG: [580]

Edition: Rossi Taibbi, Giuseppe, *Vita di Sant' Elia il Giovane*, Palermo: Istituto Siciliano di studi bizantini e neoellenici, 1962, 2-122.

DOHD:
https://www.doaks.org/research/byzantine/resources/hagiograp hy/database/dohp.asp?cmd=SShow&key=59

Empress Theodora:

Author: Anonymous

BHG: [1731]

Edition: Athanasios Μαρκόπουλος, "*Life* of the Empress Theodora (BHG 1731)" [Greek: Μαρκόπουλος, Αθανάσιος, "Βίος της αυτοκράτειρας Θεοδώρας (BHG 1731)"], *Byzantina Symmeikta* 5 (1983): 249-85, (257-71).

DOHD:
https://www.doaks.org/research/byzantine/resources/hagiograp hy/database/dohp.asp?cmd=SShow&key=15

Empress Theophano:

Author: Anonymous

BHG: [1794]

Edition: Kurtz, Eduard, *Zwei griechische Texte über die hl. Theophano die Gemahlin Kaisers Leo VI*. St. Petersburg 1898, 1-24.

DOHD:
https://www.doaks.org/research/byzantine/resources/hagiograp hy/database/dohp.asp?cmd=SShow&key=24

Eustratios of Agauros:

Author: Anonymous

BHG: [645]

Edition: Papadopoulos-Kerameus, Athanasios, *Unedited texts from the collections of Jerusalem* [Greek: Παπαδόπουλος-Κεραμεύς, Αθανάσιος, Ἀνάλεκτα Ἱεροσολυμιτικῆς σταχυολογίας], vol. 4, St. Petersburg, 1897, 367-400.

DOHD:
https://www.doaks.org/research/byzantine/resources/hagiograp hy/database/dohp.asp?cmd=SShow&key=6

Euthymios the Younger:

Author: Basil the Monk

BHG: [655]

Edition: Petit, Louis "Vie et office de saint Euthyme le Jeune", *Revue d'Orient Chrétien* 8 (1903): 155–205, 503–36.

DOHD:
https://www.doaks.org/research/byzantine/resources/hagiograp hy/database/dohp.asp?cmd=SShow&key=8

George of Amastris:

Author: Anonymous

BHG: [668]

Edition: Vasilevskij, Vasilij, *Works* [Russian: Васильевский, Василий, Труды], vol. 3, St. Petersburg, 1915, 1–71.

DOHD:
https://www.doaks.org/research/byzantine/resources/hagiograp hy/database/dohp.asp?cmd=SShow&key=10

George of Choziba:

Author: Antonius

BHG: [669]

Edition: Houze, Carolus, "Sancti Georgii Chozebitae confessoris et monachi vita auctore Antonio eius discipulo", *Analecta Bollandiana* 7 (1888), 95–144, 336–59.

DOHD: n/a

Germanos of Kosinitza:

Author: Anonymous

BHG: [698]

Edition: *AASS*, Maii tomus III, Brussels: Culture et civilisation, 1968 (repr.), 6–10 (Latin translation: 162–67).

DOHD:
https://www.doaks.org/research/byzantine/resources/hagiograp hy/database/dohp.asp?cmd=SShow&key=11

Golinduch:

Author: Eustratius Presbyterus

BHG: [700]

Edition: Papadopoulos-Kerameus, Athanasios, *Unedited texts from the collections of Jerusalem* [Greek: Παπαδόπουλος-Κεραμεύς, Αθανάσιος, Ἀνάλεκτα Ἱεροσολυμιτικῆς σταχυολογίας], vol. 4, St. Petersburg, St. Petersburg, 1897, 149–74.

DOHD: n/a

Gregory of Dekapolis:

Author: Anonymous

BHG: [711]

Edition: Makris, Georgios, *Ignatios Diakonos und die Vita des Hl. Gregorios Dekapolites* [Byzantinisches Archiv 17], Stuttgart: Teubner, 1997, 56–152.

DOHD:
https://www.doaks.org/research/byzantine/resources/hagiography/database/dohp.asp?cmd=SShow&key=12

Irene of Chrysobalanton:

Author: Anonymous

BHG: [952]

Edition: Rosenqvist, Jan, *The life of St. Irene Abbess of Chrysobalanton*, Uppsala, 1986, 2–112.

DOHD:
https://www.doaks.org/research/byzantine/resources/hagiography/database/dohp.asp?cmd=SShow&key=57

John of Gotthia:

Author: Anonymous

BHG: [891]

Edition: *AASS*, Junii tomus 7, Paris & Rome, 1867, 167–71.

DOHD:
https://www.doaks.org/research/byzantine/resources/hagiography/database/dohp.asp?cmd=SShow&key=106

Ioannikios (*Metaphr.*):

Author: Symeon Metaphrastes

BHG: [937]

Edition: MPG, vol. 116, Paris, 1863, 35–92.

DOHD: n/a

Ioannikios (*Peter*):

Author: Peter the Monk

BHG: [936]

Edition: *AASS*, Novembris tomus II.1, Brussels, 1854, 384–435.

DOHD:
https://www.doaks.org/research/byzantine/resources/hagiography/database/dohp.asp?cmd=SShow&key=23

Ioannikios (*Sabbas*):

Author: Sabbas the Monk

BHG: [935]

Edition: *AASS*, Novembris tomus II.1, Brussels, 1854, 332–83.

DOHD:
https://www.doaks.org/research/byzantine/resources/hagiography/database/dohp.asp?cmd=SShow&key=13

John Climacus:

Author: Daniel of Raitho

BHG: [882]

Edition: MPG, vol. 88, Paris, 1864, 596–608.

DOHD: n/a

John the Merciful:

Author: Leontios of Neapolis

BHG: [886-886c]

Edition: Féstugière, André-Jean, *Léontios de Néapolis. Vie de Syméon le Fou et Vie de Jean de Chypre. Édition commentée par A. Féstugiere en collaboration de L. Rydén* [Bibliothèque Archéologique et Historique 95], Paris: Librairie Orientaliste Paul Geuthner, 1974, 343–409.

DOHD: n/a

John the Psichaites:

Author: Anonymous

BHG: [896]

Edition: van den Ven, Paul, "La vie grecque de s. Jean le Psichaïte", *Muséon* 21 (1902): 103–23.

DOHD:
https://www.doaks.org/research/byzantine/resources/hagiography/database/dohp.asp?cmd=SShow&key=14

Leo of Catania:

Author: Anonymous

BHG: [981b]

Edition: Latyshev, Vasilij, *Unpublished Greek Hagiographical Texts* [Russian: Латышевъ, Василий, *Неизданные греческіе агиографическіе тексты*], St. Petersburg, 1914, 12–28.

DOHD:
https://www.doaks.org/research/byzantine/resources/hagiography/database/dohp.asp?cmd=SShow&key=109

Luke of Steiris:

Author: Anonymous

BHG: [994]

Edition: Sofianos, Demetrios, *The Life of St. Luke of Steiri* [Greek: Σοφιανός, Δημήτριος, *Ὁ βίος τοῦ ὁσίου Λουκᾶ τοῦ Στειριώτη*], Athens: Akritas, 1989, 159-223.

DOHD:
https://www.doaks.org/research/byzantine/resources/hagiography/database/dohp.asp?cmd=SShow&key=64

Makarios of Pelekete:

Author: Sabbas the Monk

BHG: [1003]

Edition: van den Gheyn, Joseph, "Macarii monasterii Pelecetes hegumeni acta Graeca", *Analecta Bollandiana* 16 (1897): 142-63.

DOHD:
https://www.doaks.org/research/byzantine/resources/hagiography/database/dohp.asp?cmd=SShow&key=18

Martyrs of Amorion (v. 3):

Author: Michael Monk and Synkellos

BHG: [1213]

Edition: Vasilevskij, Vasilij and Petr Nikitin, "Legends of the 42 Martyrs of Amorion and their Holy Service" [Russian: Васильевскій, Василій и Петр Никитин, *Сказания о 42 Аморийских мучениках и церковная служба им*], St. Petersburg, 1905, 22-36.

DOHD:
https://www.doaks.org/research/byzantine/resources/hagiography/database/dohp.asp?cmd=SShow&key=41

Martyrs of Amorion (v. 7):

Author: Euodios Monk

BHG: [1214]

Edition: Vasilevskij, Vasilij and Petr Nikitin, "Legends of the 42 Martyrs of Amorion and their Holy Service" [Russian: Васильевскій, Василій и Петр Никитин, *Сказания о 42 Аморийских мучениках и церковная служба им*], St. Petersburg, 1905, 61-78.

DOHD:
https://www.doaks.org/research/byzantine/resources/hagiography/database/dohp.asp?cmd=SShow&key=42

Melania:

Author: Gerontius

BHG: [1241]

Edition: Gorce, Denys, *Vie de Sainte Mélanie* [*Sources chrétiennes* 90], Paris: Éditions du Cerf, 1962, 124-270.

DOHD: n/a

Michael Maleinos:

Author: Theophanes

BHG: [1295]

Edition: Petit, Louis, "Vie de Saint Michael Maleinos", *Revue d'Orient Chrétien* 7 (1902), 543-94.

DOHD:
https://www.doaks.org/research/byzantine/resources/hagiography/database/dohp.asp?cmd=SShow&key=76

Michael the Synkellos:

Author: Anonymous

BHG: [1296]

Edition: Cunningham, Mary, *The life of Michael the Synkellos* [*Belfast Byzantine Texts and Translations* 1 (1991)], 44-128.

DOHD:
https://www.doaks.org/research/byzantine/resources/hagiography/database/dohp.asp?cmd=SShow&key=76

Naum of Ohrid:

Author: Anonymous

BHG: [1316Z]

Edition: "Die Viten des hl. Naum von Ohrid", ed. Erich Trapp, *Byzantine Studies* 35 (1974): 161-85.

DOHD:
https://www.doaks.org/research/byzantine/resources/hagiography/database/dohp.asp?cmd=SShow&key=85

Nicholas of Sion:

Author: Anonymous

BHG: [1347]

Edition: Ševčenko, Ihor and Nancy Ševčenko, *The Life of Saint Nicholas of Sion* [*The Archbishop Iakovos Library of Ecclesiastical and Historical Sources* 10], Brookline, Mass.: Hellenic College Press, 1984.

DOHD: n/a

Nicholas of Stoudios:

Author: Anonymous

BHG: [1365]

Edition: MPG, vol. 105, Paris, 1862, 863-925.

DOHD:
https://www.doaks.org/research/byzantine/resources/hagiography/database/dohp.asp?cmd=SShow&key=19

Nikephoros of Medikion:

Author: Anonymous

BHG: [2297]

Edition: Halkin, François, "La Vie de Saint Nicéphore fondateur de Médikion en Bithynie", *Analaecta Bollandiana* 78 (1960): 401-28.

DOHD:
https://www.doaks.org/research/byzantine/resources/hagiography/database/dohp.asp?cmd=SShow&key=27

Nikephoros of Sebaze:

Author: Anonymous

BHG: [2300]

Edition: Halkin, François, "Une victime inconnue de Léon I' Arménien? Saint Nicéphore de Sébazè", *Byzantion* 23 (1953): 11-30.

DOHD:
https://www.doaks.org/research/byzantine/resources/hagiography/database/dohp.asp?cmd=SShow&key=17

Niketas of Medikion:

Author: Theosteriktos of Medikion

BHG: [1341]

Edition: *AASS*, Aprilii tomus 1, Paris & Rome, 1866, Appendix, XVIII-XXVII.

DOHD:
https://www.doaks.org/research/byzantine/resources/hagiography/database/dohp.asp?cmd=SShow&key=30

Niketas Patrikios:

Author: Anonymous

BHG: [1342B-1342E]

Edition: Papachryssanthou, Denise, "Un Confesseur du second Iconoclasme: La Vie du Patrice Niketas", *Travaux et mémoires* 3 (1968): 325-51.

DOHD:
https://www.doaks.org/research/byzantine/resources/hagiography/database/dohp.asp?cmd=SShow&key=26

Nikon Metanoeite:

Author: Anonymous

BHG: [1366]

Edition: Sullivan, Denis, *The Life of Saint Nikon: Text, translation, and commentary* [The Archbishop Iakovos Library of Ecclesiastical and Historical Sources 14], Brooklin Mass.: Hellenic College Press, 1987: 26-271.

DOHD:
https://www.doaks.org/research/byzantine/resources/hagiography/database/dohp.asp?cmd=SShow&key=87

Pancratius of Taormina:

Author: Gregory the Pagurite

BHG: [1411]

Edition: Stallman-Pacitti, Cynthia, "The Encomium of S. Pancratius of Taormina by Gregory the Pagurite", *Byzantion* 60 (1990), 346-64.

DOHD: n/a

Patriarch Germanos:

Author: Anonymous

BHG: [697]

Edition: Lamza, Lucian, *Patriarch Germanos I. von Konstantinopel (715 – 730)*, Würzburg: Augustinus-Verlag, 1975, 200-240.

DOHD:
https://www.doaks.org/research/byzantine/resources/hagiography/database/dohp.asp?cmd=SShow&key=111

Patriarch Euthymios:

Author: Anonymous

BHG: [651]

Edition: Karlin-Hayter, Patricia, *Vita Euthymii patriarchae Constantinopolitani* [Bibliothèque de Byzantion, 3], Brussels: Editions de Byzantion, 1970, 3-147.

DOHD:
https://www.doaks.org/research/byzantine/resources/hagiography/database/dohp.asp?cmd=SShow&key=82

Patriarch Ignatios:

Author: Niketas-David Paphlagon

BHG: [817]

Edition: MPG, vol. 105, Paris, 1862, 487-575.

DOHD:
https://www.doaks.org/research/byzantine/resources/hagiography/database/dohp.asp?cmd=SShow&key=38

Patriarch Nikephoros:

Author: Ignatios the Deacon

BHG: [1335]

Edition: de Boor, Carl, *Nicephori archiepiscopi Constantinopolitani opuscula historica*, Leipzig: Teubner, 1880, 139-217.

DOHD:
https://www.doaks.org/research/byzantine/resources/hagiography/database/dohp.asp?cmd=SShow&key=31

Patriarch Tarasios:

Author: Ignatios the Deacon

BHG: [1698]

Edition: Efthymiadis, Stephanos, *The Life of the Patriarch Tarasios by Ignatios the Deacon (BHG 1698)* [*Birmingham Byzantine and Ottoman monographs* 4], New York: Routledge, 2016, 67-168 (English translation: 171-206).

DOHD:
https://www.doaks.org/research/byzantine/resources/hagiography/database/dohp.asp?cmd=SShow&key=39

Paul of Latros I:

Author: Anonymous

BHG: [1474]

Edition: Delehaye, Hippolyte, "Vita S. Pauli iunioris", in *Milet: Ergebnisse der Ausgrabungen und Untersuchungen seit dem Jahre 1899*, ed. Th. Wiegand, vol. 3.1., Berlin: Reimer, 1913, 105-135.

DOHD:
https://www.doaks.org/research/byzantine/resources/hagiography/database/dohp.asp?cmd=SShow&key=81

Paul of Latros II:

Author: Anonymous

BHG: [1474d]

Edition: Delehaye, Hippolyte, "Laudatio S. Pauli iunioris", in *Milet: Ergebnisse der Ausgrabungen und Untersuchungen seit dem Jahre 1899*, ed. Th. Wiegand, vol. 3.1., Berlin: Reimer, 1913, 136-57.

DOHD: n/a

Peter of Atroa:

Author: Sabbas the Monk

BHG: [2364]

Edition: Laurent, Vitalien, *La Vie merveilleuse de saint Pierre d'Atroa* [*Subsidia hagiographica* 29], Brussels: Société des Bollandistes, 1956, 65-225.

DOHD:
https://www.doaks.org/research/byzantine/resources/hagiography/database/dohp.asp?cmd=SShow&key=25

Peter of Atroa (v. retr.):

Author: Sabbas the Monk

BHG: [2365]

Edition: Laurent, Vitalien, *La vita retractata et les miracles posthumes de saint Pierre d'Atroa* [Subsidia hagiographica 31], Brussels: Société des Bollandistes, 1958, 134–71.

DOHD:
https://www.doaks.org/research/byzantine/resources/hagiography/database/dohp.asp?cmd=SShow&key=25

Phantinos the Younger:

Author: Anonymous

BHG: [2367]

Edition: Follieri, Enrica, *La vita di San Fantino il Giovane. Introduzione, testo greco, traduzione, commentario e indici* [Subsidia hagiographica, 77], Brussels: Société des Bollandistes, 1993, 400–470.

DOHD:
https://www.doaks.org/research/byzantine/resources/hagiography/database/dohp.asp?cmd=SShow&key=90

Philaretos the Merciful:

Author: Niketas of Amnia

BHG: [1511Z]

Edition: Fourmy, Marie-Henriette and Maurice Leroy, "La vie de s. Philarète", *Byzantion* 9 (1934): 112–67.

DOHD:
https://www.doaks.org/research/byzantine/resources/hagiography/database/dohp.asp?cmd=SShow&key=117

Plato of Sakkoudion:

Author: Theodore Studites

BHG: [1553]

Edition: MPG, vol. 99, Paris: 1860.

DOHD:
https://www.doaks.org/research/byzantine/resources/hagiography/database/dohp.asp?cmd=SShow&key=36

Sabbas the Younger:

Author: Orestes, Patriarch of Jerusalem

BHG: [1611]

Edition: Cozza-Luzi, Giuseppe, *Historia et laudes ss. Sabae et Macarii Juniorum e Sicilia*. Roma: Bibliotheca Apostolica Vaticana, 1893, 5–70, 137–42.

DOHD:
https://www.doaks.org/research/byzantine/resources/hagiography/database/dohp.asp?cmd=SShow&key=75

Sophronios of Jerusalem:

Author: Ioannes Zonaras

BHG: [1641]

Edition: Papadopoulos-Kerameus, Athanasios, *Unedited texts from the collections of Jerusalem* [Greek: Παπαδόπουλος-Κεραμεύς, Αθανάσιος, Ἀνάλεκτα Ἱεροσολυμιτικῆς σταχυολογίας], vol. 5, St. Petersburg, 1889, 136–50.

DOHD: n/a

Stephen the Thaumaturge:

Author: Leontios of Damascus

BHG: [1670]

Edition: *AASS*, Iulii tomus 3, Paris and Rome, 1867, 504–84.

DOHD:
https://www.doaks.org/research/byzantine/resources/hagiography/database/dohp.asp?cmd=SShow&key=119

Stephen the Younger:

Author: Stephen the Deacon

BHG: [1666]

Edition: Auzépy, Marie-France, *La Vie d' Étienne le Jeune par Étienne le Diacre* [Birmingham Byzantine and Ottoman monographs 3], New York: Rootledge, 2016, 87–177.

DOHD:
https://www.doaks.org/research/byzantine/resources/hagiography/database/dohp.asp?cmd=SShow&key=118

Symeon Stylites the Younger:

Author: Anonymous

BHG: [1689]

Edition van den Ven, Paul, *La Vie ancienne de saint Syméon Stylite le Jeune (521 – 592)*, vol. 1: *Introduction et texte grec* [Subsidia hagiographica 32], Brussels: Société des Bollandistes, 1962, 1–224.

DOHD: n/a

Symeon the Holy Fool:

Author: Leontios, Bishop of Neapolis in Cyprus

BHG: [1677]

Edition: Leontios of Néapolis, "Vie de Syméon le Fou", in Féstugière, André-Jean and Lenard Ryden, *Léontios de Néapolis. Vie de Syméon le Fou et Vie de Jean de Chypre*, Paris, 1974, 55-104.

DOHD: n/a

Theodora of Thessalonica:

Author: Gregory the Cleric

BHG: [1737-1738]

Edition: Kurtz, Eduard, *Des Klerikers Gregorios Bericht über Leben, Wundertaten und Translation der heiligen Theodora von Thessalonich*, Petersburg, 1902, 1-49.

DOHD:

https://www.doaks.org/research/byzantine/resources/hagiography/database/dohp.asp?cmd=SShow&key=21

Theodore Graptos:

Author: Theophanes, Bishop of Caesarea in Cappadocia

BHG: [1745z]

Edition: Featherstone, Jeffrey-Michael, "The praise of Theodore Graptos by Theophanes of Caesarea", *Analecta Bollandiana* 98 (1980): 93-150.

DOHD: n/a

Theodore of Edessa:

Author: Basil of Emesa

BHG: [1744]

Edition: Pomjalovskij, Ivan, *The Life of our father Theodore, archbishop of Edessa*, [Russian: Помяловский, Иван, *Житие иже во св. отца нашего Феодора архиепископа Эдесского*), St. Petersburg, 1892, 1-120.

DOHD:

https://www.doaks.org/research/byzantine/resources/hagiography/database/dohp.asp?cmd=SShow&key=32

Theodore Sykeotes:

Author: George, Abbot of Sykeon

BHG: [1748]

Edition: Féstugière, André-Jean, *Vie de Théodore de Sykéôn*, vol. 1 [Subsidia hagiographica 48], Brussels: Société des Bollandistes, 1970, 1-161.

DOHD: n/a

Theodore Studites:

Author: Michael Monachus

BHG: [1754]

Edition: MPG, vol. 99, Paris, 1862, 233-328.
DOHD:
https://www.doaks.org/research/byzantine/resources/hagiograp hy/database/dohp.asp?cmd=SShow&key=37
Thomas Dephourkinos:
Author: Anonymous
BHG: [2458]
Edition: Delehaye, Hippolyte, *Propylaeum ad Acta Sanctorum Novembris. Synaxarium Ecclesiae Constantinopolitanae,* Brussels: Société des Bollandistes, 1902, 293-98.
DOHD:
https://www.doaks.org/research/byzantine/resources/hagiograp hy/database/dohp.asp?cmd=SShow&key=69

OTHERS

Acta et diplomata graeca medii aevi sacra et profana, ed. Franz Miklošič and Joseph Müller, vol. 1, Athens: Spanos, 1996.

Aeschylus, "Persae", ed. Gilbert Murray, *Aeschyli septem quae supersunt tragoediae,* Oxford: Clarendon Press, 1960, 53-95.

Ammianus Marcellinus, History. Books 14-19, ed. John Rolfe [Loeb Classical Library 300], Cambridge, Mass.: Harvard University Press; William Heinemann, 1935.

Anastasios Sinaita, "De taxeota seu de milite redivivo", ed. François Nau, "Le text grec sur les récits du moine Anastase sur les saints pères du Sinai", *Oriens Christianus* 2 (1902): 83-87.

"Anthemius", ed. Ludwig Radermacher, *Griechische Quellen zur Faustsage,* Wien and Leipzig: Hölder-Pichler-Tempsky in Komm, 1927, 258-71.

Antoninus Liberalis, *Metamorphoseon synagogue,* ed. Ignatius Cazzaniga, Milan: Istituto Editoriale Cisalpino, 1962.

Aphthonios le Sophiste, "Exercices préparatoires", ed. Michel Patillon, *Corpus Rhetoricum,* vol. 1, Paris: Les Belles Lettres, 2008, 112-62.

Apocalypsis Henochi Graece, ed. Matthew Black [Pseudepigrapha veteris testamenti Graece 3], Leiden: Brill, 1970.

"Apollodori bibliotheca," ed. Richard Wagner, *Pediasimi libellus de duodecim Herculis laboribus* [Mythographi Graeci 1], Leipzig: Teubner, 1996 (repr.), 1-169.

"Apollodori epitoma," ed. Richard Wagner, *Pediasimi libellus de duodecim Herculis laboribus* [Mythographi Graeci 1], Leipzig: Teubner, 1996 (repr.), 171-237.

"Aristophanis Equites," ed. Nigel Wilson, *Aristophanis Fabulae*, Oxford: Oxford University Press, 2007, 69-128.

"Aristophanis Vespae," ed. Nigel Wilson, *Aristophanis Fabulae*, Oxford: Oxford University Press, 2007, 209-73.

Aristotle, *Nicomachean Ethics*, ed. Harris Racham [Loeb Classical Library 73], Cambridge, MA: Harvard University Press, 1926.

Aristote, *Histoire des animaux*, ed. Pierre Louis, vol. 1: *Livres I-IV*, Paris: Les Belles Lettres, 1964, 486a-538b.

Aristoteles "Physiognomonica," ed. Immanuel Bekker, *Aristotelis opera*, vol. 2, Berlin: De Gruyter, 1960, 805a1-814b8.

Artemidori Daldiani onirocriticon libri V, ed. Roger Pack, Leipzig: Teubner, 1963, 1-324.

Athanasius Alexandrinus, "Expositiones in Psalmos", in MPG, vol. 27, Paris, 1837, 60-545, 548-589.

Athenagoras, "Legatio sive Supplicatio pro christianis", ed. William Schoedel, *Athenagoras. Legatio and De resurrection*, Oxford: Clarendon Press, 1972, 2-86.

Basilius Magnus, "Homilia quod Deus non est auctor malorum", in MPG, vol. 31, Paris, 1857, 329-53.

Basilius Magnus, "De ieiunio homilia I", in MPG, vol. 31, Paris, 1857, 164-84.

Basilius Magnus, "Homiliae super Psalmos", in MPG, vol. 29, Paris, 1857, 209-494.

The Ancient Egyptian Book of the Dead, ed. and trans. Wallis Budge and Epiphanius Wilson, New York: Quarto Publishing Group, 2016.

"The Romance of Callimachos and Chrysorrhoe", ed. Emmanuel Kriaras, *Byzantine Chivalric Romances* [Greek: "Τὸ μυθιστόρημα τοῦ Καλλιμάχου καὶ τῆς Χρυσορρόης", ed. Εμμανουήλ Κριαράς, *Βυζαντινά ιπποτικά μυθιστορήματα*], Athens, 1955.

Cassii Dionis Cocceiani historiarum Romanarum quae supersunt, ed. Ursul Boissevain, vol. 1, Berlin: Weidmann, 1895; vol. 2, Berlin: Weidmann, 1898; vol. 3, Berlin: Weidmann, 1901.

"Gai Valeri Catulli Veronensis Liber", ed. Francis Cornish, John Postgate, and John Mackail, *Catullus. Tibullus. Privilegium Veneris* [Loeb Classical Library 6], Cambridge: Harvard University Press, 1921, 1-181.

"Carminum Sapphicorum Fragmenta", ed. Edgar Lobel and Dennis Page, *Poetarum Lesbiorum fragmenta*, Oxford: Clarendon Press, 1963.

[Cicero], *Ad C. Herennium de ratione dicendi (Rhetorica ad Herennium)*, ed. and trans. Harry Caplan, London: Heinemann, 1954.

Cicero, *De oratore*, ed. Eric Warmington, trans. Edward Sutton, vol. 1: *Books I, II* [Loeb Classical Library 348], London: Heinemann, 1967.

Claudii Aeliani de natura animalium libri xvii, varia historia, epistolae, fragmenta, ed. Rudolph Hercher, vol. 1, Leipzig: Teubner, 1971.

Clément d'Alexandrie, *Le protreptique*, ed. Claude Mondéser [Sources chrétiennes 2], Paris: Éditions du Cerf, 1949, 52–193.

Excerpta historica iussu imp. Constantini Porphyrogeniti confecta: *Excerpta de virtutibus et vitiis*, ed. Antoon Roos, Theodor Büttner-Wobst, Ursul Boissevain, and Carl De Boor, vol. 2: *Excerpta de virtutibus et vitiis*, ed. Antoon Roos, part 1: Berlin: Weidmann, 1906, 1–361; part 2: Berlin: Weidmann, 1910, 1–407.

Cosmas Hierosolymitanus, "Collectio et Interpretatio Historiarum quarum quarum meminit divus Gregorius in carminibus suis, tum ex Scriptura tum ex profanes Poetis atque Scriptoribus", in MPG, vol. 38, Paris, 1862, 347–670.

"The confession of Saint Cyprian", ed. Ryan Bailey, "The Confession of Cyprian of Antioch: Introduction, Text and Translation", PhD diss (McGill University, 2009), 33–107.

Constitution of the Godly and Holy Canons of the Saintly and All-Praiseworthy Apostles and of the Ecumentical and Local Synods and of the Holy Fathers, ed. Georgios Rhalles and Michael Potles [Greek: Σύνταγμα τῶν θείων καὶ ἱερῶν κανόνων τῶν τε ἁγίων καὶ πανευφήμων ἀποστόλων καὶ τῶν οἰκουμενικῶν καὶ τοπικῶν συνόδων καὶ τῶν κατὰ μέρος ἁγίων πατέρων, ed. Γεώργιος Ράλλης and Μιχαὴλ Ποτλῆς], 6 vols., Athens, 1852.

"Cyprianus und Justina", ed. Ludwig Radermacher, *Griechische Quellen zur Faustsage*, Wien and Leipzig: Hölder-Pichler-Tempsky in Komm, 1927, 76–113.

Cyrillus Alexandrinus, "De exitu animi, et de secondo adventu", in MPG, vol. 77, Paris, 1864, 1071–90.

"Anonymi narratio de aedificatione templi S. Sophiae", ed. Theodor Preger, *Scriptores originum Constantinopolitanarum*, vol. 1, Leipzig: Teubner, 1975, 74–108.

"Die Erzählung des Helladius (Proterius)", ed. Ludwig Radermacher, *Griechische Quellen zur Faustsage*, Wien & Leipzig: Hölder-Pichler-Tempsky in Komm, 1927, 117–49.

Die Kyraniden, ed. Dimitris Kaimakis [Beitrage zur Klassischen Philologie, 76], Meisenheim: Anton Hain, 1976.

Digenes Akrites, ed. John Mavrogordato, Oxford: Clarendon Press, 1956.

Diodori bibliotheca historica, ed. Immanuel Bekker, Ludwig Dindorf, and Friedrich Vogel, Stuttgart, 5 vols., 1985.

Diogenis Laertii vitae philosophorum, ed. Miroslav Marcovich, vol. 1: *Libri I-X*, Berlin: De Gruyter, 2008.

Ecloga. Das Gesetzbuch Leons III. und Konstantinos' V, ed. Ludwig Burgmann [*Forschungen zur Byzantinischen Rechtsgeschichte* Band 10], Frankfurt am Main: Löwenklau Gesellschaft, 1983.

Ephraem Syrus, "Sermo in eos, qui in Christo obdormierunt", ed. Kontantinos Frantzolas, *The Works of St. Ephraem Syrus* [Greek: Κωνσταντίνος Φραντζόλας, Ὁσίου Ἐφραὶμ τοῦ Σύρου ἔργα], vol. 6, Thessalonica, 1995, 94–118.

Ephraem Syrus, "Precationes ad Dei matrem", ed. Kontantinos Frantzolas, *The Works of St. Ephraem Syrus* [Greek: Κωνσταντίνος Φραντζόλας, Ὁσίου Ἐφραὶμ τοῦ Σύρου ἔργα], vol. 6, Thessalonica, 1995, 354–413.

Ephraem Syrus, "Sermo de secundo aduentu et iudicio," ed. Kontantinos Frantzolas, *The Works of St. Ephraem Syrus* [Greek: Κωνσταντίνος Φραντζόλας, Ὁσίου Ἐφραὶμ τοῦ Σύρου ἔργα], vol. 4, Thessalonica, 1995, 223–33.

Epiphanius Constantiensis, "Panarium, sive Arcula adversus octoginta haereses", in MPG, vol. 41, Paris, 1863, 173–1179.

"Escape from the Abominable and Unclean Gyllou" [Greek: Ἀποστροφὴ τῆς μιαρᾶς καὶ ἀκαθάρτου Γυλλοῦς"], ed. Konstantinos Sathas, *Bibliotheca Graeca Medii Aevi*, vol. 5, Venice: Phoinix, 1876, 573–75.

Eunapii vitae sophistarum, ed. Giuseppe Giangrande, Rome: Polygraphica, 1956.

Euripides, "Alcestis", ed. James Diggle, *Euripidis fabulae*, vol. 1, Oxford: Clarendon Press, 1984, 37–83.

Euripides, "Rhesus", ed. James Diggle, *Euripidis fabulae*, vol. 3, Oxford: Clarendon Press, 1994, 433–79.

Eusebius Caesariensis, "Commentaria in Psalmos", in MPG, vol. 23, Paris, 1857, 66–1396; vol. 24, Paris, 1964, 9–76.

Eusebius Caesariensis, "Contra Hieroclem", ed. Carl Kayser, *Flavii Philostrati opera*, vol. 1, Hildesheim: Olms, 1964, 369–413.

Eusebius Caesariensis, *Die Praeparatio Evangelica*, ed. Karl Mras, *Eusebius Werke*, vol. 8.1: *Einleitung. Die Bücher I bis X*, Berlin: De Guyter, 1982.

The ecclesiastical history of Evagrius with the scholia, ed. Joseph Bidez and Léon Parmentier, London: Methuen, 1979.

The Epistles of Horace, ed. Augustus Wilkins, London and New York: Macmillan, 1888.

Evagrius Ponticus, "De octo spiritibus malitiae", in MPG, vol. 79, Paris, 1865, 1045–64.

"[Exorcism] of Gyllou" [Greek: Τῆς Γυλλοῦς], ed. Émile Legrand, *Bibliothèque grecque vulgaire*, vol. 2, Paris: Maisonneuve, 1881, XVIII.

Georgii Monachi Chronicon, ed. Carl de Boor, 2 vols., Leipzig: Teubner, 1978.

Georgius Monachus, "Chronicon Breve", in MPG, vol. 110, Paris, 1863, 41-1260.

Georgii Syncelli Ecloga chronographica, ed. Alden Mosshammer, Leipzig: Teubner, 1984.

Grégoire le Grand, *Dialogues*, vol. 3, ed. Adalbert de Vogüé, trans. Paul Antin, Paris: Éditions de Cerf, 1980.

Gregorius Nazianzenus, "De daemonum pugnis", in MPG, vol. 37, Paris, 1862, 1428-30.

Gregorius Nyssenus, "De vita Gregorii Thaumaturgi", in MPG, vol. 46, Paris, 1863, 893-957.

Gregorius Pisides, "Hymnus Acathistus", in MPG, vol. 92, 1335-48.

Hérodote, *Histoires*, ed. Philippe-Ernest Legrand, 9 vols., Paris: Les Belles Lettres, 1944-92.

Hermogenes, "On types of Style" [Greek: Περὶ ἰδεῶν λόγου], ed. Hugo Rabe, *Hermogenis opera* [Rhetores Graeci 6], Stuttgart: Teubner, 1969, 93-212.

Hermogenes, *On types of Style*, trans. Cecil Wooten, Chapel Hill: The University of North Carolina Press, 1987.

Hermogène, "Exercices préparatoires", ed. Michel Patillon, *Corpus Rhetoricum*, vol. 1, Paris: Les Belles Lettres, 2008, 180-206.

Herodianus, "De prosodia catholica", ed. August Lentz, *Grammatici Graeci*, vol. 3.1: *Herodiani Technici reliquiae*, Hildesheim: Olms, 1965, 3-547.

Hesiod, "The Shield of Heracles", ed. and trans. Hugh Evelyn-White, *Hesiod. Homeric Hymns, Epic Cycle, Homerica* [Loeb Classical Library Volume 57], Cambridge, Mass.: Harvard University Press, 1982.

Hesiod, "Works and Days", ed. and trans. Hugh Evelyn-White, *Hesiod. Homeric Hymns Epic Cycle, Homerica* [Loeb Classical Library Volume 57], Cambridge, Mass.: Harvard University Press, 1982, 2-64.

Hesiod, "The Theogony", ed. and trans. Hugh Evelyn-White, *Hesiod. Homeric Hymns, Epic Cycle, Homerica* [Loeb Classical Library Volume 57], Cambridge, Mass.: Harvard University Press, 1982, 78-154.

Hesychii Alexandrini lexicon, ed. Kurt Latte and Ian Cunningham, vol. 1: Α-Δ [Sammlung griechischer und lateinischer Grammatiker 11], Berlin and Boston: De Gruyter, 2018; vol. 2: Ε-Χ, Hauniae: Munksgaard, 1966.

Hesychius Hierosolymitanus Presbyterus, "Ad Theodulum sermo compendiosus animae perutilis, de temperantia et virtute", in MPG, vol. 93, Paris, 1865, 1479-1544.

Hippocrate, "De la maladie sacrée", ed. and French trans. Émile Littré, *Oeuvres complètes d'Hippocrate*, vol. 6, Paris: Baillière, Amsterdam: Hakkert, 1962, 352-96.

"Historia Alexandri Magni. Recensio α sive Recensio vetusta", ed. Wilhelm Kroll, *Historia Alexandri Magni*, vol. 1, Berlin: Weidmann, 1926, 1-146.

Historia monachorum in Aegypto, ed. André-Jean Festugière, Brussels: Société des Bollandistes, 1971.

Homer, *The Iliad*, ed. and trans. Augustus Murray, 2 vols, Cambridge, Mass.: Harvard University Press, 1924.

Homer, *The Odyssey*, ed. and trans. Augustus Murray, 2 vols., Cambridge, Mass., Harvard University Press, 1919.

Hori Apollinis hieroglyphica, ed. Francesco Sbordone, Naples: Loffredo, 1940.

Hyginus, *De Astronomica*, ed. Ghislaine Viré, Stuttgart and Leipzig: Teubner, 1992.

Hyginus, *Fabulae*, ed. Peter Marshall, München and Leipzig: Saur, 2002.

Iamblichus, *De vita Pythagorica liber*, ed. Ludwig Deubner, Leipzig: Teubner, 1975.

Ioannis Scylitzae Synopsis Historiarum, ed. Ioannes Thurn [*Corpus fontium historiae Byzantinae* V], Berlin: De Gruyter, 1973.

Ioannis Lydi liber de mensibus, ed. Richard Wünsch, Leipzig: Teubner, 1898.

Jamblique, *Les mystères d'Égypte*, ed. Édouard des Places [Collection Budé 174], Paris: Les Belles Lettres, 1966.

Joannes Cantacuzenus, "Pro Christiana religione contra sectam Mahometicam apologiae IV", in MPG, vol. 154, Paris, 1866, 371-584.

Joannes Cassianus, "Collationum XXIV collectio in tres partes divisa", in MPL, vol. 49, Paris, 1846, 477A-1328C.

Joannes Chrysostomus, "De Baptismo Christi et de Epiphania", in MPG, vol. 49, Paris, 1862, 361-71.

Joannes Chrysostomus, "Contiones VII de Lazaro", in MPG, vol. 48, Paris, 1862, 963-1054.

Joannes Chrysostomus, *Homiliae in Genesim*, in MPG, vol. 53, Paris, 1862 (Translation: St. John Chrysostom, *Homilies on Genesis 1-17*, trans. Robert Hill [The Fathers of the Church. St. John Chrysostom. A New Translation 74], Washington: The Catholic University of America Press, 1986.

Joannes Chrysostomus, "In Matthaeum Homiliae", in MPG, vol. 57, Paris, 1862, 13-472.

Joannes Chrysostomus, "In memoriam martyrum", in MPG, vol. 52, Paris, 1862, 827-35.

Joannes Damscenus, "Epistola ad Theophilum imperatorem de sanctis et venerandis imaginibus", in MPG, vol. 95, Paris, 1864, 346-86.

Joannes Damascenus, "De draconibus et strigibus", in MPG, vol. 94, Paris, 1864, 1599-1604.

Joannes Moschus, "Beatis Joannis Eucratae liber, qui inscribitur pratum, quod floridam proferat vitarum narrationem coelestis roseti", in MPG, vol. 87.3, Paris, 1863, 2852-3112.

Julien, "Sur les actions de l'empereur ou Sur la royauté Second Éloge de Constance", ed. Joseph Bidez, L'empereur Julien. Oeuvres complètes, vol. 1.1., Paris: Les Belles Lettres, 1932, 116-80.

Julien, "Sur Hélios le Roi", ed. and trans. Christian Lacombrade, L'empereur Julien. Oeuvres completes, vol. 2.2, Paris: Les Belles Lettres, 1964, 100-138.

Julien, "Lettres", ed. and trans. Joseph Bidez, L'empereur Julien. Oeuvres completes, vol. 1.2, Paris: Les Belles Lettres, 1960, 12-23, 26, 51-77, 84-91, 133-200, 205-7.

Julien, "A Thémistius", ed. and trans. Gabriel Rochefort, L'empereur Julien. Oeuvres completes, vol. 2.1, Paris: Les Belles Lettres, 1963, 12-30.

Justinus Martyr, "Cohortatio ad Graecos", in MPG, vol. 6, Paris, 1857, 241-311.

Justinus Martyr, "Dialogus cum Tryphone Judaeo", in MPG, vol. 6, Paris, 1857, 471 — 800.

"Juvenalis Saturae", ed. and trans. Susanna Braund, Juvenal and Persius [Loeb Classical Library, 91], Cambridge, Mass.: Harvard University Press, 2004, 130-511.

"Liutprandi Relatio de legatione Constantinopolitana", ed. Immanuel Bekker, Die Werke Liutprands von Cremona [Scriptores rerum Germanicarum in usum Scholarum ex Monumentis Germanicis Historicis separatism editi], Hannover and Leipzig, 1915, 175-212.

Lucian, "The Lover of Lies, or the Doubter (Philopseudes sive Incredulus)", ed. Austin Harmon, Lucian, vol. 3 [Loeb Classical Library 130], London: Heinemann, 1960, 320-80.

Manetho, "Apotelesmatica", ed. Arminius Koechly, Poetae bucolici et didactici, Paris: Didot, 1862, 41-101.

Maximus Tyrius, Philosphoumena — ΔΙΑΛΕΞΕΙΣ, ed. George Koniaris [Texte und Kommentare 17], Berlin and New York: De Gruyter, 1995.

Menander, "Fragmenta longiora apud alios auctores servata", ed. Francis Sandbach *Menandri reliquiae selectae*, Oxford: Clarendon Press, 1972, 303–24.

Michaelis Glycae Annales, ed. Immanuel Bekker [*Corpus scriptorum historiae Byzantinae* 16], Bonn: Weber, 1836.

Michael Psellus, "De Babutzicario", ed. John Duffy and Dan O'Meara, *Michaelis Pselli philosophica minora*, vol. 2, Leipzig: Teubner, 1989, 163.

Michael Psellus, "De Gillo", ed. John Duffy and Dan O'Meara, *Michaelis Pselli philosophica minora*, vol. 2, Leipzig: Teubner, 1989, 164.

Michael Psellus, "Greek Provisions on Demons" [Greek: Ἑλληνικαὶ διατάξεις περὶ δαιμόνων], ed. John Duffy and Dominic O'Meara, *Michaelis Pselli philosophica minora*, vol. 2, Leipzig: Teubner, 1989, 123–26.

Nicolai progymnasmata, ed. Joseph Felten [Rhetores Graeci 11], Leipzig: Teubner, 1913, 1–79.

Nonni Panopolitani Dionysiaca, ed. Rudolph Keydell, 2 vols., Berlin: Weidmann, 1959.

Novellae, ed. Rudolph Scholl and Wilhelm Kroll, *Corpus iuris civilis*, vol. 3, Berlin: Weidman, 1895.

Olympiodorus, *Commentary on the first Alcibiades of Plato*, Leendert Westerink, Amsterdam: Hakkert, 1982.

O Poulologos, ed. Stamatia Krawczynski [*Berliner Byzantinische Arbeiten* 22], Berlin: Akademie Verlag, 1960.

Origen, *The Philocalia*, ed. Joseph Robinson, Cambridge: Cambridge University Press, 1893.

Origen, *The Philocalia*, trans. George Lewis, Edinburgh: Clark, 1911.

Origéne, *Contre Celse*, ed. Marcel Borret, 3 vols. [Sources Chrétiennes 132], Paris: Éditions de Cerf, 1967–1969.

Origenes, "Commentaria in Psalmos", in MPG, vol. 12, Paris, 1862, 1053–1685.

Palladius Hellenopolitanus episcopus, "Apophthegmata Patrum", in MPG, vol. 65, Paris, 1864, 71–442.

Palladius Helenopolitanus, "Historia Lausiaca", in MPG, vol. 34, Paris, 1860, 991–1278.

Pausaniae Graeciae descriptio, ed. Maria Helena Rocha-Pereira, 3 vols., Leipzig: Teubner, 1989–90.

Philochorus, "Fragmenta", ed. Felix Jacoby, *Die Fragmente der griechischen Historiker*. vol. 3B, Leiden: Brill, 1954, 98–160.

BIBLIOGRAPHY   511

Photius, *Bibliothèque*, ed. René Henry, vol. 2: *Codices 84–185* [Collection Budé 142], Paris: Les Belles Lettres, 1977.

"Physiologus (redactio prima)", ed. Francesco Sbordone, *Physiologus*, Milan: Società Anonima Editrice 'Dante Alighieri', 1936, 1–145.

"Physiologus (diversarum versionum capita disiecta in vulgare lingua)", ed. Francesco Sbordone, *Physiologus*, Milan: Società Anonima Editrice 'Dante Alighieri', 1936, 313–25.

Pindar, "Fragmenta incerta", ed. Herwig Maehler and Bruno Snell, *Pindari carmina cum fragmentis*, vol. 2, Leipzig: Teubner, 1975, 1–161.

Pindar, "Pythia", ed. Herwig Maehler and Bruno Snell, *Pindari carmina cum fragmentis*, vol. 1: *Epinicia*, Berlin and New York: De Guyter, 2008, 50–102.

Plato, "Apologia Socratis", ed. John Burnet, *Platonis opera*, vol. 1, Oxford: Clarendon Press, 1967, 17–42.

Plato, "Cratylus", ed. John Burnet, *Platonis opera*, vol. 1, Oxford: Clarendon Press, 1967, 383–440.

Plato, "Leges", ed. John Burnet, *Platonis opera*, vol. 5, Oxford: Clarendon Press, 1967, 624–969.

Plato, "Phaedo", ed. John Burnet, *Platonis opera*, vol. 1, Oxford: Clarendon Press, 1967, 57–118.

Plato, "Phaedrus", ed. John Burnet, *Platonis opera*, vol. 1, Oxford: Clarendon Press, 1967, 227–76.

Plato, "Respublica", ed. John Burnet, *Platonis opera*, vol. 4, Oxford: Clarendon Press, 1968, 327–621.

Plato, "Sophista", ed. John Burnet, *Platonis opera*, vol. 1, Oxford: Clarendon Press, 1968, 216–68.

Plato, "Symposium", ed. J. Burnet, *Platonis opera*, vol. 2, Oxford: Clarendon Press, 1967, 172–223.

Plato, *Symposium, Dialogues of Plato*, trans. Benjamin Jowett, vol. 1, Oxford: Clarendon Press, 1964.

Plotinus, *Enneads*, ed. Hans-Rudolph Swyzer and Paul Henry, trans. Arthur Armstrong, *Plotinus*, vol. 1: *Porphyry on the Life of Plotinus and the order of his books, Enneads I. 1-9* [Loeb Classical Library 440], Cambridge: Harvard University Press, 1989.

Plutarchus, "Agis et Cleomenes", ed. Konrad Ziegler, *Plutarchi vitae parallelae*, vol. 3.1, Leipzig: Teubner, 1971, 352–415.

Plutarchus, "De defectu oraculorum", ed. Wilhelm Sieveking, *Plutarchi moralia*, vol. 3, Leipzig: Teubner, 1972, 59–122.

"Poimandres", ed. Arthur Nock and André-Jean Festugière, *Corpus Hermeticum*, Paris, 1972, 7–19.

Porphyrius, "De abstinentia", ed. Johann Nauck, *Porphyrii philosophi Platonici opuscula selecta*, Leipzig: Teubner and Hildesheim: Olms, 1963, 85-269.

Porphyrii de philosophia ex oraculis haurienda: librorum relinquiae, ed. Gustav Wolff, Hildesheim, 1962.

Porphyry, "On the Life of Plotinus", ed. Hans-Rudolph Swyzer and Paul Henry, trans. Arthur Armstrong, *Plotinus*, vol. 1: *Porphyry on the Life of Plotinus and the order of his books, Enneads I. 1-9* [Loeb Classical Library 440], Cambridge: Harvard University Press, 1989, 1-88.

Proclus Constantinopolis archiepiscopus, "Orationes", in MPG, vol. 65, Paris, 1864, 679-834.

Proclus Diadochus, *Commentary on the first Alcibiades of Plato*, ed. Leendert Westerink, Amsterdam: North-Holland Publishing, 1954.

Procli Diadochi in Platonis Cratylum commentaria, ed. Georgius Pasquali, Leipzig: Teubner, 1994.

Proclus Diadochus, "De malorum substinentia liber", ed. Helmut Boese, *Procli Diadochi tria opuscula*, Berlin: De Gruyter, 1960, 173-265.

Procli Diadochi in Platonis rem publicam commentarii, ed. Wilhelm Kroll, 2 vols., Amsterdam: Hakkert, 1965.

Procli Diadochi in Platonis Timaeum commentaria, ed. Ernestus Diehl, 3 vols., Amsterdam: Hakkert, 1965.

Procopius, *On Buildings*, ed. and trans. Henry Dewing and Glanville Downey [Loeb Classical Library 343], Cambridge, MA: Harvard University Press, 1940.

Pseudo-Amphilochius, "On the life and the miracles of our father St. Basil, Bishop of Caesarea in Cappadocia [Greek: Εἰς τὸν βίον καὶ τὰ θαύματα τοῦ ἐν ἁγίοις πατρὸς ἡμῶν Βασιλείου ἀρχιεπισκόπου Καισαρείας Καππαδοκίας], in *Amphilochii Opera Omnia*, ed. François Combefis, Paris: Piget, 1644, 155-225.

Pseudo-Dionysius Areopagita, "De divinis nominibus", ed. Beate Regina Suhla, *Corpus Dionysiacum*, vol. 1 [Patristische Texte und Studien 33], Berlin and New York: De Guyter, 1990.

Pseudo-Dionysios of Tel-Mahre, *Chronicle, Part III*, ed. and trans. Witold Witakowski [Translated texts for historians 22], Liverpool, 1996.

[Pseudo-]Joannes Chrysostomus, "Homiliae in Genesim", in MPG, vol. 56, Paris, 1862, 519-538.

[Pseudo-]Joannes Chrysostomus, "In infirmos", ed. Alexander Vasiliev, *Anecdota Graeco-Byzantina*, vol. 1, Moscow, 1893, 323-27.

[Pseudo-] Michael Psellus, "Quaenam sunt Graecorum opiniones de daemonibus", in MPG, vol. 122, Paris, 1889, 875-82.

Pseudo-Psellos, "Timothée ou des demons", ed. Paul Gautier, "De daemonibus de Pseudo-Psellos", *Revue des Études Byzantines* 38 (1980): 133-77.

[Pseudo-] Sophronius Hierosolymitanus, "Triodium", in MPG, vol. 87/3, Paris, 1863, 3839-3981.

Publii Ovidii Nasonis Metamorphoses, ed. William Anderson, Stuttgart and Leipzig: Teubner, 1981

Quintilian, *The Institutio Oratoria*, ed. and trans. Harold Butler, London and New York: G.P. Putnam's Sons, 1921.

Sophocles, "Trachinae", ed. Alphonse Dain, trans. Paul Mazon, *Sophocle*, vol. 1, Paris: Les Belles lettres, 1967, 14-60.

Sozomenus. *Kirchengeschichte (Historia Ecclesiastica)*, ed. Joseph Bidez and Günther Hansen [Die griechischen christlichen Schriftsteller 50], Berlin: Akademie Verlag, 1960.

Strabonis geographica, ed. Karl Müller, Cambridge: Cambridge University Press, 2015.

Suetonius, "Caligula", ed. and trans. John Rolfe, *De vita Casarum*, vol. 1 [Loeb Classical Library 31], Cambridge, Mass.: Harvard University Press, 1913, 404-96.

Suidae lexicon, ed. Ada Adler [Lexicographi Graeci, vol. 1], Part 1: Α-Γ, München and Leipzig: Saur, 2001; Part 2: Δ-Ι, Stuttgart: Teubner, 1994; Part 3: Κ-Ο, Stuttgart: Teubner, 1967; Part 4: Π-Ψ, München and Leipzig: Saur, 2001; Part. 5: *Praefationem indices dissertationem continens*, München and Leipzig: Saur, 2001.

"The Testament of Reuben, the First-Born Son of Jacob and Leah", ed. Robert Charles, *The Apocrypha and Pseudepigrapha of the Old Testament in English*, vol. 2, Oxford, Clarendon Press, 1913, 295-300.

The Testament of Solomon, ed. Chester McCown [Untersuchungen zum Neuen Testament 9], Leipzig, 1922.

Théodoret de Cyr, *Thérapeutique des maladies helléniques*, ed. and trans. Pierre Canivet [Sources chrétiennes 57.1], Paris: Éditions du Cerf, 1958.

Théodoret de Cyr, *L'histoire des moines de Syrie* [Sources chrétiennes 234], ed. Pierre Canivet and Alice Leroy-Molinghen, 2 vols., Paris: Éditions du Cerf, 1977-1979.

Theodori Studitae Epistulae, ed. Georgios Fatouros, 2 vols. [Corpus Fontium Historiae Byzantinae. Series Berolinensis 31.1-2], Berlin: De Gruyter, 1992.

Theognis, "Elegiae," ed. Ernestus Diehl, *Theognis*, Leipzig: Teubner, 1971, 1-83.

Theonis Progymnasmata, ed. Leonhard von Spengel, *Rhetores Graeci*, vol. 2, Frankfurt am Main: Minerva, 1966, 59-130

Theophanis chronographia, ed. Carl de Boor, 2 vols., Hildesheim: Olms, 1963.

Theophylactus, "Enarratio in evangelium Lucae", in MPG, vol. 123, Paris, 1864, 683-1126.

Theophanis Continuati liber V. Vita Basilii imperatiris, ed. Ihor Ševčenko [Corpus fontium historiae Byzantinae 42], Berlin: De Gruyter, 2011.

"Theophilus nach der Bearbeitung des Eutychianus mit daraus abgeleiteten Fassungen", ed. Ludwig Radermacher, Griechische Quellen zur Faustsage, Wien and Leipzig: Hölder-Pichler-Tempsky in Komm, 1927, 182-218.

"Theophilus. Älteste Fassung", ed. Ludwig Radermacher, Griechische Quellen zur Faustsage, Wien — Leipzig: Hölder-Pichler-Tempsky in Komm, 1927, 164-177.

Thucydides, History of the Peloponnesian war, ed. and trans. Charles Smith, vol. 1: Books I and III [Loeb Classical Library 108], London: Heinemann, 1956.

"Testamentum Salomonis", ed. Chester McCown, The Testament of Solomon [Untersuchungen zum Neuen Testament 9], Leipzig, 1922,˙5 -˙76.

"Vies et récits d'anachorètes (IV-e — VII-e siècles)", ed. Léon Clugnet and François Nau, Révue d'Orient Chrétien, 8 (1903): 91-100.

"La version longue de la vision du moine Cosmas", ed. Christine Angelidi, Analecta Bollandiana 101 (1983): 73-99.

Xenopophon, "Memorabilia Socratis", ed. [James Adam], trans. Edgar Marchant, Xenophon. Memorabilia, Oeconomicus, Symposium, Apology [Loeb Classical Library 168], Cambridge, Mass. and London: Harvard University Press, 1997, 1-360.

Zenobius, "Epitome collectionum Lucilli Tarrhaei et Didymi", ed. Friedrich Schneidewin and Ernst von Leutsch, Corpus paroemiographorum Graecorum, vol. 1, Hildesheim: Olms, 1965, 1-175.

II. Secondary sources

Abrahamse, Dorothy and Douglas Domingo-Forasté, "Life of David, Symeon, and George", in Byzantine Defenders of Images. Eight Saint's Lives in English Translation, ed. Alice-Mary Talbot [Byzantine Saints' Lives in Translation, 2], Washington D.C.: Dumbarton Oaks, 1998, 143-241.

Acconcia-Longo, Augusta, "A proposito di un articolo sull'agiografia iconoclasta", Rivista di Studi Bizantini e Neoellenici 29 (1992): 10-17.

Acconcia-Longo, Augusta, "Di nuovo sull'agiografia iconoclasta", *Rivista di Studi Bizantini e Neoellenici* 30 (1993): 7-15.

Acconcia-Longo, "La vita di s. Leone vescovo di Catania e gli incantesimi del mago Eliodoro", *Rivista di Studi Bizantini e Neoellenici* 26 (1989): 3-98.

Aitken, W. "Beelzebul", *Journal of Biblical Literature* 31, no. 1 (1912): 34-54.

Alexandrova, Donka, *Metamorphoses of 20th-century Rhetoric* [Bulgarian: Александрова, Донка, *Метаморфози на реториката през XX в.*], Sofia: Sofia University Press, 2013.

Androutsos, Christos, *Dogmatics of the Eastern Orthodox Church* [Greek: Ανδρούτσος, Χρήστος, *Δογματική τῆς Ὀρθοδόξου Ἀνατολικῆς Ἐκκλησίας*], Athens, 1907.

Angelidi, Christine, "La version longue de la vision du moine Cosmas", *Analecta Bollandiana* 101 (1983): 73-99.

Angelidi, Christine, "The Life of St. Basil the Younger" [Greek: Αγγελίδη, Χριστίνα, *Ο Βίος τοῦ ἁγίου Βασιλείου τοῦ Νέου*]. PhD diss (University of Ioannina), 1980.

Anton, John, "*Theourgia* – *Demiourgia*: A Controversial Issue in Hellenistic Thought and Religion", in *Neoplatonism and Gnosticism*, ed. Richard Wallis and Jay Bregman [Studies in Neoplatonism: Ancient and Modern, 4], Albany: New York State University Press, 1992, 9-32.

Athanasiadi, Polymnia, "The Chaldean Oracles: Theology and Theurgy", in *Pagan Monotheism in Late Antiquity*, ed. Polymnia Athanasiadi and Michael Frede, Oxford: Clarendon Press, 1999, 149-185.

Auzépy, Marie-France, "A propos des vies de saints iconoclasts", *Rivista di Studi Bizantini e Neoellenici* 30 (1993): 2-5.

Auzépy, Marie-France, "De la Palestine à Constantinople (VIIIe – IXe siècles): Etienne le Sabaïte et Jean Damascène", *Travaux et Mémoires* 12 (1994): 183-218.

Auzépy, Marie-France, *La Vie d' Étienne le Jeune par Étienne le Diacre* [Birmingham Byzantine and Ottoman monographs 3], New York: Routledge, 2016.

Bailey, Ryan. "The Confession of Cyprian of Antioch: Introduction, Text and Translation". PhD diss (McGill University), 2009.

Barb, Alfons, "Antaura, the Mermaid and the Devil's Grandmother", *Journal of the Warburg and Courtauld Institutes* 29, no. 1 (1966): 1-23.

Barr, James, "The Question of Religious Influence: The Case of Zoroastrianism, Judaism, and Christianity", *Journal of the American Academy of Religion* 53, no. 2 (June 1985): 201-35.

Bartelink, Gerhardus, "Μισόκαλος, épithéte du Diable", *Vigiliae Christianae* 12, no. 1 (May 1958): 37-44.

Bassett, Edward, "Regulus and the serpent in the *Punica*", *Classical Philology*, 50/1 (January 1955): 1-20.

Bassett, Samuel, "ΔAIMΩN in Homer", *The Classical Review* 33, no. 7/8 (November – December 1919): 134-36.

Bernheim, Frederick and Ann Zener, "The Sminthian Apollo and the Epidemic among the Achaeans at Troy", *Transactions of the American Philological Association* 108 (1978): 11-14.

Bidez, Joseph and Franz Cumont, *Les Mages hellénistés*, vol. 1, Paris, 1938.

Bloomfield, Morton, "The Origin of the Concept of the Seven Cardinal Sins", *The Harvard Theological Review* 34, no. 2 (April, 1941): 121-28.

Blum, Claes, "The meaning of στοιχεῖον and its Derivatives in the Byzantine Age", *Eranos Jahrbuch*, XLIV (1946): 315-325.

Brakke, David, *Demons and the Making of the Monk. Spiritual Combat in Early Christianity*, Cambridge Mass. and London: Harvard University Press, 2006.

Böcher, Otto, *Dämonenfurcht und Dämonenabwehr. Ein Beitrag zur Vorgeschichte der Christlichen Taufe* [Beiträge zur Wissenschaft vom Alten und Neuen Testament 90], Stuttgart: Kohlhammer, 1970.

Bojadschiew, Tsotscho, *The Night in the Middle Ages* [Bulgarian: Бояджиев, Цочо, *Нощта през средновековието*], Sofia: Sofi-R, 2000.

Bouras, Laskarina, "Dragon Representations on Byzantine Phialae and their Conduits", *Gesta* 16, no. 2 (1977): 65-68.

Burkert, Walter, *Greek Religion, Archaic and Classical*, trans. J. Raffan, Oxford: Blackwell, 1985.

Burkert, Walter, *The Near-Eastern Influence Orientalizing on Greek Culture Revolution in The Early Archaic Age*, trans. Margaret Pinder and W. Burkert, Cambridge Mass.: Harvard University Press, 1992.

Burkert, Walter, *Antike Mysterien. Funktionen und Gehalt*, München: Beck, 1990.

Burnet, John, *Early Greek Philosophy*, London: Black, 1920.

Byron, Gay, *Symbolic Blackness and Ethnic Difference in Early Christian Literature*, London: Routledge, 2002.

Campbell, Joseph, *The Hero with a Thousand Faces* [Bollingen Series XVII], Princeton: Princeton University Press, 2004.

Casson, Lionel, *Ships and Seamanship in the Ancient World*, Princeton: Princeton University Press, 1971.

Chatzidakis, Nano, *Greek Art. Byzantine Mosaics*, Athens: Ekdotike Athenon, 1994.

Cheynet, Jean-Claude, "Toparque et topotèrétès à la fin du XIe siècle", *Revue des études byzantines* 42 (1984): 215-24.

Christophilopoulou, Aikaterine, *Byzantine History* [Greek: Χριστοφιλοπούλου, Αικατερίνη, *Βυζαντινή Ιστορία*], vol. I (=A'): 324–610, Thessalonica: Vanias, 1992; vol. II.1 (=B'1): 610–867, Thessalonica: Vanias, 1993; vol. II.2 (=B'2): 867–1081, Thessalonica: Vanias, 1997.

Clerc, Jean-Benoît, *Homines magici. Etude sur la sorcellerie et la magie dans la société romaine impériale*, Bern: Peter Lang, 1995.

Collard, P., "Une nouvelle *Tabula defixionis* d'Égypte", *Révue de Philologie de Littérature et Histoire Anciennes* 4 (1930): 248–56.

Comella, Annamaria, *I rilievi votivi greci di periodo arcaico e classico: diffusione, ideologia, committenza*, Bari: Edipuglia, 2002.

Connor, Carolyn, *Women of Byzantium*, New Heaven: Yale University Press, 2004.

Conybeare, Frederick, "Christian Demonology", I: *Jewish Quarterly Review*, 8, no. 4 (July 1896): 576–608; II: *Jewish Quarterly Review* 9, no. 1 (October 1896): 59–114.

Crowley, Tim "On the use of stoicheion in the sense of 'element'", *Oxford Studies in Ancient Philosophy* 29 (2005): 367–94.

Cumont, Franz, *After Life in Roman Paganism*, New Haven: Yale University Press, 1922.

Dagron, Gilbert, *Constantinolpe imaginaire. Étude sur le recueil des «patria»* [Bibliothèque byzantine: études 8], Paris: Presses Universitaires de France, 1985.

da Costa-Louillet, Germaine, "Saints de Constantinople aux VIIIe, IXe, et Xe siècles", I: *Byzantion* 24, no. 1 (1954): 179–263, 453–511; II: *Byzantion* 25–27 (1957): 783–852.

da Costa-Louillet, Germaine, "Saints de Grèce aux VIIIe, IXe et Xe siècles", *Byzantion* 31 (1961): 309–69.

da Costa-Louillet, Germaine, "Saints de Sicile et d'Italie méridionale aux VIIIe, IXe et Xe siècles", *Byzantion* 29–30 (1959–60): 89–173.

Delatte, Armand and Charles Josserand, "Contribution à l'étude de la démonologie byzantine", in *Mélanges Bidez*, ed. Georges Mathieu [Annuaire de l'institut de philologie et d'histoire orientales, vol. II (1934)], Brussels, 1934, 207–32.

Delatte, Armand, *La catoptromancie grecque et les dérivés*, Liège and Paris, 1932.

Delehaye, Hippolyte, *Les Saints Stylites*, Brussels and Paris, 1923.

Delumeau, Jean, *La peur en Occident (XVIe – XVIIIe ciècles). Une cite assiégeé*, Paris: Fayard, 1978.

Detienne, Marcel, *La notion de DAÏMÔN dans le pythagorisme ancienne* [Bibliothèque de la Fac. de Philos. et Lettres de l'Univ. de Liège, Fasc. clxv.], Paris: Les Belles Lettres, 1963.

Dickie, Matthew, "Bonds and Headless Demons in Graeco-roman magic", *Greek Roman and Byzantine Studies*, 40, no. 1 (1999): 99–104.

Diehl, Charles, *L'Afrique byzantine. Histoire de la domination byzantine en Afrique (533 – 709)*, Paris: Leroux, 1896.

Dimitrov, Theodor, "Fever-Demon or Plague-Demon? Toward a new interpretation of v. Sym. Styl. J. 231", *Etudes Balkaniques* 4 (2015): 15–22.

Dobroklonskiy, Alexander, *The Venerable Theodore, confessor and Abbot of the Stoudios Monastery* [Russian: Доброклонскій, Александръ, *Преп. Феодоръ, исповедникъ и игуменъ Студийскій*], 2 vols., Odessa: "Экономическая" типография, 1913-14.

Drandakis, Nikolaos, *Byzantine Frescoes of Mesa Mani* [Greek: Δρανδάκης, Νικόλαος, Βυζαντινές τοιχογραφίες της Μέσα Μάνης], Athens: Archeological Society of Athens, 1995.

Downey, Glanville, *A History of Antioch in Syria: From Seleucus to the Arab conquest*, Princeton: Princeton University Press, 1961.

Dujčev, Ivan, *The Bulgarian Middle Ages. Studies on the Political and Cultural History of Medieval Bulgaria* [Bulgarian: Дуйчев, Иван, *Българско средновековие. Проучвания върху политическата и културната история на на средновековна България*], Sofia: Nauka i Izkustvo, 1972.

Dujčev, Ivan, "Une ambassade byzantine auprès des Serbes au IXe siècle", *Zbornik radova Vizantoloskog Instituta Srpske akademije nauka* 7 (1961): 53–60.

Efthymiadis, Stephanos, "On the Hagiographical Work of Ignatius the Deacon", *Jahrbuch der Österreichischen Byzantinistik* 41 (1991): 73–83.

Efthymiadis, Stephanos, *The Life of the Patriarch Tarasios by Ignatios the Deacon (BHG 1698)* [Birmingham Byzantine and Ottoman monographs 4], New York: Routledge, 2016.

Else, Gerald, "God and Gods in Early Greek Thought", *Transactions and Proceedings of the American Philological Association* 80 (1949): 24–36.

Ferrante, Nicola, *Santi italogreci in Calabria*, Reggio Calabria, 1981.

Féstugière, André-Jean, *Vie de Théodore de Sykéôn*, vol. 1 and 2 [Subsidia hagiographica 48], Brussels: Société des Bollandistes, 1970.

Féstugière, André-Jean, *Léontios de Néapolis. Vie de Syméon le Fou et Vie de Jean de Chypre. Édition commentée par A. Féstugiere en collaboration de L. Rydén* [Bibliothèque Archéologique et Historique 95], Paris: Librairie Orientaliste Paul Geuthner, 1974.

Finamore, John, "Reason and Irrationality: The intersection between philosophy and magic in later Neoplatonism", in *Plato in the Third Sophistic*, ed. Ryan Fowler, Boston and Berlin: De Gruyter, 2014, 39–57.

Flusin, Bernard, *Saint Anastase le Perse et l'histoire de la Palestine au début du vie siècle*, 2 vols., Paris: Centre National de la Recherche Scientifique, 1992.

Follieri, Enrica, *La vita di San Fantino il Giovane. Introduzione, testo greco, traduzione, commentario e indici* [Subsidia hagiographica, 77], Brussels: Société des Bollandistes, 1993.

François, Gilbert, *Le Polythéisme et l'emploi au singulier des mots θεός, δαίμων dans la litterature grecque d'Homère à Platon* [Bibliothèque de la Faculté de Philosophie et Lettres de l'Université de Liège, fasc. CXLVII], Paris: Les Belles Lettres, 1957.

Fountoulis, Ioannis, "The Saints Georges, Archbishops of Mytilene" [Greek: Φουντούλης, Ιωάννης, "Οἱ ἅγιοι Γεώργιοι, ἀρχιεπίσκοποι Μυτιλήνης"], *Lesviakon Eortologion* [Greek: *Λεσβιακὸν Ἑορτολόγιον*] 1 (1959): 33–43.

Gautier, Paul, "De daemonibus de Pseudo-Psellos", *Revue des Études Byzantines* 38 (1980): 105–94.

Gay, Jules, *L'Italie méridionale et l'Empire Byzantin depuis l'avénement de Basile Ier jusqu'à la prise de Bari par les Normands (867 − 1071)*, vol. 1, Paris: Fontemoing, 1904.

Gedeon, Manuel, *Proconnesus: Church Community, Temples and Monasteries, and Bishoprics* [Greek: Γεδεών, Μανουήλ, *Προικόννησος: ἐκκλησιαστικὴ παροικία, ναοὶ καὶ μοναί, μητροπολίαι καὶ ἐπισκοπαί*], Istanbul, 1895.

Gérolymatou, Maria, "Les échanges commerciaux à Byzance du VIIIe Siècle à 1204". PhD diss (Université Paris I − Panthéon − Sorbonne), 1994.

Geyer, John, "Mice and Rites in 1 Samuel V-VI", *Vetus Testamentum* 31/3 (July 1981): 293–304.

Ginzburg, Carlo, *Ecstasies. Deciphering the witches' Sabbath*, New York: Pantheon Books, 1991.

Gioles, Nikolaos, *Early Christian Church Architecture (200-600)* [Greek: Γκιολές, Νικόλαος, *Παλαιοχριστιανική ναοδομία (π. 200 − 600)*], Athens, 1998.

Gokey, Francis, *The Terminology for the Devil and Evil Spirits in the Apostolic Fathers*, Washington DC.: Catholic University of America Press, 1961.

Grégoire, Henri, "Thomas Dephourkinos du monastère de Kyminas et le quatrième mariage de Léon le Sage", *Byzantion* 32 (1962): 381–86.

Greenfield, Richard, *Traditions of Belief in Late Byzantine Demonology*, Amsterdam: Hakkert, 1988.

Guilland, Rodolphe, *Recherches sur les institutions Byzantines*, vol. 1 and 2 [Berliner Byzantinische Arbeiten, 35], Berlin: Akademie Verlag, 1967.

Guillou, André, *Le Diable Byzantin*, Paris and Athens: Daedalus, 1997.

Guillou, André, "Grecs d'Italie du Sud et de Sicile au moyen âge: les moines", *Mélanges d'archéologie et d'histoire* 75, no. 1, (1963): 79–110.

Halkin, François, "S. Nicéphore de Médikion d'après un synaxaire du mont Sinaï", *Analecta Bollandiana* 88 (1970): 13–16.

Hatzaki, Myrto, *Beauty and the Male Body in Byzantium. Perceptions and Representations in Art and Text*, New York: Palgrave Macmillan, 2009.

Harrison, Jane, *Prolegomena to the Study of Greek Religion*, Cambridge, 1922.

Hasluck, Frederick, "The Marmara Islands", *The Journal of Hellenic Studies* 29 (1909): 6–18.

Haupt, Paul, "Asmodeus", *Journal of Biblical Litetature* 40 (1921): 174–78.

Hild, Joseph-Antoine, "Daemon", in *Dictionnaire des antiquités Grecques et Romaines*, vol. 2.1, s.v. "Daemon," Paris: Librairie de L. Hachette, 1892, 9–19.

Hild, Joseph-Antoine, *Étude sur les demons dans la litterature et la religion des Grecs*, Paris: Librairie de L. Hachette, 1881.

Hill, George, "Apollo and St. Michael: Some Analogies", *The Journal of Hellenic Studies* 36 (1916): 134–62.

Howe, Thalia, "Zeus Herkeios: Thematic Unity in the Hekatompedon Sculptures", *American Journal of Archaeology* 59, no. 4 (October 1955): 287–301.

Hristova, Boryana, *The Book of Enoch. Ethiopian Version; Slavonic (Bulgarian) Version*, [Bulgarian: Христова, Боряна, *Книга на Енох. Етиопска версия; Славянска (Българска) версия*], Sofia, 2008.

Janin, Raymond, *La géographie ecclésiastique de l'émpire Byzantin. Les églises et monastères de Constantinople*, Paris, 1953.

Janin, Raymond, *Les églises et les monastères et les grands centres byzantins (Bithynie, Hellespont, Latros, Galèsios, Trébisonde, Athènes, Thessalonique)*, Paris, 1975.

Jenkins, Romilly and Cyril Mango, "A Synodicon of Antioch and Lacedaemonia", *Dumbarton Oaks Papers* 15 (1961): 225–42.

Jenkins, Romilly, *Byzantium. The Imperial Centuries, A.D. 610 — 1071*, London: Weidenfeld & Nicolson, 1966.

Joannou, Périclès-Pierre, *La démonologie populaire à Byzance au XIe siècle. La vie inédite de S. Auxence par M. Psellos*, Wiesbaden, 1971.

Jonston, Sarah, "Defining the Dreadful: Remarks on the Child-Killing Demon", in *Ancient Magic and Ritual Power*, ed. Marvin Meyer and Paul Mirecki [Religions in the Greco-Roman World, 129], Leiden: Brill, 2001, 361-87.

Jörgensen, Ove, "Das Auftreten der Gotter in den Büchern ι-μ der Odyssee", *Hermes* 39 (1904): 357-82.

Jowett, Garth and Victoria O'Donnel, *Propaganda and Persuasion*, Los Angeles: SAGE Publications, 2012.

Kaegi, Walter, "The Byzantine armies and Iconoclasm", *Byzantinoslavica* 27 (1966): 48-70.

Kaouras, Giorgos, *Byzantium. Sexual crimes and Their Punishments* [Greek: Καουρας, Γιώργος, *Βυζάντιο. Τα ερωτικά εγκλήματα και οι τιμωρίες τους*], Athens: Periplous, 2003.

Karpozilos, Apostolos, "The position of blacks in Byzantine society," in *Marginal people in Byzantium*, ed. Chryssa Maltezou [Greek: Καρποζηλος, Απόστολος "Η θέση των μαύρων στη Βυζαντινή κοινωνία," in *Οι περιθωριακοί στο Βυζάντιο*, ed. Χρύσα Μαλτεζου), Athens, 1999, 67-81.

Kazhdan, Alexander, "Byzantine Hagiography and Sex in the Fifth to Twelfth Centuries", *Dumbarton Oaks Papers* 44 (1990): 131-43.

Kazhdan, Alexander, "The Chronicle of Symeon Logothetes" [Russian: Каждан, Александр, Хроника Симеона Логофета], *Vizantiyskiy Vremennik*, 15 (1959): 125-43.

Kazhdan, Alexander, *A History of Byzantine Literature*: vol. 1: 650-850, Athens: Institute for Byzantine Research, 1999; vol. 2: 850-1000, Athens: Institute for Byzantine Research, 2006.

Kelly, Henry, "The Metamorphoses of the Eden Serpent Durring the Middle Ages and the Renaissance", *Viator* 2 (1971): 301-27.

Kennedy, George, *A New History of Classical Rhetoric*, Princeton: Princeton University Press, 1994.

Kennedy, George, *Progymnasmata. Greek Textbooks of Prose Compilation and Rhetoric*, Atlanta: Society of Biblical Literature, 2003.

Kiessling, Nicolas, "Antecedents of the Medieval Dragon in Sacred History", *Journal of Biblical Literature* 89, no. 2 (Jun. 1970): 167-77.

Knecht, Robert Jean, *Hero or Tyrant? Henry III, King of France, 1574-89*, Burlington: Ashgate, 2014.

Koukoules, Phaidon, *Life and Culture of the Byzantines* [Greek: Κουκουλές, Φαίδων, *Βυζαντινῶν Βίος καὶ πολιτισμός*], vol. 5, Athens: Collection de l'Institut Francais d'Athènes, 1952; vol. 6, Athens: Collection de l'Institut Francais d'Athènes, 1955.

Kountoura-Galaki, Eleonora, "Two-way Relationships of an Obscure and Prominent Saint: The Case of Saint Nicholas", in *Heroes and the Nameless, Obscure and Famous on the Fringes of the History of Art* [Greek: Κουνδούρα-Γαλάκη, Ελεονώρα, "Αμφίδρομες σχέσεις αφανούς και επιφανούς αγίου: η περίπτωση του αγίου Νικολάου", in *Ήρωες και ανώνυμοι, αφανείς και επώνυμοι στις παρυφές της ιστορίας και της τέχνης*], Athens: The National Hellenic Research Foundation, 2006, 73-87.

Krappe, Alexander, "ΑΠΟΛΛΩΝ ΣΜΙΝΘΕΥΣ", *Classical Philology* 36/2 (April 1941): 133-41.

Krueger, Derek, *Symeon the Holy Fool. Leontios'Life and the Late Antique City*, Los Angeles: University of California Press, 1996.

Krumbacher, Karl, *Geschichte der byzantinischen Literatur von Justinian bis zum Ende des Oströmischen Reiches*, München: Beck, 1897.

Lambakis, Stelios, "The Descents into Hell in the Byzantine and Post-Byzantine Literarure" [Greek: Λαμπάκης, Στέλιος, "Οι καταβάσεις στον Κάτω κόσμο στη βυζαντινή και στη μεταβυζαντινή λογοτεχνία"]. PhD diss. (University of Ioannina), 1982.

Langton, Edward, *Essentials of Demonology: A Study of Jewish and Christian Doctrine, Its Origin and Development*, London: The Epworth Press, 1949.

Langton, Edward, *Satan, a Portrait*, London: Skeffington & Son, 1945.

Latyshev, Vasilij, *Unpublished Greek Hagiographical Texts* [Russian: Латышевъ, Василий, *Неизданные греческие агиографические тексты*], St. Petersburg, 1914.

Laurent, Vitalien, *La Vie merveilleuse de saint Pierre d'Atroa* [Subsidia hagiographica 29], Brussels: Société des Bollandistes, 1956.

Lausberg, Heinrich, *Handbook of Literary Rhetoric*, trans. Matthew Bliss, Annemiek Jansen, and David Orton, Leiden, Boston, and Köln: Brill, 1998.

Lazenby Francis, "Greek and Roman Household Pets", I: *The Classical Journal* 4 (January 1945): 245-250; II: *The Classical Journal* 5 (February 1949): 299-307.

Lemerle, Paul, *Le premier humanisme byzantine. Notes et remarques sur enseignement et culture à Byzance des origines au Xe siècle* [Bibliothèque Byzantine. Études 6] Paris: Presses Universitaires de France, 1971.

Lemerle, Paul, *Prolégomènes à une édition critique et commentée des "Conceils et Récits" de Kekaumenos* [Académie Royale de Belgique, Classe des Lettres et des Sciences Morales et Politiques, Mémoires, vol. LIV, fasc. 1], Brussels, 1960.

Lipschitz, Elena, *Essays on the History of Byzantine Society and Culture. 8th – first half of the 9th century* [Russian: Липшиц, Елена, *Очерки истории византийского общества и культуры. VIII-первая половина IX века*], Moskow and Leningrad: Publishing House of the Academy of Sciences of the USSR, 1961.

Loparev, Chrisanf, *Greek Saints' Lives of the eighth and ninth centuries: An attempt at a scientific classification with an overview from a historical and historical-literary point of view* [Russian: Лопарев, Хрисанф, *Греческія житія святыхъ VIII и IX вѣковъ. Опытъ научной классификаціи памятниковъ агіографіи съ обзоромъ ихъ съ точки зрѣнія исторической и историко-литературной*], vol. 1, St. Petersburg, 1914.

Luck, Georg, *Arcana Mundi. Magic and the Occult in the Greek and Roman Worlds. A Collection of Ancient Texts*, Baltimore: John Hopkins University Press, 2006.

MacLaurin, Evan, "Beelzebul", *Novum Testamentum* 20, no. 2 (April 1978): 156–60.

Malingoudis, Faidon, "Slavonic Names from Byzantine Bithynia" [Greek: Μαλιγγούδης, Φαίδων, «Σλαβικά ονόματα από τη Βυζαντινή Βιθυνία], *Hellenika* 31, no. 2 (1979): 494–96.

Mango, Cyril, "Diabolus Byzantinus", *Dumbarton Oaks Papers* 46 (1992): 215–23.

Mango, Cyril and Stephanos Efthymiadis, *The Correspondence of Ignatios the Deacon* [Dumbarton Oaks Texts 11; Corpus Fontium Historiae Byzantinae, 39], Washington D.C.: Dumbarton Oaks, 1997.

Mango, Cyril, *Byzantium. The Empire of New Rome*, London: Charles Scribner's Sons, 1980.

Mango, Cyril, "On Re-Reading the Life of St. Gregory the Decapolite", *Byzantina* 13, no. 1 (1985): 633–56.

Mango, Cyril, "A Byzantine Hagiographer at Work: Leontios of Neapolis", in *Byzanz und der Westen: Studien zur Kunst des Europäischen Mittelalters*, ed. Irmagard Hutter, Wien, 1984.

Mango, Cyril and Ihor Ševčenko, "Some Churches and Monasteries on the Southern Shore of the Sea of Marmara", *Dumbarton Oaks Papers* 27 (1973): 235–77.

Mango, Cyril, Roger Scott, and Geoffrey Greatrex, *The Chronicle of Theophanes Confessor. Byzantine and Near East History AD 284 – 813*, Oxford: Clarendon Press, 1997.

Margalith, Othniel, "The Meaning of *'plym* in 1 Samuel V–VI", *Vetus Testamentum* 33, no. 3 (1983): 339–41.

Markopoulos, Athanasios, "*Life* of the Empress Theodora (BHG 1731)" (Greek: Μαρκόπουλος, Αθανάσιος, "Βίος της αυτοκράτειρας Θεοδώρας (BHG 1731)"], *Byzantina Symmeikta* 5 (1983): 249-285.

Marrou, Henri, *A History of Education in Antiquity*, trans. George Lamb, London and New York: Sheed and Ward, 1956.

Mavropoulou-Tsioumi, Chrysanthi and A. Koyntouras, "The Church of St. Andrew at Peristera, reconstructed in the 9th century" (Greek: Μαυροπούλου-Τσιούμη, Χρυσάνθη and Ά. Κούντουρας, "Ό ναός τοῦ Ἁγίου Ἀνδρέα στὴν Περιστερά μετασκευασμένος τὸν 9ο αἰ".], *Klironomia* 13, no. 2 (1981): 487-507.

Morrison, John and Roderick Williams, *Greek Oared Ships (900 - 322 B.C.)*, Cambridge: Cambridge University Press, 1968.

Moulton, James and A. T.C. Cree, "ΣΜΙΝΘΕΥΣ, Pestilence and Mice", *The Classical Review* 15, no. 5 (June 1901): 284-85.

Muchembled, Robert, *Une Histoire du Diable. XIIe-Xxe siècle*, Paris: Éditions Du Seuil, 2000.

Murphy, George, *Rhetoric in the Middle Ages. A History of Rhetorical Theory from Saint Augustine to the Renaissance*, Berkley and Los Angeles: California University Press, 1974.

Murray, Gilbert, *Five Stages of Greek Religion*, Oxford: Clarendon Press, 1925.

Musolino, Giovanni, *Santi eremiti Italogreci: grotte e chiese rupestri in Calabria*, Soveria Mannelli: Rubbettino, 2002.

Nau, François, "Le text grec sur les récits du moine Anastase sur les saints pères du Sinai", *Oriens Christianus* 2 (1902): 58-89.

Nikolaou, Katerina, *Woman in the Middle Byzantine Period: Social Prototypes and Everyday Life in Hagiographical Texts* [Greek: Νικολάου, Κατερίνα, Η *Γυναίκα στη Μέση Βυζαντινή Εποχή. Κοινωνικά πρότυπα και καθημερινός βίος στα αγιολογικά κείμενα*], Athens: The National Hellenic Research Foundation, 2005.

Nilsson, Martin, *A History of Greek Religion*, Oxford: Clarendon Press, 1949.

Ninck, Martin, *Die Bedeutung des Wassers im Kult und Leben der Alten* [*Philologus Supplementband* XIV, II], Darmstadt, 1960.

Nock, Arthur, "The Emperor's Divine Comes", *The Journal of Roman Studies* 37 (1947): 102-16.

Nock, Arthur, "Studies in the Graeco-Roman Beliefs of the Empire", *The Journal of Hellenic Studies* 45, no. 1 (1925): 84-101.

O'Brien, Peter, "Principalities and Powers and Their Relationship to Structures in Ephesians and Colossians", *Reformed Theological Review* XL (1981): 1-10.

Oikonomides, Dimitrios, "Gello in Greek and Rumanian Literature" [Greek: Οικονομίδης, Δημήτριος, "Ἡ Γελλὼ εἰς τὴν Ἑλληνικὴν καὶ Ῥουμανικὴν λαογραφίαν"], *Journal of the Greek Folklore Society* 30 (1975), 246-78.

Oikonomides, Nicolas, "The Role of the Byzantine State in the Economy", in *The Economic History of Byzantium: From the Seventh through the Fifteenth Century*, ed. Angeliki Laiou [Dumbarton Oaks Research Library and Collection 39], vol. 3, Washington, D.C.: Dumbarton Oaks, 2002, 973-1058.

Oikonomidès, Nikolas "Silk Trade and Production in Byzantium from the Sixth to the Ninth Century: The Seals of Kommerkiarioi", *Dumbarton Oaks Papers* 40 (1986): 33-53.

Orlandos, Anastasios, "The Catholicon of the Peristera Monastery near Thessaloniki" [Greek: Ὀρλάνδος, Ἀναστάσιος, "Τὸ καθολικὸ τῆς παρὰ τὴν Θεσσαλονίκην μονῆς Περιστερῶν"], *Archeion ton Byzantinon Mnemeion tes Hellados* [=Ἀρχεῖον τῶν Βυζαντινῶν Μνημείων τῆς Ἑλλάδος] 7 (1951): 146-67.

Pallas, Dimitrios, "Zur Topographie und Chronologie von Hosios Lukas: eine kritische Übersicht", *Byzantinische Zeitschrift* 78 (1985): 94-107.

Panagiotopoulos, Ioannis, *On the Athiggani: Politics and Religion in the Byzantine Empire* [Παναγιωτόπουλος, Ιωάννης, *Περί Αθιγγάνων: πολιτική και θρησκεία στη Βυζαντινή Αυτοκρατορία*], Athens: Herodotos, 2000.

Papachryssanthou, Denise, "La vie de Saint Euthyme le Jeune et la métropole de Thessalonique à la fin du IXe et au début du Xe siècle", *Revue des Études Byzantines* 32 (1974): 225-45.

Patai, Raphael, *The Hebrew Goddess*, Detroit: Wayne State University Press, 1990.

Patillon, Michel, *Corpus Rhetoricum*, vol. 1, Paris: Les Belles Lettres, 2008.

Pease, Arthur, "Things without honor", *Classical Philology* 21, no. 1 (January 1926): 27-42.

Peeters, Paul, "Sainte Golinduch, martyre perse († 13.7.591)", *Analecta Bollandiana* 62 (1944): 74-125.

Perdrizet, Paul, *Negotium perambulans in tenebris. Études de démonologie gréco-orientale*, Strasbourg, 1922.

Petrinski, Gerasim, *The Bride-Shows in Byzantium: Rhetoric, Literature, Propaganda* [Bulgarian: Петрински, Г. *Конкурсите за красота във византийския императорски двор: реторика, литература, пропаганда*], Haskovo: Poliraph-Jug, 2015.

Petrinski, Gerasim "Faustus Byzantinus: The Legend of Faust in Byzantine Literature and Its Neo-Platonic Roots", *Sofia Philosophical Review* 13, no. 1 (2020): 48-76.

Petrinski, Gerasim, *Late Antique and Byzantine Rhetoric* [Bulgarian: Петрински, Герасим, *Късноантична и византийска канонична реторика*], Sofia: Sofia University Press, 2014.

Piccione, Peter "The Egyptian Game of Senet and the Migration of the Soul", in *Ancient Board Games in Perspective*, ed. Irving Finkel, London: British Museum Press, 2007, 54–63.

Pitsakis, Konstantinos, "Some thoughts on the 'mirror punishments' in the Medieval Greek space", in *Tolerance and Repression in the Mid-Byzantine Period*, ed. Katerina Nikolaou [Greek: Πιτσάκης, Κωνσταντίνος, "Μερικές σκέψεις για τις «ποινές-κάτοπτρο» στον Ελληνικό μεσαιωνικό χώρο," in *Ανοχή και καταστολή στους μέσους Βυζαντινούς χρόνους*, ed. Κατερίνα Νικολάου], Athens, 2002, 285-312.

Pirivatrić, Srđan, *Samuilo's state. Its extent and character* [Serbian: Пириватрић, Срђан, *Самуилова Држава. Обим и карактер*] [Serbian Academy of Sciences and Arts Studies, 21], Belgrade: Institute for Byzantine Studies, 1997.

Plamenov, Petar, *Ecstasy of the text* [Bulgarian: Пламенов, Петър, *Екстазът от текста*], Sofia: Sofia University Press, 2023.

Plamenov, Petar, *The Body Text* [Bulgarian: Пламенов, Петър, *Тялото текст*], Sofia: Sofia University Press, 2018.

Plamenov, Petar, *The Promises of the Interesting* [Bulgarian: Петър Пламенов, *Обещанията на интересното*], Sofia: Sofia University Press, 2019

Pratsch, Thomas, *Der hagiographische Topos. Griechische Heiligenviten in mettelbyzantinischer Zeit* [Millennium-Studien zu Kultur und Geschichte des ersten Jahrausends n. Chr. 6], Berlin: De Gruyter, 2005.

Provatakis, Thomas, *The Devil in Byzantine Art* [Greek: Προβατάκης, Θωμάς, *Ὁ Διάβολος εἰς τὴν βυζαντινὴν τέχνην*], Thessalonica, 1980.

Radermacher, Ludwig, *Griechische Quellen zur Faustsage*, Wien & Leipzig: Hölder-Pichler-Tempsky in Komm, 1927.

Ramsay, William, *The Historical Geography of Asia Minor* [Royal Geographical Society. Supplementary Papers 4], London, 1890.

Remes, Paulina, *Neoplatonism*, London and New York: Routledge, 2014.

Rochow, Ilse "Die Häresie der Athinganer im 8. und 9. Jahrhundert und die Frage ihres Fortlebens", in *Studien zum 8. und 9. Jjahrhundert in Byzanz*, ed. Helga Köpstein and Friedhelm Winkelmann [Berliner Byzantinische Arbeiten 51], Berlin, 1993, 163–78.

Rochow, Ilse, *Kaiser Konstantin V (741–775). Materialen zu seinem Leben und Nachleben*, Frankfurt am Main: Peter Lang, 1994.

Rydén, Lennart, "The Bride-Shows at the Byzantine Court — History or Fiction?", *Eranos Jahrbuch* 83 (1985): 175–191.

"Les Saints Kozebites", *Échos d'Orient* 1, no. 8 (1898): 228–33.

Sakkos, Stergios, *On the Anastasioses of Sinai* [Greek: Σακκος, Στέργιος, Περὶ Ἀναστασίων Σιναϊτῶν], Thessalonica, 1964.

Savvides, Alexios, "The Laconian John Aratos and the Jews in the Late Tenth Century A.D." [Greek: Σαββίδης, Ἀλέξιος, "Ὁ Λάκων Ἰωάννης Ἄρατος καὶ οἱ Ἰουδαῖοι τῆς Σπάρτης στὰ τέλη τοῦ 10 μ. Χ. αἰ."], *Byzantinai Meletai* [=Βυζαντιναὶ μελέται] 6 (1995): 201–09

Scott, Alan, "The Date of the *Physiologus*", *Vigiliae Christianae* 52, no. 4 (November 1998): 430–41.

Ševčenko, Ihor, "Hagiography of the Iconoclast Period", in *Iconoclasm. Papers given at the Ninth Spring Symposium of Byzantine Studies*, ed. Antony Bryer and Judith Herrin, Birmingham: University of Birmingham, 1975.

Sherry, Lee, "Life of St. Athanasia of Aegina", in *Holy Women of Byzantium*, ed. Alice-Mary Talbot, Dumbarton Oaks, 1996, 137–58.

Schilbach, Erich, *Byzanntinische Metrologie*, München, 1970.

Scholem, Gershom, "Demons, Demonology in Kabbalah", in *Encyclopaedia Judaica*, vol. 5, s.v. "Demons. Demonology", Jerusalem, 2007, 575–78.

Smith, Mark, "Ancient Bisexuality and the Interpretation of Romans 1:26 — 27", *Journal of American Academy of Religion* 64, no. 2 (summer 1996): 223–56.

Snell, Bruno, *The Discovery of the Mind in Greek Philosophy and Thought*, New York: Dover Publications, 2011.

Snowden, Frank, "The Negro in Classical Italy", *American Journal of Philology*, 68, no. 3 (1947): 266–92.

Sophianos, Demetrios, *The Life of St. Luke of Steiri* [Greek: Σοφιανός, Δημήτριος, Ὁ βίος τοῦ ὁσίου Λουκᾶ τοῦ Στεριώτη], Athens: Akritas, 1989.

Sophianos, Demetrios, "The Monastery of Hosios Loukas: a survey and critical analysis of the reliability of the sources" [Greek: Σοφιανός, Δημήτριος, "Ἡ μονὴ τοῦ Ὁσίου Λουκᾶ: ἔλεγχος καὶ κριτικὴ τῆς ἀξιοπιστίας καὶ ἑρμηνείας τῶν πηγῶν"), *Mesaionika kai nea ellinika* (=Μεσαιωνικὰ καὶ Νέα Ἑλληνικά) 4 (1992): 23–80.

Spyridakis, Georgios, "The Death Rituals of the Byzantines According to Archeological Sources" [Greek: Σπυριδάκης, Γεώργιος, Τὰ κατὰ τὴν τελευτὴν ἔθιμα τῶν Βυζαντινῶν ἐκ τῶν ἁγιολογικῶν πηγῶν], *Annuaire de l'association d'études byzantines* [Ἐπετηρὶς τῆς Ἑταιρίας Βυζαντινῶν Σπουδῶν] 20 (1950): 74–171.

Stathakopoulos, Dionysios, *Famine and Pestilence in the Late Roman and Early Byzantine Empire. A systematic survey of subsistence crises and epidemics* [Birmingham Byzantine and Otthoman Monographies 9], Aldershot: Ashgate, 2004.

Stewart, Charles, *Demons and the Devil. Moral Imagination in Modern Greek Culture*, Princeton: Princeton University Press, 1991.

Sullivan, Denis, "Life of St. Ioannikios", in Byzantine Defenders of Images. Eight Saint's Lives in English Translation, ed. Alice-Mary Talbot [Byzantine Saints' Lives in Translation 2], Washington D.C.: Dumbarton Oaks, 1998, 243-351.

Sullivan, Denis, The Life of Saint Nikon: Text, translation, and commentary [The Archbishop Iakovos Library of Ecclesiastical and Historical Sources 14], Brooklin Mass.: Hellenic College Press, 1987.

Sullivan, Dennis "Was Constantine VI "Lassoed" at Markellai", Greek, Roman and Byzantine Studies 35 (1994): 287-91.

Talbot, Alice-Mary, "Some observations on the Life of St. Basil the Younger", in Byzantine Hagiography: Texts, Themes & Projects, ed. Antonio Rigo, Michele Trizio, and Eleftherios Despotakis [Studies in Byzantine History and Civilization 13], Brepols Publishers, 2018, 313-25.

Talbot, Alice-Mary, "Life of St. Stephen the Younger. Introduction and translation", in Byzantine Defenders of Images. Eight Saint's Lives in English Translation, ed. Alice-Mary Talbot [Byzantine Saints' Lives in Translation 2], Washington D.C.: Dumbarton Oaks, 1998: 9-12.

Talbot, Alice-Mary, "Life of St. Theodora of Thessalonike", in Holy Women of Byzantium. Ten Saints' Lives in English Translation, ed. Alice-Mary Talbot, Dumbarton Oaks: Dumbarton Oaks Research Library and Collection, 1996, 158-237.

Tambornino, Julius, De antiquorum daemonismo, Gießen, 1909.

Taylor, Lily, "The Daimōn of the Persian King", The Journal of Hellenic Studies 48 (1928), 6.

Thomson, O. Easily Led. A History of Propaganda, Sutton Publishing, 1999.

Treadgold, Warren, "The Bride-Shows of the Byzantine Emperors", Byzantion 49 (1979): 395-413.

Treadgold, Warren, "The Bulgars' Treaty with the Byzantines in 816", Rivista di Studi Bizantini e Slavi 4 (1984): 213-20.

Triandaphyllou, Konstantinos, "Greeks from Southern Italy who escaped to Patra during the 9th century" [Τριανταφύλλου, Κωνσταντίνος, ""Ελληνες τῆς Νότιας Ἰταλίας καταφυγόντες εἰς Πάτρας τὸν θ' αι".], in La chiesa greca in Italia dall' VIII al XVI secolo. Atti del convegno storico interecclesiale, ed. Michele Maccarrone, vol. 3, Padua: Antenore, 1973.

Vakaloudi, Anastasia, *Magic as a Social Phenomenon in Early Byzantium (4th – 7th centuries)* [Greek: Βακαλούδη, Αναστασία, *Η μαγεία ως κοινωνικό φαινόμενο στο πρώϊμο Βυζάντιο (4ος-7ος αι.)*], Athens: Enalios, 2001.

Vailhé, Siméon, "Répertoire alphabetique des monastères de Palestine", *Revue d'Orient Chrétien* 4 (1899): 512-42.

van den Ven, Paul, *La Vie ancienne de saint Syméon Stylite le Jeune (521 – 592)*, vol. 1: *Introduction et texte grec* [Subsidia hagiographica 32], Brussels: Société des Bollandistes, 1962; vol. 2: *Traduction et Commentaire, Vie grecque de sainte Marthe, mère de S. Syméon, Indices*, Brussels: Société des Bollandistes, 1970.

Vasiliev, Alexander, *Byzance et les Arabes*, ed. Marius Canard and Henri Grégoire, Tome 1: *La dynastie d'Amorium (820 – 867)*, Brussels: Éditions de l'Institute de Philologie et d'Histoire Orientales, 1935; Tome 2.1.: *La dynastie Macedonienne (867 – 959)*, Brussels, 1968.

Vinson, Martha, "Gender and Politics in the Posticonoclastic Period: The Lives of Antony the Younger, the Empress Theodora, and the Patriarch Ignatios", *Byzantion* 68, no. 2 (1998): 468-515.

Vinson, Martha, "The Terms ἐγκόλπιον and τενάντιον and the Conversion of Theophilus in the *Life of Theodora* (BHG 1731)", *Greek, Roman and Byzantine Studies* 36 (1995): 89-99.

Von Falkenhausen, Vera, *Untersuchaugen über die Byzantinische Herrschaft in Suditalien vom 9. bis ins 11. Jahrhundert*, Wiesbaden, 1967.

von Oefele, Felix, "A Babylonian Representation of a jumping mouse", *Journal of the American Oriental Society* 38 (1918): 140.

Voutiras, Emmanuel, "Euphemistic names for the powers of the nether world", in *The World of Ancient Magic. Papers from the First International Samson Eitrem Seminar at the Norwegian Institute at Athens, 4 – 8 May 1997*, eds. David Jordan, Hugo Montgomery, and Einar Thomassen, Bergen: The Norwegian Institute at Athens, 1999, 73-82.

Vryonis, Speros, "St. Ioannicius the Great (754 – 846) and the "Slavs" of Bithynia", *Byzantion* 31 (1961): 245-48.

Walter, Christopher, "The Thracian Horseman: Ancestor of the Warrior Saints?", *Byzantinische Forschungen* 14 (1989): 657-73.

Wiesen, David, "Juvenal and the Blacks", *Classica et Mediaevalia* 31 (1970): 132–50.

Wilford, F. A., "ΔAIMΩN in Homer", *Numen* 12, no. 3 (September 1965): 217–32.

Wolska-Conus, Wanda, "De quibusdam Ignatiis", *Travaux et mémoires* 4 (1970): 329–60.

Wright, Archie, *The Origin of Evil Spirits. The Reception of Genesis 6:1-4 in Early Jewish Literature*, Tubingen: Mohr Siebec, 2005.